WAIVER, VARIATION AND ESTOPPEL

WAIVER, VARIATION AND ESTOPPEL

Sean Wilken
BA (Oxon); DipLaw;
Barrister of the Middle Temple

and

Theresa Villiers
LLB; BCL; Lecturer in Law, King's College, London; Barrister of the Inner Temple

JOHN WILEY & SONS
Chichester • New York • Weinheim • Brisbane • Singapore • Toronto

Published by John Wiley & Sons Ltd,
Baffins Lane, Chichester,
West Sussex PO19 1UD, England

National 01243 779777
International (+44) 1243 779777
e-mail (for orders and customer service enquiries): cs-books@wiley.co.uk
Visit our Home Page on http://www.wiley.co.uk
or http://www.wiley.com

Other Wiley Editorial Offices

John Wiley & Sons, Inc., 605 Third Avenue,
New York, NY 10158–0012, USA

WILEY-VCH Verlag GmbH, Pappelallee 3,
D-69469 Weinheim, Germany

Jacaranda Wiley Ltd, 33 Park Road, Milton,
Queensland 4064, Australia

John Wiley & Sons (Asia) Pte Ltd, 2 Clementi Loop #02–01,
Jin Xing Distripark, Singapore 129809

John Wiley & Sons (Canada) Ltd, 22 Worcester Road,
Rexdale, Ontario M9W 1L1, Canada

Library of Congress Cataloging-in-Publication Data

Wilken, Sean.
Waiver, variation, and estoppel/by Sean Wilken & Theresa Villiers.
p. cm.
Includes bibliographical references and index.
ISBN 0-471-96921-4
1. Waiver—Great Britain. 2. Estoppel—Great Britain. 3. Contracts—Great Britain.
I. Villiers, Theresa. II. Title.
KD703.W34W55 1998
346.4102—dc21 97–34885
CIP

British Library Cataloguing in Publication Data

A catalogue record for this book is available from the British Library

ISBN 0-471-96921-4

Typeset in 11/13 pt Sabon by The Midlands Book Typesetting Company, Loughborough, Leicestershire.
Printed and bound in Great Britain by Bookcraft (Bath) Ltd, Midsomer Norton, Somerset.
This book is printed on acid-free paper responsibly manufactured from sustainable forestry, in which at least two trees are planted for each one used for paper production.

"Caught by the crabbing sun I walk on fire
And cast a shadow crab upon the land,
By the sea's side, hearing the noise of birds,
Hearing the raven cough in winter sticks,
My busy heart who shudders as she talks
Sheds the syllabic blood and drains her words."

from 'Poem on his Birthday' by Dylan Thomas
(reproduced with kind permission).

CONTENTS

FOREWORD

One of the greatest strengths of the common law lies in its versatility, its responsiveness to new problems. This permits a freshness of approach, an ability to tackle a novelty without the need to force it into a codified doctrinal mould. When the responses to individual needs have been numerous enough it may be possible to detect a pattern, from which there can be deduced a general principle capable of direct application in subsequent cases.

This oft-celebrated virtue of the common law is, however, fallible in two respects. First, where an attempt to generalize imposes on the instances a unity which does not exist, representing them as examples of an underlying principle which they do not truly represent. Secondly, at the other extreme, where a common thread which really does link the individual examples goes unrecognized, perhaps because the instances are too widely scattered to fit into any but the widest perspective, or perhaps because the adversarial system of law-making cannot succeed unless all the necessary materials are before the court.

These strengths and weaknesses are a particular feature of the area (or, it may be, the areas) of law discussed in the present work. Somewhere behind all the doctrines variously identified as estoppel, waiver, and so on lies a human instinct, implicit in all developed legal systems, which finds it distasteful that the law should enable someone to have it both ways, to blow hot and cold, to change a settled course of conduct, or an expressed intention, to the unfair detriment of another. This concept is universal, but it cannot be given full rein without creating more problems than it solves. The question is to map the boundaries, and the instances have been so widely dispersed, the examples from one field so inadequately deployed in another, the language of the judgments so various, that the translation of the instinct into accurate rules of law has yet to be achieved.

This is why the topics discussed in this book are so hard to manage. All those who have handled them in practice will know that doctrines such as estoppel can be powerful and yet dangerous weapons. The challenge is to set the boundaries for their proper use, and this task requires a disciplined study of materials drawn from a wide range of sources.

The fruits of just such a study are evident in this book. It does not attempt the impossible in the shape of a fully worked-out theory, capable of reconciling all the reported cases. What it does achieve is a methodical survey of the law – and particularly of commercial law, where the doctrines are of special practical importance – from which practitioners of all kinds in many different fields may find instance and commentary ready at hand for the tasks before them.

The book will be a boon, and I am glad to commend it.

M. I. MUSTILL

PREFACE

This book has its origins in the frustration that is felt by practitioners and academics alike in tackling the doctrines that form its subject (if not its obsession). As we have pointed out, these doctrines are frequently relied on but less frequently analysed and understood. We therefore wrote the book in an attempt to provide an explanation for both the difficulty and utility of these doctrines. As far as the explanation is concerned, it has been the aim to provide the reader with coherent views and, if they should disagree with those views, with at least a starting point in the appropriate authorities from which to form their own. By this route, we hope that the book will prove to be some use to practitioners and academics alike.

We also hope that it will be read not as an exhaustive, jurisprudential analysis, but as an essay, in the true sense of the word. Therefore, such conclusions that are reached are reached in the knowledge that it is almost impossible to be dogmatic about the scope and application of these doctrines and that it would be rash for authors as professionally young as ourselves to approach this area in any other way.

Finally, we would like to thank the following for their help and support: Sue Joshua and David Wilson at John Wiley for thinking that the book was a good idea and for answering the numerous queries during writing; Kirsten Singleton for her assistance in research for chapters 8 to 12; the administrative staff and clerks at King's and Essex Street respectively for their patience, tolerance and flexibility; and our friends and colleagues for their support, for listening to, and occasionally responding to, our monomastic rants during the course of writing.

The line is drawn in the legal sand as at today's date.

Sean Wilken
39 Essex Street
London

Theresa Villiers
King's College
London

1st December 1997

As an individual note, I would like to thank: all members of my Chambers for their support, tolerance and assistance throughout the past 18 months; Richard Wilmot-Smith Q.C. for taking the time from an extremely busy practice to read and to comment on what are now chapters 2–7, 13–18, 20; Stephen Ruttle Q.C. for performing a similar task with similar burdens on Chapter 19; and my room-mate, Vincent Nelson, for an inexhaustible supply of patience and first-principles reasoning. Any errors that remain are, of course, my own.

SW

TABLE OF CASES

Cases

Legislation

United Kingdom

STATUTORY INSTRUMENTS

RULES OF THE SUPREME COURT

EUROPEAN COMMUNITY

UNITED STATES

Part I

WAIVER, VARIATION AND ESTOPPEL

Chapter 1
INTRODUCTION

'I do not doubt that I often happen to talk of things which are treated better in the writings of master-craftsmen, and with more authenticity.'[1]

This work does not pretend to completeness. Irrespective of whether, as a matter of principle, any study can achieve completeness, the 'elusive'[2] and 'vague'[3] concepts of waiver, variation and estoppel occur and are relied on in so many contexts throughout the law of obligations that to consider them all would be unhelpful. This is partly because of the tendency apparent in the case law to regard these doctrines as doctrines of last resort. This tendency leads to an unjustified use of the doctrines where their requisite elements are not made out. To consider each and every case where the doctrines were invoked, often unsuccessfully, would therefore add nothing but greater length to this work. **1.01**

This work therefore attempts to set out a series of propositions and to consider those propositions as they apply to commercial law. The work falls into two sections: an examination of the doctrines of waiver, variation and estoppel as means to establish underlying rules; and an application of those propositions to 'commercial'[4] law. **1.02**

As far as the propositions are concerned, the work moves from the most specific and concrete doctrine — the variation of contracts — through to the most general and wide ranging — proprietary estoppel. In so doing, we draw distinctions between each of the doctrines. The thesis underlying those distinctions is twofold. First, the law is reluctant to impose obligations on a party without that party's specific consent supported by consideration. However, that reluctance does not extend **1.03**

---

[1] Michel de Montaigne, *On Books*.

[2] See *Transgrain Shipping BV v Global Transporte Oceanico SA (The Mexico I)* [1990] 1 Lloyd's Rep. 507 *per* Mustill L.J. (as he then was) at 514.

[3] See, *e.g. Colley v Overseas Exporters* [1921] 3 KB 302 *per* McCardie J. at 311–2.

[4] Used in a general sense to cover not only those areas which fall within the jurisdiction of the Commercial Court but also those areas which fall outwith that jurisdiction but remain 'commercial' in a loose sense of the word — see *Commercial Law — Introduction*, Chap. 13.

to the deprivation of rights or of the benefit of obligations. A party may be deprived of those without consideration being present. Secondly, the broad distinctions between each of the doctrines result from the different but analogous limitations placed upon the circumstances in which modification occurs. Thus, consideration must be present for the variation of contracts; the requirement of knowledge is the analogous limitation in cases of waiver; and detriment performs that function in 'estoppel'.[5]

Our consideration of variation in the abstract[6] is at Chapter 2. The consideration takes two interrelated forms. First, we consider the elements necessary for a variation — tritely offer, acceptance and consideration. Those elements have been consistently required since the early nineteenth century and, subject to recent developments in the law of consideration,[7] have remained unchanged. Whilst these requirements provide certainty by determining the circumstances in which obligations will be varied; these requirements are consistently undermined by the practices they seek to regulate.[8] The resultant tension manifests itself in the legal uncertainty as to the effects of unilateral and bilateral variations. The former may automatically determine the contract[9] and the latter may operate as an implied discharge of all extant obligations.[10] Secondly, we consider the results of this tension: namely that uncertainty as to the effects of a variation[11] and the means by which the requirements for variation can be mitigated or avoided. In considering the means by which the requirements for a variation can be mitigated, two points must be borne in mind. First, the courts have no difficulty in bypassing the requirements where the parties have agreed in advance that the contract can be varied by particular means.[12] That is consistent with the traditional view that the parties' bargain is to be upheld. Secondly, greater difficulty arises as to whether a contract will **1.04**

5 'Estoppel' in this context refers to equitable forbearance, estoppel by representation, estoppel by convention, estoppel by deed and proprietary estoppel.

6 Es opposed to the role that variation plays in specific areas of the law.

7 See *Williams v Roffey Brothers* [1991] 1 QB 1.

8 Seen most notably in the numerous cases of parties' failure to comply with the formalities of the Statute of Frauds and the Sale of Goods Act 1893 discussed at *Variation*, para. 2.38 ff. and *Banking* at paras 15.02, 15.60.

9 See discussion of *White and Carter (Councils)* at *Election*, paras 7.09 ff.; and the possibility of automatic termination in employment contracts at *Employment*, para. 18.17.

10 See *Variation* at para. 2.32.

11 See *Variation* at paras 2.27 ff., 2.36.

12 For instance, by the incorporation of rules into the contract which provide for their own variation without agreement — see *Variation* at para. 2.39.

be varied in the face of events which make performance of the contract extremely difficult but do not frustrate it. The most logical resolution of this difficulty and the courts' reaction to it is to outline a nascent doctrine of variation by necessity.[13]

At Chapters 3–5, we consider the doctrine of 'waiver'. Chapter 3 is definitional. Although a definitional chapter is unusual in a book of this kind, it is, we would suggest, necessary because of the terminological difficulties associated with the doctrines. Indeed, when the correct analysis is applied, three points emerge. First, 'waiver' in its true sense[14] only applies to the loss of contractual rights. Thus, waiver cannot create additional obligations of any kind. By parity of reasoning, the elements required to establish the waiver must relate to the contractual obligations assumed by the parties. There will be no waiver, therefore, where there is no unequivocal representation as to whether or not particular contractual rights will be relied on. Secondly, there are four types of waiver, depending on the right which it lost. Waiver can range from the loss of a contractual right unique to one party; to the loss of a right of rights before breach; the loss of rights after breach; and to the loss of all rights, including that of claiming damages. Thirdly, waiver in all these forms requires knowledge — this knowledge providing the limitation on the circumstances in which a party may be alleged to have lost its rights. **1.05**

In Chapter 4, the types and elements of waiver are outlined. In each case, the basic definition is derived from waiver by election. The right most frequently lost is the right to elect arising from a fundamental breach of the contract.[15] We apply that analysis to other forms of waiver because of the similarity of the rights being lost. A party which has a waiver in any form being raised against it will usually be seeking to rely on rights analogous to the right to elect. Further, no distinction in principle can be constructed in this context between the right to elect and the other purely contractual rights being lost. Chapter 5 sets out the complications associated with waiver. In particular, we consider whether waiver is suspensory or irrevocable. Here distinctions can and should be drawn between the types of waiver: distinctions which flow from the nature of the rights being lost.[16] **1.06**

---

[13] See *Variation* at para. 2.39.
[14] Waiver of tort being a different doctrine falling outwith this work.
[15] Assuming that the contract does not automatically determine or that the right to elect has not been lost as a result of the terms of the contract — see *Election* at para. 7.09 ff. and *Employment* at para.18.17
[16] See *Waiver — Complexities* at paras. 5.02, 5.05.

Chapter 6 considers the *Panchaud Frères* doctrine. Although often cited as forming part of the doctrine of waiver, on our analysis, the doctrine has few, if any, of the necessary hallmarks. Further, as the doctrine arguably can be confined to the context of shipping law,[17] it is difficult to see how waiver in the true sense of the word is in play. We therefore suggest that *Panchaud* can only be treated as an anomaly confined, at best, to shipping law. **1.07**

Chapter 7 is concerned with election and its relation both to waiver and to acquiescence. Our analysis of waiver, being based on, but not limited to, waiver by election, leads us to suggest that election is a subset of waiver. As such, for an election to be present the elements required for a waiver — an unequivocal representation made with the requisite knowledge — must also be present. Where those elements are not present, the party seeking to establish that the right to elect has been lost has two choices: to argue that no right to elect accrued or that the innocent party has been deprived of its right to elect by acquiescence or estoppel. As to the former, it would appear that the right to elect can be excluded by the terms of the contract or, potentially, by the rule in *White and Carter (Councils) v McGregor*.[18] The former is uncontroversial and consistent with the courts' desire to uphold the terms of the bargain reached. The latter represents not a fetter on the right to elect but equity intervening to curtail the innocent party's remedies accruing on repudiatory breach.[19] **1.08**

With Chapters 8 to 11, we move from waiver to estoppel. As suggested above, the distinction between waiver and estoppel is that knowledge is required for the former, detriment for the latter. Further, within the doctrine of estoppel we draw distinctions between the various doctrines dependent on whether representations, shared assumptions or property, are at issue. Three points are common to our analysis of all types of estoppel. First, the distinctions that we seek to draw are and will remain necessary unless and until the English law adopts a unified theory of estoppel, eradicating the distinctions which have existed and at present exist. Secondly the element of detriment is common to all forms of estoppel and may well take the same form in each. Detriment is the prejudice triggered by withdrawal of the representation/assumption/promise; that prejudice itself arising from the change of position that has occurred. Thirdly, this analysis of detriment makes explicit the **1.09**

[17] See *The Panchaud Frères 'doctrine'* at paras 6.06–7, 6.11.
[18] [1962] AC 413.
[19] See *Election* at paras 7.15, 7.18–9.

conceptual underpinning of all estoppels. Estoppels operate to prevent or reduce detriment being suffered by those who rely on assumptions induced by others. In certain incarnations, namely where they operate on promises, estoppels often mitigate the harshness of the law of contract's emphasis on consideration. The relationship of estoppel and the doctrine of consideration is one which is fraught with tension and is referred to at various points in this work. It should be noted, however, that estoppels cover a range of situations which fall outside the scope of the promissory liability central to the law of contract. We have sought to set out and analyse the various different types of assumption which are capable of giving rise to an estoppel. It is clear that not all assumptions can do so, even where induced by others. One of the most controversial issues in this area of law concerns whether the current limits on the scope of actionable assumptions are coherent or justifiable.

Chapter 12 analyses equitable forbearance. The doctrine which we have labelled equitable forbearance has also been referred to as promissory estoppel. We have adopted the former term because the doctrine is inherently based on concessions and promises to forbear from enforcing existing rights. The use of this term reflects the doctrine's close affinity with waiver,[20] the main difference between them being that waiver requires informed consent for its operation whereas equitable forbearance requires detrimental reliance. We examine the elements of equitable forbearance in turn, concluding that detriment is a pre-requisite for its operation. We assess the principles which determine when the doctrine will operate to suspend the rights foregone and when it will operate to extinguish them, drawing the conclusion that the prime aim of the relief is to avert detriment to the promisee. We close with an assessment of the status of the principle restricting the doctrine to forbearance of existing rights rather than the creation of new obligations. **1.10**

Chapters 13 and following form the second section of the work — the application of the doctrines to various areas of the law. Although these chapters are designed to be free standing, some reference back will have to be made to the doctrines as we define them. As we point out in the *Commercial Law — Introduction* the areas chosen are self-selecting; the frequency with which these doctrines are considered suggesting that it is appropriate to include a particular area. Further, as the focus of this book is the modification of commercial obligations, it **1.11**

[20] The terms have often been used interchangeably by the courts — see *Waiver — Types and Elements* at para. 4.39 ff. and *Sale of Goods and Shipping* at para. 20.02 ff.

seemed appropriate to consider the interaction of these doctrines with 'commercial law' in its loosest sense. The traditional areas of commercial practice — banking, insurance and shipping — therefore appear as do agency, company, construction and employment. We also acknowledge that areas are omitted from the section which could well have been included. There is, for example, no discussion of issue estoppel. However, this work concerns itself with the substantive law and issue estoppel is relevant only to practice and procedure. Perhaps a more serious omission is that there is no chapter on local authorities. However, given the complexities which arise in relating estoppel to the public law doctrine of legitimate expectation, a consideration of the role of estoppel in public law falls outwith the present scope of the book.

Chapter 2
VARIATION

INTRODUCTION

The variation of a contract is the alteration of the obligations contained in that contract.[1] As such, it could be argued that variation has much in common with waiver and estoppel[2]. However, as will be seen below, variation of contract is a separate and distinct doctrine from waiver, election and estoppel and must be pleaded and proved as such. That distinction is demonstrated by the terminological and actual differences between waiver, estoppel and variation; the legal requirements for there to be a variation; and the difficulties associated with the doctrine. **2.01**

TERMINOLOGICAL AND ACTUAL DISTINCTIONS

Tritely, the three doctrines of waiver, variation and estoppel can absolve a party from the obligations assumed under the contract or lead to the loss of a party's rights. For this reason, all three doctrines can arise from the same facts and practitioners often plead the doctrines in the alternative.[3] This superficial similarity has caused variation to be treated as synonymous both with waiver[4] and estoppel[5] or given rise to the invocation of an overarching doctrine of 'modification'.[6] Indeed, at least one **2.02**

---

1 See *Goss v Lord Nugent* (1883) 5 B & Ad 58 at 64–5, 110 ER 713 at 716.

2 Used in a loose sense here to cover estoppel by representation, estoppel by convention and equitable forbearance.

3 See *Cowey v Liberian Operations Limited* [1966] 2 Lloyd's Rep. 45, where an attempt to plead alternative estoppel and variation cases failed.

4 See *Stead v Dawber* (1839) 10 Ad & E 58, 113 ER 22 and *WJ Alan v El Nasr Export* [1972] 2 QB 189 *per* Megaw L.J. at 218 D.

5 See *Fenner v Blake* [1900] 1 QB 426.

6 See reference to a general doctrine of 'modification' not requiring consideration — *Syros Shipping Co SA v Elaghill Trading Co The Proodos C* [1980] 2 Lloyd's Rep. 390.

commentator has attempted to rationalize difficult cases by suggesting that, in the name of variation, the court was in fact relying on 'waiver in the sense of forbearance'.[7]

2.03 However, it is submitted on analysis clear distinctions of form and substance can and should be drawn. Put at its simplest, a variation of a contract alters the obligation to be performed and can only take place before that obligation is to be performed. Waiver and estoppel do not alter the terms of the contract, merely the remedies arising from an alleged breach of that contract.[8] Further, waiver and estoppel may result in there being:

> . . . a total dissolution of the contract placing the parties in the same situation in which they stood before the agreement was entered into.[9]

Variation, by contrast, cannot result in the dissolution of all contractual ties between the parties.[10]

REQUIREMENTS FOR A VARIATION

2.04 Historically, the courts have analysed variation of contract as analogous to the entry by the parties into a new contract with the concomitant requirements of offer, acceptance and consideration.[11] Therefore, in *Goss v Lord Nugent*[12] the court stated:

> By the general rules of the common law . . . it is competent to the parties at any time before breach of it, by a new contract not in writing, either altogether to waive, dissolve, or annul the former agreements, or in any manner add to, or subtract from, or vary or qualify the terms of it and thus to make a new contract . . .

---

[7] See Treitel 1 at p. 174.

[8] *Enrico Furst & Co v WE Fischer Ltd* [1960] 2 Lloyd's Rep. 340 *per* Devlin J. at 349 col. 2 – 350 col. 1. A distinction which explains the need for consideration for a variation but not for a waiver.

[9] See *Robinson v Page* (1826) 3 Russ 114 at 119, 38 ER 519 at 521.

[10] See *Construction* 17.10 ff., for a discussion of this principle in a particular context.

[11] See, *e.g. Bret v JS* (1600) Croke, Eliz 756, 78 ER 987 and *Pinnel's Case* (1602) 5 Coke Rep. 117a; 77 ER 237 in which the alteration of a contractual obligation was viewed as the acceptance of a fresh obligation and the conferring of a fresh and therefore different benefit.

[12] (1883) 5 B & Ad 58 at 64–5; 110 ER 713 at 716.

Adopting that view, the requirements for a variation are to be drawn from the law relating to the formation of a contract[13] and the same formalities will apply to the variation of the contract as apply to its formation.[14] Therefore, where a contract is required to be in writing[15] or evidenced in writing then the variation must be in writing to have any effect[16] or if it is to be given effect by the court.[17] However, by the rules of equity, a deed is not required to vary a deed.[18] **2.05**

On this basis, three requirements emerge: there is a valid and subsisting contract on foot between the parties; there is some form of consensus between the parties as to the obligations which are to be altered; the parties have acted in some way to their benefit or detriment in either agreeing the variation or as a result of the variation. Each is considered in turn. **2.06**

A VALID AND SUBSISTING CONTRACT

Subject to one possible exception,[19] the *sine qua non* of any variation of contract is a subsisting contract to be varied. Therefore, there can be no variation once the contract has terminated.[20] **2.07**

Thus, in *Royal Exchange Assurance v Hope*[21] the plaintiff executor of Mr Barker sued on a life policy entered into by Mr Barker prior to **2.08**

---

[13] We therefore respectfully disagree with Lord Denning M.R.'s view that variation of a contract can be nothing more or less than a particular interpretation of its terms (see *Amalgamated Investment & Property Co Ltd v Texas Commerce International Bank Ltd* [1982] 1 QB 84 at 121C–D). Variation, at the least, is alteration of the physical terms of a contract.

[14] See *McCausland v Duncan Lawrie Ltd* [1997] 1 WLR 38.

[15] See, e.g. s. 40 of the Law of Property Act 1925; s. 2 of the Law of Property Act 1989; s. 52 of the Hire Purchase Act 1965; and ss. 1–2, 11 of the Employment Rights Act 1996.

[16] See *New Hart Business v Brindley* [1975] Ch 342.

[17] However, where the variation alters the contract, that variation can be relied on by way of defence to an action on the contract — see *In re a Debtor (No. 517 of 1991) TLR* 25 November 1991 and *Implied Discharge* at 2.30 below.

[18] See *Berry v Berry* [1929] 2 KB 316.

[19] See the discussion of *Brikom Investments v Carr* [1979] 1 QB 467 at paras 2.10 ff., below.

[20] See *Goss op. cit.* Therefore, in the employment context, a transfer of employment at common law from X to Y will usually not be a variation of the contract of employment, as the transfer necessarily involves the termination of employment with X *before* employment with Y begins (*de Rosa v John Barrie Ltd* [1974] 1 WLR 946 at 964D–E). Contrast the effect of the Transfer of Undertakings (Protection of Employment) Regulations 1981 — discussed at *Employment*, paras 18.10 ff.

[21] [1928] Ch 179.

his death. As originally drawn up, the life policy was to expire on 31 July 1926 and in August 1925, Mr Barker assigned the benefit of the policy to the defendant giving notice to the insurance company, Sun Life. However, shortly before the expiry of the policy, Mr Barker extended the policy until 31 October 1926, failing at the same time to enter into an assignment of the extended policy. Mr Barker then died on 1 October 1926 (within the extended life of the policy). Royal Exchange Assurance sought a declaration against the defendant that the defendant was not entitled to the benefit of the policy, there in fact being two policies, one assigned (to 31 July) and one unassigned (1 August to 31 October). The court relied on the fact that the assigned policy was subsisting to spell out both an intention to benefit the defendant and a variation of the policy. In so doing, the court expressly acknowledged that the defendant's position would be 'more difficult' if the policy had expired prior to Mr Barker's instruction to continue cover until 31 October 1926.[22]

It follows from the above, that terms of the contract which have been performed cannot be varied. The simple reason is that there can be little practical benefit in the parties altering an obligation in respect of which performance has already been offered.[23] Therefore in *Hope*, it was Sun Life's continuing and therefore executory obligation to provide cover until the new expiry date of the policy[24] or death of the assured[25] which was varied.[26] **2.09**

A possible exception — pre-contractual variation and collateral contracts

It has been suggested (relying on *Brikom Investments Ltd v Carr*[27]) that the terms of the contract can be varied *before* that contract is **2.10**

[22] *Per* Sargant L.J. at 195; *per* Lawrence L.J. at 196–7.

[23] We therefore draw a distinction between the parties' agreeing that the performance will be different and an acceptance by one party that another party's performance has been different.

[24] See *Isaacs v Royal Ins Co* (1870) LR 5 Exch. 296 at 300 and *Hirdes GmbH v Edmond* [1991] 2 Lloyd's Rep. 546.

[25] See, *e.g. Lineberger v Security Life & Trust Co* 95 SE 2d 501.

[26] In this context, it is respectfully suggested that Lawrence L.J.'s suggestion at 197 is either incorrect or merely refers to the fact that the transaction between assignor and assignee was complete once assignment had taken place and been notified.

[27] [1979] 1 QB 467.

concluded.[28] In *Carr*, the Plaintiff, a firm of managing agents of a block of flats in Harrow, entered into a number of long leases of the flats. The leases expressly provided for a landlord's repairing covenant backed by contributions from the tenants. At the time of entry into the leases, the roofs of the flats were urgently in need of repair under that landlord's covenant. Prior to entry, the landlord plaintiff's agents represented that the plaintiff would repair the roofs at its own cost. However, after the tenants had signed the leases, the plaintiff sought to recover the costs of repairing the roofs from the tenants.

The Court of Appeal held that the plaintiff could not recover. Lord Denning M.R. did so on the basis that the representations generated an estoppel which inured for the benefit of the successors in title to or assignees of the original tenants.[29] Lord Justice Roskill, as he then was, with whom Lord Justice Cumming-Bruce agreed, doubted whether the doctrine of estoppel could extend that far,[30] and found that the representations constituted a collateral contract negating the express terms of the lease.[31] As an alternative ground, Lord Justice Roskill also found that the plaintiff had waived its rights to recover from the defendants.[32] Lord Justice Cumming-Bruce found that the original tenants could rely on a collateral contract and the assignees could rely on the doctrine of waiver.[33] **2.11**

For present purposes,[34] it is Lord Justice Roskill's finding that there was a collateral contract that is of interest. The collateral contract in *Carr* only came into being because of the representations made prior to the entry into the contract. Further, in a sense the collateral contract varied the terms of the lease. Therefore, *prima facie*, it would appear that Treitel arguably is correct in saying that there was a variation prior to the entry into the main contract. However, it is respectfully submitted that the better view is that although the facts which lead to the collateral contract took place before the formation of the lease, the collateral contract only came into existence *after* the lease was signed. Therefore, there was no variation prior to the formation of the lease. The lease **2.12**

28 See Treitel 1 at p.97; contra. Chitty at para. 3–062.
29 [1979] 1 QB 467 at 484F–5C.
30 *ibid.* at 485F–6G.
31 *ibid.* at 488B–F.
32 *ibid.* at 488F–9E.
33 *ibid.* at 490G–1C.
34 We do not propose to consider Lord Denning M.R.'s *dicta* in any detail in this chapter. See *Equitable Forbearance* 12–11 for an analysis of *Carr* in so far as it relates to the doctrine of equitable Forbearance.

was entered into and then varied by the operation of the collateral contract.

We would support that suggestion by five routes. First, the lease, as is usually the case with collateral contracts, provided the consideration for the collateral contract.[35] Therefore, the collateral contract had no effect unless and until the main contract was entered into and, potentially *vice versa*.[36] Secondly, the collateral contract existed to vary the main contract.[37] Absent the main contract, an agreement not to enforce the terms of the main contract would either be an agreement to agree,[38] an incomplete agreement[39] or void for uncertainty:[40] the main contract would therefore be unenforceable.[41] Thirdly, Lord Justice Roskill reached his conclusion by reference to *Hughes v Metropolitan Railway Co*[42] which expressly limited any principle laid down in this regard to actions taking place *after* entry into the contract. Put another way, there is nothing in *Hughes* which supports an *a priori* variation of contract. Fourthly, it is perfectly possible to analyse the representations made by the plaintiff as a form of offer which was accepted by entry into the lease.[43] Therefore, the collateral contract could only come into being after the lease.[44] Fifthly, as a matter of logic, it is difficult to see how a contract can be varied prior to inception without considerable inroads being made into the English law on the formation of contracts. 2.13

---

[35] See *De Lasalle v Guildford* [1901] 2 KB 215 and *Hill v Harris* [1965] QB 601.

[36] See *De Lasalle* above at 221: '*It* [the collateral contract] *must be a collateral undertaking forming part of the contract by agreement of the parties express or implied, and must be given during the course of dealing which leads to the bargain, and should then enter into the bargain as part of it.*'

[37] In this context see *Heilbut Symons & Co v Buckleton* [1913] AC 30 at 47, where Lord Moulton stated '*Such collateral contracts,* **the sole effect of which is to vary or add to the terms of the written contract,** *are therefore viewed with suspicion by the law . . .* '

[38] *i.e.* an agreement that the plaintiff and the defendant would enter into a contract and once they did so would not enforce one particular term of that contract.

[39] See *Pagnan SpA v Feed Products Ltd* [1987] 2 Lloyd's Rep. 601 per Lloyd L.J. at 619 cols 1–2 for the test to be applied.

[40] It being impossible to say what terms were not to be complied with prior to entry into the main contract.

[41] See *Walford v Miles*[1992] 2 AC 128; *May & Butcher v R.* [1934] 2 KB 17n. Contrast *Foley v Classique Coaches* [1934] 2 KB 1; *Hillas & Co Ltd v Arcos* (1932) 43 Ll L Rep. 359 and *The Queensland Electricity Generating Board v New Hope Collieries Ltd* [1989] 1 Lloyd's Rep. 205 at 210, where Sir Robin Cooke stated that arguments based on uncertainty exert 'minimal attraction'.

[42] (1877) 2 App Cas 439 per Lord Cairns at 448.

[43] See *Record v Bell* [1991] 1 WLR 853 at 862A-B.

[44] Such an analysis would also ensure that the analysis of the requirements for a collateral contract, a contract and a variation, are consistent.

CONSENSUS AS TO THE OBLIGATIONS WHICH ARE ALTERED

2.14 Post *Felthouse v Brindley*,[45] it is axiomatic that a party cannot unilaterally vary the terms of a contract; there has to be acceptance of the variation of the contract, that acceptance being more than 'mental acceptance or mere acquiescence'. Therefore, in the same way as there must be offer and acceptance at the formation of the contract, the parties[46] to the contract must agree to the variation,[47] must agree to all material aspects of the variation[48] and must intend[49] to vary the contract.[50] Where there are numerous parties to the contract, all must agree to the proposed variation.[51] Further, as with a contract, a party's agreement must be freely given and when the consent is obtained as a result of duress, it will be of no effect.[52] Finally, the parties' consensus must be sufficiently certain and be in sufficiently clear terms so that proposed alteration of their obligations can be given effect.[53]

---

45 (1862) 11 CBNS 869, 142 ER 1037.

46 Presently, the parties to a contract are free to vary it. However, the proposed reform of the law of privity will curtail that right in respect of contracts for the benefit of third parties. Variation will not be permitted where the third party has communicated its agreement to the contract to the promisor, the promisor is aware that the third party has relied on the contract or the promisor can be reasonably expected to have foreseen that the third party would rely on the contract and the contract does not provide otherwise (see Contracts (Rights of Third Parties) Bill; Law Commission Report *Privity of Contract: Contracts for the Benefit of Third Parties* (July 1996) Cmnd. 3329 XV:(14) ff.; Professor Burrows, *Reforming Privity of Contract: Law Commission Report No. 242* (unrep) pp. 16 ff.

47 See *Morris v CH Bailey* [1969] 2 Lloyd's Rep. 215 *per* Salmon L.J. at 219 cols 1–2 and *Fairlie v Christie* (1817) 4 Taunt 416 at 420, 129 ER 166 at 168.

48 See *Hill v Patten* (1873) 8 East 373; 103 ER 386.

49 However, whether a party did or did not intend to vary the contract will be objectively derived from a consideration of the objective evidence — see, *e.g.* (albeit in the context of construing the contract) *Deutsche Genossenschaftsbank v Burnhope & Ors* [1995] 1 WLR 1580 per Lord Steyn at 1587D-F.

50 See *Grogan v Robert Meredith & or TLR* 20 February 1996.

51 See *Campbell v Christie* (1817) 2 Stark 64, 171 ER 573, where the failure to obtain the consent of one of a pool of underwriters vitiated the proposed variation of the insurance contract.

52 See *The Universe Sentinel* [1983] 1 AC 366 and *Atlas Express Ltd v Kafco (Importers and Distributors) Ltd* [1989] QB 833.

53 The variation will substitute one contract for another and therefore must comply with the contractual requirement of certainty — see *Woodhouse AC Israel Cocoa Ltd SA v Nigerian Produce Marketing* [1972] AC 741 *per* Lord Hailsham at 757; Chitty at paras 2–099 ff.

Action to Benefit or Detriment

The traditional view

The proposed variation must, as a general rule, be supported by consideration. Therefore, the rules relating to the existence or absence of consideration, in that context, apply by and large to the variation of contracts.[54] Consideration will be provided by the mutual exchange of promises and by the possible conferral of a benefit or detriment to one of the parties.[55] Where, for example, alterations are made to the currency in which payment may be made[56] or to the place where payment is to be made,[57] both parties may benefit. The fact that, as matters turn out, only one party benefits from the variation is, it is submitted, irrelevant. **2.15**

Two conclusions follow from this 'traditional' approach to consideration. First, as with the formation of contracts, the courts will not inquire into the adequacy of consideration[58] and will, on occasion, go out of their way to create consideration where it would appear to most observers that there is no[59] or at best minimal consideration.[60] **2.16**

Secondly, past consideration cannot support a variation of contract. Therefore, where a party has performed its obligations, it cannot utilize those performed obligations as any form of consideration supporting a variation of another party's obligations.[61] **2.17**

A departure from the traditional view

However, it is submitted that this traditional model has to be revised in light of two factors. The first is the gradual movement from an analysis of contracts as an exchange of promises to an analysis of contract in terms of the benefits conferred thereby.[62] The second is the Court of **2.18**

---

54 See Chitty at para. 3–004 ff.

55 See, *e.g. O'Sullivan v Management Agency & Music Ltd* [1985] QB 428 and *Re William Porter & Co* [1937] 2 All ER 361 (analysis based solely on detriment).

56 See *WJ Alan & Co Ltd v El Nasr Export and Import Co* [1972] 2 QB 189 and *Shamsher Jute Mills Ltd v Sethia (London) Ltd* [1987] 2 Lloyd's Rep. 388.

57 See *Banking* at para. 15.08.

58 See *Grisley v Lother* (1614) Hobart 10, 80 ER 161.

59 See *Shadwell v Shadwell* (1860) 9 CBNS 159, 142 ER 62; *Chitty* at para. 3–008, n. 32.

60 See, *e.g. Chappell & Co v Nestle Co Ltd* [1960] AC 87 (chocolate wrappers constitute consideration); but contrast *Lipkin Gorman v Karpnale* [1991] 2 AC 548.

61 See *Stilk v Myrick* (1809) 2 Camp 317, 170 ER 851 at 1168.

62 See, for a very early formulation of the analysis, the *Introduction* to Atiyah 1.

Appeal's decision in *Williams v Roffey Bros & Nicholas (Contractors) Ltd.*[63]

The decision in Williams v Roffey

In *Williams*, the plaintiff was engaged as a subcontractor by the defendant to carry out the carpentry works on a block of flats. The plaintiff was able to complete some flats but due to the underpricing of the subcontract and the inadequate supervision of his works by the defendant, the plaintiff was in financial difficulty affecting his ability to complete. The defendant therefore offered to pay the plaintiff an extra £575 as an incentive for the plaintiff to complete the works timeously. In other words, the Defendant offered the plaintiff extra money to persuade the plaintiff to perform that which he had already contracted to do. However, when the plaintiff had substantially and timeously completed the works under the contract, the defendant refused to pay the plaintiff. The plaintiff therefore sued the defendant and succeeded at both first instance and on appeal. **2.19**

The Court of Appeal rejected an argument based on estoppel[64] and found that the variation was supported by consideration since the defendant was to receive a 'practical benefit' from the variation.[65] That practical benefit comprised: the assurance that the plaintiff would continue to work on site, the better organisation of the plaintiff's work so as to allow the defendant to make more efficient use of the labour on site, the avoidance of an obligation to pay a penalty as a result of the failure to complete the flats timeously and the avoidance of the inconvenience of having to find a contractor to replace the plaintiff. **2.20**

The Court of Appeal buttressed the reliance on practical benefit in several ways. Lord Justice Glidewell analysed the position as follows:[66] **2.21**

> (i) if A has entered into a contract to do work for, or to supply goods or services to, B in return for payment by B; and (ii) at some stage before A has completely performed his obligations under the contract B has reason to doubt whether A will or will be able to, complete his side of the bargain; and (iii) B thereupon promises A an additional payment in return for A's promise to perform his contractual obligations on time; and (iv) as a result of giving his promise, B obtains in practice a benefit, or obviates a disbenefit; (v) B's promise is not given as a result of economic duress or fraud

---

63 [1991] 1 QB 1.
64 *ibid.* at 13E–G and 23D.
65 *ibid.* at 11, 19, 20 and 21.
66 *ibid.* at 15G–16B.

on the part of A; then (vi) the benefit to B is capable of being consideration for B's promises, so that the promise will be legally binding.

Lord Justice Russell adopted a 'pragmatic approach'[67] deciding: **2.22**

> Consideration there still must be but, in my judgment, the courts nowadays should be more ready to find its existence so as to reflect the intentions of the parties to the contract where the bargaining powers are not unequal and where the finding of consideration reflects the true intention of the parties . . . .[68]
>
> A gratuitous promise, pure and simple, remains unenforceable unless given under seal. But where as in this case a party undertakes to make a payment because by so doing it will give you an advantage arising out of the continuing relationship with the promisee the new bargain will not fail for want of consideration.[69]

Lord Justice Purchas (albeit with some doubt) came to the conclusion that there would be consideration where both parties had received some benefit even if neither party suffered a detriment.[70] **2.23**

Applying Williams v *Roffey*

Although the decision has been subject to academic criticism[71] and will not apply to straightforward debtor/creditor relationships,[72] we would suggest that the decision has four benefits and therefore should be considered to be good law. First, *Williams* recognizes that, in commercial dealings, there is an advantage to one party if it can increase the likelihood of other party completing the contract. Further, there can be no obvious public policy objection[73] to further payments being made by the parties to ensure that benefit accrues. Secondly, *Williams* also recognizes, as is the case, that the performance of a pre-existing contractual obligation may result in the party receiving a benefit from **2.24**

[67] [1991] 1 QB 1 at 19D.

[68] *ibid.* at 18H.

[69] *ibid.* at 19D–E.

[70] *ibid.* at 23D.

[71] See, *e.g.* 'Consideration: Practical Benefit and the Emperor's New Clothes' by Mindy Chen-Wishart in *Good Faith and Fault in Contract Law* ed. J Beatson and D Freidman (Clarendon Press, Oxford, 1995) at pp. 123–50.

[72] *Re Selectmove* [1995] 1 WLR 474, CA *per* Peter Gibson L.J.; at 480C–1D applying *Foakes v Beer* (1884) 9 App Cas 605. See *Equitable Forbearance* para. 12.09; *Banking* para. 15.19.

[73] Subject to the public policy caveat expressed by Russell L.J. that care must be taken where the parties do not possess equal bargaining power.

that performance other than the mere fact of performance.[74] Thirdly, the strict, traditional adherence to a formalistic doctrine of consideration does not reflect modern commercial practice. In modern commercial practice, there is both a need for fluidity to take account of changing market conditions and for the recognition that the contractual relationships between A and B can have effects on the market as a whole or on A's relationships with numerous other parties unconnected with the contract. The decision opens the way for the courts to reflect that fluidity.[75] Fourthly, the practical benefit test may serve to reduce the courts' desire or need to 'invent' consideration.

It is therefore submitted that the court should find that a variation is supported by consideration[76] in all cases where it is possible to find that the variation results in the accrual of a benefit to the parties to the contract. Further, the court should not find that a variation of contract is invalid even if the practical benefit is merely that the due performance of existing obligations under the contract is to be varied to the benefit of both parties.[77] **2.25**

DIFFICULTIES ASSOCIATED WITH THE DOCTRINE

The approach of the courts to the issue of variation gives rise to three interrelated complexities; complexities which can be expressed as three questions. What is the effect of a variation? What is the effect of a **2.26**

---

[74] Per Purchas L.J. at 21. See also *Anangel Atlas Compania Naviera SA v Ishikawajima-Harima Heavy Industries Co Ltd (No. 2)* [1990] 2 Lloyd's Rep. 526, where the defendant promised concessions to the plaintiff to persuade them to accept a hull on time *pour encourager les autres,* namely the defendant's other customers, to accept constructed hulls in a falling market.

[75] But see *Re Selectmove* [1995] 1 WLR 474, CA at 480C–1D in which Peter Gibson L.J. recognized the force of an argument that in the real world practical benefit would accrue to a creditor in allowing payment of a debt by instalments but felt himself bound by *Foakes v Beer* (1884) 9 App Cas 605.

[76] Save where a debt is concerned in which case *Foakes v Beer* would apply — see n. 69 above.

[77] But see Hudson para 7.025, where the author canvasses the possibility that the employer may agree to a variation purely to benefit the contractor. In that circumstance, there would be no bilateral exchange and *Williams* would not apply. The approach may be theoretically correct, however, in practical terms it is difficult to envisage a situation where an employer would so agree unless some benefit accrued to the employer.

unilateral variation?[78] How have the commercial difficulties, created by the above, been moderated or reduced? It is submitted that the existence of those complexities and the mechanisms which the courts have adopted to resolve them, underlie and are the rationale for the limited nature of the doctrine of variation and its distinct nature, unrelated to both estoppel and waiver.

THE EFFECT OF A VARIATION

There are two possible approaches to this question. First, a variation of the contract may operate as a 'rescission'. This approach arises from the historical requirement of formalities and is therefore supported by the older authorities. Secondly, a variation of the contract may operate as an implied discharge by agreement of the previous contract. This approach, it is submitted, is logical and consistent. However, there are suggestions that it may lead to practical difficulties. **2.27**

'Rescission'

As has already been pointed out, the courts will only find that a contract has been varied where certain requirements, namely those akin to the formation of a contract, have been met. Similarly, certain formal requirements apply where the parties attempt to vary those contracts required as a matter of law to be in writing.[79] Logically, the latter requirement flows from the former. The historical rationale for the application of formal requirements to variations is that they prevent the requirements as to the formation of contracts from being bypassed or undermined by the doctrine of variation.[80] This rationale previously extended to everyday contracts for the sale of goods. Thus, by s. 4 of the Sale of Goods Act 1893, contracts for the sale of goods where more than 10 *l* was at issue had to be in writing. Therefore, variations of those contracts **2.28**

---

[78] A variation inevitably implies a state of affairs where the requirements set out above. A unilateral variation being one where there is no consensus.

[79] See para. 2.05 above.

[80] The formal requirement also prevents the statutory requirements as to writing being bypassed by oral variations. See *Robinson v Page* (1826) 3 Russ 114, 38 ER 519; *Stead v Dawber* (1839) 10 Ad & E 58, 113 ER 22; *Noble v Ward* (1867) LR 2 Ex 135; *Morris v Baron & Co* [1918] AC 1; *British and Beningtons Ltd v NW Cachar Tea Co Ltd* [1923] AC 48 and *United Dominions Trust (Jamaica) Limited v Shoucair* [1969] 1 AC 340.

had to be in writing and, for example, if changes as to time or place of delivery were to be valid, those changes, being variations, would also have to be in writing.[81]

The immediate effect of s. 4 was that commercial arrangements should have been less flexible; it no longer being open to the parties to vary their obligations informally. However, in practice the parties to commercial contracts continued to enter into informal variations and then to seek to enforce those obligations in the courts. The courts, by s. 4, were unable to enforce the contracts but sought to find some mechanism by which the contracts could be preserved and commercial flexibility and the merits of the particular case reflected by the law. The courts sought to do this by holding that the parties to a contract could so fundamentally alter the terms of that contract by variation that the original contract was in fact 'rescinded'.[82] In such circumstances, neither party could rely on the contract. **2.29**

That approach still appears to be good law, even though the categories of contracts which must be supported by formalities have been considerably reduced over time. However, using rescission in this way creates additional complexities in ascertaining the effect of a variation. First, if 'rescission' does not occur in every case, difficult questions of fact arise as to when, and in what circumstances, a variation will lead to rescission. Secondly, there is the logical corollary of those questions of fact, which is why, as a matter of logic, do certain variations lead to a rescission of the contract whilst others do not. **2.30**

Circumstances in which rescission takes place

The courts have resolved that question thus: **2.31**

> . . . which comes nearer to their intention — to leave them with an unamended agreement or without any agreement at all . . . If the new agreement reveals an intention to rescind the old, the old goes; and if it does not, the old remains in force and unamended.[83]

This, it is submitted, creates a double uncertainty. There is the primary uncertainty as to when the courts will have recourse to the parties' intentions. There is then the secondary uncertainty as to what the courts will

---

[81] See *Morris v Baron & Co* [1918] AC 1.

[82] See *Morris v Baron & Co* [1918] AC 1 per Viscount Haldane at 20–1, *per* Lord Dunedin at 25–6, *per* Lord Atkinson at 29–33 and *British and Beningtons* [1923] AC 48 *per* Lord Sumner at 68–9.

[83] See *United Dominions Corporation (Jamaica) v Shoucar* [1969] 1 AC 340 *per* Lord Devlin at 348B–C.

determine the parties' intentions to have been. These uncertainties are compounded by the fact that the parties varying the contract do not intend either to leave the contract as it was or to vitiate the contract altogether — they wish to create a different contract. Therefore, to spell out the intention of the parties on that basis is, at best, difficult.

The logical difficulty

Axiomatically, the terms of a contract are to be taken and read together to ascertain what the bargain between the parties was.[84] That rule applies to varied and unvaried contracts. Therefore, in the normal course of events,[85] it is not possible to separate out the various terms of the contract and if one term is altered, the entire bargain is altered. Thus, logically, variation of a contract should create a new contract in all circumstances.[86] There is no reason why some variations should have that result and others do not. Additionally, 'rescission' is the dissolution *ab initio* of all contractual ties. Variation is, by its very nature, not the dissolution of all obligations but the modification of all or some of the obligations assumed. **2.32**

Implied Discharge

A valid variation of a contract replaces the obligations previously assumed by the parties with the new and varied obligations.[87] As far as the future performance of the contract is concerned,[88] the previous contract becomes irrelevant. The most accurate label for that process would be implied discharge. Further, acknowledging that all variations operate as implied discharges of the previous agreement avoids the practical and logic difficulties outlined above. No debate can arise as to **2.33**

---

[84] Hence, the canon of construction that all terms of a contract are to be construed together (the *expressio unius* principle) and the difficulty of severing contract terms — see Chitty 16–164 ff.

[85] Absent severance of a term of the contract.

[86] See *Edwin Hill & Partners v First National Plc* [1989] 1 WLR 225 *per* Nourse L.J. at 234H and *per* Browne-Wilkinson V.-C. at 235E.

[87] The courts may have tacitly allowed implied discharge to operate by permitting the parties to 'rescind' (*Coniers v Holland* (1588) 2 Leon 214; *Langden v Stokes* (1634) Cro Car 383 and *Treswaller v Keyne* (1621) Cro Jac 620) and to reconstitute the contract on different terms (*Nash v Armstrong* (1861) 10 CB NS 259).

[88] The previous contract would, of course, be relevant to any issue of breach prior to the variation.

the circumstances in which the previous agreement ceases to have effect and no logical confusion results.

In addition to the above, a number of additional reasons would suggest that implied discharge is the better approach. First, Lord Devlin in *Shoucar*[89] suggested that the English courts would adopt the logical conclusion if it could be shown that the difficulties it created either did not apply or were misconceived. In so doing, he clearly viewed implied discharge as the better option and left the way open for its reappraisal. Secondly, to the extent that the approach in *Morris v Baron*[90] and the succeeding cases was based on a need to preserve a distinction between variation and rescission, that need is, it is respectfully submitted, more apparent than real. Rescission, in the modern sense, vitiates the contract *ab initio*.[91] In no sense does a variation vitiate the original contract *ab initio*. It follows the use of the term 'rescission' in this context is a misnomer and the equation of variation and rescission a category mistake. Thirdly, if the old contract is discharged and then replaced, none of the difficulties with 'unenforceability' arise. Fourthly, to suggest that variation may, in certain circumstances, be a rescission is inconsistent with the fact that a unilateral variation can constitute a repudiation of contract which may be accepted or ignored.[92] Fifthly, and finally, the rationale for formalities has been to protect certain types of contracting parties from 'sharp practice'. It is submitted that greater protection of such parties can be achieved by examining whether that party freely and fairly contracted[93] as opposed to a reliance on formalities which may offer little or no real protection. **2.34**

However, whilst the operation of implied discharge in all cases of variation has been acknowledged as being correct 'as a matter of formal logic,'[94] the English courts have avoided reaching that conclusion to date for two reasons. First, a belief that implied discharge creates difficulties for the parties as 'a minor variation may destroy the effect of the whole transaction between the parties.'[95] Secondly, the courts may have **2.35**

---

89 [1969] 1 AC 340 at 349E–F.
90 [1918] AC 1.
91 See *McDonald v Dennys Lascelles Ltd* (1933) 48 CLR 457 at 476–7 and *Johnson v Agnew* [1980] AC 367 at 396.
92 See para. 2.36 below.
93 By reference to undue influence, duress, the Unfair Terms in Consumer Contracts Regulations 1994 (1994/3159) or Council Directive on Unfair Terms in Consumer Contracts 93/13/EEC.
94 See *British and Beningtons* [1923] AC 48 *per* Lord Sumner at 68.
95 See *United Dominions Corporation (Jamaica) v Shoucar* [1969] 1 AC 340 *per* Lord Devlin at 348A.

confused rescission and discharge giving rise to a conviction that the existence of implied discharge erodes the distinction between rescission and variation.[96]

Whilst there is some force in those objections, on balance we would suggest that the better view is that a variation which satisfies the criteria set out above,[97] operates to discharge the old contract by mutual agreement and to replace it with the new contract.[98] That approach has the benefit of certainty and simplicity. The difficulty relating to those contracts which are required to be in writing would therefore be resolved by the fact that the new contract in its entirety would be unenforceable.[99] **2.36**

THE EFFECT OF A UNILATERAL VARIATION

On one analysis,[1] a unilateral variation should have no effect whatsoever, the parties continuing with the contract as before. However, if the proposed variation makes substantial or fundamental changes to the contract, it is tantamount to a declaration by the proposing party that it does not intend to continue to perform the contract in the unvaried form. Therefore, the proposed variation may amount to anticipatory repudiatory breach of the contract or, if insisted upon, will amount to a repudiation of the contract.[2] It therefore follows that the party choosing not to accept the proposed variation will be put to its election to accept the repudiation or to call expressly for the performance of the **2.37**

96 See *Morris v Baron* [1918] AC 1.

97 A distinction is to be drawn between variation and unilateral variation.

98 See also Keating at p. 288. This approach would be consistent with the requirement that a proposed variation must be sufficiently certain so as to give it contractual effect — see *Woodhouse AC Israel Cocoa Ltd SA v Nigerian Produce Marketing* [1972] AC 741 *per* Lord Hailsham at 757.

99 There may be a further benefit to this analysis. The mutual release by the parties of their obligations under the old contract might operate as consideration for entry into the new contract thereby avoiding the difficulties associated with consideration as outlined at para. 2.15 ff., above.

1 *United Dominions Corporation (Jamaica) v Shoucar* [1969] 1 AC 340 at 348A, considered at paras 2.28 and 2.34 above.

2 See *Coleman v S&W Baldwin* [1977] IRLR 342 and *Pedersen v Camden LBC* [1981] ICR 674. In the employment context, the relationship is subject to an implied obligation of good faith and confidence. Therefore, a unilateral variation will probably amount to repudiation as a result of a breach of that obligation in any event — see *Woods v WM Car Services (Peterborough) Ltd* [1981] ICR 666, [1982] ICR 693, CA.

contract in its unaltered form.[3] In a further analogy to offer and acceptance, the innocent party must demonstrate that by its conduct it has accepted the repudiation.[4]

THE MODERATION OF COMMERCIAL DIFFICULTIES OF VARIATION

A rigid formal adherence to the requirements of variation creates difficulties in practice. Such difficulties have been mitigated by two mechanisms for variation of a contract that do not require the express consent of the parties to, or consideration for, that variation. The first mechanism is clearly established and involves construing certain agreements as if the parties had agreed to permit certain types of variation to those agreements. The second mechanism, it is submitted, is of more doubtful origin and status and may involve the court in finding that the obligations assumed by the parties have varied in the face of *force majeure* or potentially frustrating events. We refer to the former as 'agreements permitting variation' and the latter as 'variation by necessity'. 2.38

Agreements permitting variation

The courts will deem the parties to have entered into an agreement permitting variation in two cases. First, when the parties incorporate within the contract a set of rules themselves providing for their own variation or amendment.[5] In such circumstances, it would clearly be contrary to the commercial purpose of the contract, evinced by the incorporation of the rules, to allow the rules outwith the contractual context to alter and the rules actually incorporated to remain the same. Thus, in such circumstances, any amendment of the rules outwith the contract will automatically amend the incorporated rules and vary the contract. Secondly, where the parties have either expressly[6] or impliedly[7] agreed that one or both of them should have the power to vary the agreement, 2.39

[3] See *Burdett-Coutts v Hertfordshire County Council* [1984] IRLR 91.
[4] See *Vitol SA v Norelf Ltd* [1996] 3 WLR 105 *per* Lord Steyn at 113A–C.
[5] See *Page v Liverpool Victoria Friendly Society* (1927) 43 TLR 712 *per* Lord Hansworth M.R. at 713 and *Yeo v Stewart* [1947] 2 All ER 28 *per* Sellers J at 33F–G.
[6] *Robert H Dahl v Nelson, Donkin* (1881) 6 App Cas 38 at 39, 43 and *Dal v Orr* [1980] IRLR 413; *Spafax v Harrison* [1980] IRLR 413.
[7] *Millbrook v McIntosh* [1981] IRLR 309.

that party will have that power. Under this head, there are in fact two types of variation permitted — a variation of the contract *per se* and a variation of the performance of the terms of the contract. In most cases, the above distinction is one without a difference. However, the above distinction is pertinent where building contracts are concerned.[8]

Variation by necessity

In a series of extremely difficult cases,[9] the courts considered the issues arising from the Mississippi floods in 1973 and the subsequent ban imposed by the US Government on exports of American soya bean meal. At the time, the market in soya beans was extremely volatile. As a result, trading in soya bean futures could be very profitable and a specific pattern of trading emerged. A purchaser, B, would enter into a sales contract with the seller, A, for delivery of a consignment of soya beans in, for example, seven months' time. At that date, B would know that the cargo would be shipped cif under a GAFTA 100 form.[10] However, B would not know to which port the soya would be shipped, the date of the bill of lading, nor the size of the cargo. Depending on market conditions, B would sell on the benefit and burden of the contract to another purchaser, C, who would then sell on to another, D, and so on. The result was that a cargo could be the subject of a whole 'string' of sales before a final sale and purchase took place. Further, this futures market was dominated by a limited number of companies which would be involved in numerous such strings and could be involved on more than one occasion in any one string.[11] At some point during the process, the destination port, the date of the bill of lading, the name of the vessel and the total size of the consignment would be passed to B and then down the string by a Notice of Appropriation.[12] **2.40**

[8] See *Construction* at para. 17.03 ff., below.

[9] That difficulty being recognized by the courts at the time, the litigation being described as an 'unattractive piece of forensic history' (*Andre &Cie SA v Tradax Export SA* [1983] 1 Lloyd's Rep. 254 *per* Kerr L.J. at 258 cols 1–2) with those involved being the 'cognoscenti in this recondite field' (*Tradax Export SA v Cook Industries Inc* [1982] 1 Lloyd's Rep. 385 *per* Kerr L.J. at 387 col. 2).

[10] A Grain and Feed Trade Association cif contract which provided for English law to be the proper law of the shipping contract and for arbitration of the issues arising from the shipping contract to take place in London.

[11] The involvement of a company at more than one point in the string would create a 'circle': that is, the process restarting albeit at a different buying/selling price.

[12] The Notice of Appropriation had to be a particular form, defects in which led to particular issues of waiver arising — as to which see *Waiver — Types and Effects* at para. 4.26 and *Sale of Goods and Shipping* paras 20.13–15.

2.41 In mid-1973, the US Department of Commerce embargoed the shipment of soya bean from the US except for those goods afloat or in the course of being loaded. The embargo was then followed by the introduction of a licensing system. Therefore, soya bean exports were limited to a fraction of that which they had been with little or no prospect of the restrictions being relaxed. The only readily available source of soya bean was the soya bean cargoes afloat, known as the loophole cargoes. The loophole cargoes represented a fraction of the total soya bean cargoes which had already been sold by forward delivery. Therefore, a seller in the string, D, was in the difficult position of having to find soya bean from the loophole cargoes to meet its obligation to the next purchaser in the string, E. Once D had found a loophole cargo, D had a choice. D could probably satisfy one of its purchasers in one string from that cargo. However, D could not satisfy the other purchasers in other strings as well. Therefore, D could only perform its obligation to one party by deliberately not choosing to perform its obligations to others. Further, with regard to those other purchasers, D could not, on traditional principles, argue that the contract had been frustrated, as D had chosen not to perform the contract even though the choice had arguably arisen from *force majeure* or a frustrating event.

2.42 In considering these difficulties, the courts appeared to come to a number of differing conclusions. First, in two cases[13] the courts held that D could properly perform his obligation to the buyer if he delivered less than the contractual amount, if D had

> contractual commitments to more than one buyer under contracts in identical terms save as to price and quantity, and where without actionable fault on his part he has insufficient goods available to supply all his buyers

and D distributed his goods *pro rata* among all the buyers.[14] Mr Justice Goff rationalized the ability to pro rate as follows:

> . . . in the absence of any term to the contrary, the buyer under a contract containing such a clause must contemplate that the seller has other customers besides himself, and must also contemplate that the seller will take reasonable steps to fulfil the needs of other customers . . . [15]

[13] *Westfalische Central Genossenschaft GmbH v Seabright per* Goff J. (as he then was) unrep. but cited in *Bremer Handelsgessellschaft mbH v Continental Grain* [1983] 1 Lloyd's Rep. 269.

[14] See *Bremer* above *per* Mustill J. (as he then was) at 280 col. 2.

[15] *Seabright* above in *Bremer* at 292.

Secondly, the House of Lords in *Bremer Handelsgesellschaft mbH v Vanden Avenne Izegem PVBA*[16] appeared to suggest that pro rating was one form of performance but it might also be possible for the seller to perform in any reasonable way and still not be in breach.[17] However, the House of Lords formally left the question open by stating that, on the facts of that case, pro rating did not arise.[18] A small shipment of 90 tonnes was at issue and to require pro rating would have left each buyer with a *de minimis* quantity of soya bean meal and was '*destructive of commercial reality*'.[19] Thirdly, and by way of contrast, in *Pancommerce v Veecheema*[20] Lord Donaldson M.R. stated:

> There is no English authority justifying the proposition that where a seller has a legal commitment to A and a non-legal moral commitment to B and he can honour his obligation to A or B but not to both, he is justified in law in potentially honouring both obligations.[21]

From those conclusions, it is relatively, strongly arguable that the parties' obligations were altered by reason of the circumstances. D, the seller, could supply less goods than he had contracted to supply and the other parties to the contract were, it appears, obliged to accept that lesser performance as proper performance. It would appear therefore that the contract had been varied. That variation took place in order to preserve the contract in face of a potentially frustrating event. Although it would appear that these cases are anomalous, with none of the requirements for a variation being satisfied, we would submit that the better view is that these cases do fall within the law as it applies to variation. If one adopts Mr Justice Goff's analysis that the parties are deemed to have agreed to act as commercial men; commercial men in those particular circumstances agreed to vary the agreements as and when commercially appropriate. These cases are therefore akin to the agreement to vary cases referred to above. Thus, the courts spelt out, from the particular trading conditions, an agreement to pro rated or reasonable performance in the event of an embargo. Put another way, where **2.43**

---

16 [1978] 2 Lloyd's Rep. 109.

17 *ibid. per* Lord Wilberforce at 115 col. 1. See also *Intertradex SA v Lesieur-Torteaux SARL* [1978] 2 Lloyd's Rep. 509 at 513; *Bremer Handelsgesellschaft mbH v C Mackprang Jr (No. 1)* [1979] 1 Lloyd's Rep. 221 at 224, 228 and *Continental Grain Export Corp v STM Grain Ltd* [1979] 2 Lloyd's Rep. 378 at 473.

18 [1978] 2 Lloyd's Rep. 109 *per* Lord Wilberforce at 115 col. 1 and *per* Lord Salmon at 128 col. 2.

19 *Per* Lord Russell at 131.

20 [1983] 2 Lloyd's Rep. 304.

21 *ibid.* at 307 col. 1.

commercial circumstance dictated, the contracts were of necessity varied.

It follows from the above that these cases are not, on one view, anomalous. However, a further difficulty arises as to whether they lay down any rule of general application. In *Bremer* Mr Justice Mustill's (as he then was), decision was clearly premised on there being a series of identical contracts. If that is right, then the doctrine of variation by necessity would be of limited application. However, it does not appear that the doctrine is to be so limited. Thus, for example, the obligation to perform a 'standard' bipartite supply contract will be altered if there is a shortage of the relevant goods even where there is no string of identical contracts.[22] Further, it may be possible in certain circumstances for a party to suspend the performance of its obligations. Thus, in *Lawrence v Twentiman*,[23] a builder contracted to build a house within a certain period. However, before that period had started and throughout the period, the area in which the house was to be built was badly affected by plague. The court held that the obligation to build the house was suspended whilst the plague affected the area. Whilst it is doubtful that there is an established doctrine of suspension in English law,[24] *Lawrence* does suggest that the doctrine of variation by necessity is not to be confined to multi-party international trade contracts. **2.44**

We would therefore tentatively submit that a nascent doctrine of variation by necessity is present in English law. Further, the existence of such a doctrine would make practical and commercial sense for two reasons. First, in the face of unforeseen events, parties are often faced with the stark, difficult choice of either performing a contract which has materially changed from the bargain originally entered into or alleging that the contract has been frustrated.[25] Where the parties to **2.45**

---

[22] See *Sainsbury Ltd v Street* [1972] 1 WLR 834; and also *Tennants (Lancashire) Limited v CS Wilson & Co* [1917] AC 495 at 511–2 where Viscount Haldane suggested that there might be lawful pro rata performance of a supply contract.

[23] 1 Rolle's Abridgement Conditions G at p. 10 (p. 450) cited in *Hall v Wright* (1858) EB & E 746, 120 ER 688 at 758, 790, 693.

[24] It is clear that there is no right to suspend performance in the light of another party's breach — see *Channel Tunnel Group v Balfour Beatty* [1992] 1 QB 655 at 666; *Terkol Rederierne v Petroleo Brasilero SA (The Badagry)* [1985] 1 Lloyd's Rep. 395 at 399 and *Canterbury Pipelines v Christ Church Drainage* [1979] NZLR 347. However, query whether a distinction may be drawn between suspension in response to breach as opposed to suspension in the face of a potentially frustrating event.

[25] See, *e.g. British Movietonenews Ltd v London and District Cinemas* [1952] AC 166 at 185. See also 'Non-Contractual Arrangements for the Modification of Performance: Forbearance, Waiver and Equitable Estoppel' H.K. Lucke [1991] 2 *UWALR* 149 at 151–2.

the contract are two experienced commercial entities, it seems unnecessary to put the parties to that choice if some mechanism can be created for preserving their contract and allowing for some flexibility. Secondly, there is little logical reason for drawing a distinction between the Mississippi Flood cases and other, albeit less factually complex, commercial transactions.

Chapter 3

WAIVER(I) TERMINOLOGY

DIFFICULTIES IN DEFINING THE TERM

Although '*Waivers appear in almost every area of law and in connection with almost every type of legal right*',[1] commentators and the courts have found giving a precise meaning to the term difficult concluding that it is 'vague',[2] 'imprecise',[3] 'not a term of art',[4] 'flexible'[5] and covers 'a variety of situations'[6] or 'a multitude of sins'.[7] This difficulty no doubt led the editor of Spencer Bower[8] to conclude: **3.01**

> The truth is, perhaps, that whereas a fairly successful attempt may be made to state with precision what is meant by 'estoppel' and by 'election', the term 'waiver' when used in a similar connotation is not capable of definition in terms of the authorities

and further to suggest:

> Possibly it may be regarded as usefully describing an end-result; but its application to the process by which that result is brought about is almost inevitably attended with ambiguity as to the essential nature of that process. The term when so employed is used sometimes in one significance and sometimes in another, and the result is that its use has dangers which

---

1 See Edward L Rubin, 'Towards a General Theory of Waiver' *UCLA Law Review* 28 (1981) at 478.

2 See *Ross T Smyth & Co Ltd v Bailey Son & Co* (1940) 164 LT 102 *per* Lord Wright at 106; *Larratt v Bankers & Traders Insurance Co* (1941) 41 SR (NSW) 215 *per* Jordan C.J. at 216.

3 See *The Commonwealth of Australia v Verwayen* (1990) 170 CLR 394 *per* Mason C.J. at 406.

4 See *Banning v Wright* [1972] 1 WLR 972 *per* Lord Reid at 981D–E.

5 See *Mulcahy v Hoyne* (1925) 36 CLR 41 *per* Isaacs J. at 53.

6 See *Mardorf Peach & Co Ltd v Attica Sea Carriers Corporation of Liberia* [1977] AC 850 *per* Lord Wilberforce at 871B–E.

7 Corbin, 'Conditions in the Law of Contract' (1919) 28 *Yale Law Journal* 739 at 754.

8 Spencer Bower at 319–20.

can be avoided only by foregoing it as a useful term when considering either estoppel or election.[9]

One result of such pessimism might be the jettisoning of waiver in favour of a general concept of 'injurious reliance'[10] accompanied by a suggestion that any attempt to define waiver is merely an exercise in semantics.[11] However, we would suggest that such pessimism and its allied arguments should and can be discounted. The fact that the English courts regularly resort to waiver as a mechanism for altering commercial obligations[12] in all types of contractual relations[13] coupled with the need for certainty in the law governing such obligations[14] make it necessary that an attempt should be made to establish '*a firm and definite rule for* [this] . . . *particular class of legal relationship*'.[15] Further, it is submitted that rule and that attempt are not semantic[16] for two reasons. First, the decision whether or not and how to plead waiver will have an effect on the substantive rights and obligations of the parties.[17] Secondly, a continued failure to define what is meant by waiver can only result in further uncertainty which is detrimental to those parties operating in the commercial arena. **3.02**

PROVISOS TO A DEFINITION

There are four provisos to any attempt to define waiver. First, the definition must take account of the historical uses to which the doctrine has **3.03**

9 Spencer Bower at 320.
10 See para. 3.05 below.
11 *The Commonwealth of Australia v Verwayen* (1990) 170 CLR 394 *per* Deane J. at 449 *per* Dawson J at 451. See also *Mavie Fisheries Pty Ltd v Switzerland Insurance Australia Ltd* (1996) 140 ALR 57. *per* Tamberlin J at 79–80.
12 *Tyers v Rosedale* (1873) LR 8 Exch 305 *per* Martin B. at 318.
13 Thus, for example, waiver is applicable to the Crown in contracts to which it is a party — *Sykes v R.* [1939] 3 DLR 585.
14 As to the expressed need for which, see *Scandinavian Trading Tanker Co AB v Flota Petrolera Ecuatoriana ('The Scaptrade')* [1983] 2 AC 694 *per* Lord Diplock at 703E–4G; *Banco Exterior Internacional v Mann* [1995] 1 All ER 936 *per* Hobhouse L.J. at 944b and *Westdeutsche Landesbank Girozentrale v Islington London Borough Council* [1996] 2 All ER 961 *per* Lord Browne-Wilkinson at 987h.
15 See *Maredelanto Compania Naviera SA v Bergbau-Handel GmbH ('The Mihalis Angelos')* [1971] 1 QB 164 *per* Megaw L.J. at 204D–E.
16 See also Arjunan, *Waiver and Estoppel — A Distinction without a Difference? ABLR* 21 (1993) 86 at 87.
17 See *The Commonwealth of Australia v Verwayen* (1990) 170 CLR 394 *per* Toohey J. at 466 and Arjunan, *Waiver and Estoppel — A Distinction without a Difference? ABLR* 21 (1993) 86 at 110.

been put. Those uses were to bypass the doctrine of consideration and to bypass the requirement that contracts be in writing. As to the former, in *Wilson v Kingsgate Mining Industries Pty Ltd*[18] Wootten J. stated:

> A number of doctrines have been formulated separately to mitigate the unjust consequences of a rigorous application of the basic position of English law that a man is bound only by a promise given for consideration or under seal. There are peripheral matters such as the refusal of discretionary remedies on the grounds of laches and acquiescence. The most important doctrines, however, are forbearance, estoppel in pais, promissory estoppel, waiver, election and some cases of approbation and reprobation.[19]

As to the latter, and by way of example, under s. 4 of the Sale of Goods Act 1893, sales of goods contracts worth more than 10 *l* and variations to such contracts had to be in writing to be enforceable.[20] However, parties would frequently alter the terms of the contract orally. Therefore, to prevent one party taking advantage of the formalities rule and suing the other party under the terms of the original contract, the courts tacitly[21] developed the doctrine of waiver.[22] A party could rely on the waiver to defeat the claim made against it, but could not sue on the waiver unless it was in writing.[23] A similar mechanism was adopted in relation to the Statute of Frauds.[24] That historical use has meant that waiver was deployed more as a means to an end than as a free standing doctrine,[25] creating a definition of the term based on such cases and

---

[18] [1973] 2 NSWLR 713.

[19] *ibid.* at 730D–G.

[20] See *Variation* at para. 2.28 ff.

[21] In the US, the courts have explicitly recognized that they are attempting to bypass s. 87A-2–209(4) of the Statute of Frauds — see *Farmers Elevator Co of Reserve v Anderson* 552 P 2d 63 (1976) and *Imperator Realty v Tull* 228 NY 447 (1990).

[22] See *Besseler Waetcher Glover & Co v South Derwent Coal Co Ltd* [1938] 1 KB 408 *per* Goddard J. at 415–16; *Hickman v Hayes* (1875) 10 LR 10 CP 598 *per* Lindley J. at 605 and *Plevins v Downing Co* (1876) 1 CPD 220. In so doing, the courts adopted the procedural rule of *retraxit* by which rights were formally renounced in court 3 *Blackstone's Commentaries* at p. 296.

[23] This explains why the argument succeeds in *Hickman* and not in *Plevins* where, on one view, the party suing had to rely the waiver but see Treitel 1 at pp. 99–101 for an alternative view.

[24] See, *e.g. Cuff v Penn* (1813) 1 M & S 21, 105 ER 8; *Thresh v Rake* (1793) 1 Esp 53, 170 ER 277; *Goss v Lord Nugent* (1833) 5 B & Ad 558, 110 ER 713; *Stead v Dawber* (1839) 10 Ad & E 57; 113 ER 22 and Stoljar, 'The Modification of Contracts' *Canadian Bar Review* 35 (1957) 485 at 494, 497–8.

[25] *Cf.* Stoljar *op. cit.* at 504. A further result was that waiver was a one-sided doctrine with the doctrine of estoppel being developed to protect the waivee *cf.* Stoljar *op. cit.* at 502.

defining waiver in a more modern context where such devices are not necessary can therefore prove difficult.

Secondly, the term has been '*indiscriminately used by the Courts as means of relieving parties from bargains or the consequences of bargains which are thought to be harsh or deserving of relief*'[26] or '*to prevent a man in certain circumstances from taking up two inconsistent positions*'.[27] Therefore, again 'waiver' may more often describe an end which is achieved rather than the process by which that end is achieved.[28] Further, it may well be that the underlying rationale for the courts' decisions has not been juridical analysis but a view of the merits of the case and an attempt to achieve a just result in light of those merits. Thus, although it is possible to analyse the extent to which those conclusions were justified on the facts of the case, drawing conclusions of principle from such cases proves difficult. **3.04**

Thirdly, to avoid defining waiver, estoppel, election, affirmation and, potentially, variation, the courts have relied on broad formulations of single all-inclusive principles. Thus, an overarching doctrine has been posited so that: **3.05**

> If the defendant, as he did, led the plaintiffs to believe that he would not insist on the stipulation as to time, and that, if they carried out the work, he would accept it, and they did it, he could not afterwards set up the stipulation as to the time against them. Whether it be called waiver or forbearance on his part or an agreed variation or substituted performance does not matter. It is a kind of estoppel. By his conduct he evinced an intention to affect their legal relations. He made, in effect, a promise not to insist on his strict legal rights. That promise was intended to be acted upon and was in fact acted upon. He cannot afterwards go back on it.[29]

Similarly, reference has been made to a 'general principle' loosely based on the doctrine of estoppel[30] and the idea that:

> The rule that neither party can rely on his own failure to communicate accurately to the other party his own real intention by what he wrote or

---

[26] *Mardorf Peach & Co Ltd v Attica Sea Carriers Corporation of Liberia* [1977] AC 850 *per* Lord Wilberforce at 871B–E.

[27] *Craine v Colonial Mutual Fire Insurance Co* (1920) 28 CLR 305 *per* Isaacs J. at 326.

[28] See *Commonwealth of Australia v Verwayen* (1990) 170 CLR 394 *per* Mason J. at 406.

[29] *Charles Rickards Ltd v Oppenhaim* [1950] 1 KB 616 *per* Denning L.J. at 623.

[30] The principle of 'injurious reliance' is closer to estoppel than waiver because estoppel operates only where detrimental reliance has occurred whereas there is no such requirement in waiver cases.

> said or did, as negativing consensus ad idem, is an example of a general principle of English law that injurious reliance on what another person did may be a source of legal rights against him. I use the broader expression "injurious reliance" in preference to "estoppel" so as to embrace all circumstances in which A can say to B: "You led me reasonably to believe that you were assuming particular legally enforceable rights to me . . ."[31]

The result of both approaches is, it is submitted, to generate further confusion in this difficult area; the courts still recognizing that there are differences between the doctrines but on occasion applying them as if they were one and the same doctrine.[32] Notwithstanding that criticism, we would suggest that any definition of waiver must acknowledge the existence and effect of both approaches on this area of the law.

Fourthly, we would suggest that any definition of waiver must **3.06** recognize that as a matter of practice it may be easier to describe the results of the application of the doctrine, that a party is precluded from a particular course of action, than to describe the elements which comprise the doctrine. That fact gives the doctrine of waiver the flexibility set out above. However, it also means that the doctrine of waiver could be described as 'context specific' or even 'parasitic' on other doctrines.[33] Again it is difficult to give waiver a precise definition in principle in isolation from the facts and the other doctrines.

DEFINITION

We would therefore suggest that a preliminary definition of waiver can **3.07** be arrived at by using two interdependent methods — a process of exclusion, identifying the circumstances in which the courts have drawn a distinction between waiver and some other doctrine; and a process of inclusion, identifying the circumstances in which the courts have found that there was a waiver. Those circumstances can then be used to analyse the elements which constitute the doctrine.

[31] *Paal Wilson & Co A/S v Partenreederei Hannah Blumenthal* [1983] 1 AC 854 *per* Lord Diplock at 916A–C.

[32] See *Wilson v Kingsgate Mining Industries Pty Ltd* [1973] 713 *per* Wootten J. at 730D–G where the court recognized the tendency to create and apply one doctrine but emphasized that there remained clear differences between the doctrines.

[33] See Carter para. 1042.

The Exclusionary Process

Waiver can simply be distinguished from variation. It is a distinction which, in principle,[34] the courts have consistently drawn: **3.08**

> Waiver does not vary the terms of the contract . . . Waiver is conduct on the part of a party to a contract which affects his remedies for a breach of contract by the other party[35]

further holding that variation is '*wholly distinct from the doctrine of forbearance...*'.[36] The maintenance of that distinction would accord with the fact that a waiver is unsupported by consideration,[37] whereas a variation requires consideration in some form or another;[38] the fact that variation requires there to be offer and acceptance,[39] whereas waiver may not; the fact that the parties by varying the contract can restrict their ability to waive requirements of that contract;[40] and the fact that variation will affect the substantive performance by both parties under the contract as opposed merely affecting the remedies[41] which one party can seek in relation to breach of the contract.[42] Thus, although a party may be forced to accept different performance under the contract by virtue of a waiver, the obligations under the contract have not in fact

[34] In practice, the distinction may be less easy to draw; the practical results of applying the two doctrines may be indistinguishable — see *Watson v Healy Lands Ltd* [1965] NZLR 511 *per* Woodhouse J. at 513, 11 10–20.

[35] *Enrico Furst & Co v WE Fischer Ltd* [1960] 2 Lloyd's Rep. 340 *per* Devlin J. at 349 col. 2–350 col. 1.

[36] *Levey & Co v Goldberg* [1922] 1 KB 688 *per* McCardie J. at 690. See also *Impala Distributors v Taunus Chemical Manufacturing Co (Pty) Ltd* (1973) (3) SA 273; *Van As v du Preez* 1981 (3) SA 760 and *Waimor Holdings Ltd v Dean* [1981] 2 NZLR 416.

[37] Stoljar, 'The Modification of Contracts' *Canadian Bar Review* 35 (1957) 485 at 492.

[38] See *Variation* at para. 2.15 ff.

[39] See *Variation* at para. 2.14.

[40] See *SN Kurkjian (Commodity Brokers) Ltd v Marketing Exchange for Africa Ltd* [1986] 2 Lloyd's Rep. 614 at 615 col. 2; the parties could, for instance, vary the contract to introduce a 'no-waiver' agreement — see *Insurance* at para. 19.71 and *Banking Law* at para. 15.20.

[41] Even where the courts have found that a particular waiver had contractual status, it was still only an '*agreement to release or not to assert a right*' *Nippon Menkwa Kabushiki Kaisha (Japan Cotton Trading Company Ltd) v Dawsons Bank Ltd* (1935) 51 Ll L R 147 *per* Lord Russell at 150 col. 2.

[42] Thus even in cases of unilateral or pure waiver which may operate *in futuro* (see *Waiver — Types and Elements* at para. 4.27–35 below), the waivor is foregoing its remedies where the waivee proffers different performance at the later date.

changed. As Mr Justice Mustill (as he then was), pointed out in *Cook Industries Inc v Meunerie Legois SA*:[43]

> It may seem a paradox to assert that even if, by virtue of a waiver, the sellers could properly tender July bills of lading in fulfilment of a June instalment, it does not follow that the contract became one under which the obligation to ship in June was replaced by one which required the sellers to ship or procure shipment in June or July. I am not convinced however that this is a paradox, nor to my mind is it clear that the question of waiver (which is relevant to the liability of the buyers for a refusal to accept an appropriation) is the same as the question of variation (which is relevant to the liability of the sellers for failing to effect or procure a timely shipment)[44]

Drawing the distinction between waiver and 'estoppel' appears to cause more difficulty.[45] In *Kammins Ballroom Co. v Zenith Investments*[46] Lord Diplock stated: **3.09**

> 'Waiver' is a word which is sometimes used loosely to describe a number of different legal grounds on which a person may be debarred from asserting a substantive right which he once possessed or from raising a particular defence to a claim against him which would otherwise be available to him. We are not concerned in the instant appeal with the first type of waiver. This arises in a situation where a person is entitled to alternative rights inconsistent with one another. If he has knowledge of the facts which give rise in law to these alternative rights and acts in a manner which is consistent only with his having chosen to rely on one of them, the law holds him to his choice even though he was unaware that this would be the legal consequence of what he did. He is sometimes said to have 'waived' the alternative rights . . . but this is better categorised as 'election' rather than as 'waiver' . . . . The second type of waiver which debars a person from raising a particular defence to a claim against him arises when he either agrees with the claimant not to raise that defence or so conducts himself as to be estopped from raising it . . . The ordinary principles of estoppel apply to it.[47]

---

[43] [1981] 1 Lloyds Rep. 359.

[44] *ibid. per* Mustill J. *ibid.* at 368 col. 2–369 col. 2. Compare the early cases of waiver where the doctrine was considered to be akin to accord and satisfaction — *Cuff v Penn* (1813) 1 M l S 21 *per* Lord Ellenborough C.J. at 27; *Moore v Campbell* (1854) 10 Ex 323 per Parke B at 333. See the discussion as to whether a waiver irrevocably changes the terms of the contract in *Waiver — Complexities* at para. 5.02.

[45] See *Free Grammar School of John Lyon v Mayhew* (1997) HLR 219 for a recent example of this difficulty.

[46] [1971] AC 850.

[47] *ibid.* at 882H–3D.

Kammins was applied in *Motor Oil Hellas (Corinth) Refineries SA v Shipping Corporation of India ('The Kanchenjunga')*.[48] There, Lord Goff relied on *Kammins* in discussing the principles underlying the doctrine of 'election'[49] and stated:

> Election is to be contrasted with equitable estoppel . . . There is an important similarity between the two principles, election and equitable estoppel, in that each requires an unequivocal representation, perhaps because each may involve a loss, permanent or temporary, of the relevant party's rights. But there are important differences as well. In the context of a contract, the principle of election applies when a state of affairs comes into existence in which one party becomes entitled to exercise a right, and has to choose whether to exercise the right or not. His election has generally to be an informed choice, made with the knowledge of the facts giving rise to the right. His election once made is final; it is not dependent upon reliance on it by the other party. On the other hand, equitable estoppel requires an unequivocal representation by one party that he will not insist upon his legal rights against the other party, and such reliance by the representee as will render it inequitable for the representor to go back upon his representation. No question arises of any particular knowledge on the part of the representor, and the estoppel may be suspensory only. Furthermore, the representation itself is different in character in the two cases. The party making his election is communicating his choice whether or not to exercise a right which has become available to him. The party to an equitable estoppel is representing that he will not in future enforce his legal rights. His representation is therefore in the nature of a promise which, though unsupported by consideration, can have legal consequences; hence it is sometimes referred to as promissory estoppel.[50]

It follows that there is powerful authority for contrasting waiver, in the sense of waiver by election, with all forms of 'estoppel' creating a simple twofold categorization. However, on balance, we would suggest that this twofold categorization is too simplistic. By suggesting that all cases where a party loses its rights are either a waiver by election or an estoppel, Lord Goff omits those categories of waiver which are not waiver by election. It is further submitted that, although it may be **3.10**

---

48 [1990] 1 Lloyd's Rep. 391.

49 See *Election, Affirmation and Acquiescence passim* below

50 *Motor Oil Hellas (Corinth) Refineries SA v Shipping Corporation of India ('The Kanchenjunga')* [1990] 1 Lloyd's Rep. 391 *per* Lord Goff at 399 col. 2. For a discussion of the relationship between the two cases see *Waiver — Types and Elements* para. 4.06 below.

difficult to give a precise definition to such a wide-ranging doctrine,[51] 'estoppel' proper can be distinguished from all types of waiver[52] by reference to the basic principles underlying the doctrine. Thus:

> When its true foundations are stated, it will be seen that estoppel is separated from waiver in point of principle by a very broad line of demarcation. First of all, the law of estoppel looks chiefly at the situation of the person relying on the estoppel; next, as a consequence of the first, the knowledge of the person sought to be estopped is immaterial; thirdly as a further consequence, it is not essential that the person sought to be estopped should have acted with any intention to deceive; fourthly conduct short of positive acts is sufficient.[53]

As well as distinctions of basic principle, other distinctions can be drawn. **3.11**
A waiver[54] will only operate in a contractual context whereas an estoppel or equitable forbearance may operate where the parties are not in a contractual relationship.[55] As set out below, it is clear that waiver in all senses involves the abnegation of contractual rights and therefore can only come into play where there is a contract between the parties. Further, it may be possible for a party to claim that the other is estopped by silence or inaction where the other was under a duty to inform that party of certain facts and did not.[56] As set out below,[57] waiver in any form requires a clear unequivocal representation by words or conduct, silence or inaction do not suffice. Finally, a claim relying on an estoppel may permit equity to intervene on other grounds to assist the party raising the estoppel.[58] A claim in waiver will succeed or fall on its own terms and does not lead to the general intervention of equity. We would therefore suggest that waiver is certainly to be distinguished from variation and, albeit with more difficulty, from estoppel/equitable forbearance.

---

51 See 12.24–7 below.
52 Including this second type.
53 *Craine v Colonial Mutual Fire Insurance Co* (1920) 28 CLR 305 *per* Isaacs J. at 327.
54 Whether a waiver by election, a pure waiver, a unilateral waiver or a total waiver.
55 See *Evenden v Guildford City FC* [1975] QB 917 *per* Denning M.R. at 924B–C; *Waltons Stores (Interstate) Ltd v Maher* (1988) 164 CLR 387 *per* Deane J. at 399–406; *The Commonwealth of Australia v Verwayen* (1990) 170 CLR 394 *per* Mason C.J. at 410.
56 See *Pacol Ltd & ors v Trade Lines and R/I Sif IV ('the Henrik Sif')* [1982] 1 Lloyd's Rep. 456 *per* Webster J. at 465 col. 2.
57 See *Waiver — Types and elements* at para. 4.44 ff.
58 See *BICC v Burndy* [1985] Ch 232 *per* Kerr L.J. at 253B–C.

THE INCLUSIONARY PROCESS

From the above, it is clear that the courts have utilized two broad categories of 'waiver'.[59] The first, we would suggest, is waiver in the proper sense of the word. The second is Lord Goff's second category, a hybrid which may have elements in common with waiver and estoppel proper but capable of distinction from both. Given the concept's hybrid nature, we would suggest that this second category be termed equitable forbearance.[60] There is forbearance as rights are foregone, however, as there is reliance by the other party on that forbearance, equity intervenes to protect the other party.[61] **3.12**

Waiver in the true sense of the word can be crudely described as 'a voluntary or intentional relinquishment of a known right,[62] claim or privilege'.[63] On a more complex level, we would suggest that there are four types of waiver. The first and main type is waiver by election. There are, however, three additional types of waiver. These can be best described by the situations in which they occur: where X has not been put to its election but, nevertheless, decides to accept different future performance by Y under the contract ('pure waiver');[64] where Y has failed to perform its obligations under the contract and X accepts that non-performance as proper performance under the contract foregoing X's right to repudiate **and** to sue for damages ('total waiver';)[65] and X's foregoing of a right under the contract which inures solely for X's benefit ('unilateral waiver').[66] **3.13**

---

[59] See also *State Trading Corporation of India v Compagnie Francaise D'Importation et de Distribution* [1983] 2 Lloyd's Rep. 679 *per* Lloyd J. at 681 col. 2; *Telfair Shipping Corporation v Athos Shipping Co SA* [1981] 2 Lloyd's Rep. 74 at *per* Neill J. at 87 col. 2 — 88 col; [1983] 1 Lloyd's Rep. 127, CA *per* Kerr L.J. at 134 col. 2 and *Craine v Colonial Mutual Fire Insurance Co* (1920) 28 CLR 305 *per* Isaacs J. at 326.

[60] See Treitel 1 p. 100 ff., and *Waiver — Types and elements* at para. 4.10 below and following. However, a full analysis of equitable forbearance falls outwith the scope of this chapter and is dealt with in *Equitable Forbearance passim.*

[61] See Hudson at para. 1.255.

[62] The rights foregone can be legal or equitable — see J Glover, *Commercial Equity: Fiduciary Relationships* (Butterworths, Sydney, 1995) at paras 3.29–30, pp. 46–7.

[63] See *Northwestern Fire & Marine Insurance Co v Pollard* 238 P 594 at 596; *Hoxie v Howe Insurance Co* 32 Conn 21 (1864); *Clark v West* 193 NY 349 (1908); *Acetylene Gas Co v Oliver* 939 S.W. 2d 404 (1996); *Majernicek v Hartford Cas Ins Co* 688 A.2d 1330 (1997); *State v Crabtree* 482 S.E. 2d 605; *Flipps Nine, Inc v Missouri Property and Gas Insurance Guarantee Association* 941 S.W. 2d 564 (1997); *Breeden v Breeden* 678 N.E. 2d 423 (1997) and *F.D.I.C. v U.S. Fire Insurance Co* 956 F. Supp. 701.

[64] As to which see *Waiver — Types and elements* at para. 4.26.

[65] See *Waiver — Types and elements* at para. 4.28.

[66] See *Waiver — Types and elements* at para. 4,34.

Adopting this categorization has four main benefits. First, it enables distinctions to be drawn between the type of defective performance being excused.[67] Secondly, it allows for an analysis of the extent to which the waivor's remedies are lost.[68] Thirdly, by outlining four related categories of waiver and one of equitable forbearance, it draws a broad distinction between those cases where there is reliance by one party on the other's actions and those where there is not. The latter, cases in which the courts have examined the conduct and knowledge of one party alone, are examples of the four related categories of waiver and not examples of equitable forbearance. Fourthly, while it might be said that the practical results of the application of any of the doctrines will be the same, a party loses its rights, the position is clarified so that a party wishing to avoid losing its rights may be able to moderate its actions to achieve that end. 3.14

[67] Whether past or future.
[68] Total waiver as opposed to waiver by election and pure waiver.

Chapter 4

WAIVER (II) TYPES OF WAIVER AND THEIR ELEMENTS

WAIVER BY ELECTION

In *Kammins Ballroom Co. v Zenith Investments*,[1] Lord Diplock stated that the fundamental requirement of waiver by election is that X, the party alleged to have waived a right,[2] has made an election in the sense that: **4.01**

> where a party in his own mind has thought that he would choose one of two remedies, even though he has written it down in a memorandum or has indicated it in some other way, that alone will not bind him; but so soon as he has not only determined to follow one of his remedies but has communicated it to the other side in such a way as to lead the opposite party to believe that he has made that choice, he has completed his election and can go no further; and whether he intended it or not, if he has done an unequivocal act — I mean an act which would be justifiable if he had elected one way and would not be justifiable if he had elected another way — the fact of his having done that unequivocal act to the knowledge of the persons concerned is an election.[3]

A number of points follow. First, election[4] and waiver are intimately linked[5] so that '*The consequence of the election, if established, is the*

---

1 [1971] AC 850.

2 For the purposes of the analysis in this chapter we refer at all times to the party who is waiving the right as X and the other party to the contract as Y.

3 *Scarf v Jardine* (1882) 7 App Cas 345 *per* Lord Blackburn at 360–1.

4 Election in the sense used by us encompasses equitable and common law election — see *Election, Affirmation and Acquiescence* at para. 7.03.

5 See *Van Schalkwyk v Griesel* 1948 (1) SA 460 *per* Tindall J.A. at 463; *contra. Ex p Sussen* 1941 TPD 15 *per* Murray J. at 20.

abandonment, i.e. the waiver, of a right'.[6] Secondly, waiver by election is a reaction on the part of X to non-contractual performance by Y; that is to previously defective performance or a refusal to perform by Y under the contract.[7] Thirdly, a waiver by election will curtail the remedies which X may have arising out of the conduct complained of; X will not be allowed to repudiate the contract.[8] Therefore, this type of waiver:

> applies to an election as to something in futuro; it is not a term to describe an answer to a right which is complete in praesenti.[9]

It follows that waiver by election cannot affect X's complete and accrued right to damages.[10] Fourthly, as with election,[11] the primary function of waiver by election is to prevent there being inconsistency in the manner in which a party to a contract asserts its rights. Waiver by election therefore ensures that X does not 'approbate and reprobate' the contract.[12] Fifthly, the analogy or link with election assists the analysis of the elements required to found a waiver by election.

ELEMENTS OF WAIVER BY ELECTION

The leading analysis of waiver by election is that of Lord Goff in *Motor Oil Hellas (Corinth) Refineries SA v Shipping Corporation of India ('The Kanchenjunga')*.[13] The facts of the case were as follows. Under a charterparty dated 8 August 1978, the owners chartered the vessel *The Kanchenjunga* for four consecutive voyages subject to a warranty given **4.02**

---

6 *China National Foreign Trade Transportation Corporation v Evlogia Shipping Co SA of Panama* [1979] 1 WLR 1018 *per* Lord Scarman at 1034H.

7 A distinction is therefore to be drawn between waiver by election which is retrospective and pure waiver which waives the future performance of a particular obligation. Waiver by election does include, however, X's reaction to Y's anticipatory breach (as to which see *Stocznia v Latvian Shipping Co.* [1997] 2 Lloyd's Rep. 228; Treitel 'Affirmation after Repudiatory Breach' (1998) 114 *LQR* 22).

8 See *Enrico Furst & Co v WE Fischer Ltd* [1960] 2 Lloyd's Rep. 340 *per* Devlin J. at 349 col. 2–350 col. 1.

9 *Atlantic Shipping and Trading Co Ltd v Louis Dreyfus & Co* [1922] 2 AC 250 *per* Lord Sumner at 262.

10 This conclusion is also supported by logic — if X were to elect in a particular way (for instance to accept the non-contractual performance as proper performance) X might forego any right to damages that it might have.

11 As to which see *Commonwealth of Australia v Verwayen* (1990) 170 CLR 394 *per* Brennan J. at 423.

12 See *Craine v Colonial Mutual Fire Insurance Co* (1920) 28 CLR 305 *per* Isaacs J. at 320.

13 [1990] 1 Lloyd's Rep. 391.

by the charterers as to the safety of any port which the vessel might visit. The charterers then sub-chartered the vessel to Varnima Chartering Compania Naviera SA. The sub-charterers, on 19 November 1980, sub-sub-chartered the vessel for one voyage from one or two safe ports to Refineria de Petroleos del Norte SA (Petronor). One of the nominated safe ports was Kharg Island in the Gulf. On 20 November, the charterers ordered the vessel to Kharg Island, the order being repeated on 21 November. At the time, however, due to the Iran-Iraq war, Kharg Island had been bombed on more than one occasion by Iraq. Therefore, Kharg Island arguably was not a safe port. On 21 November, the owners instructed the vessel to proceed to Kharg Island and it arrived on 23 November giving notice of readiness to load on that date. On 25 November, the owners ordered the vessel away from Kharg Island on the basis that Kharg Island was not a safe port. This was the first indication by the owners that they did not consider the nominated port to be safe and therefore that the safe port warranty in the main charterparty had not been complied with. However, the vessel remained where it was. By 1 December, the vessel still had not reached its berth at Kharg Island and Kharg Island was bombed. The master of the vessel then took the vessel away from Kharg Island. The owners then called on the charterers to nominate another safe port but the charterers insisted on Kharg Island. The owners then instructed vessel to Kharg Island and the master refused. As a result there was a failure to load the vessel and the charterers suffered loss and damage.

The dispute proceeded to arbitration where the arbitrators found that Kharg Island could not at any time be said to have been a safe port. **4.03**
Therefore the charterers, in theory, had acted in breach of contract in nominating Kharg Island and insisting that *The Kanchenjunga* berth at Kharg Island. That finding of the arbitrators therefore inevitably lead to a consideration of whether the owners' conduct constituted an election or estoppel. The arbitrators rejected the charterers' argument that there had been an election or estoppel and the charterers appealed, the case eventually reaching the House of Lords.

Lord Goff found that there had been an election on the part of the **4.04**
owners by their instruction to the vessel to proceed to Kharg Island. He analysed the position as follows:

> 'waiver' . . . may refer to a forbearance from exercising a right or to an abandonment of a right. Here we are concerned with waiver in the sense of abandonment of a right which arises by virtue of the party making the election. Election itself is a concept which may be relevant in more than one context. In the present case, we are concerned with an election which may arise in the context of a binding contract, when a state of affairs

comes into existence in which one party becomes entitled, either under the terms of the contract or by the general law, to exercise a right, and he has to decide whether or not to do so. His decision, being a matter of choice for him, is called in law an election . . . . Characteristically, the effect of the new situation is that a party becomes entitled to determine or to rescind the contract, or to reject an uncontractual tender of performance; but, in theory at least, a less drastic course of action might become available to him, under the terms of the contract. In all cases, he has in the end to make his election, not as a matter of obligation, but in the sense that, if he does not do so, the time may come when the law takes the decision out of his hands, either by holding him to have elected not to exercise the right which has become available to him, or sometimes by holding him to have elected to exercise it . . . In particular, where with knowledge of the relevant facts a party has acted in a manner which is consistent only with his having chosen one of the two alternative and inconsistent courses of action then open to him — for example, to determine a contract or alternatively to affirm it — he is held to have made his election accordingly . . . It can be communicated to the other party by words or conduct; though, perhaps because a party who elects not to exercise a right which has become available to him is abandoning that right, he will only be held to have done so if he has so communicated his election to the other party in clear and unequivocal terms . . . Once an election is made, however, it is final and binding . . . Moreover, it does not require consideration to support it, and so it is to be distinguished from an express or implied agreement, such as a variation of the relevant contract, which traditionally requires consideration to render it binding in English law.[14]

Lord Goff made one additional point, he stressed that a waiver by election could only properly exist where X at least had knowledge of the facts giving rise to his choice.[15] It follows that two elements must be present for there to be a waiver by election: an unequivocal representation by X in relation to the right allegedly being waived and at least knowledge by X of the facts which show that it has to choose between two inconsistent courses of conduct. **4.05**

It has been suggested[16] that Lord Goff's analysis differs from that of Lord Diplock in *Kammins*. On one level Lord Diplock distinguishes between waiver and estoppel by pointing out that waiver is the choice **4.06**

[14] [1990] 1 Lloyd's Rep. 391 at 397 col. 2–398 col. 2.

[15] *ibid* at 398 col. 2–399 col. 1.

[16] See Clarke at para. 26–4A2 for this analysis.

between rights whereas estoppel is the loss of a defence.[17] Lord Goff, on the other hand, may be said to distinguish between waiver and estoppel by reference to the breaches which have led to the rights which X is allegedly losing. Waiver relates to past breaches; estoppel/equitable forbearance to the excusing of future non-performance. The difficulty with this analysis is that it reduces all forms of waiver to waiver by election; that is, to X's reaction to a past repudiatory breach. Further, complications in the relationship between waiver and estoppel are created. If waiver only relates to past breaches and a waiver takes place, it becomes impossible for there to be a waiver and an estoppel/equitable forbearance arising from the same facts; X's rights will be altered by the waiver and there will be nothing for an alleged estoppel to bite on.[18] However, it appears that a waiver can lead to an estoppel/equitable forbearance.[19] One way of resolving this difficulty is to distinguish between waiver and estoppel/equitable forbearance by reference to the fact that estoppel/equitable forbearance is based on the actual or potential detriment suffered by Y.[20] In this way the elements of the relevant doctrines are examined and potentially difficult questions of the relationship between the loss of rights and the loss of defences are avoided. Further, it is suggested that, on this level, there is no inconsistency between Lord Diplock and Lord Goff.

Unequivocal representation

An election must be communicated or conveyed[21] to the other party,[22] 4.07
therefore X's waiver by election must also be communicated to Y.

---

[17] See *The Athos* [1981] 2 Lloyd's Rep. 74 *per* Neil J. at 87–8; *Cia Tirrena di Assicurazioni SpA v Grand Union Insurance Co* [1991] 2 Lloyd's Rep. 143 *per* Waller J. at 153 compared with *The Scaptrade* [1983] QB 529 *per* Goff L.J. at 536 and *Janred Properties Ltd v ENIT* [1989] 2 All ER 444.

[18] A similar difficulty may arise if waiver is confined to an accepting of different future performance as again it is X's rights arising from Y's change of position which are being waived — see Stoljar, 'The Modification of Contracts' *Canadian Bar Review* 35 (1957) 485 at 491; compare 3 *Corbin on Contracts* (1951) s 752.

[19] See, *e.g. Ficom SA v Sociedad Cadex Limitada* [1980] 2 Lloyd's Rep. 118 *per* Goff J. at 132 col. 2. Further a waiver, equitable forbearance or estoppel may arise from the same facts allowing one claim to succeed and the other to fail — see *Commonwealth of Australia v Antonio Giorgio Pty Ltd* (1986) 67 ALR 244.

[20] That is the analysis in *Craine v Colonial Mutual Fire Insurance Co* (1920) 28 CLR 305 *per* Isaacs J. at 326.

[21] *Vitol SA v Norelf Ltd* [1996] 3 WLR 105 *per* Lord Steyn at 113B–14E.

[22] See *Election, Affirmation and Acquiescence* at para. 7.04 and cases there cited. See

Further, as election is an unequivocal act, the communication must be unequivocal.[23] However, X's waiver does not have to be orally communicated, provided that there has been an election,[24] a waiver by election can be implied from X's conduct. Thus:

> A party can represent that he will not enforce a specific legal right by words or conduct. He can say so expressly – this of course he can only do if he is aware of the right. Alternatively he can adopt a course of conduct which is inconsistent with the exercise of that right. Such a course of conduct will only constitute a representation that he will not exercise the right if the circumstances are such to suggest either that he was aware of the right when he embarked on the course of conduct inconsistent with it or that he was content to abandon any rights that he might enjoy which were inconsistent with that course of conduct.[25]

Conduct required

It is important to note that even though a waiver may be spelled out from conduct, that conduct must be unequivocal in the true sense of the word. The conduct must be capable of one construction only, namely that X has chosen to forego its rights. Thus, examples of unequivocal conduct will include: agreeing in advance that X will not exercise specific rights which might accrue on breach;[26] an insist- **4.08**

also *David Blackstone v Burnetts (West End) Ltd* [1973] 1 WLR 1487 *per* Swanwick J. at 1499C *Sargent v ASL Developments Ltd* (1974) 131 CLR 634 *per* Mason J. at 656; *Newbon v City Mutual Life Assurance Society Ltd* (1935) 52 CLR 723 *per* Rich, Dixon, Ewatt J.J. at 733; *Khoury v Government Insurance Office of NSW* (1984) 165 CLR 622 *per* the court at 633 and *Zucker v Straightlace Pty Ltd* (1986) 11 NSWLR 87 *per* Young J. at 94F–6E.

23 See *Finagrain SA Geneva v P Kruse Hamburg* [1976] 2 Lloyd's Rep. 508 *per* Megaw L.J. at 534 col. 1; *Mardorf Peach & Co Ltd v Attica Sea Carriers Corp of Liberia* [1977] AC 850 *per* Lord Wilberforce at 871C; *Bremer Handelsgesellschaft v C Mackprang Jr* [1979] 1 Lloyd's Rep. 221 *per* Stephenson L.J. at 228; *Avimex SA v Dewulf & Cie* [1979] 2 Lloyd's Rep. 57 *per* Goff J. at 67 col. 2–68 col. 1; *Sea Calm Co SA v Chantiers Navals de L'Esterel SA ('The Uhenbels')* [1986] 2 Lloyd's Rep. 294 *per* Hirst J. at 298 col. 1. See also *Berry v Hodsdon* [1989] 1 Qd R 361 *per* Derrington J. at 365; *Hawler Pacific Pty Ltd v Helicopter Charter Pty Ltd* (1991) 22 NSWLR 298 *per* Priestley J.A. at 304 and *Spelson v George* (1992) 22 NSWLR 666 *per* Handley J.A. at 672.

24 *Tropical Traders Ltd v Goonan* (1964) 111 CLR 41 *per* Kitto J. at 55.

25 *Youell & Ors v Bland Welch & Co Ltd & ors ('The 'Superhulls Cover' Case) (No. 2)* [1990] 2 Lloyd's Rep. 431 *per* Phillips J. at 450 col. 1. See also *Bremer Handelsgesellschaft mbH v Westzucker GmbH* [1981] 1 Lloyd's Rep. 207 *per* Goff J. at 212 col. 2 and *Cerealmangimi SpA v Toepfer ('The Eurometal')* [1981] 1 Lloyd's Rep. 337 *per* Lloyd J. at 341 col. 2.

26 Thus, for example, X can, by prior agreement, waive any rights accruing from a

ence after breach that Y continue to perform the contract;[27] X's voluntary[28] acceptance after breach of benefits arising from the contract;[29] commencing an action for specific performance only;[30] and obtaining an order for specific performance.[31] By parity of reasoning, claiming damages and specific performance in the alternative or requesting that Y perform the contract pending X's review of Y's conduct[32] are not sufficiently unequivocal.

Two difficulties arise: whether silence or delay can amount to a waiver and whether X's reservation of its rights will in all cases protect it from a finding that it has waived its rights. **4.09**

Silence or delay

There is authority to suggest that silence, delay or a failure to act can constitute a sufficiently unequivocal representation so as to found waiver.[33] However, in both cases the court stated that X had 'waived' its rights because Y had suffered prejudice as a result.[34] It is submitted **4.10**

---

breach of fiduciary duty by Y — see J Glover, *Commercial Equity: Fiduciary Relationships* (Butterworths, Sydney, 1995) paras 3.29–30, pp. 46–7.

27 See *Trustees of Henry Smith's Charity v Wilson* [1983] QB 316 *per* Slade L.J. at 331; and also *O'Connor v SP Bray Ltd* (1936) 36 SR (NSW) 248 *per* Jordan C.J. at 261 and *Holland v Wiltshire* (1954) 90 CLR 409. This would embrace anticipatory breach by Y — see *Stocznia v Latvian Shipping Co.* [1997] 2 Lloyd's Rep. 228; Treitel 'Affirmation after Repudiatory Breach' (1998) 114 *LQR* 22.

28 See *Metcalfe v Britannia Ironworks Co* (1877) 2 QBD 423 *per* Lord Coleridge C.J. at 427 and *Forman & Co Pty Ltd v The Ship Liddesdale* [1900] AC 190 *per* Lord Hobhouse at 204.

29 See *Davenport v R.* (1877) 3 App Cas 115; *R. v Paulson* [1921] 1 AC 271 *per* Lord Atkinson at 286; *Fuller's Theatre v Musgrove* (1923) 31 CLR 524 *per* Isaacs and Rich J.J. at 541; *Mulcahy v Hoyne* (1925) 26 CLR 41 *per* Starke J. at 57; *Wendt v Bruce* (1931) 45 CLR 245; *Tropical Traders Ltd v Goonan* (1964) 111 CLR 41 *per* Kitto J. at 42; *Sargent v ASL Developments Ltd* (1974) 131 CLR 634 and *Expert Clothing Service & Sales Ltd v Hillgate House Pty Ltd* [1986] Ch 340 *per* Slade L.J. at 359D.

30 *Ogle v Comboyuro Investments Pty Ltd* (1976) 136 CLR 444. The claim must be for specific performance alone, *i.e.* not for specific performance and damages in lieu.

31 See *Johnson v Agnew* [1980] AC 367.

32 See *Insurance* at para. 19.45.

33 See *Allen v Robles* [1969] 1 WLR 1193 *per* Fenton-Atkinson L.J. at 1196G–H and *Wahbe Tamari & Sons and Jaffa Trading Co v Colprogeca-Sociedade General de Fibras, Cafes e Produtos Colonias Lda* [1969] 2 Lloyd's Rep. 18 *per* Megaw J. at 23 col 1.

34 See, also *Becker v Sunnypine Park Pty* 1982 (1) SA 958 *per* Goldstone J. at 965. Thus, it is not the immediate failure by X to elect which leads to the loss of rights but a delay such as to trigger some detriment to Y — see *Crabb v Gleeson* [1920] VLR 189; *Owendale Pty Ltd v Anthony* (1967) 117 CLR 539 *per* Windeyer J. at 557 and *Turner v Labafox International Pty Ltd* (1974) 131 CLR 660 *per* Mason J. at 671.

that in fact both cases were, therefore, decided on estoppel/equitable forbearance principles, namely Y's detriment, rather than on a finding that X made unequivocal representation foregoing its rights. It follows that the better view is that silence, delay or a failure to act cannot form an unequivocal representation such that X will be held to have waived its rights.[35]

Reservation of rights

By a reservation of rights,[36] X seeks to preserve the rights it possesses. That must be an unequivocal representation that it is not making its election. Therefore, common sense and logic would suggest that an express reservation of rights would defeat any suggestion of waiver by X.[37] In the main, we would suggest that is a correct approach. However, there are two caveats to the above. **4.11**

First, the fact that X has reserved its rights in one regard will not protect X in relation to other rights which might be waived. Thus, if X reserves its rights in relation to late in delivery of goods which are also defective, X may be taken to have waived its rights in relation to the defects in the goods.[38] Secondly, there is authority to suggest that a reservation of rights cannot protect X from a finding that it has waived its rights.[39] Those authorities adopt three approaches to the issues. First, where the Court has concluded that X in reserving its rights and calling for performance under the contract has acted inconsistently, the court has been reluctant to allow X the benefit of that inconsistency.[40] **4.12**

---

[35] *Selwyn v Garfit* (1888) 38 ChD 273. See also (by analogy to affirmation) *Aaron's Reefs v Twiss* [1896] AC 273; *Oelkers v Ellis* [1914] 2 KB 139; *Leaf v International Galleries* [1950] 2 KB 86 and *Oscar Chess v Williams* [1957] 1WLR 370.

[36] We do not consider here the use of 'non-waiver' agreements, *i.e.* agreements entered into before breach or any right of election arises, as such, agreements are confined, by and large, to and have effect in, sophisticated commercial agreements between experienced parties — see, *e.g. Insurance* at para. 19.71 and *Banking* at para. 15.20.

[37] See *Finagrain SA Geneva v P Kruse Hamburg* [1976] 2 Lloyd's Rep. 508 *per* Roskill L.J. at 541 col. 2; *Cook Industries Inc v Meunerie Legois SA* [1981] 1 Lloyd's Rep 359 *per* Mustill J. at 368 col. 1; *Peter Cremer v Granaria BV* [1981] 2 Lloyd's Rep 583 *per* Goff J. at 590 col. 1 and *Nichimen Corporation v Gatoil Overseas Inc* [1987] 2 Lloyd's Rep 46 *per* Sir John Megaw at 56 col. 2.

[38] Provided that X has knowledge of the defects.

[39] See *Bremer Handelsgesellschaft mbH v C Macprang JR* [1979] 1 Lloyd's Rep. 221 *per* Lord Denning M.R. at 225 col. 1–2.

[40] See, *e.g. Oceanic Freighters Corporation v MV Libyaville Reederei und Schiffahrts* GmbH [1975] 1 Lloyd's Rep. 537 *per* Mocatta J. at 554; *Bremer v Macprang* above *per* Shaw L.J. at 230 col. 2–231 col. 1; *Finagrain v Kruse above per* Mocatta J. at 525 col. 1. See also *Croft v Lumley* (1856) 5 E & B 648 at 652; *Davenport v R.*

Secondly, it has been suggested that waiver is a 'conclusion of law' reached by the courts when the necessary facts are established.[41] If so, then the court can find that there has been a waiver notwithstanding X's protestations to the contrary and override the reservation of rights. Thirdly, in certain cases, the courts appear to have been reluctant to allow X to evade the provisions of the contract where it would be unmeritorious[42] or impracticable[43] for it do so.

It is submitted that all three approaches should be treated with caution. **4.13**
On one analysis, if an unequivocal representation is required to found a waiver, the only way in which a reservation of rights cannot preserve X's position is if the court were to conclude, on the particular facts of the case, that the reservation of rights was a sham, X intending it to have little or no effect. On that view, the first two approaches would be legitimate and would apply in extreme cases. The alternative analysis would be to view these cases as in fact cases on estoppel/equitable forbearance where it might be arguable that a reservation of rights would not protect X.[44]

Knowledge

Whether or not knowledge is required to found a waiver by election **4.14**
can be broken down into four related questions: is knowledge of the facts giving rise to the right to elect required? Is knowledge of the right itself required? And can either of the above forms of knowledge be imputed to X?[45] Is an intention to waive one's rights required?

Is knowledge of the facts required?

Lord Diplock in *Kammins* clearly envisaged that there could only be waiver **4.15**
by election where X has knowledge of the facts underlying the choice which

(1877) 3 App Cas 115 *per* Sir Montague E Smith at 132; *Stone v Stringer* (1880) 61 LT 470; *R. v Paulson* [1921] 1 AC 271 *per* Lord Atkinson at 286; *Haynes v Hirst* (1927) 27 SR (NSW) 480 *per* Long Innes J.; *Carter v Green* [1950] 2 KB 76; *Antaios Naviera SA v Salen Rederierna AB* [1983] 1 WLR 1362 *per* Lord Donaldson M.R.1370H–1C and *per* Fox L.J. at 1377 A–C.

41 See *Craine v Colonial Mutual Fire Insurance Co* (1928) 28 CLR 305 *per* Isaacs J. at 326.

42 *Bremer v Macprang per* Lord Denning M.R. at 225 cols 1–2; 226 col. 1.

43 *Antaios Naviera SA v Salen Rederierna AB* [1983] 1 WLR 1362 *per* Lord Donaldson M.R. at 1370H–1371C; *per* Fox L.J. 1377 A–C.

44 As to which see 12.20.

45 'Imputed' does not connote in this context the imputation of knowledge to a company or principal via its employee or agent.

it is required to make.[46] In *Bremer Handelsgesellschaft mbH v Vanden Avenne-Izegem PVBA*,[47] however, Lord Salmon, in considering notices, provided under cl. 22 of the GAFTA 100[48] contract[49] stated that the buyers by their conduct '*necessarily waived any defect* . . . [the notice] *might contain whether they were aware of it or not*'[50] thereby suggesting that knowledge was not a requirement for at least certain types of waiver.

It is submitted that the better view is that at least knowledge of the facts is required for a number of reasons. First, the courts have repeatedly held that a waiver by election requires knowledge.[51] Thus, in *Matthews v Smallwood*,[52] Mr Justice Parker stated that the law on the subject was 'reasonably clear' before going on to state that: **4.16**

> Waiver of a right of re-entry can only occur where the lessor, with knowledge of the facts on which his right to re-enter arises, does some unequivocal act recognizing the continued existence of the lease. It is not enough that he should do an act which recognizes, or appears to recognize, the continued existence of the lease, unless, at the time when the act is done, he has knowledge of the facts under which, or from which, his right of entry arose. Therefore we get the principle that, though an act of waiver operates with regard to all known breaches, it does not operate with regard to breaches which were unknown to the lessor at the time when the act took place.[53]

Matthews was expressly approved by the House of Lords[54] and is of general application.[55] On the other hand, Lord Wilberforce stated in

---

46 *Kammins Ballrooms Co Ltd v Zenith Investments (Torquay) Ltd* [1971] AC 850 at 883B–C.

47 [1978] 2 Lloyd's Rep. 109.

48 The Grain and Feed Trade Association contract; the provisions of which are considered in more detail at *Variation* at paras 2.39 ff.

49 See para. 4.26 below for a further consideration of the case.

50 *Bremer Handelsgesellschaft mbH v Vanden Avenne-Izegem PVBA* [1978] 2 Lloyd's Rep. 109 at 127 col. 1.

51 See *Earl of Darnley v Proprietors of London, Chatham and Dover Railway* (1867) LR 2 HL 43 *per* Lord Chelmsford L.C. at 57 'A waiver must be an intentional act with knowledge.' More recently see *Bristol and West Building Society v Mothew* [1996] 4 All ER 698 *per* Millett L.J. at 703a–b, 704 where a plea of waiver unsupported by any allegation of X's knowledge was held not to amount to a defence to an application for summary judgment under RSC Ord 14.

52 [1910] 1 Ch 777.

53 *ibid.* at 786.

54 *Fuller's Theatre and Vaudeville Co v Rofe* [1923] AC 435 *per* Lord Atkinson at 443.

55 See, *e.g.* *Craine v Colonial Mutual Fire Insurance Co* (1920) 28 CLR 305 a case on insurance law in which *Matthews* was applied — see also *Aquis Estates Ltd v Minton* [1975] 1 WLR 1452 at 1458E.

Bremer that he felt that the case raised no points of principle.[56] If *Bremer* was intended to cast doubt on the principle set out in *Matthews* and *Kammins*, it would be reasonable to expect that the House of Lords would have made that clear and not overturned the principle by a 'side-wind'. Secondly, on analysis, we would suggest that Lord Salmon was in fact considering equitable forbearance and therefore did not lay down any rules in respect of waiver by election.[57] Thirdly, as pointed out above, for X to elect, X must have knowledge of the facts creating his rights. If waiver is the consequence of election,[58] it would be anomalous if knowledge were required for one and not the other. Finally, waiver is a limited mechanism by which the courts have bypassed the need for consideration. Given the courts' reluctance to 'emasculate'[59] the doctrine of consideration, it would be natural for the courts to impose a requirement that would act as a substitute for consideration and limit the application of waiver. Knowledge, like consideration, would suggest that X intended the unequivocal representation to have legal effect. Thus, knowledge is a suitable substitute for the doctrine of consideration.[60]

Is Knowledge of the right required?

Although it is therefore reasonably clear that knowledge of the facts is required to found a waiver by election, what is less clear is whether X must also be aware of the *right* to elect or indeed whether knowledge or an intention to waive can be imputed to X. This point was considered at length in *Peyman v Lanjani*.[61] **4.17**

The facts of *Peyman* are complex. In brief, the case concerned the entry into a lease of a restaurant and flats by the first defendant and the subsequent assignment of that lease to the plaintiff by the first defendant. **4.18**

[56] *Bremer Handelsgesellschaft mbH v Vanden Avenne — Izegem PVBA* [1978] 2 Lloyd's Rep. 109 at 116 col. 2.

[57] See para. 4.26 below.

[58] As to which see *Waiver — Terminology* at 3.09; *Election, Affirmation and Acquiescence* at para. 7.04 and cases there cited. See also *Thomas v Henry* 1985 (3) SA 889 *per* Van Heerden J.A. at 896.

[59] *Drexel Burnham Lambert International NV v Mohamed Schaker Salim Abou el Nasr and Establissement Abou Nasr el Bassatni* [1986] 1 Lloyd's Rep. 356 *per* Staughton J. at 366 col. 2.

[60] Similarly, in equitable forbearance, the requirements that Y relied on the representation and that it would be inequitable for X to resile would also act as substitutes for the doctrine of consideration — see 12.08 and 12.52.

[61] [1985] 1 Ch 457.

As the lessors were two of Imperial Tobacco Plc's pension companies, the lease was subject to covenants restricting assignment. The first defendant, an Iranian who spoke no English and of 'scruffy appearance,'[62] doubted that the landlords would assign title to the restaurant to a person like him, therefore, to procure entry into the lease by the lessors, the first defendant arranged for his impersonation by a Mr Moustashari at all meetings with the landlords. Further, that deception was repeated to persuade the lessors to consent to the assignment to the plaintiff. The plaintiff was aware of the impersonation but not of its effects, being advised by the second defendant, his solicitor, that the impersonations need not give him cause for concern.[63] However, the result of the impersonation was that the first defendant's title to the lease was defective and therefore the assignment from the first defendant to the plaintiff was null and void. When the plaintiff, via his new solicitors, discovered this fact, he rescinded the contract for the assignment and left the property. In the subsequent litigation, the defendants argued that the plaintiff had knowledge of the facts which would have entitled him to repudiate the contract at an very early stage and therefore the plaintiff had waived the defects in the assignment. The judge at first instance agreed and the plaintiff appealed on this point to the Court of Appeal.

On these facts, the Court of Appeal addressed two questions, the first of which was whether X was required to have knowledge of the right to elect.[64] This question in essence turned on whether Lord Diplock's statement in *Kammins*[65] that: **4.19**

> If he has knowledge of the facts which give rise in law to these alternative rights and acts in a manner which is consistent only with his having chosen to rely on one of them, the law holds him to his choice even though he was unaware that this would be the legal consequence of what he did[66]

had the result that X was not required to have knowledge of the right to elect. Lord Justice Stephenson considered that it did not. Relying on *Coastal Estates Pty Ltd v Melevende*[67] and authorities relating to the waiver of statutory rights,[68] he concluded that Lord Diplock was in

---

[62] *ibid.* at 464F–G *per* Stephenson L.J.
[63] *ibid.* at 481B *per* Stephenson L.J.
[64] [1985] 1 Ch 457 *per* Stephenson L.J. at 482C.
[65] [1971] AC 850.
[66] *ibid.* at 883B–C; see para. 4.09.
[67] [1965] VR 433.
[68] *Young v Bristol Aeroplane Co Ltd* [1946] AC 163 at 176 and *Evans v Bartlam* [1937] AC 473 at 479.

fact merely stating that X does not need to know that the court may treat the consequences of his election as irrevocable.[69] Further, relying on the analogy or link with election,[70] Lord Justice Stephenson went on to emphasize that common principles applied to waiver by election notwithstanding the particular area in which the doctrine was operating[71] before stating:

> I therefore feel free . . . to hold that knowledge of the facts which give rise to the right to rescind is not enough to prevent the plaintiff from exercising that right, but he must know that the law gives him the right yet choose with that knowledge not to exercise it.
>
> The Plaintiff can therefore rely on his own unchallenged ignorance of the law, unless he is precluded from doing so either by what he has done or by his solicitor's knowledge of the law. Those decisions lay down what a person in his position must know before he loses his right to rescind; they do not go far into what he must not do if he is to keep the right, or what the effect on it of his having legal advice may be.[72]

Lord Justice Stephenson's conclusions were supported by Lord Justice May and Lord Justice Slade. Both Lord Justices were concerned to emphasize that a distinction had to be drawn between the principles which would apply in estoppel and those which would apply in election. Further, it is clear that both Lord Justices were using the term 'election' to cover 'waiver by election' drawing a category distinction between estoppel or 'waiver by conduct' which required there to be detriment and the type of 'election' at issue in *Peyman*.[73] Further, Lord Justice Slade suggested that if Y alleges in its pleadings that X is precluded from relying on a right as a result of an election (and therefore pleads out a waiver by election), Y must plead that X had knowledge of the right to rescind[74] and if necessary particularize that allegation.[75] It would follow, *prima facie*, that *Peyman* is clear authority for the proposition that knowledge of the right to elect is required. **4.20**

However, the decision in *Peyman* is not without difficulty. Although the case has not been expressly distinguished or overruled, the House of **4.21**

---

69 [1985] 1 Ch 457 at 486G.
70 See para. 4.01 above and *Election, Affirmation and Acquiescence* at para. 7.01 and *ibid*. at 487C.
71 *ibid*. at 487C–E.
72 *ibid*. at 487F–H.
73 *ibid*. *per* May L.J. at 493G–H; *per* Slade L.J. 500D–E.
74 *ibid*. at 500H–1B.
75 Under RSC Ord. 18, r. 12(4), a party is not required to particularize the facts and matters on which it relies in support of an allegation that the other party knew a fact unless and until it is requested to do so by the other party.

Lords in *The Kanchenjunga*[76] left the question open.[77] Further, in *Bliss v South East Thames Regional Health Authority*[78] Lord Justice Dillon in response to a submission that based on *Peyman* a party had to have knowledge of its rights before a waiver by election could be found stated:

> This is a formidable argument, and the acceptance of it could have considerable repercussions in employment law. But I do not find it necessary to express any opinion on it in the present case . . . [79]

Additionally, the authority relied on in *Peyman* as supporting at least Lord Justice Stephenson's view of the requirements to found a waiver, *Coastal Estates Pty Ltd v Melevende*,[80] has been impliedly doubted and not followed in subsequent Australian cases.[81] Either of those two facts would suggest that *Peyman* goes too far in requiring there to be knowledge of the right to elect. Further difficulties may arise from the practical effect of the decision in *Peyman*. Outside commercial transactions, in a great many cases the parties will not be legally advised[82] and therefore it will be very difficult to say that X was aware of its rights. As Lord Justice Dillon pointed out, that could have considerable ramifications by considerably curtailing the circumstances in which the courts will find that there has been a waiver of rights.

Notwithstanding the above, we would suggest that *Peyman* is correctly decided and that for there to be a waiver, X must have knowledge both of the facts and the rights consequent on those facts.[83] That this point has been left open in other, subsequent cases at the appellate level does **4.22**

---

[76] [1990] 1 Lloyd's Rep. 391.

[77] *ibid.* at 398 col. 2.

[78] [1987] ICR 700.

[79] *ibid.* at 717F–G. As to the application of waiver to the employment context see *Employment* at paras 18.13 ff.

[80] [1965] VR 433.

[81] See *Sargent v ASL Developments Ltd* (1974) 131 CLR 634; *Khoury v Government Insurance Office of New South Wales* (1984) 165 CLR 622; *Zucker v Straightlace Pty Ltd* (1986) 11 NSWLR 87 at 93 and *Hill v Canberra Centre Holdings Ltd* (1995) 122 FLR 434.

[82] Therefore, there will be no presumption that they know of their rights — *Peyman* [1985] 1 Ch 457 *per* Stephenson L.J. at 487D.

[83] In *Insurance Corporation of the Channel Islands v The Royal Hotel Ltd* (unrep. 30/7/97 Comm Ct) Mr Justice Mance explicitly adopted this test. See also *National Insurance and Guarantee Corp Plc v Imperio Reinsurance Co (UK) Ltd* (unrep. 30/9/97 Comm Ct Colman J). Put colloquially, 'the penny must drop' when X becomes aware of the facts.

not affect the correctness of the decision. In any event, there is long-standing authority to support the approach adopted in *Peyman.*[84] Further, the proposition that *Coastal Estates v Melvende*[85] has been doubted in subsequent Australian cases, is itself not without difficulty. It may well be that there is a long-standing rule in Australia that knowledge of the right is not required,[86] however, it is also clear that the courts will examine X's knowledge of its rights in certain contexts to ascertain whether X's conduct was sufficiently unequivocal.[87] That examination is only explicable if X's knowledge of its rights is an element of waiver. Finally, as a matter of principle, there is no reason why X should be prejudiced by having a waiver found where X was ignorant of its rights. That would be contrary both to logic (how else can X be said to have made a choice unless X is aware that there is a choice to be made) and to relationship between waiver by election and election. As for Y, if Y has neither relied on X's conduct nor suffered any detriment, there is no reason why Y should be able to argue that X is precluded from exercising its rights. Put another way, if Y has suffered by its reliance on X's conduct (which was suggestive of a waiver by election), Y could be protected by pleading and proving that there had been an equitable forbearance of X's rights or that X was estopped from asserting those rights.

Can knowledge be imputed so as to found a waiver?

This was the second question considered in *Peyman.* There the court reformulated the issue into two further questions: did X's conduct '*amount to an affirmation of his contract, an abandonment of his right to rescind?*' and '*Is he precluded, or estopped, by his conduct from denying that he has abandoned his contract?*'[88] The court answered those questions by considering X's intention and whether **4.23**

---

[84] See *Vyvyan v Vyvyan* (1861) 30 Beav 655, 54 ER 813 and *Kendall v Hamilton* (1879) 4 App Cas 504 *per* Lord Blackburn at 542. More recently, see *Simner v New India Assurance Co* [1995] LRLR 240 *per* Judge Diamond Q.C. at 258 col. 2.

[85] [1965] VR 433.

[86] See, *e.g. O'Connor v SP Bray Ltd* (1936) 36 SR (NSW) 248 *per* Jordan C.J. at 262–4 and *Elder's Trustee and Executor Co Ltd v Commonwealth Homes and Investment Co Ltd* (1941) 65 CLR 603 *per* Rich A.C.J. Dixon, McTiernan J.J. at 617–8.

[87] *Sargent v ASL Developments Ltd* (1974) 131 CLR 634 *per* Stephen J. at 643–6 and *Elder's Trustee and Executor Co Ltd v Commonwealth Homes and Investment Co Ltd* (1941) 65 CLR 603 *per* Rich A.C.J.; Dixon, McTiernan JJ. at 618.

[88] [1985] 1 Ch 457 *per* Stephenson L.J. at 488A–B.

or not X's intention was to be objectively or subjectively ascertained[89] then deciding:

> Waiver or election is always a question of intention to be decided on the evidence as a question of fact . . . In fact and law men's intentions must be judged by their actions, and a man's acts may convey to any reasonable person standing in the shoes of the other party to a contract, as clearly as any words, an intention to repudiate or affirm the contract. If the other party, relying on acts having the latter effect, suffers detriment or prejudice, there is unequivocal, and irrevocable, affirmation.[90]

The court therefore appeared to fuse four separate issues: was there an affirmation, was there an estoppel, what was the relevance of X's intention and can intention be deduced from X's conduct.

It follows that the court in *Peyman* did not give a clear answer to the question. However, the court's reformulation of the question and its subsequent analysis suggest that the court came to the conclusion that whether or not knowledge could be imputed was relevant in one of two ways. First, the issue was relevant to the question of whether X's conduct was sufficiently unequivocal to found either a waiver by election or equitable forbearance.[91] Put another way, the more unequivocal X's conduct was, the more likely (in real terms) it would be that Y would rely on it and the more likely it is that X intended to elect in the manner suggested by the conduct. That the question was analysed in terms of waiver by election and equitable forbearance would suggest that the Court of Appeal was concerned with the elements common to both. Direct and actual knowledge is not, on any view, required to found an equitable forbearance[92] but is required for waiver. By contrast, inferred knowledge is relevant to equitable forbearance where Y seeks to spell out the appropriate unequivocal promise from X's conduct.[93] Put simply, the Court of Appeal's analysis **4.24**

---

89 [1985] 1 Ch 457 *per* Stephenson L.J. at 488C.

90 *ibid. per* Stephenson L.J. at 488C–D

91 *ibid. per* Stephenson L.J. at 491C. In *Insurance Corporation of the Channel Islands v The Royal Hotel Ltd* (unrep. 30/7/97 Comm Ct) Mr Justice Mance adopted this view. See also *National Insurance and Guarantee Corp Plc v Imperio Reinsurance Co (UK) Ltd* (unrep. 30/9/97 Comm Ct Colman J). For Commonwealth support of this view see *Sargent v ASL Developments Ltd* (1974) 131 CLR 634 *per* Stephen J. at 645–6 and *Elder's Trustee and Executor Co Ltd v Commonwealth Homes and Investment Co Ltd* (1941) 65 CLR 603 *per* Rich A.C.J., Dixon, McTiernan JJ. at 618.

92 Due to its links to estoppel, equitable forbearance looks to the conduct of X and its effect on Y, X's knowledge is strictly speaking irrelevant.

93 See *Equitable Forbearance* at paras 12.26–7.

was directly relevant to equitable forbearance only. It therefore appears that the Court of Appeal was in fact considering equitable forbearance and not setting out the principles which should apply to waiver by election. Secondly, and related to the first point, by the reference to estoppel and reliance, the court appeared to suggest that if Y has to rely on imputed knowledge, Y should put its case on the basis of an equitable forbearance not waiver by election.[94] It is therefore submitted that although the decision is unclear, the Court of Appeal decided that imputed knowledge was not sufficient to found a waiver by election. We would submit that such a decision was correct and would make practical sense as where, for instance, X is being deliberately obtuse as to its rights, Y will be protected by equitable forbearance.

Is an intention to waive rights required?

Peyman appears to suggest that an intention to waive rights will always be required[95] and it is implicit in the finding that there was an *unequivocal* representation that X must be taken by its conduct to have intended to waive its rights. There is, it is submitted, nothing objectionable in such a requirement. However, we would suggest that it does not follow that X's *subjective* intention is a necessary element of waiver.[96] Such a requirement would run contrary to the established rule that a party's intention is to be objectively deduced from its conduct.[97] **4.25**

---

[94] The primary thrust of Y's case would then be based on Y's actions in response to X's conduct.

[95] [1985] 1 Ch 457 *per* Stephenson L.J. at 488C–D.

[96] At least in English and Australian law. Compare *Palmer v Poulter* 1983 (4) SA 11 *per* Ackerman J. at 20; *Thomas v Henry* 1985 (3) SA 889 at 898; *Boyer v American Casualty Company* 332 F 2d 708 (1964) *per* Smith C.J. at 711; *Richmond v Grabowski* 781 P 2d 192 (1989); *Shane v WCAU-TV, CBS Televisions, Div of CBS Inc* 719 F Supp 353 (1989); *Lone Mountain Production Co v Natural Gas Pipeline Co of America* 710 F Supp 305 (1989); contra *Community Convalescent Center of Naperville Inc v First Interstate Mortgage Co of Illinois* 537 NE 2d 1162; app denied 545 NE 2d 106 (1989); *Ebrahimi v EF Hutton & Co Inc* 794 P 2d 1015 (1989) which suggest that the position is less clear in other jurisdictions.

[97] *Tropical Traders v Goonan* (1964) 111 CLR 41 *per* Kitto J. at 55; *Watson v Healy Lands Ltd* [1965] NZLR 511 *per* Woodhouse J. at 514 ll 33–5; *Central Estates (Belgravia) Ltd v Woolgar (No. 2)* [1972] 1 WLR 1048 at 1052, 1054, 1056; *Sargent v ASL Developments* (1974) 131 CLR 634 *per* Stephen J. at 646; *Champtaloup v Thomas* [1976] 2 NSWLR 264 *per* Glass J.A. at 268E; but see *Earl Darnley v London, Chatham & Dover Rly Co (Properties etc)* (1867) LR 2 HL 43 at 47 for the contrary view.

EXAMPLES OF WAIVER BY ELECTION

Typical examples of waiver by election will include:[98] where X waives the right to forfeit a lease[99] or, in a sale of goods contract, Y delivers late or makes it clear by its conduct that it will not deliver timeously and X does not repudiate the contract,[1] or X and Y have agreed that payment for the goods will be in a particular form and Y tenders payment which is accepted in a different form,[2] or Y fails to serve appropriate notices under the contract and X accepts those notices as good notwithstanding the defects in them.[3] **4.26**

PURE WAIVER

Pure waiver can be summed up as '*the unilateral divesture of certain rights*'[4] or: **4.27**

---

[98] For further examples see *Wallis, Son & Wells v Pratt & Haynes* [1911] AC 394; *Bowes v Chaleyer* (1923) 32 CLR 159; *Wendt v Bruce* (1931) 45 CLR 245 at 253; *Hain Steamship Co Ltd v Tate and Lyle Ltd* (1936) 41 Comm Cas 350; *Tramways Advertising Pty Ltd v Luna Park NSW Ltd* (1938) SR (NSW) 632 *per* Jordan C.J. at 644; *Chandris v Isbrandtson-Moller Co Inc* [1951] 1 KB 240 *per* Devlin J. at 248; *Carr v JA Berriman Pty Ltd* (1953) 89 CLR 327 *per* Fullagar J. at 349; *Gange v Sullivan* (1966) CLR 418; *Suisse Atlantique Société d'Armement Maritime SA v NV Rotterdamsche Kolen Centrale* [1967] 1 AC 361 *per* Viscount Dilhorne at 395B and *Compagnie de Renflouement de Recuperation et de Travaux Sous Marins VS Baroukh et Cie v W Seymour Plant Sales & Hire Ltd* [1981] 2 Lloyd's Rep. 466 *per* Mustill J. at 482 col. 2.

[99] See *Telfair Shipping Corporation v Athos Shipping Co SA* [1981] 2 Lloyd's Rep. 74 *per* Neill J. at 87 col. 2; *Owendale Pty Ltd v Anthony & Or* (1967) 117 CLR 539 *per* Windeyer J. at 556; *Matthews v Smallwood* [1910] 1 Ch 777 *per* Parker J. at 786 and *Fuller's Theatre and Vaudeville Co v Rofe* [1923] AC 435 *per* Lord Atkinson at 443.

[1] See, *e.g. Charles Rickards* v *Oppenhaim* [1950] 1 KB 616 (on its facts as opposed to the analysis of waiver set out in the case). See also *Stocznia v Latvian Shipping Co.* [1997] 2 Lloyd's Rep. 228 for the corollary of the refusal to supply — the refusal to pay.

[2] See, *e.g.* the facts as set out in *Ficom SA v Sociedad Cadex Limitada* [1980] 2 Lloyd's Rep. 118 *per* Goff J. at 131 col. 2; *Panoutsos v Raymond Hadley Corporation of New York* [1917] 2 KB 473 *per* Bailhache J. at 475; *Cape Asbestos v Lloyd's Bank* [1921] WN 274 *per* Bailhache J. at 276 and *Nichimen Corporation v Gatoil Overseas Inc* [1987] 2 Lloyd's Rep. 46.

[3] See, *e.g. Bremer Handelsgesellschaft mbH v Vanden Avenne-Izegem PVBA* [1978] 2 Lloyd's Rep. 109 and *Bunge GmbH v Alfred C Toepfer* [1978] 1 Lloyd's Rep. 506.

[4] See *Commonwealth of Australia v Verwayen* (1990) 170 CLR 394 *per* Brennan J. at 423.

> the abandonment of a right in such a way that the other party is entitled to plead the abandonment by way of confession and avoidance if the right is thereafter asserted.[5]

The only distinction between pure waiver and waiver by election is that X has not been put to its election. Therefore, X can expressly or by its conduct suggest that Y need not perform its future obligations under the contract. There is no need for Y to have acted in breach of the contract.[6] Put another way, waiver by election is in the main retrospective and pure waiver is prospective. Thus, where X and Y had contracted for Y to arrange primary and mezzanine financing for the purchase of ships by X, and X, having obtained primary finance through Y, intimated to Y that no further meetings between X and Y were necessary, the court held that X had waived the future performance by Y of its obligations under the contract. Y could therefore claim all its fees under the contract notwithstanding the fact that mezzanine finance had not been obtained.[7] Put another way, the pure waiver will amount to a 'dissolution *pro tanto* of the [particular] contractual tie between the parties'[8] with both parties retaining their accrued obligations[9] but being discharged from the *future* performance of particular obligations under the contract.

The circumstances in which pure waiver will occur will be few. This **4.28**
is because in most cases for X or Y's conduct to be sufficiently serious to merit the costs and risks associated with litigation, there will either have been a breach by X or Y of the contract or Y will have suffered significant detriment. The former case would fall under the rubric of waiver by election and the latter under equitable forbearance. However, it is submitted that the recognition of the doctrine is important for three reasons. First, the doctrine of election is limited to those circumstances where there has been repudiatory breach of the contract. To suggest that is the sum total of the situations in which waiver will arise would, we suggest, give too narrow a scope for the application of the doctrine of waiver. Thus, there are circumstances where absent repudiation or

---

[5] *Banning v Wright* [1972] 1 WLR 972 *per* Lord Hailsham L.C. at 979C–D.
[6] Hence, the use of the term 'pure waiver'.
[7] *Tufton Associates Ltd v Dilmun Shipping* [1992] 1 Lloyd's Rep. 71 *per* Judge Diamond Q.C. at 80 col. 2.
[8] *Mulcahy v Hoyne* (1925) 36 CLR 41 *per* Isaacs J. at 53.
[9] Namely such of their primary obligations to perform under the contract which have accrued and the secondary obligation to pay damages in respect of the failure to perform the primary obligations — see *e.g. Photo Production Ltd v Securicor* [1980] AC 827 at 849 and *State Trading Corp of India v Golodetz* [1989] 2 Lloyd's Rep. *per* Kerr L.J. at 285–7.

consideration X accepts alternative performance by Y.[10] Secondly, we would suggest that this analysis is the only way to reconcile cases like *Kammins*[11] which are concerned with waiver by election and *Banning v Wright*[12] in which their Lordships spoke of waiver in wider terms than the abandonment of a right to accept the repudiatory breach of the contract by Y.[13] Thirdly, acknowledging the two doctrines is consistent with the fact that in broad terms the courts will prevent a party acting inconsistently in respect of its rights under the contract, each of the doctrines represents a different mechanism for achieving this end.

TOTAL WAIVER

It is trite law that where Y has acted in breach, X can sue for damages and/or treat the breach as repudiatory and treat itself as discharged from further performance under the contract. If a waiver by election precludes X from subsequently treating itself as discharged, in theory it should be possible for X to be precluded by a different type of waiver from claiming damages and from treating itself as discharged. This supposition is supported by s. 11(2) of the Sale of Goods Act 1979 which states that where Y has breached a condition, X may 'waive' the breach *or* elect to treat itself as discharged. In drawing the distinction it appears that Parliament was at least accepting the possibility that X could forego all its rights. This putative loss of all rights has been called a total waiver,[14] terminology which we adopt. **4.29**

4.30 It can be seen from the above that total waiver has much in common with waiver by election, being a reaction to a breach of contract. However, total waiver may also be identical to accord and satisfaction where X's rights arising as a result of breach are compromised by a agreement between X and Y, that agreement being supported by consideration. If that is correct, total waiver would not be a 'waiver' at all being supported by consideration.[15] This difficulty has led to some debate as to whether total waiver exists at all.

[10] See *Tufton* above.
[11] [1971] AC 850 above.
[12] [1972] 1 WLR 972.
[13] *ibid.* at 979.
[14] Treitel 1 at p. 726.
[15] *Mulcahy v Hoyne* (1925) 36 CLR 41 *per* Isaacs J. at 55, 56 and *Orr v Ford* (1989) 167 CLR 316 *per* Deane J. at 337–8.

In *ETS v Soules & Cie International Trade Development Co Ltd*[16] the court considered the submission that the buyer under a cif contract had elected to accept defective documents, that acceptance constituting a total waiver. The court held that the submission was: **4.31**

> wholly untenable. True the buyers could have rejected these documents on each occasion when they were presented. But if they do not reject them, either because (as was the case here) they did not know at the time of the matters which gave rise to invalidity, or because, knowing that they could reject, they nevertheless decide not to do so, there is no basis on which it can be said that merely by electing not to reject the documents they have in any way given up their right to claim damages in respect of whatever damage may have been caused to them by the breach of contract involved in the tendering of wrong documents.[17]

It is noticeable that the court did not reject the possibility of a total waiver in theory, the court merely held that it was not possible to create a total waiver from the acceptance of documents under the contract. It would therefore follow that, in appropriate circumstances, Y might succeed in showing that there had been a total waiver of X's rights.

The difficulty with the above is that in *Kwei Tek Chao & Ors v British Traders and Shippers LD*[18] the court went further and held that for there to be a total waiver there would have to be **4.32**

> a separate agreement binding on the buyer by which he had agreed to surrender the right to damages which automatically vested in him at the time of breach[19]

It would appear from the court's reference to a separate, binding agreement that the court felt that for Y to succeed in alleging that X had waived its right to damages, Y had to show that the contract between X and Y had been varied or that a collateral contract had been entered into.[20] As total waiver cannot be a variation of a contract or a collateral contract as it is unsupported by consideration, *Kwei Tek* would be authority for the proposition that total waiver is nothing more than accord and satisfaction.[21]

On balance, we would suggest that the better view is that set out in **4.33**

---

16 [1980] 1 Lloyd's Rep. 129.
17 *ibid. per* Megaw L.J. at 137 col. 2–138 col. 1.
18 [1954] 2 QB 459.
19 *ibid. per* Devlin J. at 477.
20 See also *The Democritos* [1975] 1 Lloyd's Rep. 368 *per* Kerr J. at 398 col. 1.
21 For waiver in this sense see *Ledingham v Bermejo Estancia Co Ltd* [1947] 1 All ER 749.

ETS.[22] As a matter of principle we can see no reason why a total waiver requires a separate agreement supported by consideration whilst the waiver which took place in *Tufton* did not. If consideration is not required where X waives the future performance of Y's primary obligations, there is no reason why consideration should be required where there is a waiver of Y's secondary obligation to pay damages.[23] Further, s. 11(2) of the Sale of Goods Act 1979 does not appear to be introducing out any unusual or new principle in English law in and by its reference to the possibility of total waiver.[24]

What should be borne in mind in this area, however, is that it will be extremely unlikely for a party to a contract to forego its rights to claim any damages altogether.[25] Therefore, it would be reasonable to expect the courts to view Y's allegations of total waiver with some scepticism and to require both knowledge of the right to waive Y's secondary obligations and the clearest unequivocal conduct or representation on the part of X. It also follows that cases of total waiver will be very rare. The courts may often follow the easier routes of finding that there was a variation of the contract[26] or an equitable forbearance.[27] Only in exceptional circumstances will Y be able to point to circumstances which **4.34**

---

[22] See Benjamin at para 12–34. Although Benjamin appears to support this analysis, it is possible that Benjamin does so as a result of confusing waiver and estoppel — see para. 12–35.

[23] *Robophone Facilities Ltd v Blank* [1966] 1 WLR 1428 *per* Diplock L.J. at 1446A–C; *C Czarnikow Ltd v Koufos* [1966] 2 QB 695 *per* Diplock L.J. at 730F–731B; *RV Ward Ltd v Bignall* [1967] 1 QB 534 *per* Diplock L.J. at 548B–E; *Banning v Wright* [1972] 1 WLR 972 *per* Lord Simon at 990C-D; *Moschi v Lep Air Services* [1973] AC 331 *per* Lord Diplock at 350C–D; *per* Lord Simon at 355G; *Photo Production Ltd v Securicor Transport Ltd* [1980] AC 827 *per* Lord Diplock at 848–50; *Bremer Vulkan Schiffbau und Maschinenfabrik v South India Shipping Corp Ltd* [1981] AC 909 *per* Lord Diplock at 982C-E; *Sudbrook Trading Estate Ltd v Eggleton* [1983] 1 AC 444 *per* Lord Diplock at 478F-G; *Paal Wilson & Co A/S v Partenreederei Hannah Blumenthal* [1983] 1 AC 854 *per* Lord Diplock at 915D-E; *Afovos Shipping Co v Pagnan* [1983] 1 WLR 195 *per* Lord Diplock at 203C-G and *State Trading Company of India v M Golodetz Ltd* [1989] 2 Lloyd's Rep. 285 per Kerr L.J. at 285 col. 2–286 col. 1.

[24] See, *e.g. Sullivan v Constable* (1932) 48 TLR 369. See also *Cuff v Penn* (1813) 1 M&S 21 per Lord Ellenborough C.J. at 27; and *Moore v Campbell* (1854) 10 Ex 323 *per* Parke B. at 333.

[25] Thus, for example, in construction law, the courts are extremely unwilling to find that there has been a waiver of a right to claim damages due to the contractor's defective work by architect acceptance of the building as complete — see *East Ham BC v Bernard Sunley Ltd* [1966] AC 406; Hudson 8.116.

[26] *Compagnie de Renflouement de Recuperation et de Travaux Sous Marins VS Baroukh et Cie v W Seymour Plant Sales & Hire Ltd* [1981] 2 Lloyd's Rep. 466 per Mustill J. (as he then was) at 482 col. 2.

[27] Benjamin at para. 12–035 p. 571–2 and cases there cited.

are sufficiently compelling to override the commercial unlikelihood of X foregoing a valuable right to claim damages.[28]

UNILATERAL WAIVER

A unilateral waiver will arise where X alone has the benefit of particular clauses in the contract and decides unilaterally to forego the benefit of those clauses.[29] As with the other types of waiver, X must have knowledge of the relevant terms and be aware that it has the benefit of those terms. Further, as with other types of waiver, the unilateral waiver must be communicated to Y. Unilateral waiver, however, can be clearly distinguished from waiver by election and total waiver in that it is not a reaction to breach of contract on the part of Y. Further, unilateral waiver is different from pure waiver in that the waiver of a term wholly for X's benefit may not affect Y's performance of the contract, a pure waiver by releasing Y from future performance under the contract may have that effect. **4.35**

It follows that unilateral waiver can only arise in very limited circumstances — where the term waived is purely for X's benefit. There can be no such waiver where bilateral obligations or benefits exist.[30] Thus, for example X may unilaterally waive powers granted to it pursuant to the contract which it could exercise at its sole discretion.[31] **4.36**

Two difficulties arise. First, given the English theory of contract as a mutual exchange of promises, it is difficult to see how any term can be purely for the benefit of one party.[32] Associated with this difficulty is the fact that, practically speaking, it will be very rare for Y to agree a term **4.37**

---

[28] See *e.g. Finagrain SA Geneva v P Kruse Hamburg* [1976] 2 Lloyd's Rep. 508 per Roskill L.J. at 541 col. 2.

[29] *Hawksley v Outram* [1892] 3 Ch 359 *per* Lindley L.J. at 376; *per* Lopes L.J. at 378; *Morell v Studd & Millington* [1913] 2 Ch 648 *per* Astbury J. at 660; *Panoutsos v Raymond Hadley Corporation of New York* [1917] 2 KB 473 *per* Viscount Reading C.J at 477; *North v Loomes* [1919] 1 Ch 378 and *Napier v Dexters Ltd* (1926) 26 Ll LR 184 at 187–8. See also *In the Matter of the Estate of Clark* 447 NW 2d 549 (1989); *Gesell v Reeves* 429 NW 2d 363 (1988) and *WWW Associates Inc v Gianconteri* 548 NYS 2d 580, 559 NYS 2d 983, 565 NYS 2d 440.

[30] *Lloyd v Nowell* [1895] 2 Ch 744 *per* Kekewich J. at 746 (the exercise of the powers being the condition precedent to any obligations accruing under the contract); *Heron Garage v Moss* [1974] 1 WLR 148 *per* Brightman J. at 153D–F.

[31] See *Hawksley v Outram* [1892] 3 Ch 359 *per* Lindley L.J. at 376.

[32] This difficulty is encountered in other jurisdictions — see *Margo v Seegers* 1980 (3) SA 708 *per* Goldstone J. at 712; compared with *Phillips v Townsend* 1983 (3) SA 403 *per* Schock J. at 409A–C and *Meyer v Barnardo* 1984 (2) SA 580 *per* Kumleben J. at 584.

which gives a benefit solely to X. Secondly, there are the difficulties associated with *Barrett Bros (Taxis) Ltd v Davies*[33] in which Lord Denning M.R.[34] appeared to find that there was a unilateral waiver by an insurer of a condition precedent to liability under the policy that the insured notify it of the results of any criminal proceedings against the insured. The unilateral waiver was the insurer's failure to request further documentation from the insured given the insured's statement that it had received a police information. The decision is curious for a number of reasons. First, it is difficult to see how an omission, without more, can constitute the unequivocal representation required to found a waiver.[35] Secondly, the notification requirements of contracts of insurance can usually be expressed as 'If Y does a particular act, X will indemnify Y'. These requirements therefore form part and parcel of the mutual obligations owed by X and Y. Thirdly, if *Barrett* is correctly decided, the doctrine is considerably wider than as originally set out in *Hawksley v Outram*[36] where X was held to have waived powers under the contract which were exercisable only by X. Fourthly, a condition precedent by definition forms the basis of the bargain between X and Y and goes to the root of the contract. There is and was at the time that *Barrett Bros* was decided established authority that a term which goes to the root of the contract cannot be unilaterally waived.[37] We would therefore respectfully suggest that *Barrett* was wrongly decided. It therefore follows that unilateral waiver is properly to be confined to a limited range of circumstances equivalent to those which were found to exist in *Hawksley.*

EQUITABLE FORBEARANCE[38]

For the purposes of this chapter,[39] the elements of equitable forbearance and therefore the distinction between equitable forbearance and waiver can be stated quite shortly: **4.38**

---

[33] [1966] 1 WLR 1334.

[34] *ibid.* at 1339F–G with whom the other Lord Justices agreed.

[35] See para. 4.24 above.

[36] [1892] 3 Ch 359 *per* Lindley L.J. at 376.

[37] See *Lloyd v Nowell* [1895] 2 Ch 744 *per* Kekewich J. at 746. See also *Meyer v Barnardo* 1984 (2) SA 580 *per* Kumleben J. at 584.

[38] Although equitable forbearance is considered in this section for the sake of completeness, it is clear from our analysis above that equitable forbearance is not 'waiver' within the true meaning of the word.

[39] For an fuller explication see Chapter 12 *passim* and in particular paras 12.23–7. See also H.K. Lucke 'Non-Contractual Arrangements for the Modification of Performance: Forbearance, Waiver and Equitable Estoppel' UWALR 149 21 (1991) for a discussion of the distinctions to be drawn.

> It will therefore be seen that both species of waiver require proof by the party alleging waiver of some kind of unequivocal statement or representation from the opposite party. In relation to election it is crucial to show both knowledge of the facts and knowledge of the right of choice, but once all those are shown there is no need to establish reliance or detriment. In estoppel,[40] however, the essential ingredients are the unequivocal representation coupled with the reliance to the opposite parties' detriment.[41]

The contrast between the two doctrines is relatively clear.[42] In practice, however, the relationship between waiver and equitable forbearance has been blurred with both advocates and judges using the terms interchangeably.[43] Additional confusion has been created by the use of the term 'estoppel' where the proper term should be equitable forbearance. Tritely, this confusion leads to further terminological uncertainty, an uncertainty which it is submitted is to be '*deprecated*'.[44] A further result is that it becomes easier to identify a '*broad principle*' of '*fair dealing and justice*' to the effect that:

> If one party, by his conduct, leads another to believe that the strict rights arising under the contract will not be insisted upon, intending that the other should act on that belief, and he does act on it, then the first party will not afterwards be allowed to insist on the strict rights when it would be inequitable for him so to do.[45]

Whilst the existence of such an overarching doctrine may have the virtue of simplicity, it takes no account, we would suggest, of the complexity of this area of the law nor does it accurately reflect the present state of the cases in this area.[46]

It might also be said that these cases support an argument that the distinctions which we have drawn and seek to draw are invalid.[47] We **4.39**

---

[40] Used here in the sense of equitable forbearance.

[41] *Sea Calm Shipping Co SA v Chantiers Navals de L'Esterel SA ('The Uhenbels')* [1986] 2 Lloyd's Rep. 294 *per* Hirst J. at 298 col. 1.

[42] See para. 4.09 above.

[43] See *e.g. Bremer Handelsgesellschaft mbH v Bunge Corporation* [1983] 1 Lloyd's Rep. 476 *per* Goff J. at 484 col. 2; *Peter Cremer v Granaria BV* [1981] 2 Lloyd's Rep. 583 *per* Goff J. at 586 col. 1, 587 col. 2 and *Free Grammar School of John Lyon v Mayhew* (1997) 29 HLR.

[44] *Ross T Smyth & Co Ltd v Bailey, Son & Co* (1940) 164 LT 102 *per* Lord Wright at 106.

[45] *Plasticmoda Societa per Azioni v Davidsons (Manchester) Ltd* [1952] 1 Lloyd's Rep. 527 *per* Denning L.J. at 538–9 cols 2–1.

[46] This conclusion must follow from the fact that several doctrines can be seen to be operating in this area.

[47] See *Waiver — Terminology* at paras 3.10 ff.

would submit that such an argument is misconceived for two reasons. First, as pointed out elsewhere,[48] the court's blurring of the boundaries between waiver and equitable forbearance has arisen from the inability of one party to show that the alleged waivor possessed the requisite knowledge to found a waiver by election not from an intention to fuse these doctrines.[49] Secondly, the courts in these cases have founded the analysis on the concepts of representation and reliance or detriment. The application of those concepts suggests that, far from ruling that waiver and estoppel are to be viewed as the same doctrine, the courts were relying on the principle of equitable forbearance. If that analysis is adopted, then much of the confusion and difficulty is resolved.

The leading decision on this point is *Bremer Handelsgesellschaft mbH v Vanden Avenne-Izegem PVBA*.[50] *Bremer* was a Mississippi Flood case[51] in which issue was taken as to validity of force majeure notices served under clause 22 of the GAFTA 100 contract. Lord Salmon held that the defects in the notices had been 'waived' by the buyers as: **4.40**

> There was no suggestion of any kind either in that telex or any of the others that there was anything else wrong with the notice, e.g., that it was defective or served out of time. I think that any reasonable sellers would have rightly inferred that the buyers were accepting the notice as a valid and effective notice under cl. 22 save that the reference to 500 tonnes should be altered to 280 tonnes. To put it another way, the buyers made an unequivocal representation that they were treating the notice as a valid and effective notice under cl. 22.[52]

Lord Salmon then proceeded to consider whether or not the sellers had suffered any detriment as a result of the representation and stated that whether or not the buyers had any knowledge of their rights was irrelevant.[53]

Bremer was considered extensively in *Bremer Handelsgesellschaft mbH v C Macprang JR*.[54] However, the court in *Bremer v Macprang* differed as to their interpretation of what the House of Lords had really meant in *Bremer*. Lord Salmon's analysis was adopted by Lord Denning **4.41**

---

[48] See *Sale of Goods and Shipping* at para. 20.02.

[49] See, however, *Free Grammar School of John Lyon v Mayhew* (1997) HLR 219 where the Court of Appeal relied on estoppel despite an express finding of requisite knowledge.

[50] [1978] 2 Lloyd's Rep. 109.

[51] See *Variation* at para. 2.39 for an explanation of the facts underlying these cases.

[52] [1978] 2 Lloyd's Rep. 109 at 126 col. 1–2.

[53] *ibid.* at 127 col. 1.

[54] [1979] 1 Lloyd's Rep. 221.

M.R. and used as the basis of a contention[55] that *Bremer* was the 'final step' in a line of cases derived from *Central London Property Trust Ltd v High Trees House Ltd*,[56] those cases establishing the principle that:

> If a buyer, who is entitled to reject goods or documents on the ground of a defect in the notices or the timing of them, so conducts himself as to lead the seller reasonably to believe that he is not going to rely on any such defect — whether he knows it or not — then he cannot afterwards set up the defect as a ground for rejecting the goods or documents when it would be unfair or unjust to allow him to do so. It is unfair and unjust to allow it when the sellers all down the line have acted on the belief that the notices were good and have presented shipping documents accordingly. The sellers here allowed the buyers to have the goods at the very low contract price instead of the higher market price which they might otherwise have obtained.[57]

Lord Justice Stephenson, however, held:

> . . . what matters is the conduct of the 'waiving' or 'estopped' party, these buyers, and its effect on a reasonable seller, or a reasonable person in the position of the other party, these sellers. And if the buyer so acts as to lead a reasonable seller in these sellers' shoes to believe that he was waiving his rights or accepting a non-contractual shipment as a fulfilment of their contract, and the seller does believe it, the buyer cannot be heard to say 'I did not notice the obvious breach of contract on your part which gave me a right to complain or refuse'. But this has no application to matters peculiarly within the seller's knowledge or matters of which he can more easily obtain knowledge than can the buyer.[58]

Further Lord Justice Shaw stated:

> If in the prevailing conditions affecting the position of the parties to a contract the conduct of one of them affords a reasonable foundation for the inference that he is prepared to forego any right or rights he may have in a certain regard and the other contracting party does draw the inference and persists in the residual contractual relationship upon that

[55] It is respectfully submitted that Lord Denning's contention ought to be treated with some caution for two reasons. First, the contention is based on a reading of the House of Lords in *Bremer* as laying down a general doctrine of waiver and overturning allegedly inconsistent Court of Appeal decisions (at 225 col. 2). The former is inconsistent with Lord Wilberforce's express disavowal of any intent to change the law and the latter is, unfortunately incorrect. Secondly, it is not possible to fuse estoppel and waiver as set out at *Waiver — Terminology* at paras 3.09 ff.

[56] [1947] KB 130.

[57] [1979] 1 Lloyd's Rep. 221 at 226 col. 1.

[58] [1979] 1 Lloyd's Rep. 221 at 229 col. 1.

basis, then whether it be regarded as waiver or estoppel the foregoing of those rights cannot thereafter be gainsaid.[59]

Two points arise. First, the Court of Appeal in *Bremer v Macprang* was divided. Whilst Lord Denning advanced a wide doctrine in which knowledge was not required,[60] Lord Justice Shaw being in ' complete agreement' with him,[61] Lord Justice Stephenson stated: **4.42**

> I do not understand Lord Salmon's reference to waiving any defect in the notice . . . 'whether they were aware of it or not' as laying down any general principle that there can be a waiver or equitable estoppel on the part of someone who does not know that his rights have been infringed or has not at the least such obvious means of knowing that his rights have been infringed that the other party can reasonably assume that the party waiving or estopped is acting with knowledge of their infringement. Lord Salmon was I think referring to a patent defect which could only be missed by not reading the notice or not knowing the law.[62]

It follows that it is difficult to suggest that *Bremer v Macprang* advanced any coherent analysis of *Bremer*. Further, as pointed out elsewhere,[63] of the two views, Lord Justice Stephenson's would appear to be correct. Secondly, it is noticeable that despite that disagreement between the three members of the Court of Appeal, all referred to the objective effect of the buyer's conduct on the sellers and all three appeared to blur waiver and estoppel. Additionally, in both *Bremer* and *Bremer v Macprang*, to found the alleged waiver, the court relied heavily on the representations made, the inferences drawn by the representee and the reasonableness of the representee's reliance on those representations or inferences. The courts' reliance is more consistent with the intervention of an equitable doctrine more closely related to estoppel than with waiver in the true sense of the word. Further and as pointed out above,[64] if Lord Salmon was considering any of the forms of waiver set out above, then his decision is at odds with the established authorities.[65] Finally, it is submitted

[59] [1979] 1 Lloyd's Rep. 221 at 231 col. 1.

[60] *ibid.* at 225. The doctrine being the Denningnite overarching concept which we have rejected elsewhere.

[61] *ibid.* at 231.

[62] *ibid.* at 229.

[63] *Equitable Forbearance* at paras 12.24 ff., and *Sale of Goods and Shipping* at paras 20.02, 20.05.

[64] See para. 4.21 above.

[65] The alternative approach is to suggest that there was a waiver, the requisite knowledge being provided by the patent nature of the defect — see *Bremer Handelsgesellschaft mbH v C Macprang JR* [1979] 1 Lloyd's Rep. 221 at 229 and *Sale of Goods and Shipping* at paras 20.02, 20.05.

that this re-categorization of these cases as ones of equitable forbearance is the only way of rationalizing the cases in which the courts have used the term waiver 'in the sense of estoppel'[66] or in which the court having analysed the facts found that Y was entitled to succeed under one head but not the other.[67]

It is therefore submitted that not only are the distinctions set out above correct but also that it is appropriate to refer to a doctrine of equitable forbearance which is distinct from the doctrine of waiver in its various forms. **4.43**

ELEMENTS COMMON TO ALL FORMS OF WAIVER

Drawing on the above, it is submitted that the elements which are common to all forms of waiver in the true sense of the word are: **4.44**

(1) an unequivocal representation by X either by words or conduct that it will forego certain rights; and
(2) X makes that representation when it is aware of the facts that give rise to the rights which are being foregone, of the right to forego those rights and the connection between the two.

PRACTICAL EFFECT

The practical effect of the types of waiver outlined above is dealt with in more detail in the specific subject chapters. For present purposes, it falls to consider in general terms how X can conduct itself so as to prevent a finding of waiver against it. In brief, X must be astute to ascertain whether Y is complying with the terms of the contract and as to what performance is to be expected of X and Y. As soon as X detects **4.45**

---

[66] See *e.g. Finagrain SA Geneva v P Kruse Hamburg* [1976] 2 Lloyd's Rep. 508 *per* Megaw L.J. at 534; *Bunge GmbH v Alfred C Toepfer* [1978] 1 Lloyd's Rep. 506; *EDM Mertens & Co PVBA v Veevoeder Import Export Vimex BV* [1979] 2 Lloyd's Rep. 272 *per* Lloyd J. at 284 col. 2; *Peter Cremer v Granaria BV* [1981] 2 Lloyd's Rep. 583 and *Bremer Handelsgesellschaft mbH v Bunge Corporation* [1983] 1 Lloyd's Rep. 476 *per* Goff L.J. at 484 col. 2.

[67] See, *e.g. Nippon Yusen Kaisha v Pacifica Navegacion SA ('The Ion')* [1980] 2 Lloyd's Rep. 245.

that there may be some change in performance under the contract, X should decide whether it wishes to respond or not. X will have three choices: to do nothing and risk foregoing its rights; to repudiate the contract; or to reserve its rights. Usually, and provided that the reservation is not a sham, the best method would be for X to reserve its rights until such time as it is clear to X whether it wishes to continue with the contract as being currently performed.

Chapter 5

WAIVER (III) COMPLEXITIES

Although our analysis of terminology and the types and elements of waiver has been aimed at clarifying this difficult area, five additional questions remain which require analysis. First, the effect of a waiver *per se* and the extent to which it is suspensory. Secondly, the extent to which all forms of waiver are 'case specific', or put another way, the extent to which a waiver of one particular right may lead to other rights being waived. Thirdly, the evidence required to establish a waiver. Fourthly, the extent to which X can be said to have waived its rights as a result of the actions of its agent. Fifthly, the extent to which a waiver will have any effect on third parties. **5.01**

THE EFFECT OF WAIVER

The doctrine of waiver has been viewed as a mechanism of bypassing the doctrine of consideration.[1] In this respect, a waiver is to be contrasted with a variation which has to be supported by consideration.[2] Further, as variation permanently alters X and Y's obligations under the contract, it would follow that waiver cannot permanently alter X and Y's obligations under the contract. In other words, waiver is only suspensory of X's rights. Thus: **5.02**

> As a general rule, an existing legal right is not destroyed by mere waiver, in the sense of an express or implied intimation that the person in whom the right is vested does not intend to enforce it . . . Thus if a party to a contract becomes entitled to avoid it by reason of a breach by the other party of an essential promise, the fact that, with knowledge of the facts

---

[1] See *Waiver — Types and elements* at para. 4.16.
[2] See *Waiver — Terminology* at para. 3.08.

> which give rise to the right to avoid, he says or does something which recognises the continued existence of the contract does not necessarily amount to a binding waiver of his right to avoid . . . The effect is, however, produced if his act is of an unequivocal nature affecting the other party, and one which he would not be entitled to do if the contract were not subsisting, or one which leads the other party to do or abstain from doing something on the footing that the contract is still subsisting . . . to be effectual, the conduct relied upon as an effective waiver must comply with the general condition stated . . . as the basis of all forms of estoppel in pais.[3]

It is submitted that it follows that, absent an estoppel/equitable forbearance, whilst pure waiver and unilateral waiver are only suspensory,[4] waiver by election and total waiver generally are not.[5] Therefore, care must be taken to analyse which rights are being waived. In, for example, *Hickman v Hayes*[6] a waiver by election of the right to repudiate arising from non-timeous performance merely suspended the right to claim damages.[7] Thus, on a further repudiation, the original right to repudiate had been lost but damages became payable as from the original date for performance under the contract.[8] **5.03**

There are two reasons for that distinction. First, waiver by election[9] and total waiver are choices which in the main can only be made once **5.04**

[3] *Larratt v Bankers & Traders Insurance Co* (1941) 41 SR (NSW) 215 *per* Jordan C.J. at 216–7.

[4] See *Cape Asbestos v Lloyd's Bank* [1921] WN 274 *per* Bailhache J. at 276; *Ficom SA v Sociedad Cadex Limitada* [1980] 2 Lloyd's Rep. 118 *per* Goff J. at 132 col. 1.

[5] See, *e.g. The Kanchenjunga* [1990] 1 Lloyd's Rep. 391. Compare, however, Benjamin at paras 12.035–12.037.

[6] (1875) LR 10 CP 598 at 607.

[7] See also *Dowling v Rae* (1927) 39 CLR 363 *per* Isaacs J. at 370.

[8] *Ogle v Earl Vane* (1868) LR 3 QB 272; *Hickman v Haynes* (1875) LR 10 CP 598 at 607; *Levey & Co v Goldberg* [1922] 1 KB 688 *per* McCardie J. at 691–2 and *Besseler Waechter Glover & Co v South Derwent Coal Co Ltd* [1938] 1 KB 408 *per* Goddard J. at 418.

[9] For examples see *Wallis, Son & Wells v Pratt & Haynes* [1911] AC 394; *Bowes v Chaleyer* (1923) 32 CLR 159; *Wendt v Bruce* (1931) 45 CLR 245 at 253; *Hain Steamship Co Ltd v Tate and Lyle Ltd* (1936) 41 Comm Cas 350; *Tramways Advertising Pty Ltd v Luna Park NSW Ltd* (1938) SR (NSW) 632 *per* Jordan C.J. at 644; *Chandris v Isbrandtson-Moller Co Inc* [1951] 1 KB 240 *per* Devlin J. at 248; *Carr v JA Berriman Pty Ltd* (1953) 89 CLR 327 *per* Fullagar J. at 349; *Gange v Sullivan* (1966) CLR 418; *Suisse Atlantique Société d'Armement Maritime SA v NV Rotterdamsche Kolen Centrale* [1967] 1 AC 361 *per* Viscount Dilhorne at 395B and *Compagnie de Renflouement de Recuperation et de Travaux Sous Marins VS Baroukh et Cie v W Seymour Plant Sales & Hire Ltd* [1981] 2 Lloyd's Rep. 466 *per* Mustill J. at 482 col. 2.

and once made there is no right which can be resurrected.[10] Put another way, waiver by election and total waiver relate to X's accrued remedies when there has already been a breach of the primary obligations under the contract. Once those remedies have been foregone, they cannot be resurrected.[11] Secondly, and by contrast, pure waiver or unilateral waiver relates to the future performance of future obligations under the contract and it is possible for the future obligations under the contract to be altered.[12]

IS WAIVER CASE SPECIFIC?

Given the analysis of the knowledge required to found a waiver, it is unsurprising that a waiver by X of one particular right does not mean that another, albeit connected right, has also been waived.[13] Thus, if in a cif contract X waives its rights in relation to the documents required under the contract, that does not mean that X has waived its rights in relation to the time at which the goods are to be delivered[14] or if X is taken to have waived its rights in respect of defects in a notice served under one clause, that does not mean that the X has waived its rights in respect of the same notice under a different clause of the contract[15] or if X waives its right to reject the tender of documents under a cif contract, that does not amount to a waiver of its right to sue for damages in respect of the defective goods.[16] The proposition can be extended to a waiver of particular obligations under the contract provided that the 5.05

---

10 For an argument to the contrary see Lucke, 'Non-Contractual Arrangements for the Modification of Performance: Forbearance, waiver and equitable estoppel' *University of Western Australia Law Review* 21 (1991) 149 at 163. See also Treitel 'Affirmation after Repudiatory Breach' (1998) 114 *LQR* 22.

11 See, *e.g. Alexander v Gardner* (1835) 1 Bing NC 671, 131 ER 1276. The position may be different where there is a continuing anticipatory breach — see *Stocznia v Latvian Shipping Co.* [1997] 2 Lloyd's Rep. 228; Treitel *op. cit.*

12 Subject always to the parties' implied obligations to act so as not to frustrate or defeat the purpose of the contract *Electronic Industries Ltd v David Jones Ltd* (1954) 91 CLR 288 at 297; Chitty at para. 13–010 nn. 62, 64.

13 See, *e.g. R v Paulson* [1921] 1 AC 271 *per* Lord Atkinson at 280, but not those outwith knowledge *Matthews v Smallwood* [1910] 1 Ch 777 *per* Parker J. at 786 and *Elders Trustee and Executor Co Ltd v Commonwealth Homes and Investment Co Ltd* (1941) 65 CLR 603 *per* Rich A.C.J., Dixon, McTiernan JJ. at 616.

14 *Finagrain SA Geneva v P Kruse Hamburg* [1976] 2 Lloyd's Rep. 508 *per* Megaw L.J. at 534 col. 1.

15 See *Bunge GmbH v Alfred C Toepfer* [1978] 1 Lloyd's Rep. 506 *per* Brandon J. at 510 col. 2.

16 *ETS Soules & Cie International Trade Development Co Ltd* [1980] 1 Lloyd's Rep. 129 *per* Megaw L.J. at col. 2–138 col. 1.

terms imposing those obligations are severable.[17] It follows that care must be taken to ascertain the facts that X knew and the precise representation made in order to determine the rights that X has waived and the breach which has allegedly been waived.[18] Particular care must be taken where there is a continuing breach. In such cases, one instance of breach may be waived but not the others.[18a]

THE EVIDENCE REQUIRED TO SUPPORT A WAIVER

In variation[19] and with estoppel[20] it is clear that Y must be able to show that the proposed variation or representation was clear, precise and sufficiently certain to found a contract. It is submitted that the same rule applies to all types of waiver,[21] it not being possible to draw a distinction between waiver and variation or estoppel on the basis that a waiver may merely preserve the status quo as opposed to altering the terms of the contract.[22] Therefore, to establish a waiver, as well as **5.06**

---

[17] *Waimiha Sawmilling Co Ltd v Howe* [1922] NZLR 339.

[18] *Tramways Advertising Pty Ltd v Luna Park (NSW) Ltd* (1938) SR (NSW) 632 *per* Jordan C.J. at 645; but have to have another breach *Monigatti v Minchen* [1937] NZLR; *Larking v Great Western (Nepean) Gravel Ltd* (1940) 64 CLR 221; *Carr v JA Berriman Pty Ltd* (1953) 89 CLR 327 *per* Fullagar J. at 349; *Wood Factory Pty Ltd v Kiritos Pty Ltd* (1985) 2 NSWLR 105 *per* McHugh J. at 145G; *Lombok Pty Ltd v Supetina Pty Ltd* (1987) 71 ALR 333 *per* Pincus J. at 349; *UCB Leasing Ltd v Holtum* (1987) 137 New LJ 614 at 615; *Re Emanuel* [1988] 2 Qd R 514; *Ogle v Comboyuro Investments Pty Ltd* (1976) 136 CLR 444; *Foran v Wright* (1989) 168 CLR 385; *Loughridge v Lavery* [1969] VR 912; *Berger v Boyles* [1971] VR 321 *per* Gillard J. at 326 ll 5–10; *The Millstream Pty Ltd v Schultz* [1980] 1 NSWLR 547; *Sibbles v Highfern Pty Ltd* (1987) 164 CLR 214 and *Construction Law* at para. 16.15–16.

[18a] See discussion in Treitel 'Affirmation after Repudiatory Breach' (1998) 114 *LQR* 22 for a different analysis. Compare *Stocznia v Latvian Shipping Co.* [1997] 2 Lloyd's Rep. 228 in which the Court held that there could be an irrevocable waiver of a continuing breach.

[19] See *Variation* at para. 2.14.

[20] See *Woodhouse AC Israel Cocoa Ltd SA v Nigerian Produce Marketing* [1972] AC 741 at 762C–D.

[21] See *Carolan v Brabazon* (1846) 3 Jo & Lat 200 *per* Sugden L.C at 209 '*this Court requires as clear evidence of the waiver as of the existence of the contract itself*'; *Robinson v Page* (1826) 3 Russ 114 at 119, 38 ER 519 at 521 and *ex p. Schumann* (1877) 19 LR Ir 240.

[22] See *Food Corporation of India v Antclizo Shipping Corporation ('The Antclizo')* [1987] 2 Lloyd's Rep. 130 at 142 cols 1–2 where Lord Justice Buckley rejected a submission that a waiver required a lower standard.

knowledge, Y must show that there was a clear and unequivocal representation either by words or conduct which directly affected particular terms of the contract in a specific way.[23]

Where a representation is made expressly little difficulty arises.[24] 5.07
Where the representation is implied from X's conduct, the position is less clear. It is submitted that a number of principles can be drawn from the authorities. First, in all types of waiver, there must be as a minimum conduct which is referable to the right being foregone. Thus, where, for example, a notice served under the contract is defective but neither party takes any action in response to that notice, there will be no waiver.[25] Secondly, in waiver by election, if, after X possesses the requisite knowledge, X performs some act under the contract, a waiver will be made out. Therefore, where Y has acted in fundamental breach of the contract by, for example, tendering the wrong goods or the wrong documents or paying in the incorrect manner, X will probably be taken to have waived if with the requisite knowledge it accepts the goods, or accepts the monies,[26] or requests Y to carry out further actions under the contract.[27] Similarly, if X rejects the goods or the payment as soon as it is aware of the defect, there will be no waiver.[28] Thirdly, if Y acts in a way that is patently at odds with the terms of the contract and X responds to that behaviour otherwise than by stating that the behaviour is in breach of the contract, a waiver will be made out. Thus, if in a cif contract Y tenders documents which are patently bad on their face and X does not on receipt point out that the documents are bad on their face, X will be taken to have waived the defects.[29] Fourthly, generally a

---

[23] *Feinstein v Niggli & another* 1981 (2) SA 684 *per* Trollip J.A. at 698; see also *Laws v Rutherford* 1924 AD 261 *per* Innes C.J. at 263; *Netlon Ltd v Pacnet Pty Ltd* 1977 (3) SA 840 at 872G–873H; in Australia *Larratt v Bankers and Traders Insurance Co Ltd* (1941) 41 SR (NSW) 215 *per* Jordan C.J. at 217 and *Tiplady v Gold Coast Carlton Pty Ltd* (1984) 8 FCR 438 at 451.

[24] Exception where the possibility of a waiver is excluded by a no-waiver clause.

[25] *Bunge GmbH v Alfred C Toepfer* [1978] 1 Lloyd's Rep. 506 *per* Brandon J. at 510 col. 2.

[26] See *Texas Steamship Co Ltd v The Brimnes (owners) ('The Brimnes')* [1979] 1 QB 929; *Panoutsos v Raymond Hadley Corporation of New York* [1917] 2 KB 473 and *Tankexpress A/S v Compagnie Financiere Belge des Petroles SA ('The Petrofina')* [1949] AC 76 at 93, 98, 103.

[27] See, *e.g.* *Cerealmangimi SpA v Toepfer ('The Eurometal')* [1981] 1 Lloyd's Rep. 337.

[28] See *e.g.* *Mardorf Peach & Co v Attica Sea Carriers Corporation of Liberia* [1977] AC 850 *per* Lord Wilberforce at 871B–E.

[29] See, *e.g.* *Bremer Handelsgesellschaft mbH v Vanden Avenne-Izegem PVBA* [1978] 2 Lloyd's Rep. 109; but see *Avimex SA v Dewulf & Cie* [1979] 2 Lloyd's Rep. 57 where the defect was not apparent from the face of the notices *per* Goff J. at 67 col. 2–68 col. 1.

failure to act or respond by X will not be enough to found a waiver unless X's failure amounts to an unequivocal representation that in fact X was aware of the facts and chose to do nothing about them.[30] urther, it is more unlikely that the court will find that there has been a waiver by election as a result of X's silence, failure to act or a mere lapse of time.[31] Fifthly, X will not be taken to have waived a right merely because in the past it has waived that right. Therefore, where X has allowed Y to present a revocable letter of credit in payment for goods in the past and the contract provides for a revocable letter of credit, X is perfectly entitled to reject the next revocable letter of credit presented by Y.[32] Finally, it is submitted that the very uncertainty as to whether or not X has waived by its conduct has led the courts to rely more heavily on equitable forbearance or estoppel.[33] This tendency explains why in *Larratt v Bankers & Traders Insurance Co*[34] the court explained the authorities by stating that a waiver based on a representation by conduct would only be effective if an estoppel was present.

WAIVER BY X'S AGENT

Where X engages an agent, that agent can waive X's rights.[35] However, a waiver will be based on X's actions, a waiver can only take place where the agent has the appropriate authority.[36] The circumstances in **5.08**

---

[30] See *Tyrer & Co v Hessler & Co* (1902) 7 Com Cas 166 *per* Romer L.J. at 171; *Allen v Robles* [1969] 1 WLR 1193 *per* Fenton-Atkinson L.J. at 1196G-H; *Buckland v Farmar &* Moody [1979] 1 WLR 221 *per* Goff L.J. at 236D and *Pearl Carriers Inc v Japan Line Ltd ('The Chemical Venture')* [1993] 1 Lloyd's Rep. 508 *per* Gatehouse J. at 521 col. 2.

[31] *Bremer Handelsgesellschaft mbH v Deutsche Conti-Handelsgesellschaft mbH* [1983] 2 Lloyd's Rep. 45 *per* Lord Donaldson M.R. at 49 col. 2 and *State Trading Corporation of India Ltd v M Golodetz Ltd* [1989] 2 Lloyd's Rep. 277 *per* Lloyd L.J. at 286 col. 2. On analysis, if the court does so find, it is more likely than not that the court is applying estoppel principles and there should be some requirement of prejudice.

[32] See *Cape Asbestos v Lloyd's Bank* [1921] WN 274 *per* Bailhache J. at 276.

[33] See the approach adopted in *Bremer v Vanden Avenne-Izegem* [1978] 2 Lloyd's Rep. 109 and *Cook Industries Inc v Meunerie Legois SA* [1981] 1 Lloyd's Rep. 359 *per* Mustill J. at 368 col. 1.

[34] (1941) 41 SR (NSW) 215 at 216–7 *op. cit.*

[35] See, *e.g. Evans v Employers' Mutual Insurance Association Ltd* [1936] 1 KB 505; *FAME Insurance Co v Spence* [1958] NZLR 735 and *Mardorf Peach & Co Ltd v Attica Sea Carriers Corporation of Liberia* [1977] AC 850 *per* Lord Wilberforce at 871B–E.

[36] As opposed to estoppel which looks at the effect on Y.

which an agent will possess authority will vary and we therefore deal with questions arising under this head in the individual subject chapters.[37]

WAIVER AND THIRD PARTIES

Waiver is a contractual doctrine. It follows that a waiver can only affect a third party, A, if the contract is assigned to A. In two cases, *Brikom Investments Ltd v Carr*[38] and *Tenax Steamship Co Ltd v Owners of The Brimnes ('The Brimnes')*,[39] the courts have suggested that where A takes an assignment of a contract, A will be bound by any previous waiver. Both cases create difficulty. We have argued elsewhere that *Brikom* was an unusual case. The principles applied are uncertain[40] and the conclusion runs contrary to the established principles of landlord and tenant law.[41] Further, on analysis, it would appear that rights were foregone in that case as a result of an equitable forbearance. *The Brimnes*,[42] although a case of waiver in the true sense, is similarly difficult for three reasons. First, the case on assignment was raised late and, as a result, at least one member of the Court of Appeal felt that the issues had not been fully explored.[43] Secondly, it is at least arguable that it was conceded and therefore not in issue that a waiver could affect third parties as a result of an assignment.[44] Thirdly, the majority of the Court of Appeal appeared to accept that a waiver could affect third parties as a result of an assignment almost as a matter of course.[45] The issue was not considered in detail. It follows that there are at least respectable arguments that neither *Brikom* nor *The Brimnes* should be followed on this point. **5.09**

otwithstanding the difficulties with *Brikom* and *The Brimnes*, we would suggest that a third party, A, can be affected by waiver where **5.10**

[37] See *Insurance* at para. 19.58; *Banking* at para. 15.16 and *Agency passim.*
[38] [1979] QB 467, CA.
[39] [1975] 1 QB 929.
[40] See *Equitable Forbearance* at para. 12.11, 12.30.
[41] See *Equitable Forbearance* at para. 12.71.
[42] [1975] 1 QB 929.
[43] *ibid. per* Megaw L.J. at 960D ff.
[44] *ibid. per* Edmund Davies L.J. (as he then was) 956B.
[45] See, *e.g. per* Edmund Davies L.J (as he then was) 948D–E, 955H–956B; *per* Cairns L.J. 971H.

there is an assignment for two reasons.[46] First, there is no reason why A should be in a better position than X merely as a result of an assignment. If contractual rights have been foregone, an assignment, which transfers the benefits accruing under the contract, cannot alter that position.[47] If an assignment negated a waiver, X would be able to assign the contract to A with a provision for re-assignment back to X, thereby avoiding the waiver. Secondly, an assignment could take place in two situations: before or after breach. Before breach, the only waivers which could have taken place are pure and unilateral waivers which are suspensory.[48] A can therefore reverse those waivers on assignment. As the only argument against a waiver affecting A is the detriment that A would suffer, that argument falls away in these circumstances. After breach, either A will take the assignment to force Y to perform the contract or to pursue Y for damages. In the former case, A will wish to rely on X's waiver and to argue that the contract is in force. In the latter, a clear issue arises as to the benefits that A is receiving as a result of the assignment. If A is aware of the breach, A will knowingly be taking an assignment of a cause of action and will therefore face the difficulties arising from the doctrine of champerty.[49] If A is unaware of the breach, the very fact of assignment will suggest that A wishes to be bound by the contract. In either event, A is not materially prejudiced by X's waiver and there can be no reason why the waiver should not transfer on assignment to A.

---

[46] We reach the same conclusion in relation to equitable forbearance — see *Equitable Forbearance* at para. 12.68.

[47] A similar position is reached in subrogation — see *Insurance* at para. 19.97.

[48] See para. 5.04 above.

[49] For the most recent explanation and application of those rules see *Giles v Thompson* [1994] 1 AC 142.

Chapter 6

THE PANCHAUD FRÈRES 'DOCTRINE'

INTRODUCTION

6.01 Much commercial litigation is triggered by changes in market prices or conditions which have led one party to a contract to change its conduct or to refuse to perform the contract as originally agreed. That change or refusal will often mean that that party has acted inconsistently. In the ensuing litigation, the aggrieved party will wish to rely on that inconsistency either to provide it with a substantive remedy or to focus the court's attention on the perceived merits of its case. In this context, the aggrieved party will probably rely on the substantive doctrines of waiver and estoppel and may also seek to rely on various statements made by the Court of Appeal in *Panchaud Frères SA v Etablissements General Grain Co.*[1]

PANCHAUD FRÈRES

6.02 The facts of the case are relatively simple. By a contract dated 14 May 1965, the plaintiff sellers sold 5,500 tons of yellow maize to the defendant buyers cif Antwerp, payment by telegraphic transfer against documents on first presentation and the shipment was to be in June or July 1965. 5,300 tons were shipped in June or July. However, in breach of the contract, 200 tons were not shipped until 11 or 12 August 1965. Notwithstanding the late shipment, the plaintiff sellers amended the bill of lading covering that late shipment to state that the 200 tons had been shipped on 31 July 1965 in compliance with the contract. However, the certificate of quality which was supplied as part of the documents stated

[1] [1970] 1 Lloyd's Rep. 53.

that shipment had been on 11 or 12 August. Whilst the shipment was at sea, the buyers took up the documents without making any complaint as to date on the bill of lading as compared with that on the certificate. When the shipment arrived the goods were defective and litigation ensued. During the arbitration, the defendant buyers discovered that the shipment had been made late and that the bill of lading had been altered. The defendant buyers therefore purported to reject the shipment on that basis. The Court of Appeal held that the defendant buyers were not entitled so to do.

Lord Denning M.R. reached that conclusion by finding that the buyers were estopped by their conduct from relying on the late shipment and: **6.03**

> The basis of it is that a man has so conducted himself that it would be unfair or unjust to allow him to depart from a particular state of affairs which another has taken to be settled or correct . . . If a man, who is entitled to reject goods on a certain ground, so conducts himself as to lead the other to believe that he is not relying on that ground, then he cannot afterwards set it up as a ground of rejection, when it would be unfair or unjust to allow him to do so[2]

It appears from the judgment that Lord Denning presumably felt that, notwithstanding the deliberate alteration of the bill, the buyers should have known from the certificate of quality that the shipment was late and therefore went on to hold that:

> By taking up the documents and paying for them, they are precluded afterwards from complaining of the late shipment or of the defect in the bill of lading[3]

Lord Justice Winn agreed and stated: **6.04**

> In my own judgment it does not seem possible in this case to say affirmatively that there was here either a fresh agreement to rescind or vary the original contract, or anything which, within the scope of the doctrine as hitherto annunciated, could be described as an estoppel or a quasi estoppel. I respectfully agree with my Lord that what one has here is something perhaps in our law not yet wholly developed as a separate doctrine — which is more in the nature of a requirement of fair conduct — a criterion of what is fair conduct between the parties. There may be an inchoate doctrine stemming from the manifest

[2] [1970] 1 Lloyd's Rep. 53 at 57 col. 1.
[3] *ibid.* at 58 col. 1.

> convenience of consistency in pragmatic affairs, negativing any liberty to blow hot and cold in commercial conduct.[4]

The case therefore would appear to be authority for two general propositions. The first is a restatement of the general Denningite concept of estoppel stated and restated in numerous cases.[5] The principle and the relevant cases are discussed elsewhere.[6] The second is Lord Justice Winn's statement that parties in a commercial relationship owe each other some form of duty to act consistently. The two principles can be loosely stated as an 'inchoate' principle that the courts will intervene to prevent a party taking an unmeritorious and inconsistent, albeit commercially justified and possibly lawful, course of action. It is that loose principle which, if correct, could be referred to as the *Panchaud Frères* doctrine. **6.05**

APPLICATION OF THE DOCTRINE

The doctrine has been considered on several occasions.[7] Thus, where notices are issued under the contract which are defective and the other party has appeared to accept those notices, that other party has been precluded from later relying on the defects in the notices.[8] In addition to this narrow application of the decision to similar factual situations,[9] the case has been applied in other areas of the law. Thus, where the parties had conducted their affairs on the basis that there was a concluded contract between them, it was held to be unfair and unjust to permit one party to resile from that position and contend that there **6.06**

---

[4] *ibid.* 59 col. 1.

[5] See, *e.g. Plasticmoda Societa per Azioni v Davidsons (Manchester) Ltd* [1952] 1 Lloyd's Rep. 527 at 538 col. 2 – 539 col. 1 and *Bremer Handelsgesellschaft mbH v C Macprang JR* [1979] 1 Lloyd's Rep. 221 at 225 cols 1–2, 226 col. 1.

[6] See *Equitable Forbearance passim.*

[7] See Benjamin at para. 12–037. *Panchaud* — type reasoning (but not the case itself) has been applied in *The Astraea* [1971] 2 Lloyd's Rep. 494; 502; *The Vladimir Illich* [1975] 1 Lloyd's Rep. 322; *Alfred C Toepfer v Peter Cremer* [1975] 2 Lloyd's Rep. 118; *The Shackleford* [1978] 1 WLR 1080; *Bunge GmbH v Alfred C Toepfer* [1978] 1 Lloyd's Rep. 506; [1979] 1 Lloyd's Rep. 554; *Avimex SA v Dewulf & Cie* [1979] 2 Lloyd's Rep. 57; and *Bunge AG v Fuga AG* [1980] 2 Lloyd's Rep. 513.

[8] See *Alfred C Toepfer v Cramer* [1975] 2 Lloyd's Rep. 118 and *Warren Import Gesellschaft Krohn & Co v Alfred C Toepfer* [1975] 1 Lloyd's Rep. 322 *per* Donaldson J. at 329 col. 2.

[9] These cases could equally well, we suggest, have been decided on waiver or equitable forbearance principles — see the analogous cases discussed at *Waiver— Types and Elements* paras 4.48 ff. and *Sale of Goods and Shipping* at paras 20.02, 20.05.

was no concluded contract.[10] Further, *Panchaud Frères* has been relied on as authority for the proposition that no detriment or reliance is required to create an estoppel when the parties involved are experienced commercial operators. Thus, in *Surrey Shipping Co Ltd v Compagnie Continentale (France) SA ('The Shackleford'),*[11] a dispute as to laytime under a charterparty, Mr Justice Donaldson pointed out that both the plaintiff and the defendant had considerable experience in chartering vessels and therefore were to be taken as being aware of their rights.[12] Therefore, *Panchaud Frères* would apply to all notices served by either party. In applying *Panchaud Frères*, the judge held:

> I do not understand these judgments as requiring any evidence of positive or active reliance. If a man so conducts himself that another could reasonably regard a particular state of affairs as existing or settled, the only question is whether or not in all the circumstances it would be just and fair to allow him to resile. It is in this context that the position of the other party has to be considered. Deliberate action or inaction in reliance upon the alleged estopping conduct will provide good, and probably overwhelming reason for holding that it would be unfair or unjust to allow any resilement. Evidence that the conduct was unnoticed or disregarded or treated as of no importance might well lead to the opposite conclusion.[13]

All of the above would suggest that there is a valid and subsisting doctrine which has been termed the '*so-called Panchaud principle of fair dealing*'.[14]

However, it has also been suggested that *Panchaud Frères* is to be confined to its facts[15] and that the case laid down no new principles of law[16] or indeed no principle of law at all.[17] Further in *BP Exploration Co v Hunt (No. 2)*[18] Mr Justice Goff stated that: **6.07**

> All that the Panchaud case decided was that if, in a cif contract, the documents show that the goods were shipped late, and the buyer nonetheless accepts the documents, then, even if he has failed to notice the late shipment

---

[10] See *Mitsui Babcock Energy Ltd v John Brown Engineering Ltd* (1997) 51 Con LR 129 *per* H.H. Judge Esyr Lewis Q.C. at 186.
[11] [1978] 1 Lloyd's Rep. 191.
[12] *ibid.* at 195 col. 2. – 196 col. 1.
[13] *ibid* at 198 col. 1.
[14] *V Berg & Son Ltd v Vanden Avenne — Izegem PVBA* [1977] 1 Lloyd's Rep. 499 at 504.
[15] *Alma Shipping Corporation v Union of India ('The Astraea')* [1971] 2 Lloyd's Rep. 494 at 502.
[16] *V Berg & Son Ltd v Vanden Avenne — Izegem PVBA* [1977] 1 Lloyd's Rep. 499 at 504.
[17] *Tracomin SA v Sudan Oil Seeds Co Ltd* [1983] 1 All ER 404 *per* Staughton J. at 415.
[18] [1979] 1 WLR 783; *contra Mitsui Babcock Energy Limited v John Brown Engineering Ltd* (1997) 51 Con LR 129.

> date when he took up the documents, he will thereafter be precluded from rejecting the goods for that reason. The decision stems from the need for finality in commercial transactions . . . [19]

before going on to hold that Lord Justice Winn's dictum was not of '*general application*' and that the Lord Justice '*was merely expressing the principle of finality which underlies the doctrine of acceptance in contracts of sale of goods*'.[20] All of the above would suggest that the nature and scope of the 'doctrine' are far from clear.

DIFFICULTIES WITH THE DECISION

It is submitted that the confusion described above can be in part resolved by an examination of the decision itself in an attempt to ascertain what the Court of Appeal actually held. What is clear is that the case was not one of waiver in any form. The defendant buyers did not have the appropriate knowledge of the defect.[21] It follows that either the case was decided on the basis of estoppel or some other principle. As far as estoppel is concerned, it is possible that the buyers were prevented from relying on a defect in the documents by reason of the explicit contradiction between the certificate of quality and the bill of lading. The alternative view was that the buyers made some form of representation as to their future conduct which created an equitable forbearance and they thereby lost their right to reject. It is submitted that neither view is satisfactory especially as it is difficult to spell out any form of representation which would found an estoppel/equitable forbearance.[22] Similarly, **6.08**

[19] [1979] 1 WLR 783 at 811B–C. See also *Glencore Grain Rotterdam BV v Lebanese Organisation for International Commerce* [1997] 4 All E.R. 514.

[20] *ibid.* at 811G.

[21] We would suggest that defect was not sufficiently clear to fall within the concept of waiver which was advanced in *Bremer Handelsgesellschaft mbH v Vanden Avenne-Izegem PVBA* [1978] 2 Lloyd's Rep. 109; *Bremer Handelsgesellschaft mbH v C Macprang JR* [1979] 1 Lloyd's Rep. 221 at 229 (see *Waiver — Types and Elements* para. 4.41 and *Sale of Goods and Shipping* at paras 20–02, 20.05). However, the defect probably would have sufficed for the broad Denningite concept of 'waiver' articulated in *Bremer v Macprang* at 226. As argued elsewhere, we do not think that Lord Denning M.R.'s view is supportable.

[22] See *Avimex SA v Dewulf & Cie* [1979] 2 Lloyd's Rep. 57 at 67 col. 2–68 col. 1 where on similar facts Goff J. held that there was no representation and no patent defect in the notices. Further, as there was no express promise to forego rights, any equitable forbearance would have to be inferred from conduct and the buyer's knowledge of their rights would probably have to be established (see *Equitable*

in considering *Panchaud* the courts have found it difficult to identify the basis of the decision. Mr Justice Goff in *BP Exploration Co* c *Hunt* was of the view that *Panchaud* did not raise any point of equitable estoppel[23] and in *Avimex SA v Dewulf & Cie*[24] the judge appeared to treat the case as one raising a common law estoppel. We therefore are driven to conclude that the better view is that *Panchaud* is not a case on estoppel in the proper sense of the word.[24a]

The other possibility, that *Panchaud* sets out a new doctrine, is also fraught with difficulty. On the one hand, on more than one occasion the courts have suggested that it might be appropriate to create one doctrine which would prevent a party acting opportunistically. Thus, there are references to a developing concept of 'injurious reliance'[25] or to unconscionability in addition to the Denningite attempt to instil a loose concept of 'fairness' into the English law. *Panchaud* would therefore form part and parcel of these attempts.[26] The arguments in support of such a doctrine are straightforward — that it would simplify what is an allegedly over complex or unclear area of the law. **6.09**

However, it is submitted that objections of principle can be made in respect of each of the concepts. The Denningite view is exposed at least to the criticism that it creates uncertainty and valorizes the individual judge's view of the merits of the particular case. The interpolation of a general principle of 'unconscionability' whilst potentially simplifying the law is therefore to be resisted.[27] Finally, although there are suggestions that waiver has been subsumed by estoppel,[28] as discussed in the chapters on waiver and estoppel, those suggestions do not reflect the law and cannot overturn the mass of authority to the contrary. Further, even if the above is incorrect, it would be anomalous if the parties to a commercial contract were protected against each other's inconsistent actions whereas consumers were not. In traditional models, it is usually the latter group which are protected against another's unmeritorious **6.10**

Forbearance at paras 12.26 ff.). Axiomatically, that knowledge was not present and therefore there could be no equitable forbearance.

23 [1979] 1 WLR 783 at 810.

24 [1979] 2 Lloyd's Rep. 57 at 69–71.

24a But see *Glencore Grain Rotterdam BV v Lebanese Organisation for International Commerce* [1997] 4 All E.R. 514 *per* Evans L.J. at 530; in which the Learned Judge appeared to accept that a form of estoppel was operating in *Panchaud*.

25 *Paal Wilson & Co A/S v Partenreederei Hannah Blumenthal* [1983] 1 AC 854 *per* Lord Diplock at 916 A–C.

26 See *Mitsui Babcock Energy Ltd v John Brown Engineering Ltd* (1997) 51 Con LR 129 *per* H.H. Judge Esyr Lewis Q.C. at 185.

27 See *Sunbird Plaza Pty Ltd v Maloney* (1988) 166 CLR 245 at 263.

28 See *The Commonwealth of Australia v Verwayen* (1990) 170 CLR 394 at 449.

actions rather than the former. Finally, the *Panchaud* principle suggests that the parties to a contract owe reciprocal obligations to each other in addition to those set down in the contract. Those reciprocal obligations are equivalent to the parties being obliged to act 'fairly'. Apart from the limited circumstances in which the law imposes an obligation to act fairly or in good faith,[29] the law is antipathetic to the imposition of such obligations as it runs contrary to the *laissez faire* attitude adopted towards parties' freedom to contract. If the Court of Appeal in *Panchaud* intended to take such a step, there is no doubt that it would have done so explicitly.[29a]

EFFECT OF THE DECISION

It follows from the above that *Panchaud* is an unsatisfactory decision **6.11**
which accords neither with principle nor with logic. However, *Panchaud* has not been overruled and therefore must be treated as good law. We are therefore reluctant to suggest that *Panchaud* was wrongly decided.[30] It is therefore submitted that the proper view is that suggested by Mr Justice Goff in *BP Exploration Co.*, *Panchaud* is authority for the proposition that, in certain extreme circumstances, a party to a shipping and/or supply contract will be precluded from relying on an otherwise valid ground for repudiating the contract.[30a] Viewed in this light, *Panchaud* forms part of a line of cases to this effect[31] which are extremely difficult to explain[32] and limited to their particular facts.

---

[29] Contracts *uberrimae fides* and as set out in Council Directive 93/13/EEC on Unfair Terms in Consumer Contracts, Art. 3.

[29a] In *Glencore Grain Rotterdam BV v Lebanese Organisation for International Commerce* [1997] 4 All E.R. the Court of Appeal considered whether there was a *Panchaud* doctrine before adopting Goff J's approach in BP.

[30] For a contrary view see Dugdale and Yates (1976) 39 MLR 680 at 691.

[30a] A view supported by the *ratio* of *Glencore Grain Rotterdam BV v Lebanese Organisation for International Commerce* [1997] 4 All E.R. 514 *per* Evans L.J. at 530i–j.

[31] See, for example, *Braithwaite v Foreign Hardwood Co* [1905] 2 KB 543.

[32] In *Esmail v J Rosenthal & Sons Ltd* [1964] 2 Lloyd's Rep. 447, Salmon L.J. was the only one of the three Lord Justices who felt able to attempt even a tentative explanation of *Braithwaite*.

Chapter 7

ELECTION, AFFIRMATION AND ACQUIESCENCE

INTRODUCTION

It is axiomatic in our analysis of waiver above, in particular in the use of the category of 'waiver by election', that there is a substantial overlap in theory between one type of waiver and election. For present purposes, four additional points must be made. First, in practice, a distinction may be drawn between waiver by election and election. The former will only lead to rights being lost while the latter may lead to the preservation or loss of rights dependent on circumstances.[1] Notwithstanding this practical difference, analytically, however, there is no distinction between the doctrines.[2] Secondly, as election is but one type of waiver, election is a subset of an overall category 'waiver' by which a party foregoes its rights.[3] Thirdly, it follows that the principles which are applicable to election can also be applied to waiver and, to a limited degree, *vice versa*. Fourthly, it also follows that the effect of an election will be the same as the effect of a waiver by election.[4] **7.01**

We would additionally suggest that election is, in one sense, synonymous with affirmation;[5] affirmation in the sense of a decision of a party to be bound by the contract notwithstanding a repudiatory breach of the contract by the other party.[6] Further, these three synonymous concepts[7] are capable of distinction from the similar **7.02**

---

1 For example, whether the party chooses to accept the repudiation and rely on its accrued rights to do so or chooses to remain bound by the contract.

2 See paras 7.04 ff., below.

3 For a contrary view see Carter at para. 1041, p. 352.

4 See *Waiver — Complexities* at para. 5.03.

5 *Bliss v South East Thames Regional Health Authority* [1987] ICR 700 *per* Dillon L.J. at 715 G and H and *Tropical Traders Ltd v Goonan* (1964) 111 CLR 41 at 55.

6 That is the 'positive' aspect of election; the negative aspect being the decision to accept the repudiatory breach.

7 Referred to for convenience's sake as 'election'.

equitable doctrine of acquiescence. This chapter is therefore concerned with establishing the contiguity of the three doctrines by setting out the elements of election; analysing the limits on the application of the doctrine; and considering the relationship between election and acquiescence.[8]

ELECTION

ELEMENTS OF THE DOCTRINE

The doctrine can be outlined as: **7.03**

> where a party in his own mind has thought that he would choose one of two remedies, even though he has written it down in a memorandum or has indicated it in some other way, that alone will not bind him; but so soon as he has not only determined to follow one of his remedies but has communicated it to the other side in such a way as to lead the opposite party to believe that he has made that choice, he has completed his election and can go no further; and whether he intended it or not, if he has done an unequivocal act — I mean an act which would be justifiable if he had elected one way and would not be justifiable if he had elected another way — the fact of his having done that unequivocal act to the knowledge of the persons concerned is an election.[9]

Therefore, at root, the doctrine is based on simple considerations of common sense and equity.[10] Two points flow. First, the distinction which was once drawn between the 'equitable' doctrine of election (where a

[8] In so doing, our analysis is confined to the doctrine of election as substantively applied. No consideration is given the use of the term in civil procedure where the plaintiff may *elect* between two particular remedies (see, e.g. *Lordsvale Finance plc v Bank of Zambia* [1996] 3 All ER 156) or between two particular defendants by entering judgment against one of them (Rules of the Supreme Court, Sweet & Maxwell, London, 1997 at para. 14/8/2. In either case, the plaintiff must, before judgment (see *Neilson v Betts* LR 5 HL) have made an informed choice to that end (*Island Records Ltd v Tring International Ltd* [1995] 3 All ER 444 *per* Lightman J. at 447; *Bonus Garment Company v Karl Rieker GmbH & Co KG* [1995] 3 HKC 721 *Tang Man Sit v Capacious Investments Ltd* [1996] 2 WLR 192) and be choosing between two alternative remedies (see Professor P Birks, 'Inconsistency between Compensation and Restitution' (1996) 112 *Law Quarterly Review* pp. 375–9).

[9] *Scarf v Jardine* (1882) 7 App Cas 345 *per* Lord Blackburn at 360–1.

[10] *Johnson v Agnew* [1980] AC 367 *per* Lord Wilberforce at 398.

party seeking to approbate and reprobate a will or other legal document[11]) and the common law doctrine (where a party decides '*whether he will affirm a contract induced by fraud or avoid it, whether he will in certain cases waive a tort and claim as in contract*'[12]) is no longer valid. Both the so-called common law and equitable doctrines are to be viewed as one.[13] That doctrine is applicable to documents and transactions[14] and will be invoked when a party with knowledge of its rights chooses between two inconsistent rights.[15] Secondly, that doctrine is based on considerations of equity only in the loosest sense; namely,[16] preventing a party from adopting inconsistent positions.[17] Thus, the doctrine will apply to a vendor's attempt to revoke the purchase of land whilst taking the benefit of the harvests from that land[18] or a litigant's attempt to pursue a different remedy when it has already obtained judgment claiming a different and inconsistent remedy.[19]

Unequivocal representation

A party will be taken to have elected where it has a choice between two or more courses of action and has so acted that it is plain that it has chosen one course of action as opposed to another.[20] The act of election does not 7.04

[11] *Lissenden v CAV Bosch* [1940] AC 412 *per* Viscount Maugham at 418.

[12] *ibid. per* Viscount Maugham at 418.

[13] *ibid. per* Lord Atkin at 429.

[14] *Verschures Creameries Ltd v Hull and Netherlands Steamship Co Ltd* [1921] 2 KB 608 *per* Scrutton L.J. at 612.

[15] *Lacy v Anderson* (1581–2) Choyce Cases in Chancery 155, 156 and see e.g. *Dillon v Parker* (1818) 1 Swans 539, 36 ER 422 *per* Plumer M.R. at 403.

[16] Once its elements are satisfied.

[17] *Craine v Colonial Mutual Fire Insurance Co Ltd* (1920) 28 CLR 305 *per* Isaacs J. at 326; *Wendt v Bruce* (1931) 45 CLR 245 *per* Gavan Duffy C.J. at 253 and Starke J.; *per* Dixon J. at 257 and *Grundt v Great Boulder Pty Gold Mines Ltd* (1937) 59 CLR 641 at 657 *per* Latham C.J.

[18] *Wendt v Bruce* (1931) 45 CLR 245 *per* Gavan Duffy C.J. at 253 and Starke J. and *per* Dixon J. at 257.

[19] *United Australia Ltd v Barclays Bank* [1941] AC 1 *per* Lord Atkin at 30 and *Meng Leong Development Pte Ltd v Jip Hong Trading Co Pte Ltd* [1985] AC 511 *per* Lord Templeman at 522B–D. See also *Port of Melbourne Authority v Anshun Pty Ltd* (1981) 147 CLR 589 *per* Brennan J. at 611–2 and *Ciaverella v Balmer* (1983) 153 CLR 438 *per* the court at 449.

[20] *Heyman v Darwins Ltd* [1942] AC 356 *per* Viscount Simon L.C. at 361 and *State Trading Corp of India v M Golodetz* [1989] 2 Lloyd's Rep. 277 *per* Kerr L.J. at 286 col. 2. The same test applies to affirmation — see *Car and Universal Finance Co Ltd v Caldwell* [1965] 1 QB 525 *per* Sellers L.J. at 550B.

have to be in any particular form[21] and can arise from a result of a failure to perform in response to breach.[22] However, as a minimum, the election must be conveyed[23] to the other party either by being communicated to it[24] orally or in writing or by conduct.[25] Put simply, there must be an objective manifestation of the choice.[26] Silence or delay, however, will not suffice. We stress, however, that the requirement that the election be conveyed does not mean that any element of detrimental reliance is required for the other party to argue successfully that there was an election.[27] The requirement exists to give some empirical foundation to the doctrine as a marker of the decision which the electing party has reached.[28]

It follows that, in the contractual context,[29] whilst a prudent[30] party **7.05**

---

21 *Vitol SA v Norelf Ltd* [1996] 3 WLR 105 *per* Lord Steyn at 113B.

22 *ibid. per* Lord Steyn at 113F–14E.

23 The word used in *Vitol* above. It is submitted that the reference to the election being 'conveyed' to the other party avoids a false dichotomy between the cases where there is overt communication and those where the courts have inferred election from conduct. The key issue is whether the other party has become aware of the election. See also *Pacific & General Insurance v Hazell* Moore-Bick J. (Com Ct unrep. 17 October 1996.

24 *Lakshmijit v Sherani* [1974] AC 605 *per* Lord Cross at 616C–D; *China National Foreign Trade Transportation Corporation v Evlogia Shipping Co SA of Panama (The Mihalios Xilas)* [1979] 1 WLR 1018 *per* Lord Diplock at 1024D–E and *per* Lord Scarman at 1034H–5B. The communication need not be by a party to contract (see *Wood Factory Pty Ltd v Kiritos Pty Ltd* (1985) 2 NSWLR 105 at 146; *MSC Mediterranean Shipping Co SA v BRE Metro Ltd* [1985] 2 Lloyd's Rep. 239 *per* Saville J. at 240 col. 2 and *Vitol SA v Norelf Ltd* [1996] 3 WLR 105 *per* Lord Steyn at 113C–D).

25 Where there is no overt communication, whether or not there has been an election may be a conclusion of law drawn by the courts (see *State Trading Corp of India v M Golodetz* [1989] 2 Lloyd's Rep. 277 *per* Kerr L.J. at 286 col. 2; *Tropical Traders Ltd v Goonan* (1966) 115 CLR 41 at 55 and *Gator Shipping Corp v Trans-Asiatic Oil SA (The Odenfield)* [1978] 2 Lloyd's Rep. 357 *per* Kerr J. at 379 col. 1. Where the court does so infer it will do so because in the context, one of the party's actions demonstrate objectively and unequivocally that it is making the alleged election (see *Insurance Corporation of the Channel Islands v The Royal Hotel Limited* (unrep. 30/9/97 Comm Ct Mance J.).

26 See *Insurance Corporation of the Channel Islands v The Royal Hotel Limited* (unrep. 30/7/97 Comm Ct Mance J)

27 Detrimental reliance only being required where there is an estoppel. However, an election may give rise in limited circumstances to an estoppel.

28 See *Insurance Corporation of the Channel Islands v The Royal Hotel Limited* (unrep. 30/9/97 Comm Ct Mance J)

29 As pointed out above (n. 8), this work only deals with election as part of the substantial law.

30 In *Insurance Corporation of the Channel Islands v The Royal Hotel Limited* (unrep. 30/7/97 Comm Ct) Mr Justice Mance noted that there may be a distinction between what the reasonable party (alleging the election) may infer and what the prudent

will communicate its election orally or in writing,[31] a party may convey its election to accept a repudiatory breach by: entering into an alternative contract covering the same subject matter as the repudiated contract;[32] discussing settlement options arising from the repudiatory conduct;[33] preventing the other party[34] or itself[35] from performing contract; or by issuing and serving a writ claiming one specific remedy[36] be taken to have elected[37] to pursue that remedy alone and be precluded from pursuing the alternate remedy.[38]

Knowledge

7.06 For there to be an election, the party alleged to have elected must have knowledge of the facts giving rise to the right to elect and of its rights.[39] As with the requirement that there be an unequivocal representation, there is no distinction in this respect between waiver by election[40] and election.

---

party (alleged to have elected) may have thought. That distinction created a 'conundrum' that Mr Justice Mance was not required to resolve. We would suggest, however, that the distinction (a) may only arise in insurance law; (b) and even if it does arise, may be more apparent than real.

31 *Car and Universal Finance Co Ltd v Caldwell* [1965] 1 QB 525 *per* Sellers L.J. at 550D–F.

32 See *State Trading Corp of India v M Golodetz* [1989] 2 Lloyd's Rep. 277.

33 *MSC Mediterranean Shipping Co SA v BRE Metro Ltd* [1985] 2 Lloyd's Rep. 239 *per* Saville J. at 240 col. 2.

34 *Chatterton v Maclean* [1951] 1 All ER 761 *per* Parker J. at 764C–D.

35 *RV Ward v Bignall* [1967] 1 QB 534 *per* Diplock L.J. at 548E-F and *Gator Shipping Corp v Trans-Asiatic Oil SA ('The Odenfield')* [1978] 2 Lloyd's Rep. 357 *per* Kerr L.J. at 379 col. 1.

36 *Heyman v Darwins* [1942] AC 356 *per* Viscount Simon L.C. at 362.

37 The alternative view is that one cause of action has merged with the other — see *Kendall v Hamilton* (1879) 4 App Cas 504 at 513–5 and *Brostoff v Clark Kenneth Leventhal* (unrep 11 March 1996, Dyson J.).

38 *United Australia Ltd v Barclays Bank* [1941] AC 1 *per* Lord Atkin at 30; *Express Newspapers v News (UK) Ltd* [1990] 1 WLR 1320 *per* Browne-Wilkinson V.C. at 1329G and *Meng Leong Development Pte Ltd v Jip Hong Trading Co Pte Ltd* [1985] AC 511 *per* Lord Templeman at 522B–D. See also *Port of Melbourne Authority v Anshun Pty Ltd* (1981) 147 CLR 589 *per* Brennan J. at 611–2 and *Ciaverella v Balmer* (1983) 153 CLR 438 *per* the court at 449.

39 *Kendall v Hamilton* (1879) 4 App Cas 504 *per* Lord Blackburn at 542; and *Insurance Corporation of the Channel Islands v The Royal Hotel Limited* (unrep. 30/9/97 Comm Ct Mance J)

40 For the elements of waiver by election see *Waiver — Types and Elements* at para. 4.01

LIMITS OF THE DOCTRINE

The common law doctrine outlined above may be limited in two main ways: by the terms of the contract and, more doubtfully, by the effect of the rule outlined in *White and Carter (Councils) v McGregor*.[41] **7.07**

The effect of the terms of the contract

The parties can provide for a mechanism by which the innocent party can terminate the contract on repudiatory breach. That mechanism will usually take the form of a notification of breach and election to terminate[42] or initial notification of breach followed by further notification of a failure to cure that breach and subsequent termination[43] or, in shipping cases, withdrawal of the vessel.[44] The purpose of such mechanisms will be to allow a party in breach to cure that breach[45] or to prevent a party from electing to terminate the contract for purely 'formal' or 'technical' breaches of its terms.[46] Where the parties have laid down such notification provisions, the election must strictly comply with said provisions. Therefore, where the contract provides for notice of breach at a certain time or in a certain form, that provision must be complied with.[47] If it is not complied with, the right to elect to terminate the contract for the particular breach, the subject of the notice, will be lost.[48] In those circumstances, if there is no other breach on which the innocent party can rely, its election which does not comply with the contractual provisions will be wrongful.[49] **7.08**

---

41 [1962] AC 413.

42 See, *e.g.* *Steedman v Drinkle* [1916] 1 AC 275 at 278.

43 See, *e.g.* *Hyundai Heavy Industries Co Ltd v Papadopoulos* [1980] 1 WLR 1129 at 1132.

44 *Afovos Shipping Co SA v Pagnan* [1983] 1 WLR 195 at 198A-B; *Rawson v Hobbs* (1961) 107 CLR 466 *per* Dixon C.J. at 477–8; *The Mihalis Angelos* [1971] 1 QB 164 and *Tradax Export SA v Dorada Compania Naviera SA (The Lutetian)* [1982] 2 Lloyd's Rep. 140 *per* Bingham J. at 154 col. 2–155 col. 2.

45 *Afovos Shipping Co SA v Pagnan* [1982] 1 WLR 848 *per* Griffiths L.J. at 856D–G.

46 See *Sale of Goods and Shipping* at para. 20.31 for a discussion of 'anti-technicality' clauses.

47 *Afovos Shipping Co SA v Pagnan* [1982] 1 WLR 848 *per* Lord Griffiths at 858A–B, 859.

48 *Green v Sommerville* (1979) 141 CLR 595 *per* Barwick C.J. at 600.

49 *Tankexpress A/S v Compagnie Financiere Belge des Petroles SA ('The Petrofina')* [1949] AC 76.

The rule in White and Carter (Councils)

In *White and Carter (Councils)*, the House of Lords stated that the innocent party faced with a repudiatory breach could elect either to accept the breach as repudiatory or to remain bound by the contract. If the party chose to remain bound by the contract, the contract would remain on foot and the other party to that contract would remain obliged to perform.[50] The principle makes analytical sense; there is no reason in principle why the innocent party's right to performance under the contract should be curtailed by the other's breach. However, one result is that the contract could be indefinitely prolonged after one party had clearly stated that it did not intend to perform. An indefinite prolongation of that nature gives rise to practical difficulties.[51] Those difficulties may be resolved by creating two exceptions on the rule. First, the House of Lords acknowledged that the innocent party would be forced to accept the repudiation where the continued performance of the contract required the cooperation of the party in breach.[52] This rule covers all contracts where there are bilateral obligations or where the innocent party's rights are dependent on further performance or cooperation[53] by the party in breach.[54] Thus, for example, a party may well be forced to accept the repudiation of a sale of goods contract where the payment of the price will be dependent on the other party accepting delivery.[55] Whilst it might be said that this exception undermines the rule, the exception has the benefit of being founded on common sense[56] and of generating legal certainty. **7.09**

---

[50] [1962] AC413 at 427, 429, 430, 445. See also *Fullers' Theatres Limited v Musgrove* (1923) 31 CLR 524 at 543–4; *Dyke v McLeish Estates Ltd* (1927) 27 SR (NSW) 74 at 76; *Tramways Advertising Pty Ltd v Luna Park (NSW) Ltd* (1938) 38 SR (NSW) 632 *per* Jordan C.J. at 645 and *Ahmed v Estate & Trust Agencies* [1938] AC 624 at 639.

[51] The most obvious being that it makes little sense to keep a contract alive where one party has made it perfectly clear that it will not perform its obligations under the contract.

[52] [1962] AC 413 at 429.

[53] Including passive cooperation (*Hounslow London Borough Council v Twickenham Garden Developments Ltd* [1971] 1 Ch 233 *per* Megarry J. at 253–4) or assistance (*Finelli v Dee* (1968) 67 DLR (2d) 393 *per* Laskin J.A. at 395).

[54] For a discussion of the difficulties arising in employment contracts see *Employment* at paras 18.19.

[55] The principle applies in employment (where the right to be paid wages is only triggered by the offer by the employee to provide services) and potentially to charterparties — see *Clea Shipping Corp v Bulk Oil International (No. 2) ('The Alaskan Trader')* [1984] 1 All ER 129 *per* Lloyd J. at 138a; contra *Gator Shipping Corp v Trans-Asiatic Oil SA ('The Odenfeld')* [1978] 2 Lloyd's Rep. 357.

[56] *cf.* the pragmatic approach of Sachs L.J. in *Decro-Wall International SA v Practitioners in Marketing* [1971] 1 WLR 361 at 375G–H.

Greater difficulties arise, it is submitted, with the second exception. In *White and Carter,* Lord Reid formulated the exception as follows: **7.10**

> It may well be that, if it can be shown that a person has no legitimate interest, financial or otherwise, in performing the contract rather than claiming damages, he ought not to be allowed to saddle the other party with an additional burden with no benefit to himself. If a party has no interest to enforce a stipulation, he cannot in general enforce it, so it might be said that, if a party has no interest to insist on a particular remedy, he ought not to be allowed to penalise the other party by taking one course when another is equally advantageous to him.[57]

Lord Reid then added to this statement by stating that the court might exercise its '*general equitable discretion*' where the innocent party had no '*substantial or legitimate interest*' in continuing with the contract.[58]

Lord Reid's tentative and technically *obiter* statement,[59] it is submitted, left the existence of the exception, the basis on which and the circumstances in which, it would operate unclear. This lack of clarity was not resolved in *White and Carter* nor has it been resolved in subsequent cases. **7.11**

The existence of the exception

The high water mark of the exception was in *Attica Sea Carriers Corp. v Ferrostaal Poseidon Bulk Reederei GmbH,*[60] where the then Master of Rolls examined whether the innocent party had a legitimate interest in not exercising the right to terminate; whether '*in all reason*' the innocent party should have accepted the repudiation, damages being an inadequate remedy.[61] Lord Denning M.R. concluded that if the innocent party did not have that legitimate interest, then the contract terminated. Similarly, in *Clea Shipping Corp v Bulk Oil International Limited ('The Alaskan Trader')*[62] Mr Justice Lloyd, as he then was, held that there must be some fetter '*in extreme cases*' on the innocent party's rights.[63] However, rather than curtail the innocent party's right of election, Mr **7.12**

[57] [1962] AC 413 *per* Lord Reid at 431.
[58] [1962] AC 413 at 431.
[59] See *Clea Shipping Corp v Bulk Oil International (No 2) (The Alaskan Trader')* [1984] 1 All ER 129 *per* Lloyd J. at 132j.
[60] [1976] 1 Lloyd's Rep. 250.
[61] *ibid.* at 255.
[62] [1984] 1 All ER 129.
[63] See also the similar statement by Kerr J. in *Gator Shipping Corporation v Trans-Asiatic Oil Ltd SA ('The Odenfeld')* [1978] 2 Lloyd's Rep. 357 at 374 col. 1 '*It follows that any fetter on the innocent party's right of election whether or not to accept a repudiation will only be applied in extreme circumstances, viz. where*

Justice Lloyd stated that in extreme cases the courts would exercise their equitable jurisdiction and refuse to allow the innocent party a remedy.[64]

7.13 On the other side of the equation, the exception has not been applied where, by keeping the contract on foot, the innocent party would possess a secured, as opposed to an unsecured, claim in a liquidation[65] or would avoid liability to a third party in damages.[66] Further, in *White and Carter* itself Lord Hodson stated

> There is no duty laid upon a party to a subsisting contract to vary it at the behest of the other party so as to deprive himself of the benefit given to him by the contract. To hold otherwise would be to introduce a novel equitable doctrine that a party was not to be held to his contract unless the court in a given instance thought it reasonable so to do. In this case it would make an action for debt a claim for a discretionary remedy. This would introduce uncertainty into the field of contract which appears to be unsupported by authority.[67]

This dictum contradicts the foundation of Lord Reid's formulation — the intervention of equity — and provides a strong policy reason as to why the exception should not exist. It is not possible, in our submission, to reconcile Lord Hodson with Lord Reid by suggesting that the statement '*unless the court in a given instance thought it reasonable to do so*' means that equity could intervene where the innocent party was acting unreasonably.[68] That reading would be to contradict the thrust of Lord Hodson's peech; to take that particular phrase out of its grammatical context and would be contrary to Lord Reid's own rejection of a reasonableness test.[69] As far as *Attica Sea Carriers* is concerned, Lord Justice Orr decided the case primarily by application of the principle that cooperation was necessary[70] with Lord Justice Browne agreeing with both Lord Justice Orr and Lord Denning.[71] It follows that what *Attica Sea Carriers* actually decided

---

damages would be an adequate remedy **and** *where an election to keep the contract alive would be wholly unreasonable.'*

64 At 137b–g. Lloyd J. founded that conclusion on an analogy with the American law of contract (where even in cases of repudiation the innocent party must mitigate its loss) and on the fact that the innocent party's refusal to accept the repudiation was equivalent to its being granted specific performance of the contract.

65 *George Barker (Transport) Ltd v Eynon* [1974] 1 WLR 462.

66 *Ahmed v Estate and Trust Agencies, (1927) Ltd* [1938] AC 624 at 639–40 and *Gator Shipping Corp v Trans-Asiatic Oil SA ('The Odenfeld')* [1978] 2 Lloyd's Rep. 357 *per* Kerr J. at 374.

67 [1962] AC 413 at 445.

68 Carter para. 1125, p 417.

69 [1962] AC 413 at 430.

70 [1976] 1 Lloyd's Rep. 250 at 256.

71 It has also been suggested that *Attica Sea Carriers* is an extreme case which should

is unclear.[72] Additional difficulties arise from *Fercometal v Mediterranean Shipping Co*[73] in which Lord Ackner stated[74] that a party facing repudiatory breach had two choices to affirm or terminate, there being '*no via media*' of some rights remaining in force whilst others do not.[75] Those stark alternatives do not permit the operation of an exception to or fetter on the right of election.

It follows that the status of the exception is far from clear.[76] On balance, we would suggest that there may well be no place for such an exception in English law for four reasons.[77] First, the party in breach should not be permitted, by the mere fact of breach, to relieve itself of the obligations under the contract. Secondly, the obligations assumed under a contract can be analysed into a primary obligation to perform and a secondary obligation to pay damages on breach.[78] The application of the exception erodes that distinction by holding that the innocent party can be satisfied with compliance with the secondary obligation only. Put another way, the primary obligation is to perform and the fact of breach should not allow the party in breach to replace that primary obligation with the secondary. Thirdly, the rights of the party in breach can be adequately protected either by the 'cooperation exception' or by the doctrines set out in this work. The party in breach does not, it is submitted, require further protection. Fourthly, allowing the exception creates uncertainty as to when and in **7.14**

---

be confined to its particular facts — see *Gator Shipping Corp v Trans-Asiatic Oil SA ('The Odenfeld')* [1978] 2 Lloyd's Rep. 357 *per* Kerr J. at 373.

72 For the contrary view see *Clea Shipping Corp v Bulk Oil International (No. 2) ('The Alaskan Trader')* [1984] 1 All ER 129 *per* Lloyd J. at 135f–g.

73 [1989] AC 788.

74 Albeit in a slightly different context.

75 [1989] AC 788 at 805 D–F.

76 *cf. Decro-Wall International SA v Practitioners in Marketing* [1971] 1 WLR 361 at 370E, where Salmon L.J. thought that Lord Reid was paraphrasing an argument addressed to their Lordships without commenting on the quality of that argument.

77 We reject the argument that the doctrine forces the innocent party to accept the repudiation — see *Clea Shipping Corp v Bulk Oil International (No. 2) ('The Alaskan Trader')* [1984] 1 All ER 129 *per* Lloyd J. at 136c.

78 *Robophone Facilities Ltd v Blank* [1966] 1 WLR 1428 *per* Diplock L.J. at 1446A–C; *C Czarnikow Ltd v Koufos* [1966] 2 QB 695 *per* Diplock L.J. at 730F–731B; *RV Ward Ltd v Bignall* [1967] 1 QB 534 *per* Diplock L.J. at 548 B–E; *Banning v Wright* [1972] 1 WLR 972 *per* Lord Simon at 990C–D; *Moschi v Lep Air Services* [1973] AC 331 *per* Lord Diplock at 350C–D and *per* Lord Simon at 355G *Photo Production Ltd v Securicor Transport Ltd* [1980] AC 827 *per* Lord Diplock at 848–50; *Bremer Vulkan Schiffbau und Maschinenfabrik v South India Shipping Corp Ltd* [1981] AC 909 *per* Lord Diplock at 982C–E; *Sudbrook Trading Estate Ltd v Eggleton* [1983] 1 AC 444 *per* Lord Diplock at 478F–G; *Paal Wilson & Co A/S v Partenreederei Hannah Blumenthal* [1983] 1 AC 854 *per* Lord Diplock at 915D–E; *Afovos Shipping Co v Pagnan* [1983] 1 WLR 195 *per* Lord Diplock at 203C–G and *State Trading Company of India v M Golodetz Ltd* [1989] 2 Lloyd's Rep. 285 *per* Kerr L.J. at 285 col. 2–286 col. 1.

what circumstances the innocent party will lose its rights without any act on its part but merely as the result of a conclusion of law reached by the courts as to its 'legitimate interests'.[79]

The difficulty with an outright rejection of the exception is that it is relatively well established in English Law.[80] Therefore, unless and until the point is reviewed by the House of Lords, it must be given some effect. Given the difficulties associated with the exception and the uncertainty generated by it, the most appropriate course would be to confine the exception to those cases where the continuation of the contract would be '*wholly unreasonable . . . quite unrealistic, unreasonable and untenable*'.[81] Put another way, it may well be that the exception enunciated by Lord Reid amounts, and should amount, to no more than a reflection of the practicalities of the case[82] or the fact that the innocent party can only continue the contract with the repudiating party's non-existent cooperation. **7.15**

The basis of the exception

Lord Reid appeared to give two bases for the exception. First, by analogy with the law on penalties, the court could intervene to protect the party being penalized. Secondly, there was a general equitable discretion vested in the court to prevent the innocent party from exercising its rights in such circumstances. Both, it is submitted, are problematic. **7.16**

The analogy with penalties

The analogy with penalties is, it is submitted, flawed. A clause will be penal if it is not a genuine pre-estimate of loss on breach.[83] Therefore, a clause will be penal if it does not accord with the party's secondary obligation to pay damages; it must be the 'imposition of an additional **7.17**

---

[79] The certainty argument was considered and rejected in *Clea Shipping Corp v Bulk Oil International (No. 2) ('The Alaskan Trader')* [1984] 1 All ER 129 *per* Lloyd J. at 137f–g.

[80] *Attica Sea Carriers Corp. v Ferrostaal Poseidon Bulk Reederei GmbH* [1976] 2 Lloyd's Rep. 250; *Gator Shipping Corp v Trans-Asiatic Oil SA ('The Odenfeld')* [1978] 2 Lloyd's Rep. 357 and *Clea Shipping Corp v Bulk Oil International (No. 2) ('The Alaskan Trader')* [1984] 1 All ER 129. As to the American position see *Rockingham County v Luten Bridge Co* 35 F 2d 301 (CA, 4th Cir, 1929) at 308.

[81] *Clea Shipping Corp v Bulk Oil International (No. 2) ('The Alaskan Trader')* [1984] 1 All ER 129 *per* Lloyd J. at 135j citing *The Odenfeld.*

[82] This was the approach taken in *Decro-Wall International SA v Practitioners in Marketing Ltd* [1971] 1 WLR 361.

[83] *Dunlop Pneumatic Tyre Co Ltd v New Garage and Motor Co Ltd* [1915] AC 79 *per* Lord Dunedin at 86–8 and *Bridge v Campbell Discount Co Ltd* [1962] AC 600.

or different liability on breach'[84] and a clause requiring that sums then due under the contract are paid is not penal.[85] Further, the exercise of the power to strike down penalty clauses is a '*blatant interference with freedom of contract and is designed for the sole purpose of providing relief against oppression . . . It has no place where there is no oppression.*'[86] The exception in *White and Carter* relates to the sums due under the contract, there is no need for oppression before it comes into play and (by its substitution of the secondary obligation for the primary obligation) is confined to the damages payable under the contract. It is therefore submitted that no proper analogy can be drawn between the two.

A general equitable discretion

Although election now comprises both equitable election and election at common law,[87] there must, it is submitted, be some doubt as to the extent to which equitable principles can or should operate to mitigate the stark legal choice between the termination or the continuation of the contract. Further, applying the exception has the practical effect[88] of rewriting the bargain by substituting secondary for primary obligations. Absent mistake or rectification, equity will not rewrite the parties' bargain,[89] therefore, it is conceptually difficult to see what role equity can play in this area. Finally, if election is based on common sense,[90] common sense usually implies some form of certainty. The implication of a general, undefined equitable discretion assists, it is submitted, neither certainty nor common sense. **7.18**

That said, if the exception is to continue to exist in English law, its most natural basis must be an unspecified equitable discretion only exercised in limited circumstances for two reasons. First, for the reasons set out above, the doctrine is not founded on the law on penalties. Secondly, equity is a sufficiently flexible and therefore the most appropriate tool for the task. **7.19**

84 *Legione v Hateley* (1983) 152 CLR 406 at 446.

85 See, *e.g. Thompson v Hudson* (1869) LR 4 HL 1 *per* Lord Westbury at 28 and *The Atlantic Star* [1988] 1 Lloyd's Rep. 122 at 125, 127.

86 *Elsey v JG Collins Insurance Agencies Ltd* (1978) 83 DLR (3d) 1 *per* Dickson J. at 15 and *Philips Hong Kong Ltd v Attorney General of Hong Kong* (1993) 61 BLR 49 at 58.

87 See para. 7.03 above.

88 By denying the innocent party its remedy of continuing with the contract — see *Clea Shipping Corp v Bulk Oil International (No. 2) ('The Alaskan Trader')* [1984] 1 All ER 129 *per* Lloyd J. at 136c.

89 See *White and Carter* [1962] AC 413 *per* Lord Hodson at 445. Equity will be particularly reluctant to intervene to alter commercial bargains – see *Scandinavian Trading Tanker Co AB v Flota Petrolera Ecuatoriana ('The Scaptrade')* [1983] 2 All ER 763, [1983] 3 WLR 203.

90 *Johnson v Agnew* [1980] AC 367 *per* Lord Wilberforce at 398.

The circumstances in which the exception would operate

7.20 Given the dubious nature of the exception and the uncertainty of its foundation, it is unsurprising that the circumstances in which it operates are also unclear.[91] There appear to be four possibilities: the innocent party will not be entitled to elect to keep the contract on foot: where it 'ought in all reason' to terminate, damages being an adequate remedy;[92] where it does not have a legitimate interest *simpliciter* in so doing; where it does not have a substantial interest in so doing;[93] and where, in an extreme case, continued performance of the contract is impracticable and unreasonable given the need for cooperation between the parties. The first possibility, it is submitted, draws the ambit of the exception too widely. The innocent party's right to elect is unnecessarily curtailed and no regard is had to the remedial aspects of the issue.[94] As to the second two: the difference between 'legitimate' and 'substantial' interests, is purely semantic and either test generates practical and analytical uncertainty. We would therefore suggest that the proper approach is the fourth allowing the courts to reflect the commercial practicalities of the case and to prevent oppressive or wholly unreasonable conduct.[95]

ACQUIESCENCE

7.21 In *De Bussche v Alt*[96] the court stated the elements of waiver by election as set out above[97] and then queried whether short of waiver by election there was some form of acquiescence whereby:

---

[91] See para. 7.12 above.

[92] *Attica Sea Carriers Corp v Ferrostaal Poseidon Bulk Reederei GmbH* [1976] 1 Lloyd's Rep. 250 *per* Lord Denning M.R. at 255.

[93] [1962] AC 413 *per* Lord Reid at 431.

[94] The exception in *White and Carter* requires examination of the remedies available to the innocent party – see 7.12 above; *Decro Wall International SA v Practitioners in Marketing* [1971] 1 WLR 361 *per* Salmon L.J. at 370D–E and *per* Sachs L.J. at 375H; *Clea Shipping Corp v Bulk Oil International ('The Alaskan Trader')* [1984] 1 All ER 129 *per* Lloyd J, at 137 and *Lusograin Comercio Internacional de Cereas Ltd v Bunge AG* [1986] 2 Lloyd's Rep. 654 at 658.

[95] See para 7.15 above; *Gator Shipping Corp v Trans-Asiatic Oil SA ('The Odenfeld')* [1978] 2 Lloyd's Rep. 357 *per* Kerr J. at 374 and *Clea Shipping Corp v Bulk Oil International ('The Alaskan Trader')* [1984] 1 All ER 129 *per* Lloyd J. at 135j.

[96] (1877) 8 ChD 286.

[97] *ibid. per* James, Baggallay, Thesiger L.JJ. at 313.

> If a person having a right, and seeing another person about to commit, or in the course of committing an act infringing upon that right, stands by in such a manner as to induce the person committing the act, and who might otherwise have abstained from it, to believe that he assents to its being committed, he cannot afterwards be heard to complain of the act. This as Lord Cottenham said in the case already cited[98] is the proper sense of the term "acquiescence", and in that sense may be defined as quiescence under such circumstances as that assent may be reasonably inferred from it, and is no more than an instance of the law of estoppel by words or conduct.[99]

The court expressly distinguished acquiescence from waiver by election[1] thereby raising the question as to what in fact it is.

7.22 It is submitted that it is clear that acquiescence does not form part of the law of waiver for three reasons. First, as set out above, there can be no waiver as a result of a party's mere silence or delay in making its election.[2] Acquiescence by contrast is purely based on silence or a failure to act. Secondly, acquiescence, as enunciated in *De Bussche,* is clearly a wider doctrine than waiver. Thirdly, acquiescence relates to the conduct and belief of the representee, that conduct and belief being irrelevant in cases of waiver.[3] We would therefore suggest that acquiescence has more in common with the law of estoppel [4] which is a flexible doctrine[5] which will prevent a party from relying on its strict legal rights.[6]

---

98 *Duke of Leeds v Earl Amherst* 2 Ph 117 at 123.

99 (1877) 8 ChD 286 *per* James, Baggallay, Thesiger L.JJ. at 314.

1 *ibid.*

2 See *Waiver — Types and elements* para. 4.10.

3 See *Waiver — Terminology* paras. 3.09 ff.

4 *Taylor Fashions Ltd v Liverpool Trustees Co* [1982] 1 QB 133 *per* Oliver J. at 147C–D; *Amalgamated Property Co v Texas Bank* [1982] QB 84 *per* Goff J. at 103B–D and *Habib Bank Ltd v Habib Bank AG* [1981] 1 WLR 1265 *per* Oliver L.J. at 1285B–F. However acquiescence in this sense operates differently from estoppel proper: see para. 11.08 below.

5 *In Re Pauling's Settlement Trusts* [1964] 1 Ch 303 *per* Upjohn L.J. at 353; *Shaw v Applegate* [1977] 1 WLR 970 *per* Buckley L.J. at 977H–8B and *Taylor Fashions Ltd v Liverpool Trustees Co* [1982] 1 QB 133 *per* Oliver J. at 148E–G, 154F–G, 155C–D.

6 See *Willmott v Barber* (1880) 15 ChD 96 *per* Fry J. at 105–6 (party will not be allowed to rely on its rights where it would be fraudulent to do so). Thus, for example, knowledge may be required in certain contexts — see, e.g. *Life Association of Scotland v Siddal* (1861) 3 De GF & J 58, 45 ER 800 at 72–3, 74 at 806 and *per* Turner L.J. *In Re Pauling's Settlement Trusts* [1964] 1 Ch 303 *per* Upjohn L.J. at 353.

Chapter 8

ESTOPPEL BY REPRESENTATION

INTRODUCTION TO THE DIFFERENT TYPES OF ESTOPPEL

The term estoppel originates from the same root as the word stopped, namely the French 'estoup'. The doctrine of estoppel was so named because it originally operated to prevent the party estopped from adducing evidence to contradict its previous representation. As Coke put it: **8.001**

> . . . a man's owne act or acceptance stoppeth or closeth his mouth stoppeth or closeth his mouth to alleage or plead the truth.

The fact that the doctrine led to the suppression of the truth led some earlier judges to stigmatize it as 'odious'.[1] However, it has come to be recognized as an exceptionally useful legal device, being described as '*a simple and wholly untechnical conception, perhaps the most powerful and flexible instrument to be found in any system of court jurisprudence.*'[2] It has also been characterized as a principle of honesty,[3] common sense[4] and common fairness.[5]

---

1 See, for example, *Baxendale v Bennet* (1878) 3 QBD 578 *per* Bramwell L.J. at 529 ('Estoppels are odious, and the doctrine should never be applied without a necessity for it').

2 *Canada and Dominion Sugar Company, Limited v Canadian National (West Indies) Steamships, Limited* [1947] AC 46, PC (Canada) at 56, quoting Sir Frederick Pollock. See also *Simm v Anglo American Telegraph* (1879) 5 QBD 188, CA *per* Bramwell L.J. at 202.

3 *Re Exchange Securities & Commodities Ltd* [1988] Ch 46 *per* Harman J. at 54.

4 *London Joint Stock Bank Ltd v Macmillan* [1918] AC 777 *per* Lord Haldane at 818.

5 *Lyle-Meller v A Lewis & Co* [1956] 1 WLR 29, CA *per* Morris L.J. at 44.

ESTOPPEL IN PAIS

Historically, estoppel was divided into three categories,[6] estoppel by record, estoppel by deed[7] and estoppel in pais.[8] Estoppel by record covers the principles of *res judicata* which determine when parties will be bound by judgments issued in previous proceedings between them. This subject has developed independently of the other two types of estoppel. Its principles are beyond the scope of this work and we make no further reference to them. Estoppel in pais may be further subdivided. It contains both estoppel by convention, which originated in common law, and estoppel by representation.[9] The latter doctrine developed at a later stage. It originated in equity but was subsequently recognized by the common law.[10] Although there is some doubt,[11] estoppel in pais is now commonly regarded as also including the equitable doctrines of promissory estoppel and proprietary estoppel.[12] The latter two doctrines have sometimes been referred to, individually or jointly, as equitable estoppel in order to distinguish them from estoppel by representation.[13] However, the use of the term equitable estoppel is misleading since estoppel by representation is also recognized by the rules of equity. The divide between law and equity plays no significant classificatory role in the law of estoppel. **8.002**

The individual inter-relationships between the various estoppels are discussed in the relevant chapters, to which reference should be made for further detail. Here we seek only to give a brief guide as to the general affiliations between them. **8.003**

---

[6] See Coke, *A Commentary on Littleton* (11th ed., London 1719) at p. 352a.

[7] Coke used the term estoppel by writing but his text makes it is clear that he was referring to the doctrine now known as estoppel by deed (as to which see generally chap. 10 below).

[8] See Coke, *A Commentary on Littleton* (11th ed., London 1719) at para. 352a. The term estoppel by conduct has been used as an alternative to estoppel in pais. This term has also been used to describe estoppel by representation, where the relevant representation is made by conduct rather than by express statement or by silence. See para. 8.52 below. Because of the terminological inconsistency we have avoided the use of this term in our text.

[9] Meagher, at para. 17.02 and *Legione v Hateley* (1983) 152 CLR 406 at 430.

[10] *Legione v Hateley* (1983) 152 CLR 406 at 430.

[11] As to proprietary estoppel, see para. 11.03 and as to promissory estoppel see paras 12.05–7.

[12] *Legione v Hateley* (1983) 152 CLR 406 at 430.

[13] *Roebuck v Mongovin* [1994] 1 All ER 568, HL *per* Lord Brown Wilkinson at 975.

COMMON FEATURES OF THE VARIOUS ESTOPPELS: DETRIMENTAL RELIANCE

In the following analysis, we have used W to signify the party seeking to raise the estoppel and M to signify the party sought to be estopped. Three factors appear to be common to all forms of estoppel. First, that M's conduct led to W forming a certain belief or fortified a belief W already held. Secondly, W, with M's knowledge, changed its position in reliance on the belief. Thirdly, that change of position will lead W to suffer detriment if the truth of the belief is subsequently denied. Fourthly, M seeks to deny the truth of the belief. 8.004

There are some inconsistencies between the operation of these requirements under the respective doctrines. For example, it is by no means clear that detriment is a requirement of promissory estoppel. Additionally, in both promissory and proprietary estoppel significant emphasis is placed on whether it would be inequitable or unconscionable for M to resile from the assumption induced. Such broad concepts have played little, if any, role in estoppel by representation. 8.005

DISTINGUISHING FEATURES OF THE VARIOUS ESTOPPELS: THE CLAIMANT'S BELIEF

The most fundamental point at which the estoppels diverge is as to the nature of the belief or assumption which M's conduct has led W to form. Estoppel by representation and by convention operates where M leads W to believe that a certain state of facts exist. Promissory estoppel operates where M leads W to believe that M's legal rights under a contract or other legal relationship will not be enforced. Proprietary estoppel operates where M leads W to believe that W has, or will obtain, an interest or right over M's property. 8.006

A SINGLE ESTOPPEL DOCTRINE?

There are influential dicta suggesting that a single principle underlies all the forms of estoppel, other than estoppel by record. It has been argued that the doctrines are all examples of a general principle which operates to prevent M's unjust denial of an assumption or belief which it has 8.007

permitted or encouraged W to act upon to its detriment.[14] A significant difficulty with this theory is that there are inconsistencies between the reliance and detriment requirements of the various doctrines. However, as far as these matters are concerned, there is sufficient evidence of convergence to make the single estoppel theory at least tenable.[15]

The main difficulty with the theory is that, as paragraph 8.06 shows, **8.008** estoppel will operate only when certain circumscribed and specified types of assumption or belief are formed by W. In particular, assumptions as to M's *future intention* will give rise to an estoppel only in the limited circumstances where promissory or proprietary estoppel apply. This restriction was imposed to preserve the boundary between estoppel and contract: representations as to future intention amount to promises and, according to orthodox contract theory, are only enforceable if given for consideration.[16] Three main methods of overcoming this difficulty have been advocated. First, although both estoppel by representation and estoppel by convention are supposedly confined to assumptions of fact, this limiting factor is so elastic as to make it ineffectual. For example, M may be estopped, under either of these doctrines, from denying that a legally binding obligation has been entered into. The distinction between promising to undertake such an obligation and representing that such an obligation has in fact been entered into seems illusory. Hence, it is argued, estoppel is operating on promises as to future intentions and obligations. Although the line between fact and intention may not always be drawn with consistency or clarity, it is still one which the courts seek to draw. Hence, these estoppels are still restricted to representations of fact.[17] Secondly, it has been argued that promissory estoppel can and should operate to create new rights rather than merely to include promises to forbear from enforcing existing ones. This approach has been adopted by the Australian High Court.[18] The issue

---

[14] *Amalgamated Investment & Property Co. Ltd, (in liquidation) v Texas Commerce International Bank Ltd* [1982] 1 QB 84 *per* Lord Denning M.R. at 122a–d; *Lyle-Meller v A Lewis & Co* [1956] 1 WLR 29, CA *per* Denning L.J. at 35 and *Moorgate Mercantile Co Ltd v Twitchings* [1976] 1 QB 225, CA *per* Lord Denning M.R. at 241. For dicta suggesting that the distinctions between certain limited categories should be removed see *Crabb v Arun DC* [1976] Ch 179 *per* Lord Scarman at 193b and *Taylors Fashions Ltd* v *Liverpool Victoria Trustees Co Ltd* [1982] 1 QB 133 *per* Oliver J. at 151.

[15] At para. 8.04 above.

[16] *Jorden v Money* (1854) V HLC, 185 10 ER 868 and paras 8.27–9.

[17] See generally paras 8.28 to 8.34 below.

[18] *Waltons Stores (Interstate) Ltd v Maher* [1988] 164 CLR 387 and *Commonwealth of Australia v Verwayen* [1990] 170 CLR 394.

is discussed further at paragraphs 12.61 to 12.67. For the reasons we there put forward, we submit that the promissory estoppel doctrine is correctly confined to forbearances. To assert that the doctrine may be used to create new rights is to mistake its inherent nature. Promissory estoppel is essentially analogous to a waiver with insufficient knowledge for the operation of the latter doctrine.[19] Hence, we have chosen generally to use the term equitable forbearance to describe this doctrine rather than the more common designation of promissory estoppel.[20] Thirdly, it has been submitted that proprietary estoppel may operate in relation to assurances unrelated to property. Although the cases offer some support for such an approach, for the reasons given at paragraphs 11.87 and 11.96 to 11.101 we submit that the scope of proprietary estoppel is still confined to instances where W believes that it has or will be granted a right in M's property. The final difficulty with the theory is that estoppel by representation and convention probably admits of only one remedial response, namely that M is prevented from denying the facts which it has led W to believe.[21] In marked contrast, the relief granted under promissory and proprietary estoppel will not always lead to M's being required to make good W's belief, though it may sometimes do so. In proprietary estoppel, the court will award the minimum equity necessary to avert detriment to W.[22] Although the position is less clear with respect to promissory estoppel, it is submitted that the same approach is applicable.[23] For assimilation to occur, some adjustment has to be made to the remedial approaches currently adopted in the various doctrines. Adopting the flexible detriment based approach in cases of estoppel by representation and convention would involve a fundamental reappraisal of the nature of the two doctrines. It would necessitate acknowledging that they are not merely evidential doctrines but principles of substantive law.[24]

---

[19] See paras 4.38–43 above and para. 12.24 below.

[20] See further para. 12.05–7.

[21] See paras 8.118 to 8.119 and 9.05 below.

[22] See paras 11.51–4 below.

[23] See paras 12.55–6 below.

[24] It should be noted that even the radical developments recently seen in the Australian jurisdiction have not extended to the assimilation of all types of estoppel. According to the majority of the High Court, the estoppel by representation doctrine remains distinct from the equitable estoppel principle recently developed and expanded in that jurisdiction: *Waltons Stores (Interstate) Ltd v Maher* [1988] 164 CLR 387; *Commonwealth of Australia v Verwayen* [1990] 170 CLR 394 and *McCraith v Fraser* (1991) 104 FLR (Aus) 227. But see the minority judgments of Deane J. in *Waltons Stores* above and of Mason C.J. and Deane J. in *Verwayen* above.

In summary, it is clear that the rules governing the various types of estoppel analysed in this work remain distinct. The assimilation approach has not been accepted in English law. This was recently emphasized by Lord Justice Millet: **8.009**

> [The attempt] to demonstrate that all estoppels other than estoppel by record are now subsumed in a single and all embracing estoppel by representation and that they are all governed by the same requirements has never won general acceptance. Historically unsound, it has been repudiated by academic writers and is unsupported by authority.[25]

Similarly Lord Steyn recently declined an invitation to formulate a single general principle to cover the two types of estoppel with which he was faced in the *'The Indian Endurance' (No 2) Republic of India v India Steamship Company*:[26]

> The question was debated whether estoppel by convention and estoppel by acquiescence are but aspects of one overarching principle. I do not underestimate the importance of the continuing development of the law and the search for simplicity. I also accept that at a high level of abstraction such an overarching principle could be formulated. But . . . [I am persuaded] . . . that to restate the law in terms of an overarching principle might tend to blur the necessarily separate requirements and distinct terrain of application, of the two kinds of estoppel.[27]

Theoretical issues and future developments

One criticism which may be made of the continued separation of estoppel into categories is that there seem to be no sensible or intelligible criteria to distinguish which types of assumptions are capable of giving rise to an estoppel and which are not. There is some substance to this criticism, but arguably, a coherent dividing line can be identified. Generally, any assumptions may trigger an estoppel except promises as to future intention. These should be generally be governed by the law of contract and so be incapable of giving rise to an estoppel,[28] except in **8.010**

---

[25] *First National Bank v Thompson* [1996] 1 All ER 140, CA at 144h–j.

[26] [1997] 4 All ER 380. See also *Dun & Bradstreet Software Services (England) Ltd v Provident Mutual Life Assurance Association* [1997] EGCS 89 CA, lexis transcript, discussed at para. 12.67 below.

[27] [1997] 4 All ER 380 at 392c–e (Lords Hoffmann, Lord Cooke of Thorndon, Lord Hope of Craighead and Lord Browne-Wilkinson concurring). For problems surrounding the term estoppel by acquiescence see para. 8.57 below.

[28] See para. 8.08 above and 8.27–33 below.

special circumstances. Those special circumstances cover instances where a promise is made to forbear from enforcing a positive subsisting legal right, whether a proprietary[29] or contractual one.[30] The rationale for this division is that people expect to be able to retract gratuitous promises and should normally be allowed to do so. However, where those promises relate to subsisting entitlements, more caution may reasonably be expected of the promisor. The promisor only enjoys those pre-existing rights by virtue of the law's enforcement mechanisms. Hence the promisor may be expected to exercise them in a responsible manner, if it is to continue to retain them. If detrimental reliance occurs, it is reasonable for the courts to modify or extinguish the rights it previously accorded to the promisor. We suggest below[31] that the differences in the effects of promissory estoppel/equitable forbearance and proprietary estoppel have been exaggerated. They both operate only to reduce the pre-existing rights of the promisor and not to impose new burdens on it.

If a single all embracing estoppel does emerge, a new theory will have to be developed to demonstrate which assumptions should be capable of giving rise to an estoppel and which should not. It has been frequently asserted that the governing criteria should be whether it would be unconscionable for M to deny the assumption it has induced W to form.[32] The danger of this approach rests in the fact that unconscionability may provide such vague and undefined criteria for the imposition of liability, as to lead to uncertainty. As we set out generally in this work, the case-law indicates that certain core requirements must be met before a finding of unconscionability may be made for the purposes of estoppel. These consist of three elements. Firstly, M has played some role in inducing M to form or retain a certain belief or assumption. Secondly, We has relied to detriment on that assumption or belief. Thirdly, M knew of the reliance or intended that the assumption should be relied on. Put simply, the unconscionability concept has been used as a shorthand to describe the orthodox elements of the estoppel doctrine. **8.011**

---

29 Potentially giving rise to a proprietary estoppel.

30 Potentially triggering the equitable forbearance/promissory estoppel doctrine.

31 See further paras 11.96–101 and in particular 11.116–7 below.

32 *Taylors Fashions Ltd v Liverpool Victoria Trustees Co Ltd* [1982] 1 QB 133 per Oliver J. at 151, *Commonwealth of Australia v Verwayen* [1990] 170 CLR 394 per McHugh J. at 501; Halliwell 'Estoppel: Unconscionability as a Cause of Action' (1994) 14 *LS* 15; Lunney 'Towards a Unified Estoppel — The Long and Winding Road' [1992] *Conv* 239; Joshua Getzler 'Unconscionable Conduct and Unjust Enrichment' (1990) 16 *Mon ULR* 283 at 305–6 and Mason 'The Place of Equity and Equitable Remedies on the Contemporary Common Law World' [1994] 110 *LQR* 238 at 253–6.

In particular detriment to W is essential for a finding of unconscionability.[33] The only point of difficulty is whether other factors can and should also be taken into account once the threshold requirements described have been established.[34] According to the unconscionability theorists, the scope of estoppel is not limited at all by the content of the assumption but only by the other elements necessary to establish the doctrine. Put simply, any assumption would be capable of triggering estoppel if qualifying reliance and detriment is shown. This might well be thought to extend the doctrine too widely. Alternatively, it has been suggested that an estoppel should arise only where the assumption was one on which it was reasonable to rely.[35] Such a requirement has only been clearly articulated in relation to estoppel by representation.[36] Arguably, however, English law imposes such a requirement across all the estoppel categories. The orthodox limits on the scope of actionable assumptions may be restated in terms of reasonableness. While it might often be reasonable to rely on another's statement of fact, it is seldom reasonable to rely on a promise which is not supported by consideration.[37] Special factors have to be demonstrated to justify such reliance, namely where the promise is made in relation to existing and positive entitlements.[38] In our view, neither the courts nor academics have so far come up with an alternative convincing and workable rationale to determine which assumptions it is reasonable to rely on and which it is not.[39]

---

[33] See paras 8.04 to 8.05 (general principles), 8.85 to 8.107 (estoppel by representation), 9.04 (estoppel by convention), 11.31 to 11.47 (proprietary estoppel), 12.33 to 12.48 (promissory estoppel/equitable forbearance).

[34] See paras 8.91 to 8.92 (estoppel by representation — only detriment is relevant), 11.34 and 11.70 (proprietary estoppel — other factors can be taken into account), 12.49 to 12.50 (promissory estoppel/equitable forbearance — other factors can be taken into account).

[35] Robertson, Situating Equitable Estoppel Within the Law of Obligations [1997] Syd LR 32. Others suggest estoppel should operate to fulfil the reasonable expectations of the parties: Steyn, Contract Law: Fulfilling the Reasonable Expectations of Honest Men [1997] 113 LQR 433, Baker, From Sanctity of Contract to Reasonable Expectation? (1979) CLP 17 and Thompson, From Representation to Expectation: Estoppel as a Cause of Action [1983] CLJ 257.

[36] See paras 8.80 to 8.82 below.

[37] *Amalgamated Investment & Property Co. Ltd, (in liquidation) v Texas Commerce International Bank Ltd.* [1982] QB 84 per Goff J. at 107a–c and *Waltons Stores (Interstate) Ltd v Maher* [1988] 164 CLR 387 *per* Mason C.J. and Wilson J. at 406.

[38] See the rationalization of the current scope of assumptions triggering estoppel suggested in para. 11.10 above.

[39] Although see the interesting attempt to do so by Michael Spence in his article, Australian Estoppel and the Protection of Reliance, (1997) JCL 203. Robertson, in his article 'Situating Equitable Estoppel Within the Law of Obligations' [1997] *Syd L.R.* 32 acknowledges at page 57 that Australian High Court failed to deal with this

Recent attention has focused on where estoppel should be positioned within the sub-divisions of the law of obligations.[40] Professor Burrows has identified the divisions which flow from the three most important principles in the law of obligations: *'the fulfilment of expectations engendered by a binding promise, the compensation of wrongful harm and the reversing of unjust enrichment'*.[41] These categories reflect the orthodox categories of contract, tort and restitution. Estoppel may be distinguished from restitution in that it may operate where no enrichment has passed to the defendant.[42] There is, however, a considerable overlap between the two areas because the acts of detrimental reliance frequently do enrich the defendant.[43] Where, for example, benefits are conferred by one party on another in anticipation of a contract, it is possible for both estoppel and restitution to operate.[44] Given the defining importance of enrichment to the law of restitution, its secondary importance in estoppel cases must rule out a joint categorisation of the two areas of law. It has been suggested that estoppel should be categorized as part of the law of promises and grouped together with, or included in, the law of contract.[45] This issue is considered in detail in relation to proprietary estoppel. The similarity of estoppel and contract is at its most obvious in relation to this type of estoppel since proprietary estoppel can clearly be used as a cause of action to give effect to promises unsupported by consideration.[46] As we later point out,[47] estoppel has a **8.012**

---

question in *Waltons Stores (Interstate) Ltd v Maher* [1988] 164 CLR 387: although the requirement that the parties be in a pre-existing legal relationship was abandoned (see para. 8.08 above), the court did not reveal whether *any* and if so what type of pre-existing relationship was necessary.

40 Robertson 'Situating Equitable Estoppel Within the Law of Obligations' [1997] *Syd LR* 32.

41 Burrows 'Contract, Tort and Restitution — A Satisfactory Divide or Not?' [1983] 99 *LQR* 217.

42 See *Avon CC v Howlett* [1983] 1 WLR 605 CA (estoppel by representation), *Crabb v Arun DC* [1976] Ch 179 (proprietary estoppel) and *Cerealmangimi SpA v Toepfer* [1981] 3 All ER 533 (equitable forbearance/promissory estoppel).

43 See for example *Inwards v Baker* [1965] 2 QB 29 CA where the promisee had built a house on the land of the promisor and generally Goff and Jones at 559–563 who appear to categorize a number of estoppel cases as part of the law of restitution.

44 See, for example the type of situation in issue in *Regalian Properties* v *London Docklands Development Corpn* [1995] 1 WLR 212 (noted McKendrick 'Negotiations Subject to Contract' [1994] *RLR* 100) where estoppel received surprisingly little consideration from either the parties or the judge. *Ibid* at p. 227.

45 Burrows 'Contract, Tort and Restitution — A Satisfactory Divide or Not?' [1983] 99 *LQR* 217 at 243–4; Birks 'Equity in the Modern Law: An Exercise in Taxonomy' (1996) 26 UWALR 1, Hugh Collins *The Law of Contract*, Butterworths, London, 1997, 3rd Ed. chapter 5.

46 See paras 11.12–15 and 11.102–7 below.

47 *ibid.*

much wider scope than contract, since it may operate on assurances and statements which are not promises. This objection need not be insurmountable, given the elasticity of the concept of the promise. The more important issue revolves around the relief available in estoppel cases. If the aim of the remedy is to make good the expectation or enforce the promise, it becomes plain that estoppel does fit within the first of Professor Burrows' categories. If, however, the remedy available is aimed at reversing the detriment suffered, namely the claimant's reliance loss, estoppel is operating to compensate wrongful harm. In that case, the appropriate categorisation for estoppel is as part of the law of wrongs. There is considerable controversy as to which of these approaches to relief is the correct one. As we set out above,[48] the expectation approach is adopted in estoppel by representation and convention, whilst we consider that the correct approach in promissory and proprietary estoppel is the reliance approach. A further complication is provided by the fact that promissory estoppel is arguably a specific response to the inadequacies of the contractual doctrine of waiver.[49] This illustrates the premature nature of this debate. Unless there is a single estoppel doctrine, it is difficult or impossible to place it in one category. It has been suggested simply that some estoppel cases fall into the contract or consensual category and some fall into the wrongs category.[50]

By way of contrast the Australian High Court has gone further than the English Courts towards merging the estoppel categories. It has been accepted that estoppel can operate on promises as to future intention and can give rise to a cause of action and create new rights. The restriction of substantive equitable estoppel to promises not to enforce subsisting contractual or proprietary rights has been abandoned.[51] Although this new type of 'equitable estoppel' seems to be capable of subsuming the area currently covered by estoppel by representation, the majority of the court has yet to accept the complete abandonment of the old distinctions.[52] **8.013**

[48] At para. 8.09.

[49] See paras 4.38–43 and 8.08 above and 12.06 below.

[50] P.D. Finn 'Unconscionable Conduct' (1994) *JCL* 37, commenting that *Waltons Stores (Interstate) Ltd v Maher* [1988] 164 CLR 387 was a contractual type case and that *Commonwealth of Australia v Verwayen* [1990] 170 CLR 394 was a case based on the commission of a wrong. Note also McBride's interesting suggestion that estoppel falls within a new category of common law obligation namely one which imposes a duty to prevent detrimental reliance on a promise: see McBride 'A Fifth Common Law Obligation' (1994) 14 *LS* 35 at pp. 45–50.

[51] *Waltons Stores (Interstate) Ltd v Maher* [1988] 164 CLR 387 and *Commonwealth of Australia v Verwayen* [1990] 170 CLR 394. See para. 8.08 above.

[52] A minority in *Waltons Stores (Interstate) Ltd v Maher* [1988] 164 CLR 387 and *Commonwealth of Australia v Verwayen* [1990] 170 CLR 394 took the view that estoppel by representation could be merged with the new estoppel. See para. 8.08, n. 24 above.

However, it seems that a single detriment based estoppel doctrine is emerging, designed to compensate the detriment suffered by the claimant rather than necessarily fulfilling its expectation.[53] Given the compensatory approach to relief, this doctrine would seem to fit more neatly into the wrongs category than the contract one.[54] Further, it may be possible to describe the doctrine using the duty based terminology usually associated with the law of tort. For example, the estoppel might arise as a result of breach of a duty to ensure the reliability of its representations[55] or a duty to prevent harm flowing from reliance on its conduct.[56] This 'equitable estoppel' as developed in the Australian courts is thus best viewed as part of the law of wrongs. An analogy with tort may give useful insight into, for example, issues of causation and quantum. However, it might also provide a salutary example of the difficulties which flow from attempting to formulate broad general principles to replace pre-existing discrete legal categories.[57] Where as in the English law of estoppel, there is no established general principle, the analogy and model breaks down. Certainly the substantive English doctrine of proprietary estoppel displays elements in common with the Australian doctrine and might most appropriately placed within the law of wrongs because of its remedial consequences. However, promissory estoppel/ equitable forbearance is more realistically viewed as contractual, being analogous to an extended form of waiver (see paragraph 8.08 above). It is impossible to classify all of the English estoppel doctrines under a single category because the significant internal differences between them.

INTRODUCTION TO ESTOPPEL BY REPRESENTATION

Estoppel by representation is a doctrine recognized by both law and equity. **8.014**
Moreover, since *Jorden v Money*,[58] it has been clear that the doctrine operates in the same way in both the jurisdictions. Considerable difficulty has,

[53] *Waltons Stores (Interstate) Ltd v Maher* [1988] 164 CLR 387 at 423 and *Commonwealth of Australia v Verwayen* [1990] 170 CLR 394 at 413.

[54] Robertson 'Situating Equitable Estoppel Within the Law of Obligations' [1997] *Syd LR* 32 and Spence 'Australian Estoppel and the Protection of Reliance' (1997) *JCL* 203.

[55] Spence 'Australian Estoppel and the Protection of Reliance' (1997) *JCL* 203.

[56] Robertson 'Situating Equitable Estoppel Within the Law of Obligations' [1997] *Syd LR* 32. See also McBride 'A Fifth Common Law Obligation' (1994) 14 *LS* 35 at 45–50.

[57] See the painful history of the tort of negligence, in particular *Anns v Merton LBC* [1978] AC 728, *Caparo Industries v Dickman* [1990] 2 AC 605, *Murphy v Brentwood DC* [1991] 1 AC 398 and *White v Jones* [1995] 2 AC 207.

[58] *Jorden v Money* (1854) V HLC 185, 10 ER 868.

however, arisen in this area in relation to the concept generally referred to as estoppel by negligence. As we set out below,[59] most, and probably all, of the so-called estoppel by negligence cases are better explained by other legal principles. We submit that estoppel by negligence is neither a valid legal principle nor one that falls within the law of estoppel or of estoppel by representation. However, we have continued to cite a number of these authorities in support of general points on estoppel by representation. Only where the relevant point is a controversial one, have we flagged the estoppel by negligence cases. We have approached the cases in this way for two reasons. First, the estoppel by negligence principle is highly controversial and the general conclusions we draw are certainly open to contrary argument. It is therefore possible our view of the issue is incorrect and that the cases do form part of the law of estoppel. Secondly, the analysis used in many of the cases does utilize estoppel principles. These principles are frequently correctly stated, although we dispute the correctness of their application in estoppel by negligence cases.

SUMMARY OF ELEMENTS

An estoppel by representation will arise between A and B if the following **8.015**
elements are made out. Firstly, A makes a false[60] representation of fact to B or to a group of which B was a member. Secondly, in making the representation, A intended or knew that it was likely to be acted upon. Thirdly, B, believing the representation, acts to its detriment in reliance on the representation. Fourthly, A subsequently seeks to deny the truth of the representation. Fifthly, no defence to the estoppel can be raised by A.

A RULE OF EVIDENCE OR SUBSTANTIVE LAW: MAY ESTOPPEL BY REPRESENTATION GIVE RISE TO A CAUSE OF ACTION?

The weight of authority favours the view that estoppel by representa- **8.016**
tion is a rule of evidence rather than of substantive law.[61] The doctrine

[59] At paras 8.146 to 8.160.

[60] As is set out at para. 8.72 below, it is not necessary to demonstrate that A knew that the representation was untrue.

[61] *Low v Bouverie* [1891] 3 Ch 82 CA at 105; *Oliver v Bank of England* [1902] 1 Ch.

does not, in itself, amount to a cause of action.[62] Once the constituent elements of the estoppel are established, the court will not allow the representor to adduce evidence which contradicts the truth of the representation which it has made. The legal relationship of the parties is then assessed according the facts as represented and not according to the true state of affairs. In other words, estoppel by representation operates only to set up a state of facts. The result of the case will be determined according to the legal consequences flowing from the state of facts set up. Hence, it is the facts set up and not the estoppel, which are the source of the substantive legal obligation.

The doctrine may have a crucial, albeit indirect, effect on the result of a case. It may be 'a step on the way'[63] to establishing a cause of action. The doctrine will have a decisive effect if the existence of the fact, which the representor is estopped from denying, determines whether the action will succeed or fail.[64] Thus, the doctrine may, and frequently does, give rise indirectly to a cause of action, where it operates to set up a state of facts which themselves vest a cause of action in the representee. **8.017**

For example, in *Farrow v Orttewell,*[65] D served a notice to quit on P, who was an agricultural tenant. Such tenants, who left as a result of a **8.018**

610, CA at 628 (affd without comment on the point at *Starkey v Bank of England* [1903] AC 114); *Lyle-Meller v A Lewis & Co* [1956] 1 WLR 29, CA *per* Hodson L.J. at 40 and *per* Lord Denning M.R. at 36 (contrasting the doctrine with promissory estoppel); *Bell v Marsh* [1903] 1 Ch 528, CA *per* Lord Collins M.R. at 540; *London Joint Stock Bank Ltd v Macmillan* [1918] AC 777 *per* Lord Haldane at 818; *Greenwood v Martins Bank Ltd* [1932] 1 KB 371, CA *per* Scrutton L.J. at 379 and [1933] AC 51 at *per* Lord Tomlin at 59 ('a procedural matter'); *Nippon Menkwa Kabushiki Kaisha (Japan Cotton Trading Co Ltd) v Dawson's Bank Ltd* (1935) 51 Lloyd's Rep. 147, PC (India) *per* Lord Russell at 150 col. 2; *Avon CC v Howlett* [1983] 1 WLR 605, CA *per* Slade L.J. at 622c–d; *Evans v Bartlam* [1937] AC 473 *per* Lord Wright at 484; *Re Exchange Securities & Commodities Ltd* [1988] Ch 46 at *per* Harman J. at 54 and *Hopgood v Brown* [1955] 1 WLR 213 *per* Evershed M.R. at 223.

[62] *Low v Bouverie* [1891] 3 Ch 82, CA *per* Bowen L.J. at 105; *In re Ottos Kopje Diamond Mines Ltd* [1893] 1 Ch 618 CA at 628; *Seton, Laing v Lefone* (1887) 19 QBD 68, CA at 70 and 618 *Nippon Menkwa Kabushiki Kaisha (Japan Cotton Trading Co Ltd) v Dawson's Bank Ltd* [1935] 51 Lloyd's Rep. 147, PC (India) *per* Lord Russell at 150 col. 2.

[63] *Low v Bouverie* [1891] 3 Ch 82, CA at 105. See also *Lyle-Meller v A Lewis & Co* [1956] 1 WLR 29, CA *per* Hodson L.J. at 40 and *Canada and Dominion Sugar Company, Limited v Canadian National (West Indies) Steamships, Limited* [1947] AC 46, PC (Canada) at 56.

[64] *Low v Bouverie* [1891] 3 Ch 82 CA at 112 and *Nippon Menkwa Kabushiki Kaisha (Japan Cotton Trading Co Ltd) v Dawson's Bank Ltd* [1935] 51 Lloyd's Rep. 147, PC (India) *per* Lord Russell at 150 col. 2. See also the examples cited below.

[65] [1943] Ch 480, CA.

valid notice, had a statutory right to apply for compensation.[66] In fact, the notice was invalid because it was served by D prior to his acquiring legal title to the premises in issue. D was estopped from denying that the notice was valid. P therefore had a cause of action against D because of the statute applied to the *assumed* state of affairs set up by the estoppel, namely the situation where a tenant leaves agricultural land after receiving a valid notice to quit. In *TCB Ltd v Gray*[67] a contract of guarantee was drawn up. Acting under a power of attorney granted by the guarantor, R consented to the removal of a clause limiting the liability under the guarantee. The power of attorney had not been properly executed but the guarantor was estopped from denying that it was valid. The bank could sue for the full amount of the principal debt rather than the lesser sum due under the unamended agreement. The cause of action flowed from the assumed state of facts namely a that a contract had been entered into in the amended rather than the original form.

Similarly, estoppel by representation may provide a defence to a cause of action which would otherwise have succeeded. For example, in *Daejan Properties Ltd v Mahoney*,[68] a landlord was estopped from denying that it had entered into a contract which gave the tenant protection equivalent to that of a statutory tenancy under the Rent Act 1977. Such a tenancy precluded an action for possession, giving the tenant a defence to the landlord's action. In *Ismail v Polish Ocean Lines*,[69] a cargo owner was not allowed to claim damages for improper storage because his agent had represented that the method used was adequate. **8.019**

The issue under consideration has frequently been debated in terms of whether estoppel by representation may be used as a sword or a shield. Such terminology may mislead in this context. It should be noted that estoppel by representation may be used both offensively and defensively, in the manner set out above. What it cannot be used to do is to create new rights independent of a collateral and subsisting cause of action arising from the facts which the representor is estopped from denying. It is only in this sense that it is true to say that estoppel by representation may not be used as a sword. **8.020**

66 Agricultural Holdings Act 1923.
67 [1986] Ch 621.
68 [1995] 2 EGLR 75, CA.
69 [1976] QB 893, CA.

Difficulties with the evidential analysis

Some have classified estoppel by representation as a principle of substantive law[70] because it may have the decisive impact adverted to above.[71] Further, as is set out in paragraph 8.30 below, estoppel by representation may operate to prevent the representor denying 'the fact' that a legally binding obligation has been entered into. The distinction between promising to undertake such an obligation and representing that such an obligation has in fact been entered into seems illusory. Arguably, it is disingenuous to assert that the representation sets up the facts which give rise to the cause of action. It looks very much as if estoppel by representation is operating substantively to impose legal obligations.[72] This matter is discussed further at paragraphs 8.30 to 8.33 below. Despite the attractions of this argument, on balance, we consider that estoppel by representation remains tied to its evidential roots. **8.021**

It should be noted, however, that the issue is not merely academic. It has a critical impact on the relief available in estoppel by representation cases. If the doctrine is purely evidential, the only possible outcome is that the representor is prevented from denying the truth of what it has represented.[73] There is no intermediate position or alternative remedy. **8.022**

---

[70] *Canada and Dominion Sugar Company, Limited v Canadian National (West Indies) Steamships, Limited* [1947] AC 46, PC (Canada) at 56 (the doctrine may be described as rule of evidence but is more properly viewed as substantive rule of law) and *Moorgate Mercantile Co Ltd v Twitchings* [1976] 1 QB 225, CA (rev. on appeal on another point at [1977] AC 890) *per* Lord Denning M.R. at 241g–h (estoppel is a principle of justice and equity).

[71] See paras 8.17 to 8.20 above.

[72] See Jackson 'Estoppel as a sword Part 1' (1965) 81 *LQR* 84 and Part 2 (1965) 81 *LQR* 223, Thompson 'From Representation to Expectation: Estoppel as a Cause of Action' [1983] *CLJ* 257.

[73] The following cases affirm this outcome without expressly indicating that it is the only remedy available: *Maclaine v Gatty* [1921] 1 AC 376, HL Sc *per* Lord Birkenhead at 386; *Knights v Wiffen* (1870) LR 5 QB 660, CA *per* Blackburn J. at 665; *Carr v London and North Western Rly Co* (1875) LR 10 CP 307 *per* Brett and Denman JJ. at 317; *Dixon v Kennaway & Co* [1990] 1 Ch 833 *per* Farwell J. at 838; *Farrow v Orttewell* [1943] Ch 480, CA *per* Lord Hanworth M.R. at 498; *Evans v Bartlam* [1937] AC 473 *per* Lord Wright at 484; *Jorden v Money* (1854) V HLC 185, 10 ER 868 *per* Lord Cranworth L.C. at 210; *Pickard v Sears* (1837) 6 A&E 469, 112 ER 179 at 474; *Re Exchange Securities & Commodities Ltd* [1988] Ch 46 *per* Harman J. at 54; *Algar v Middlesex County Council* [1945] 2 All ER 243, DC *per* Humphreys J. at 250f–g and *Hopgood v Brown* [1955] 1 WLR 213 *per* Evershed M.R. at 224.

Either the representation is deemed to be true or it is not.[74] This matter is discussed further at paragraph 8.108 below. Increasing doubts as to the appropriateness of this remedial inflexibility[75] may force a reappraisal of the doctrine and a recognition that it should be reclassified as a substantive one, whereby certain legal consequences flow from allowing representations to be relied on to the detriment of those to whom they are made.

MUTUALITY

It has been asserted that estoppels must be mutual[76] but there is very limited scope for the operation of this principle in relation to estoppel by representation. It is clear that the doctrine may operate where there has been a unilateral representation by one party: there is no need to establish the agreement or co-operation of the representee.[77] **8.023**

There are three contexts in which an element of mutuality is required. First, the representation must have been made to the party seeking to raise the estoppel.[78] A third party cannot take advantage of, or be burdened by, the estoppel (except in the limited circumstances set out in paragraphs 8.131 to 8.143 below). Secondly, the representee is not free to rely both on the true facts and those as represented to it. It cannot both deny and aver the representation but must instead elect between the remedies available under the competing versions of the facts. For example, in *Scarf v Jardine*,[79] the representee entered into a contract with A, who had for many years acted as agent for B. B was estopped from denying that A was his (B's) agent. In fact, A was no longer acting for B but was instead acting as agent for C. The representee sought to sue both B and C under the contract. It was held that he could sue either A, on the facts as presupposed by the estoppel, or C, on the true facts. **8.024**

[74] It is no coincidence that one of the more recent reaffirmations of the evidential nature of the doctrine is contained in *Avon CC v Howlett* [1983] 1 WLR 605, CA *per* Slade L.J. at 622c–d which is authority for the controversial proposition that estoppel cannot operate pro tanto.

[75] See in particular the authorities cited at 8.116 to 8.119 below.

[76] Coke, *A Commentary on Littleton*, (11th ed., London 1719), at p. 352a.

[77] See, for example, *In re Ottos Kopje Diamond Mines Ltd* [1893] 1 Ch 1892, CA and *Lyle-Meller v A Lewis & Co* [1956] 1 WLR 29, CA. This is an important distinction between estoppel by representation and estoppel by convention, which requires mutual dealings between the parties. See para. 9.03.

[78] See para. 8.45 below.

[79] [1882] 7 App Cas 345, HL.

He could not hold both jointly liable.[80] Thirdly, once the estoppel has been established it may give rise to a bilateral arrangement, giving rise to mutual rights and duties, by which both parties are thereafter bound, for example, the relationship of landlord and tenant.[81]

ELEMENTS OF ESTOPPEL BY REPRESENTATION

REPRESENTATION

To establish an estoppel by representation it is necessary to show that a representation was made[82] by the party sought to be estopped[83] or by its agent, authorized according to the general rules of agency.[84] An expression of opinion is insufficient to give rise to an estoppel by representation.[85] This may amount to a free standing limitation on estoppel or it may be an application of the rule that it must be reasonable to rely on the representation. It will seldom be reasonable to rely on the mere opinion of another.[86] A representation made in response to a question by the representee may give rise to an estoppel.[87] However, in certain circumstances **8.025**

---

80 *Scarf v Jardine* [1882] 7 App Cas 345, HL at 350, 359, 363, 364.

81 *Daejan Properties Ltd v Mahoney* [1995] 2 EGLR 75, CA.

82 *Lipkin Gorman v Karpnale* [1991] 2 AC 548 *per* Lord Goff at 578, reducing the usefulness of the doctrine as a defence to a restitutionary claim. See further para. 8.150–8 below.

83 *Re Exchange Securities & Commodities Ltd* [1988] Ch 46 at *per* Harman J. at 54.

84 *Moorgate Mercantile Co Ltd v Twitchings* [1976] 1 QB 225, CA *per* Lord Denning M.R. at 243f (rev. on appeal on another point at [1977] AC 890); *De Tchihatchef v. Salerni Coupling Ltd* [1932] 1 Ch 330; *Ismail v Polish Ocean Lines* [1976] QB 893, CA *per* Lord Denning M.R. at 903, *per* Ormrod L.J. at 907 and *per* Shaw L.J. at 911; *Gresham Life Assurance Society v Crowther* [1914] 2 Ch 219 *per* Astbury J. at 228 (affd on other grounds [1915] 1 Ch 214, CA); *Nippon Menkwa Kabushiki Kaisha (Japan Cotton Trading Co Ltd) v Dawson's Bank Ltd* [1935] 51 Lloyd's Rep. 147 PC (India) and *Trane (UK) Ltd v Provident Mutual Life Assurance* [1995] EGLR 33 *per* Judge Cooke at 38–39.

85 *Algar v Middlesex County Council* [1945] 2 All ER 243, DC *per* Humphreys J. at 251e–f and *George Whitechurch Ltd v Cavanagh* [1902] AC 117 *per* Lord James at 133.

86 See below at para. 8.80.

87 *Avon CC v Howlett* [1983] 1 WLR 605, CA where the defendant asked his former employer whether he was entitled to the payments which he had received from them. He was informed that everything was in order and that he was so entitled. See also George Whitechurch Ltd v Cavanagh [1902] AC 117, *Ashpitel v Bryan* (1863) 3 B & S 474, 122 ER 179, *Algar v Middlesex County Council* [1945] 2 All ER 243, DC

the fact that the representee procured the representation complained of will prevent an estoppel from arising (see paragraph 8.120 below).

Apart from the principle set out in paragraph 8.39 below, the representation will be interpreted according to ordinary principles of construction. No special technical rules apply.[88] **8.026**

Representation of fact

In order to give rise to an estoppel by representation it is necessary to show that a representation of fact[89] was made which is untrue.[90] A representation as to future[91] intention does not give rise to an estoppel by representation.[92] Hence, a promise to do something in the future **8.027**

---

per Cassels J. at 248d–e and *per* Humphreys J. at 251a–b; *Holt v Markham* [1923] 1 KB 504; *Hopgood v Brown* [1955] 1 WLR 213 *per* Evershed M.R. at 224 and *Low v. Bouverie* [1891] 3 Ch 82, CA. No estoppel arose in the last case but would have done so were it not for the fact that the response to the enquiry was equivocal.

88 *Canada and Dominion Sugar Company, Limited v Canadian National (West Indies) Steamships, Limited* [1947] AC 46, PC (Canada) at 55.

89 *Jorden v Money* (1854) V HLC 185, 10 ER 868 *per* Lord Cranworth L.C. at 215 and *per* Lord Brougham at 226, contra. Lord St Leonards at 248 and 250; *Citizens' Bank of Louisiana v First National Bank of New Orleans* (1873) LR 6 HL 352 *per* Lord Selbourne at 360 (existing fact); *Gresham Life Assurance Society v Crowther* [1914] 2 Ch 219 *per* Astbury J. at 228 (affd on other grounds [1915] 1 Ch 214, CA); *Maddison v Alderson* (1883) 8 App Cas 467 *per* Lord Selbourne L.C. at 473; *Covell v Sweetland* [1968] 1 WLR 1466 *per* Hinchcliffe J. at 1474; *Freeman v Cooke* (1848) 2 Ex 654, ER 652 at 656; *Farquharson Bros and Co v C King and Co* [1902] AC 325 at 330; *Chadwick v Manning* [1896] AC 231 *per* Lord Macnaughton at 238; *Yorkshire Insurance Co v Craine* [1922] 2 AC 541 at 553; *Veitch v Caldicott* (1945) 173 LT 30 at 33; *Carr v London and North Western Rly Co* (1875) LR 10 CP 307 *per* Brett and Denman JJ. at 317; *Dixon v Kennaway & Co* [1990] 1 Ch 833 *per* Farwell J. at 838; *Re Bankruptcy Notice* [1924] 2 Ch 76, CA *per* Lord Pollock M.R. at 89 and *per* Atkin L.J. at 96; *Evans v Bartlam* [1937] AC 473 *per* Lord Russell at 483; *George Whitechurch Ltd v Cavanagh* [1902] AC 117 *per* Lord Macnaughton at 130; *Algar v Middlesex County Council* [1945] 2 All ER 243, DC *per* Humphreys J. at 250f–g and 251e–h; *Nippon Menkwa Kabushiki Kaisha (Japan Cotton Trading Co Ltd) v Dawson's Bank Ltd* [1935] 51 Lloyd's Rep. 147, PC (India) *per* Lord Russell at 150 col. 2; *Kelsen v Imperial Tobacco Co of Great Britain & Ireland Ltd* [1957] 2 All ER 343 *per* MacNair J. at 349d–f and *TCB Ltd v Gray* [1986] Ch 621 *per* Sir Nicholas Browne-Wilkinson V.C. at 634.

90 *Piggot v Stratton* (1859) 1 De GF&J 33, 45 ER 271 *per* Lord Campbell L.C. at 50, 277 and *Moorgate Mercantile Co Ltd v Twitchings* [1977] AC 890 *per* Lord Edmond Davies at 917.

91 See para. 8.34 below for the principles applying to representations of present intention.

92 *Roebuck v Mongovin* [1994] 1 All ER 568, HL *per* Lord Browne-Wilkinson at 975 and *Argy Trading Co Ltd v Lapid Developments Ltd* [1977] 1 WLR 444 *per* Croom Johnson J. at 457a–e. See also the cases cited in note 89 above, including, in particular, *Evans v Bartlam* [1937] AC 473 *per* Lord Russell at 483 and *Jorden v Money* (1854) V HLC 185, 10 ER 868 *per* Lord Cranworth L.C. at 215.

does not trigger the operation of the doctrine, even where detrimental reliance has taken place. If such representations are to have legal effect, it must be in contract,[93] waiver,[94] proprietary estoppel[95] or equitable forbearance. This proposition was first clearly established in the controversial House of Lords decision *Jorden v Money*,[96] but has been frequently repeated.[97] In our view, it formed part of the ratio of the case and still forms part of English law.[98] This restriction of estoppel by representation has contributed to the development of other doctrines, in particular, that of equitable forbearance. *Jorden v Money* has been heavily criticised and the decision gives rise to a number of difficulties which are discussed below.[99]

Representations of future intention: is Jorden *v* Money *still good law?*

The equitable forbearance doctrine[1]

There are significant similarities between estoppel by representation and **8.028**
equitable forbearance. The following elements are arguably common to both. First, the representor's conduct led to the representee forming a certain belief or fortified a belief it already held. Secondly, the representee

---

[93] *Jorden v Money* (1854) V HLC 185, 10 ER 868 *per* Lord Cranworth L.C. at 215 and *per* Lord Brougham at 226 contra. Lord St Leonards at 248 and 250; *Maddison v Alderson* (1883) 8 App Cas 467 *per* Lord Selbourne L.C. at 473; *George Whitechurch Ltd v Cavanagh* [1902] AC 117 *per* Lord MacNaughton at 130; *Nippon Menkwa Kabushiki Kaisha (Japan Cotton Trading Co Ltd) v Dawson's Bank Ltd* [1935] 51 Lloyd's Rep. 147, PC (India) *per* Lord Russell at 150 col. 2; *Re Bankruptcy Notice* [1924] 2 Ch 76, CA *per* Lord Pollock M.R. at 89 and *Evans v Bartlam* [1937] AC 473 *per* Lord Wright at 484.

[94] *Nippon Menkwa Kabushiki Kaisha (Japan Cotton Trading Co Ltd) v Dawson's Bank Ltd* [1935] 51 Lloyd's Rep. 147, PC (India) *per* Lord Russell at 150 col. 2.

[95] *Kelsen v Imperial Tobacco Co of Great Britain & Ireland Ltd* [1957] 2 All ER 343 *per* MacNair J. at 349e–f.

[96] (1854) V HLC 185, 10 ER 868.

[97] See the cases cited at n. 89 above.

[98] See *per* contra. Lord Denning M.R. in *Lyle-Meller v A Lewis & Co* [1956] 1 WLR 29, CA at 35 and *Moorgate Mercantile Co Ltd v Twitchings* [1976] 1 QB 225, CA at 242b (rev. on appeal on another point at [1977] AC 890) positing a broad all embracing estoppel doctrine operating on representations of fact, law or intention and going beyond the confines of traditional estoppel by representation. See also the minority judgments of Deane J. in *Waltons Stores (Interstate) Ltd v Maher* [1988] 164 CLR 387 and of Mason C.J. and Deane J. in *Commonwealth of Australia v Verwayen* [1990] 170 CLR 394.

[99] See paras 8.28 to 8.33.

[1] As to which see generally chapter 12. The relationship of equitable forbearance and *Jorden v Money* is discussed further at paras 12.61–7.

changed its position in reliance on the belief. Thirdly, that change of position will lead the representee to suffer detriment if the truth of the belief is subsequently denied. Fourthly, the representee seeks to deny the truth of the belief. The most important divergence between the two is that estoppel by representation operates on a representation of fact whereas equitable forbearance operates on a representation as to future intention or promise. Thus, it is argued that a single estoppel doctrine is in play, which is triggered by both representations of fact and intention.

There are number of possible responses to this argument. First, it could be contended that the equitable forbearance doctrine is inconsistent with *Jorden v Money* and is therefore founded on an illegitimate and incorrect line of authority. Although not without its difficulties, the equitable forbearance doctrine is now well established in English law and this position is no longer tenable. Secondly, only promises to forbear from exercising existing legal rights will trigger the operation of the equitable forbearance doctrine. Thus, the scope of representations of future intention which will bring the doctrine into play is very limited. Rather than undermining the *Jorden v Money* rule, the equitable forbearance doctrine amounts to a limited exception to it which has developed as a means of mitigating the defects of the law of waiver and election.[2] Thirdly, there are distinctions between the ways in which the two doctrines operate.[3] In particular, the effects of equitable forbearance are more limited than those of estoppel by representation. The remedy for the former doctrine will go no further than is necessary to restore the representee to its previous position. Thus, it may often operate merely to suspend the representor's right to resile from its representation.[4] Although the issue is highly controversial, the latter doctrine probably requires the representation to be made good.[5] For the last two reasons, we submit that the development of the equitable forbearance doctrine has left the principle of *Jorden v Money* intact. **8.029**

Difficulties in distinguishing representations of fact and representations of intention

Representations of fact capable of giving rise to an estoppel by representation include a representation as to the legal effect of a **8.030**

[2] See paras 4.38–43, 12.12 and 12.24.
[3] See paras 8.162–8.
[4] See paras 12.51–6 below.
[5] See paras 8.108–119.

document[6] including a contract[7] and a representation that a contract has been entered into.[8] In such cases, the representor is estopped from denying that a legally binding obligation has been entered into. The distinction between promising to undertake such an obligation and representing that such an obligation has in fact been entered into seems illusory. Hence, it is argued, estoppel by representation is operating on promises as to future intentions and obligations. Arguably, it is disingenuous to assert that the representation sets up the facts which give rise to the cause of action. It looks very much as if the representation itself is being given effect to, giving rise in itself to substantive legal consequences.

For example, in *Yorkshire Insurance Co v Craine*[9] an insurer was estopped from denying the fact that a valid claim had been made under a contract of insurance.[10] In *Ismail v Polish Ocean Lines*,[11] a cargo owner was estopped from denying that its goods had been improperly stored during the shipment because its agent had insisted on the method used. This representation would seem to be capable of analysis either as a representation of fact, namely that the method of storage used was the correct one, or as a representation of intention, namely that the cargo owner would not insist on its right to demand proper storage. Similarly, a number of cases involve the representation of fact that notice required **8.031**

[6] *Sidney Bolsom Investment Trust Ltd v E. Karmios & Co. (London) Ltd* [1956] 1 QB 529, CA *per* Denning L.J. at 540 and *per* Harman L.J. at 545. It was held in *Dun & Bradstreet Software Services (England) Ltd v Provident Mutual Life Assurance Association* [1997] EGCS 89 CA, lexis transcript, that the representation that notices served under a tenancy agreement were valid was one of fact. In *Kaliszewska v John Clage and Partners* (1984) 5 Con LR per HH Judge White QC at 87–88, it was held that the representation that a property was sound and had no defects in it was a representation of fact. See Ungar 'The High Trees Case: Promise or Gift?' (1965) 28 *MLR* 231 suggesting that the means of reconciling the equitable forbearance doctrine with *Jorden v Money* (1854) V HLC 185, 10 ER 868 (as to which see para. 8.29 above) would be to construe all forbearances as representations of fact.

[7] *De Tchihatchef v Salerni Coupling Ltd* [1932] 1 Ch 330 *per* Luxmoor J. at 342 and *Covell v Sweetland* [1968] 1 WLR 1466 *per* Hinchcliffe J. at 1474.

[8] *Daejan Properties Ltd v Mahoney* [1995] 2 EGLR 75, CA *per* Sir Thomas Bingham M.R. at 77 and *per* Hoffman L.J. at 79. The case might alternatively be explained as a one of proprietary estoppel. See also *Janred Properties Ltd v ENIT* [1989] 2 All ER 444.

[9] [1922] 2 AC 541 at 546–7.

[10] See also *Lyle-Meller v A Lewis & Co* [1956] 1 WLR 29, CA, where the defendant was estopped from denying certain products which it had manufactured fell within a royalty agreement entered into with the plaintiff.

[11] [1976] QB 893, CA. See also *Brikom Investments v Seaford* [1981] 1 WLR 863, CA *per* Ormrod L.J. at 896b–g where the representation of 'fact' was that the landlord was responsible for performing repairs to the demised premises.

by a contract has been validly served.[12] There would seem to be little to distinguish a representation that the notice was in fact validly served and a promise or representation of intention that the representee would not enforce its right to compliance with formalities required for notice.[13]

Further, while a promise *not to enforce* a debt cannot give rise to an estoppel by representation,[14] a representation that a debt *has been released* may do so.[15] Doubt has been expressed as to whether the latter line of authority has survived *Jorden v Money*.[16] However, in that case, it was emphasized by the majority that Louisa Jorden had never represented that she had actually released the debt. Had she done so, the result might well have been different. **8.032**

Such cases show the difficulty of distinguishing between representations of fact and representations of future intention. Consequently, the outcome of cases may depend on the precise form of the representation rather than its substance. Further, there is considerable scope for judicial discretion. The fact/intent dichotomy is easily manipulated and may be used by the courts to mask policy decisions.[17] Despite these difficulties, *Jorden v Money* still forms part of English law. It is the means by which estoppel by representation is prevented from undermining the contractual doctrine of consideration. If estoppel by representation applied to representations as to future intention, it would thereby render enforceable promises unsupported by consideration.[18] **8.033**

Representations of present intention

A representation of present intention may amount to a representation of fact. As Bowen L.J. memorably put it: 'The state of a man's mind is **8.034**

[12] *Trane (UK) Ltd v Provident Mutual Life Assurance* [1995] EGLR 33 *per* Judge Cooke at 38–9.

[13] See also *Piggot v Stratton* (1859) 1 De GF&J 33, 45 ER 271, where S represented to H that the terms of S's lease prevented his building on his land. In reliance on this, H built houses on a neighbouring plot. At 52 and 278 Lord Campbell C.J. distinguished *Jorden v Money* on the grounds that S had stated that he had no power to build during the currency of the lease. This was a representation of fact not future intention.

[14] The very point in issue in *Jorden v Money*.

[15] *Eden v Smith* (1800) 5 Ves 341 and *Reeves v Bryner* (1801) 6 Ves 516.

[16] Treitel at pp. 120–1.

[17] See, for example, *Nippon Menkwa Kabushiki Kaisha (Japan Cotton Trading Co Ltd) v Dawson's Bank Ltd* [1935] 51 Lloyd's Rep. 147, PC (India) *per* Lord Russell at 150 col. 2 where it was held that a representation that goods were unencumbered could not give rise to an estoppel as it was construed as a promise not to enforce security over goods.

[18] See further paras 8.21 to 8.22.

as much a fact as the state of his digestion.'[19] Hence, theoretically, such a representation may trigger the application of the doctrine under discussion. However, such a representation is seldom likely to do so in practice. The fact that or/the representor later acted inconsistently with the professed intention may frequently be attributable to its having changed its mind rather than its having misrepresented its original intention. An estoppel precluding the denial of the fact that a certain intention was once held, will not preclude any subsequent change of mind.[20] In such a case, the representee would have to depend on other causes of action (such as fraud or negligence) in which an estoppel precluding assertion of the falsity of the original representation would be a hindrance rather than an aid.[21]

Representations of mixed fact and law

A representation of mixed fact and law may give rise to an estoppel by representation.[22] To restrict the scope of the doctrine to pure representations of fact would give rise to significant difficulties for two reasons. First, in a number of legal contexts,[23] it has proved notoriously difficult to delineate clearly between issues of fact and law. Secondly, such a restriction would severely limit the scope of the doctrine because the contexts in which it arises frequently give rise to legal questions: the doctrine's intention and reliance requirements,[24] mean that the doctrine may only operate in comparatively formal situations where significant rights are in issue. **8.035**

[19] *Edgington v Fitzmaurice* (1885) 29 ChD 459 at 483.

[20] *Veitch v Caldicott* (1945) 173 LT 30 at 33.

[21] See the comments of Deane J. in *Waltons Stores (Interstate) Ltd v Maher* [1988] 164 CLR 387 at 450.

[22] *Covell v Sweetland* [1968] 1 WLR 1466 *per* Hinchcliffe J. at 1474 (construction of a contract); *De Tchihatchef v. Salerni Coupling Ltd* [1932] 1 Ch 330 (same); *Algar v Middlesex County Council* [1945] 2 All ER 243, DC *per* Humphreys J. at 251g–h (representation that an employee had the same pension rights under new job as under old); *Lyle-Meller v A Lewis & Co* [1956] 1 WLR 29, CA *per* Hodson L.J. at 40 (whether goods produced by D fell within the terms of a licence agreement entered into with P) and *Gresham Life Assurance Society v Crowther* [1914] 2 Ch 219 *per* Astbury J. at 227 (affd on other grounds [1915] 1 Ch 214, CA) (whether house mortgaged was trust property or not).

[23] In particular in administrative law and in restitution.

[24] See paras 8.74 and 8.80 below.

Representations of law

8.036 A representation of pure law is not sufficient to give rise to an estoppel by representation.[25] There are two alternative reasons for this approach. First, both parties are deemed to be in a good as position as one another to investigate the legal position;[26] in such a situation it is not reasonable for one party to rely on the other. This would breach the principle discussed at paragraph 8.80 below. Secondly, a representation of law is arguably only ever an expression of opinion and as such incapable of giving rise to an estoppel.[27]

8.037 There is conflicting authority as to whether a representation as to the validity of a deed is a one of law[28] or fact.[29] However, it may be possible to reconcile the cases if it is recognized that such a representation may be *either* one of fact or law, depending on the circumstances. For example, a representation that a deed had been sealed would amount to one of fact[30] whereas a representation that registration under statutory insolvency provisions was not required would amount to one of law.[31]

---

25 *Lyle-Meller v A Lewis & Co* [1956] 1 WLR 29, CA *per* Hodson L.J. at 41; *London County Territorial and Auxiliary Forces Association v Nicholls* [1949] 1 KB 35; *Kai Nam v Ma Kam Cham* [1956] AC 358, PC (Hong Kong) *per* Lord Cohen at 367; *Algar v Middlesex County Council* [1945] 2 All ER 243, DC *per* Humphreys J. at 251e–f and *Gresham Life Assurance Society v Crowther* [1914] 2 Ch 219 *per* Astbury J. at 228 (affd on other grounds [1915] 1 Ch 214, CA). Contra. *Lyle-Meller v A Lewis & Co* [1956] 1 WLR 29, CA *per* Lord Denning M.R. at 35; *Moorgate Mercantile Co Ltd v Twitchings* [1976] 1 QB 225, CA *per* Lord Denning M.R. at 242b (rev. on appeal on another point at [1977] AC 890) and *Harnam Singh v Jamal Pirbhai* [1951] AC 688 at 691. The last mentioned case may be better interpreted as one of equitable forbearance rather than estoppel by representation.

26 *Lyle-Meller v A Lewis & Co* [1956] 1 WLR 29, CA *per* Hodson L.J. at 41.

27 *Algar v Middlesex County Council* [1945] 2 All ER 243, DC *per* Humphreys J. at 251e–f. See also *Perring v Draper* [1997] EGCS 109 where a lease had been entered into on behalf of the trust. Prior to entering the lease, the trustees had corresponded with the landlord's surveyor and they claimed that he had assured that their personal liability under the lease would be confined to the extent of the trust assets. Mantell J. held that the surveyor's expression of his erroneous opinion as to the liabilities of trustees in general could not give rise to any estoppel preventing the landlord from pursuing the trustees for the full extent of their personal liability under the lease. There was no substitute for independent legal advice.

28 *Re Bankruptcy Notice* [1924] 2 Ch 76, CA *per* Atkin L.J. at 96.

29 *TCB Ltd v Gray* [1986] Ch 621.

30 *ibid.*

31 *Re Bankruptcy Notice* [1924] 2 Ch 76, CA *per* Atkin L.J. at 96.

Admissions of liability

An admission of liability may give rise to an estoppel[32] if the relevant issue involves mixed fact and law but not if it comprises a pure question of law.[33] It should be noted, however, that to satisfy the detriment[34] requirements in such a context, the representee must demonstrate that it has incurred expense or suffered damage which cannot be compensated in a costs order.[35] **8.038**

The representation must be clear and unequivocal

In view to the serious consequences of establishing an estoppel by representation, fairly stringent clarity requirements are imposed in order to restrict the operation of the doctrine.[36] The same requirement has been expressed in a number of slightly different ways. It has been frequently held that the representation must be clear and unequivocal.[37] An alternative formulation is that the representation must be clear and unqualified, precise and unambiguous.[38] There is some uncertainty as to whether the representation will be construed objectively or not. The traditional rule was stated in *Low v Bouverie*[39] as follows: **8.039**

> The language upon which the estoppel is founded, must be precise and unambiguous. That does not necessarily mean that the language must be

[32] *H. Clark (Doncaster) Ltd v Wilkinson* [1965] Ch 694, CA *per* Lord Denning M.R. at 702 and *per* Salmon L.J. at 704.

[33] *Lyle-Meller v A Lewis & Co* [1956] 1 WLR 29 CA *per* Hodson L.J. at 41.

[34] As to which, see generally para. 8.88.

[35] *H. Clark (Doncaster) Ltd v Wilkinson* [1965] Ch 694, CA *per* Lord Denning M.R. at 702.

[36] *Low v Bouverie* [1891] 3 Ch 82, CA at 113.

[37] *Low v. Bouverie* [1891] 3 Ch 82, CA at 113; *Sidney Bolsom Investment Trust Ltd v E. Karmios & Co. (London) Ltd* [1956] 1 QB 529, CA *per* Denning L.J. at 540; *Lowe v Lombank* [1960] 1 WLR 196, CA *per* Diplock J. at 205; *Nippon Menkwa Kabushiki Kaisha (Japan Cotton Trading Co Ltd) v Dawson's Bank Ltd* [1935] 1 Lloyd's Rep. 147, PC (India) *per* Lord Russell at 151 col. 2; *Moorgate Mercantile Co Ltd v Twitchings* [1977] AC 890 *per* Lord Wilberforce at 902 (dissenting, but not on this point) and *Bute (Marquess) v Barclays Bank Ltd* [1955] 1 QB 202 per McNair J. at 213.

[38] *Canada and Dominion Sugar Company, Limited v Canadian National (West Indies) Steamships, Limited* [1947] AC 46, PC (Canada) at 56. See also *Maclaine v Gatty* [1921] 1 AC 376, HL Sc *per* Lord Shaw at 394 ('clear and continuous') and *Weld Blundell v Synott* [1940] 2 KB 107 *per* Asquith J. at 114 ('definite and unequivocal').

[39] [1891] 3 Ch 82, CA.

> such that it cannot possibly be open to different constructions, but that it must be such as will be reasonably understood in a particular sense by the person to whom it is addressed.[40]

This dictum was considered at length by the House of Lords in *Woodhouse AC Israel Cocoa Ltd v Nigerian Produce Marketing Co Ltd.*[41] Their lordships held that it was not necessary to show that the representation was capable of only one possible interpretation.[42] It was sufficient if any interpretation, other than that formed by the representee, was far fetched and strained.[43] The representation had to be sufficiently clear to justify the representee's having no doubt that the words meant what it took them to mean.[44] We consider that their lordships did not disapprove the approach of Bowen L.J. They merely refined the applicable test by making it clear that it is not sufficient to show that the representee *might* reasonably have interpreted the words in the way it did: it is necessary to show that it was very unlikely that any reasonable person would have interpreted them differently, hence Bowen L.J.'s use of the word '*will*' rather than other more qualified terms such as '*may*', '*might*' or '*could*'.

Spencer Bower[45] attempts to limit the scope of *Woodhouse* in two **8.040**
ways. First, he distinguishes it on the grounds that it was a case of promissory estoppel/equitable forbearance and not estoppel by representation. This cannot be supported. The comments referred to were clearly directed at analysis of the authorities on estoppel by representation. Lords Hailsham and Salmon thereby intimated that the applicable principles were the same for both doctrines. Lord Cross considered there to be a distinction. For promissory estoppel, he posited a stricter test more closely linked to the subjective intention of the representor.[46] It is submitted that the two doctrines do apply the same test, Lord Cross's subjective approach having failed to gain acceptance in

---

40 *ibid.* at 106. See also *Carr v London and North Western Rly Co* (1875) LR 10 CP 307 *per* Brett and Denman JJ. at 317; *Dixon v Kennaway & Co* [1990] 1 Ch 833 *per* Farwell J. at 838; *Algar v Middlesex County Council* [1945] 2 All ER 243, DC *per* Humphreys J. at 250f–g and *Nippon Menkwa Kabushiki Kaisha (Japan Cotton Trading Co Ltd) v Dawson's Bank Ltd* [1935] 51 Lloyd's Rep. 147, PC (India) *per* Lord Russell at 151 col. 2.

41 [1972] AC 741.

42 *ibid. per* Lord Salmon at 771.

43 *ibid. per* Lord Hailsham L.C. at 756.

44 *ibid. per* Lord Cross at 768.

45 At para. 83.

46 Lord Cross did, however, make some additional comments on *Low v Bouverie* and the estoppel by representation cases. These are referred to above at para. 8.39.

subsequent equitable forbearance cases.[47]

Secondly, Spencer Bower suggests that the *Woodhouse* approach is confined to representations which are solely express rather than those inferred from conduct or those which are partly express and partly inferred from conduct. It is possible to read *Woodhouse* in this way; the case concerned the interpretation of an express written representation. The authorities which use the phraseology of *Low v Bouverie* have tended to involve representations which are at least partially inferred from conduct.[48] Further, it might seem difficult to attain a sufficient degree of clarity from mere conduct. As we set out above, however, we consider that there is little substantive difference between the dictum of Bowen L.J. and the approach adopted in *Woodhouse*. In our view, the same test applies to all types of representation, namely that of *Woodhouse*.[49] **8.041**

Analogy with equitable forbearance

For the reasons set out above,[50] we consider that, in this context, estoppel by representation is governed by the same principles as equitable forbearance. Hence, useful guidance on this issue may be found at paragraphs 12.13 to 12.15 where the test is discussed in relation to the latter doctrine. **8.042**

Burden of proof

In *George Whitechurch Ltd v Cavanagh*,[51] Lord Brampton averred[52] that *the evidence* supporting an estoppel must be clear and unequivocal. It is probable that this was merely a restatement of the principle under **8.043**

[47] See the cases listed at para. 12.14.

[48] See the equitable forbearance/promissory estoppel cases of *Bremer Handelsgeselleschaft Schaft v Vanden Avenne-Izegem* [1978] 2 Lloyd's Rep 109, HL at 126 *per* Lord Salmon; *Bremer Handelsgesellschaft mbH v C Macprang JR*. [1979] 1 Lloyds Rep. 221, CA at 228; *'The Chemical Venture'* [1993] 1 Lloyd's Rep. 509 at 521 and *Societe Italio-Belge v Palm & Vegetable Oils (Malaysia), The Post Chaser* [1982] 1All ER 19 at 25c–d.

[49] See also *Goldsworthy v Brickell* [1987] Ch 378, CA at 410, 411, which concerned a representation inferred from conduct where an approach very similar to that of *Woodhouse* was adopted. Further, in *Peyman v Lanjani* [1985] Ch 457, CA, Slade L.J. held at 502g–h that if a representation is to be inferred from conduct the acts must be consistent only with the position alleged and be inconsistent with other positions.

[50] At para. 8.40.

[51] [1902] AC 117.

[52] *ibid*. at 145.

discussion rather than any modification of the normal burden of proof. Therefore, it suffices to prove on the balance of probability that the alleged representation was in fact made. Once this is done, it is necessary to construe the terms of the representation to establish whether they are sufficiently clear.

Equivocal representations

It is possible to negative the effect of a clear statement by immediately contradicting it.[53] However, where the representor deliberately expresses its representation in equivocal terms in order to lull the representee into a false sense of security while endeavouring to preserve its (the representor's) legal position, an estoppel may arise despite the lack of clarity.[54] **8.044**

The representation must have been made to the party raising the estoppel or to a group of which it was a member

The representation must have been made to the representee[55] or to a group of which it was a member.[56] It is possible to make a representation to the general public. It is difficult to discern a general principle which determines what sort of conduct gives rise to such wide ranging representations. The issue seems to be at least partly determined by the intention of the representor. If the representor intended members of the general public to rely on its representation, this will probably be sufficient.[57] Further, it may be sufficient if the representor knew that it **8.045**

---

[53] *Freeman v Cooke* (1848) 2 Ex 654, ER 652 at 657.

[54] *'The Stolt Loyalty'* [1993] 2 Lloyd's Rep. 281 and *Piggott v Stratton* (1859) 1 De GF&J 33, 45 ER 271 at 48. If the representor wishes to preserve its legal position, it can do so without resorting to such underhand tactics. If it expressly disclaims responsibility for the accuracy of its representation, no estoppel will arise. See *Hammersmith and Fulham BC v Top Shop Centres Ltd* [1990] Ch 237 *per* Warner J. at 257c–d.

[55] *Jorden v Money* (1854) V HLC 185, 10 ER 868 *per* Lord Cranworth L.C. at 212; *Gresham Life Assurance Society v Crowther* [1914] 2 Ch 219 *per* Astbury J. at 227 (affd on other grounds [1915] 1 Ch 214, CA); *Knights v Wiffen* (1870) LR 5 QB 660, CA *per* Mellor J. at 666 and *Jones Bros v Holloway Ltd v Woodhouse* [1923] 2 KB 117, DC *per* Bailhache J. at 124.

[56] *Hammersmith and Fulham BC v Top Shop Centres Ltd* [1990] Ch 237 *per* Warner J. at 257c–d and *Bell v Marsh* [1903] 1 Ch 528 *per* Lord Collins M.R. at 541.

[57] *Bishop v Balkis Consolidated Co* (1890) 25 QBD 77 *per* Vaughan Williams J. at 83 (affd on other grounds at 512).

was probable that the general public[58] would have rely on the representation.[59]

Examples of representations to the general public

An important example occurs when a company issues a share certificate in the name of an applicant, X. It thereby represents that X is the owner of the shares in issue.[60] If a member of the public acts to its detriment in reliance on the share certificate (typically by paying X for the shares), the company will be estopped from denying X's title. The representation is probably also made to X.[61] This will be of practical relevance where, for example, X has purchased shares on the strength of a genuine certificate but a forged transfer. It will seldom be possible for X to raise an estoppel for two reasons. First, X will be precluded from raising the estoppel if it had any reason to doubt the veracity of the documents which it submitted to the company on its application for registration or where it was in as good as position as the company to know that the transfer was forged.[62] This will prevent an estoppel arising because of the role of the representee in procuring the representation (see paragraph 8.120 below). Secondly, in proving detrimental reliance, X will not be able to rely on the money spent on purchasing the shares because this pre-dates the issuing to the certificate (and thus the representation). Other acts of detriment will have to be established such as entering into a contract to sell the shares to a third party or failing to pursue the person who executed the original forged transfer. If the certificate states that **8.046**

[58] Or such smaller group to whom the representation is alleged to have been made.

[59] There is some similarity between this issue and the vexed question of when a duty of care in tort arises. An approach analogous with tort was taken in *Seton, Laing v Lefone* (1887) 19 QBD 68, CA *per* Lord Esher M.R. at 72. The defendant issued a statement on which it was probable that other tradespeople would rely. Hence, the plaintiff could raise the estoppel despite intercepting the statement, which the representor actually intended to go to another. However, as we set out below, at para. 8.160, this case may not be an example of estoppel at all. It may be a case of simple negligence and hence it is of only limited use in assessing the issue under consideration.

[60] *Simm v Anglo American Telegraph* (1879) 5 QBD 188, CA: *In re Ottos Kopje Diamond Mines Ltd* [1893] 1 Ch 1892, CA and *Dixon v Kennaway & Co* [1900] 1 Ch 833.

[61] *Dixon v Kennaway & Co* [1900] 1 Ch 833 at 840 although Farwell J.'s reasons for distinguishing *Simm v Anglo American Telegraph* (1879) 5 QBD 188, CA are not entirely convincing.

[62] *Dixon v Kennaway & Co* [1900] 1 Ch 833 at 840, distinguishing *Simm v Anglo American Telegraph* (1879) 5 QBD 188, CA.

the shares are fully paid up, the issuing company thereby represents to the general public that this is the case.[63]

Similarly, statements made in bills of lading are made to the general public and a variety of individuals relying on such documents may be able to raise estoppels.[64] **8.047**

Successive representees

It should be emphasized that although it is possible to make a representation to the general public, no representor may be estopped as against the whole general public.[65] The estoppel will only arise in favour of those who can make out the other essentials of estoppel by representation. It is necessary for anyone seeking to rely on the estoppel to establish that they believed the representation and relied on this belief to their detriment.[66] Take, for example, the share certificate example referred to above. If Y purchased the shares from X, in order to raise an estoppel, it must prove that it believed the representation, *i.e.* that it believed that X was the owner of the shares. If Y sells on the shares to Z, Z too must establish anew the components of estoppel by representation. If Z knew that X was not the true owner, no estoppel will arise.[67] The fact that Z purchased the shares from someone who did not can make no difference. Conversely, if Y bought the shares knowing that they did not belong to X, and sells them on to a purchaser who did not, the purchaser may be able to raise an estoppel. Y's knowledge is irrelevant. A estoppel will arise in favour of the purchaser if it believed the representation and acted to its detriment on it.[68] **8.048**

It was held in *Re Stapleford Colliery Co (Barrow's case)*[69] that a contrary rule applies to cases where the company has represented that shares are fully paid up. In that case, X purchased the shares without knowledge of the true facts. X sold them on to Y who was aware of the **8.049**

---

63 See *Burkinshaw v Nicholls* (1878) 3 App Cas 1004 and para. 16.11 below.

64 See, for example, *Canada and Dominion Sugar Company, Limited v Canadian National (West Indies) Steamships, Limited* [1947] AC 46, PC and further authorities cited at para. 20.35–7 under 'Shipping'. In *MacFisheries Ltd v Harrison* (1924) 132 LT 22 *per* Swift J. at 26, a representation to the general public was made via a sign hung outside a pub. No estoppel arose however, because the party seeking to rely on the doctrine had not noticed the sign. See further para. 8.79 below.

65 Just as it is not possible to contract with the whole general public.

66 See generally paras 8.88 to 8.92 on the necessity for detrimental reliance.

67 Any other result would contravene the principle that estoppel does not operate to pass title, as to which see para. 8.127 below and paras 16.11–12 below.

68 *Burkinshaw v Nicholls* (1878) 3 App Cas 1004.

69 (1880) 14 ChD 432.

truth and knew that the shares were not fully paid up. This is further discussed at paragraph 16.12 below. For the reasons we there set out, we submit that the case was probably wrongly decided.

Examples of representations

Representation by express statement

Express statements which have given rise to estoppel by representation are many and varied. Cases involving such express representations are sometimes referred to as instances of estoppel by statement, but no special principles apply to them. Estoppel by statement is merely a subdivision of estoppel by representation. It is not possible or useful to attempt a comprehensive listing of all the different express statements which have given rise to estoppel but some of the more important and common examples should be noted. Further examples, arising in particular specialist areas, are discussed in Chapters 14 to 20 below. **8.050**

Representations may be made orally or in writing. The court may be prepared to construe a succession of different documents in order to ascertain the representation made, if the documents are sufficiently linked.[70] Particularly important practical examples of express representations are statements made in bills of lading. These concern matters such as the nature[71] and condition[72] of the goods shipped. Both statutory and common law estoppels may arise as a result of the statements contained in bills of lading. The applicable principles are discussed in detail at paragraphs 20.35 to 20.37 below. Further important examples are statements contained in share certificates, which are discussed at paragraphs 16.10 to 16.12. Additionally, admissions made by counsel in legal proceedings may give rise to an estoppel,[73] as may representations by a warehouse owner that he holds goods in store, to the order **8.051**

---

[70] *London County Territorial and Auxiliary Forces Association v Nicholls* [1949] 1 KB 35 *per* Scott L.J. at 49.

[71] *Parsons v New Zealand Shipping Co* [1901] 1 KB 548.

[72] *Compania Vascongada v Churchill* [1906] 1 KB 237; *The Skarp* [1935] P 134 and *The Tromp* [1912] P 337.

[73] *H. Clark (Doncaster) Ltd v Wilkinson* [1965] Ch 694, CA *per* Lord Denning M.R. at 702 and *per* Salmon L.J. at 704, although see para 8.35 to 8.36 above for the difficulties arising where the representation is not purely one of fact.

of the representee,[74] statements made by planning officers in correspondence,[75] statements by a landlord that the tenancy was a joint one between the representee and another person[76] or that a break clause was exercisable by a certain date,[77] a statement by a customer that a cheque to be drawn on its account was genuine and properly executed[78] or by an employer that its former employee was entitled to the payments he had received,[79] a statement by the agent of cargo owner that method of stowage he had recommended was adequate[80] and a statement by an alleged signatory that the signature on a deed was genuine.[81]

Representation by conduct

It is possible to make a representation by conduct[82] so long as it is sufficiently unequivocal (as to which see paragraph 8.39 above). This is probably the most common way of making a representation for the purposes of estoppel. Such cases have sometimes been referred to as involving estoppel by conduct but no special principles apply to them. Estoppel by conduct is, in this context,[83] used merely to signify a subdivision of estoppel by representation.[84] As with estoppel by express statement, the types of conduct which have been held to give rise to estoppel **8.052**

---

[74] *Knights v Wiffen* (1870) LR 5 QB 660, CA.

[75] *Graham v Secretary of State for the Environment and another* [1993] JPL 353 *per* David Widdicombe Q.C. at 354 and *Wells v Minister for Housing and Local Government* [1967] 2 All ER 1041 but see para. .000 below for the limitations on the scope of estoppel against public authorities.

[76] *Daejan Properties Ltd v Mahoney* [1995] 2 EGLR 75, CA.

[77] *Trane (UK) Ltd v Provident Mutual Life Assurance* [1995] EGLR 33.

[78] *Bank of England v Vagliano Bros* [1891] AC 107 at 117 *per* Lord Halsbury L.C. and *per* Lord Selborne at 123–4. Such express representations should be contrasted with the so-called estoppel by negligence cases, where liability arises from a mere negligent failure in preparation or custody of the relevant cheque.

[79] *Avon CC v Howlett* [1983] 1 WLR 605, CA, the employee had queried the level of payments received but was assured that they were in order.

[80] *Ismail v Polish Ocean Lines* [1976] QB 893, CA.

[81] *Ashpitel v Bryan* (1863) 3B & S474, 122 ER 179.

[82] *Carr v London and North Western Rly Co* (1875) LR 10 CP 307 *per* Brett and Denman JJ. at 317; *Dixon v Kennaway & Co* [1990] 1 Ch 833 *per* Farwell J at 838; *Pickard v Sears* (1837) 6 A&E 469, 112 ER 179 at 474 and *Hopgood v Brown* [1955] 1 WLR 213 *per* Evershed M.R. at 224.

[83] As we set out above in para 8.02, the term has also been used as an alternative to the term estoppel in pais which covers estoppel by representation, by convention and, possibly, equitable forbearance and proprietary estoppel as well. Given this terminological inconsistency, we have avoided the use of the term.

[84] See, however, *Yorkshire Insurance Co v Craine* [1922] 2 AC 541, PC at 553 where the privy council, somewhat confusingly, rejected a claim based on estoppel by representation but accepted one based on estoppel by conduct.

are so varied as to make a comprehensive listing neither possible nor particularly useful. We have therefore selected a number of the more important examples. Further examples are discussed in chapters 14 to 20 below.

A representation may be made by gestures[85] or through the use of a map[86] or flag.[87] Agreeing with a statement made by another and communicating that agreement to the representee can amount to a representation in terms of the original statement.[88] If a representor is empowered to do X by a contract on condition that certain facts existed, it cannot deny those facts once it has actually done X, since this would be to aver that its own conduct had been unlawful.[89] One of the most important instances of conduct giving rise to a representation is where a party 'holds out' another as its agent having authority to carry out a particular function. For further detail on this type of representation and the relationship of such cases with general agency principles, see paragraphs 14.10 to 14.24 below. **8.053**

In a number of cases, representations have been inferred from a course of mutual dealings.[90] In *Pickard v Sears,*[91] goods were seized by W in execution of a debt owed to him by Y. In fact the goods belonged to Z. Z at no point objected to their seizure, even when he and Y subsequently visited the offices of W's lawyer and attempted to negotiate a compromise. Z was estopped from asserting his title to the goods. Similarly, in *Sarat Chunder Dey v Ghopal Chunder Laha,*[92] H represented his mother in negotiations for a mortgage over certain property[93] she was believed to own. It later transpired that H had a claim to the property. His conduct in negotiating on behalf of his mother was amounted to a representation that he had no claim to the property. He was consequently estopped from asserting priority over the mortgagee. **8.054**

---

85 *Walters v Morgan* (1861) 3 De GF&J 718, 45 ER 1056: a representation could be made by 'a nod and a wink'. Note, however, that the case did not concern estoppel but the misrepresentation sufficient to bar specific performance.

86 *Hopgood v Brown* [1955] 1 WLR 213.

87 *Dionissis v R 'the Laura'* (1865) 3 Moo PCCNS 181, 16 ER 68.

88 *Hopgood v Brown* [1955] 1 WLR 213 and *De Tchihatchef v Salerni Coupling Ltd* [1932] 1 Ch. 330.

89 *Yorkshire Insurance Co v Craine* [1922] 2 AC 541, PC at 546–7.

90 Such cases have much in common with estoppel by convention and it may be possible for both doctrines to operate on the same facts.

91 (1837) 6 A&E 469, 112 ER 179 at 474.

92 (1892) LR 19 Ind App 203, PC (India), *cf. Bell v Marsh* [1903] 1 Ch 528.

93 Even to the extent of signing the eventual mortgage agreement on her behalf.

In *Jennings v Great Northern Rly Co*,[94] it was held that a sale of train tickets to an employer, for the use of his employees, estopped the railway authority from enforcing a by-law against those employees requiring the passengers to produce their tickets. Service of a notice to quit has been held to amount to a representation that the notice was valid and that the person issuing it was in fact the landlord who had power to issue it.[95] Clearing a cheque and paying out funds on it, does not amount to representation by the bank that the cheque is genuine, even where the special collection method is used. At most, such conduct can amount to a representation only that the bank believes the cheque to be genuine.[96] **8.055**

Delay in prosecuting legal proceedings

Whether representations may be inferred from delay in prosecuting legal proceedings has been extensively canvassed in relation to the equitable forbearance doctrine. The same approach is applicable in estoppel by representation cases and therefore reference should be made to paragraph 12.17 below for further detail on this issue. Mere delay or inactivity will seldom give rise to an inferred representation sufficient to amount to an estoppel since such conduct will almost always be equivocal.[97] However, in *Covell v Sweetland*,[98] a dispute arose as to the construction of a maintenance agreement. The wife asserted that the agreement obliged the husband to pay maintenance for the duration of her life. The husband averred that his liability, under the agreement, ended with the marriage. The judge found as a fact that the latter construction was the correct one. However, he held that, in any event, the wife would have been estopped from asserting the contrary because of her failure for five years to enforce the maintenance provisions or assert her right to payments under it. Further, in *National Westminster Bank Ltd v Barclays Bank International Ltd*,[99] Kerr J. held that the delay in claiming back money paid out on a forged cheque did not estop a bank from maintaining an action for money paid under mistake. He conceded, however, that different considerations might apply to longer delays.[1] **8.056**

---

94 (1865) LR 1 QB 7 *per* Cockburn C.J. at 9–10.
95 *Farrow v Orttewell* [1943] Ch 480, CA.
96 *National Westminster Bank Ltd v Barclays Bank International Ltd* [1975] 1 QB 654 *per* Kerr J. at 674c–g.
97 See para. 12.17 below.
98 [1968] 1 WLR 1466 *per* Hinchcliffe J. at 1474.
99 [1975] 1 QB 654 at 676b–c.
1 See also *Holt v Markham* [1923] 1 KB 504, CA *per* Scrutton L.J. and *Pearl Mill Co v Ivy Tannery Co* [1919] 1 KB 78, DC *per* Rowlatt J. at 82 and *per* McCardie J. at 84.

No estoppel will arise where the alleged representor continues to assert its rights during the period of delay.[2]

Representation by silence

Cases where the representation is made by purely passive conduct are sometimes referred to as involving estoppel by silence or estoppel by acquiescence.[3] The latter term has been used to signify those proprietary estoppel cases where the property owner passively acquiesces in the claimant's belief, rather than giving it active encouragement.[4] Although the principles applicable in such cases have elements in common with this head of estoppel by representation, there are important differences between them.[5] To minimize confusion we have avoided the use of the term estoppel by acquiescence. An important difficulty is caused by the tendency in the cases to deal with estoppel 'by silence' or 'acquiescence', as if it were a separate free standing head of estoppel.[6] Consequently, in some cases there is no attempt to analyse the nature of the assumption formed by the representee as a result of the silence or acquiescence of the alleged representor. There are strict limitations on the scope of assumptions which can give rise to an estoppel (as to which see paragraph 8.08 above). Only those which fall within the limited scope of the various different estoppel doctrines will trigger an estoppel. This means that the assumption induced by the silence of the representor must fall within the scope of those covered by one or more of those doctrines, namely proprietary estoppel, estoppel by convention, estoppel by representation or equitable forbearance.[7] The silence cases can generally be fitted within one of the other heads but there is often room to **8.057**

---

[2] *Bristol Corporation v Sinnott* [1918] 1 Ch 62, CA *per* Swinfen Eady L.J.

[3] For example, in *Pacol Ltd v Trade Lines Ltd ('the Henrik Sif')* [1982] 1 Lloyd's Rep. 456 at 465 and *De Tchihatchef* v *Salerni Coupling Ltd* [1932] 1 Ch 330.

[4] See, for example, *Taylors Fashions Ltd v Liverpool Victoria Trustees Co Ltd* [1982] 1 QB 133.

[5] As to which see para 8.171 below.

[6] See *e.g. Pacol Ltd v Trade Lines Ltd ('the Henrik Sif')* [1982] 1 Lloyds Rep. 456 and *'The Indian Endurance' (No 2) Republic of India v India Steamship Company* [1997] 4 All ER 380 HL per Lord Steyn at 392c–e.

[7] Lord Steyn specifically declined to subsume the categories of estoppel by acquiescence and convention in *'The Indian Endurance' (No 2) Republic of India v India Steamship Company* [1997] 4 All ER 380 HL at 392e–g. We do not consider our position to be inconsistent with this case. We agree that estoppel by acquiescence and estoppel by convention are not simply two different terms for the same doctrine. We positively aver that the term estoppel by acquiescence has been used in cases involving doctrines *other than* estoppel by convention. Our view merely entails that there may be an

doubt as to which is the correct one. In particular, the cases discussed at paragraph 8.63 below may be more properly categorized as falling within the scope of equitable forbearance or estoppel by convention. They generally involve assumptions about whether legal rights will be enforced rather than assumptions as to a particular fact or facts. This would take them out of the scope of the estoppel by representation. However, the general principles applicable to cases where an assumption is induced by silence appear to be the same for both equitable forbearance and estoppel by representation.[8] The cases in the respective areas have often been cited interchangeably.[9] Hence we have included some authorities which may fall under the head of equitable forbearance and reference should also be made to the discussion of this issue at paragraphs 12.18–9 below.

It is difficult to divide the cases in this category from those falling within the general head of representations by conduct. The distinguishing feature of this head is that there is some active conduct in the previous category as opposed to mere silence in the category under consideration. However, the two categories tend to blend into one another. Thus, in *Pickard v Sears*[10] Z's failure to bring his rights to the attention of W formed an important part of the finding that a representation had been made. However, his conduct went beyond mere silence as to his contrary rights and involved active negotiations with W and Y. The case thus involves a representation by conduct and not mere silence. **8.058**

overlap between estoppels by acquiescence and convention and Lord Steyn's judgement did not rule this out. The assumption in issue in the *Indian Endurance* was that a party to legal proceedings would not insist on its right to take a particular defence based on the fact of judgment in another jurisdiction. This would, we suggest, fall under the scope of equitable forbearance, as an alleged promise to forego legal rights. See further at para. 12.18–9 below.

8 However, equitable forbearance operates on representations as to legal rights and between parties in a legal relationship; as is pointed out below at para. 8.63, the special characteristics of the relationship of parties to legal proceedings mean that the application of the general principles will seldom give rise to a duty to speak.

9 See *Pacol Ltd v Trade Lines Ltd ('the Henrik Sif')* [1982] 1 Lloyds Rep. 456, *The 'Superhulls Cover' Case (No. 2)* [1990] 2 Lloyd's Rep. 431, *'The Indian Endurance' (No 2) Republic of India v India Steamship Company* [1997] 4 All ER 380 HL, none of which cannot sensibly be categorized as falling within estoppel by representation. All concerned promises to forbear form enforcing legal rights. All included reference to authorities featuring estoppel by representation and/or estoppel by negligence.

10 (1837) 6 A&E 469, 112 ER 179 at 474.

The duty to speak: general principles

No representation will be inferred from silence unless the representor is under a legal[11] duty to disclose a particular fact or facts.[12] Inaction or silence, by contrast with positive conduct or statement, is said to be colourless:[13] it cannot influence a person to act to his detriment unless it acquires a positive content such that that person is entitled to rely on it.[14] This positive content is acquired as follows: where a person is under a legal duty to disclose some fact to another and does not do so, the other is entitled to assume the non-existence of the fact. The omission amounts to a representation that the fact does not exist.[15] The duty must be owed to the person seeking to raise the estoppel,[16] or to a group of which he was a member. **8.059**

There is some controversy as to precisely when such a duty arises. In *Moorgate Mercantile v Twitchings*[17] the House of Lords considered the circumstances in which the owner of a car could be estopped from asserting title against a third party who had purchased the car in good faith. Lord Wilberforce held: **8.060**

> What I think we are looking for here is an answer to the question whether, having regard to the situation in which the relevant transaction occurred, as known to both parties, a reasonable man, in the position of the 'acquirer' of the property, would expect the 'owner' acting honestly and responsibly, if he claimed any title in the property, to take steps to make that claim known to, and discoverable by, the 'acquirer' and whether, in the face of an omission to do so, the 'acquirer' could reasonably assume that no such title was claimed.[18]

---

[11] *The 'Superhulls Cover' Case (No. 2)* [1990] 2 Lloyd's Rep. 431 *per* Phillips J. at 452.

[12] *Greenwood v Martins Bank Ltd* [1933] AC 51 *per* Lord Tomlin at 57; *Chadwick v Manning* [1896] AC 231 *per* Lord MacNaughton at 238; *The Indian Endurance (No 2) Republic of India and another v India Steamship Co Ltd* [1996] 3 All ER 641, CA *per* Staughton L.J. at 653j; (aff without express reference to this particular point in at [1997] 4 All ER 380 HL); *Jones Bros v Holloway Ltd v Woodhouse* [1923] 2 KB 117, DC *per* Bailhache J. at 124 and *per* McCardie J. at 128 and *Hopgood v Brown* [1955] 1 WLR 213 *per* Evershed M.R. at 224.

[13] *Moorgate Mercantile Co Ltd v Twitchings* [1976] 1 QB 225 *per* Lord Wilberforce at 903.

[14] *ibid.*

[15] *Spiro v Lintern* [1973] 1 WLR 1002, CA at 1010.

[16] *Jones Bros v Holloway Ltd v Woodhouse* [1923] 2 KB 117, DC *per* Bailhache J. at 124.

[17] [1977] AC 890.

[18] [1977] AC 890 at 903, approved in *'The Indian Endurance' (No 2), Republic of India v India Steamship Company* [1997] 4 All ER 380 HL.

In *Pacol Ltd v Trade Lines Ltd ('the Henrik Sif')*,[19] Webster J. adopted this dictum and reformulated it in the following general terms: **8.061**

> . . . the duty necessary to raise an estop by silence or acquiescence arises where a reasonable man would expect person against whom the estoppel is raised, acting honestly and responsibly to bring the true facts to the attention of the other party known by him to be under a mistake as to their respective rights.

Mr Justice Webster's decision gives rise to a number of difficulties. First, the doctrine in issue in *Moorgate* was the controversial principle of estoppel by negligence, which may not form part of the law of estoppel at all (see further paragraphs 8.144 to 8.160 below). Secondly, Lord Wilberforce dissented on the relevant question namely, in what circumstances did a duty to speak arise? Despite these difficulties the *Pacol* test has been approved in subsequent authorities[20] and now appears to be a correct general statement of the law.[21]

Two aspects of the *Pacol* test should be noted. First, there is no need to establish a pre-existing legal duty to speak, arising from, for example, tort or contract. The circumstances of the case and the relationship of the parties can generate the necessary duty. Secondly, it is necessary to show that the representor knew of *a mistake* made by the representee as to the parties' respective legal entitlements. Thus, it is necessary to show not only that the representor knew of the representee's belief but also that the representor knew (or at least suspected)[22] that the belief was mistaken. It must therefore be established that the representor knew the true facts or had at least a suspicion of true position.[23] Hence, such **8.062**

---

19 [1982] 1 Lloyd's Rep. 456.

20 *'The Stolt Loyalty'* [1993] 2 Lloyd's Rep. 281 and *The Indian Endurance (No 2) Republic of India and another v India Steamship Co Ltd* [1996] 3 All ER 641, CA *per* Staughton L.J. at 653j and 654a-c. In affirming the decision of the Court of Appeal in *'The Indian Endurance' (No 2) Republic of India v India Steamship Company* [1997] 4 All ER 380 HL at 392c–e, Lord Steyn did not refer to *Pacol* but did approve the dictum of Lord Wilberforce in *Moorgate Mercantile Co Ltd v Twitchings* [1977] AC 890 (quoted at para. 8.60 above) on which the later case was based.

21 Although see para. 12.64 below for the difficulties flowing from Webster J.'s application of the test to the facts of the case.

22 See also the *'The Stolt Loyalty'* [1993] 2 Lloyd's Rep. 281.

23 See, *per* contra., *Spiro v Lintern* [1973] 1 WLR 1002, CA at 1011. The facts of *Spiro* are outlined below at para. 8.67. Arguably the defendant's conduct went beyond the purely passive in this case. For example, the defendant agreed to sell furniture to the plaintiff to be used in the property under dispute. It is uncontroversial that knowledge of the falsity of the representation is not necessary where there has been some active conduct on the part of the alleged representor. See para. 8.72 below.

cases are an exception to the general rule[24] that it is unnecessary to establish that the representor knew that the representation was false. It is submitted that the terms of the duty presuppose such knowledge. It can scarcely be reasonable to expect even the most reasonable and honest party to bring to the attention of another facts of which the first party was unaware.

The duty to speak: examples

Parties to legal proceedings

While the general principle set out in *Pacol* may be correct, its application to the facts of the case is controversial. The duty to speak in that case was extended to a duty to point out to the opponent in legal proceedings that it had sought time extensions from the wrong party. The decision has therefore been circumscribed. We would submit that the decision is to be limited to its facts.[25] In *The Stolt Loyalty*[26] Mr Justice Clark applied *Pacol* but stated that each case must depend on its own facts and that opponents in litigation do not normally owe a duty to point out one another's errors. It was appropriate to impose the *Pacol* duty in *The Stolt Loyalty*, because the defendants had responded to the requests for an extension in deliberately equivocal terms in order to prolong the plaintiff's error. The duty to speak will not be lightly imposed in new situations, particularly in legal proceedings: the parties are not expected to 'nurse maid' their opponents, at least where they are well used to commercial litigation, otherwise the client might well ask which side its lawyer is on.[27] It is therefore submitted that the application of the duty to speak to parties in legal proceedings in *Pacol* and *The Stolt Loyalty* was exceptional and triggered only by their special facts. Alternatively, it is submitted that the duty will be imposed only where one party has been guilty of sharp practice in the conduct of the litigation.[28] **8.063**

---

[24] As to which see below at para. 8.72.

[25] In *RPPC v Bank Leumi* [1992] Lloyd's Rep. 515 at 542, Hirst J. stated that *Pacol* turned on its peculiar facts.

[26] [1993] 2 Lloyd's 281 at 288–9.

[27] *The Indian Endurance (No 2) Republic of India and another v India Steamship Co Ltd* [1996] 3 All ER 641, CA *per* Staughton L.J. at 654b–d (aff. in *'The Indian Endurance' (No 2) Republic of India v India Steamship Company* [1997] 4 All ER 380 HL without reference to *'The Stolt Loyalty'*) approving the approach taken in *'The Stolt Loyalty'*.

[28] In effect where one party has led the other 'up the garden path'. See further *Dun & Bradstreet Software Services (England) Ltd v Provident Mutual Life Assurance*

Failure to assert and inconsistent legal right

In *Spiro v Lintern*[29] the Court of Appeal held that: **8.064**

> If A having some right or title adverse to B, sees B, in ignorance of that right or title, acting in a manner inconsistent with it in a way which would be to B's disadvantage if the right or title were asserted against him thereafter, A is under a duty to disclose the existence of his right or title. If he stands by and allows B to continue in his course of action A will not be allowed, if the other conditions of estoppel are satisfied, to assert his right or title against B.[30]

Hence, the duty to correct B's mistake arises wherever A is aware that B is acting to its detriment in reliance on a belief which is inconsistent with A's right or title. This potentially wide ranging principle bears a superficial similarity to the doctrine generally referred to as estoppel by negligence (see paragraphs 8.144 to 8.160 below). It is distinguishable however. The *Spiro* principle clearly operates only where A is aware that B is acting inconsistently with his right or title. Estoppel by negligence may occur where A is not aware of B's conduct but is simply negligent in arming another with ostensible title to the property.[31]

Although the case was not cited, the *Spiro* principle probably underlies the decision in *Bristol and West Building Society v Henning*.[32] A claimed a beneficial interest in the family home, title to which was registered in the name of her boyfriend. She claimed to be able to enforce this interest in priority to Bristol and West, who held a legal charge over it. A was aware that the property was to be charged to the building society. She was also aware that the society was relying on obtaining security over the premises, without any prior encumbrances. Having stood by while the building society advanced the loan on this assumption, A was prevented from asserting priority **8.065**

Association [1997] EGCS 89 CA (lexis transcript) and paras 12.18–9 where the same principle is discussed in the context of equitable forbearance. See above at para. 8.57 above for the relationship of estoppel by representation, equitable forbearance and estoppel by silence/acquiescence.

[29] [1973] 1 WLR 1002, CA *per* Buckley L.J. at 1010.

[30] See also *Re Safety Explosives Ltd* [1904] 1 Ch 226, CA and *Pickard v Sears* (1837) 6 A&E 469, 112 ER 179 although there was a representation by conduct in the latter case as well as a duty to speak.

[31] See para. 8.145 below.

[32] [1985] 1 WLR 778.

over them.[33] This principle is applicable both to unregistered[34] and registered land.[35]

It was held in *Fung Kai Sun v Chan Fui Hing* that if A finds out that a deed has been forged in its name, A is under a duty to inform the holder of the deed that it was forged. It is not clear whether this case is an example of the *Spiro* principle or the doctrine generally referred to as estoppel by negligence (see further, paragraph 8.147 below). **8.066**

In *Spiro v Lintern*,[36] it was further held that if A sees B acting in the mistaken belief that A is under some binding obligation to him and in a manner consistent only with the existence of such obligation which would be to B's disadvantage of A were thereafter to assert that no such binding obligation existed, A is under a duty to disclose the non-existence of the obligation. In that case, the defendant's wife had entered a contract to sell the family home to the plaintiff. The house was actually owned by the defendant and his wife had no authority to sell it on his behalf. The defendant failed to inform the plaintiff of the wife's lack of authority. On the contrary, the defendant stood by and allowed the plaintiff to act to his detriment in reliance on the belief that he had the benefit of a binding contract.[37] This conduct was held to have amounted to a representation that the wife had sufficient authority to enter the contract. Hence, an estoppel arose to prevent the defendant's raising the want of authority point. **8.067**

Other examples

Where a representation is made, by any one of the three methods outlined in this section,[38] it is deemed to continue until retracted by the representor and that retraction is communicated to the person to whom the representation was made. Hence, the representor comes under a duty to communicate the retraction to the representee.[39] **8.068**

The failure to reply to enquiries or correspondence has been held to give rise to an implied representation. For example, in *Algar v Middlesex County* **8.069**

---

33 See also *Equity and Law Home Loans v Prestidge* [1992] 1 WLR 137; *Midland Bank v Farmpride Hatcheries* (1981) 260 EG 493, CA *per* Shaw L.J. at 497 and *per* Oliver L.J. at 497 and *Sarat Chunder Dey v Ghopal Chunder Laha* (1892) LR 19 Ind App 203, PC (India). *cf.* the similar approach used by the House of Lords in *Abbey National Building Society v Cann* [1991] AC 56 at 94b–g.

34 *Bristol and West Building Society v Henning* [1985] 1 WLR 778.

35 *Paddington Home Loans v Mendelsohn* (1985) SO P&CR 44.

36 [1973] 1 WLR 1002, CA at *per* Buckley L.J. at 1101.

37 Arguably there was also some active conduct.

38 *i.e.* by statement, conduct or silence.

39 See, for example, *Scarf v Jardine* [1882] 7 App Cas 345, HL.

Council[40] the employee of a local authority wrote to it asking it to confirm that its pension rights were unaffected by a proposed job change. The authority's failure to reply estopped it from asserting that the employee's rights were prejudicially affected by the change. Similarly, in *Holt v Markham*[41] a government department wrote to the defendant asserting that he was not entitled to certain sums paid to him. The ground specified was incorrect. The defendant pointed this out to them and heard nothing more for three months when the authority claimed back the money on a different and correct ground. The authority was estopped from asserting that the sums were improperly paid. It should be noted that this approach effectively allows one party to impose a duty to speak on another by addressing enquiries to it.[42]

A trustee owes no duty to give information to the beneficiary as to encumbrances which the beneficiary has entered into with respect to its beneficial interest. Consequently, the trustee owes no such duty to those authorized by the beneficiary to enquire about such encumbrances.[43] A guarantor owes no duty to its co-surety to remind it of an indemnity agreed between them which both parties had every reason to recall.[44] **8.070**

Representation by negligence

It has been averred in a number of cases that a representation may be inferred from negligence. Because of particular difficulties raised by the so-called estoppel by negligence cases we consider them in a separate section at paragraphs 8.144 to 8.160 below. **8.071**

KNOWLEDGE AND INTENTION

Subject to one possible caveat,[45] it is not necessary to establish that the representor was dishonest[46] or that it knew that the representation was **8.072**

[40] [1945] 2 All ER 243, DC *per* Cassels J. at 248d–e and *per* Humphreys J. at 251a–b.
[41] [1923] 1 KB 504, CA.
[42] For criticism of such an approach see Spencer Bower at para. 71. Note also the divergence of opinion on the principle applicable to the equitable forbearance doctrine — see *Wallis Holiday Camp v Shell-Mex* [1974] 3 All ER 575 *per* Lord Denning at 580–1 and *per* Stamp L.J. at 586g–587d and para. 12.19.
[43] *Low v Bouverie* [1891] 3 Ch 82, CA at 99.
[44] *Chadwick v Manning* [1896] AC 231 *per* Lord Macnaughton at 238.
[45] As we set out in para. 8.62 above, we consider that it is probably necessary to show awareness of the the true position where a representation is inferred solely from silence, *i.e.* where a duty to speak is imposed.
[46] *Roberts & Co. Ltd v Leicestershire County Council* [1961] Ch 555 *per* Pennycuick J. at 570.

false.[47] Innocence of the truth is no defence and an estoppel may arise even where the representor never knew or has forgotten the true facts.[48] However, if it is possible to demonstrate knowledge of the truth, the representee may have useful remedies[49] arising in other areas of law such as misrepresentation and fraud.

It is necessary to demonstrate one of the slightly differing mental states listed below. Although the need to establish the relevant mental element has been frequently repeated,[50] it has not proved to be of great practical significance. Once it has been established that the representee acted in reliance on the representation, the requisite mental element has almost invariably been found to exist. There seems to be only one case where an estoppel argument failed for want of the latter factor alone.[51] **8.073**

A representation intended to be acted upon

An estoppel may arise if it can be shown that the representor intended its representation to be acted upon.[52] An objective approach is taken to **8.074**

---

47 *Spiro v Lintern* [1973] 1 WLR 1002 CA at 1012b–d; *Jorden v Money* (1854) V HLC 185, 10 ER 868 at 210 *per* Lord Cranworth L.C. at 212; *Sarat Chunder Dey v Ghopal Chunder Laha* (1892) LR 19 Ind App 203, PC (India) *per* Lord Shand at 215; *Citizens' Bank of Louisiana v First National Bank of New Orleans* (1873) LR 6 HL 352 *per* Lord Selbourne at 360–361; *Freeman v Cooke* (1848) 2 Ex 654, ER 652 at 663; *Greenwood v Martins Bank Ltd* [1932] 1 KB 371, CA *per* Scrutton L.J. at 379 and *Farrow v Orttewell* [1943] Ch 480, CA *per* Lord Hanworth M.R. at 499.

48 *Low v Bouverie* [1891] 3 Ch 82, CA at 107, 111.

49 As to which see specialist texts.

50 See for example the cases in n. 15 below.

51 See the comments of Spencer Bower at para. 99, citing *Pierson v Altrincham UDC* (1917) 86 LJ KB 969 where Ridley J. held at 317 col. 2, that '*it may be inferred as a fact, . . . in many and perhaps most cases in which the court comes to a conclusion that a person has been reasonably induced to believe, as a reasonable man, that a certain state of facts existed,* [that] *the court would find that he was intended so to believe, or . . . that he believed that it was intended that he should act on such a belief.*'

52 *Low v Bouverie* [1891] 3 Ch 82, CA at 111; *Covell v Sweetland* [1968] 1 WLR 1466 *per* Hinchcliffe J. at 1474; *Citizens' Bank of Louisiana v First National Bank of New Orleans* (1873) LR 6 HL 352 *per* Lord Selbourne at 360–1; *Freeman v Cooke* (1848) 2 Ex 654, ER 652 at 663; *Bishop v Balkis Consolidated Co* (1890) 25 QBD 77 *per* Vaughan Williams L.J. at 82 (affd on other grounds at 512); *Carr v London and North Western Rly Co* (1875) LR 10 CP 307 *per* Brett and Denman JJ. at 317; *De Tchihatchef v Salerni Coupling Ltd.* [1932] 1 Ch 330 *per* Luxmoor J. at 342 (sufficient that representation was made with the purpose of its being acted upon); *Dixon v Kennaway & Co* [1990] 1 Ch 833 *per* Farwell J. at 838; *Sidney Bolsom Investment Trust Ltd v E. Karmios & Co. (London) Ltd* [1956] 1 QB 529, CA *per* Denning L.J. at 540 and *per* Morris L.J. at 544; *Algar v Middlesex County Council*

the issue and therefore it will suffice to show that the representor has so conducted itself that a reasonable person would believe that the representor held the requisite intention.[53] Thus, intention to induce may be presumed.[54] This requirement has seldom been considered in any detail. In *Trane (UK) Ltd v Provident Mutual Life Assurance*[55] such an intention was presumed where, in course of negotiations concerning a lease, a landlord made a clear representation which it was pointless to make unless the representee was to be able to assume it was seriously meant. This case gives useful insight into the principle underlying the rule under discussion. It seems to be designed to prevent casual or informal statements from forming the basis of an estoppel. A similar function is performed in relation to the equitable forbearance/promissory estoppel doctrine by the requirement that the representor must intend to create legal relations,[56] although the latter requirement is not itself applicable in estoppel by representation cases.

8.075 It is probably also sufficient to demonstrate that the representor knew that a reasonable person would be likely to act in reliance on the

---

[1945] 2 All ER 243, DC *per* Humphreys J. at 250f–g; *Lowe v Lombank* [1960] 1 WLR 196, CA *per* Diplock J. at 205; *Customs & Excise Commissioners v Hebson Ltd* [1953] 2 Lloyd's Rep. 382 at *per* Pearson J. at 397 col. 1; *Gresham Life Assurance Society v Crowther* [1914] 2 Ch 219 *per* Astbury J. at 227 (affd on other grounds [1915] 1 Ch 214, CA); *Nippon Menkwa Kabushiki Kaisha (Japan Cotton Trading Co Ltd) v Dawson's Bank Ltd* (1935) 51 Lloyd's Rep. 147, PC (India) *per* Lord Russell at 150 col. 2; *TCB Ltd v Gray* [1986] Ch 621 *per* Sir Nicholas Browne-Wilkinson V.C. at 634; *Hopgood v Brown* [1955] 1 WLR 213 *per* Evershed M.R. at 224 and *Trane (UK) Ltd v Provident Mutual Life Assurance* [1995] EGLR 33 *per* Judge Cooke at 38–9.

53 *Citizens' Bank of Louisiana v First National Bank of New Orleans* (1873) LR 6 HL 352 *per* Lord Selbourne at 360–1; *Sidney Bolsom Investment Trust Ltd v E. Karmios & Co. (London) Ltd* [1956] 1 QB 529, CA *per* Denning L.J. at 541 and *per* Morris L.J. at 544; *Freeman v Cooke* (1848) 2 Ex 654, ER 652 at 663; *Carr v London and North Western Rly Co* (1875) LR 10 CP 307 *per* Brett and Denman JJ. at 317; *Dixon v Kennaway & Co* [1990] 1 Ch 833 *per* Farwell J. at 838; *Farrow v Orttewell* [1943] Ch 480, CA *per* Lord Hanworth M.R. at 499; *Jorden v Money* (1854) V HLC 185, 10 ER 868 *per* Lord Cranworth L.C. at 214–5; *Algar v Middlesex County Council* [1945] 2 All ER 243, DC *per* Humphreys J. at 250f–g; *Lowe* v *Lombank* [1960] 1 WLR 196, CA *per* Diplock J. at 205; *Greenwood v Martins Bank Ltd* [1932] 1 KB 371, CA *per* Scrutton L.J. at 379; *Customs & Excise Commissioners v Hebson Ltd* [1953] 2 Lloyd's Rep. 382 *per* Pearson J. at 397 col. 1 and *Trane (UK) Ltd v Provident Mutual Life Assurance* [1995] EGLR 33 *per* Judge Cooke at 38–9.

54 *Re Exchange Securities & Commodities Ltd* [1988] Ch 46 at *per* Harman J. at 54 and *Hopgood v Brown* [1955] 1 WLR 213 *per* Evershed M.R. at 224.

55 [1995] EGLR 33 *per* Judge Cooke at 39.

56 As to which see para. 12.22 below.

representation[57] or had reasonable grounds to believe that the representee would so act.[58]

Knowledge of the representee's detrimental reliance

8.076 It can be seen from the previous paragraphs that the focus of the intention or knowledge requirement is at the point of representation rather than at the point of reliance. The authorities fail to deal expressly with the situation where the representor makes the representation without the requisite intention but later learns that the representee is acting in reliance on it. In the parallel areas of equitable forbearance and proprietary estoppel, it is clear that mere knowledge of the representee's acts in reliance[59] is sufficient, without establishing any particular prior intention.[60] It is submitted, however, that such knowledge probably would also suffice for estoppel by representation. Once the representor becomes aware of the acts of the representee and of the fact that they are being performed in reliance on its representation, the representor comes under a duty to retract the representation if it does not intend it to be relied on. Unless the representor retracts the representation or advises the representee not to rely on it, it will probably be presumed to have intended the representee to continue to rely on it. Except in certain controversial instances,[61] it is not generally necessary to show that the representation was made negligently,[62] although if it was this may give rise to parallel remedies in tort.[63]

8.077 Intention and knowledge are alternatives. It is not necessary to establish both. Once an intention to induce reliance is demonstrated, it is not necessary to go on to establish that the representor actually knew[64]

[57] *Dixon v Kennaway & Co* [1990] 1 Ch 833 *per* Farwell J. at 837, applying *Knights v Wiffen* (1870) LR 5 QB 660, CA *per* Blackburn J. at 665.

[58] *Jorden v Money* (1854) V HLC 185, 10 ER 868 *per* Lord Cranworth L.C. at 212.

[59] Knowledge of acts in reliance logically requires that the representor knows both of the acts performed and of the fact that they are being performed in reliance on the representee's belief in the truth of the representation.

[60] See para. 12.23 and 11.21.

[61] As to which see para. 8.144 ff below.

[62] *Moorgate Mercantile Co Ltd v Twitchings* [1977] AC 890 *per* Lord Salmon at 913.

[63] As to which see specialist texts.

[64] Arguably, the intentional mental element required of the representor, as set out in para 8.74 above, in any event involves constructive knowledge or notice of the acts of the representee. Such knowledge or notice arises where the representor has reasonable grounds to suspect the relevant facts or has actual knowledge of facts which would put him on notice of the existence of the relevant facts.

that the representee was so acting. For example, if a company issues a share certificate to X, it makes a representation to the general public that X is the owner of the shares. It is deemed to intend that representation to be acted upon by any member of the public. In none of the cases where this principle has been applied has the company actually known of the representee's acts in reliance (namely contracting to buy the shares from X and paying the purchase price accordingly).[65]

No specific acts need be intended

In the following paragraph, we consider, in more detail, precisely what the representor must intend or have knowledge of, in the sense set out above. For clarity, we have tended to use the term intention to describe collectively, the slightly differing mental states referred to above. There is some suggestion in the case law that it is necessary to establish that the requisite mental element in relation to a specific course of conduct, *i.e.* that the representor intended the representee to act specifically in the way which it in fact acted.[66] In our view, this approach is too restrictive; it is probably sufficient merely to show an intention to induce conduct of some sort. As is set out below, in order to establish an estoppel, the representee must prove that its conduct was reasonable in the circumstances. This principle prevents unexpected or eccentric acts from amounting to detrimental reliance and provides an adequate limitation on the scope of qualifying conduct. It has been held in some cases that it must be shown that the representor intended the representee to act to his *detriment*.[67] It is unlikely that such dicta impose a requirement that prejudice capable of amounting to detriment was intended. It is probably necessary only to show an intention to induce the representee to act and that the acts in question gave rise to detriment.[68] **8.078**

[65] *In re Ottos Kopje Diamond Mines Ltd* [1893] 1 Ch 1892, CA and *Dixon v Kennaway & Co* [1990] 1 Ch 833.

[66] *Carr v London and North Western Rly Co* (1875) LR 10 CP 307 *per* Brett and Denman JJ. at 317 and *Dixon v Kennaway & Co* [1990] 1 Ch 833 *per* Farwell J. at 838. See also *Sidney Bolsom Investment Trust Ltd v E. Karmios & Co. (London) Ltd* [1956] 1 QB 529, CA *per* Morris L.J. at 544 (no estoppel because nothing in the representor's conduct amounted to 'an invitation to the representee to act in the way it did').

[67] *Re Bankruptcy Notice* [1924] 2 Ch 76, CA *per* Pollock M.R. at 88 and *Re Exchange Securities & Commodities Ltd* [1988] Ch 46 *per* Harman J. at 54.

[68] As to which see para. 8.88 below.

RELIANCE

It is necessary to show that the representation was communicated to the representee[69] and that the representee believed that it was true.[70] The representee must also have acted in reliance on representation.[71] 8.079

It must have been reasonable to rely on the representation

While the representee is under no general duty to investigate the truth of the representation,[72] it cannot rely blindly on any representation made to it. It is necessary to show that the representation was of such a nature as would have misled a reasonable person.[73] It must have been reasonable to believe that the representation was true[74] and reasonable to have acted on it in the way the representee did.[75] Whether it is so reasonable will depend on the circumstances of the case. There may be facts which should cause the representee to enquire as to the truth of the representation or the authority of the person 8.080

---

69 *Macfisheries Ltd v Harrison* (1924) 132 LT 22, 40 TLR 709.

70 *Pickard v Sears* (1837) 6 A&E 469, 112 ER 179 at 474; *Low v Bouverie* [1891] 3 Ch 82, CA at 113; *Canada and Dominion Sugar Company, Limited v Canadian National (West Indies) Steamships, Limited* [1947] AC 46, PC (Canada) at 56; *Bell v Marsh* [1903] 1 Ch 528, CA *per* Lord Collins M.R. at 541 and *per* Omer L.J. at 544; *Farrow v Orttewell* [1943] Ch 480, CA *per* Lord Hanworth M.R. at 498; *Re Bankruptcy Notice* [1924] 2 Ch 76, CA *per* Atkin L.J. at 96; *Jorden v Money* (1854) V HLC 185, 10 ER 868 *per* Lord Cranworth L.C. at 210, 212; *Lowe v Lombank* [1960] 1 WLR 196, CA *per* Diplock J. at 205; *Gresham Life Assurance Society v Crowther* [1914] 2 Ch 219 *per* Astbury J. at 228 (affd on other grounds [1915] 1 Ch 214 CA) and *The 'Superhulls Cover' Case (No. 2)* [1990] 2 Lloyd's Rep. 431 *per* Phillips J. at 448.

71 See the cases listed at para. 8.84.

72 *Trane (UK) Ltd v Provident Mutual Life Assurance* [1995] EGLR 33 *per* Judge Cooke at 39b and *Gresham Life Assurance Society v Crowther* [1914] 2 Ch 219 *per* Astbury J. at 227 (affd on other grounds [1915] 1 Ch 214, CA).

73 *Low v Bouverie* [1891] 3 Ch 82, CA at 113 and *Canada and Dominion Sugar Company, Limited v Canadian National (West Indies) Steamships, Limited* [1947] AC 46, PC (Canada) at 55.

74 *Canada and Dominion Sugar Company, Limited v Canadian National (West Indies) Steamships, Limited* [1947] AC 46 PC (Canada) at 56. See also *Maclaine v Gatty* [1921] 1 AC 376, HL Sc *per* Lord Birkenhead at 386 (the representee must have been 'justified' in believing representation).

75 *Freeman v Cooke* (1848) 2 Ex 654, ER 652 at 656; *Seton, Laing v Lefone* (1887) 19 QBD 68, CA at 73 and *Trane (UK) Ltd v Provident Mutual Life Assurance* [1995] EGLR 33 *per* Judge Cooke at 39b.

communicating it. For example, it would be unreasonable to rely on a representation by a junior administrator, working in a branch of a large multinational, that the company had stocks of green cheese extracted from the moon.[76] A highly important general factor is whether the subject matter of the representation fell within the representor's particular scope of knowledge or expertise or whether it was something concerning which the representee could reasonably be expected to form its own view.[77]

For example, in *Sidney Bolsom Investment Trust Ltd v E. Karmios & Co. (London) Ltd*[78] a tenant served notice of a request to extend its tenancy pursuant to rights under statute. The landlord in turn served a notice of opposition, one of the grounds of which was a challenge to the validity of the original notice served on it by the tenant. As a result of a failure on the tenant's part to prosecute its claim within the statutory time limits, the tenant later claimed that its notice was indeed invalid or alternatively, that the landlord was estopped from denying this. The representation contained in the landlord's notice of opposition did not give rise to an estoppel. It was for both parties to form their own opinion as to the validity of the notice.[79] Hence, it was unreasonable for the tenant to rely on the landlord's opinion in the matter. It should have applied to the court to ascertain whether it was valid or not.[80] **8.081**

By contrast, in *Trane (UK) Ltd v Provident Mutual Life Assurance*[81] the landlord's managing agent had represented that the date for the exercise of the break clause in the lease was later than it in fact was. Although the tenant had acted somewhat casually in failing to obtain legal advice on the matter, Judge Cook[82] held that the representation went against the interests of the landlord. It was therefore one which the landlord could not be expected to make unless it was likely to be true. Hence, it was reasonable to believe the representation made and to act on it. **8.082**

[76] This example was used in *Trane (UK) Ltd v Provident Mutual Life Assurance* [1995] EGLR 33 *per* Judge Cooke at 39b.
[77] *cf.* the principle that a representation of law cannot be the basis of an estoppel, as to which see para. 8.36 above.
[78] [1956] 1 QB 529, CA.
[79] [1956] 1 QB 529, CA *per* Morris L.J. at 544.
[80] *ibid. per* Denning LJ at 541. See also *Perring v Draper* [1997] EGCS 109, discussed at para. 8.36 above.
[81] [1995] EGLR 33 *per* Judge Cooke at 39b.
[82] Sitting as a deputy High Court judge.

Disclaimers

8.083 If the representor expressly disclaims responsibility for accuracy of representation, no estoppel will arise.[83] It will not be reasonable to rely on a representation thus qualified.

The representee must have acted in reliance on the representation[84]

8.084 It is not necessary to show that the representee has performed a positive act. It is sufficient if the representee refrained from acting in a particular way as a result of the representation.[85] What is essential is that the representee has been led to act differently from the way in which it would have

---

[83] *Hammersmith and Fulham BC v Top Shop Centres Ltd* [1990] Ch 237 *per* Warner J. at 257c–d.

[84] *Low v Bouverie* [1891] 3 Ch 82, CA at 111; *Oliver v Bank of England* [1902] 1 Ch 610, CA at 628 (affd without comment on the point at *Starkey v Bank of England* [1903] AC 114); *Canada and Dominion Sugar Company, Limited v Canadian National (West Indies) Steamships, Limited* [1947] AC 46, PC (Canada) at 56; *Covell v Sweetland* [1968] 1 WLR 1466 *per* Hinchcliffe J. at 1474; *Greenwood v Martins Bank Ltd* [1933] AC 51 *per* Lord Tomlin at 57; *Sarat Chunder Dey v Ghopal Chunder Laha* (1892) LR 19 Ind App 203, PC (India) *per* Lord Shand at 215; *Bell v Marsh* [1903] 1 Ch 528, CA *per* Lord Collins M.R. at 541 and Romer L.J. at 544; *Hammersmith and Fulham BC v Top Shop Centres Ltd* [1990] Ch 237 at 259a; *Carr v London and North Western Rly Co* (1875) LR 10 CP 307 *per* Brett and Denman JJ. at 317; *Dixon v Kennaway & Co* [1990] 1 Ch 833 *per* Farwell J. at 838; *Avon CC v Howlett* [1983] 1 WLR 605, CA *per* Slade L.J. at 620f–g; *H. Clark (Doncaster) Ltd v Wilkinson* [1965] Ch 694, CA *per* Lord Denning M.R. at 702 and *per* Salmon L.J. at 704; *Farrow v Orttewell* [1943] Ch 480, CA *per* Lord Hanworth M.R. at 491; *Re Bankruptcy Notice* [1924] 2 Ch 76, CA *per* Lord Pollock M.R. at 88; *Re Exchange Securities & Commodities Ltd* [1988] Ch 46 *per* Harman J. at 54; *Jorden v Money* (1854) V HLC 185, 10 ER 868 *per* Lord Cranworth L.C. at 210; *Daejan Properties Ltd v Mahoney* [1995] 2 EGLR 75, CA *per* Sir Thomas Bingham MR at 77; *Civil Aviation Authority v Internationale Nederlanden Aviation Lease BV and the European Organisation for the Safety of Air Navigation (Interveners)* [1997] 1 Lloyd's Rep. 96 *per* Judge Diamond Q.C. at 104 col. 2; *De Tchihatchef v Salerni Coupling Ltd* [1932] 1 Ch 330 *per* Luxmoor J. at 342; *Algar v Middlesex County Council* [1945] 2 All ER 243, DC *per* Humphreys J. at 250f–g; *Lowe v Lombank* [1960] 1 WLR 196, CA *per* Diplock J. at 205; *Gresham Life Assurance Society v Crowther* [1914] 2 Ch 219 *per* Astbury J. at 228 (affd on other grounds [1915] 1 Ch 214, CA); *Nippon Menkwa Kabushiki Kaisha (Japan Cotton Trading Co Ltd) v Dawson's Bank Ltd* [1935] 51 Lloyd's Rep. 147, PC (India) *per* Lord Russell at 151 col. 2; *Knights v Wiffen* (1870) LR 5 QB 660, CA *per* Blackburn J. at 665 and *per* Lush J. at 667; *Hopgood v Brown* [1955] 1 WLR 213 *per* Evershed M.R. at 224 and *Keith v R. Gancia and Co Ltd* [1904] 1 Ch 774, CA *per* Vaughan Williams L.J. at 789.

[85] *Hammersmith and Fulham BC v Top Shop Centres Ltd* [1990] Ch 237 *per* Warner J. at 259a. See, for example, *Covell v Sweetland* [1968] 1 WLR 1466 *per* Hinchcliffe

done had the representation never been made.[86] Put another way, the representee must have changed its position in reliance on the representation. Both positive acts and passive omissions amount to a change of position in the legal sense and arguably in the literal sense as well. A passive omission may give rise to a change of position because external events may alter the position of the representee. Were it not for the representation, the representee would have adjusted its affairs to take into account these external events and thus preserve its original position.

It is not necessary to show that the change of position falls into any pre-existing category but a limiting criterion is provided by the requirement of detriment.[87] Any act will suffice so long as it involves a change of position which is such as to give rise to detriment, in the event that the representor later denies the truth of the representation. There are certain restrictions inherent in this apparently flexible approach: some general categories of acts may be incapable of giving rise to detriment.[88] **8.085**

There must have been a causative link between the representee's belief that the representation was true and the acts which gave rise to detriment. This link has been described and analysed in various different ways. It has been averred that the representation must have been the real or proximate cause of the relevant conduct[89] or that the conduct must have resulted from the representation.[90] However, the cases where such an approach has been adopted have tended to involve the so-called estoppel by negligence principle to which different rules may apply.[91] It is probably unnecessary to show that the actions were caused solely by the representation. It is sufficient if it influenced the representee's decision to act in the way which it did.[92] It is necessary to establish that the **8.086**

J. at 1474 (failure to apply to divorce court to get a maintenance agreement set aside); *Dixon v Kennaway & Co* [1990] 1 Ch 833 *per* Farwell J. at 839 (failure to pursue the fraudulent vendor of shares) and *Knights v Wiffen* (1870) LR 5 QB 660, CA *per* Blackburn J. at 665 (failure by a buyer to ask for its money back under a sale of goods transaction where the buyer was legally entitled to do so).

86 *Citizens' Bank of Louisiana v First National Bank of New Orleans* (1873) LR, 6 HL 352 *per* Lord Selbourne at 360 and *Bell v Marsh* [1903] 1 Ch 528 CA *per* Lord Collins M.R. at 541, 543 and *per* Cozens Hardy L.J. at 545.

87 As to which see below at paras 8.88 to 8.107 below.

88 See para. 8.93, 11.33 and 11.45.

89 *Seton, Laing v Lefone* (1887) 19 QBD 68, CA at 71.

90 *Greenwood v Martins Bank Ltd* [1933] AC 51 *per* Lord Tomlin at 57.

91 See paras 8.144 to 8.160 below.

92 *Amalgamated Investment & Property Co. Ltd, (in liquidation) v Texas Commerce International Bank Ltd* [1982] 1 QB 84 *per* Goff J. at 105a.

representation encouraged or induced[93] the representee to act in the way it did. The fact that it was material to the decision so to act is insufficient.[94] The causative link may exist where a belief already held is strengthened or the representee is lulled into a false sense of security.[95]

Proving causation

The burden lies on the representee to prove that its conduct was caused by the representation in the sense just described.[96] The doctrine thus operates differently from proprietary estoppel. Under the latter doctrine, the normal burden is, in the certain circumstances, reversed and the onus is placed on the representor to show that the conduct was not caused or influenced by the representation made.[97] The burden was so reversed in *Hammersmith and Fulham BC v Top Shop Centres Ltd.*[98] It is difficult to establish clearly whether this was a case of proprietary estoppel or estoppel by representation or both. The authorities[99] cited in support of the reversal of the burden concerned proprietary estoppel and therefore the cases provide little, if any, support for the application of this principle to estoppel by representation. There is some authority to suggest, however, that where the action taken by the representee is the obvious and expected consequence of his having been influenced by the representation, a prima facie inference of causation may be drawn **8.087**

93 *Freeman v Cooke* (1848) 2 Ex 654, ER 652 at 656; *Re Bankruptcy Notice* [1924] 2 Ch 76, CA *per* Lord Pollock M.R. at 88; *Lowe v Lombank* [1960] 1 WLR 196, CA *per* Diplock J. at 205; *Pickard v Sears* (1837) 6 A&E 469, 112 ER 179 at 474; *Farrow v Orttewell* [1943] Ch 480, CA *per* Lord Hanworth M.R. at 491; *Hopgood v Brown* [1955] 1 WLR 213 *per* Evershed M.R. at 224 and *Re Exchange Securities & Commodities Ltd* [1988] Ch 46 *per* Harman J. at 54.

94 *Credit Suisse v Allerdale BC* [1996] 1 Lloyd's Rep. 315 at 369 (affd on other grounds [1996] 2 Lloyd's Rep. 241). Colman J. was there referring to estoppel by convention but was applying the same test adopted in *Amalgamated Investment & Property Co. Ltd, (in liquidation) v Texas Commerce International Bank Ltd* [1982] 1 QB 84.

95 *Dixon v Kennaway & Co* [1900] 1 Ch 833. See also the equitable forbearance case of *Lark v Outhwaite* [1991] 2 Lloyd's Rep. 132 at 142.

96 See the following authorities where the burden seemed to be placed squarely on the shoulders of the representee: *Nippon Menkwa Kabushiki Kaisha (Japan Cotton Trading Co Ltd) v Dawson's Bank Ltd* (1935) 51 Lloyd's Rep. 147, PC (India) *per* Lord Russell at 150 col. 2; *Lowe v Lombank* [1960] 1 WLR 196, CA *per* Diplock J. at 207 and *Trane (UK) Ltd v Provident Mutual Life Assurance* [1995] EGLR 33 (*obiter*) *per* Judge Cooke at 39d-e.

97 See para. 11.26.

98 [1990] Ch 237 *per* Warner J. at 262c-d.

99 *Greasley v Cook* [1980] 1 WLR 1306, CA and *Re Basham decd* [1986] 1 WLR 1498.

without the claimant adducing further evidence.[1] The mere fact that the conduct followed the representation is insufficient evidence of causation.[2]

DETRIMENT

In order to raise an estoppel by representation, the representee must establish detriment[3] or prejudice.[4] It is commonly said that the representee must have acted to its detriment.[5] This formulation has led to **8.088**

---

1 See Spencer Bower at para. 109 and *Newbon v City Mutual Life Insurance Society Ltd* (1935) 52 CLR 723 at 734–5.

2 *Lowe v Lombank* [1960] 1 WLR 196, CA *per* Diplock J. at 207.

3 *Spiro v Lintern* [1973] 1 WLR 1002, CA at 1010h–11a, 1012h–13d; *Canada and Dominion Sugar Company, Limited v Canadian National (West Indies) Steamships, Limited* [1947] AC 46, PC (Canada) at 56; *Covell v Sweetland* [1968] 1 WLR 1466 *per* Hinchcliffe J. at 1474; *Greenwood v Martins Bank Ltd* [1933] AC 51 *per* Lord Tomlin at 57; *Bell v Marsh* [1903] 1 Ch 528, CA *per* Lord Collins M.R. at 541; *per* Romer L.J. at 544 and *per* Cozens Hardy L.J. at 545; *Carr v London and North Western Rly Co* (1875) LR 10 CP 307 *per* Brett and Denman JJ. at 317; *Dixon v Kennaway & Co* [1990] 1 Ch 833 *per* Farwell J. at 838; *Avon CC v Howlett* [1983] 1 WLR 605, CA *per* Slade L.J. at 621g–2c; *H. Clark (Doncaster) Ltd v Wilkinson* [1965] Ch 694, CA *per* Lord Denning M.R. at 702 and *per* Salmon L.J. at 704; *Fung Kai Sun v Chan Fui Hing* [1951] AC 489, PC (Hong Kong) *per* Lord Wright at 503; *Re Bankruptcy Notice* [1924] 2 Ch 76, CA *per* Lord Pollock M.R. at 88; *Re Exchange Securities & Commodities Ltd* [1988] Ch 46 *per* Harman J. at 54; *M'Kensie v British Linen Co* (1881) 6 App Cas 82 HL Sc *per* Lord Selbourne L.C. at 92, *per* Lord Blackburn at 101 and *per* Lord Watson at 109; *Norfolk CC v Secretary of State for the Environment* [1973] 3 All ER 673 *per* Lord Widgery C.J. at 677d–g; *Weld Blundell v Synott* [1940] 2 KB 107 *per* Asquith J. at 114; *TCB Ltd v Gray* [1986] Ch 621 *per* Sir Nicholas Browne-Wilkinson V.C. at 634; *George Whitechurch Ltd v Cavanagh* [1902] AC 117 *per* Lord Robertson at 135; *Trane (UK) Ltd v Provident Mutual Life Assurance* [1995] EGLR 33 (*obiter*) *per* Judge Cooke at 39d–e; *Peyman v Lanjani* [1985] Ch 457, CA *per* Slade L.J. at 500d-e, *per* May L.J. 496d–e and *per* Stephenson L.J. at 488d-e; *Hopgood v Brown* [1955] 1 WLR 213 *per* Evershed M.R. at 224 and *Simm v Anglo American Telegraph* (1879) 5 QBD 188, CA (representee had to show that he was damaged by his reliance on the representation).

4 *Jones Bros v Holloway Ltd v Woodhouse* [1923] 2 KB 117, DC *per* Bailhache J. at 124 and *per* McCardie J. at 128; *Tarmac Construction Ltd v Esso Petroleum Co Ltd*, 51 Con LR 187 ORB *per* H.H. Judge Humphrey Lloyd Q.C. at 223 and *Algar v Middlesex County Council* [1945] 2 All ER 243, DC *per* Humphreys J. at 250f–g.

5 *Farquharson Bros and Co v C King and Co* [1902] AC 325 *per* Lord Halsbury L.C. at 330; *Bell v Marsh* [1903] 1 Ch 528 *per* Lord Collins M.R. at 541; *R.E. Jones v Waring & Gillow* [1926] AC 670 *per* Viscount Cave L.C. at 683; *H. Clark (Doncaster) Ltd v Wilkinson* [1965] Ch 694, CA *per* Lord Denning M.R. at 702 and *per* Salmon L.J. at 704; *Covell v Sweetland* [1968] 1 WLR 1466 *per* Hinchcliffe J. at 1474; *Norfolk CC v Secretary of State for the Environment* [1973] 3 All ER 673 *per* Lord Widgery C.J. at 677d–g and *Peyman v Lanjani* [1985] Ch 457, CA *per* Slade L.J. at 501a–d.

some confusion; as was pointed out by Mr Justice Dixon on *Grundt v Great Boulder Pty Gold Mines Ltd*, whilst it is not strictly incorrect, it '. . . *does not bring out the basal purpose of the doctrine*'.[6] The detriment, which it is the aim of estoppel to prevent, is that which would flow from the representee's change of position, were the representor to be permitted to deny the truth of the representation.

> . . . the real detriment or harm from which the law seeks to give protection is that which would flow from the change of position if the assumption were deserted that led to it. So long as the assumption is adhered to, the party who altered his situation on the faith of it cannot complain. His complaint is that when afterwards that other party makes a different state of affairs the basis of an assertion of rights against him, then if it is allowed, his own original change of position will operate as a detriment. His action or inaction must be such that, if the assumption on which he proceeded is shown to be wrong and an inconsistent state of affairs was accepted as the foundation of the rights and duties of himself and the opposite party, the consequence would be to make his original act or failure to act a source of prejudice.[7]

Two aspects of the *Grundt* formulation should be noted. First, since **8.089** the representee needs to establish only that it will suffer detriment or prejudice *if the representor resiles* from the assumption, the change of position, itself, need not be onerous, unpleasant or damaging. So long as the assumption is adhered to, the representee suffers no prejudice. On the contrary, it may benefit from its change of position. For example, in *De Tchihatchef v Salerni Coupling Ltd*,[8] Fitzgerald entered into a contract with Salerni Coupling Ltd. He represented that the contract contained certain lucrative terms. In reliance on his representation, the company referred to these favourable terms in a share prospectus. While the representation was adhered to, this act by the company enured to its benefit: the relevant item in the prospectus would amount to an important inducement to subscribe to the share issue. Detriment is assessed, however, not at the point of performance of the relevant change of position, but at the point when the representor seeks to resile from its representation. Denial of the representation in *Salerni*'s case left the

---

[6] *Grundt v Great Boulder Pty Gold Mines Ltd* (1937) 59 CLR 641 *per* Dixon J. at 674. This was an estoppel by convention case but the relevant principle would seem to be equally applicable in this context: see *Re Exchange Securities & Commodities Ltd* [1988] Ch 46 at *per* Harman J. at 55.

[7] *Grundt v Great Boulder Pty Gold Mines Ltd* (1937) 59 CLR 641 at 674–5 and *Waltons Stores (Interstate) Ltd v Maher* [1988] 164 CLR 387 (HC of Australia) *per* Brennan J. at 419.

[8] [1932] 1 Ch 330.

company vulnerable to legal action by those who had bought shares in reliance on the statement contained in the prospectus.

Secondly, the representee might be said to suffer harm as a result of the mere fact of denial of the truth of the representation. This type of detriment, alone, is insufficient to raise an estoppel by representation. Some additional disadvantage is necessary, caused by the representee's change of position. Take, for example, the case of *Norfolk CC v Secretary of State for the Environment*,[9] where a company applied for planning permission to build a factory. The application was rejected by the authority but one of its agents mistakenly represented to the company that its application had been successful. The company thereafter commenced preparations for the development by placing orders for necessary machinery. The authority discovered the error. No estoppel arose to prevent the authority asserting the true facts, namely that planning permission had not been granted. The company was worse off under the true facts than under the facts as represented: under the latter it was the recipient of planning permission and under the former, it was not. Thus, the company could be said to have suffered harm as a result of the authority's resiling from the representation made. This was, however, insufficient. There was no estoppel because no detriment flowed from the company's change of position, namely the ordering of the machinery: the company had been able to cancel the orders without incurring any penalty.[10] **8.090**

Detriment and inequity

In marked contrast to other forms of estoppel, the concept of inequity is seldom referred to in estoppel by representation cases. The vast majority of such cases involve a fairly mechanistic application of the requirements of representation reliance and detriment. However, in *Lipkin Gorman v Karpnale*,[11] Lord Goff held that: **8.091**

> . . . estoppel normally depends upon the existence of a representation by one party, in reliance upon which the representee has so changed his position that it is inequitable for the representor to go back upon his representation.

---

9 [1973] 3 All ER 673.

10 See also the example referred to in the preceding para., *De Tchihatchef v. Salerni Coupling Ltd* [1932] 1 Ch 330. The mere denial of the representation would have harmed the representee because the contractual terms would have been less favourable to it. This harm would have been insufficient. It was necessary to go on to demonstrate harm resulting from the company's acts in reliance on the representation, namely including the representation in its share prospectus.

11 [1991] 2 AC 548.

Similar statements have been made in a limited number of other authorities.[12] It has been frequently averred that equitable forbearance and proprietary estoppel are based on the prevention of unconscionable or inequitable conduct.[13] As is set out in paragraphs 12.50 and 11.34, this has led the courts to take into account, in addition to the orthodox requirements of belief, reliance and detriment, a number of other random factors in assessing whether liability has been established. There is no suggestion that this flexible approach is applicable in estoppel by representation cases. On the contrary, Lord Justice Slade has warned of the dangers of resorting to broad concepts of equity with the consequent uncertainty that this can generate.[14] A move towards a more flexible approach may occur, particularly if the various different types of estoppel are to converge or at least draw closer together, but the sacrifice of certainty that this would involve may be too high a price to pay for uniformity of approach.[15] **8.092**

Examples of detriment

Apart from two possible caveats,[16] an identical detriment requirement seems to be imposed by both the doctrines of proprietary estoppel and estoppel by representation. Reference should therefore be made to paragraph 11.31 to 11.47 below, where we set out the general principles which determine what type of conduct is capable of giving rise to detriment. It should be noted that, while it is not necessary to show that the acts performed fall within any pre-existing category, some conduct may be inherently incapable of giving rise to detriment.[17] For convenience we have selected some examples of detriment occurring specifically in the context of estoppel by representation. We adopt the same threefold **8.093**

---

[12] *Holt v Markham* [1923] 1 KB 504, CA *per* Warrington L.J. at 512; *Avon CC v Howlett* [1983] 1 WLR 605, CA *per* Cumming-Bruce L.J. at 608e–h; *Ismail v. Polish Ocean Lines* [1976] QB 893, CA *per* Lord Denning M.R. at 903 and *Civil Aviation Authority v Internationale Nederlanden Aviation Lease BV and the European Organisation for the Safety of Air Navigation (Interveners)* [1997] 1 Lloyd's Rep. 96 *per* Judge Diamond Q.C. at 104 col. 2.

[13] See paras 11.01 and 12.33 below.

[14] *Avon CC v Howlett* [1983] 1 WLR 605, CA *per* Slade L.J. at 621g–h.

[15] See further para. 8.10–3 above.

[16] As to which see paras 8.102 to 8.107 below, discussing the two anomalous instances where detriment has been found to exist, contrary to orthodox principles. The cases in issue involve estoppel by representation. There is no reason to apply these dubious lines of authority to proprietary estoppel. Hence, this may be a point of distinction between the operation of the two doctrines.

[17] See paras 11.43–5 below.

classification of detriment[18] as we have in relation to proprietary estoppel and equitable forbearance. We do so with two reservations. First, the categorization is merely a useful analytical tool which we have adopted in order to identify the common characteristics of detriment cases. It may not be comprehensive although there is no example of detriment which we have been unable to fit within it. Secondly, the categories are not mutually exclusive and overlap with one another.

The representee foregoes something of value

8.094 The detriment in this category results from the loss of money, labour or other assets of financial value. Examples include: advancing money by way of loan in reliance on the representation that the loan was supported by a valid unlimited personal guarantee by the managing director;[19] failing to withdraw funds from an investment scheme in reliance on the representation that large profits had been made and were being held by the scheme managers for the benefit of the representee;[20] giving up the tenancy of a farm, selling off neighbouring properties and entering the tenancy of new premises in reliance on the representation that a valid notice to quit had been served;[21] rejecting an offer of local authority accommodation and consequently being removed from the authority's priority need list in reliance on the representation that the representee had a tenancy protected by statute;[22] paying for extensive damp proofing works to be carried out on a property in reliance on the representation that the representee had the benefit of a valid contract to purchase the premises;[23] purchase of goods in reliance on the representation by a warehouse owner that it was holding them for the seller;[24] building sea front houses in reliance on the representation that a neighbour was

---

18 The categorization adopted is derived, subject to some modifications, from Malcolm Clarke's article 'Banker's Commercial Credits among the High Trees' [1974] *CLJ* 260 at 283.

19 *TCB Ltd v Gray* [1986] Ch 621 *per* Sir Nicholas Browne-Wilkinson V.C. at 634.

20 *Re Exchange Securities & Commodities Ltd* [1988] Ch 46, although no estoppel was made out in the case, partly because the alleged representation was not established.

21 *Farrow v Orttewell* [1943] Ch 480, CA. The protective statute which governed the case, Agricultural Holdings Act 1923, gave the tenant a right to compensation if it left as a result of a valid notice to quit but not if it left voluntarily.

22 *Daejan Properties Ltd v Mahoney* [1995] 2 EGLR 75, CA *per* Sir Thomas Bingham M.R. at 78a–b.

23 *Spiro v Lintern* [1973] 1 WLR 1002, CA at 1013a–d.

24 *Seton, Laing v Lefone* (1887) 19 QBD 68, CA.

legally disabled from building so as to obstruct the view from them;[25] paying the purchase price for shares in reliance on the representation that the purported vendor was the owner of the shares;[26] and failing to apply for social security payments in reliance on the representation that the representee was legally entitled to a specified level of pay from his employer.[27]

There are a number of cases where the detriment alleged to have been suffered consists of failure to pursue a legal claim against a third party.[28] Three points should be considered in relation to such cases. First, it may be possible to categorize them either under the first of the second of our detriment categories. We have chosen to include them under this head because the second category concerns conduct which leaves the representee vulnerable to legal penalties rather than merely undermining its remedies against others. Secondly, as is discussed below at paragraph 8.102, there is considerable controversy as to whether it is necessary to establish only that it is no longer practical to pursue the claim (because, for example, the wrongdoer has become bankrupt or fled the jurisdiction) or whether it is necessary also to show that the claim would have been successful had it been prosecuted in due time. Thirdly, a number of the cases in which this issue has been considered concern the controversial doctrine of estoppel by negligence.[29] As is set out in paragraph 8.144, there is some doubt as to whether such cases actually form part of the law of estoppel at all. Any general principles extracted from them may, therefore, be suspect. **8.095**

The representee fails to safeguard its legal position

The detriment in this category results from positive acts (or more usually omissions) on the part of the representee which would make it vulnerable to legal proceedings in the event that the truth of the **8.096**

[25] *Piggot v Stratton* (1859) 1 De GF&J 33, 45 ER 271.

[26] *Re Bahia and San Francisco Railway Co Ltd* (1868) LR 3 QB 584 and *In re Ottos Kopje Diamond Mines Ltd* [1893] 1 Ch 1892, CA.

[27] *Avon CC v Howlett* [1983] 1 WLR 605, CA. By the time the true facts came to light, it was too late to apply for the relevant benefits.

[28] *Knights v Wiffen* (1870) LR 5 QB 660, *CA; Simm v Anglo American Telegraph* (1879) 5 QBD 188, CA; *Weld Blundell v Synott* [1940] 2 KB 107 *per* Asquith J. at 114; *Fung Kai Sun v Chan Fui Hing* [1951] AC 489 PC (Hong Kong); *M'Kensie v British Linen Co* (1881) 6 App Cas 82 HL and *Hammersmith and Fulham BC v Top Shop Centres Ltd* [1990] Ch 237.

[29] See, for example, *Greenwood v Martins Bank Ltd* [1933] AC 51.

representation is denied. For example, in *Ismail v Polish Ocean Lines*[30] shippers stowed a cargo defectively in reliance on the representation by the cargo owners agent that the method used was adequate. Had the cargo owner been permitted to deny the truth of his representation, he would have been able to claim damages for defective stowage, against the shippers. In *De Tchihatchef v Salerni Coupling Ltd*,[31] a company stated in a share prospectus that it had the benefit of a contract on lucrative terms, in reliance on the representation that the contract included the specified terms. Denial of the representation would have rendered the company vulnerable to legal proceedings by those who subscribed to the issue in reliance on the contents of the prospectus.

Further examples include contracting to sell shares to a third party in reliance on the representation that the representee was the owner of the shares. The denial of the representation leaves the representee vendor liable to an action for breach of contract by the person to whom it purported to sell the shares.[32] Failing to apply to the family court to have a maintenance agreement varied or set aside in reliance on the representation that maintenance was only payable for a limited period,[33] will suffice as will failing to serve notice to exercise break clause within the time specified in a lease.[34] **8.097**

The representee alters its budget or expenditure

The detriment in this category is relevant where the representor has led the representee to believe that the latter is legally entitled to some benefit received. The most usual example is where A makes a payment to B and represents that B is legally entitled to that payment and is thus free to spend the money as it wishes. B therefore needs to establish that it would suffer detriment if the representation is withdrawn, namely where A denies B's entitlement and asks for the return of the money.[35] To establish detrimental reliance, three requirements must be satisfied.[36] **8.098**

---

30 *Ismail v Polish Ocean Lines* [1976] QB 893, CA.

31 *De Tchihatchef v Salerni Coupling Ltd.* [1932] 1 Ch. 330 *per* Luxmoor J. at 342.

32 *Dixon v Kennaway & Co* [1900] 1 Ch 833 *per* Farwell J. at 838–839.

33 *Covell v Sweetland* [1968] 1 WLR 1466 *per* Hinchcliffe J. at 1474.

34 *Trane (UK) Ltd v Provident Mutual Life Assurance* [1995] EGLR 33 *per* Judge Cooke at 38–9.

35 Usually in an action for restitution. For further discussion of this type of case see paras 8.150 to 8.158 below. Such cases usually arise where A has mistakenly paid B a sum of money to which the latter is not entitled and subsequently seeks its return in an action in restitution.

36 For further analysis of detrimental reliance in this context see Beatson and Bishop, 'Mistaken payments in the law of restitution' (1986) *University of Toronto Law Journal* 149.

8.099 First, B has spent money.[37] There is no need to establish that the money spent was that actually received from the representor, nor is there any need to show that the money spent was the traceable proceeds of the money so received.[38] Secondly, B has spent money in reliance on the representation. Put simply, the representee must have spent the money in a way it would have done but for a representation. If the money has been spent on ordinary day to day expenses, which the representee would have been obliged to meet anyway, the requirement of reliance has not been satisfied. The representee has done nothing which it would not have done in any event.[39] Thirdly, B has spent the money in a way which cannot be recouped: it is necessary to show that the money has been spent in a way which leaves the representee with no retained value. Examples might include spending the money on a holiday, paying it to charity or, in the case of a company, issuing a special one-off dividend to shareholders. If the money has been used to purchase a saleable asset which is retained by B, no detriment will result from its being asked to refund the money. B can sell the asset and return the money.[40]

8.100 Thus, in *Avon CC v Howlett*[41] the defendant was overpaid by his former employer, who represented that the payments had been correctly made. The defendant and his wife altered their budget accordingly. It was found as a fact that they increased their spending in accordance with their perceived income. The money was thus spent on a number of small improvements to their daily life.[42] Some goods bought with the

---

[37] As to how much money must be spent see paras 8.109 to 8.119 below.

[38] As Birks points out at p. 408, in *National Westminster Bank Ltd v Barclays Bank International Ltd* [1975] 1 QB 654, the money paid to the alleged representee had never been touched. It was held in an account which had been frozen by an injunction awarded to the plaintiff bank. This did not, however, prevent the possibility of an estoppel arising.

[39] *cf.* the closely related restitutionary defence of change of position — see *Lipkin Gorman v Karpnale* [1991] 2 AC 548 *per* Lord Goff at 580.

[40] *Spiro v Lintern* [1973] 1 WLR 1002, CA at 1013a–d. See also *Lipkin Gorman v Karpnale* [1991] 2 AC 548 *per* Lord Templeman at 560 commenting on the change of position defence.

[41] [1983] 1 WLR 605 CA. See also *Holt v Markham* [1923] 1 KB 504, CA *per* Warrington L.J. at 512 and *per* Scrutton L.J. at 514–5; *Deutsche Bank (London Agency) v Beriro & Co* (1895) 73 LT 669, CA; *Skyring v Greenwood* (1825) 4 B&C 281; *Weld Blundell v Synott* [1940] 2 KB 107 and *Larner v LCC* [1949] 2 KB 1, [1949] All ER 964, CA (although see para 8.144 to 8.160 below as to whether all of these cases actually involve estoppel by representation).

[42] Sheldon J. found as a fact that all the money had been so spent. The pleadings alleged that only a proportion of the money had been spent. Counsel for the defendant declined the judge's invitation to adjust the pleadings accordingly, since the defendant's trade union wished to use the proceedings as a test case to ascertain whether it was possible to defeat the entirety of employer's claim to overpayments,

money were retained but they were of minimal value. Although the defendant had received a benefit from the increased spending, to have required him to refund the overpayments would have been to impose an onerous and unexpected liability, which he would have been unable to meet. The employer's action to recover the money failed.

There is some authority to suggest that it is sufficient merely to show that the money has been spent.[43] Unless the second and third requirements are made out, no harm can flow to the representee as a result of it being required to refund money to which it was never entitled in the first place. This head of detriment is closely related to the restitutionary defence of change of position from which useful analogies may be drawn (see paragraphs 8.156 to 8.158 below). **8.101**

Points of difficulty

Loss of a chance: hypothetical loss

The application of the principles set out above necessarily involves an element of speculation as to what would have happened in a hypothetical situation. The court is required to compare what actually happened with what would have happened had the representation never been made. To establish detriment, the representee must show that it was worse off under the latter situation than under the former. This has sometimes given rise to difficulties, particularly where the representee's acts in reliance consist of foregoing some opportunity, such as a omitting to prosecute a cause of action. In theory, it should be necessary to show that the opportunity foregone had some intrinsic value, *i.e.* that there was a chance of a successful outcome for the representee. If, for example, there was no chance that the representee would have obtained an enforceable judgment had it prosecuted the cause of action, it is difficult to aver that it suffered any detriment as a result of refraining from so doing. However, the courts have sometimes seemed reluctant to investigate whether there was any chance of a successful outcome for the representee. **8.102**

---

by demonstrating the requisite change of position in relation to some but not all of the money in issue. See further para. 8.109 below.

[43] *London and River Plate Bank v Bank of Liverpool* [1896] 1 QB 7 *per* Mathew J. at 11; *Skyring v Greenwood* (1825) 4 B&C 281 *per* Bayley J. at 290 and *Holt v Markham* [1923] 1 KB 504, CA *per* Warrington L.J. at 512.

In *Knights v Wiffen*,[44] Wiffen sold some of the goods which he held in his warehouse to Maris who sold them on to Knights. Wiffen told Knights that he had appropriated goods to the contract (which would have had the effect of passing title to the goods to Knights). Maris later became bankrupt. Wiffen had not in fact appropriated goods to Knights' contract but was estopped from denying that he had. If Knights had not received the assurance from Wiffen, he would have terminated the contract and asked for his money back, although it was '*very likely he might not have derived much benefit if he had done so*'.[45] Their lordships held that this conduct gave rise to detriment, despite their doubts as to his chances of successfully retrieving his money from Maris. **8.103**

Some doubt as to the correctness of the decision was expressed in *Simm v Anglo American Telegraph*,[46] where the alleged detriment consisted of failing to pursue a third party who had executed a forged transfer of shares to the representee. The Court of Appeal emphasized that it was necessary to show not just that the representee had refrained from pursuing the wrongdoer but that it had been prejudiced by so doing.[47] No such prejudice existed in *Simms* because the stock exchange rules gave the representee a watertight claim against the dealer through whom the forger had sold the shares. **8.104**

There are four possible views on this issue. First, the rationale behind *Knights* rests simply on the courts' reluctance to engage in speculation as to the outcome of hypothetical proceedings. Once the representee has allowed the the opportunity to be lost to the representor, uncertainty should be resolved in the latter's favour and detriment is assumed. The result of *Simms* may be reconciled with such an approach because there was no such uncertainty in that case. The Court of Appeal was not **8.105**

---

[44] (1870) LR 5 QB 660, CA.

[45] *ibid. per* Blackburn J. at 665. This finding is understandable given the impending insolvency of Maris. A similar approach was applied in *M'Kensie v British Linen Co* (1881) 6 App Cas 82, HL Sc *per* Lord Blackburn at 100. More recently, in *Hammersmith and Fulham BC v Top Shop Centres Ltd* [1990] Ch 237 *per* Warner J. at 261a–c, it was held that a tenant's foregoing the opportunity to negotiate for a new sub-under-lease or apply for relief against forfeiture of a sub-under-lease, amounted to detriment, regardless of whether such conduct was likely to result in a successful outcome. This case is discussed further at para. 11–37 below.

[46] (1879) 5 QBD 188, CA *per* Brett L.J. at 212, although these reservations are largely concerned with the issue of whether title can pass as a result of estoppel rather than detriment. See also *Re Goldcorp Exchange Limited* [1994] 2 All ER 806 *per* Lord Mustill at 817b.

[47] (1879) 5 QBD 188, CA *per* Brett L.J. at 211; *Weld Blundell v Synott* [1940] 2 KB 107 *per* Asquith J. at 114 and *Fung Kai Sun v Chan Fui Hing* [1951] AC 489, PC (Hong Kong) *per* Lord Wright at 506.

required to assess what would have happened had the original claim been prosecuted, since it was clear that there was an alternative and cogent remedy against a third party. Secondly, the representee might be said to have suffered prejudice because it forever lost the opportunity to take a reasoned decision on the transaction, in the light of all the circumstances, unfettered by the the misapprehension caused by the representation. The loss of a chance, in itself, might amount to detriment, regardless of the prospects of success.[48] Thirdly, in *Dixon v Kennaway & Co*,[49] Mr Justice Farwell analysed the problem in terms of the onus of proof. The burden fell on the representee to prove that it had refrained from prosecuting its claim. Once it had done this, the onus shifted to the representor to prove that no prejudice or detriment resulted from the delay, *i.e.* that the wrongdoer had never been worth suing in the first place. Fourthly, *Knights* is wrongly decided. On balance, we consider the first view to be the most convincing explanation of the case law.

Granting or entering a sub-lease

In *Keith v R. Gancia and Co Ltd*[50] it was held that granting or entering a sub-lease gives rise to detriment regardless of the terms. There are two circumstances where such conduct could amount to detriment. First, detriment would occur if the benefit gained from the arrangement was affected by the withdrawal of the representation.[51] Take, for example, the case where a sub-lease is entered in reliance on the representation that a neighbour had no power to build so as to obstruct the view from the sub-let property. If the representation is denied, detriment occurs in that the view expected is lost. The asset purchased is less valuable as a result of withdrawal of the representation.[52] Secondly, detriment would be suffered if the sub-lessor and sub-lessee were restricted as to the terms on which they could transfer their interests. Thirdly, if denial of the **8.106**

[48] This may explain the finding that granting an underlease amounted to detriment regardless of its terms. Potentially, such a transaction might result in benefit to the claimant. Such cases cannot sensibly be explained in terms of the court's distaste for speculation because the consequences the tenant's decision may be clearly analysed by reference to the terms of the under lease. See further para. 8.106 below.

[49] [1900] 1 Ch 833 *per* Farwell J. at 839–40.

[50] [1904] 1 Ch 774, CA applied in *Hammersmith and Fulham BC v Top Shop Centres Ltd* [1990] Ch 237.

[51] See para. 11.41 below on the necessity of showing that expenditure or valuable assets have been wasted.

[52] *cf.* the similar facts of *Piggot v Stratton* (1859) 1 De GF&J 33, 45 ER 271.

representation means that the the sub-lessor cannot give good title to the sub-lessee, the detriment suffered is clear. The lessor will be liable to the sub-lessee for breach of contract should the representation be denied. Absent one of these factors, it is hard to see why the granting or entering of the sub-lease should necessarily give rise to detriment. If the representee was left with a valuable disposable asset, arguably no detriment is suffered: the representee has got what it paid for.[53] However, according to *Keith*, none of the three factors listed is necessary.

The reasoning in that case is somewhat obscure. It might be possible to explain the apparent lack of detriment in one of two ways. The representee might be said to have suffered prejudice because it forever lost the opportunity to take a reasoned decision on the transaction, in the light of all the circumstances, unfettered by the the misapprehension caused by the representation. Perhaps the better explanation of this line of authority is that it forms an anomalous instance where deemed[54] rather than actual detriment suffices to give rise to an estoppel.[55] **8.107**

RELIEF

It has been frequently averred that the effect of estoppel by representation is to prevent the representor from setting up the true facts.[56] Instead **8.108**

---

[53] *Spiro v Lintern* [1973] 1 WLR 1002, CA at 1013a–d. *cf.* the proprietary estoppel case of *Christian v Christian* (1981) NLJ 43 discussed at para. 11.41 below.

[54] A possible parallel is provided by the cheque cases such as *Cocks v Masterman* (1829) 9 B&C 902.

[55] At para. 112, Spencer Bower suggests that *Keith v R Gancia* stands for the proposition that the assumption of legal liabilities to which the representee would not otherwise have been subject is sufficient to amount to detriment. We can see no justification for interpreting the case so widely. If the case is correct at all, it is submitted that it should be limited to the sub-lease of sub-lease situation. Such a limitation at least reduces the conflict with conventional principles which is adverted to in this paragraph.

[56] The following cases affirm this outcome without expressly indicating that it is the only remedy available: *Maclaine v Gatty* [1921] 1 AC 376 HL Sc *per* Lord Birkenhead at 386; *Knights v Wiffen* (1870) LR 5 QB 660, CA *per* Blackburn J. at 665; *Carr v London and North Western Rly Co* (1875) LR 10 CP 307 *per* Brett and Denman JJ. at 317; *Dixon v Kennaway & Co* [1990] 1 Ch 833 *per* Farwell J. at 838; *Farrow v Orttewell* [1943] Ch 480, CA *per* Lord Hanworth M.R. at 498; *Evans v Bartlam* [1937] AC 473 *per* Lord Wright at 484; *Jordon v Money* (1854) V HLC 185, 10 ER 868 *per* Lord Cranworth L.C. at 210; *Pickard v Sears* (1837) 6 A&E 469, 112 ER 179 at 474; *Re Exchange Securities & Commodities Ltd* [1988] Ch 46 *per* Harman J. at 54 and *Algar v Middlesex County Council* [1945] 2 All ER 243, DC *per* Humphreys J. at 250f–g.

the representor is bound by its representation or estopped from denying its truth. If absolute and unqualified, this approach has one very significant drawback. Either the representation is deemed to be true or it is not. There is no intermediate position. Hence, the establishment of any detriment, regardless of its seriousness or extent,[57] will give rise to an estoppel and trigger the consequence referred to. It is not possible, if this analysis is correct, to reflect the extent of the detriment suffered in the order made. The doctrine cannot operate to give partial, or *pro tanto*, relief to the representee. The consequence of holding the representor to its representation may result in a benefit to the representee which far outweighs the detriment sustained by the representee.

CAN ESTOPPEL BY REPRESENTATION OPERATE *PRO TANTO*?

Arguments against the pro tanto approach: the decision in *Avon CC v Howlett*[58]

The issue was raised in *Avon CC v Howlett*,[59] where the plaintiff local authority had repeatedly overpaid one of its employees, the defendant. The total overpayment amounted to £1007 and the authority sought the return of this sum as money paid under a mistake of fact. Estoppel was raised as a defence to this restitutionary claim. At first instance, Mr Justice Sheldon found as a fact that all the money had been spent in a way which could not be recouped. He found that the defendant and his wife had spent the money on a number of small improvements to their daily lives. It is uncontroversial that such conduct would be sufficient to give rise to detriment in the event of the recipient's being called upon to repay the funds in issue.[60] However, the pleaded case only covered spending and other acts of detriment to the value of £546.61. Counsel declined to amend his pleadings because the parties wished to use the proceedings as a test case to establish whether the lesser acts of detriment amounted to a complete defence. When the matter came before **8.109**

[57] So long as the detriment suffered is not *de minimis*. See para. 11.33 below, where the *de minimis* rule is stated in relation to proprietary estoppel. It is submitted that the same approach is applicable in estoppel by representation cases.
[58] [1983] 1 WLR 605, CA.
[59] *ibid.*
[60] See above at paras 8.98 to 8.101.

the Court of Appeal, both Lords Justice Slade and Eveleigh held that it did:[61] estoppel generally could not operate *pro tanto* to give a partial defence to the claim. Lord Justice Cumming Bruce refused to decide the case on the pleaded facts but expressed himself in obiter agreement with Lord Justice Slade's judgment on them.[62]

The authorities considered in Avon

8.110 It is at least doubtful whether the authorities cited in *Avon* stand for the proposition that estoppel by representation can never operate *pro tanto*. Reliance was placed on *Ogilvie v West Australian Mortgage & Agency Corporation*[63] and *Greenwood v Martins Bank Ltd.*[64] Both of these cases concerned instances where a bank customer discovered that cheques on his account had been forged but failed to inform the bank of this until a significant period had elapsed. In both cases, it was held that there was no need to investigate whether the bank could actually have recovered any money from the forger had it acted immediately. It was enough to show that it was no longer possible or practical to recover money from the wrongdoer. The two cases involved the application of the principle generally referred to as estoppel by negligence. As we set out below,[65] there is some doubt as to whether such cases fall within the scope of estoppel at all. In our view, they are more accurately characterized as examples of circuity of action. The customer was in breach of a duty to inform the bank promptly of any forgeries and the bank owed a duty to not to make payments for which it had no mandate. The mutual breaches of duty, in effect, cancelled one another out.

8.111 Less controversially, both cases may be explained as examples of the application of the principle of *Knights v Wiffen*,[66] whereby the court refuses to speculate as to the outcome of hypothetical proceedings. Once it is shown that the opportunity to pursue the claim has been lost, uncertainty is resolved in the representee's favour. Thus, the detriment suffered covered the entire extent of the claim since it was presumed that the bank would have succeeded in recovering the full amount from the forger. *Ogilvie* can clearly be explained in this way as probably can

[61] [1983] 1 WLR 605, CA *per* Eveleigh L.J. at 611b–h and *per* Slade L.J. at 622–4.
[62] [1983] 1 WLR 605, CA at 609h.
[63] [1896] AC 257, PC (WA) *per* Lord Watson at 270.
[64] [1932] 1 KB 371, CA *per* Scrutton L.J. at 383–4.
[65] At paras 8.144 to 8.160.
[66] (1870) LR 5 QB 660, CA.

the judgment of Lord Justice Greer in *Greenwood*.[67] It is conceded, however, that it is not possible to explain all of the general comments of Lord Justice Scrutton on this basis.

Further reliance was placed on *Skyring v Greenwood*[68] and *Holt v Markham*,[69] on the basis that in neither case did the court assess exactly how much of the money had been spent. In *Skyring*, there appeared to be no evidence of *any* detrimental reliance. The court seemed prepared to assume that it had taken place. It is submitted therefore that the case can give no assistance on the point. In *Holt*, it was clear that not all the money had been spent[70] but there was no indication as to whether a substantial amount remained unspent. Further, detrimental acts, *additional* to the mere spending, of the money were established.[71] **8.112**

The principles applied in Avon

Lord Justice Slade based his judgment on two reasons. First, his lordship held that to require the representee to prove precisely the extent of its acts of detriment, would be to impose too harsh an obligation. However, there is no reason to believe that the application of the normal civil burden of proof would cause such difficulty: proof on the balance of probabilities would not require the representee to account for every penny spent[72] or to equate precisely the detriment suffered with the benefit which would be bestowed by holding the representor to its representation. Further, the House of Lords has held that such a process will have to be performed in relation to the restitutionary defence of change of position.[73] We would therefore suggest that the comments of Lord Justice Slade on this point must be subject to some doubt.[74] **8.113**

Secondly, his lordship held that, as estoppel was a rule of evidence, its consequence must simply be that the representor was precluded from averring facts which contradict its representation. In *Avon*'s case, the employer authority had represented that its employee was entitled to £1007. It was estopped from denying that the employee was so entitled. **8.114**

---

67 See, in particular, [1932] 1 KB 371, CA at 386–7.
68 (1825) 4 B&C 281.
69 [1923] 1 KB 504, CA.
70 *ibid. per* Warrington L.J. at 512.
71 The defendant parted with his War Savings certificates. See [1923] 1 KB 504, CA *per* Bankes L.J. at 511.
72 See Burrows *The Law of Restitution*, Butterworths, London 1993 at p. 437.
73 *Lipkin Gorman v Karpnale* [1991] 2 AC 548. As to the relationship between the estoppel by representation and change of position see para. 8.156 below.
74 See Paul Key 'Estoppel as a defence to restitution' (1995) *CLJ* 525.

It is on this ground that the result of the case can be justified. For the reasons given in paragraph 8.108 above, while estoppel by representation remains an evidential doctrine, the conclusion reached in *Avon* must inexorably follow. As is set out below, *Avon* itself may be of limited weight in terms of precedent.[75] It is those cases where estoppel by representation is an evidential, rather than a substantive, doctrine[76] which effectively rule out a *pro tanto* approach.

Subsequent authorities

Avon has been approved in subsequent authorities.[77] In *Lipkin Gorman v Karpnale*,[78] Lord Goff accepts the correctness of the *Avon* principle in relation to estoppel by representation. In his view, this aspect of the doctrine made it an unsuitable tool with which to deal with the problems he was discussing. It was one of a number of reasons which led his lordship to recognize the restitutionary defence of change of position.[79] **8.115**

Arguments in favour of the pro tanto approach

Notwithstanding the above, there may be a number of reasons why the *Avon* should not be regarded as conclusively excluding the possibility that estoppel by representation may operate *pro tanto*. First, their Lordships were considering a hypothetical state of facts rather than an actual case. This must limit the case's value in terms of precedent.[80] Secondly, all three of their Lordships contemplated that there might be circumstances when the doctrine could operate *pro tanto*.[81] Unfortunately, they gave little indication as to what those circumstances would be and failed to reconcile their comments with their general rejection of the *pro tanto* approach. **8.116**

It has been further suggested a representation may subdivide the **8.117**

---

[75] See para. 8.116.
[76] Cited at para. 8.16 above.
[77] *Re Exchange Securities & Commodities Ltd* [1988] Ch 46 *per* Harman J. at 56.
[78] [1991] 2 AC 548.
[79] *ibid.* at 578.
[80] As pointed out by Cumming Bruce L.J. in *Avon CC v Howlett* [1983] 1 WLR 605, CA at 608e–g.
[81] *Avon CC v Howlett* [1983] 1 WLR 605, CA *per* Cumming Bruce L.J. at 609e–f, *per* Eveleigh L.J. at 611g–612b and *per* Slade L.J. at 622b–c.

representation.[82] Hence, in cases such as *Avon*, the representor might be estopped from denying that the representee was free to spend £546 but free to retract his representation as to the sum which remained unspent. This would involve rewriting the representation and is inconsistent with the evidential approach to the doctrine. It has been alternatively suggested that in cases where the result of the estoppel might confer a benefit exceeding the detriment suffered, the court might extract an undertaking from the representee to refund the excess to the representor.[83] It is submitted, however, that it would be improper to enable the court to effect by means of undertakings what it could not do under substantive principles of law.

Conclusion

If the *Avon* principle is to be abandoned, it can only be by reformulating the doctrine of estoppel by representation as one of substantive law rather than of evidence. This would involve recognizing the doctrine as a source of legal obligation in itself and not merely a means of setting up a state of facts on which ordinary principles of law then operate. Such an approach would have three primary advantages. First, it would reflect more accurately the fundamental and decisive effect which the doctrine can have on the substantive legal position between the parties. Secondly, it would bring estoppel by representation into line with equitable forbearance and proprietary estoppel which are substantive doctrines. Thirdly, it would avoid the unfairness inherent in the *Avon* principle and enable the courts to choose a remedy which is proportionate to the detriment suffered. Additionally, the adoption of a more flexible remedial approach further facilitates consistency between estoppel by representation and proprietary estoppel. This is particularly desirable because the two doctrines may operate on the same set of facts (see paragraphs 8.137 and 8.172), namely where representations have been made as to the ownership of property. Both doctrines are triggered by similar acts of detrimental reliance, albeit that estoppel by representation is limited to a narrower range of representations.[84] If a proprietary estoppel is established, the court has a wide remedial discretion. The party estopped is sometimes held to its representation or assurance, but this is not the invariable outcome. Often a lesser remedy is deemed **8.118**

[82] Burrows, *The Law of Restitution*, Butterworths, London, 1993, at p. 437.

[83] This was suggested in the dissenting judgment of Viscount Cave L.C. (with whom Atkin J. concurred) in *R.E. Jones v Waring & Gillow* [1926] AC 670 at 683. The point was left open by Slade L.J. in *Avon* at 625a–b.

[84] See para. 8.172 for a comparison between the requirements of the two doctrines.

appropriate (see paragraphs 11.54 to 11.48 below). Arguably, it would be unfortunate if a claimant could demand a greater measure of relief simply by satisfying the stricter requirements of estoppel by representation. There would seem to be little to justify the differential measure of relief and such an approach undermines those proprietary estoppel cases which emphasize the width of the courts' discretion.

There is a degree of support for a more flexible approach, although the difficulty in clearly distinguishing estoppel by representation from other estoppels casts doubt on the strength of that support. In *Brikom Investments v Seaford*,[85] an estoppel arose in relation to the representation by the landlords that they and not the tenant were responsible for repairs. A statutory rent was fixed based on this assumption. The rent would have been fixed at a lower level had the rent officer believed that the tenant was responsible for repairs. In fact the lease did place the obligation on the tenant. It was held that the landlord could enforce the repair obligation and thus retract its representation, *once it had refunded the past rent overpayments*. Hence, so long as the detriment, namely the payment of the higher rent, was reversed the true facts could be adduced. Although this case is probably best viewed as one of equitable forbearance, it is susceptible to analysis as one of estoppel by representation. It therefore gives some support to a more flexible approach. Similarly, in *Civil Aviation Authority v Internationale Nederlanden Aviation Lease BV and the European Organisation for the Safety of Air Navigation (Interveners)*,[86] one of the reasons for Judge Diamond's rejection of the estoppel claim was that the results of its operation would be wholly disproportionate to the mischief suffered by the representee. **8.119**

DEFENCES

THE REPRESENTATION WAS IMPROPERLY INDUCED

The mere fact that the the representation was made in response to a question by the representee does not prevent its giving rise to an **8.120**

[85] [1981] 1 WLR 863, CA.
[86] [1997] 1 Lloyd's Rep. 96 *per* Judge Diamond Q.C. at 105 col. 1.

estoppel.[87] However, no estoppel will arise where the representation was extracted under duress, whether the relevant pressure was exerted by the representee or a third party.[88] Nor will an estoppel arise where the representation has been induced by the concealment of some material fact by the representee. The general principle was stated by Lord Brampton in *George Whitechurch Ltd v Cavanagh*.[89]

> No representations can be relied on as estoppels if they have been induced by the concealment of any material fact on the part of those who seek to use them as such; and if the person to whom they are made knows something which, if revealed, would have been calculated to influence the other to hesitate or seek for further information before speaking positively, and that something has been withheld, the representation ought not to be treated as an estoppel.[90]

For example, by issuing a share certificate to Z, a company thereby represents to Z that it is the owner of the shares. An estoppel may arise in favour of Z if it later acts to its detriment in reliance on the belief that it is the true owner of the shares.[91] The *George Whitechurch* principle will prevent an estoppel arising where the circumstances of the original transfer to Z were sufficiently suspicious to put Z on enquiry.[92] In this situation, a duty is imposed on the representee, Z, to make the relevant inquiries and pass the information obtained on to the company. If it fails to do so, no estoppel can be founded on the representation subsequently made by the company. It may be sufficient merely to show that the representee was in a better position to evaluate the propriety of the transaction and thus the truth of the representation.[93] This 'defence' may simply be a manifestation of the principle that it must have been reasonable for the representee to have relied on the representation.[94] Arguably, it can never be reasonable for a party to rely on a representation the truth of which it has clear grounds to doubt.

---

[87] *George Whitechurch Ltd v Cavanagh* [1902] AC 117 and the cases cited at n. 87 para. 8.25 above.

[88] *Debs v Sibec Developments Ltd* [1990] RTR 91 *per* Simon Brown J. at 98.

[89] [1902] AC 117 at 145.

[90] [1902] AC 117 at 145, applied in *National Westminster Bank Ltd v Barclays Bank International Ltd* [1975] 1 QB 654 at 676e–7b. See also *Simm v Anglo American Telegraph* (1879) 5 QBD 188, CA *per* Bramwell L.J. at 204.

[91] See para 8.46 above.

[92] *George Whitechurch Ltd v Cavanagh* [1902] AC 117 *per* Lord Brampton at 145. See also *National Westminster Bank Ltd v Barclays Bank International Ltd* [1975] 1 QB 654 at 676e–7b where the circumstances 'reeked of suspicion'.

[93] See *Simm v Anglo American Telegraph* (1879) 5 QBD 188, CA *per* Brett L.J. at 209 as explained in *Dixon v Kennaway & Co* [1900] 1 Ch 833 *per* Farwell J. at 840.

[94] As to which see para. 8.80 above.

UNDERMINING THE EFFECT OF A STATUTE

No estoppel by representation will arise if its effect would be to undermine the operation of a statute.[95] Hence, no party can be estopped from denying that invalidity of a deed of arrangement rendered void by statute.[96] Similarly, in *Re Exchange Securities & Commodities Ltd*[97] an investment company had represented to its clients that large profits had been made using their respective capital stakes and that these profits were being held for them in accounts with the company. No such profits had actually been made. The company went into liquidation. The clients asserted that the company's representations would have estopped it from denying that the profits had been made. Consequently, they attempted to prove in the insolvency proceedings for both their original capital investment and for the profits which the company had represented had been made. Mr Justice Harman held that the liquidator had a statutory duty to assess the true liabilities of the company, and could not be bound by estoppel which would prevent or hinder the carrying out of this duty.[98] **8.121**

If a statute prohibits a certain type of express agreement or contract, estoppel cannot be used to achieve the same effect indirectly. Put simply, a party cannot be estopped from denying something which it could not lawfully have agreed to expressly.[99] Hence, just as it is impossible expressly to contract out of the Rents Acts and the Housing Acts, no party can be estopped from asserting that its tenancy falls within the scope of the statutes.[1] Conversely, it is not possible to contract into the statutory scheme of protection. If the terms of the tenancy do not fall within the scope of the relevant statute, the tenancy is not a protected **8.122**

[95] *Re Bankruptcy Notice* [1924] 2 Ch 76, CA *per* Atkin L.J. at 97–8 and *Re Exchange Securities & Commodities Ltd* [1988] Ch 46 at *per* Harman J. at 57–60.

[96] *Re Bankruptcy Notice* [1924] 2 Ch 76, CA *per* Atkin L.J. at 97–8.

[97] [1988] Ch 46.

[98] *ibid. per* Harman J. at 57–60.

[99] *Daejan Properties Ltd v Mahoney* [1995] 2 EGLR 75, CA *per* Sir Thomas Bingham M.R. at 77d and *per* Hoffman L.J. at 79l.

[1] *Daejan Properties Ltd v Mahoney* [1995] 2 EGLR 75, CA *per* Hoffman L.J. at 79l. See also *Campbell Discount Co v Gall* [1961] 1 QB 431, CA *per* Holroyd Pearce at 442–3 doubting whether a hire purchase agreement protected under consumer credit legislation could be removed from it by estoppel. A tenant may, it seems, agree to give up any additional rights which it may have under a contractual tenancy. Hence, in *Harnam Singh v Jamal Pirbhai* [1951] AC 688 the tenant was estopped from relying on its contractual tenancy. The tenant had represented that he was only a statutory tenant and had no additional rights under contract.

one. Hence, the representation that the tenancy falls within the statute cannot give rise to an estoppel so as to bring the tenancy within the scope of legislative protection.[2] The parties cannot by contract or estoppel give a tribunal jurisdiction which it does not have.[3]

Public authorities and ultra vires

An important example of the principle that estoppel may not be used to nullify the effect of a statute concerns public authorities. Estoppel by representation cannot be used where its effect would be to force a public authority to do something which is beyond its powers.[4] No authority can be estopped from denying something which it could not lawfully have agreed to expressly. An *ultra vires* agreement cannot become intra vires by estoppel, lapse of time, acquiescence or delay.[5] If an authority had no power to enter a particular agreement or give an undertaking, it cannot give itself the power through estoppel.[6] Estoppel cannot be raised to prevent the exercise of a statutory discretion or excuse the failure to perform a statutory duty.[7] This strict approach may lead to some harsh results,[8] where members of the **8.123**

[2] *Daejan Properties Ltd v Mahoney* [1995] 2 EGLR 75, CA *per* Sir Thomas Bingham M.R. at 77e–f and *per* Hoffman L.J. at 79l–m.

[3] *Daejan Properties Ltd v Mahoney* [1995] 2 EGLR 75, CA *per* Sir Thomas Bingham M.R. at 77e–f and *per* Hoffman L.J. at 79l–m and *Secretary of State for Employment v Globe Elastic Thread Co Ltd* [1980] AC 506 *per* Lord Wilberforce at 519. The parties may, however, agree to grant contractual rights equivalent to those granted by statute and an estoppel can therefore arise to prevent one party from denying that it has granted such rights. See *Daejan per* Sir Thomas Bingham M.R. at 77g–h and *per* Hoffman L.J. at 79m.

[4] *Islington Vestry v Hornsey UDC* [1900] 1 Ch 695, CA per Lord Lindley M.R. at 704–5.

[5] *York Corp v Henry Lethal & Sons* [1924] 1 Ch 557 *per* Russell J. at 573.

[6] *Minister of Agriculture Fisheries and Food v Matthews* [1950] 1 KB 148 *per* Cassels J. at 153–4.

[7] *Western Fish Products v Penwith DC* [1981] 2 All ER 204, CA *per* Megaw at 219b (the estoppel alleged in the case was proprietary but the comments made cover all types of estoppel considered in this work); *Southend-on-Sea Corporation v Hodgson (Wickford) Ltd* [1961] 2 WLR 806, DC *per* Lord Parker C.J. at 423–4; *Graham v Secretary of State for the Environment and another* [1993] JPL 353 *per* David Widdicombe Q.C. at 354 and *Customs & Excise Commissioners v Hebson Ltd* [1953] 2 Lloyd's Rep. 382 *per* Pearson J. at 396 col. 2. See also Re Exchange Securities [1988] Ch 46 discussed at paras 8.134–5 below.

[8] Leading some to suggest that statutory compensation should be available to members of the public who suffer detriment as a result of reliance on *ultra vires* representations by public authorities. See Sir William Wade, *Administrative Law* (7th ed., Clarendon Press, Oxford, 1994) at pp. 375–7.

public have relied to their detriment on *ultra vires* representations. It has been held, however, that the duty of an authority to obey the law and stay within the limits of its statutory powers is more important than any duty not to cause injury by inadvertent representations.[9] The damage to the general public which would result from permitting an authority to go beyond the powers granted by parliament is deemed to outweigh the damage to individual representees.[10]

8.124 It should be noted, however, that in cases where an estoppel would have arisen but for the *ultra vires* principle, the authority may have breached a public law duty, such as the duty to act fairly or the duty not to undermine legitimate expectations. Such public law principles may have some elements in common with private law estoppel.[11] The similarity is limited, however, and comparisons between the public and private law doctrines can be misleading.[12]

Extent of the use of estoppel by representation against public authorities

8.125 It can therefore be seen that the scope for the use of estoppel against[13] public authorities (particularly those dealing with planning issues) is very limited.[14] In *Western Fish Products v Penwith DC*,[15] Lord Justice Megaw confined its use to two situations.[16] First, where an authority

[9] *Maritime Electric Co Ltd v General Dairies Ltd* [1937] AC 610, PC (Canada) *per* Lord Maugham at 620–1.

[10] For example, in *Western Fish Products v Penwith DC* [1981] 2 All ER 204, CA it was alleged that the officer of a planning authority had represented that the development contemplated was covered by the established use of the premises. It was noted by Megaw L.J. at 219e–f that if the authority was bound by its officer's representation it would be forced to take the decision without taking into account any public objection to the development. His Lordship was also concerned that public authorities should be allowed to advise the public freely without anxiety that every careless statement might give rise to an estoppel; see 222a–b.

[11] See, for example, the public law doctrine outlined in *R v Inland Revenue Commissioners, ex p. Unilever plc* [1996] STC 681, CA *per* Simon Brown L.J. at 693c–d, commenting on *R v IRC, ex p. MFK Underwriting Agents Ltd* [1990] 1 WLR 1545.

[12] *R. v Inland Revenue Commissioners, ex p. Unilever plc* [1996] STC 681, CA *per* Simon Brown L.J. at 695b–d.

[13] For an example of an equitable forbearance/promissory estoppel working in favour of an authority see *Augier v Secretary of State for the Environment* (1979) 38 P&CR 219 at 226.

[14] *Graham v Secretary of State for the Environment and another* [1993] JPL 353 *per* David Widdicombe Q.C. at 354.

[15] [1981] 2 All ER 204, CA.

[16] This twofold classification was adopted in *Graham v Secretary of State for the Environment and another* [1993] JPL 353 *per* David Widdicombe Q.C. at 354.

validly delegates its functions to an officer, it will be bound by the decision made by the officer.[17] Secondly, if an authority waives a procedural requirement relating to an application made to it for the exercise of its statutory powers, it may estopped from relying on lack of formality.[18]

EFFECT OF ESTOPPEL BY REPRESENTATION ON THIRD PARTIES

The effect of estoppel by representation in third parties is an area of considerable difficulty and uncertainty. A number of broad general principles have been formulated in the cases. For example, it has been held that estoppel binds the representor and its '*privies in title*'[19] and that estoppel binds only the original representor and those claiming '*in right*' of the original representor.[20] Unfortunately, these principles have not always provided a reliable guide, particularly those laid down before the development of modern principles as to the transmissibility of commercial rights and interests. The difficulties in this area have been compounded because it is possible to analyse this problem from two different angles. Some cases have addressed the issue by asking simply whether the effect of the estoppel is transferred to the third party while others have asked whether the estoppel is effective to pass title to the third party.[21] **8.126**

PASSING TITLE

A relatively common instance of estoppel concerns representations as to title to goods or other property. Where X represents to Y that Y is the owner of the goods, an estoppel may arise, under normal principles, **8.127**

---

17 [1981] 2 All ER 204, CA *per* Megaw at 219j, explaining *Lever Finance Ltd v Westminster (city) London Borough Council* [1971] 1 QB 222 as an example of the application of this principle.

18 [1981] 2 All ER 204, CA *per* Megaw at 221b-d citing *Wells v Minister for Housing and Local Government* [1967] 2 All ER 1041 as an example.

19 *Eastern Distributors v Goldring* [1957] 2 QB 600 CA *per* Devlin J. at 607; *Hopgood v Brown* [1955] 1 WLR 213 *per* Evershed M.R. at 225. See also the estoppel by deed case of *Taylor v Needham* (1810) Taunt 278.

20 [1988] Ch 46 at 53.

21 See the comments of Devlin J. in *Eastern Distributors v Goldring* [1957] 2 QB 600 at 607.

to prevent X denying its representation. The estoppel does not, however, operate actually to pass title to Y in this situation since it has no effect upon the real nature of the transaction. As Lord Mustill put in *Re Goldcorp Exchange Limited*,[22]

> . . . it seems to me that an estoppel gives no title to that which is the subject matter of estoppel. The estoppel assumes that the reality is contrary to that which the person is estopped from denying, and the estoppel has no effect at all upon the reality of the circumstances . . . a person may be estopped from denying that certain goods belong to another; he may be compelled by a suit in the nature of an action of trover to deliver them up, if he has them in his possession and under his control; but if the goods, in respect of which he has estopped himself, really belong to somebody else, it seems impossible to suppose that . . . he can be compelled to deliver over another's goods to the person in whose favour the estoppel exists against him: that person is entitled to maintain a suit in the nature of an action of trover against him; but that person cannot recover the goods, because no property has really passed to him, he can recover only damages. In my view estoppel only creates a cause of action between the person in whose favour the estoppel exists and the person who is estopped.

Two particular aspects of this approach should be noted. First, if the goods, which X has represented belong to Y, actually belong to a third party, Y cannot use estoppel by representation to claim them. The third party has real title whereas Y has merely a pretence of title which cannot prevail.[23] The estoppel will prevent X's adducing evidence contrary to Y's title but it will not so prevent the third party.[24] Secondly, although X may be estopped as against Y from denying Y's title, Y is unable to *pass title* of the goods to a third party, Z. This principle is applicable whether or not X is the owner of the goods. If Z is to claim the goods it **8.128**

[22] [1994] 2 All ER 806 *per* Lord Mustill at 817f–818c, citing with approval the comments of Brett L.J. in *Simm v Anglo American Telegraph* (1879) 5 QBD 188, CA at 206–7. See also the remarks of Cotton L.J. in *Simm* at 215–6 and *Eastern Distributors v Goldring* [1957] 2 QB 600, CA *per* Devlin J. at 606.

[23] *Re Goldcorp* [1994] 2 All ER 806 *per* Lord Mustill at 817f–g. See also *Re Exchange Securities & Commodities Ltd* [1988] Ch 46 *per* Harman J. at 57–8, contrasting the debt created by estoppel by representation with the 'real debt' (*i.e.* one generated by ordinary substantive principles of law such as contract, without the assistance of any estoppel) which it was the duty of the liquidator to ascertain in order that the correct distribution of funds should be available on winding up. For further detail on this case, see 8.134–5. This approach was recently approved in *Re: Harvard Securities Ltd. (In Liquidation), Holland v Newbury The Times* 18 July 1997 by Neuberger J.

[24] *Knights* v *Wiffen* (1870) LR 5 QB 660, CA *per* Mellor J. as approved in *Re Goldcorp* [1994] 2 All ER 806 *per* Lord Mustill at 817f–j.

must establish afresh the requirements of estoppel by representation. Specifically, Z must prove that X *represented to* Z that Y was the owner of the goods. The original representation to Y will not suffice to raise an estoppel in Z's favour.

This analysis gives rise to three difficulties. First, there are a number of cases decided under the controversial principle of estoppel by negligence which suggest that estoppel can operate to pass title. The most important examples are where a principal represents that its agent has authority to sell its goods (typically by arming the agent with the documents sufficient to enable it to represent that it was the owner of the goods)[25] and where a principal gives a completed and signed bill or security, with the express purpose of allowing the agent to sell or negotiate the bill or security.[26] As is explained below,[27] the principle applied in these cases is best analysed as falling outwith the law of estoppel. The principle is better viewed as a free standing exception to the *nemo dat* rule, generated by commercial expediency. **8.129**

Secondly, some confusion may result from the fact that it is possible to make a representation to the general public. For example, in the issuing of a share certificate in the name of X, the company thereby represents to the general public that X is the owner of the shares. If X purports to sell the shares to Y, the company will be estopped from denying X's title.[28] It looks superficially as if title has passed as a result of the estoppel. However, the estoppel in favour of Y has generated the renewed and continuing representation *to Y* contained in the share certificate. Hence, this line of authority is consistent with the general position we have taken. This is endorsed by the fact that, in such cases, Y is not entitled to the shares but only for compensation for the company's failure to register Y as their owner.[29] If a company issues a share certificate, in favour of X, stating that the shares are fully paid up, it thereby represents to the the general public that this is the case. In *Re Stapleford Colliery Co, Barrow's case* (1880) 14 ChD 432, it was held that the purchaser from X could claim the benefit of the estoppel even where it (the purchaser) knew that the shares were not fully paid up. No new estoppel could arise in favour of a representee who knows **8.130**

---

[25] As to which see paras 14.17–18 (*Agency*) below and particularly *Eastern Distributors v Goldring* [1957] 2 QB 600, CA *per* Devlin J. at 607.

[26] As to which see paras 15.64–5 (*Banking*) and 16.13 (*Company*) below.

[27] At paras 14.17–18, 15.65 and 16.13.

[28] See paras 8.46 to 8.49.

[29] *In re Bahia and San Francisco Railway Company* [1893] AC 396 at 403–5 *per* Lord Herschell at 408.

the representation to be false hence it appears that the estoppel is here having a substantive effect and transferring rights and title to a third party. As we explain further below (at paragraph 16.12) we consider that the case was probably wrongly decided.

TRANSFERRING THE BENEFIT OF THE ESTOPPEL

The executors or personal representatives of the representee may take advantage of any estoppel arising in favour of the deceased as a result of events taking place during his or her lifetime.[30] Similarly, a trustee in bankruptcy can take advantage of estoppels arising in favour of the bankrupt[31] and a liquidator can take advantage of those arising in favour of the company.[32] **8.131**

TRANSFERRING THE BURDEN OF THE ESTOPPEL

Liquidators and trustees in bankruptcy

There is some uncertainty as to the circumstances in which a company liquidator or trustee in bankruptcy may be bound by an estoppel arising against the company or bankrupt, respectively. The same principles apply to both types of officer.[33] It is clear that a liquidator will be bound by an estoppel arising as a result of the representation, in a share certificate issued by the company, that shares are fully paid up.[34] Assuming all the components of estoppel are made out, the liquidator cannot claim a **8.132**

---

[30] *Skyring v Greenwood* (1825) 4 B&C 281. See also *Mackley v Nutting* [1949] 1 All ER 413 at 417 and *Whitmore v Lambert* [1955] 2 All ER 147, CA, although these cases concerned tenancies by estoppel. Such cases give rise to special considerations and it may not be possible to extrapolate the principles applied in them outside the specific context of tenancies by estoppel.

[31] *Harnam v Anderson* (1809) 2 Camp 243.

[32] *Re Central Klondike Gold Mining and Trading Co* (1898) 5 Mans 336.

[33] *Re Exchange Securities & Commodities Ltd* [1988] Ch 46 *per* Harman J. at 58.

[34] *Re British Farmers Pure Linseed Cake Co* (1878) 7 ChD 533; *Bloomenthal v Ford* [1897] AC 156; *Re London Celluloid Co* (1888) 39 ChD 190 and *Burkinshaw v Nicholls* (1878) 3 App Cas 1004.

contribution from the representee, even where the shares were not in fact fully paid up.

In *Re Exchange Securities & Commodities Ltd*,[35] Mr Justice Harman held that the liquidator was not bound by an estoppel arising from a representation made by the company as to the amount it owed its creditors. Mr Justice Harman's decision was based on two grounds which may be described as a wide ground and a narrow ground respectively. The wide ground was that there was a general principle that the representation had to have been made by the party against whom the estoppel was raised. Since the liquidator had not made the representation, he could not be bound. This approach gives rise to some difficulties, given his Lordship's general assertion that an estoppel could arise against someone claiming in right of the representor. Earlier authority, of considerable weight,[36] had suggested that the liquidator can be in no better a position than that of the company, suggesting that it was indeed someone claiming in right of the representor. The narrower ground was that the the liquidator had a statutory duty to ascertain the true debts owed by the company, rather than the fictional ones as represented by it. He distinguished the earlier line of cases referred to above on the grounds that they concerned the liquidator's recovery of money owed to the company rather than his paying out what the company owed to others.[37] **8.134**

Three different general approaches are possible. First, a liquidator is not bound by estoppels arising in respect of how much the company owed but is bound by estoppels arising as to how much was owed to the company. Secondly, the liquidator is bound by estoppels arising against the company except where the effect would hinder the carrying out of a statutory duty.[38] Thirdly, the liquidator is not bound by estoppels arising against the company,[39] the explanation of the share cases being that the representation made in the certificate is a continuing one **8.135**

---

[35] [1988] Ch 46.

[36] See, for example, *Harris v Truman* (1882) 9 QBD 264 *per* Coleridge C.J. at 267, 269, *per* Brett L.J. at 274 and *per* Holker L.J. at 276 and *Re London Celluloid Co* (1888) 39 ChD 190, CA *per* Bowen L.J. at 205.

[37] [1988] Ch 46 per Harman J. at 57–60. See also *Re Harvard Securities Ltd. (In Liquidation), Holland v Newbury The Times* 18 July 1997, where the narrower ground was adopted and approved. Neuberger J. also relied on *British Eagle International Airlines Ltd v Companie Nationale Air France* [1975] 1 WLR 758 where it was held that companies were not able to contract out of the provisions of the Companies Act 1948 which provided for *pari passu* distribution to non-preferential creditors.

[38] See Harman J.'s narrower ground outlined above and the cases cited at n. 36 above.

[39] See Harman J.'s wider ground outlined above.

which is impliedly adopted by the liquidator. Hence, such cases are not examples of where the liquidator was bound by a pre-existing estoppel but examples of a new estoppel arising against the liquidator. In our view, the second approach is the correct one. It reflects Mr Justice Harman's narrower ground and is the most effective means of reconciling the case with what was said in the earlier authorities. In our view, *Exchange Securities* is simply an application of the principle that estoppel cannot be used to prevent the carrying out of a statutory duty (as to which see paragraph 8.123 above).

Purchasers of real property

As is set out above,[40] it has been held that an estoppel binds the representor and its privies. There is no clear principle, however, which determines who is a privy.[41] In some circumstances, the term has been used to cover the situation where the representation is made through an agent.[42] We do not consider this to be a true third party situation. Alternatively, those deriving title from or under the representor have been described as its privies.[43] **8.136**

An estoppel by representation may arise in relation to real property, for example, where X represents to Y that the boundary between two properties is at a certain point and Y relies on this representation and constructs a building which adjoins the perceived boundary. If X's representation is untrue and in fact Y's building extends on to X's neighbouring plot, an estoppel will clearly arise to prevent X from complaining of Y's trespass.[44] The difficult question, however, is what happens if X sells the neighbouring plot to a third party? These facts arose in *Hopgood v Brown*,[45] where the Court of Appeal held that the third party was bound because he claimed title through X. The purchaser gave value for the land. There was no express finding as to whether he had actual notice but it is clear that he had constructive notice because Y was in occupation of the land, namely the disputed strip. However, their Lordships made no reference to these factors. It was sufficient that **8.137**

---

40 At para. 8.126.
41 *Eastern Distributors v Goldring* [1957] 2 QB 600 CA *per* Devlin J. at 607.
42 *ibid.*
43 *ibid. See also Re Exchange Securities & Commodities Ltd* [1988] Ch 46 *per* Harman J. at 54.
44 *Hopgood v Brown* [1955] 1 WLR 213.
45 *ibid.* See also *Gresham Life Assurance Society v Crowther* [1914] 2 Ch 219 *per* Astbury J. at 228 (affd on other grounds [1915] 1 Ch 214, CA).

the purchaser derived title through X because X could grant no more than he actually owned. Their Lordships applied *Taylor* v *Needham*.[46]

There are three significant difficulties with this approach. First, *Taylor v Needham*[47] concerned the application of estoppel by deed rather than estoppel by representation. Secondly, such an approach is premised on the assumption that the estoppel operates to strip X of some of his property rights, namely the ownership of the disputed strip of land. Unless the doctrine has this substantive effect, there is nothing to disable X from selling the entirety of the property, including the strip, to the purchaser. This approach thus conflicts with the principle that estoppel by representation does not operate actually to pass title but only to prevent the representor from contradicting his earlier statement.[48] Thirdly, such an approach creates a potentially lethal lacuna in the conveyancing system. Rights of fundamental importance may be created informally, and may bind unwary purchasers without the need for registration or even notice. To allow, as the Court of Appeal appeared to do, such an important doctrine to operate wholly outwith the registration schemes of the English law of real property is little short of astonishing.[49] **8.138**

In our view, obligations created by estoppel by representation are purely personal in nature and will not pass with conveyance of the property. This is a bold approach but we consider that *Hopgood v Brown* cannot be reconciled with the authorities cited at paragraphs 8.127 to 8.130 above. At the highest, we would submit that such rights can only pass in the same limited circumstances as those created by proprietary estoppel (as to which see paragraphs 11.71 to 11.83 below). This would accord with the suggestions in the case law that the bona fide purchaser for value without notice of the estoppel is not a 'privy' to the estoppel and therefore not bound by it, whereas other purchasers are.[50] Such an approach involves an application of the doctrine of notice.[51] This doctrine has received significant statutory modification. Although the analogy is by no means precise, proprietary estoppel interests generally bind in the same circumstances as those which were governed by the doctrine of notice before its statutory modification. **8.139**

---

46 (1810) Taunt 278.
47 *ibid.*
48 See para. 8.127 above.
49 See *National Provincial Bank v Ainsworth* [1965] AC 1175, HL and *Midland Bank v Green* [1981] AC 513 for general comments on the importance of the integrity of the land registration schemes.
50 *Eastern Distributors v Goldring* [1957] 2 QB 600, CA *per* Devlin J. at 607.
51 As to which see specialist texts and paras 11.79 to 11.81 below.

However, *Hopgood* may be partially explained as a proprietary estoppel case. If the owner of land X, represents to a third party, Y, that Y owns the land, a proprietary estoppel may arise in favour of Y. In contrast to estoppel by representation, this type of estoppel is substantive in nature and may affect the actual ownership, rather than merely creating a 'pretence' of ownership in favour of the representee.[52] Although the issue is by no means clear, it seems that rights created by proprietary estoppel may pass to transferees of land in the circumstances set out in paragraphs 11.77 to 11.81. **8.140**

Other third parties

The executors or personal representatives of the representor are bound by any estoppel arising as a result of a representation made by the deceased during his or her lifetime.[53] **8.141**

Where a company makes a representation concerning its property, no estoppel thereby arising will bind a debenture holder, even where the representation takes place prior to the crystallization of the floating charge over the assets in question.[54] Under the terms of such a charge, the company is free to deal with its assets. The chargor's rights will be affected only where the company creates and transfers *property* interests in those assets. The chargor's security interest will therefore not be affected by the company's entering into *personal* obligations relating to the property.[55] As we set out above,[56] estoppel by representation does not operate to create property rights or transfer ownership but only to give rise to personal rights and obligations between representor and representee. Hence, the debenture holder is unaffected by an estoppel by representation arising against the company. It should be noted, however, that where the company's representation concerns the ownership of its property, a proprietary estoppel may arise in favour of the representee, as well as an estoppel by representation. The latter doctrine operates substantively and is **8.142**

---

52 See para. 11.73 below.

53 *De Tchihatchef v Salerni Coupling Ltd* [1932] 1 Ch 330. See also *Bell v Marsh* [1903] 1 Ch 528 where an estoppel would have been made out against the executors but for the lack of detrimental reliance by the representee.

54 *Re Goldcorp* [1994] 2 All ER 806 *per* Lord Mustill at 818c–g. See also *RW Tasker & Sons Ltd* and *Hoare v W Tasker & Sons Ltd* [1905] 2 Ch 587, CA *per* Stirling L.J. at 599 and *per* Cozens Hardy L.J. at 601.

55 *Re Goldcorp* [1994] 2 All ER 806 *per* Lord Mustill at 818f–g.

56 At para. 8.127.

probably capable of passing ownership interests to the representee.[57] Hence, the representee may be able to attain priority over the debenture holder using this doctrine.

In *Hammersmith and Fulham BC v Top Shop Centres Ltd*,[58] an estoppel arose between the landlords of a property and their sub-tenants. The landlords sold the reversion to a purchaser for value. The conveyance was made expressly subject to such rights as the sub-tenant might have.[59] Mr Justice Warner held that an estoppel bound the purchaser of the reversion. The case may not be of general application for two reasons. First, it is by no means clear whether the doctrine applied was estoppel by representation or proprietary estoppel. As is set out elsewhere, proprietary estoppel may create transmissible interests in circumstances where estoppel by representation cannot. Secondly, the point was not disputed by the parties. 8.143

ESTOPPEL BY NEGLIGENCE

Estoppel by negligence is a further possible variant of estoppel by representation. Just as a representation may be made by conduct, so, it is averred, may a representation be made by negligence.[60] We have dealt with this doctrine in brief because we consider that most, and probably all, of the cases thought to involve the doctrine, are more satisfactorily explained using alternative legal principles. 8.144

ELEMENTS

In order to establish what is termed an estoppel by negligence it is necessary to establish the following elements. First, the representor 8.145

---

57 See para. 11.73 below.

58 [1990] Ch 237 *per* Warner J. at 258f–h. See also *Keith v R. Gancia and Co Ltd* [1904] 1 Ch 774, CA.

59 The terms of the transfer were not sufficient to give rise to a constructive trust in favour of the sub-tenants since they amounted to a negative 'subject to' clause rather than a positive one: for an explanation of the distinction and of the operation of such trusts see *Ashburn Anstaldt v Arnold* [1988] 2 WLR 706.

60 *Greenwood v Martins Bank Ltd* [1932] 1 KB 371, CA *per* Greer L.J. at 388; *Bell v Marsh* [1903] 1 Ch 528, CA *per* Lord Collins M.R. at 541 and *Freeman v Cooke* (1848) 2 Ex 654, ER 652.

owed a duty to the representee to take reasonable care.[61] It is sufficient if this duty was owed to the general public or to a group of which the representee was a member.[62] Secondly the representor negligently failed to perform the duty.[63] Thirdly, the negligence of the 'representor' must have led the representee to believe a certain state of facts.[64] Fourthly, the negligence was the proximate or real cause of loss to the representee.[65] The consequence of establishing the estoppel is to prevent the 'representor' from alleging facts contrary to the belief induced by its negligence.

POINTS OF DIFFICULTY

Considerable confusion has surrounded this area of law. First, there is no clear principle determining when a duty will be imposed. Secondly, according to some authorities, duty, breach and damage will suffice. In such cases, it is difficult to discern any representation made or belief induced.[66] Hence, it is difficult to fit such cases within the general framework of estoppel or estoppel by representation. Thirdly, in the majority of alleged estoppel by negligence cases, the party sought to be estopped never intended or knew that others would act on its representations. Thus, a further essential component of estoppel seems to be missing. It may be possible to get round this difficulty using a strictly objective approach to the question[67] but this seems artificial. Fourthly, **8.146**

---

[61] *Moorgate Mercantile Co Ltd v Twitchings* [1977] AC 890 *per* Lord Fraser at 924 and *per* Lord Salmon at 912; *Johnson v Credit Lyonnaise Co* (1877) 3 CPD 32 *per* Cockburn C.J. at 42 (Bramwell L.J. concurring at 48) and *Campbell Discount Co v Gall* [1961] 1 QB 431, CA *per* Holroyd Pearce at 442–3.

[62] *Bell v Marsh* [1903] 1 Ch 528, CA *per* Lord Collins M.R. at 541.

[63] *Moorgate Mercantile Co Ltd v Twitchings* [1977] AC 890 *per* Lord Fraser at 924 and *per* Lord Salmon at 912.

[64] *Dixon v Kennaway & Co* [1990] 1 Ch 833 *per* Farwell J. at 238; *Carr v London and North Western Rly Co* (1875) LR 10 CP 307 *per* Brett and Denman JJ. at 318; *Coventry v Great Eastern Railway Co* (1883) 11 QBD 776, CA *per* Brett L.J. at 789 and *per* Lindley L.J. at 781 and *Seton, Laing v Lefone* (1887) 19 QBD 68, CA *per* Fry L.J. at 73.

[65] *Moorgate Mercantile Co Ltd v Twitchings* [1977] AC 890 *per* Lord Fraser at 924 and *per* Lord Salmon at 912; *Debs v Sibec Developments Ltd* [1990] RTR 91 *per* Simon Brown J at 99; *Campbell Discount Co v Gall* [1961] 1 QB 431, CA *per* Holroyd Pearce at 442–3 and *London Joint Stock Bank Ltd v Macmillan* [1918] AC 777 *per* Lord Haldane at 815.

[66] See, for example, *Moorgate Mercantile Co Ltd v Twitchings* [1977] AC 890 and *Abigail v Lapin* [1934] AC 481 PC (NSW) at 504.

[67] See para. 8.74 above.

in certain cases the doctrine has operated to pass title to third parties.[68] As we set out above,[69] this conflicts with well established principles of estoppel by representation.

AN ALTERNATIVE EXPLANATION OF THE SO-CALLED 'ESTOPPEL BY NEGLIGENCE' CASES

Negligence in the custody or preparation of cheques and other bills of exchange

8.147 The bank's mandate is only to pay out funds in accordance with the instructions of the customer. Therefore, if a bank pays out on a forged cheque, it has breached its mandate and the customer can generally sue for the return of the funds wrongly paid out.[70] It has been held in a number of cases, however, that negligence in the preparation or custody of the cheque will prevent the customer complaining of the breach of mandate. These cases are discussed under '*Banking*' at paragraphs 15.55 to 15.59. For the reasons there set out, we submit that estoppel is not the doctrine in play in these cases. Rather, they are examples of circuity of action: no action lies against the bank because it has a corresponding negligence claim against the customer. The latter claim provides a complete answer to the first.

8.148 This situation must be contrasted, however, with that in which the customer actually represents, expressly or by conduct, that the cheque is genuine and correct.[71] Where the customer does make such an express representation and the bank pays, it is highly likely that the elements of an estoppel by representation will be made out. The customer will not be able to sue for the monies paid out, not as a result of an alleged 'estoppel by negligence' but as the result of an estoppel by representation.

[68] *Eastern Distributors v Goldring* [1957] 2 QB 600, CA *per* Devlin J. at 610–11.
[69] At para. 11.126.
[70] See para. 15.55 below.
[71] *Bank of England v Vagliano Bros* [1891] AC 107.

Negligently entrusting a third party with ostensible ownership of goods or securities

According to the *nemo dat* rule, where X purports to sell goods to Z, which in fact belong to Y,[72] Y can assert title to the goods against Z. In a number of authorities, it has been held that Y is prevented from asserting title against Z where it has negligently armed X with apparent ownership of the goods or securities and thereby represented that X has authority to sell them. These cases are discussed at below at paragraphs 14.17, 14.18, 15.64 and 16.13. For the reasons there set out, we submit that such cases do not involve the application of estoppel principles but rather a free standing exception to the *nemo dat* rule, driven by commercial expediency. **8.149**

Estoppel as a defence to restitutionary claims[73]

Estoppel has been used to provide a defence to a restitutionary claim for money paid under a mistake of fact. As is discussed below, there is some doubt as to whether estoppel should continue function in this context. If estoppel continues to operate at all in this area,[74] there seems to be no reason why it should not apply to other restitutionary claims, such as those for money paid under contracts which fail. It will not be applicable to those claims where the recipient is aware of the existence of the relevant vitiating factor, such as duress. In such cases, the defendant knows that it is not entitled to the money and hence the third essential element (as set out in the next paragraph) of the estoppel is missing. **8.150**

Elements of the estoppel defence

After the components of a claim in restitution have been made out,[75] the estoppel defence has arisen in following circumstances. First, the **8.151**

[72] Subject to a number of limited exceptions, as to which see specialist texts.

[73] See generally on this subject, paras 15.66–8 below, Andrew Burrows, *The Law of Restitution* (Butterworths, London 1993) at 431–9, P.B.H. Birks, *An Introduction to the Law of Restitution* (Clarendon Press, Oxford 1988) at p. 402–10; Goff and Jones, *The Law of Restitution* (Sweet and Maxwell, London, 1993) at p. 739–60; Beatson and Bishop 'Mistaken Payments in the Law of Restitution' (1986) *University of Toronto LJ* 149 and Paul Key 'Estoppel as a defence to restitution' (1995) *CLJ* 525.

[74] As to which see below at paras 8.153 to 8.159.

[75] As to which see specialist texts.

plaintiff payor represented, expressly or impliedly, that the money had been correctly paid to the defendant payee and that it was free to spend the money as it wished. Secondly, the defendant believed this representation. Thirdly, the defendant acted to its detriment in reliance on the representation, usually by spending the money in a way which cannot be recouped.[76]

Representation and duty

It is necessary to show either that there was a genuine (or collateral) representation, made by express statement or inferred from conduct,[77] or that the payor was under a duty to the payee to calculate the sum accurately.[78] In the latter type of case, the requisite representation may be inferred merely from the fact of payment to the defendant. The cases falling within the former category clearly do not form part of the law of estoppel by negligence whereas those in the latter category may do. **8.152**

Problems with the estoppel defence

The problems which have beset other variants of so-called estoppel by negligence have occurred in this context. Three particular difficulties should be noted. First, there is no coherent principle which determines those relationships where a duty of accuracy is imposed. Arguably, a duty should be imposed only where the parties are unequal and the payor has a great deal more information and expertise in the relevant matters than the payee. However, there is no consistency between the cases. For example, in *Weld Blundell v Synott*,[79] the first mortgagee, pursuant to its statutory rights, took possession of the secured property and sold it to meet its outstanding debt. After deducting the sums due to it, the first mortgagee is under a duty to remit the proceeds to the holder of any second mortgage or charge. Such mortgagees are in a vulnerable **8.153**

---

[76] See further paras 8.98 to 8.101 under *Detriment.*

[77] *Deutsche Bank (London Agency)* v *Beriro & Co* (1895) 73 LT 669 *per* Mathew J. affd by CA (Lindley, Smith, Rigby L.JJ. at 671) (where there was an express representation and a breach of duty) and *Holt v Markham* [1923] 1 KB 504, CA.

[78] *Deutsche Bank (London Agency)* v *Beriro & Co* (1895) 73 LT 669 *per* Mathew J. affd by CA (Lindley, Smith, Rigby L.JJ. at 671) (where there was an express representation and a breach of duty); *Weld Blundell v Synott* [1940] 2 KB 107 *per* Asquith J. at 114–5, *R.E. Jones* v *Waring & Gillow* [1926] AC 670 *per* Viscount Cave L.C. at 683 and *per* Lord Sumner at 693 and *Skyring v Greenwood* (1825) 4 B&C 281.

[79] [1940] 2 KB 107.

position and have very limited rights to information on the repossession sale. In *Weld*, the first mortgagee mistakenly overpaid the second. No duty of accuracy arose despite the inequality between the parties. By contrast, in *Avon CC v Howlett*,[80] it was held that an employer owed a duty to its employees to calculate their remuneration accurately. Arguably, an employee is in as good a position as his or her employer to know the level of remuneration due to him or her. If there is a degree of inequality in such cases, it is not nearly as marked as that present in *Weld*.[81]

Secondly, the content of the inferred representation is uncertain. If the payor is deemed to represent that the payment is correct and immediately final, this imposes a very severe burden. It is more likely that the representation is only that such care has been taken that any error will be brought to light within a reasonable time.[82] If the inferred representation is so limited, the defence will not operate immediately on receipt of the payment. **8.154**

Thirdly, a fundamental difficulty flows from the inherent nature of the estoppel by the representation concept. Although the matter is highly controversial, it seems that estoppel cannot operate *pro tanto* but only as a complete defence. Once the elements of the doctrine are made out, the result is that the payor is estopped from denying the representation previously made, namely that the money had been correctly paid to the defendant. Hence, if the defendant can establish that it has spent part of the money in the requisite manner, it has a complete defence to the action.[83] The court is faced with an unattractive choice. If there has been no representation there is no possibility of a defence to the claim, regardless of whether the defendant had relied to its detriment on receipt and spent the money. Alternatively, if representation has been made and some detrimental reliance established, the plaintiff is wholly deprived of a remedy. **8.155**

Interrelationship with the defence of change of position

According to Lord Goff, the first and third difficulties referred to provide 'a strong indication' that estoppel is not an appropriate concept with **8.156**

---

80 [1983] 1 WLR 605, CA *per* Slade L.J. at 622.

81 It should be noted that the finding as to duty was not essential to the outcome of *Avon* as the employer had expressly represented to the employee that the payments he had received were correct.

82 See *Introduction to the Law of Restitution*, P.B.H. Birks, Clarendon Press, Oxford, 1988 at p. 404.

83 See paras 8.108–115 above.

which to deal with this situation.[84] In *Lipkin Gorman v Karpnale*,[85] the House of Lords recognized the existence of the defence of change of position. In summary

> the defence is available to a person whose position has so changed that it would be inequitable in all the circumstances to require him to make restitution, or alternatively to make restitution in full.[86]

Both estoppel and change of position will be triggered by detrimental reliance but it is clear from *Lipkin Gorman*, the latter doctrine differs in two ways. First, there is no need to establish any express or implied representation. It is sufficient if the payee formed the belief that the money was its own and that it was free to spend it as it liked. The source of that belief is not material. Secondly, it is clear that change of position can and often will operate as a partial rather than a complete defence. Hence, if the defendant still retains some of the money paid to him he will be obliged to disgorge it even if the remainder cannot be recouped.

The question is whether the change of position defence has wholly **8.157** supplanted that of estoppel or whether the two doctrines will operate in tandem, with the 'all or nothing' defence being available where the requisite representation is made out.[87] This issue is discussed further under *Banking* at paragraphs 15.66 to 15.68. There are sensible arguments in favour of retention of the estoppel defence where there is a genuine collateral representation.[88] However, in the light of Lord Goff's dictum,[89] the status of even these cases must be open to doubt.

There seems very little justification for survival of the duty cases, given **8.158** the particular difficulties associated with them.[90] It is submitted this line of authority should not survive *Lipkin Gorman*. Arguably, the cases were, in fact, early and crude manifestations of the change of position defence laid down in *Lipkin Gorman*. The remedial effects of estoppel by representation are by no means clear. As is set out above,[91] it is possible that the doctrine may operate *pro tanto*. If so, the boundary between the two defences hinges solely on the unsatisfactory concept

---

84 *Lipkin Gorman v Karpnale* [1991] 2 AC 548 *per* Lord Goff at 579.
85 [1991] 2 AC 548.
86 *ibid. per* Lord Goff at 580.
87 See the discussion of this issue by Paul Key in 'Estoppel as a Defence to Restitution' (1995) '*CLJ*' 525 and, in particular, the materials cited at nn. 16–18 at p. 528.
88 But see Paul Key's interesting suggestion that such cases are better dealt with using principles of election: 'Estoppel as a Defence to Restitution' (1995) *CLJ* 525 at 532.
89 Referred to above in para 8.156.
90 As set out in para. 8.146 above.
91 At paras 8.117 to 8.119.

of the representation inferred from breach of duty. Alternatively, it is submitted that, if the cases do involve the application of a different principle, they are inconsistent with the new and more limited defence laid down by the House of Lords. This issue has not yet been settled by the courts and it is therefore possible that such cases remain good law.

Conclusion

In summary, we would submit that a further category of the so-called estoppel by negligence doctrine, namely those where a duty of accuracy is placed on a payor, rests on distinctly dubious foundations. Such cases are better explained as early examples of change of position rather than estoppel. **8.159**

The remaining cases

The preceding paragraphs demonstrate that the bulk of the cases on this subject can be excluded from the law of estoppel. This leaves a fairly negligible rump of authorities which may be governed by the estoppel by negligence doctrine. Examples include the negligent issue of mercantile documents such as delivery orders on which others are likely to rely. Such cases may be explicable in terms of ordinary principles of the modern law of tort.[92] Further, if a party discovers that a deed has been forged in its name, it has a duty to inform the holder of the deed of the forgery.[93] It is not entirely clear whether it is necessary to establish negligence on the part of the original party. If not, such cases are no more than a further instance where the law imposes a duty to speak, as discussed in paragraph 8.59 above. If negligence is a requirement, it may be possible (and indeed preferable) to accommodate them within the law of tort rather than of estoppel. **8.160**

---

[92] *Coventry v Great Eastern Railway Co* (1883) 11 QBD 776, CA and *Seton, Laing v Lefone* (1887) 19 QBD 68, CA. In the latter case, an express representation was made, but not to the party claiming the benefit of the estoppel.

[93] *Fung Kai Sun v Chan Fui Hing* [1951] AC 489, PC (Hong Kong) *per* Lord Reid at 501.

RELATIONSHIP OF ESTOPPEL BY REPRESENTATION WITH OTHER DOCTRINES

In the following comparison sections, we have used W to signify the party seeking to set up the estoppel and M to signify the party bound by the estoppel. **8.161**

EQUITABLE FORBEARANCE OR PROMISSORY ESTOPPEL

The general nature of the doctrines

For the reasons set out at paragraphs 12.05 to 12.07 below we have chosen to refer to the doctrine under discussion in this section as equitable forbearance rather than using the more common designation, promissory estoppel. Estoppel by representation is recognized both by equity and common law[94] whereas equitable forbearance is a purely equitable principle.[95] Estoppel by representation is an evidential doctrine operating only to prevent a party to litigation denying the truth of a certain set of facts. The outcome of the case depends on the application of ordinary legal principles to the facts thus set up by the doctrine. In contrast, equitable forbearance operates substantively and is a source of legal obligation in itself, giving limited effect to certain promises.[96] **8.162**

Pre-existing relationship

Equitable forbearance can operate only between parties who, at the time of the representation, were in pre-existing relationship giving rise to legal **8.163**

[94] See para. 8.14 above.
[95] See para. 11.01 below.
[96] *Silovi Pty Ltd v Barbaro* (1988) 13 NSWLR 466 *per* Priestley J.A. at 472. The comments were directed towards Australian doctrine of promissory or equitable estoppel but the distinction drawn between the evidential and the substantive principles is equally applicable to the more limited English equivalent.

rights and duties.[97] No such relationship is necessary in estoppel by representation cases.[98]

Promise or representation

It is a requirement of both doctrines that M has made a representation to W. Subject to one possible caveat,[99] the principles governing the manner in which a representation may be made are the same in both doctrines. Specifically, a representation may be made by express statement,[1] conduct[2] or silence.[3] In both doctrines, silence will probably only give rise to a representation where there is a duty to disclose the fact in issue. It is a requirement of both doctrines that the representation is clear and unequivocal.[4] **8.164**

The most important point of difference between estoppel by representation and equitable forbearance concerns the nature of the representation made. Estoppel by representation will operate only where M has made a representation of fact,[5] or of mixed fact and law.[6] Equitable forbearance will operate only where M has promised not to enforce its pre-existing legal rights against M.[7] The latter doctrine is therefore triggered by a representation of future intention, which is incapable of generating an estoppel by representation. As is set out at paragraphs 8.30 to 8.33 above, however, it is sometimes difficult to draw a coherent line between the two types of representation. **8.165**

Reliance

Both doctrines require W to have acted to in reliance on the representation made by M. Further, it is necessary to show that M intended W so **8.166**

---

[97] See paras 12.10–11 below.
[98] See, for example, *Knights v Wiffen* (1870) LR 5 QB 660, CA; *In re Ottos Kopje Diamond Mines Ltd* [1893] 1 Ch 618 CA and *TCB Ltd v Gray* [1986] Ch 621.
[99] As to which see paras 8.40 above and 12.14 below on the application of the requirement that the representation must be clear and unequivocal.
[1] As to equitable forbearance see para. 12.16 below; as to estoppel by representation see para. 8.50 above.
[2] As to equitable forbearance see para. 12.16 below; as to estoppel by representation see para. 8.52 above.
[3] As to equitable forbearance see paras 12.17–19 below; as to estoppel by representation see para 8.59 above.
[4] As to equitable forbearance see paras 12.13–14 below; as to estoppel by representation see para 8.39 above.
[5] See para. 8.27–29 above.
[6] See para. 8.35 above.
[7] See para. 12.12 below.

to act or was aware that W was so acting.[8] For both doctrines there must have been a causative link between W's acts and the representation made, *i.e.* W must have been led to act differently by the representation.[9] In cases of estoppel by representation, the burden is placed on W to establish causation.[10] The onus of proof is probably the same with respect to equitable forbearance, although there is some authority to suggest the burden may occasionally be reversed.[11]

Detriment

In order to establish estoppel by representation, it is essential to demonstrate detriment. Specifically, it is necessary to show that W's change of position in reliance on the representation will cause W to suffer detriment in the event that the correctness of the representation[12] is denied.[13] There is some doubt as to whether detriment is a necessary component of equitable forbearance. It is clear that it is essential to establish that resiling from the promise made would be inequitable having regard to the dealing between the parties.[14] On balance, we submit that detriment is an essential pre-requisite for establishing inequity.[15] Detriment is therefore required by both doctrines. However, in equitable forbearance cases, additional factors may be taken into account in assessing whether it would be inequitable to resile from the representation. Put simply, detriment is a pre-condition but not a guarantee of the operation of the equitable forbearance doctrine. By contrast, and subject to some limited exceptions,[16] detriment will guarantee the operation of estoppel by representation. **8.167**

Measure of relief

It is clear that the effect of equitable forbearance will often be temporary, **8.168**
the doctrine operating only to suspend M's right to resile from the

[8] As to equitable forbearance see para. 12.23 and 12.29; as to estoppel by representation see para. 8.74 and 8.84.
[9] As to equitable forbearance see paras 12.28–9; as to estoppel by representation see paras 8.84 to 8.87.
[10] See para. 8.84 above and 12.28.
[11] See paras 12.30–1.
[12] See para. 8.88 above.
[13] See paras 12.33–4 below.
[14] See paras 12.33–8 below.
[15] See paras 12.34–8 below.
[16] As to which see paras 8.120 to 8.125 above.

representation made rather than to extinguish it. It is also clear that the doctrine may operate permanently in exceptional cases. Although the issue is not settled, it is submitted that the guiding principle is that the measure of relief will go no further than the minimum necessary to prevent detriment to the representee.[17] Sometimes this may only be achieved by requiring M to make good its representation, *i.e.* abide by the terms of its promise, although this is by no means always the case. By contrast, in estoppel by representation cases, establishing detrimental reliance leads automatically[18] to M being required to make good its representation. Although the issue is highly controversial, it seems that this outcome will follow regardless of whether the benefit thereby accruing to W will be greater than the detriment suffered. The differential remedial outcomes reflect a deeper division: equitable forbearance is frequently said to concern the prevention of inequitable conduct[19] whereas reference to such abstract concepts of fairness have been noticeably rare in estoppel by representation cases.[20]

PROPRIETARY ESTOPPEL

The general nature of the doctrines

Estoppel by representation is recognized both by equity and common law[21] whereas proprietary estoppel is an equitable doctrine.[22] Estoppel by representation is an evidential doctrine operating only to prevent a party to litigation denying the truth of a certain set of facts. The outcome of the case depends on the application of ordinary legal principles to the facts thus set up by the doctrine.[23] In contrast, proprietary estoppel operates substantively and is a source of legal obligation in itself.[24] It may create positive rights to property. **8.169**

[17] See paras 12.51–4 and, in particular, paras 12.55–6.
[18] Subject to the defences set out in paras 8.120–5 above. See generally paras 8.109–119 on the relief available in estoppel by representation cases.
[19] See para. 12.34 below.
[20] See para. 8.91.
[21] See para. 8.14 above.
[22] See para. 11.01 below.
[23] See above at para. 8.16.
[24] *Silovi Pty Ltd v Barbaro* (1988) 13 NSWLR 466 *per* Priestley J.A. at 472. The comments were directed towards the Australian doctrine of equitable estoppel but the distinction drawn between the evidential and the substantive principles is equally applicable to the English proprietary estoppel doctrine.

ASSURANCE AND REPRESENTATION

It is a requirement of both doctrines that M has caused W to form a belief of some kind or confirmed a belief already held. Both impose similar requirements as to the manner in which the belief may be fostered. These include express statement, conduct and silence. For silence to suffice to give rise to an estoppel by representation, it is clear that the circumstances must impose a duty to speak on the silent party.[25] The terminology of duty has not been frequently employed in proprietary estoppel cases but it is submitted that a similar approach is used: silence or purely passive acquiescence will suffice to raise a proprietary estoppel where the party sought to be estopped stood by in the knowledge that the party seeking to raise the estoppel was acting under a mistake. These circumstances raise a duty to speak.[26] **8.170**

Proprietary estoppel is, however, somewhat more flexible than estoppel by representation: it can arise as a result of mutual dealings between parties in which both have formed a shared expectation as to the outcome of the transaction or underlying basis of their relationship.[27] In such cases, it is very difficult to identify any clear cut representation by either party. It is not necessary to show a clear or unequivocal representation in proprietary estoppel cases[28] whereas this is an essential component of an estoppel by representation claim.[29] **8.171**

The nature of the qualifying belief differs with respect to the two doctrines. For estoppel by representation it is necessary to show that the party sought to be estopped made a representation of fact which was believed by the party seeking to raise the estoppel. By contrast, proprietary estoppel will operate on representations of fact *or intention* so long as they relate to the ownership of property. To establish a proprietary estoppel claim, it is necessary to show that M led W to believe either that W was or would become the owner of property which M in fact owned.[30] If M clearly represents to W that W is the owner of property, this amounts to a sufficient assurance to give rise to proprietary estoppel. It is also a representation of fact capable of giving rise to an **8.172**

[25] See para. 8.59 above.
[26] See para. 11.19 below.
[27] See para. 11.13 below.
[28] See para. 11.07 and *Sledmore v Dalby* [1996] P&CR 196, CA *per* Hobhouse L.J. at 207.
[29] See para. 8.39 above.
[30] See paras 11.08–15 below.

estoppel by representation. There is therefore an overlap between the operation of the two doctrines.[31]

8.173 Proprietary estoppel will also operate where M promised that it would transfer ownership[32] of its property to W.[33] In such cases, the doctrine is operating on promises or representations as to future intention, neither of which are capable of giving rise to an estoppel by representation.[34] Neither doctrine requires that M knew the representation to be false,[35] except where M's conduct has been purely passive.[36] For convenience, in the remainder of this section, we have used the term representation to refer to the different assurances which are capable of triggering the operation of the doctrines under consideration.

Reliance

8.174 Both doctrines require W to have acted to its detriment in reliance on the representation made by M. Further, it is necessary to show that M intended W so to act or was aware that W was so acting.[37] For both doctrines there must have been a causative link between W's acts and the representation made, *i.e.* W must have been led to act differently by the representation.[38] However, the onus of proof differs between the doctrines: in cases of estoppel by representation the burden is always placed on W to establish causation, whereas in proprietary estoppel the burden is, in certain circumstances, reversed.[39] M is required to prove that W would have acted in the same way even had the representation never been made.

[31] See, for example, *Hopgood v Brown* [1955] 1 WLR 213 considered at para. 8.137 above.
[32] Or some lesser proprietary interest or use right.
[33] See paras 11.12–14.
[34] See para. 8.27 above.
[35] As to proprietary estoppel see para. 11.20; as to estoppel by representation see para. 8.72.
[36] See para. 8.170 above.
[37] As to proprietary estoppel see paras 11.21–2; as to estoppel by representation see paras 8.74–7.
[38] As to proprietary estoppel see para. 11.24; as to estoppel by representation see para. 8.84.
[39] See para. 11.26, both generally on this point and for the circumstances which will cause the reversal of the normal burden.

Detriment

Subject to two possible caveats,[40] the detriment requirement is the same in both doctrines: it is necessary to show that, as a result of her acts in reliance, W will suffer detriment if the truth of M's representation is denied.[41] In proprietary estoppel cases, the court may take into account a number of factors additional to detriment, in assessing whether it would be inequitable for M to deny the correctness of W's belief. Detriment is a precondition not a guarantee of relief. By contrast, such factors will not be taken into account in estoppel by representation cases. Subject to some limited exceptions, detriment will guarantee relief.[42] **8.175**

Measure of relief

As regards proprietary estoppel, once detrimental reliance is established, the court has a flexible discretion as to what, if any, relief to grant. All the circumstances of the case may be taken into account.[43] However, the overriding guiding principle is that the remedy should not exceed the minimum necessary to avert detriment.[44] Sometimes this may only be achieved by requiring M to make good its representation but this is by no means always the case. By contrast, in estoppel by representation cases, establishing detrimental reliance leads automatically[45] to M being required to make good its representation. Although this matter is far from settled, it seems that this outcome will follow regardless of whether the benefit thereby accruing to W will be greater than the detriment suffered. The differential remedial outcomes reflect a deeper division: proprietary estoppel is frequently said to concern the prevention of unconscionable or inequitable conduct[46] whereas reference to such abstract concepts of fairness have been noticeably rare in estoppel by representation cases.[47] **8.176**

---

[40] As to which see para. 11.37 below and paras 8.102 and 8.106 above.
[41] As to proprietary estoppel see paras 11.31–8; as to estoppel by representation see para. 8.88.
[42] See para. 8.91 above. The exceptions are discussed at paras 8.120–5.
[43] See paras 11.50 and 11.58–63 below.
[44] See paras 11.51–4 below.
[45] Subject to the defences set out in paras 8.120–5 above. See generally paras 8.109–119 on the relief available under estoppel by representation.
[46] See paras 11.01, 11.34, 11.49 and 11.55–63 below.
[47] See para. 8.91.

Effect on third parties

Estoppel by representation, being merely evidential, does not affect the reality of the dealings between the parties. Hence, where M represents to W that W is the owner of property, estoppel by representation will not operate actually to transfer title to W but only to prevent M from denying that W is the owner. This means that W has no ownership right which it can transfer to third parties.[48] The estoppel affects only the personal rights and liabilities arising between M and W. By contrast, it is submitted that proprietary estoppel does vest property rights in W although their precise nature and the point at which they arise is highly controversial.[49] **8.177**

[48] See generally paras 8.127–8 above.
[49] See paras 11.71–85.

Chapter 9

ESTOPPEL BY CONVENTION

INTRODUCTION

On one level, the elements of estoppel by convention can be simply stated. Thus, the estoppel will arise where: (i) the parties have established, by their construction of their agreement or a common apprehension as to its legal effect, a convention basis; (ii) on that basis, the parties have regulated their subsequent dealings; and (iii) one party would suffer detriment if the other were to be permitted to resile from that convention.[1] As such estoppel by convention can, on this level,[2] be relatively easily distinguished from estoppel by representation and equitable forbearance. Estoppel by convention depends on a shared assumption[3] which can be one of fact or law[4] and not on either a representation as to a state of facts[5] or a promise **9.01**

---

[1] *Hamel-Smith v Pycroft & Jervase Ltd* (QBD unrep. 5 February 1987 *per* Peter Gibson J.) applying *Keen v Holland* [1984] 1 WLR 251 per Oliver L.J. at 261F–G approved *Norwegian American Cruises A/S v Paul Mundy Ltd ('The Vistafjord')* [1988] 2 Lloyd's Rep. 343 *per* Bingham L.J. at 351–2. See also *Shearson Lehman Hutton Inc v Maclaine Watson & Co Ltd* [1989] 2 Lloyd's Rep. 570 *per* Webster J. at 596 col. 2; *Bank of Scotland v Wright* [1991] BCLC 244 *per* Brooke J. at 261e–f; *Lovett v Fairclough* (1991) 61 P&CR 385 *per* Mummery J. at 401; *Credit Suisse v Beegas Nominees* [1994] 4 All ER 803 *per* Lindsay J. at 831e–h; *W Middlesex Golf Club Limited v London Borough of Ealing* (1994) 68 P&CR 461, *per* Roger Kaye Q.C. at 480; *Republic of India v India Steamship Co Ltd ('The Indian Endurance') (No. 2)* [1996] 3 All ER 641 *per* Staughton L.J. at 651j; [1997] 3 WLR 818 *per* Lord Steyn at 829F–H; and *John v George and Walton* (1996) 71 P&CR 375 *per* Simon Brown L.J. at 394–5.

[2] But see 9.06 ff., below.

[3] *Amalgamated Investment and Property Co Ltd v Texas Commerce International Bank Ltd* [1982] QB 84 *per* Eveleigh L.J. at 126A-B; and *per* Brandon L.J. at 130G–131B adopting Spencer Bower para. 157; p. 157.

[4] See *Hiscox v Outhwaite (No. 1)* [1992] 1 AC 562 *per* Lord Donaldson M.R. at 575G and *W Middlesex Golf Club Limited v London Borough of Ealing* (1994) 68 P&CR 461 *per* Roger Kaye Q.C. at 482.

[5] Giving rise to an estoppel by representation — see Chap. 8.

as to future obligations.[6] Estoppel by convention is, as the law currently stands, therefore to be distinguished from equitable forbearance or estoppel by representation.[7]

However, there are three complications to the above analysis. First, when as a matter of fact[8] will the doctrine apply. Secondly, can estoppel by convention provide the party relying on it with a cause of action. Thirdly, can or could estoppel by convention be viewed as part of an overarching doctrine of estoppel. **9–02**

APPLICATION OF THE DOCTRINE

There are two limitations on the operation of the doctrine. First, there must be a *shared* assumption. This requirement has two elements. First, one party must have acted so that '*across the line*' between it and the other party, a belief or expectation is created in the mind of the other party.[9] Secondly, the conduct required for there to be a 'crossing of the line' is '*mutually manifest conduct*'[10] which if it is not the formation of a contract must be '*something very close to it*'.[11] It follows that an estoppel by convention will only arise in limited circumstances. However, the requirement of a shared assumption does not mean that one party must have induced or encouraged the other to act on a particular assumption.[12] An estoppel by **9.03**

---

[6] Giving rise to equitable forbearance — see Chap. 12.

[7] Lord Steyn expressly accepted this point in *Republic of India v India Steamship Co Ltd* [1997] 3 WLR 818 at 830D–E whilst noting that '*at a high level of abstraction*' an '*overarching principle*' of estoppel could be formulated.

[8] Estoppel by convention being essentially a question of evidence — see *Cooperative Bank v Tipper* [1996] 4 All ER 366 *per* H.H.Judge Roger Cooke at 372a–d.

[9] See *K Lokumal & Sons (London) Ltd v Lotte Shipping Co Pte Ltd ('The August Leonhardt')* [1985] 2 Lloyd's Rep. 28 *per* Kerr L.J. at 35 col. 1; *Companie Portorafti Commerciale SA v Ultramar Panama Inc ('The Captain Gregos') (No. 2)* [1990] 2 Lloyd's Rep. 395 *per* Bingham L.J. at 405 col. 2 and *The Stolt Loyalty* [1993] 2 Lloyd's Rep. 281 *per* Clarke J. at 290 cols 1–2.

[10] *K Lokumal & Sons (London) Ltd v Lotte Shipping Co Pte Ltd ('The August Leonhardt')* [1985] 2 Lloyd's Rep. 28 *per* Kerr L.J. at 34 col. 1—35 col. 2 and *Republic of India v India Steamship Co Ltd ('The Indian Endurance') (No. 2)* [1996] 3 All ER 641 *per* Staughton L.J. at 652d; [1997] 3 WLR 818.

[11] *Republic of India v India Steamship Co Ltd ('The Indian Endurance') (No. 2)* [1996] 3 All ER 641 *per* Staughton L.J. at 652e; upheld on different reasoning [1997] 3 WLR 818. As to the evidence required/admissible — see *Skywest Aviation Pty Ltd* v *Commonwealth* (1995) 126 FLR 61.

[12] *Republic of India v India Steamship Co Ltd ('The Indian Endurance') (No. 2)* [1996] 3 All ER 641 *per* Staughton L.J. at 652a–b; [1997] 3 WLR 818; and *John v George and Walton* (1996) 71 P&CR 375 *per* Morritt L.J. at 385.

convention can arise out of conduct or silence.[13] By parity of reasoning, where there is no shared assumption, there will be no estoppel by convention;[14] even if one party has acted unjustly. The party seeking to establish the estoppel will therefore have to fall back on estoppel by representation. By contrast, an estoppel by representation cannot arise from silence/acquiescence unless one party is under a duty to speak.[15] Therefore, the party which fails in establishing an estoppel by convention, which can arise from a failure to act, may find establishing an estoppel by representation difficult.

The second limitation is that it must be 'unjust' or 'unconscionable' **9.04**
to allow one party to resile from the common assumption.[16] This limitation is nothing more or less than the detriment necessary for estoppels.[17] For present purposes, four points should be noted. First, the party seeking to establish detriment must show it acted on the basis that the shared assumption was correct.[18] Secondly, provided that the party seeking to establish the estoppel has so acted, detriment may well be suffered by the mere fact that there has been a change from the presumed position.[19] This is because the party seeking to establish the estoppel must already have shown that: (i) the other party has acted unjustly in

---

[13] *Republic of India v India Steamship Co Ltd ('The Indian Endurance') (No. 2)* [1996] 3 All ER 641 *per* Staughton L.J. at 652e. However, where such an estoppel is sought to be established care must be taken to ascertain exactly *what* is to be inferred from the conduct complained of — see *The Indian Endurance (No. 2)* [1997] 3 WLR 818.

[14] See *Shearson Lehman Hutton Inc v Maclaine Watson & Co Ltd* [1989] 2 Lloyd's Rep. 570 *per* Webster J. at 606 cols 1–2 and *Republic of India v India Steamship Co Ltd ('The Indian Endurance') (No. 2)* [1996] 3 All ER 641 *per* Staughton L.J. at 653e.

[15] See *Moorgate Mercantile Co Ltd v Twitchings* [1977] AC 890 *per* Lord Wilberforce at 903 (dissenting on the decision at issue but not on this particular point); *Pacol Ltd v Trade Lines Ltd ('The Henrik Sif')* [1982] 1 Lloyd's Rep. 456 *per* Webster J. at 465 cols 1–2 and *The Stolt Loyalty* [1993] 2 Lloyd's Rep. 281 *per* Clarke J. at 290 cols 1–2.

[16] See *Norwegian American Cruises A/S v Paul Mundy Ltd ('The Vistafjord')* [1988] 2 Lloyd's Rep. 343 *per* Bingham L.J. at 352 col. 1; *Shearson Lehman Hutton Inc v Maclaine Watson & Co Ltd* [1989] 2 Lloyd's Rep. 570 per Webster J. at 596 col. 2; *Furness Withy (Australia) Pty Ltd v Metal Distributors (UK) Ltd ('The Amazonia')* [1990] 1 Lloyd's Rep. 236 *per* Dillon L.J. at 251 and *Hiscox v Outhwaite (No. 1)* [1992] 1 AC 562 *per* Lord Donaldson M.R. at 575G-H.

[17] See para 8.04–05, 8.85–107, 11.31–47 and 12.33–48 for description.

[18] See, *e.g. Lovett v Fairclough* (1991) 61 P&CR 385 *per* Mummery J. at 401 and *The Stolt Loyalty* [1993] 2 Lloyd's Rep. 281 *per* Clarke J. at 291 col. 2 This type of 'reliance' may be relatively easily inferred — see by analogy *Nationwide Building Society v Lewis* (ChD unrep. 23 May 1997 *per* Rimer J.).

[19] See, *e.g. Mitsui Babcock Energy Ltd v John Brown Engineering Ltd* (1997) 51 Con LR 129 per H.H. Judge Esyr Lewis Q.C. at 185–6.

allowing the belief or expectation to 'cross the line' and arise in its mind;[20] and (ii) it has engaged in mutual dealings, those mutual dealings axiomatically requiring a change of position. These elements almost inevitably carry with them a finding that detriment has been suffered.[21] Therefore, a consideration of the third element of the doctrine necessarily must take into account the detriment implicit in the first two elements.[22] Thirdly, it does not follow that the requirement of detriment necessary in all estoppels is reduced in estoppel by convention. The same three-stage analysis[23] applies here as it does elsewhere. Fourthly, although many of the authorities suggest that 'unconscionability' will trigger an estoppel by convention, at best 'unconscionability' forms a hurdle *additional* to that of detriment which the party seeking to establish the estoppel must overcome.[24] On any view, 'unconscionability' does not replace detriment. However, we would suggest that the better view is that there is no separate requirement of 'unconscionability', at least so far as estoppel by convention is concerned. The term is used to describe the overall effect of the convention; mutual dealings and detriment. Put another way, where the three elements of estoppel by convention are made out, withdrawal from the convention will be 'unconscionable' without more.[25]

ESTOPPEL BY CONVENTION AS A SWORD

Our consistent and uncontroversial approach in this work has been that 9.05
estoppel (with the exception of proprietory estoppel) is an evidentiary

[20] *i.e.* in allowing a mistaken view of the common assumption to 'cross the line' – *K Lokumal & Sons (London) Ltd v Lotte Shipping Co Pte Ltd ('The August Leonhardt')* [1985] 2 Lloyd's Rep. 28 *per* Kerr L.J. at 34 col. 1–35 col. 2 and *John v George and Walton* (1996) 71 P&CR 375 *per* Simon Brown L.J. at 396.

[21] The position can be contrasted with estoppel by representation where there may be a representation and reliance without the change of position to the representee's detriment.

[22] See *Norwegian American Cruises A/S v Paul Mundy Ltd ('The Vistafjord')* [1988] 2 Lloyd's Rep. 343 *per* Bingham L.J. at 353 col. 1 and *John v George and Walton* (1996) 71 P&CR 375 *per* Simon Brown L.J. at 396.

[23] Action (whether representation or shared assumption), reliance and detriment.

[24] See *Equitable Forbearance* at para. 12.33 ff.; esp. para. 12–38.

[25] This, we would suggest, is clear from *K Lokumal & Sons (London) Ltd v Lotte Shipping Co Pte Ltd ('The August Leonhardt')* [1985] 2 Lloyd's Rep. 28 *per* Kerr L.J. at 34 col. 1–35 col. 2. See also *Norwegian American Cruises A/S v Paul Mundy Ltd ('The Vistafjord')* [1988] 2 Lloyd's Rep. 343 *per* Bingham L.J. at 351–3 col. 1.

doctrine that does not create substantive rights. It follows that an estoppel by convention cannot create, in the proper sense of the word, a cause of action. However, estoppel by convention will preclude a party from arguing that a particular state of affairs does not exist. Therefore, the party may be precluded from denying that it is a party to a guarantee;[26] or that there was a concluded contract between the parties;[27]or that it is obliged to indemnify the facts at issue falling within the indemnity provided.[28] In such circumstances, the estoppel is purely defensive — the other party is precluded from contending that the claim must fail. However, the effect of that preclusion is that the party relying on the estoppel must succeed. This will be the case even if the effect of the estoppel is to grant a party greater rights than existed under the contract.[29] Thus, although as a matter of analysis, the estoppel is acting as a shield, as a matter of reality, it is at least a sharp-edged shield.

AN OVERARCHING DOCTRINE OF ESTOPPEL?

In *Amalgamated Investment & Property Co Ltd v Texas Commerce International Bank Ltd,*[30] the Master of the Rolls, Lord Denning, articulated an extremely wide doctrine of estoppel, subsuming estoppel by representation, equitable forbearance and proprietary estoppel.[31] A subsequent Master of the Rolls, Lord Donaldson, suggested that this wide doctrine encompassed estoppel by convention.[32] There is therefore powerful authority to suggest that it would be wrong to treat estoppel by convention as a separate doctrine.[33] **9.06**

26 See *Amalgamated Investment & Property Co Ltd (in liquidation) v Texas Commerce International Bank Ltd* [1982] 1 QB 84 *per* Robert Goff J. at 105D–6A.
27 See *Mitsui Babcock Energy Ltd v John Brown Engineering Ltd* (1997) 51 Con LR 129 *per* H.H. Judge Esyr Lewis Q.C. at 185–6.
28 See *Hiscox v Outhwaite (No. 3)* [1991] 2 Lloyd's Rep. 524 *per* Evans J. at 535 cols 1–2.
29 See *Sarat Chunder Dey v Gopal Chunder Laha* (1892) 19 LR Ind App 203; *Calgary Milling Co Ltd v American Surety Co of New York* [1919] 3 WWR 98 and *De Tchihatchef v Salerni Coupling Ltd* [1932] 1 Ch 330.
30 [1982] QB 84.
31 *ibid.* at 122A–D.
32 *Hiscox v Outhwaite (No. 1)* [1992] 1 AC 562 at 574H–5 D. See also *John v George and Walton* (1996) 71 P&CR 375 *per* Morrit L.J. at 385.
33 A proposition which also has academic support — see 'From representation to expectation: estoppel as a cause of action' Thompson [1983] *CLJ* 257; Finn, Chap. 4 *passim.*

However, as we have suggested elsewhere,[34] the better view is that the English law has not at present gone so far as to create such overarching doctrines.[35] Given that the courts still regard estoppel by convention and estoppel by representation, for example, as different doctrines[36] it is necessary and appropriate to consider the elements of each of the doctrines. That approach has two additional advantages. First, the creation of an overarching doctrine does not bypass the requirement that a party must plead and prove that it acted in a particular way on the strength of a particular representation, assumption or promise.[37] Therefore, it is imperative that these individual doctrines and their separate elements are recognized. Secondly, 'estoppel' has been much criticized as a vague or uncertain doctrine. The recognition that separate doctrines are at work removes much of that uncertainty. **9.07**

The main criticism of this approach is that it could be atomistic: fragmenting a flexible doctrine into a series of inflexible categories. However, we would suggest that such criticism is misplaced for three reasons. First, there is sufficient flexibility in each of the categories to cover all factual situations. Secondly, if an atomistic approach leads to clarity and certainty then that approach should be adopted especially where, as here, the approach does not over-complicate the issues.[38] Thirdly, the English law still recognizes (due to the doctrine of consideration) fundamental differences between promises and representations. If a clear and consistent law of obligations is to exist, those differences must be reflected across the board. **9.08**

---

34 See, in the context of waiver, *Waiver — Terminology* at para. 3.02 ff.

35 A view that was confirmed by the House of Lords in *Republic of India v India Steamship Co Ltd* [1997] 3 WLR 818 *per* Lord Steyn at 830D-E.

36 Compare, for example, Lord Denning M.R. with Eveleigh and Brandon L.JJ. in *Amalgamated Investment & Property Co Ltd v Texas Commerce International Bank Ltd* — whilst Lord Denning decided the case on the basis of a broad principle, the majority of the court clearly regarded estoppel by convention as a separate and distinct phenomenon.

37 See, *e.g. Cooperative Bank v Tipper* [1996] 4 All ER 366 *per* H.H. Judge Roger Cooke at 372a–d.

38 See *Republic of India v India Steamship Co Ltd* [1997] 3 WLR 818 per Lord Steyn at 830 E.

Chapter 10

ESTOPPEL BY DEED

INTRODUCTION

Estoppel by deed is a rule of evidence[1] whereby parties are bound by the solemn and unambiguous statements contained in a deed which they have executed.[2] It will not itself give rise to a cause of action but will merely prevent the party estopped from contradicting the statement in issue. The legal outcome between the parties will then be determined according the state of facts set up by the doctrine.[3] That state of facts may give either a valid defence[4] or cause of action[5] to the party raising the estoppel. Hence, estoppel by deed may have a material impact on the outcome of a case. It may thus be used indirectly, but not directly, as something more than a mere shield. **10.01**

The doctrine's underlying rationale was originally as follows: deeds were to be taken so seriously as not to admit of any evidence contradicting the statements which they contained. This absolutist approach has been mitigated in two ways. First, the statement must have formed the basis on which the parties contracted with one another.[6] Secondly, the parties will not be bound by statements contained in void or voidable deeds or by statements in those parts of a deed which a court is prepared to rectify.[7] In 1878, the doctrine was criticized by **10.02**

---

[1] *Greer v Kettle* [1938] AC 156 *per* Lord Maugham at 171 (*obiter*); *Re Distributors and Warehousing Ltd* [1986] BCLC 129 *per* Walton J. at 139c–d (*obiter*); *Williams v Pinckney* (1897) 67 LJ Ch 34.

[2] *First National Bank v Thompson* [1996] All ER 144, CA *per* Ward L.J. at 149J; *Greer v Kettle* [1938] AC 156 *per* Lord Maugham at 171 (*obiter*), *Re Distributors and Warehousing Ltd* [1986] BCLC 129 *per* Walton J. at 139c–d (*obiter*) and *Williams v Pinckney* (1897) 67 LJ Ch 34.

[3] In this respect, the doctrine operates in the same way as estoppel by representation. For further discussion of the evidential/substantive and sword/shield controversies see para. 8.22 above.

[4] *Wiles v Woodward* (1850) 1 Exch 557, 155 ER 244.

[5] *Rudd v Bowles* [1912] 2 Ch 60.

[6] See below at para. 10.40.

[7] See generally paras 10.49–51 below.

Lord Jessel, who averred that it ought not to be extended.[8] Considerable problems arise because so many of the relevant principles and cases date from the Victorian and pre-Victorian era.[9] Applying such rules to modern commercial and conveyancing situations is often difficult. However, some welcome light has recently been shed on this subject by the Court of Appeal in *First National Bank v Thompson*.[10]

Estoppel by deed operates in both common law and equity.[11] Equity differs in that it will recognize a wider range of circumstances in which the doctrine will not be applied.[12] This reflects the wider range of circumstances in which equity will set a contract or deed aside. **10.03**

Terminology

There is no term which accurately describes the parties to an estoppel by deed. Representor and representee are not quite accurate because of the mutuality of many of the statements which give rise to an estoppel by deed.[13] In this chapter we have therefore used W to signify the party seeking to raise the estoppel and M to signify the party it is sought to estop. **10.04**

Summary of Elements

W will be able to raise an estoppel by deed against M if the following elements are made out. First, M executes a formally valid deed to which **10.05**

---

[8] *General Finance, Mortgage, and Discount Company v Liberator Permanent Benefit Building Society* (1878) 10 ChD 15 *per* Jessel M.R. at 24–5 and *Onward Building Society v Smithson* [1893] 1 Ch 1 *per* Lindley L.J. at 13.

[9] As far back as 1893, Bowen L.J. was moved to remark that the law on estoppel by deed was 'as old as the hills': *Onward Building Society v Smithson* [1893] 1 Ch 1 at 14. Examples of early cases which still exert profound and lasting effects on the modern law include: *Right de Jefferys v Bucknell* (1831) 2 B&Ad 278, 109 ER 1146; *Bowman v Taylor* (1834) 2 AD&E 279, 111 ER 108; *Webb v Austin* (1844) 7 Man & G 701, 135 ER 282; *Carpenter v Buller* (1841) 8 M&W 209, 212, 151 ER 1013 and *Cuthbertson v Irving* (1859) 4 H&N 742, 157 ER 1034. Prior to *First National Bank v Thompson* [1996] All ER 144, CA, the leading case was *Greer v Kettle* [1938] AC 156 which was decided in 1937.

[10] [1996] All ER 144, CA, discussed further at paras 10.66–8 below.

[11] *Greer v Kettle* [1938] AC 156 *per* Lord Maugham at 171 (*obiter*). Contra. *First National Bank v Thompson* [1996] All ER 144, CA *per* Millet L.J. at 145a–d.

[12] *Greer v Kettle* [1938] AC 156 *per* Lord Maugham at 171 (*obiter*). See further at para. 10.49 below.

[13] See below at para. 10.08.

W is named as a party.[14] Secondly, the deed contains a statement of fact, intended by the parties to be attributed either to both M and W or to M alone. Thirdly, the statement forms the basis on which the parties contract. Fourthly, M seeks to deny that statement of fact in an action on the deed by any party to it. Fifthly, no defence to the estoppel can be raised, in particular, the deed is neither void, voidable nor rectifiable.

CATEGORIZING ESTOPPEL BY DEED

Under Coke's classification,[15] estoppel by deed formed the second limb of his threefold division of estoppel into estoppel by record, estoppel by writing[16] and estoppel in pais. There is a considerable overlap between estoppel by deed and estoppel by representation and convention. This has led some to aver that estoppel by deed no longer forms a useful or independent category.[17] **10.06**

Two different types of estoppel by deed

In *First National Bank v Thompson,*[18] the Court of Appeal held that it is not possible to subsume estoppel by deed into the category of estoppel by representation.[19] Their Lordships identified two distinct doctrines, both of which have been referred to as estoppel by deed. The first type they described as technical estoppel and characterized as an instance of estoppel by representation. It can only operate on express and positive **10.07**

---

14 Those named as parties to a deed and those executing it need not necessarily be the same people. Our formulation of the first element of the doctrine reflects two principles. First, a party is only bound by an estoppel by deed arising from an instrument which it has executed: see para. 10.54 below. Secondly, an estoppel may only arise in an action on the deed. Only someone named as a party to the deed may maintain an action on it (apart from certain limited exceptions). Hence, W must be a party to the deed: see paras 10.36 and 10.53 below.

15 Coke, *A Commentary on Littleton* (11th ed., London, 1719) at para. 352a.

16 Para. 325b. *ibid* shows that Coke, in using the term 'estoppel by writing', meant to signify the doctrine (or doctrines) now generally referred to as estoppel by deed.

17 Chitty at para. 1–037 (*'there seems little point in preserving any separate category of estoppel by deed since the basis of the estoppel appears now to be covered by estoppel by representation or by convention'*), Spencer Bower at paras 171–3 (estoppel by deed is merely an example of estoppel by convention). Some support for Spencer Bower's approach is to be found in *Taylors Fashions Ltd v Liverpool Victoria Trustees Co. Ltd* [1982] 1 QB 133 *per* Oliver J. at 159.

18 [1996] All ER 144, CA.

19 *First National Bank v Thompson* [1996] All ER 144 CA *per* Millet L.J. at 144h–5d.

statements contained in a deed. The second is an older and more broadly based doctrine, which operates where M has purported to transfer to W an estate or interest in property which M does not in fact own. It does not depend on any express statement or representation, but on the mere fact of defective grant. The relationship between the two types of estoppel is discussed at paragraph 10.63–75 below. The bulk of this chapter concerns the first type of estoppel identified by the Court of Appeal. In the following section and for the remainder of the chapter, unless otherwise indicated, references to estoppel by deed are meant to signify that technical estoppel doctrine.

The relationship of estoppel by deed and estoppels by representation and convention

Statements and representations

There seems to be no situation where this type of estoppel by deed will be raised which would not also give rise to an estoppel by representation. First, both depend on a statement of fact communicated by M to W. In estoppel by deed cases the statement is contained in a mutually agreed document. This is slightly different from the unilateral representation by M to W, which generally characterizes the estoppel by representation doctrine. Superficially, it has much more in common with the mutual assumption which triggers the operation of estoppel by convention.[20] However, in reality, neither estoppel by deed nor estoppel by representation will operate unless the statement is attributable to M. As far as estoppel by deed is concerned, such an attribution will frequently be effected almost automatically by the fact that M has executed the deed in which the statement was contained. However, this is not invariably the case. If it can be shown that the parties intended the statement to be attributable to a person other than M, no estoppel by deed will arise.[21] **10.08**

Estoppel by deed imposes much stricter construction requirements than either estoppel by representation or estoppel by convention. An estoppel by deed will not arise as a matter of inference from the words of the deed. **10.09**

---

[20] See paras 9.03–4.

[21] See paras 10.46–8 below.

Only a direct and positive statement will trigger the operation of the doctrine.[22] No such rule applies in respect of estoppel by representation or estoppel by convention.

Detrimental reliance

In order to establish estoppel by representation, it is necessary to show that W relied on the statement to its detriment. Little, if any, reference is made to such requirements in estoppel by deed cases. However, the scope of estoppel by deed is limited in two significant ways. First, it is restricted to actions on the deed.[23] Secondly, it will arise only where the statement forms the basis on which the parties entered the transaction.[24] Arguably, these limitations amount to a requirement of detrimental reliance, albeit that only of a narrow and specifically defined type, namely where W has entered into a contract in reliance on the statement made. This matter is discussed at paras 10.39–44 below. **10.10**

Effect on third parties

The only point at which there is, or should be, a clear difference between estoppel by representation and estoppel by deed concerns the effect of the doctrine on third parties. It is fairly certain that estoppel by deed may bind all those claiming through the parties even the bona fide purchaser for value without notice. As is set out at paragraphs 10.53–61 below, such an approach is justifiable[25] by reference to characteristics peculiar to estoppel by deed, specifically its inherent link with a solemn and formally executed document. This approach is indefensible as far as estoppel by representation is concerned.[26] **10.11**

Conclusion on categorization

We submit that estoppel by deed of the technical type described in the greater part of this chapter is capable of being explained as merely an instance of estoppel by representation. The doctrine has a much narrower **10.12**

---

[22] See paras 10.30 below.
[23] See para. 10.36 below.
[24] See para. 10.40 below.
[25] Albeit not exactly desirable.
[26] Although it is not wholly unsupported by authority — see *Hopgood v Brown* [1955] 1 WLR 213. On this issue, generally, see paras 8.126–143 and in particular 8.136–40.

scope, but, as regards the original parties,[27] there seems to be no situation where estoppel by deed will operate where either estoppel by convention or representation will not also apply.

Given this conclusion, it is debatable whether any exposition of estoppel by deed should go beyond the specific and distinct doctrine which depends on an imperfect grant rather than an express statement or representation.[28] We have included a separate discussion of both types of estoppel by deed for two reasons. First, even the technical estoppel by deed continues to be referred to as a distinct doctrine in the cases. Secondly, there is some difficulty in reconciling all aspects of technical estoppel by deed with either estoppel by representation or convention; in particular the effect on third parties. In particular, estoppel by deed binds third parties in circumstances where it would be unjustifiable to apply estoppel by representation. Until the rules relating to transmission are assimilated, there will be instances where estoppel by deed will operate in relation to third parties where estoppel by representation will not. 10.13

ELEMENTS OF ESTOPPEL BY DEED

A STATEMENT OF FACT CONTAINED IN A DEED

The deed must be valid

No estoppel by deed will arise if the deed has not been properly created by the execution of the relevant formalities.[29] However, statements contained in invalid deeds may give rise to an estoppel by convention or by representation. A party who makes use of a document, purporting on its face to be a deed, may thereby represent that the deed had been 10.14

---

[27] As opposed to their transferees as to which see the preceding paragraph.

[28] As to which see paras 10.63–75 below.

[29] *Re Balkis Consolidated Co Ltd* (1888) 58 LT 300 *per* North J. at 301. There must be some doubt as to whether this is good authority for the point since the case concerned estoppel by negligence which may not be part of the law of estoppel at all. Even assuming that it is a species of estoppel, it has traditionally been categorized as an example of estoppel by representation rather than estoppel by deed. The principle is sound, however, particularly in the light of those cases which make it clear that no estoppel will lie in respect of a deed which is void or voidable, for reasons other than lack of form. See paras 10.49–51 below.

validly executed. Hence, an estoppel by representation will arise to prevent the party relying on the defective execution.[30]

Creation of a deed

The following is a brief guide to deeds and their creation, aimed at giving some background information. A more detailed account lies beyond the scope of this work. Reference should be made to specialist texts on contract, deeds and conveyancing.[31] A deed must perform one of three functions. First, it may transfer an interest, a right or property. Secondly, it may create an obligation binding on a party or parties. Thirdly, it may confirm some act by which an interest, a right or property has passed. Thus, many documents under seal, such as share certificates, are not deeds.[32] **10.15**

Deeds created before 31 July 1990 must have been signed, sealed and delivered. Delivery could be actual or constructive. Deeds created on or after 31 July 1990 need not be sealed if they are created by an individual.[33] Instead, it is sufficient if the signature of the individual is attested and the document states on its face that it is intended to be a deed.[34] The delivery requirement is retained.[35] From the same date, companies may create deeds without sealing, so long as the requirements of section 36A of the Companies Act 1985[36] are complied with. Other legal persons, such as corporations sole,[37] must continue to use seals. The sealing requirement has been liberally interpreted.[38] **10.16**

Which types of deed may give rise to an estoppel?

Deeds have traditionally been divided into indentures and deeds poll. A deed poll may be made, either by a single party expressing its intention or, alternatively, by two or more parties all of whom express *the same* **10.17**

[30] See, for example, *TCB v Gray* [1986] Ch 62 discussed at para. 8.18 above.
[31] See, in particular, *Halsbury's Laws*, Vol. 12, 'Deeds and other instruments'.
[32] See Chitty at para. 1.026.
[33] Law of Property (Miscellaneous Provisions) Act 1989, s.1(1).
[34] *ibid.* s.1(2)–(3).
[35] *ibid.* s.1(3)(b).
[36] As added by s.130 of the Companies Act 1989.
[37] Law of Property (Miscellaneous Provisions) Act 1989, s.1(10).
[38] See, for example, *First National Securities v Jones* [1978] Ch 109.

single common intention.[39] There is some doubt as to whether such a deed can give rise to an estoppel. There are dicta[40] to suggest that it can. However, estoppel by deed only applies in actions on the deed.[41] The scope for such actions on a deed poll is very limited. Consequently, deeds poll will rarely give rise to estoppel by deed.[42] Indentures are deeds to which two or more persons are party and which evidence some act or agreement between them, other than the single common intention which gives rise to a deed poll.[43] Such deeds are clearly capable of giving rise to an estoppel.[44]

A statement of fact or mixed fact and law

This type of estoppel will operate only on a statement contained in a deed.[45] The statement must be one of fact[46] or of mixed fact and law.[47] The doctrine probably does not apply to promises or to statements of intention. The same restriction applies to estoppel by representation. As regards the latter doctrine, the restriction is necessary to hold the line between estoppel and contract. If estoppel by representation could **10.18**

---

[39] Halsbury's Laws, Vol. 12, 'Deeds and other instruments', para. 1303.

[40] *Right de Jefferys v Bucknell* (1831) 2 B&Ad 278, 109 ER 1146 *per* Lord Tenterden at 281–2, 1147–8.

[41] See below at para. 10.36.

[42] It should be noted, however, that estoppel by representation may operate on statements made to others, whether they are parties to a particular transaction or not. Thus statements contained in a deed poll could readily give rise to such an estoppel so long as they were directed towards and communicated to another who has relied on them to its detriment. See, for example, *TCB Ltd* v Gray [1986] Ch 621 and paras 8.18–10.60.

[43] Halsbury's Laws, Vol. 12, 'Deeds and other instruments', para. 1303.

[44] *Right de Jefferys v Bucknell* (1831) 2 B&Ad 278, 109 ER 1146 *per* Lord Tenterden at 281–2, 1147–8, *Greer v Kettle* [1938] AC 156 and *Taylors Fashions Ltd v Liverpool Victoria Trustees Co. Ltd* [1982] 1 QB 133.

[45] *Greer v Kettle* [1938] AC 156 *per* Russell of Killowen at 166–7 (app. *Young v Raincock* 7 CB 310 *per* Coltman J. at 338) and *Re Distributors and Warehousing Ltd* [1986] BCLC 129 *per* Walton J. at 139e (*obiter*).

[46] *Greer v Kettle* [1938] AC 156 *per* Russell of Killowen at 338 (app. *Young v Raincock* 7 CB 310 *per* Coltman J. at 338); *Re Distributors and Warehousing Ltd* [1986] BCLC 129 *per* Walton J. at 139e (*obiter*), *Onward Building Society v Smithson* [1893] 1 Ch 1 *per* A.L. Smith L.J. at 15; *Taylors Fashions Ltd v Liverpool Victoria Trustees Co. Ltd* [1982] 1 QB 133 *per* Oliver J. at 159c–d; *Right de Jefferys v Bucknell* (1831) 2 B&Ad 278, 109 ER 1146 *per* Lord Tenterden at 282, 1148; and *Salter v Kidley* (1688) 1 Show Rep. 58, 89 ER 447 *per* Holt C.J. at 59, 448.

[47] *Taylors Fashions Ltd v Liverpool Victoria Trustees Co. Ltd* [1982] 1 QB 133 — the relevant statement was that a neighbour had a valid option to renew its lease which involves questions both of fact and law.

operate on statements of future intention, this would allow promises to be enforced which are unsupported by consideration.[48] In the case of estoppel by deed, no such difficulty arises, given that the doctrine will only operate on statements contained in a deed. Promises contained in deeds are enforceable whether or not they are given for consideration.[49] Practical rather than doctrinal factors explain why estoppel by deed does not operate on promises: there is no need to resort to estoppel, since any promise contained in a deed will be enforceable in contract.

Estoppel by deed operates where the parties agreed that a certain statement of fact or facts would form the basis of the transaction which they **10.19**
were about to enter.[50] It may not even be necessary to show that the party seeking to raise the estoppel believed that those stated facts were actually true. It is probably sufficient if W believed that they would be *regarded as true for the purposes of the agreement* between the parties.[51] Nor must the statement necessarily have been untrue.[52] The rationale of the doctrine is that a party cannot deny the terms of the contract on which it is suing,[53] reducing it almost to a principle of construction.[54]

Where the deed contains a true but incomplete statement of the facts **10.20**
no estoppel will arise to prevent the parties adducing evidence of additional facts necessary to establish the true position.[55]

Examples

Statements which may give rise to an estoppel by deed are many and **10.21**
varied. They include the statement that certain goods had been delivered

48 See paras 8.27–33 above.

49 *Cannon v Hartley* [1949] Ch 213. The remedies available will be confined to common law damages. Equitable remedies such as an injunction or specific performance will not be available since equity does not recognize the formality of a deed as a substitute for consideration: *ibid.*

50 *Greer v Kettle* [1938] AC 156 *per* Russell of Killowen at 166–7 (app. *Young v Raincock* 7 CB 310 *per* Coltman J. at 338) and *Taylors Fashions Ltd v Liverpool Victoria Trustees Co. Ltd* [1982] 1 QB 133 *per* Oliver J. at 159c–d.

51 *Grundt v Great Boulder Pty Gold Mines* (1937) 59 CLR 641 at 676.

52 *Greer v Kettle* [1938] AC 156 *per* Lord Maugham at 169–70 and *Bowman v Taylor* (1834) 2 AD&E 279, 111 ER 108 *per* Lord Denman C.J. at 289–90, 112.

53 *Foster v Mentor Life Assurance Co* (1854) 3 El & Bl 48, 118 ER 1058 *per* Erle J. at 65,1066.

54 See the comments of Brett L.J. in *Simm v Anglo American Telegraph* (1879) 5 QBD 188, CA at 206.

55 *Re Maddy's Estate* [1901] 2 Ch 820 *per* Joyce J. at 820 and *Lovett v Lovett* [1898] 1 Ch 82 *per* Romer J. at 87–8.

to a party to the deed,[56] that W was the inventor of various improvements to industrial machinery,[57] that a particular price was paid for the purchase of property,[58] that a particular person was the owner of, or seised of, a legal estate in fee simple absolute in possession, free from encumbrances,[59] that a neighbouring tenant had a valid option to renew its lease,[60] that the deed was effective from specified date[61] and that a debt has been secured on specified property.[62]

Statements concerning the title of the party sought to be estopped

The most important practical application of estoppel by deed concerns the title of the party sought to be estopped. The doctrine may apply wherever M has purported to grant or transfer property by deed.[63] It may arise in relation to general conveyances of property but has been most frequently applied where M has mortgaged property.[64] It may be used to prevent M from subsequently asserting an ownership right or interest inconsistent with that previously granted.[65] Mortgagees and purchasers may derive significant advantages if a positive assertion of title is included in a conveyance or other deed. Such statements are necessary to give rise to the type of technical estoppel by deed under consideration in the greater part of this chapter. In the absence of such an express recital of title, mortgagees and purchasers may still derive benefits from **10.22**

---

56 *Wiles v Woodward* (1850) 1 Exch 557, 155 ER 244.

57 *Bowman v Taylor* (1834) 2 AD&E 279, 111 ER 108 *per* Patteson J. at 292 *per* Lord Denman C.J. at 289–90, 112 *per* Taunton J. at 291 and *per* Williams J. at 294, 114 (although see below at para. 10.30–5 as to whether it was proper to construe the deed as containing this statement).

58 *Davis v Stone* [1992] 2 EGLR 222 Lands Tribunal (Chair D.P. Flynn) at 223e–f.

59 *Doe de Gaisford v Stone* (1846) 3 CB 176, 136 ER 71; *Onward Building Society v Smithson* [1893] 1 Ch 1 *per* Lindley L.J. at 13–14 *per* Bowen L.J. at 14 and *per* A.L. Smith at 15 and *Bensley v Burdon* (1830) 8 LJOS Ch 85. See further paras 10.33–5 below on the principles applicable to construction of such statements.

60 *Taylors Fashions Ltd v Liverpool Victoria Trustees Co. Ltd.* [1982] 1 QB 133 *per* Oliver J. at 159.

61 See para. 10.27 below.

62 *Greer v Kettle* [1938] AC 156, although the estoppel claim failed for the reasons set out in para. 10.47 below.

63 *Poulton v Moore* [1915] 1 KB 400, CA (release of a right of way); *District Bank Ltd v Webb* [1958] 1 WLR 148 (conveyance of real property) and *Williams v Pinckney* (1897) 67 LT 34 (conveyance of property to a settlement).

64 Or, more frequently, M's successors in title.

65 *General Finance, Mortgage, and Discount Company v Liberator Permanent Benefit Building Society* (1878) 10 ChD 15.

the wider species of estoppel by deed discussed at paragraphs 10.63–76 below. As we there set out, however, the benefits are not as extensive as those which accrue in express assertion cases.

Which parts of a deed may give rise to an estoppel?

Deeds are conventionally divided into various sections, all of which may give rise to an estoppel by deed. **10.23**

Recitals

Recitals follow the introduction to the deed and usually begin with the word '*WHEREAS*'. They are generally used to explain or narrate the factual background and purposes of the deed. Statements contained in recitals may give rise to an estoppel.[66] Recitals are the most common foundation for estoppel by deed.[67] **10.24**

Operative words

The operative part of the deed follows the recitals and is usually introduced with the words '*NOW THIS DEED WITNESSETH AS FOLLOWS*'. This section of the deed contains the provisions accomplishing the purpose of the instrument, such as the promises which go to make-up the relevant contract or transaction. In *Taylors Fashions Ltd v Liverpool Victoria Trustees Co. Ltd,*[68] Mr Justice Oliver held, *obiter*, that the operative part could give rise to an estoppel, so long as it was sufficiently clear and precise. A tenant's option to renew was expressed to operate only in the event of the tenants of a neighbouring property 'exercising their option to renew'.[69] This was held to amount **10.25**

---

[66] *Bowman v Taylor* (1834) 2 AD&E 279, 111 ER 108 *per* Lord Denman C.J. at 289–90, 112, *per* Taunton J. at 291 and *per* Williams J. at 294, 114 (departing from a statement in Coke, *A Commentary on Littleton* (11th ed., London 1719) at 352b); *Re Distributors and Warehousing Ltd* [1986] BCLC 129 *per* Walton J. at 139c–g (*obiter*) and *Poulton v Moore* [1915] 1 KB 400, CA *per* Buckley L.J. at 412–3 and *per* Phillimore L.J. at 415.

[67] *Taylors Fashions Ltd v Liverpool Victoria Trustees Co. Ltd* [1982] 1 QB 133 *per* Oliver J. at 159d–e.

[68] *ibid. per* Oliver J. at 159d–e.

[69] See para. 11.19 below for an account of the facts of the case.

to a statement that the neighbouring tenant had a valid option. They could not exercise it if they did not have it.

10.26 Court of Appeal *dicta* suggest that the operative part cannot give rise to an estoppel.[70] The better view is that the operative part may give rise to an estoppel although it will seldom do so because of the restrictive approach taken to construction.[71] In particular, it should be noted that a promise by M to convey or transfer property does *not* amount to a statement that M is the owner of that property.[72]

Other parts of the deed

10.27 The remaining parts of the deed are the introduction and the testimonium. The introduction states what type of deed is being created (a lease, mortgage, conveyance, etc.), the date and the parties. The testimonium is premised by the words '*IN WITNESS* whereof' and links the signatures[73] to the remainder of the document. It is theoretically possible for an estoppel to arise as a result of these parts of the deed, although such cases will be rare, given the limited scope of their contents.[74] However, an estoppel may arise as a result of the date specified in the deed. The language of the deed generally speaks from the date of delivery and not from the date of execution[75] but a party may be estopped from denying that a date later than that of delivery is to govern. In *Rudd v Bowles*,[76] various leases were executed with incomplete dates. The parties subsequently agreed to insert dates later than those of actual execution and delivery. The parties were estopped from denying that the inserted ones were the relevant governing dates. Hence, the court was able to construe the deed according the circumstances existing at the later dates.

---

70 *General Finance, Mortgage, and Discount Company v Liberator Permanent Benefit Building Society* (1878) 10 ChD 15 *per* Jessel M.R. at 24 and *First National Bank v Thompson* [1996] All ER 144, CA *per* Staughton L.J. at 151b–c.

71 As to which see below at para. 10.30.

72 See further para. 10.33 below.

73 For deeds executed before 31 July 1990, it also links the seal to the remainder of the document. See para. 10.16 above for the formalities required for the creation of deeds.

74 Further, some doubt as to whether the testimonium formed part of deed was expressed in *Pearse v Morrice* (1834) 2 AD&E 84, 111 ER 32 *per* Lord Denman C.J. at 94, 36, Taunton J. at 95, 37, Patteson J. at 95, 38. If it is not part of the deed, it cannot give rise to an estoppel by deed.

75 *Taylor v McCalmont* (1855) 4 WR 59 *per* Pollock C.B. at 59 (*ratio*).

76 [1912] 2 Ch 60 *per* Neville J. at 65.

The statement must be clear and unequivocal

No statement may give rise to estoppel by deed unless it is clear and unequivocal.[77] This requirement of clarity has been variously expressed in the authorities. It has been held that the statement must be certain to every intent,[78] distinct, precise and unambiguous.[79] We submit that the statement will be construed objectively, according the principles laid down in *Low v Bouverie*[80] and refined in *Woodhouse AC Israel Cocoa Ltd v Nigerian Produce Marketing Co Ltd.*[81] Hence, it is sufficient if any reasonable person would have interpreted the statement in the way contended, even if M did not itself subjectively form that understanding. This approach is applied in estoppel by representation cases and is discussed at paragraphs 8.39 and 8.40 above. This issue does not appear to have been directly considered in the context of estoppel by deed. We submit that in this respect,[82] the doctrines are the same.[83] **10.28**

No estoppel will arise where the truth appears in the instrument which contained the statement relied on.[84] Nor will an estoppel arise where **10.29**

[77] *Low v Bouverie* [1891] 3 Ch. 82, CA *per* Kay L.J. at 113. His Lordship's comments on estoppel by deed were technically *obiter*, since the case concerned estoppel by representation.

[78] *Right de Jefferys v Bucknell* (1831) 2 B&Ad 278, 109 ER 1146 *per* Lord Tenterden at 281–2, 1147–8.

[79] *Re Distributors and Warehousing Ltd* [1986] BCLC 129 *per* Walton J. at 139e (certain, precise and unambiguous); *District Bank Ltd v Webb* [1958] 1 WLR 148 *per* Dankwerts J. at 149–50 (same); *Williams v Pinckney* (1897) 67 LT 34 *per* Chitty, Lindley and Vaughan Williams L.JJ. at 40 (distinct and precise); *General Finance, Mortgage, and Discount Company v Liberator Permanent Benefit Building Society* (1878) 10 ChD 15 *per* Jessel M.R. at 23 (precise, clear and unambiguous); *Poulton v Moore* [1915] 1 KB 400, CA *per* Buckley L.J. at 412 (precise and unambiguous); *Poulton v Moore* [1915] 1 KB 400, CA *per* Phillimore L.J. at 415 (unambiguous); *Onward Building Society v Smithson* [1893] 1 Ch 1 *per* Bowen L.J. at 14 (clear and precise) and *Taylors Fashions Ltd v Liverpool Victoria Trustees Co. Ltd* [1982] 1 QB 133 *per* Oliver J. at 159d (clear and distinct language necessary).

[80] [1891] 3 Ch 82, CA.

[81] [1972] AC 741.

[82] As we set out below, the doctrines differ as regards inferences from the express statements contained in the deed.

[83] See *Low v Bouverie* [1891] 3 Ch 82, CA *per* Kay L.J. at 113.

[84] *Right de Jefferys v Bucknell* (1831) 2 B&Ad 278, 109 ER 1146 *per* Lord Tenterden at 281, 1147; *Saunders v Merryweather* (1865) 3 H&C 902, 159 ER 790 *per* Martin B. at 908, 792 and *per* Channell B. at 909, 793. By contrast, the broader based doctrine of estoppel by deed which is based on a defective grant rather than a representation is not barred by such conflicting statements. See below at para. 10.68.

the truth is contained in an earlier deed which is recited in the instrument relied on.[85]

Inferences and implied statements will not give rise to an estoppel

A general statement is insufficient to raise an estoppel; a statement of a specific fact is required.[86] Further, in *Onward Building Society v Smithson*,[87] it was held that no estoppel could arise where the state of facts relied on was a matter of mere inference from the words of the deed.[88] Hence, it is said that nothing is to be taken by way of intendment[89] and that there is no such thing as an estoppel by something implied.[90] The parties will be estopped from denying only facts directly and positively asserted in the deed.[91] **10.30**

A more flexible approach was adopted in *Taylors Fashions Ltd v Liverpool Victoria Trustees Co. Ltd.*[92] A tenant's option to renew was expressed to operate only in the event of the tenants of a neighbouring property 'exercising their option to renew'.[93] Mr Justice Oliver held, obiter, that this was a statement that the neighbouring tenant *had such an option* and that it was legally valid. He distinguished *Smithson* on **10.31**

---

85 *Saunders v Merryweather* (1865) 3 H&C 902, 159 ER 790 *per* Martin B. at 908, 792 and *per* Channell B. at 909, 793 and *Gillet v Abbott* (1838) Ad&El 783, 112 ER 665.

86 *Right de Jefferys v Bucknell* (1831) 2 B&Ad 278, 109 ER 1146 *per* Lord Tenterden at 282, 1148; *Doddington's Case, Hall d Doddington v Peart* (1594) 2 Co Rep. 32b, 76 ER 684 *per* Popham C.J. and Clench J., Gawdy J. and Fenner J. at 34a, 488; *Salter v Kidley* (1688) 1 Show Rep. 58, 89 ER 447 *per* Holt C.J. at 59, 448 and *Re Distributors and Warehousing Ltd* [1986] BCLC 129 *per* Walton J. at 139f (*obiter*).

87 [1893] 1 Ch 1.

88 [1893] 1 Ch 1 *per* Lindley L.J. at 13–14, *per* Bowen L.J. at 14 and *per* A.L. Smith at 15; *Right de Jefferys v Bucknell* (1831) 2 B&Ad 278, 109 ER 1146 *per* Lord Tenterden at 281, 1147 and *Re Distributors and Warehousing Ltd* [1986] BCLC 129 *per* Walton J. at 139e–f.

89 *Bowman v Taylor* (1834) 2 AD&E 279, 111 ER 108 *per* Patteson J at 292, 113 and *Re Distributors and Warehousing Ltd* [1986] BCLC 129 *per* Walton J. at 139e–f.

90 *Re Distributors and Warehousing Ltd* [1986] BCLC 129 *per* Walton J. at 139e–f.

91 *Harris v Hooper* (1847) 10 LTOS 137 and *Onward Building Society v Smithson* [1893] 1 Ch 1 *per* Lindley L.J. at 13–14, *per* Bowen L.J. at 14 and *per* A.L. Smith at 15.

92 [1982] 1 QB 133. See also *Bowman v Taylor* (1834) 2 AD&E 279, 111 ER 108 *per* Patteson J. at 292, *per* Lord Denman C.J. at 289–290, 112, *per* Taunton J. at 291 and *per* Williams J at 294, 114. A recital in licensing agreement under seal, stated that P had invented a power loom which he licensed D to exploit in exchange for payment of certain fees. D was estopped from denying that the loom was a new invention.

93 See para. 11.19 below for an account of the facts of the case.

the grounds that it was not simply a matter of inference that the neighbour's option was valid, it was a matter of *necessary* inference. Unless the neighbour had such an option, the relevant clause could be given no sensible operation at all.[94] However, the strict approach was reaffirmed by Mr Justice Walton in *Re Distributors and Warehousing Ltd.*[95] M had guaranteed to liability of Y under a lease. The reversion was assigned to W but not the guarantee. Subsequently, Y and W agreed new lease terms and both M and Y executed deeds of variation to reflect them. His Lordship held that it was a clear inference from the wording of the deed of variation that W had the benefit of the guarantee. If it did not, the terms were meaningless as they related to an unenforceable obligation. Despite this, his Lordship applied *Smithson* and rejected the plea of estoppel.

There is a conflict between *Taylors* and *Re Distributors*:[96] in both cases, the clause in issue could be given no sensible operation without drawing the inference relied on by the claimant. The flexible *Taylors* approach would bring estoppel by deed more into line with estoppel by representation. It is clear that mere inferences may give rise to an estoppel by representation.[97] Hence, the case is consistent with those authorities which suggest that this type of estoppel by deed is an example of estoppel by representation.[98] In our view, the stricter approach of *Smithson* and *Re Distributors* remains good law. However, if this type of estoppel is to be subsumed within the wider category of estoppel by representation, the principle will have to be modified accordingly. **10.32**

An important application of the *Smithson* principle concerns cases where W seeks to prevent M from denying a statement that M is the owner of particular property. This type of case is discussed further below.[99] Because of the strict approach laid down in *Smithson*,[1] considerable care needs to be taken in drafting such express statements **10.33**

---

94 [1982] 1 QB 133 at 159d–f.

95 [1986] BCLC 129.

96 *Taylors* and *Smithson* might reasonably be reconciled by restricting the latter case to the representations as to title. They formed the subject matter of the case and there are clear reasons why such statements should be narrowly construed: they create a clog on the title to property which may be a hazard to subsequent purchasers. See paras 10.53–62 below for the effect of estoppel by deed on purchasers. We have rejected this approach, however, because it does not explain the application of the strict test in *Re Distributors* which was not a title case.

97 See, for example, paras 8.52–70 on statement inferred from conduct or silence.

98 *First National Bank v Thompson* [1996] All ER 144, CA *per* Millet L.J. at 145a–b and *per* Staughton L.J. at 151a–c. Their Lordships made no comment on this specific point.

99 At paras 10.66–8.

1 [1893] 1 Ch 1, discussed in the preceding para.

of title. The more useful type of technical estoppel by deed[2] will arise to prevent M's denying ownership of property only where there is a direct and positive statement of M's title,[3] for example a statement that M is the owner, or seised, of, a legal estate in fee simple absolute in possession, free from encumbrances.[4] A covenant or promise that M has a particular thing does not amount to a positive statement that M has that thing.[5] It merely represents an agreement that M shall be treated as having the property and shall be liable for damages if this proves to be untrue.[6] The ordinary operative words of a conveyance, namely the promise to transfer property, do not therefore give rise to an estoppel.[7] Further, the statement that M has power to convey the property, does not amount to a positive statement that M is the legal owner of it. There are a number of circumstances in which a party might have power to convey without being the legal owner of property.[8] Hence, the usual implied covenants of title are not sufficient to raise an estoppel.[9]

A statement that M is entitled to the legal *or* the equitable title is insufficient to raise this type of estoppel.[10] It is necessary to specify the legal estate or interest held, hence a statement that M was '*well and sufficiently entitled to the property, . . . free from encumbrances*' will not raise an estoppel.[11] However, in *Poulton v Moore*[12] the majority[13] held that the statement that M was entitled to a right of way was **10.34**

[2] Of the sort under consideration in the bulk of this chapter, namely that identified with estoppel by representation in *First National Bank v Thompson* [1996] All ER 144, CA as opposed to the wider doctrine depending purely on a grant discussed at paras 10.63–5 below.

[3] *Onward Building Society v Smithson* [1893] 1 Ch 1 *per* Lindley L.J. at 13–4, *per* Bowen L.J. at 14 and *per* A.L. Smith at 15. See, for example, *Doe de Gaisford v Stone* (1846) 3 CB 176, 136 ER 71 and *Bensley v Burdon* (1830) 8 LJOS Ch 85.

[4] See generally *Emmet On Title,* 19th ed. loose leaf (Release 34), JT Farrand, Pearson, London, 1997 para. 14.006.

[5] *General Finance, Mortgage, and Discount Company v Liberator Permanent Benefit Building Society* (1878) 10 ChD 15 *per* Lord Jessel M.R. at 24 and *Re Distributors and Warehousing Ltd* [1986] BCLC 129 *per* Walton J. at 139e–f.

[6] *General Finance, Mortgage, and Discount Company v Liberator Permanent Benefit Building Society* (1878) 10 ChD 15 *per* Lord Jessel M.R. at 24.

[7] *Re Distributors and Warehousing Ltd* [1986] BCLC 129 *per* Walton J. at 139e–f.

[8] *General Finance, Mortgage, and Discount Company v Liberator Permanent Benefit Building Society* (1878) 10 ChD 15 *per* Lord Jessel M.R. at 23.

[9] *Onward Building Society v Smithson* [1893] 1 Ch 1 *per* Lindley L.J. at 13.

[10] *Right de Jefferys v Bucknell* (1831) 2 B&Ad 278, 109 ER 1146 *per* Lord Tenterden at 281–2, 1147–8; *General Finance, Mortgage, and Discount Company v Liberator Permanent Benefit Building Society* (1878) 10 ChD 15 *per* Jessel M.R. at 21–2.

[11] *General Finance, Mortgage, and Discount Company v Liberator Permanent Benefit Building Society* (1878) 10 ChD 15 *per* Jessel M.R. at 21–22.

[12] [1915] 1 KB 400, CA.

[13] *ibid. per* Buckley L.J. at 412–3 and *per* Phillimore L.J. at 415.

sufficient to raise an estoppel to prevent M's denying that she was the owner. Given the failure to specify the type of estate or interest to which M was entitled, this decision is questionable.[14] In *Williams v Pinckney*,[15] in a conveyance to W, M and C stated that they 'hereby convey' their respective interests together with 'all right, title, claim and demand whatsoever', subject to certain specified encumbrances. No estoppel was raised to prevent M's claiming the benefit of a mortgage granted by C over his share of the property conveyed. The deed had not stated that the listed encumbrances were the only existing ones.[16]

According to *District Bank Ltd v Webb*,[17] a statement that A and B were seised of an unencumbered fee simple absolute in possession did not amount to a representation that the premises were free from tenancies. Mr Justice Dankwerts held that no estoppel arose to prevent B's asserting that she had been granted a tenancy of the property by A and B. The judge held that the term encumbrance was the one generally being used to describe mortgages. The words 'in possession' were used to distinguish the fee simple from one in reversion and were not meant to signify 'vacant possession'. It is at least doubtful whether the same conclusion would be reached in a modern case, given the modern usage of the term encumbrance. Vendors or mortgagors should be cautioned before agreeing to such clauses. **10.35**

ESTOPPEL BY DEED ONLY OPERATES IN ACTIONS ON THE DEED AND DOES NOT COVER COLLATERAL ISSUES BETWEEN THE PARTIES

Estoppel by deed may only be used in actions on the deed in which the statement relied on was contained. It does not apply to separate or collateral actions between the parties to the deed.[18] In such cases, the deed may be relied on as evidence of the facts asserted in it, but there is nothing to stop the parties adducing contradictory evidence. For **10.36**

---

[14] See also the dissent of Pickford L.J.: [1915] 1 KB 400, CA at 416.
[15] (1897) 67 LT 34.
[16] *Williams v Pinckney* (1897) 67 LT 34.
[17] [1958] 1 WLR 148 *per* Dankwerts J. at 149–50.
[18] *Carpenter v Buller* (1841) 8 M&W 209, 212, 151 ER 1013 *per* Parke B. at 212–3, 1014–5; *South Eastern Rly Co v Warton* (1861) 6 H&N 520, 158 ER 214 *per* Martin B. at 527, 217.

example, in *Carpenter v Buller*,[19] the plaintiff and defendant executed a deed pursuant to various building works which they were carrying out. The deed recited that the defendant was the owner of a specified plot of land. The plaintiff later sued the defendant for trespass over the land specified. No estoppel arose to prevent the plaintiff from asserting his own title to the land. The action in trespass was wholly collateral to the deed and was not an action founded upon it.[20]

The line between actions on the deed and collateral actions is not always easy to draw. For example, in *Wiles v Woodward*[21], the plaintiff and the defendant entered into a deed dissolving a partnership. The deed recited that paper to the value of £898 4s 11d had been delivered to the plaintiff. By the deed, the plaintiff assigned the stock in trade of the partnership paper manufacturing business to the defendant, apart from the aforementioned paper. The plaintiff later sued the defendant for failure to deliver the paper. The claim was not collateral to the deed and the parties were estopped from denying that the paper had been delivered. **10.37**

This restriction is an important limitation on the operation of estoppel by deed. Generally, only those named as parties to the deed may sue on it.[22] Hence, benefit of estoppel by deed enures only to those named parties. **10.38**

DETRIMENTAL RELIANCE

A common factor which appears to link most forms of estoppel is detrimental reliance. This requirement may be broken down into two parts. First, W has changed its position, in reliance on the statement or representation in issue. Secondly, that change of position will lead W to suffer detriment if the truth of the statement or representation is subsequently denied. References to reliance and detriment are noticeably lacking in estoppel by deed cases.[23] However, the rationale of the **10.39**

---

[19] (1841) 8 M&W 209, 212, 151 ER 1013.

[20] (1841) 8 M&W 209, 212, 151 ER 1013 *per* Parke B. at 213, 1014.

[21] (1850) 1 Exch 557, 155 ER 244.

[22] *Chesterfield and Midland Silkstone Colliery Co Ltd v Hawkins* (1865) 3 H&C 677 at 692.The general rule admits of two limited exceptions. First, a non party may sue where the provisions of the deed constitute that party the beneficiary of a trust of the benefit of the covenant: *Gandy v Gandy* (1885) 30 ChD 57. Secondly, a non party may sue where s.56 (1) of the Law of Property Act 1925 applies.

[23] But see *Foster v Mentor Life Assurance Co* (1854) 3 El & Bl 48, 118 ER 1058 *per* Lord Campbell C.J. at 79 referring to one of the parties having acted to its prejudice. See also *Re King's Settlement* [1931] 2 Ch 294 where Farwell J. held that estoppel can only operate in favour of those who have acted on faith of the representation, although *quaere* whether this was an estoppel by deed case at all. See further at para. 10.60–1 below.

doctrine seems to be that the statements set out in the deed form the mutually agreed basis of the transaction entered into by the parties. For the following reasons, we submit that the requirements of reliance and detriment are effectively built into the existing and uncontroversial elements of the doctrine.[24]

Reliance and knowledge

The operation of the estoppel is confined to actions on the deed.[25] Only those who are named as parties to the deed may maintain an action on it.[26] An estoppel will therefore arise only in favour of those who are parties to an agreement containing the relevant statement.[27] This principle limits the scope of estoppel by deed but only to a limited extent, it is possible to be named as a party to an deed without executing it.[28] Thus an individual may become a party to the deed without being aware of even the existence of the deed, let alone the statements it contains. However, such parties probably would not be able to raise an estoppel by deed. The doctrine does not operate in such an inflexible manner: in *Greer v Kettle* it was emphasized that only statements which form the basis on which the parties contract will give rise to an estoppel by deed. Thus, it is necessary to demonstrate a causative link between entering the contract and the statement relied on to raise the estoppel. Where W has executed the deed, reliance can effectively be presumed: it is only to be expected that the parties will have relied on the contents of the agreement in deciding whether to enter into it or not. Hence, in such cases, the requirement of reliance or change of position is satisfied. 10.40

A further factor common to other estoppel doctrines is that M should have knowledge that W is acting in reliance on the statement in issue.[29] 10.41

[24] Detrimental reliance is clearly essential to establishing an estoppel by representation (see paras 8–79–107). Our analysis in this section is therefore consistent with those suggestions that the species of estoppel by deed under consideration is part of the law of estoppel by representation, as to which see, for example, *First National Bank v Thompson* [1996] All ER 144, CA *per* Millet L.J. at 145a–b and *per* Staughton L.J. at 151a–b. See further, para. 10.10–3 above for the relationship of estoppel by deed and estoppel by representation.

[25] Or those claiming in right of those parties. See, generally, paras 10.36 and 10.55–9.

[26] As to which see below at para. 10.53.

[27] See above at para. 10.36 (estoppel by deed may only be relied on in actions on the deed in question).

[28] *Webb v Spicer* (1849) 13 QB 886, 116 ER 1502 and 1505.

[29] See, for example, the principles applicable to estoppel by representation set out at paras 8.72–7.

This requirement is also satisfied on the above analysis of change of position: the required change of position includes being named as a party to the deed, in executing the deed M will invariably obtain knowledge of which other parties are named in it.

Detriment

Further problems arise in applying the second stage of the test set out above, namely the detriment requirement. Under the orthodox analysis, it would be insufficient for W to show that it entered the contract in reliance on the truth of the statements it contained. It is necessary to go further and demonstrate that the benefits received under the contract are reduced as a result of the denial of the truth of the representation. If the contract provided a good bargain in any event, no detriment will have been suffered as a result of the change of position: W will have got what it paid for.[30] The problem is compounded by the fact that parties to the deed need give no consideration for the benefits received under it. The deed may confer purely gratuitous benefits on W without imposing any obligations. It is difficult to characterize W being named as a party to such a deed as detrimental. **10.42**

There are three possible ways to explain this anomaly. First, the cases have invariably involved instances where the benefits under the deed have been diminished as a result of the denial of the correctness of the statement. This is a realistic supposition, given the close connection between the statement and the contract entered. By contrast, there may be a much more tenuous link between the contract and the statement or representations capable of triggering other more flexible types of estoppel. This issue has simply never arisen for consideration. If it did the court might well reject the plea of estoppel where the benefits conferred by the deed are not diminished by the denial of the statement it contains. Secondly, there is authority to suggest that, for the purposes of estoppel by representation, the mere undertaking of a legal obligation is sufficient to amount to deemed detriment.[31] Although the validity of this proposition is doubtful, this would explain most estoppel by deed cases. Thirdly, the analysis used in **10.43**

---

[30] See the proprietary estoppel case of *Christian v Christian* (1981) NLJ 43 and para. 11.41 below.

[31] See paras 8.106–7 above and, in particular, *Keith v R Gancia and Co Ltd* [1904] Ch 774, CA.

estoppel by convention could be applied whereby the mutual dealings inherent in entering a contract and acting under it almost necessarily carry with them a finding that detriment has been suffered.[32] We prefer the first explanation.

Unconscionability or inequity

10.44 Broad principles of inequity or unconscionability have played a significant role in related doctrines such as proprietary estoppel or equitable forbearance.[33] Such concepts seemingly play no part in the law of estoppel by deed. However, in our view, it is possible to analyse the requirements of estoppel by deed as involving detrimental reliance.[34] Arguably, to allow M to resile from the statement, after W has relied on it to its detriment, would, in itself, be inequitable. Hence, estoppel by deed could be said to require inequity in this indirect sense. As far as equitable forbearance and proprietary estoppel are concerned, the concept of inequity has been used to allow the court take into account a number of random factors, other than detrimental reliance, in assessing liability between the parties. There is no authority to suggest that such an approach is applicable in estoppel by deed cases.

RELIEF

10.45 If the component elements of estoppel by deed are made out, M will be estopped from denying the truth of the statement.[35] The legal relationship between the parties and the outcome of the case will then be determined according to the facts contained in the statement.[36] There is

[32] See para. 9.04 above.

[33] For the reasons set out at paras 12.05–7, we have chosen to use this term to signify the doctrine more commonly referred to as promissory estoppel.

[34] See paras 10.40–3 above.

[35] *Greer v Kettle* [1938] AC 156 *per* Lord Maugham at 171 (*orbiter*), *Re Distributors and Warehousing Ltd* [1986] BCLC 129 *per* Walton J. at 139c-d (*obiter*); *Williams v Pinckney* (1897) 67 LJ Ch 34 and *Onward Building Society v Smithson* [1893] 1 Ch 1 *per* Lindley L.J. at 14.

[36] *cf.* estoppel by representation — see para. 8.16.

no authority to suggest that any other remedy is possible.[37] This inflexible approach results from the evidential nature of the doctrine.[38] Its result is to prevent the party estopped from adducing evidence to contradict the statement in issue. This admits of only one remedial outcome. Either the statement is true or it is not. There is no intermediate position.

DEFENCES

THE STATEMENT WAS NOT INTENDED BY THE PARTIES TO BE ATTRIBUTABLE TO THE PARTY IT IS SOUGHT TO ESTOP

Not all statements in deeds are intended by the parties to be attributable to all those executing the document. If the parties intended the statement to be that of one particular party,[39] the estoppel may be raised only against that party.[40] The other party executing the deed will not be bound by it[41] and may adduce evidence to contradict it. Whether the statement is intended to be that of a specific party, is a question of construction of the deed[42] as a whole. It will depend partly on whether the relevant matter was particularly within the knowledge of a single party. **10.46**

For example, in *Greer v Kettle,*[43] in a contract under seal, Z agreed to guarantee a debt owed by A to Y which was secured on shares issued by X Ltd. Unknown to either party, the X shares had not been correctly issued. No liability could arise on ordinary contract principles: Z had agreed to guarantee a debt which did not exist, namely one owed by A to Y which was secured in the manner required by the guarantee. However, the deed recited that A did owe Y a debt secured on the X **10.47**

[37] Although there is some doubt on the matter, it seems that the same approach applies in estoppel by representation; see paras 8.108–19 above. The problems which may be caused by such an inflexible approach are discussed at para. 8.108 above.

[38] As to which see the cases cited at n. 1 at para. 10.01 above and compare the same rule applied in estoppel by representation cases; paras 8.108–19.

[39] Or parties.

[40] Or those parties.

[41] *Greer v Kettle* [1938] AC 156 *per* Russell of Killowen at 167 and *per* Maugham at 170 (*ratio*) and *Stroughill v Buck* (1850) 14 QB 781, 117 ER 301.

[42] *Greer v Kettle* [1938] AC 156 *per* Russell of Killowen at 167.

[43] [1938] AC 156.

shares. Y argued that Z was estopped from denying the truth of the recital and hence was contractually liable under the facts as stated in the deed. The House of Lords held that the relevant recital was intended by the parties to be that of Y alone. The recital concerned matters which could be expected to be within the knowledge of Y rather than Z. Z had certainly requested that the security be taken but was not present when the transaction supposedly took place.

In analytical terms, this principle negatives the whole existence of estoppel so it may not be strictly correct to include it in a section concerning defences. **10.48**

THE DEED IS VOID, VOIDABLE OR RECTIFIABLE

No estoppel will arise as a result of statements contained in a deed which is void.[44] No estoppel can result from a void deed because there is no deed to estop the parties.[45] The parties are free to adduce evidence to establish vitiating factors such as *non est factum*[46] or failure to comply with registration requirements.[47] Nor will an estoppel arise where the deed is voidable, for example where procured through fraud or misrepresentation, nor where there is a right to rescind the deed in equity.[48] **10.49**

No estoppel will arise if the deed itself is valid and enforceable but the court is prepared to rectify the part which contains the statement in issue.[49] Hence, the parties will not be bound by statements in a deed which were included as a result of a common mistake sufficient to merit rectification.[50] Instead of going through the two stage process of rectifying and thus preventing the estoppel from arising, the court may be prepared to short circuit this process and give direct relief by declaring that the parties are not bound by the relevant statement.[51] **10.50**

---

44 *Saunders v Anglia Building Society* [1971] AC 1004; *Mitchel v Renolds* (1711) 1 P Wms 181, 24 ER 347 *per* Parker C.J. and *Norfolk's Case* (1667) Hard 464, 145 ER 549.

45 *Saunders v Anglia Building Society* [1971] AC 1004 *per* Lord Hodson at 1019d–h.

46 *Saunders v Anglia Building Society* [1971] AC 1004.

47 *Doe d Preece v Howells* (1831) 2 B & Add 744, 109 ER 1320 *per* Lord Tenterden C.J. at 750, 1323.

48 *Greer v Kettle* [1938] AC 156 *per* Maugham at 171 (*obiter*). See also *Norwich and Peterborough Building Society v Steed* [1993] 1 All ER 330, CA *per* Scott L.J. at 340b–d (no estoppel where deed procured by fraud).

49 *Greer v Kettle* [1938] AC 156 *per* Maugham at 171 (*obiter*).

50 *Re Distributors and Warehousing Ltd* [1986] BCLC 129 *per* Walton J. at 139d–e (*obiter*).

51 *Wilson v Wilson* [1969] 1 WLR 1470 *per* Buckley J. at 1417b–d, appl. in *Pink v Lawrence* (1978) 36 P&CR 98, CA *per* Buckley L.J. at 101.

It is beyond the scope of this work to set out the circumstances in which deeds will be void, voidable or rectifiable. Specialist works on contract should be consulted on these issues. **10.51**

The Estoppel Would Contravene or Undermine a Statute

No estoppel by deed will arise if its effect would be to undermine the operation of a statute.[52] The relevant principles are the same as those applicable to estoppel by representation. These are set out at paragraphs 8.121 to 8.125 to which reference should be made for a detailed consideration of the relevant issues. **10.52**

Parties Affected by Estoppel by Deed

The Original Parties

The benefit

Estoppel by deed operates only in actions on the deed and not in other disputes between the parties.[53] Generally, only those named as parties to the deed may sue on it.[54] Hence, benefit of estoppel by deed enures only to those named parties. Strangers to the deed cannot use the statements it contains to raise estoppel by deed.[55] **10.53**

---

[52] *Maritime Electric Co Ltd v General Dairies Ltd* [1937] AC 610, PC (Canada) *per* Lord Maugham at 623 and *Doe d Chandler v Ford.* (1835) 3 A & E 649.

[53] See above at para. 10.36.

[54] *Woodard v Battersea BC* [1911] 51 LT 51; *Chesterfield and Midland Silkstone Colliery Co Ltd v Hawkins* (1865) 3 H&C 677 at 692.The general rule admits of two limited exceptions. First, a non party may sue where the provisions of the deed constitute that party the beneficiary of a trust of the benefit of the covenant — *Gandy v Gandy* (1885) 30 ChD 57. Secondly, a non party may sue where s.56 (1) of the Law of Property Act 1925 applies.

[55] Coke, *A Commentary on Littleton* (11th ed., London 1719) at p. 352a; *Doe de Marchant v Errington* (1839) 6 Bing (NC) 79, 133 ER 31 *per* Tindal C.J. at 83, 33 and *Gaunt v Wainman* (1836) 3 Bing (NC) 69, 132 ER 335 *per* Tindal C.J.

The burden

10.54 Subject to one caveat,[56] those who executed the deed are bound by estoppel arising from it.[57] Strangers will not be bound by an estoppel by deed.[58] Those who have not executed the deed will not generally be bound by it.[59] This remains true even where the deed is part of a chain of conveyances making good that party's title to land.[60] However, those who have acted on the deed and received a benefit under it may be bound by the statements it contains.[61]

THE PRIVIES OF THOSE WHO EXECUTED THE DEED

10.55 As we set out in detail below, two doctrines commonly operate under the title estoppel by deed. The following analysis applies to the technical estoppel by deed which requires an express representation rather than the more broadly based doctrine which is dependent on a defective grant of title. The latter doctrine has a more limited effect on third parties.[62]

The benefit

10.56 The benefit of estoppel by deed may be passed to the privies in title[63] of the original parties raising the estoppel.[64] Privies seeking to take advantage of the estoppel do not have to establish the requisite elements

[56] The caveat is discussed at para. 10.46 above: if the parties intended to attribute the statement, on which the estoppel is founded, to one particular party to the deed, the other parties will not be bound by it.

[57] *Greer v Kettle* [1938] AC 156 *per* Lord Maugham at 171 (*obiter*).

[58] Coke, *A Commentary on Littleton* (11th ed., London 1719) at p. 352a; *Doe de Marchant v Errington* (1839) 6 Bing (NC) 79, 133 ER 31 *per* Tindal C.J. at 83, 33; *Gaunt v Wainman* (1836) 3 Bing (NC) 69, 132 ER 335 *per* Tindal C.J. and *Woodard v Battersea BC* [1911] 51 LT 51 *per* Neville J. at 53.

[59] *Doe de Shelton v Shelton* (1835) 3 AD&E 265, 111 ER 413 *per* Lord Denman C.J. at 283, 420 and *Foster v Mentor Life Assurance Co* (1854) 3 El & Bl 48, 118 ER 1058 *per* Lord Campbell C.J. at 79, 1071.

[60] *Doe de Shelton v Shelton* (1835) 3 AD&E 265, 111 ER 413 *per* Lord Denman C.J. at 283, 420.

[61] *Webb v Spicer* (1849) 13 QB 886, 116 ER 1502 and 1505 and *cf. Dalton v Fitzgerald* [1897] 2 Ch 86, CA.

[62] See paras 10.72–3 below.

[63] For the meaning of privy in title, see below under *The burden* at paras 10.57–9.

[64] *Mackley v Nutting* [1949] 2 KB 55, CA.

of estoppel *de novo* in their own favour. It is necessary only to demonstrate that the party from whom the privy derives its title could have raised the estoppel. If no estoppel could have arisen in favour of the original party, none will enure to the benefit of its privies. Take, for example the situation where the original party, X, could not have raised an estoppel because the deed was fraudulently procured. X's privy cannot take the benefit of any estoppel even if innocent of the fraud.[65]

The burden

The burden of estoppel by deed[66] will bind the privies of the original parties estopped.[67] Privies are those who claim under, or in right of, the original parties and include personal representatives,[68] legatees[69] and volunteers (including beneficiaries under a settlement).[70] They also include those purchasing[71] from the original parties even where they are bona fide purchasers of the legal estate, for value, without notice.[72] **10.57**

Compared to related doctrines such as proprietary estoppel,[73] estoppel by deed has far reaching and enduring effects. Where estoppel by deed **10.58**

---

65 *Norwich and Peterborough Building Society v Steed* [1993] 1 All ER 330, CA *per* Scott L.J. at 340b–d but see *Re King's Settlement* [1931] 2 Ch 294 *per* Farwell J. at 299 discussed at paras 10.60–1 below. *cf. Doe d Williams v Lloyd* (1839) 5 Bing NC 741 *per* Bosanquet, Coltman and Erskine JJ. at 744, 1287, where the heir of an original party to the deed was allowed to challenge it on the grounds that it contravened a statute. This was permitted despite the fact that the heir claimed through a person who had deliberately set out to evade the statute.

66 Of the technical type described in the bulk of this chapter, as distinguished from the doctrine which depends purely on a defective grant rather than an express recital, as to which see below.

67 *Greer v Kettle* [1938] AC 156 *per* Lord Maugham at 171 (*obiter*); *Doe de Marchant v Errington* (1839) 6 Bing (NC) 79, 133 ER 31 *per* Tyndall C.J. at 83, 33 and *Taylor v Needham* (1810) Taunt 278.

68 *Mackley v Nutting* [1949] 2 KB 55, CA.

69 *Dalton v Fitzgerald* [1897] 2 Ch 86, CA *per* Lindley L.J. at 92, *per* Lopes L.J. at 93 and *per* Rigby L.J. at 94. See also the estoppel by record case of *R v Hebdon* (1738) Andrews 388, 95 ER 447 at 390, 448.

70 *Re King's Settlement* [1931] 2 Ch 294 *per* Farwell J. at 301 but see below at paras 10.60–1 as to whether this is truly an estoppel by deed case.

71 *Doe de Gaisford v Stone* (1846) 3 CB 176, 136 ER 71 *per* Tindal C.J., Coltman, Maule and Cresswell JJ. We have here used the term purchase to refer generally to the acquisition for value of *any* interest, right or estate from the relevant party whether by way of a full fee simple, mortgage, lease, etc.

72 *First National Bank v Thompson* [1996] All ER 144, CA *per* Millet L.J. at 147d–f; *Taylor v Needham* (1810) Taunt 278 and *Sumner v Schofield* (1880) 43 LT 763 *per* Kelly C.B. at 767.

73 For an account of the transmissibility of rights created by proprietary estoppel, see paras 11.71–85 below.

arises in relation to real property, it may create durable encumbrances and provide a significant hazard for purchasers. Such an approach is at odds with the preference for certainty in English conveyancing law.[74] The likely explanation is twofold. First, a significant manifestation of this preference for certainty concerns the manner in which rights are created. Specifically, informal right creation is disliked. The estoppel by deed doctrine presupposes the existence of a formal document, namely a deed. The rights in issue are being created formally. There is therefore no conflict with the aspect of the certainty principle adverted to. Secondly, the doctrine was developed during a period when deeds were viewed with such seriousness as almost to amount to public documents.[75] It was reasonable to hold third parties to the statements contained in such significant documents, even those outside the body of deeds forming the root of title of the property purchased.[76]

A number of points flow from this analysis. First, the durability of the rights created by estoppel by deed can and should be specifically linked to its unique characteristics. It is neither desirable nor correct to transplant the relevant principles to other forms of estoppel, such as estoppel by representation, which do not share those characteristics. Secondly, and as a consequence, we submit that this remains a point of divergence between estoppel by deed and estoppel by representation.[77] Consequently, if estoppel by deed is to be subsumed within estoppel by representation, some review of the transmissibility of interests will have to be conducted in order to determine which set of principles governs. Thirdly, it is at least doubtful whether rules formulated in the seventeenth and eighteenth centuries should continue to operate in the radically altered framework of modern English land law. The bulk of estoppel by deed cases pre-date the introduction of widespread registration of title in 1925. There is almost no guidance as to how the doctrine will operate in relation to registered land, if at all. The general principles set out in paragraph 10.57 above are probably confined to the diminishing amount of property governed by unregistered conveyancing. However, the Court **10.59**

[74] See *National Provincial Bank v Ainsworth* [1965] AC 1175, HL and *Midland Bank v Green* [1981] AC 513 for general comments on the importance of certainty and the integrity of the land registration schemes.

[75] Hence, the important role they continue to play in unregistered conveyancing.

[76] As to which see specialist texts.

[77] In *Hopgood v Brown*[1955] WLR 213, CA, the Court of Appeal applied estoppel by deed principles to estoppel by representation. As we set out at paras 8.136–40 above, we consider that this approach was incorrect.

of Appeal has recently held that estoppel by deed and its companion doctrine that of feeding the estoppel has at least some role to play in registered conveyancing.[78]

OTHER PARTIES

There is some authority to suggest that those who have relied to their detriment on the deed may raise an estoppel by deed, even if they were neither parties to it nor the privies of someone who was.[79] In *Re King's Settlement*,[80] M transferred property to A and B. The conveyance was expressed to be absolute and 'in consideration of love and affection'. In reality, A and B had agreed to hold the property on various trusts. The trust deed was separately executed and the transfer was absolute on its face. A and B granted an equitable mortgage to W. M was estopped from denying A and B's title was absolute. Although W derived its interest from A and B, it could not rest its claim on conventional ground that it was the privy of A and B. No estoppel had arisen in favour of A and B: they knew that the statement was untrue and was never meant to represent the true position between the parties. Hence, W was neither a party to the deed nor was it the privy of someone who could raise an estoppel and yet was still able to invoke the doctrine. Further, in no sense could the action be described as one 'on the deed' in the sense set out in paragraph 10.36 above. Thus, fundamental principles of estoppel by deed were breached. **10.60**

The case is best explained simply as an instance of estoppel by representation.[81] The latter doctrine may operate in favour of all those to whom the representation was made, who have acted to their detriment in the reliance on the belief in the truth of the representation.[82] Unlike estoppel by deed, its scope is not confined to those parties executing a particular document or to their privies. **10.61**

---

[78] *First National Bank v Thompson* [1996] All ER 144, CA. See further paras 10.74–5 below.
[79] *Re King's Settlement* [1931] 2 Ch 294 *per* Farwell J. at 299.
[80] [1931] 2 Ch 294.
[81] *cf. TCB Ltd v Gray* [1986] Ch 621and the estoppel by representation cases discussed at paras 8.64–7 and the so-called estoppel by negligence cases discussed at paras 8.149, 14.17, 14.18, 15.64 and 16.13.
[82] See generally paras 8.45–9 above.

PASSING TITLE

10.62 Estoppel by deed does not operate to pass ownership. However, the doctrine may create rights which are, in almost every respect, equivalent to title. They do not amount to genuine title. If it is stated in the deed that X is the owner of property, the other parties bound by the estoppel[83] will not be able to dispute this fact. If however, the actual owner of the property is not one of those parties, there is nothing to stop its claiming the property from X.[84]

ESTOPPEL ARISING IN PROPERTY TRANSACTIONS

ESTATES OR INTERESTS CREATED BY ESTOPPEL

10.63 Where M purports to grant an interest or estate in property which it does not in fact own, it will be estopped thereafter from denying the title of the grantee.[85] M cannot use its own lack of title to undermine the purported grant. This fundamental rule of English property law has manifested itself in the familiar law that the mortgagor cannot dispute the title of its mortgagee[86] and vice versa. Similarly a tenant cannot dispute the title of its landlord.[87] Nor may a landlord dispute the title

---

[83] Either because they executed the deed or claim the rights through someone who did, in accordance with the principles set out in paras 10.56–7 above.

[84] See paras 10.63–4 below where this issue is discussed in detail.

[85] *Industrial Properties (Barton Hill) Ltd v Associated Electrical Industries Ltd* [1977] 1 QB 580 *per* Lord Denning M.R. at 596 and *per* Roskill L.J. at 599 and *Cuthbertson v Irving* (1859) 4 H&N 742, 157 ER 1034 *per* Martin B. at 754–5, 1039. It was pointed out in *Bruton v London & Quadrant Housing Trust* [1997] 4 All E.R. 970 CA, the principle developed when title to land was often uncertain, particularly where there was a mortgage. Most mortgages then involved a conveyance of absolute title to the land to the lender, leaving the borrower with only the right to reclaim the property on repayment of the loan. The principle presumably developed to give a degree of security to grantees in these uncertain conditions.

[86] *Goodtitle d Edwards v Bailey* (1777) 2 Cowp 597 at 600–1 and *Right de Jefferys v Bucknell* (1831) 2 B&Ad 278, 109 ER 1146.

[87] *Cuthbertson v Irving* (1859) 4 H&N 742, 157 ER 1034 *per* Martin B. at 754–5, 1039; *E.H. Lewis & Son Ltd v Morelli* [1948] 2 All ER 1021, CA *per* Harman J. and Asquith L.J. at 1024–5; *Industrial Properties (Barton Hill) Ltd v Associated Electrical Industries Ltd* [1977] 1 QB 580 *per* Lord Denning M.R. at 596, *per* Roskill L.J. at 599 and *per* Lawton L.J. at 613.

of its tenant, merely by citing its own want of title to create the tenancy.[88] A tenant cannot defend an action on the covenants in a lease by disputing the title of the landlord,[89] unless the actual owner of the premises has interfered with the tenant's use of the premises during the term.[90] This restriction continues even after the tenant has left possession of the premises at the end of the term.[91]

This principle operates to vest rights in the grantee which are equivalent to a valid grant of title, except that they will not prevail against the actual owner of the property.[92] Hence, it is said that the grantee acquires an estate or interest by estoppel,[93] which is equivalent to genuine title, save in the one crucial respect mentioned. **10.64**

Although the principle has operated paradigmatically in relation to real property, there no reason why it should be restricted to this type of property.[94] There is authority to suggest that it applies to other types of property such as patent rights[95] and chattels.[96] **10.65**

---

[88] *Cuthbertson v Irving* (1859) 4 H&N 742, 157 ER 1034 *per* Martin B. at 754–5, 1039; *E.H. Lewis & Son Ltd v Morelli* [1948] 2 All ER 1021, CA *per* Harman J. and Asquith L.J. at 1024–5. No estoppel will arise unless the owner of the property has purported to grant a tenancy. If the terms of the grant conferred only a licence, the estoppel does not arise, even where exclusive possession for a term at a rent has been granted: *Bruton v London & Quadrant Housing Trust* [1997] 4 All E.R. 970 CA. The Court of Appeal rejected an ingenious attempt to combine the principle of estoppel by deed with that of *Street v Mountford* [1985] AC 809 whereby the grant of exclusive possession for a term at a rent is presumed to give rise to a tenancy unless one of a number of limited exceptional circumstances can be demonstrated: *ibid.*

[89] *Cuthbertson v Irving* (1859) 4 H&N 742, 157 ER 1034 *per* Martin B. at 757–8, 1041.

[90] *Industrial Properties (Barton Hill) Ltd v Associated Electrical Industries Ltd* [1977] 1 QB 580 *per* Lord Denning M.R. at 596 and *per* Roskill L.J. at 599. It is not necessary for the holder of paramount title actually to have evicted the tenant nor is it necessary to demonstrate that legal proceedings have been taken to obtain an order for eviction. The estoppel between landlord and tenant ends as soon as a threat of eviction occurs: *Sadiq v Hussein* [1997] NPC 19 CA, lexis transcript. The estoppel will continue, however, if the third party evicting the tenant is not acting in good faith but under some collusive arrangement with the landlord, designed to give him possession which he would not otherwise have had a right to: *ibid* and *Quennel v Maltby* [1979] 1 WLR 568.

[91] *Industrial Properties (Barton Hill) Ltd v Associated Electrical Industries Ltd* [1977] 1 QB 580 *per* Lord Denning M.R. at 596 and *per* Roskill L.J. at 599.

[92] *First National Bank v Thompson* [1996] All ER 144, CA *per* Millet L.J. at 14b–c.

[93] *Cuthbertson v Irving* (1859) 4 H&N 742, 157 ER 1034 *per* Martin B. at 754–5, 1039.

[94] Contra. *E.H. Lewis & Son Ltd v Morelli* [1948] 2 All ER 1021, CA *per* Harman J. at 1024–5.

[95] *Greer v Kettle* [1938] AC 156 *per* Lord Maugham at 169, commenting on *Clark v. Adie* (1877) 2 App Cas 423 and *Bowman v Taylor* (1834) 2 AD&E 279, 111 ER 108.

[96] *Biddle v Bond* (1865) 6 B & S 225. See also Benjamin paras 4.009–10 on the 'feeding title' doctrine which operates in respect of sale of goods transactions in a manner similar to the 'feeding of the estoppel' doctrine described below at paras 10.71–7.

Distinguishing the two types of estoppel which may arise: express representation of title

Some difficulty has been caused because the above analysis has been used in relation to two distinct common law doctrines, both of which have been referred to as estoppel by deed.[97] The relevant principles were discussed by the Court of Appeal in *First National Bank v Thompson*.[98] The first of these doctrines requires the original grant to have contained an express statement that the grantor is entitled to the interest or estate transferred.[99] This doctrine is the one which has been discussed generally in this chapter. It was categorized by their Lordships as an instance of estoppel by representation and described as a technical estoppel. 10.66

Their Lordships also identified an older and more widely based doctrine also referred to as estoppel by deed. This doctrine operates even in the absence of an express statement of title.[1] All that is necessary for its operation is a purported grant of ownership rights by a party lacking title to the subject property. It may operate in the absence of a deed, where it is possible to grant the estate or interest without one. For example, a legal tenancy of three years or less may be created where the property owner, M, with the intention of creating a tenancy, lets another take possession of the premises and pay rent.[2] If M does not own the premises at the time when these events take place, a tenancy by estoppel will be created, despite the lack of express recital or deed of grant.[3] 10.67

In *E.H. Lewis & Son Ltd v Morelli*,[4] the Court of Appeal expressed 10.68

---

[97] *First National Bank v Thompson* [1996] All ER 144, CA *per* Millet L.J. at 145b–d and *per* Staughton L.J. at 151a–c.

[98] [1996] All ER 144, CA.

[99] [1996] All ER 144, CA *per* Millet L.J. at 145a-b and *per* Staughton L.J. at 151a–b. See, for example, *Doe de Gaisford v Stone* (1846) 3 CB 176, 136 ER 71.

[1] See, for example, *Universal Permanent Building Society v Cooke* [1951] 1 Ch 95 and *Cuthbertson v Irving* (1859) 4 H&N 742, 157 ER 1034 *per* Martin B. at 757–8, 1041.

[2] Law of Property Act 1925 sections 52 (1) (d) and 54 (2); *Javad v Aqil* [1991] 1 WLR 1007. Such an intent is likely to be lacking where the parties have been negotiating for the sale of the freehold or for a long lease and the purchaser is let into possession pending finalization of term: *Javad v Aqil* [1991] 1 WLR 1007.

[3] *Universal Permanent Building Society v Cooke* [1951] 1 Ch 95; *E.H. Lewis & Son Ltd v Morelli* [1948] 2 All ER 1021, CA *per* Harman J. and Asquith L.J. at 1024–5 and *Mackley v Nutting* [1949] 2 KB 55, CA *per* Cohen L.J. at 62.

[4] [1948] 2 All ER 1021, CA *per* Harman J. (giving the judgment of the court) at 1024–5.

doubts as to whether the doctrine depending on mere grant, rather than express recital, is a species of estoppel at all. In particular, Mr Justice Harman referred to the fact that the doctrine does not require the tenant to have believed that the landlord was the true owner of the property. His Lordship held that an essential for the operation of the doctrine was thus missing, namely reliance on the truth of the representation made. As we set out above,[5] such a belief may not be essential, even in technical estoppel by deed cases where there is an express recital of title. However, the estoppel by defective grant doctrine has much in common with the principle that a party cannot take the benefit of the agreement without the burden.[6] Once the landlord has accepted rent under the purported tenancy, it cannot deny the validity of the arrangement. Further, once the tenant has accepted possession and made use of possession of the premises, it cannot dispute the tenancy unless that use is interrupted by the real owner.

FEEDING THE ESTOPPEL

If the grantor acquires title after the defective grant, the estoppel is said to be fed and the estate by estoppel is converted into an estate in interest. Put simply, the grantee thereby acquires genuine title as soon as the grantor obtains it.[7] There is no need for the grantor to execute a fresh conveyance.[8] Once the estoppel is fed the grantee's title is as effective as if it had been granted in the orthodox manner. There is no longer any paramount title which can displace it.[9] Both the estoppels referred to above may be fed by this companion doctrine.[10] However, its consequences differ slightly according to which estoppel is operating.[11] **10.69**

The doctrine of feeding the estoppel has generally operated in relation to legal estates. However, the House of Lords, in *Abbey National* **10.70**

[5] At para. 10.19 above.
[6] *ER Ives Investment Ltd v High* [1967] 2 QB 379, CA at 394, 399 and 405 and *Halsall v Brizell* [1957] 1 All ER 90.
[7] *Webb v Austin* (1844) 7 Man & G 701, 135 ER 282 *per* Tyndall C.J. at 724, 291; *Cuthbertson v Irving* (1859) 4 H&N 742, 157 ER 1034 *per* Martin B. at 754–5, 1039; *Mackley v Nutting* [1949] 2 KB 55, CA *per* Cohen L.J. at 62–63 and *First National Bank v Thompson* [1996] All ER 144, CA.
[8] *First National Bank v Thompson* [1996] All ER 144, CA.
[9] *ibid. per* Millet L.J. at 147b–d.
[10] *ibid. per* Millet L.J. at 147c–d and *per* Staughton L.J. at 151a–b.
[11] See para. 10.71 below.

v Cann,[12] assumed that it was capable of applying where the grantor has purported to confer an equitable interest on another party. There was no discussion on the point. Further, although the doctrine has operated paradigmatically in relation to real property, a similar 'feeding title' principle operates with respect to goods.[13]

DISTINCTIONS BETWEEN THE OPERATION OF THE TWO ESTOPPEL DOCTRINES

Grantor's legal title at the time of the grant

The two species of estoppel operate differently where, at the date of purported transfer, the grantor possesses legal ownership rights which are insufficient to support the grant. Where there is an express recital of title, the grantor will be estopped from denying that it had *the particular* legal title averred. Consequently, the grantee's title will be fed on the acquisition of sufficient title by the grantor, whether or not the grantor had some lesser legal estate at the time of grant.[14] Where there is no express recital, the grantor will be estopped only from denying that it had *some form of* legal title. Consequently, no estoppel will arise if the grantor owned *any* legal[15] estate in the property at the time of the grant, even if it was insufficient to support the grant. In such cases, the grantee obtains an estate in interest immediately on grant but the title acquired cannot exceed that of the **10.71**

[12] [1991] 1 AC 56. Had this assumption not been made there would have been no reason to discuss the *scintilla temporis* point on which Mrs Cann's case ultimately foundered (as to which see below at para. 10.77). If the doctrine does operate on grants of equitable interests, this throws some doubt on the emphasis in *First National Bank v Thompson* [1996] All ER 144, CA at 145a–c and 151a–c that the relevant doctrines were the product of the common law and not equity.

[13] As to which see Benjamin paras 4.009–10.

[14] *First National Bank v Thompson* [1996] All ER 144, CA *per* Millet L.J. at 147d–f.

[15] *Cuthbertson v Irving* (1859) 4 H&N 742, 157 ER 1034 *per* Martin B. at 757–8, 1041; *Universal Permanent Building Society v Cooke* [1951] 1 Ch 95 *per* Evershed M.R. at 102–3 and *First National Bank v Thompson* [1996] All ER 144, CA *per* Millet L.J. at 147f–h. The estoppel is not barred and may operate in the normal manner where the grantor has only an equitable interest in the property: *Cooke*. As is set out at para. 10.70 above, there is authority to suggest that the purported grant of equitable title may be fed by this doctrine. Presumably in such a situation the estoppel *would be* defeated where the grantor had some equitable title, albeit insufficient to make good the grant.

grantor. There is no estoppel to be fed. Consequently, the grantor's subsequent acquisition of a larger title capable of supporting the grant does not benefit the grantee.

Effect on third parties

Both types of estoppel vest title which is precarious to the extent that it is vulnerable to displacement by the genuine owner of the property.[16] However, the two types of estoppel differ in their effect on purchasers of the legal estate *from the grantor*. As is set out in paragraph 10.57 above, in cases where there is an express recital to title, the estoppel binds all those claiming including assignees and purchasers. The grantee is protected even from the bona fide purchaser for value without notice.[17] Equity is not able to intervene to protect such a purchaser in this situation. If there is no express recital, the estoppel binds all *except* the bona fide purchaser for value from the grantor without notice of the earlier transaction. Such purchasers take the legal estate free from the rights of the earlier grantee.[18] **10.72**

In summary, if the grantor made successive grants of legal title for value, one before and one after the acquisition of title, the earlier grantee prevails only where there was an express recital of title.[19] **10.73**

FEEDING TITLE TO REGISTERED LAND

It was held in *First National Bank v Thompson*,[20] that the doctrine of feeding the estoppel could apply to registered land. In that case, in July 1991, Mr Thompson purported to grant a charge over a property to First National. He did not acquire title to the property until December 1991. First National registered their charge in July 1992. The chargees had an unquestionable contractual right to **10.74**

---

16 See para. 10.64 above.

17 *First National Bank v Thompson* [1996] All ER 144, CA *per* Millet L.J. at 147d–f (*obiter*) and *Poulton v Moore* [1915] 1 KB 400, CA *per* Phillimore L.J. at 415.

18 *First National Bank v Thompson* [1996] All ER 144, CA *per* Millet L.J. at 147j and *per* Staughton L.J. at 151f-g (*obiter*), *Right de Jefferys v Bucknell* (1831) 2 B&Ad 278, 109 ER 1146 and *General Finance, Mortgage, and Discount Company v. Liberator Permanent Benefit Building Society* (1878) 10 ChD 15 *per* Jessel M.R.

19 *First National Bank v Thompson* [1996] All ER 144, CA *per* Millet L.J. at 147j–8a (*obiter*).

20 [1996] All ER 144, CA *per* Millet L.J. at 148g–9j, *per* Ward L.J. at 150b–c and *per* Staughton L.J. at 151g–j.

demand the execution of a fresh charge, which they could then register. However, because the priority of charges is determined by the date of registration, First National sought to uphold the validity of the earlier one.

According to the Court of Appeal, there was no good reason why the doctrine of feeding the estoppel should not apply to registered land. Charges over registered land can only be created if the requirements of section 25 of the Land Registration Act 1925 are met. The section grants power to execute a charge only if two preconditions are satisfied. First, an appropriate instrument of charge has been executed. Secondly, the person executing the charge is the registered proprietor. Usually the second of these two preconditions will be satisfied before the first but the section does not require this. So long as both preconditions are satisfied, a registerable charge is created. Hence charge is registerable from the point at which the later of the two events occur.[21] **10.75**

PRACTICAL LIMITATIONS ON THE FEEDING TITLE PRINCIPLE

Estoppels may only be fed by such title as the grantor acquires. The practical scope of the feeding doctrine was consequently restricted by the House of Lords in *Abbey National v Cann.*[22] In that case, the grantor had purchased the relevant property using funds secured by a mortgage over it. In an earlier decision, *Church of England Building Society v. Piskor*,[23] the Court of Appeal analysed such a transaction as follows. Although the actual transfer and mortgage might, in reality, take place simultaneously, such transactions were held to involve a series of steps taking place in a logically predetermined manner. These steps flowed from the fact that only the owner of property could grant a mortgage over it. Once the funds had been paid to the vendor, and the deed of conveyance executed, the unencumbered legal title vested in the purchaser for a notional moment in time (or *scintilla temporis*). The purchaser could then grant the charge to the mortgagee who had **10.76**

[21] Millet L.J. commented that the particular provisions of the registration system might require modifications to be made to the application of the doctrine: [1996] All ER 144, CA at 148g–h.

[22] [1991] 1 AC 56.

[23] [1954] Ch 553, CA.

provided the funds for the transaction. Hence, if the purchaser had previously purported to grant an interest in the property to W, W's title was fed during the notional moment when the purchaser owned the unencumbered legal estate. W's interest therefore pre-dated that of the mortgagee and was capable of taking priority over it.

In *Abbey National v Cann*,[24] the House of Lords disapproved this approach. Their Lordships held there that in the following circumstances, any estoppel fed by the doctrine will be automatically subordinated to the interests of mortgagees. First, all or some of the money used to fund the purchase was raised by way of a loan. Secondly, the loan was to be secured by a mortgage over the property to be acquired. Thirdly, the mortgage was executed simultaneously with, or in rapid succession to, the sale transaction. If these three conditions are satisfied, the purchaser never obtains the unencumbered legal ownership of the property, even for a *scintilla temporis*. The purchaser only ever acquires the equity of redemption. Hence any estoppels arising out of previous grants are fed only by the equity of redemption and not by full legal title.[25] The interests created as a result of the process are inherently subordinate to those of the lender and can never take priority over the mortgage. If the property is purchased without mortgage finance, the estoppel may be fed in the normal manner and will take priority over mortgages executed at a later date.[26] In such cases, there is insufficient connection between the acquisition and the mortgage for the *Cann* principle to apply. **10.77**

[24] [1991] 1 AC 56.

[25] In *Church of England Building Society v Piskor* [1954] Ch 553, CA, the Court of Appeal based their decision on the additional subordinate ground that the mortgage deed had recited that the purchaser was the owner of the property. It was held that the mortgagee could not contradict this express statement (at 559, 562 and 565). It is possible that this part of the decision survived *Abbey National v Cann*. Lord Oliver considered that *Piskor* might be justified on this ground although Lord Jauncey disagreed: [1991] 1 AC 56 at 92 and 99.

[26] According to the principles set out in para. 10.72 and 10.76 above.

Chapter 11

PROPRIETARY ESTOPPEL

INTRODUCTION

The doctrine of proprietary estoppel has its origins in equity's traditional jurisdiction to prevent fraudulent assertion of legal rights. Fraud in the sense of dishonesty is not, however, a requirement: '. . . *the plaintiff has to establish as a fact that the defendant, by setting up his right, is taking advantage of him in a way which is unconscionable, inequitable or unjust*'.[1] The courts have continued to stress the flexible discretionary nature of the doctrine, emphasizing the need for a broad approach directed '. . . *at ascertaining whether, in particular individual circumstances, it would be unconscionable for a party to be permitted to deny that which, knowingly, or unknowingly, he has allowed or encouraged another to assume to his detriment* [rather] *than to inquiring whether the circumstances can be fitted within the confines of some preconceived formula serving as a universal yardstick for every form of unconscionable behaviour*'.[2] **11.001**

SUMMARY OF ELEMENTS

The criteria for triggering the operation of the doctrine (that is 'unconscionability') have, however, crystallized into fairly settled principles. It **11.002**

---

1 Scarman L.J. in *Crabb v Arun DC* [1976] Ch 179 at 195C.

2 *Taylors Fashions Ltd v Liverpool Victoria Trustees Co. Ltd* [1982] 1 QB 133 at 151g–2a; *Lim v Ang* [1992] 1 WLR 113, PC; *Amalgamated Investment & Property Co. Ltd (in liquidation) v Texas Commerce International Bank Ltd* [1982] 1QB 84 *per* Goff J. at 104; *Shelley & Others v United Artists Corporation Ltd* (1990) 59 P&CR 34; *Nationwide Anglia Building Society v Ahmed and Balakrishnan* [1995] 70 P&Cr 381 CA; *Habib Bank Ltd* v *Habib Bank A.G. Zurich* [1981] WLR 1265 CA; *Elitestone v Morris* (1997) 73 P&CR 259 CA (rev. on other grounds at [1997] 1 WLR 687 HL); *Lloyds Bank v Carrick* [1996] 4 All ER 630 CA; *Barclays Bank v Zavoorabli* [1997] 2 All ER 19 and *Film Investors Overseas SA v Home Video Channel (trading as the Adult Channel)* [1997] EMLR 347.

is essential to demonstrate assurance, reliance and detriment. A claim in proprietary estoppel will only arise where a claimant has acted to his or her detriment in reliance on a belief or expectation that he or she has, or will, be granted, rights over an item of property and its owner acquiesces in, or encourages, that belief or expectation. Once this is established, the court will take into account 'all the circumstances of the case'[3] to ascertain whether it would be unconscionable to deny the claimant a remedy. The court will carry out a balancing exercise between the parties, based on general conceptions of fairness. This discretion, though flexible, is not wholly unstructured. In so far as it is possible, we have endeavoured to extract some general propositions from the cases. As regards the measure of relief, the flexibility of the court's discretion has again been emphasized. However, it is increasingly clear that the courts will seek to grant the minimum remedy necessary to avert detriment to the claimant. This may involve making good the expectation or assumption but it will not *necessarily* do so. The emergence of a more principled approach is, we consider, welcome evidence of the increasing maturity of the doctrine.

TERMINOLOGY

For a number of reasons, it may not be appropriate to refer to the doctrine under consideration as a species of estoppel. First, traditional estoppels such as estoppel by representation and convention operate only to set up a state of facts which determine the legal outcome between the parties, whereas proprietary estoppel is a source of legal obligation in itself and may give rise to a cause of action.[4] The effect of the doctrine was originally described as preventing or estopping the owner from enforcing his strict legal rights, namely his property rights. The modern doctrine, however, appears to go beyond mere restriction on enforcement and operates to transfer enforceable property rights to the claimant.[5] Secondly, estoppels have traditionally prevented the party estopped from denying the truth of the assumption that he has encouraged the claimant to adopt to her detriment. By contrast, the courts have a wide remedial discretion in proprietary estoppel cases. For example, the **11.003**

[3] See below at para. 11.50.
[4] See para. 11.86 below.
[5] See however 11.96–101 and in particular 11.115–7 below where we argue that the doctrine is still effectively confined to the prevention of enforcement of rights, albeit that this will *result* in the transfer of ownership to claimant.

original owner may be permitted to exercise his property rights but only after granting some lesser ownership or right to the claimant or paying compensation. Thus, it is possible to characterize the doctrine simply as a species of liability generated by detrimental reliance, with elements in common with contract or tort as well as with estoppel.[6]

We have, however, continued to refer to this doctrine by the term proprietary estoppel for three reasons. First, the term is so well established as to make departure from it impractical and pedantic. Secondly, the estoppel concept has progressed beyond its original evidential emphasis on estopping or preventing the assertion of the strict legal position, and now may be sensibly used to describe liability based on detrimental reliance. Thirdly, although this trend is manifested to differing degrees between the various species of estoppel,[7] there remains a sufficient overlap between the doctrine under consideration and other species of estoppel to make a common *classification* both feasible and useful. However, we do not go as far as suggesting that all estoppels are sufficiently similar to amount to aspects of a single unified doctrine.[8] **11.004**

Difficulties of both a semantic and substantive nature have flowed from the fact that proprietary estoppel covers two slightly different situations: (i) where the claimant has made a *mistake* as to the extent of her legal rights in a particular piece of property; and (ii) where she has been *promised* additional legal rights in such property. Some have concluded that there are two wholly different doctrines operating in this area, one based on mistake and one on promises or expectations. The term proprietary estoppel has therefore been described as *'an amalgam of doubtful utility'*.[9] In our view, it is possible to identify a single principle, albeit that the principle operates slightly differently according to whether the property owner has engaged in active encouragement or whether his conduct has been purely passive. However, adopting that single doctrine approach still leaves a terminological problem in referring to the conduct of the party sought to be estopped. We have used the word *assurance* as an umbrella term to describe the conduct of that party in **11.005**

---

6 See paras. 8.12–3 above and 11.48–54 below.

7 See paras 8.04–13 above.

8 Indeed, there have been indications that the boundaries between the various estoppel doctrines are collapsing, although we consider that there continue to be significant distinctions between them — see *Taylors Fashions Ltd v Liverpool Victoria Trustees Co. Ltd* [1982] 1 QB 133 at 151g–2a and *Amalgamated Investment & Property Co. Ltd, (in liquidation) v Texas Commerce International Bank Ltd* [1982] 1 QB 84 *per* Denning M.R. at 122 and paras 8.04–13 above and 11.96–101 below.

9 *Amalgamated Investment & Property Co. Ltd, (in liquidation) v Texas Commerce International Bank Ltd* [1982] 1 QB 84 at 103d–g.

either of the situations described. It actually involves a two-fold hurdle. Claimants must show, both that they formed the requisite belief or expectation, *and* that the same was acquiesced in or encouraged by the party to be estopped. Although the term is not particularly apt to describe the passive conduct which acquiescence entails, it is the best available shorthand.

Similarly, there is no obvious term by which to describe the respective parties in a case of proprietary estoppel. Terms such as representor and representee are inappropriate because the cases often lack any communication which could sensibly be characterized as a representation. For ease of analysis, we have used W and M to represent the respective party seeking to raise the estoppel and the party it is sought to estop. We have abandoned our gender neutral approach in this chapter: of all the principles considered in this work, proprietary estoppel has the most substantial impact on individuals outside a business context. We found it artificial to refer to such parties as 'it' against the background of the personal relationships the cases so often involve. We have endeavoured to remain even handed by referring to our hypothetical M and W as male and female respectively. **11.006**

ELEMENTS

ASSURANCE

Proprietary estoppel claims may be established only where W has acted to her detriment in reliance on a belief either that she already owned or had legal rights over some item of M's property[10] or that she would be granted such ownership or rights in the future.[11] The former case involves a *mistake* as to existing legal entitlement, whereas the second involves an expectation (or *promise*) that rights will be granted in the future. The claimant must also establish that her belief was acquiesced in, or actively encouraged by, the property owner. It is not necessary to show intent to create legal relations in the strict contractual sense.[12] **11.007**

---

[10] See paras 11.08–11 (the 'mistake' cases) below.

[11] See paras 11.12–5 (the 'expectation' cases) below.

[12] *Dodsworth v Dodsworth* (1973) 228 EG 1115, CA and *Voyce v Voyce* (1991) 62 P&CR 290, CA at 296; *Layton v Martin* [1986] 2 FLR 227 (where Scott J. considered the lack of such an intent in relation to the contract claim but not that in proprietary estoppel).

However, a specific assertion that the dealings between the parties are not intended to affect the legal position between them is likely to negate a claim in proprietary estoppel.[13] It is not necessary that the arrangements comply with any contractual certainty requirement.[14] Further, there is no need to comply with the formalities required for transfer of the property in issue.[15]

Examples

Unilateral mistake and acquiescence

W mistakenly believes that she owns property which, in fact, belongs to M. For example: **11.008**

> If a stranger builds on my land supposing it to be his own, and I, perceiving his mistake abstain from setting him right, and leave him to persevere in his error, a court of equity will not allow me afterwards to assert my title to the land on which he had expended money on the supposition that the land was his own. It considers that, when I saw the mistake into which he had fallen, it was my duty to be active and to state my adverse title; and that it would be dishonest of me to remain wilfully passive on such an occasion, in order, afterwards to profit by the mistake which I might have prevented[16]

The mistake is not induced or caused by M but is made independently and unilaterally by W. It is not necessary to demonstrate M's active encouragement of the mistake or expenditure. Passive but knowing[17]

---

[13] See Lindgren, *Estoppel in Contract* (1989) 12 UNSWLJ 153 at 173 and paras 11.08–10 below under 'Pre-Contract Negotiations.'

[14] *Holiday Inns Inc v Broadhead* (1974) 232 EG 951 at 1087 and *Lim v Ang* [1992] 1 WLR 113, PC (Brunei) where the assumption relied on was contained in the recital of a contract void for uncertainty.

[15] *Pascoe v Turner* [1979] 1 WLR 43, CA; *Re Basham decd* [1986] 1 WLR 1498 and *Lim v Ang* [1992] 1 WLR 113, PC (Brunei).

[16] *Ramsden v Dyson* (1866) LR 1 HL 129, HL *per* Lord Cranworth at 140–1. See also *AG to Prince of Wales v Collom* [1916] 2 KB 193 and *Hamilton v Geraghty* (1901) 1 SRNSW Eq 81.

[17] See para 11.19 below, where we conclude that it is necessary that M knows that W's belief is mistaken (*i.e.* knows of his own inconsistent property right). If we are correct in this conclusion, the five probanda of *Willmott v Barber* (1880) 15 ChD 96 at 105 (set out at para. 11.16 below) are still a fairly accurate description of the pre-requisites of this head of proprietary estoppel. As we there point out, however, the application of the probanda to the other heads listed in paras 11.12–5 is not appropriate.

acquiescence[18] suffices. This type of conduct is sometimes referred to as passive encouragement; for clarity we have used the term encouragement only to describe the active conduct type referred to below.[19] The mistake may be one of fact or law (questions of property ownership inevitably involving issues of both types).[20] In *Godfrey v Lees*,[21] for example, the relevant mistake was one of law. The claimant had jointly authored various musical works with the members of a pop band. The members mistakenly considered that only the person who had the original idea for a song was its composer; the claimant had not had the original idea but did take a sufficient part in its composition to be a joint owner of the rights in it.

Encouragement of mistake or expectation

In these cases, M's conduct goes beyond the merely passive and involves active conduct amounting to encouragement. It is certainly sufficient if W is encouraged to perform *acts in reliance* on the relevant belief.[22] It probably also suffices to demonstrate encouragement of the belief.[23] To distinguish the two types of encouragement would be extremely difficult, particularly in the light of the requirement that M has knowledge of the reliance.[24] In a very real sense, to encourage W in the belief that she has or will acquire an ownership interest is indirectly to encourage her to act accordingly. In encouragement cases, the state of mind of the claimant may take a number of slightly different forms, all of which are capable of giving rise to a proprietary estoppel. **11.009**

[18] This head of proprietary estoppel has sometimes been referred to simply as acquiescence or estoppel by acquiescence. It should be distinguished from the acquiescence doctrine of cases such as *Holder v Holder* [1968] Ch 353 and *De Bussche v Alt* (1877) 8 ChD 286 which may be used to bar an equitable, but not a legal, claim. There are close parallels between proprietary estoppel and this doctrine but they are not identical. See further paras 7.21–2 above.

[19] See paras 11.12–5.

[20] *Taylors Fashions Ltd v Liverpool Victoria Trustees Co. Ltd* [1982] 1 QB 133 at 148e.

[21] *Godfrey v John Lees* [1995] EMLR 307 at 333–34 and *West Middlesex Golf Club Limited v Ealing London Borough Council* (1993) 68 P&CR 461 at 482.

[22] *Willmot v Barber* (1880) 15 ChD 96 at 105. As to the categories of qualifying belief, see below at para. 11.86–95.

[23] *Ramsden v Dyson* (1866) LR 1 HL 129 HL at 170 and *Elitestone Ltd v Morris* (1997) 73 P&CR 259, CA (rev. on other grounds at [1997] 1 WLR 687 HL).

[24] See para. 11.21–2.

Mistake formed independently of M's conduct

W forms the mistaken view that she owns the property in question as a result of factors unrelated to M's conduct[25] and M encourages her to act in reliance on this belief. A practical example would include the situation where W builds on M's land thinking it to be her own and M takes on the contract to perform the works in question. In *Matharu v Matharu*,[26] W believed that property in dispute belonged to her husband, as a result of what he had told her. In fact it belonged to her father-in-law, who subsequently encouraged her mistake by referring to the house as belonging to her and his son. This category shades almost seamlessly into the unilateral mistake and acquiescence category referred to above. There is one significant distinction between the two: actionable mistakes under this head can include those shared by *both* W and M rather than being confined to those which are truly unilateral, that is confined to W.[27] If M has no knowledge of his own right to the property and thus shares the mistake made by W, he may be liable where he has actively encouraged W. By contrast, if his conduct is purely passive (as the acquiescence cases set above), no liability arises if M is ignorant of his own legal rights.[28] **11.010**

Mistake arising as a result of M's conduct: the imperfect gift cases

W's mistaken belief that she owns the property is caused by M stating explicitly or implicitly that this is the case. Put simply, M tells W that he has transferred the property to her. Such cases involve active encouragement of W's mistaken belief since M has actually authored it. If M's declaration that W is the owner is accompanied or followed by the appropriate execution of the relevant formality requirements, title passes and there is no need or scope for the operation of estoppel. It is only where these requirements are not satisfied, and hence the gift **11.011**

---

[25] Only the added element of active encouragement by M which distinguishes these cases from those described under the *Unilateral Mistake* above.

[26] *Matharu v Matharu* (1994) 68 P&CR 93, CA. See also *Huning v Ferrars* Gilb 85 (1711) 25 ER 59; *Handel v St Stephen's Close Ltd* [1994] EGLR 70 and *West Middlesex Golf Club Limited v Ealing London Borough Council* (1993) 68 P&CR 461.

[27] *Taylors Fashions Ltd v Liverpool Victoria Trustees Co. Ltd* [1982] 1 QB 133. See further para. 11.20 below.

[28] See below at para. 11.19 and *Kammins Ballrooms Co. Ltd v Zenith Investments (Torquay) Ltd* [1971] AC at 884d–h.

imperfect, that estoppel may operate. In, for example, *Pascoe v Turner*,[29] after a period of cohabitation between M and W, the former left stating '*the house is yours and everything in it*'. No formal transfer was ever executed. An estoppel arose as a result of W spending £230 on the house in the belief that it was her own.

Expectation: promises unsupported by consideration

W believes that she will, in the future, be granted an interest or right over M's property: **11.012**

> If a man, under a verbal agreement with a landlord for a certain interest in land, or, what amounts to the same thing, under an expectation, created or encouraged by the landlord, that he shall have a certain interest, takes possession of such land with the consent of the landlord, and upon the faith of such promise or expectation, with the knowledge of the landlord and without objection by him, lays out money on the land, a Court of equity will compel the landlord to give effect to such a promise or expectation.[30]

The claimant's belief may be formed by one of two slightly different methods: either it results simply from an express promise by M that such an right will be granted[31] or as a result of the mutual dealings between the parties:

> Short of an actual promise, if [M], by his words or conduct so behaves as to lead another to believe that he will not insist on his strict legal rights — knowing or intending that the other will act on that belief — and he does so act, that again will raise an equity in favour of the other.[32]

For example, in *ER Ives Investment Ltd v High*[33] and in *Crabb v Arun DC*,[34] the claimant was clearly promised an interest in M's property,

[29] [1979] 1 WLR 43, CA. See also *Dillwyn v Llewellyn* (1862) De G F and J 517, 45 ER 1285 and *Voyce v Voyce* (1991) 62 P&CR 290, CA.

[30] *Ramsden v Dyson* (1866) LR 1 HL 129, HL *per* Lord Kingsdown at 170. His dissent was on the facts not the law. See *Crabb v Arun* DC [1976] Ch 179, CA at 194a-d. *Note* that Lord Kingsdown's approach to the appropriate remedy *viz* the enforcement of the promise, is no longer the invariable or indeed even the preferred approach of the courts — see paras 11.50–4.

[31] See, for example, *Sledmore v Dalby* (1996) P&CR 196, CA; *Wayling v Jones* (1993) P&CR 170, CA; *Price v Hartwell* [1996] EGCS 98; *Durant v Heritage* [1994] EGCS 134, lexis transcript; *Re Basham decd* [1986] 1 WLR 1498. It is in this area that the potential conflict between proprietary estoppel and the contractual doctrine of consideration is at its most obvious since the court is giving legal effect to promises unsupported by consideration. See further at para. 11.102–7 below.

[32] *Per* Scarman L.J. in *Crabb v Arun* DC [1976] Ch 179, CA at 188c–d.

[33] [1967] 2 QB 379.

[34] [1976] Ch 179 at 195C.

specifically a right of way over it. In *Plimmer v Wellington Corporation,*[35] the understanding was less explicit: M (the government) was the owner of a harbour that requested W to extend the harbour's jetty and wharf and build a warehouse and shed to accommodate immigrants there. Both parties used the facilities harmoniously and to their mutual advantage for, at least, the following 16 years. It was held that the dealings between the parties showed clearly that both must have intended that the claimant should have an indefinite and irrevocable right to remain on the premises. There was no evidence that the parties had ever actually discussed the matter. A similar approach was applied in *Inwards v Baker.*[36] W was considering building a house; his father said *'why don't you build it on my land and make it a bit bigger?'*; the father's conduct must have generated an expectation in the son that he would be allowed to remain in occupation of the land for as long as he wanted.

It may be possible to characterize the so-called expectation cases as involving promises whether explicit or implicit. The expectation, by definition, must relate to the acquisition of rights in M's property.[37] Where qualifying mutual dealings take place, M, as the prior holder of the interest or right in question, must, at least implicitly, undertake to transfer it to W. However, the process which gives rise to liability may be much more subtle than a simple promissory analysis would seem to suggest. The mutual understanding may have emerged as a result of a number of factors occurring over a period of time, rather than as a result of a clear indication by M that an interest is to be transferred. What is crucial is the existence of some '. . . *unilateral or a shared assumption as to the future conduct of one or other party*'.[38] It is sufficient if the parties have dealt with one another and conducted business on the mutual assumption that a relevant right will eventually be granted, even if neither the precise nature of the right[39] nor the terms of grant have been finalized or even considered. Indeed, the necessity to **11.013**

[35] (1884) 9 Ap Cas 699, PC.

[36] *Inwards v Baker* [1965] 2 QB 29, CA at 37b.

[37] See para. 11.87 below.

[38] *Taylors Fashions Ltd v Liverpool Victoria Trustees Co. Ltd* [1982] 1 QB 133 at 148e. It is in this area that the proprietary estoppel doctrine shades almost imperceptibly into estoppel by convention, although the differing effects of the two doctrines may make it important to distinguish which one is operating in a particular case. See *West Middlesex Golf Club Limited v Ealing London Borough Council* (1993) 68 P&CR 461 at 482 and *John v George and Walton* (1996) 71 P&CR 375, CA.

[39] *Inwards v Baker* [1965] 2 QB 29, CA.

resort to an estoppel claim is generally resorted to where for some unforeseen reason, the latter terms are never, in fact, agreed.[40]

Proprietary estoppel may operate, in this instance, to relieve the parties of the harsher consequences which would otherwise flow from the unforeseen collapse of a joint enterprise, where they themselves have failed to allocate the risk of such an eventuality.[41] Explicit assumption of risk by one or other of the parties therefore negatives the operation of the doctrine. If W considered the possibility that the interest would not be granted but decided to go ahead with the acts in question, regardless, *in the hope* that the interest would be granted, no proprietary estoppel will arise. Conversely, it is necessary that M indicates, whether explicitly or implicitly, that he considers himself bound to grant the relevant interest and that therefore it is safe and risk free to act in reliance on the assumption.[42] Any reservation of position by M is fatal to an estoppel claim.[43] The unconscionability is not to be found in the transaction itself but in the subsequent attempt to go back on the basic assumptions which underpin the transaction.[44] The doctrine will operate to prevent a party from taking unfair advantage of the collapse of a scheme in which it has actively participated by, for example, engaging in protracted relationship involving mutual dealings. This type of situation is discussed further at paragraph 11.108 to 11.110 in the context of pre-contract negotiations. **11.014**

The distinction between the expectation and the imperfect gift cases is minimal. It depends partly on the nature of the representation made by W and partly on the belief formed by W as a result. A promise to transfer in the future can give rise to liability only under the expectation head. A statement of present gift or entitlement, for example 'the house is yours and everything in it' may lead to liability under either head. If W consequently forms the belief that the gift *has been perfected*, either by mistake of law (she believed an averment of gift was sufficient) or one of fact (she knew formalities were required but believed that **11.015**

---

40 Though see below, at para. 11.102–7, for instances where an estoppel claim may be used to supplement or replace one in contract.

41 See, *e.g. Lim v Ang* [1992] 1 WLR 113 PC (Brunei).

42 *Holiday Inns Inc v Broadhead* (1974) 232 EG 951 where W thought that it had a gentlemen's agreement and M showed an intention to be bound by the arrangement.

43 *Boxbusher Properties v Graham* (1976) 240 EG 463 at 465 where W took '*a calculated business risk*' knowing that the landlord might enforce his rights at any time. See generally AG for Hong Kong v Humphries Estate (Queen's Gardens) Ltd [1987] 1 A.C. 114, PC (Hong Kong).

44 *Crabb v Arun DC* [1976] Ch 179, CA *per* Scarman L.J. at 195c and *Taylors Fashions Ltd v Liverpool Victoria Trustees Co. Ltd* [1982] 1 QB 133 at 147g–h.

they had been carried out), the case falls within the first head. If, however, she knew that further formalities were necessary to perfect the gift, the case falls under the latter head and involves the expectation of future grant of an interest, a statement of present gift being readily construed as including an undertaking that formal requirements had or would be complied with.

Mistake requirement

As is set out above, proprietary estoppel may operate in a number of slightly different situations. In particular, it may operate either where W has made a mistake as to the extent of her present rights or where she expects to be granted an interest in the future. Some confusion has been caused by failure properly to distinguish these two situations. In *Willmot v Barber*,[45] Mr Justice Fry laid down five probanda which he perceived to be vital in establishing proprietary estoppel: **11.016**

> In the first place the plaintiff must have made a mistake as to his legal rights. Secondly, the plaintiff must have expended some money or must have done some act (not necessarily on the defendant's land) on the faith of his mistaken belief. Thirdly, the defendant, the possessor of the legal right must know of the existence of his own right which is inconsistent with the right claimed by the plaintiff. If he does not know of it then he is in the same position as the plaintiff and the doctrine of acquiescence is founded upon conduct with knowledge of your legal rights. Fourthly, the defendant, the possessor of the legal right, must know of the plaintiff's mistaken belief of his rights. If he does not there is nothing which calls upon him to assert his own legal rights. Lastly, the defendant, the possessor of the legal right, must have encouraged the plaintiff in his expenditure of money or in other acts which he has done, either directly or by abstaining from asserting his legal right. Where all these elements exist there is fraud of such a nature as will entitle the court to restrain the possessor of the legal right from exercising it, but, in my judgment, nothing short of this will do . . .[46]

The first of the five probanda requires W to have made a mistake as to her legal rights. It is semantically possible to characterize the expectation cases as involving a mistake: W mistakenly thought that **11.017**

[45] (1880) 15 ChD 96.

[46] At 105; arguably the fourth probanda encompasses the third since the latter requires that M knew not only of W's belief, but also that it was a mistaken one; logically it is difficult to see how M could know that the belief was mistaken without knowledge of the true position *viz* that M owned the property and not W.

M would keep his promise or that the plans made by the parties would come to fruition. To analyse such situations as mistake in this way is not, however, helpful and according to Professor Finn requires '*a willing suspension of disbelief*'.[47] It masks the problem with which the courts are seeking to deal in this type of case, namely the situation where W has relied on M's promise in such circumstances that it would be unconscionable for M to be permitted to resile from it:

> In Lord Kingsdown's example . . . for instance, there is no room for the literal application of the probanda, for the circumstances there postulated do not presuppose a mistake on anybody's part but the fostering of an expectation in the minds of both parties at the time but from which once it had been acted upon, it would be unconscionable to permit the landlord to depart.[48]

At the time the promise was made, both parties may and frequently do intend that the promise should be fulfilled. The *Willmot* probanda were not devised to deal with this type of case and their application to such cases is inappropriate.[49] They have, however, been frequently and incorrectly applied even in fairly recent expectation cases.[50] The difficulty in identifying a mistake in an expectation case may explain

---

47 *Finn, 'Equitable estoppel'* Chap. 4 of *Essays in Equity* ed. Finn (1985); *Holiday Inns Inc v Broadhead* (1974) 232 EG 951 at 1081, 1087 and *Central Street Properties Ltd v Mansbrook Rudd and Co Ltd* (1986) 276 EG 414.

48 *Taylors Fashions Ltd v Liverpool Victoria Trustees Co. Ltd* [1982] 1 QB 133 at 147g–h. See text at n. 30 para. 11.12 above for the example referred to by Lord Kingsdown.

49 *Taylors Fashions Ltd v Liverpool Victoria Trustees Co. Ltd* [1982] 1 QB 133 at 147, 151–2; *Lloyds Bank v Carrick* [1996], CA 4 All ER 630 CA *per* Morrit L.J. at 640c–g; *Shaw v Applegate* [1977] 1 WLR 970, CA at 977c–g, 978c–d, 980b–d; *Griffiths v Williams* (1977) 248 EG at 949 and *Re Basham dec'd* [1986] 1 WLR 1498 at 1507g.

50 *Coombes v Smith* [1986] 1 WLR 808 at 818a; *Crabb v Arun DC* [1976] Ch 179, CA *per* Scarman L.J. at 195a–e; *Swallow Securities Ltd v Isenberg* [1985] EGLR 132, CA (the probanda were '*guidelines*' which would probably prove to be '*necessary and essential*' to assist the court in establishing whether unconscionable conduct had occurred); *Salvation Army Trustee Co Ltd v West Yorkshire Metropolitan County Council* (1981) P&CR 179 at 194 and *Gloucestershire CC v Farrow* [1983] 2 All ER 1031 at 1036. See also *Matharu v Matharu* (1994) 68 P&CR 93, CA *per* Roche L.J. at 102 (Hurst L.J. concurring) where the active encouragement of the property owner made the application of the probanda inappropriate albeit that the case was an example of mistake: Milne [1995] MLR Vol. 58(3) 412. See further *Veitch v Caldecott* (1945) 173 LT 30 at 34 and *Stilwell v Simpson* (1983) 133 NLJ 894 which referred generally to a mistake requirement without direct reference to *Willmot*.

some of the harsher decisions in this area, particularly those occurring in a family context where a firm belief in legal entitlement is often lacking.[51]

THE PROPERTY OWNER'S KNOWLEDGE

The knowledge requirements may be satisfied via an agent, where the knowledge may be imputed to M on ordinary principles of attribution.[52] **11.018**

Knowledge of inconsistent rights

Unilateral mistake and acquiescence cases

In passive acquiescence cases, M will incur no liability unless he knew, not only of W's belief,[53] but of his (M's) own legal rights (*i.e.* of M's title and right to object to alterations to the property). Put simply, M must know that W's belief is mistaken.[54] Some doubt has been expressed as to whether such knowledge is an essential prerequisite of liability or merely one of a number of factors to be taken into account.[55] We consider that such knowledge is essential in passive acquiescence cases. The underlying basis of the doctrine is unconscionability or unfairness. More specifically, M will be prevented from taking unfair advantage of W's mistake. There seems little warrant for making M bear the consequences of this mistake unless he played some part in its formation or continuance. Where M has knowledge of his own rights, by failing to correct W's error, he has played a genuine role in its continuance. It is reasonable to expect M, in such circumstances, to take positive action to correct the error. Thus, a duty to speak out or to protest **11.019**

---

[51] See Gray at p. 322 and the authorities there cited at n.17.

[52] *Swallow Securities Ltd v Isenberg* [1985] EGLR 132, CA; *AG to Prince of Wales v Collom* [1916] 2 KB 193.

[53] As to which see below at para. 11.86–9.

[54] *Willmot v Barber* (1880) 15 ChD 96 at 105. *Taylors Fashions Ltd v Liverpool Victoria Trustees Co. Ltd* [1982] 1 QB 133 at 147b. Goff and Jones, at 168, describe Lord Cranworth's formulation as the '*equitable analogue*' of free acceptance; the existence of this doctrine is highly controversial but it should be noted that one of its essential prerequisites is that the recipient of the benefit must have an opportunity to reject the service rendered. No such opportunity is available unless the recipient knows that it owns the property in issue.

[55] *Taylors Fashions Ltd v Liverpool Victoria Trustees Co. Ltd* [1982] 1 QB 133 at 147b.

at the performance of the relevant works is generated;[56] such a duty cannot arise unless M believes that he has a right over the property in question;[57] it cannot be unreasonable to refrain from correcting a belief which you do not know is mistaken.[58] It may not be necessary to demonstrate that M had actual knowledge of his rights so long as it could be shown that he had *'at least a suspicion of the true position'*.[59]

Encouragement cases

Where active encouragement has taken place, it is not necessary to establish that M knew of his own inconsistent right.[60] The reason for the distinction between passive acquiescence and active encouragement cases is as follows. Whereas it cannot be unconscionable to refrain from asserting rights which you do not know you own,[61] it may well be unconscionable to assert those rights when you have actively encouraged another to rely on an assumption inconsistent with them. This may involve taking unfair advantage of the parties' mutual mistake by throwing the whole of the loss caused by the collapse of their joint enterprise on to one of the parties. The remedial flexibility of the doctrine **11.020**

---

[56] In fulfilling his duty to disabuse W of her error, M presumably needs to take only such steps as are reasonable in the circumstances.

[57] See Pawlowsky at p. 125.

[58] Although Oliver J expressed some reservations as to this knowledge requirement, even in the context of pure acquiescence, in *Taylors Fashions* above it was clearly material to the actual decision made in the two cases in issue. LV were the assignees of the reversion of numbers 20 to 22 Westover Road, all of which were shop premises. TF had been granted an option to renew its tenancy of number 22 by LV's predecessor in title. LV did not wish to be left in the position where the lease on one of the shops was extended but not the other two; in subsequently letting numbers 20 and 21 to OC, LV therefore agreed that the duration of OC's lease would be dependent on whether LV exercised their option to renew. None of the parties realized, until after extensive works had been performed on the properties, that TF's option was void against LV for want of registration as an estate contract under the Land Charges Act 1972. LV had not encouraged TF to carry out the works on the premises and '*. . . so far as acquiescence is concerned the defendants could not lawfully object to the work and could be under no duty to TF to communicate that which they did not know themselves, namely that the non-registration of the option rendered it unenforceable*'. In contrast, LV had encouraged OC to expend a considerable sum both on alterations to the premises and in purchasing the two leases, upon faith of the assumption that it was at least possible that LV's option might be exercised. LV were thus estopped from pleading the invalidity of the option against OC but not TF (although TF also failed to establish detrimental reliance; see para. 11.25 below).

[59] *Taylors Fashions Ltd v Liverpool Victoria Trustees Co. Ltd* [1982] 1 QB 133.

[60] *ibid.* at 147b and *West Middlesex Golf Club Limited v Ealing London Borough Council* (1993) 68 P&CR 461.

[61] See above at para. 11.19.

is such that it can divide the loss caused by the parties' misapprehension between them.

Knowledge of W's acts in reliance

A proprietary estoppel may only be established against a party who either intended[62] W to act on the assurance or knew that she was in fact so acting.[63] This requires knowledge both of W's actions and of the fact that they were performed in reliance[64] on a belief or expectation relating to the disputed property. It is not always necessary to show that M knew of the actual commission of the relevant conduct, so long as he was aware of the intention so to act: in *Crabb v Arun District Council,*[65] W sold a portion of his land without retaining a right of way over it and did so in reliance on the expectation of a right of access over the property of the Council. The latter's subsequent refusal to allow such access left the claimant's property landlocked. The claim succeeded, despite the fact that the Council was not notified of the actual sale transaction. It was sufficient that the Council knew that Mr Crabb intended to sell the plots separately and that he would consequently need the access point which its agents had promised him. Lord Denning's judgment[66] suggests that this is a general principle while Lord Justice Scarman was more cautious: **11.021**

> . . . the court must be careful to avoid generalization. I can conceive of cases in which it would be absolutely appropriate for a defendant to say: 'But you should not have acted to your detriment until you had had a word with me and I could have put you right.' But there are cases in which it is far too late for a defendant to get himself out of his pickle by

[62] *Crabb v Arun* DC [1976] Ch 179, CA at 194a–d.

[63] *Grant v Edwards* [1986] Ch 638, CA *per* Browne-Wilkinson V.C. at 656g (*dicta*); *Ward v Gold* (1969) 211 EG 155 at 161; *Costagliola v English* (1969) 210 EG 1425 at 1431; *Appleby v Cowley, The Times* 14 April 1982, lexis transcript; *Coombes v Smith* [1986] 1 WLR 808 at 812a; *Griffiths v Williams* (1977) 248 EG 947 *per* Goff L.J. at 949; *JT Developments v Quinn* (1991) 62 P&CR 33, CA at 46; *Holiday Inns Inc v Broadhead* (1974) 232 EG 951 at 1087; *Barclays Bank plc v Zaroovabli* [1997] 2 All ER 19 and *Film Investors Overseas Services SA v The Home Video Channel (trading as the Adult Channel),* [1997] EMLR 347.

[64] *Costagliola v English* (1969) 210 EG 1425 at 1431 and *Gross v French* (1976) 238 EG 39, CA at 41.

[65] [1976] 1 Ch 179, CA.

[66] *ibid.* at 189c–d.

> putting upon the plaintiff that sort of duty; and this, in my judgment, is one of those cases.[67]

The Council could no longer complain about Mr Crabb's failure to inform it of the impending transaction for two reasons. First, it had failed, for 13.5 months, to inform Mr Crabb that no right of way would or could be granted without a decision of the Council itself (rather than the employees with whom Mr Crabb had discussed the matter). Secondly, it had reaffirmed Mr Crabb's expectation by erecting gates at the point where access had been agreed in principle.[68]

There is some uncertainty as to whether it is is necessary to show that M had actual knowledge of the relevant acts or whether it is sufficient to show that he ought, in all the circumstances, to have known that they were taking place. It was held in both *Salvation Army Trustee Co Ltd v West Yorkshire Metropolitan County Council*[69] and *Swallow Securities Ltd v Isenberg*[70] that it suffices to show that M *ought to have known* that W was acting in reliance on the relevant expectation. However, in neither case was the point addressed in any detail. Further, a contrasting approach was taken in *Ward v Gold*[71] where W prepared building plans, involving an encroachment on M's airspace. M was given the plans to examine and expressed herself delighted with them, as they would not obstruct her view. Despite this, no proprietary estoppel claim arose, since the question of boundaries had not been raised and M's attention was not drawn to the projection over her property. Arguably, individuals should not be at risk of being divested of their property rights, in the absence of conscious knowledge of the relevant facts.[72] On balance, however, we consider that all that should be necessary is that M be put on notice of W's belief and reliance. The mere fact of expenditure disproportionate to W's actual interest may be sufficient **11.022**

---

67 *ibid.* at 198c–d and *JT Developments v Quinn* (1991) 62 P&CR 33, CA.

68 [1976] 1 Ch 179, CA at 198d–g.

69 (1981) P&CR 179 *per* Woolfe J. at 196.

70 [1985] EGLR 132, CA *per* Cumming Bruce L.J. These two cases are cited both by Gray at 331 text and n. 13 and by Goff and Jones at 170 as authority for the proposition referred to in the text; also cited is *Watson v Goldsbrough* [1986] 1 EGLR 265 at 266–7 but it was found as a fact in that case that M *actually knew* about the works; they were so substantial that he could not possibly have failed to notice them. Hence, the case was one of actual conscious knowledge albeit inferred from evidence of the surrounding circumstances. See also *AG to Prince of Wales v Collom* [1916] 2 KB 193 at 199.

71 (1969) 211 EG 155 at 161.

72 Compare also the requirement of conscious knowledge in cases of election as to which see para. 4.23–4.

to put M on enquiry.[73] The absence of actual knowledge therefore should not bar a proprietary estoppel claim although it may be taken into account applying the flexible test advocated in *Taylors Fashions*,[74] particularly where M has benefited from W's acts in reliance.[75]

Knowledge of detriment

It is not necessary to show that M realized that detriment was likely to flow from W's conduct, were she to resile from the assurance made. Often, such an inference will be obvious to anyone who knows of the acts performed, for example, where money is spent on improving M's property. Qualifying detriment may, however, take diverse and sometimes unexpected forms.[76] The proprietary estoppel doctrine is probably flexible enough, however, to permit M's failure to appreciate the possibility of harm to the claimant to be taken into account in determining the final outcome between the parties. **11.023**

RELIANCE

A proprietary estoppel claim will arise only where W has acted in reliance on the assurance.[77] She must have been led to change her position in the sense of acting differently from the way in which she would otherwise have done. It is not necessary to establish that the acts performed fall within some pre-existing recognized category.[78] Any act will suffice so long as it involves a change of position which is such as to cause W to suffer detriment in the event of M's resiling from the assumption made.[79] There are certain general restrictions inherent in this apparently flexible approach: certain categories of acts have been **11.024**

[73] Although only if M knew that the expenditure was being made for W's own benefit as opposed to that of some third party — see *Swallow Securities Ltd v Isenberg* [1985] EGLR 132, CA.

[74] [1982] 1 QB 133. See para. 11.01–2 above.

[75] See *Finn*, 'Equitable estoppel' Chap. 4 of *Essays in Equity* ed. Finn (1985) at p.81.

[76] See para. 11.39–46 below.

[77] *AG for Hong Kong v Humphreys Estate (Queen's Gardens) Ltd* [1987] 1 AC 114 PC HK *per* Lord Templeman at 124d–c; *Sledmore v Dalby* [1966] P&CR 196 CA *per* Hobhouse L.J. at 207; *Pascoe v Turner* [1979] 1 WLR 43 CA; *Wayling v Jones* [1993] P&CR 170 CA and *Greasley v Cook* [1980] 1 WLR 1306 CA.

[78] '*. . . the categories of detriment are not closed*': *Watts v Story* (1984) 134 NLJ 631, CA *per* Dunn and Slade L.JJ.

[79] See para. 11.31.

held to be incapable of giving rise to detriment.[80] Reliance is essential to a claim for proprietary estoppel because it provides the causative link between the conduct of M and the harm suffered by W.[81]

The assurance need not have been the single or primary motivating factor behind W's actions. It is sufficient if the assurance induced[82] or influenced[83] W's decision to perform the relevant acts but not if it was merely material to it.[84] The rule is illustrated by contrasting the results in the two cases in issue in *Taylors Fashions Ltd v Liverpool Victoria Trustees Co. Ltd*,[85] in which Taylors and Olds were both tenants of Liverpool Victoria. The terms of Olds' lease made its duration dependent on that of Taylors'. Both tenants mistakenly believed that Taylors had a valid option to extend its lease by 14 years. Both performed extensive works on their respective demised premises: the works carried out by Taylors were virtually essential for the use of the building and the capital cost would have been written off by the end of the unextended term of the lease. Further, the works would, in all likelihood, have been performed even had the assumption never been made. Put simply, the works were performed *in the belief* that the term could be extended but not *on faith of that belief*. In contrast, it was obvious that Olds would neither have performed their works nor entered the lease in the terms which they did, were it not for their belief that the Taylors lease could be extended. Olds therefore succeeded and Taylors failed. **11.025**

Burden of proof

In certain circumstances, once W has shown that she has acted to her detriment,[86] she does not have to prove, affirmatively, the causal link between **11.026**

---

[80] See paras 11.43–5 below.

[81] It thus links the moral culpability of M with the moral claim of W.

[82] *Swallow Securities Ltd v Isenberg* [1985] EGLR 132, CA *per* Cumming Bruce L.J. at 134.

[83] *Amalgamated Investment & Property Co. Ltd, (in liquidation) v Texas Commerce International Bank Ltd* [1982] 1 QB 84 *per* Goff J. at 105a; *Layton v Martin* [1986] 2 FLR 227 at 235f–g and *Wayling v Jones* (1993) P&CR 170 CA *per* Balcombe L.J. at 173.

[84] *Credit Suisse v Allerdale BC* [1996] 1 Lloyd's Rep. 315 at 369 (affd on other grounds [1996] 2 Lloyd's Rep. 241).

[85] [1982] 1 QB 133. As to the facts of the case see further para. 11.20.

[86] See generally paras 11.31–8 on detriment. There is some confusion as to whether the reversal of the burden applies to proof of detriment or proof of reliance, probably resulting from a failure to distinguish clearly between the two concepts. In our view, the onus of proving detriment remains, in all cases, with the claimant — *Coombes v Smith* [1986] 1 WLR 808 at 821b–f; contra. *Durant v Heritage* [1994] EGCS 134. The underlying rational of the principle, under discussion, lies in the court's

her actions and her belief or expectation. Put simply, she does not have to prove that she would not have performed the acts *but for* her assumption: there is a rebuttable presumption that they were so performed. The burden of proof shifts to M to show that W's acts were *not* so performed.[87] In precisely what circumstances the burden shifts is not, however, clear. In *Greasley v Cook*,[88] it was held to be sufficient to show that M's statements[89] were '. . . *calculated to influence* . . .'[90] W or '. . . *would be of such a nature as would induce, . . . tend to induce* . . .[W] *or would be a part of the inducement* . . .'[91] on W to perform the relevant acts. The mere fact that M intended so to influence W would seem to be insufficient if the particular circumstances suggest that M was unlikely, in fact, to have been so influenced. In *Watkins v Emslie*,[92] the tenant had a statutory right to extend her tenancy but failed to serve the requisite notice in the correct form. The Court of Appeal doubted[93] whether the tenant's clear assertions that her tenancy was subsisting were calculated to make the landlord believe that the notice to extend was a valid one, as the wording of the relevant statute made it clear that it was not and the landlord had been

---

reluctance to engage in speculation as to what the claimant would have done in a hypothetical situation *viz* one where the promise had not been made: *Greasley v Cook* [1980] 1 WLR 1306, CA at 1311d. Investigating what acts were performed and what harm will flow from them involves no such speculation.

87 *Greasley v Cook* [1980] 1 WLR 1306, CA *per* Lord Denning M.R. at 1311b–d, *per* Waller L.J. at 1313c–f and *per* Dunn L.J. at 1314a; *Hammersmith and Fulham BC v Top Shop Centres Ltd* [1990] Ch 237 at 262c–d; *Grant v Edwards* [1986] Ch 638, CA *per* Browne-Wilkinson V.C. at 657c–d (*dicta*); *Maharaj v Chand* [1986] AC 898, PC (Fiji) at 907g–h (referring to constructive trusts rather than estoppel); *Re Basham decd* [1986] 1 WLR 1498 at 1507f–g (*dicta*); *Wayling v Jones* (1993) P&CR 170, CA (*ratio*) *per* Balcombe L.J. at 173 (Hoffmann and Leggat L.JJ. concurring); *Coombes v Smith* [1986] 1 WLR 808 *per* Jonathan Parker Q.C. at 821b–f; *Hamp v Bygrave* (1983) 266 EG 720 *per* Boreham J. at 726 (*ratio*); *Habib Bank Ltd v Habib Bank A.G. Zurich* [1981] 1 WLR 1265, CA *per* Oliver L.J. at 1287a–c. Lord Templeman in *AG for Hong Kong v Humphreys Estate (Queen's Gardens) Ltd* [1987] 1 AC 114, PC (Hong Kong) at 124c–d might be taken to suggest the contrary position (see Gray at p. 333) but W failed in that case because there was affirmative proof that it performed the relevant acts in reliance, not on the alleged assumption but on a different basis, insufficient to found an estoppel (127g–h); the burden of proof point was not discussed.

88 [1980] 1 WLR 1306, CA at 1311.

89 The authorities tend to refer to statements or promises but there is no indication that the burden can never be reversed where M's conduct has been solely passive; it would obviously be more difficult to establish in such cases.

90 [1980] 1 WLR 1306, CA at 1311d *per* Lord Denning M.R. and *Re Basham decd* [1986] 1 WLR 1498 at 1506a.

91 [1980] 1 WLR 1306, CA at 1313c–e *per* Waller L.J.; see also *Grant v Edwards* [1986] Ch 638, CA *per* Browne-Wilkinson V.C. at 657c–d (*dicta*).

92 (1981) 261 EG 1192, CA at 1194.

93 The landlord's estoppel claim also failed on a number of other grounds.

advised throughout by solicitors (though there was no evidence that the validity of the notice had been considered by the landlord or his advisers). In *Wayling v Jones,*[94] the Court of Appeal appeared to shift the emphasis away from examination of the nature the communication made by M to analysis of the nature of the acts performed by W. Their Lordships held that the burden would only be reversed where W's *'conduct is of such a nature that inducement may be inferred'*. No guidance is given as to what type of conduct suffices but presumably if W's acts were of such a nature as would probably have been done anyway, the burden will not be reversed.[95] An alternative formulation is to require W to prove that she acted in a way no reasonable person could be expected to, in the absence of reliance on the belief in issue. There seems no doubt that the burden will be reversed if W can discharge the onus, both in respect to the nature of the communication *and* the acts performed; whether these distinct conditions are cumulative or alternative is not clear.

Rebutting the presumption

To rebut the presumption, it should be sufficient to demonstrate that W would have acted in the same way even if she had never formed the belief or expectation in issue.[96] Put simply, it would suffice if M positively proved that W acted in the way she did because of some reason other than her expectation of an interest in disputed property. In *Wayling v Jones,*[97] W stated, in cross examination, that he would have performed the relevant acts and services, even had M *never made* the promise in issue. Despite this finding, W's claim succeeded, because of his evidence that he would have left M and ceased the relevant services, had the **11.027**

[94] (1993) P&CR 170, CA *per* Balcombe L.J. at 173 (Hoffmann and Leggat L.JJ. concurring).

[95] The requirement is reminiscent of that applicable to acts in support of part performance of a contract under the now repealed Law of Property Act 1925, s. 40: see *Davies C, Estoppel — reliance and remedy* [1995] Conv 409 at 411–12. There are also close parallels with the conditions which will cause a court to infer reliance in constructive trust cases — see *Grant v Edwards* [1986] Ch 638, CA *per* Nourse L.J. at 648g.

[96] *Greasley v Cook* [1980] 1 WLR 1306, CA *per* Lord Denning M.R. at 1311d, *per* Waller L.J. at 1313a–b, and *per* Dunn L.J. at 1314a and *Re Basham decd* [1986] 1 WLR 1498 at 1506f–g.

[97] *Wayling v Jones* (1993) P&CR 170, CA *per* Balcombe L.J. at 175 (Hoffmann and Leggat L.JJ. concurring).

promise *been withdrawn*. This approach seems out of line with the earlier authorities cited above[98] and is probably incorrect.

A claimant cannot establish a proprietary estoppel on the basis of acts which it was under a statutory duty to perform in any event.[99] Deliberate attempts to obtain an interest through proprietary estoppel by performing acts in response to an assurance given will probably fail[1] because the conduct is not motivated by the relevant belief but by the hope of a legal remedy. **11.028**

The commission of domestic services will rarely give rise to a successful proprietary estoppel claim because of the practical difficulties in establishing a causative link with the relevant belief or expectation.[2] Such acts are frequently performed because of love and affection rather than because of any belief in or anticipation of an interest in property.[3] The presumption of reliance is thus fairly readily rebutted. The courts have been reluctant, however, to penalize those with altruistic motives and have devised various (sometimes dubious) ways of avoiding the application of strict causation principles. For example, in *Griffiths v Williams*,[4] W succeeded despite failing consciously to connect her work on the property with M's promise and *'being reluctant to admit even to herself that she was spending money with a view to her own inheritance rather than the comfort of her mother* [M]'. It was enough that M's assurance prevented W from considering the long-term position; if she had, she might not have effected the improvements which she did.[5] **11.029**

Although substantial financial contributions to household expenses **11.030**

---

[98] See also the comment made in Hayton and Marshall at p. 68, n. 89 that the claimant in *Coombes v Smith* [1986] 1 WLR 808 would surely have walked out on her lover, had he told her that he was reneging on his promise to provide her with a home for life. Such an incident would have undermined their whole relationship. See further para. 11.43 on the facts and result of *Coombes*.

[99] *Gloucestershire CC v Farrow* [1983] 2 All ER 103, CA.

[1] *Thomas v Fuller-Brown* [1988] 1 FLR 237, further, such claimants would have difficulty establishing that it would be unconscionable to deny them a remedy. See para. 11.58.

[2] Further, there is some doubt as to whether domestic services are capable of constituting sufficient acts in reliance, *i.e.* whether performance of such tasks can ever be said to give rise to detriment. See, further, under *Detriment* at paras 11.43–6 below.

[3] *Coombes v Smith* [1986] 1 WLR 808 at 820a–1b; *Re Basham decd* [1986] 1 WLR 1498 at 1505E–H and *Layton v Martin* [1986] 2 FLR 227 at 235F–H. See, however, *Greasley v Cooke* [1980] 1 WLR 1306 where a claim was successfully based on performance of domestic services.

[4] (1977) 248 EG 947, CA. See para. 11.26 above on the benevolent approach taken to rebutting the presumption in *Wayling v Jones* (1993) P&CR 170, CA *per* Balcombe L.J. at 175.

[5] (1977) 248 EG 947, CA at 949.

(including repairs) are capable of giving rise to a proprietary estoppel,[6] such payments will frequently, though not invariably,[7] be viewed as paid for reasons other than any expectation of an interest in that property. Specifically, where W is in occupation of property to which the outgoings relate, such payments are often found to be made in exchange for the benefit of being allowed to live in the property,[8] to enhance the enjoyment of the use of the property[9] or as a contribution to shared common expenses (where there is shared occupancy).[10] Even substantial redecoration and renovation, where performed against the background of a personal relationship, has been frequently found to be motivated by a wish to benefit the family and contribute to family life[11] rather than by any belief in legal entitlement.

DETRIMENT

Detriment is a vital component of a successful claim of proprietary estoppel.[12] It has often been said that a claimant must have 'acted to her detriment'. This formulation has led to some confusion: as was pointed **11.031**

---

6 *Grant v Edwards* [1986] Ch 638, CA; *Lloyds Bank v Rosset* [1991] 1 AC 107 and *Risch v McFee* [1991] FLR 105. The courts are particularly ready to recognize such contributions as founding a claim to M's property where they have facilitated M's discharging the mortgage on the asset to which the assumption relates.

7 *Pascoe v Turner* [1979] 1 WLR 43, CA and *Veitch v Caldecott* (1945) 173 LT 30.

8 *Griffiths v Williams* (1977) 248 EG 947, CA at 947 and *Stratulatos v Stratulatos* [1988] 2 NZLR 424 at 432–3.

9 *Bostock v Bryant and Another* (1991) 61 P&CR 23, CA; *Stilwell v Simpson* (1983) 133 NLJ 894; *E and L Berg Homes Ltd v Grey* (1979) 253 EG 473, and *Costagliola v English* (1969) 210 EG 1425 at 1431: *cf.* the grounds on which Taylors failed in their claim in *Taylors Fashions Ltd v Liverpool Victoria Trustees Co. Ltd* [1982] 1 QB 133 as explained in para. 11.25 above.

10 *Hannaford v Selby* (1976) 239 EG 811, where only the possibility of a constructive trust was considered but the same approach would be likely to be applied in relation to proprietary estoppel.

11 *Philip Lowe (Chinese Restaurant) Ltd v Sau Man Lee* (CA unrep. 9 July 1985) lexis transcript and *Lloyds Bank v Rosset* [1991] 1 AC 107 at 131d–f.

12 *Sledmore v Dalby* (1996) P&CR 196 CA at 207; *Godfrey v John Lees* [1995] EMLR 307; *Wayling v Jones* (1993) P&CR 170, CA; *Lim v Ang* [1992] 1 WLR 113, PC (Brunei); *Taylors Fashions Ltd v Liverpool Victoria Trustees Co. Ltd* [1982] 1 QB 133; *Elitestone Ltd v Morris* (1997) 73 P&CR 259, CA (rev. on other ground [1997] 1 WLR 687 HL). In our view both the doctrines of estoppel by representation and equitable forbearance impose the same detriment requirements as proprietary estoppel. The only difference between the three doctrines seems to be the anomolous cases discussed at paras 8.102–7 and 11.37 which, if correct must, we submit, be confined to estoppel by representation. Further useful discussion of the detriment principle may therefore be found at paras. 8.88–107 above and 12.33–50 below.

out by Mr Justice Dixon in *Grundt v Great Boulder Pty Gold Mines Ltd*, whilst it is not strictly incorrect, it '*. . . does not bring out the basal purpose of the doctrine*'.[13] The detriment, which it is the aim of proprietary estoppel to prevent, is that which would flow from W's change of position, were M to be permitted to resile from the relevant assurance or deny the truth of W's belief:

> . . . the real detriment or harm from which the law seeks to give protection is that which would flow from the change of position if the assumption were deserted that led to it. So long as the assumption is adhered to, the party who altered his situation on the faith of it cannot complain. His complaint is that when afterwards that other party makes a different state of affairs the basis of an assertion of rights against him, then if it is allowed, his own original change of position will operate as a detriment. His action or inaction must be such that, if the assumption on which he proceeded is shown to be wrong and an inconsistent state of affairs were accepted as the foundation of the rights and duties of himself and the opposite party, the consequence would be to make his original act or failure to act a source of prejudice.[14]

Two aspects of the *Grundt* formulation should be noted. First, since W **11.032**
needs to establish only that she will suffer detriment or prejudice *if M resiles* from the assumption, the change of position, itself, need not be onerous, unpleasant or damaging. So long as the assumption is adhered to, W suffers no prejudice. On the contrary, she will often benefit from her change of position, for example, where she has made improvements to a property which she occupies and in which she believes she has, or will be granted, an interest.[15] Secondly, claimants may be said to suffer a detriment as a

[13] *Grundt v Great Boulder Pty Gold Mines Ltd* (1937) 59 CLR 641 *per* Dixon J. at 674 (an estoppel by convention case but the relevant principle would seem to be equally applicable in this context).

[14] *ibid.* at 674–5, *Waltons Stores (Interstate) Ltd v Maher* [1988] 164 CLR 387 (HC of Australia) *per* Brennan J. at 419, *Sledmore v Dalby* (1996) P&CR 196 CA *per* Hobhouse L.J. at 208.

[15] A benefit is received via the enhanced enjoyment of the property even if the expected interest, or long term right of occupation, is denied: *Pascoe v Turner* [1979] 1 WLR 431 CA. See para. 11.30 above for the difficulty in establishing reliance in such situations. In *Brinnand v Ewens* [1987] 2 EGLR 67, CA *per* Nourse L.J. at 68B–C (Sir Roualeyn Cumming-Bruce concurring), it was held that the interest which the claimant expects must be of sufficient magnitude to justify the expenditure made; this suggests that expenditure which is not so justifiable and is therefore genuinely detrimental to W (even where the assumption is adhered to) is insufficient to raise a proprietary estoppel. This approach seems inconsistent with *Baker v Baker* [1993] 25 HLR 408, CA where W's contribution was not commensurate with the advantages which it was contemplated that he would receive; this did not prevent an estoppel arising but did restrict the relief awarded. We consider the latter approach to be the correct one.

result of the mere fact of a broken promise, that is, the denial of the promised benefit. This type of detriment, alone, is insufficient to bring the proprietary estoppel doctrine into play; some additional disadvantage is necessary, caused by W's change of position.[16] This limitation on the scope of the doctrine is necessary to prevent the undermining of the doctrine of consideration. Were such detriment to be sufficient for an estoppel claim, all promises relating to the grant of an interest in property would become legally enforceable, whether supported by consideration or not.[17]

The detriment must have been suffered by the claimant rather than another person. We would suggest that the acceptance by the Court of Appeal in *Matharu v Matharu*[18] that works and expenditure carried out by W's husband could be used to support her claim to proprietary estoppel is questionable.[19] Further, it seems that no proprietary estoppel claim will lie where the detriment suffered is trifling or *de minimis*.[20] In assessing the gravity of the detriment, however, the court will be prepared to take into account W's personal circumstances and means.[21] Mere personal distress, however, cannot give rise to a claim[22]: in this context '. . . *.equity is concerned with the protection of property and proprietary interests, not with the protection of people's feelings*'.[23] **11.033**

There is a considerable overlap between detriment and unconscionablity. It will be impossible in our view to establish sufficiently unconscionable conduct in the absence of detriment. The two concepts are distinguishable, however, since the court will take into account a **11.034**

[16] *Commonwealth of Australia v Verwayen* [1990] 170 CLR 394 *per* Brennan J. at 429.

[17] See further para. 11.102–7 below.

[18] *Matharu v Matharu* (1994) 68 P&CR 93, CA at 102, Roch L.J. justified this conclusion on the grounds that the husband's expenditure '. . . *meant that the amount of his income available to benefit* [W] *and her children was reduced..it would be wrong to consider that the money belonged solely to* [W's husband]'. As Welstead points out, this amounts to a somewhat surprising introduction of community of property into English matrimonial law — see 'Proprietary Estoppel — a Flexible Familial Equity' [1995] *Conv* 6.

[19] See *Stevens v Stevens* (CA unrep. 1989) lexis transcript.

[20] *Lloyds Bank v Rosset* [1991] 1 AC 107 *per* Lord Bridge at 131g–h considering the closely analogous area of express common intention constructive trusts. Compare *Coombes v Smith* [1986] 1 WLR 808.

[21] *Pascoe v Turner* [1979] 1 WLR 431, CA at 436f.

[22] Though it seems that where orthodox detriment is established, the additional presence of personal distress may be taken into account in assessing what remedy is appropriate — see *Pascoe v Turner* and para. 11.58 below.

[23] *Christian v Christian* (1981) 131 NLJ 43, CA, lexis transcript, *per* Brightman L.J.

number of factors other than detriment in establishing whether unconscionable conduct has occurred.[24]

Is it necessary to show detriment?

Obiter comments of Lord Denning, in *Greasley v Cook*[25] might be taken to suggest that detriment is not a necessary component of a claim in proprietary estoppel. However, we would suggest that these comments actually related to obviating the need to prove the *causal link* between the acts performed and the assumption,[26] that is as referring only to the reversal of the burden of proof of reliance.[27] Alternatively, these comments may refer to financial expenditure, confirming that other types of conduct are capable of amounting to sufficient change of position.[28] In any event, Lord Denning averred that '*It is sufficient if the party to whom the assurance is given, acts on faith of it, in such circumstances that it would be unjust and inequitable for the party making the assurance to go back on it*'; unless some detriment flows from the change of position, it is difficult to conceive of circumstances where it would be unconscionable for M to resile from the assurance.[29] **11.035**

It has been suggested that the cases display a shift away from detriment to a wider concept of alteration of position.[30] There is some indication that the courts may now be prepared to accept an alteration of position as triggering liability, even in the absence of detriment. Most notably, Lord Bridge in *Lloyds Bank v Rosset*[31] held that, once the relevant assurance or belief has been demonstrated, it will only be necessary for the claimant to show that '*. . . he or she has acted to his or her detriment* or *significantly altered his or her position in reliance on the agreement*' (our emphasis). Although of weighty authority, we do not consider that undue weight should be given to his Lordship's *dicta:* it may well be that his Lordship was merely stating the same proposition in two slightly different ways and using '*or*' accordingly. There is no warrant for examining his Lordship's words with the precision required for statutory construction. **11.036**

---

[24] See below at paras 11.55–63.
[25] [1980] 1 WLR 1306, CA at 1311.
[26] *Watts v Story* (1984) 134 NLJ 631, CA *per* Dunn and Slade L.J.J. and *Coombes v Smith* [1986] 1 WLR 808 *per* Jonathan Parker Q.C. at 821b–f.
[27] As to which see para. 11.26 above.
[28] Snell at p. 575 n. 74.
[29] *Watts v Story* (1984) 134 NLJ 631, CA, lexis transcript.
[30] See Gray at p. 338 and Pawlowsky at p. 57 and the authorities there cited.
[31] [1991] 1 AC 107 *per* Lord Bridge at 132f–h.

More significantly, the courts have sometimes been reluctant to examine precisely whether an opportunity foregone had any value, that is whether there was any chance of a successful outcome, had W taken up the opportunity sacrificed. Thus, in *Hammersmith and Fulham BC v Top Shop Centres Ltd*,[32] it was held that a tenant's foregoing the opportunity to negotiate for a new sub-under-lease or to apply for relief against forfeiture of a sub-under-lease, amounted to detriment, regardless of whether such conduct was likely to result in a successful outcome. Unless there was some chance of success, it is difficult to see how W's conduct could have been a source of detriment to her. Therefore, W ought to have been required to show that there was some prospect of success. On this analysis, there are three ways of explaining *Top Shop Centres*. First, the simplest explanantion of the case is estoppel by representation principles were in play. In such cases slightly different detriment principles may operate.[33] Secondly, an alternative explanation may rest in the court's notorious reluctance to engage in speculation as to the outcome of hypothetical proceedings. Once the landlord allowed the opportunity to be lost to the tenant, uncertainty should be resolved in the latter's favour.[34] Thirdly, the tenant might be said to have suffered prejudice because she has forever lost the opportunity to take a reasoned decision on the transaction, in the light of all the circumstances, unfettered by the belief fostered or acquiesced in by M. That loss of a chance, in itself, might amount to detriment, regardless of the prospects of success.[35] **11.037**

The need to show detriment has been frequently stressed in the cases and remains an essential pre-requisite of a proprietary estoppel claim.[36] Further, the requirement that W act on faith of the assumption, makes little sense unless some detriment is likely to result from the change of position.[37]. In our view, change of position will give rise to liability **11.038**

---

[32] [1990] Ch 237 at 261a–c.

[33] See paras 8.10–5.

[34] *cf.* the position where the transaction entered into involves an element of risk. Hobhouse J. suggested in *The Vistafjord* [1988] 2 Lloyds Rep. 343 at 368 (an estoppel by convention case) that the fact of taking the risk was sufficient detriment and that the court would not investigate whether the transaction had been a successful one.

[35] This may explain the finding that granting an underlease amounted to detriment regardless of its terms. Potentially, such a transaction might result in benefit to the claimant. Such cases cannot sensibly be explained in terms of the court's distaste for speculation because the consequences of the tenant's decision may be clearly analysed by reference to the terms of the underlease.

[36] See the cases at n. 12, para. 11.31 above.

[37] As pointed out in Woodman 'Estoppel by Part Performance' (1981) 44 *LQR* 461 at 463–4.

only where it gives rise to detriment in the orthodox sense. It is a means of demonstrating detriment, not an alternative to it. The shift identified by the commentators is probably semantic only, amounting simply to a clearer recognition that it is not the conduct itself which amounts to detriment but the fact that W has acted in such a way that she can no longer be restored to the position in which she was before the relevant assurance was made or the belief formed.

Examples of detriment

General

It is not necessary to establish that the acts performed fall within some **11.039**
pre-existing recognized category.[38] Whether detriment has been suffered is a question of fact and degree.[39] The qualifying change of position may involve positive acts or mere forbearance.[40] It need not involve expenditure of money,[41] though it will often do so. It need not be located on M's property[42] nor be referable or related to it[43] (in any other sense than that inherent in the causation requirement discussed above at paras 11.24–50 under *Reliance*). It is not necessary that any benefit or enrichment is conferred on M.[44] In *Crabb v Arun DC*,[45] for example, W owned a plot of land with an access point A leading on to M's road, together with a right of way. W decided to divide his property and to sell the part where access point A was located. Consequently, he required a further means of entry for his retained land. M's agents undertook to grant a new access point at B, knowing of W's plans. In reliance on this

---

38 '*. . . the categories of detriment are not closed*': *Watts v Story* (1984) 134 NLJ 631, CA *per* Dunn and Slade L.JJ.

39 *Watts v Story* (1984) 134 NLJ 631, CA, lexis transcript.

40 *Hammersmith and Fulham BC v Top Shop Centres Ltd* [1990] Ch 237 at 259c–d.

41 *Greasley v Cooke* [1980] 1 WLR 1306 at 1311–12 and *Re Basham decd* [1986] 1 WLR 1498 *per* Edward Nugee Q.C. at 1509c.

42 *Rochdale Canal Co v King* (No. 2) (1853) 16 Beav 630, 51 ER 924 and *Crabb* v *Arun DC* [1976] Ch 179, CA.

43 *Jones v Jones* [1977] 1 WLR 438, CA and *Grant v Edwards* [1986] Ch 638, CA *per* Browne Wilkinson at 657b; this used to be a point where proprietary estoppel and the express common intention constructive trust diverged but it is now clear that the requirement applies to neither doctrine.

44 Thus, preventing the classification of proprietary estoppel within the scope of the law of restitution.

45 [1976] Ch 179, CA. See also *Ward v Kirkland* [1966] 1 WLR 601; *Ives v High* [1967] 2 QB 379, CA; and *Tanner v Tanner* [1975] 1 WLR 1346, CA and *Habib Bank Ltd v Habib Bank A.G. Zurich* [1981] WLR 1265.

undertaking, W sold half of his land, without securing a right of way over it, from point A, to his retained property. Without access point B, W's retained property was wholly landlocked. W's act was sufficient to estop M from blocking access point B. The council were liable despite the fact that they gained no benefit from (and indeed were entirely indifferent to) Mr Crabb's dealings with his land. Indeed, it seems probable that liability could arise even where the claimant's acts in reliance were positively harmful to M. There seems to be no case where this has occurred, however, presumably because such circumstances would prompt M to intervene and correct W's misapprehension. Where the claimant gratuitously confers any benefit on M, whether by way of expenditure, labour or other means, she has sacrificed the opportunity to require payment from him.[46] Hence, although benefit or enrichment to M is not a necessary component of a proprietary estoppel claim, it is factually relevant to many circumstances and may be a useful tool in determining marginal cases.

Specific categories[47]

The claimant fails to safeguard her legal position

W will be able to establish detriment where her change of position **11.040**
exposes her to legal penalties. Hence, the doctrine will operate where W has trespassed on M's land in reliance on an assurance that she had rights over it.[48] Alternatively, her change of position may leave her in a less favourable legal position. Examples include failing to reserve a right of way over land sold,[49] failing to apply for relief against forfeiture proceedings[50] and failing to object to a planning application.[51] Such conduct may also fall under the next head, since the claimant may well

---

46 She has thus foregone something of value in the sense set out in paras. 11.41–2 below.

47 The categorization adopted is derived, subject to some modifications, from Malcolm Clarke's article 'Banker's Commercial Credits among the High Trees' [1974] *CLJ* 260 at 283. See para 8.98–101 for a third category whereby the claimant has altered her budget and expenditure in reliance on the windfall promised by the property owner. This type of detrimental reliance has arisen most frequently in estoppel by representation and equitable forbearance cases but there is no reason to suppose it would not suffice in a proprietary estoppel claim.

48 *Armstrong v Sheppard and Short* [1959] 2 QB 384 and *Ward v Kirkland* [1966] 1 WLR 601.

49 *Crabb v Arun DC* [1976] Ch 179, CA.

50 *Hammersmith and Fulham BC v Top Shop Centres Ltd* [1990] Ch 237.

51 *John v George and Walton* (1996) 71 P&CR 375, CA. See also *Stevens v Stevens* (CA unrep. 1989) lexis transcript.

have foregone a valuable opportunity to bargain or secure some advantage for herself, in reliance on her belief.

The claimant foregoes something of value

Where the conduct performed in reliance on W's belief involves expenditure or labour, it is necessary to show that W received no adequate value for the expenditure or remuneration for the labour. Put simply, it must be shown that they were wasted,[52] thus demonstrating the loss of a valuable asset (the money or hours of labour) and/or that were it not for W's belief, she would have spent her money on profitable activities or demanded remuneration for her labour in the job market.[53] Thus, in *Ives v High*,[54] Mr High built a garage on his property which could be accessed only by using a right of way which he believed that he had acquired over the land of Ives. The garage became unusable (and the expenditure wasted) once the right of way was denied. By contrast, in *Christian v Christian*,[55] M and W were proposing jointly to purchase a farm. W feared that the plot might be too small to be financially viable, given a planning restriction to agricultural use. To allay her anxieties, M promised to transfer a neighbouring plot into their joint names so that the two properties could be run as a single unit. No detriment[56] flowed from the purchase of the farm, since the land was discounted to reflect the planning restriction and there was no evidence that it was unsaleable. W had not foregone anything of value; she had not in any sense 'lost' her money since she had got what she had paid for. Similarly, the courts have been reluctant to recognize a mere change of lifestyle as sufficient change of position, since no loss of value can generally be shown. W's moving into M's house and giving up the chance of a job in his home city were not sufficient in **11.041**

[52] *Re Basham decd* [1986] 1 WLR 1498 at 1505e–h.

[53] *cf. Windeler v Whitehall* [1990] 2 FLR 505 *per* Millet J. at 516c–e: W's conduct (acting as M's escort and hostess at social functions connected with his business as a theatrical agent and supervising builders renovating the home) could not support a claim to M's house or business since it had no real financial value; '. . . [M] *would not have paid anyone to do what* [W] *did*'; to characterize what W was contributing to the business represented *'a schoolgirl's view'* of what she did.

[54] [1967] 2 QB 379, CA.

[55] (1981) 131 NLJ 43. *Smith v Halpin* [1997] 2 IRLM 38 is inconsistent with the principle laid down in *Christian v Christian*. We submit that the latter cases is to be preferred.

[56] The only disadvantage suffered by W was that she was not given the land she was promised. As stated above (at para. 11.32), such hardship is insufficient to raise a proprietary estoppel. *cf.* the position where the transaction entered into involves an element of risk. Hobhouse J. suggested in *The Vistafjord* [1988] 2 Lloyds Rep. 343 at 368 (an estoppel by convention case) that the fact of taking the risk was sufficient and that the court would not investigate whether the transaction had been a successful one.

Watts v Story.[57] However, where the conduct is accompanied by additional detriment, the position may be different. Therefore in *Tanner v Tanner*,[58] where W had given up her rent controlled flat, an asset of value, W succeeded. Similarly, in *Stevens v Stevens*[59] W succeeded because, by the time M sought to resile from his assurance, the reduction in the public housing stock had seriously impaired W's prospects of obtaining council accommodation.

Acts held to be capable of supporting a claim for proprietary estoppel include: **11.042**

- expenditure of money on building[60] on M's land or effecting alterations,[61] improvements, redecoration[62] or repairs[63] to it;

---

[57] (1984) 134 NLJ 631, CA; *Coombes v Smith* [1986] 1 WLR 808. See also the similar approach in the contractual licence case, *Horrocks v Foray* [1976] 1 WLR 231. Such conduct has, however, been taken into account where accompanied by other acts which are capable of amounting to detriment: *Jones v Jones* [1977] 1 WLR 438, CA (contribution to the purchase price of the property) and *Maharaj v J Chand* [1986] AC 898, PC (Fiji) (supporting an application to the housing authority, financial contributions to the household, domestic services and child care).

[58] *Tanner v Tanner* [1975] 1 WLR 1346, CA.

[59] *Stevens v Stevens* (CA unrep. 1989) lexis transcript. Sir Roger Ormrod suggested *obiter* that detriment is established once it is shown that W moved into the property in the expectation of obtaining a secure home for life, whereas, in fact, M's change of mind makes the right to occupy tenuous. However, his Lordship's approach of comparing that which W had been promised with that to which she was legally entitled, seems to equate detriment with the prejudice flowing simply from a broken promise which is generally accepted as insufficient to raise a proprietary estoppel — see para. 11.132 above.

[60] *Dillwyn v Llewellyn* (1862) De G F and J 517, 45 ER 1285; *Huning v Ferrars* (1711) Gilb 85, 25 ER 59; *Stiles v Cowper* (1748) 3 Atk 382, 26 ER 1198; *Unity Joint Stock Mutual Banking Association v King (a bankrupt)* (1858) 25 Beav 72, 53 ER 563; *Inwards v Baker* [1965] 2 QB 29, CA and *Salvation Army Trustee Co Ltd v West Yorkshire Metropolitan County Council* (1981) P&CR 179 (where the land in question had passed to a successor authority).

[61] There seems to be no requirement that the works objectively enhance the value of the land — see the comments in Pawlowski at p. 63 on *Pennine Raceway v Kirklees MBC* [1983] QB 382, CA.

[62] *Duke of Beaufort v Patrick* (1853) 17 Beav 59, 51 ER 954 (building a canal); *Voyce v Voyce* (1991) 62 P&CR 290, CA (modernization and decoration); *Durant v Heritage* [1994] EGCS 134 (improvements including constructing an extension and new garage); *Pascoe v Turner* [1979] 1 WLR 43, CA (sums spent on improvement, decoration and repair were all taken into account, without distinction). The refusal of Jonathan Parker Q.C., in *Coombes v Smith* [1986] 1 WLR 808, to accept that commission of works of redecoration and alteration as giving rise to detriment is questionable and is probably best explained as an example of detriment which is too trifling or *de minimis* to give rise to liability — see para. 11.43–4 below.

[63] *Pascoe v Turner* [1979] 1 WLR 43, CA and *Stevens v Stevens* (CA unrep. 1989) lexis transcript; in the latter case, the claimant failed to establish reliance, because she admitted in her evidence that she would have carried them out even in the absence of M's assurance. See further paras 11.29–3 and 11.46 for the problems relating to reliance and detriment in repairs cases.

- physical labour on such works on M's land;[64]
- expenditure of money or physical labour on such works carried out on the claimant's land;[65]
- contributing towards the purchase price,[66] mortgage payments or other outgoings due in respect of M's property;[67]
- working in M's business gratuitously[68] or for inadequate[69] financial remuneration;
- building up goodwill under a particular trade name and style;[70]
- promoting various musical works (six pop songs) through 14 years of arduous and financially unrewarding concert tours;[71]
- expenditure in support of M's planning application, with a view to a joint building venture to be carried out on M's land;[72]
- refraining from demanding repayment of or interest on a loan to M;[73]
- refraining from serving notice to quit under the Landlord and Tenant Act 1925, s. 25 and thereby delaying date on which possession might have been obtained;[74]
- granting an under-lease (regardless of its terms[75]);
- payment of premiums due on M's insurance policy[76]

---

64 *Jones v Jones* [1977] 1 WLR 438, CA; *Ungurian v Lessnoff* [1990] Ch 206 and *cf. Eves v Eves* [1975] 1 WLR 1338, CA applying the same approach to constructive trust principles.

65 *Rochdale Canal Co v King* (No. 2) (1853) 16 Beav 630, 51 ER 924; *Willmot v Barber* (1880) 15 ChD 96 at 104; *ER Ives Investment Ltd v High* [1967] 2 QB 379 and *Ward v Kirkland* [1966] 1 WLR 601.

66 *Jones v Jones* [1977] 1 WLR 438, CA and *Abbey National BS v Cann* [1991] AC 56; in the latter case W's contribution took the form of an owner occupier discount rather than cash.

67 *Price v Hartwell* [1996] EGCS 98; *Burrows v Sharpe* [1991] Fam Law 67, CA, [1989] 23 HLR 82; *Preston and Henderson v St Helens Metropolitan Borough Council, lands tribunal* (1989) 58 P&CR 500; *Veitch v Caldecott* (1945) 173 LT 30 but see the particular problems associated with payments of day to day outgoings discussed at para. 11.30 above.

68 *Hammond v Mitchell* [1992] 4 All ER 109 and *cf. Windeler v Whitehall* [1990] 2 FLR 505.

69 *Wayling v Jones* (1993) P&CR 170, CA.

70 *Habib Bank Ltd v Habib Bank A.G. Zurich* [1981] WLR 1265 and *Film Investors Overseas Services SA v The Home Video Channel (trading as the Adult Channel)*, [1997] EMLR 347.

71 *Godfrey v John Lees and others* [1995] EMLR 307 at 332–5.

72 *E and L Berg Homes Ltd v Grey* (1979) 253 EG 473, CA.

73 *Risch v McFee* [1991] FLR 105 *per* Balcombe L.J. at 110f–h.

74 *Watkins v Emslie* (1981) 261 EG 1192, CA, *per* Sir David Cairns (Donaldson and Dunn L.JJ. concurring) at 1194.

75 *Hammersmith and Fulham BC v Top Shop Centres Ltd* [1990] Ch 237 at 261f–2c.

76 *Re Foster, Hudson v Foster (No. 2)* [1938] 3 All ER 610.

Domestic services

The margins of qualifying change of position have been canvassed largely in the area of domestic services and have yet to be clearly defined.[77] There is no doubt that the detriment necessary for a claim in proprietary estoppel may arise, even where the change of position occurred against a background of a personal or family relationship with M. Sir Nicholas Brown Wilkinson, Vice Chancellor, (as he then was) stated in such a context that '. . . *any act done by* [W] *to her detriment relating to their* [M and W's] *joint lives, is in my judgment, sufficient to qualify*'.[78] However, a restrictive approach to detriment was taken by Jonathan Parker Q.C. in *Coombes v Smith*.[79] W left her husband and moved into a property owned by M; she gave up her job, as a van driver, after becoming pregnant by M; she looked after their child and the house and was ready for M's visits; she took no steps to find a job. The relationship broke down after 10 years. None of W's acts were sufficient to cause her detriment.[80] In contrast, the Court of Appeal, in *Greasley v Cooke*,[81] held that W acting as M's housekeeper and mistress and looking after his disabled sister for 28 years, without payment, was sufficient '. . . *when otherwise she might have left and got a job elsewhere*'.[82] Two points emerge from these cases. First, the courts are concerned not merely with the qualitative nature of the relevant conduct *but* also with quantitative issues; weak acts of reliance may, it seems, be compensated for by prolonged periods of acting.[83] Secondly, the more commercial the context in which domestic services are provided, the easier it is to establish an estoppel (W had originally joined the Greasley household as a salaried maid and later as housekeeper). **11.043**

---

[77] The English courts have been notoriously reluctant to reward purely domestic services (*cf. Burns v Burns* [1984] 1 Ch 317, CA), in marked contrast to other commonwealth jurisdictions. See, for example, *Gillies v Keogh* [1989] 2 NZLR 327 (CA New Zealand) *per* Richardson J. at 346 (no presumption that domestic contributions are any less valuable than financial ones) and the use of the unjust enrichment principle in Canada: *Peter v Beblow* (1993) 101 DLR (4th) 621 (Canadian Supreme Court).

[78] *Grant v Edwards* [1986] Ch 638, CA at 657b.

[79] [1986] 1 WLR 808 at 820b–1a.

[80] W also failed to establish that the acts were done in reliance on her belief that M would provide her with a permanent home. As far as ending her marriage is concerned, it is not quite clear whether W failed on the reliance ground alone or whether she also failed to establish detriment (see 820c–f) but the latter view seems to be the most likely, given the approach in the remainder of the judgment.

[81] *Greasley v Cooke* [1980] 1 WLR 1306. See also *Re Basham dec'd* [1986] 1 WLR 1498.

[82] *Per* Lord Denning MR at 1312a.

[83] *cf.* the analysis used by Howard and Hill in their article 'The Informal Creation of Interests in Land' (1995) 15 *LS* 356.

11.044 Commission of housekeeping and child care services is probably conduct capable of giving rise to detriment. Such services have a clear financial value; in performing them gratuitously in the home, W has sacrificed the opportunity, either to ask M for payment, or to sell those services in the job market. There is no justification for treating such labour differently to that performed outside the home, for example, in a business run by M or in works carried out on his property. Work in such an enterprise is clearly capable of giving rise to detriment.[84] This view is supported by *Greasley* but not by *Coombes*. *Greasley,* as the decision of the superior court, is to be preferred. The conflict may, in any event, be reconciled by characterizing *Coombes* as laying no general principle as to domestic services but only establishing that detriment had not occurred on the facts of the particular case. In concluding that W had actually benefited from the arrangement rather than suffered detriment, the judge stressed that M had supported W throughout the relationship. The provision of domestic services by one partner will often, though not invariably, be accompanied by conferral of benefits by the other, such as general financial support. As is set out below, such benefits may be taken into account when assessing whether net hardship has occurred and may often outweigh the detriment suffered as a result of commission of the services. The benefits conferred on Win Coombes outweighed any detriment she had suffered in providing the services. This will significantly limit the number of cases which are likely to arise in this area, as will the difficulties inherent in establishing reliance.[85] It should be noted that a claimant will seldom be credited with the entire value of the services, since generally they will have been rendered partly for her own convenience.

11.045 However, where value cannot be ascribed to the services or detriment, the detriment being emotional or a change in purely personal circumstances, the claim should be rejected. We would therefore suggest that the judge in *Coombes* was probably correct to reject W's claim that detriment flowed from ending her marriage, becoming pregnant by M and giving birth to his child. Not only is it difficult to value such conduct in financial terms but it would be almost impossible for the court to establish whether the claimant was harmed or benefited by such

[84] See para. 11.42 above.

[85] The problems faced by claimants in establishing that detriment has occurred as a result of the commission of domestic services should not be confused with those faced in establishing that such services were rendered *in reliance* on the expected interest in property *viz* the expectation that such services are performed by reason of love and affection (as to which see above at para. 11.29).

conduct. To do so would require an analysis of intangible emotional issues with which the doctrine of proprietary estoppel is manifestly ill-equipped to deal. However, rendering domestic services often involves foregoing a valuable opportunity to work outside the home. Arguably, even becoming pregnant and having a baby might then qualify as detriment, since they would inevitably involve a career interruption of at least a short duration. The courts would be extremely unlikely to recognise such a broad range of circumstances as triggering a legal rights. *Quaere* whether the approach in *Coombes* might have been different had W given up a more prestigious and highly paid job.[86] Similar justiciability difficulties, combined with a understandable delicacy, probably mean that the more intimate spousal, or quasi spousal, services do not qualify either. Admittedly, however, W's '*looking after [M]*' was taken into account in the calculation of detriment in *Greasley*.[87]

Repairs

Some doubt exists as to whether repairs to or paying of outgoings on a property occupied by W is conduct capable of triggering detriment, since such acts seem to inure solely to W's benefit. On the one hand, accrual of incidental benefit does not negate the possibility that overall W has suffered a net detriment.[88] Even where the claimant receives the bulk of the practical benefit of payments, they may still have been met by her in reliance on her expectation. For example, W may view money spent on repairs to, or outgoings on, a property which she occupies as contributing to the long-term preservation of the property and thus more appropriately met by its owner rather than by a transient occupier.[89] W may well have been happy to occupy the premises without carrying out such repairs; in completing them, in reliance on her belief, arguably she has suffered a detriment and her expenditure has been wasted. On the other hand, no distinction should be drawn between a benefit received by way of an enhanced environment and money spent in other ways. In either case, W received the benefit of her expenditure rather than wasting it in the sense required for establishing detriment. W would only be able to establish detriment, in such a case, if the court was prepared to **11.046**

[86] *Jones v Jones* [1977] 1 WLR 438, CA and *Greasley v Cook* [1980] 1 WLR 1306, CA at 1312a.

[87] [1980] 1 WLR 1306 at 1512a.

[88] See above at para. 11.32.

[89] *Stevens v Stevens* (CA unrep. 1989) lexis transcript. See also *Pascoe v Turner* [1979] 1 WLR 431, CA, where sums spent on improvement, decoration and repair were all taken into account, without distinction.

make a subjective evaluation which it would be unwilling to do. If the court were to engage in that exercise, W could contend that she would have preferred to live in the unrepaired house and spend the money in other ways. That argument would probably be unsustainable if the repairs were essential to make the property habitable.[90] Even if, in theory, expenditure on ongoing repairs may possibly be capable of amounting to detriment, as a matter of practice, claimants face considerable difficulties in establishing *reliance* in such cases.[91]

Benefits received

Benefits received by W from M may be taken into account when assessing whether W has suffered detriment.[92] W must show that she has suffered net detriment after the relevant benefits are taken into account. In our view, this principle is confined to benefits which are conferred on W by M (i) as part of the transaction giving rise to the estoppel or (ii) are otherwise connected with the assumption or with the property in issue. To allow more remote benefits to be taken into account would involve both undesirable uncertainty and forensic difficulty (viz the examination of the entirety of the relationship between the parties[93]). No doubt the defendant in *Inwards v Baker*[94] received all the benefits from his father (both financial and otherwise) that parents normally confer on their children; there was no suggestion, however, that these should be taken into account in assessing whether he should succeed in his estoppel **11.047**

[90] Although Megarry V.C. in *Appleby v Cowley, The Times*, 14 April 1982, lexis transcript, was prepared to take such expenditure into account, albeit acknowledging that it could carry little weight.

[91] As to which see para. 11.30 above. We consider that failure to establish reliance was the reason why expenditure on outgoings and repairs was disregarded in *Griffiths v Williams* (1977) 248 EG 947, CA at 947.

[92] *Baker v Baker* [1993] 25 HLR 408 CA at 413–14; *Watts v Story* (1984) 134 NLJ 631; *E and L Berg Homes Ltd v Grey* (1979) 253 EG 473, CA *per* Brandon L.J. at 479; *Coombes v Smith* [1986] 1 WLR 808 820h–1b; *Lovett v Fairclough* (1991) 61 P & CR 385 and *Durant v Heritage* [1994] EGCS 134 (though doubts were expressed by Andrew Park Q.C.). In *Appleby v Cowley, The Times*, 14 April 1982 Megarry V.C. held that no remedy should be granted because W had had sufficient satisfaction for their expenditure. His Lordship declined to decide whether the benefits received prevented an estoppel arising or whether one arose but deserved no remedy.

[93] Although it is conceded that such an examination will, in certain cases, be necessary even if the restrictive approach recommended is the correct one: in particular, cases where the alleged detriment consists of domestic services rendered in the expectation of an interest in the family home, the duration of the reliance and assumption may often cover several years of a relationship. See *Coombes v Smith* [1986] 1 WLR 808.

[94] [1965] 2 QB 29, CA.

claim against his father's estate. Benefits taken into account have usually involved the gratuitous or discounted use of the property in dispute.[95] The only case where more remote benefits were in issue is *Coombes v Smith*[96] where the general financial support given by M to W was taken into account. We submit that the case is consistent with our general proposition, given that it involved commission of domestic services in the expectation of an interest in the family home. In such cases, both belief and reliance are so inter-connected with general family living arrangements that general financial support by M may legitimately be characterized as part of a single ongoing transaction.

REMEDIES

Once it is established that W has acted to her detriment in reliance on a belief or expectation that she has, or will be granted, rights over an item of property and its owner acquiesces in, or encourages, that belief or expectation, the courts have a wide discretion as to what remedy, if any, should be awarded.[97] There is some reluctance to interfere with decisions at first instance without clear justification.[98] **11.048**

It is thus clear that establishing the threefold requirements of assurance, reliance and detriment is no guarantee of a particular remedy and may be no guarantee of a remedy at all.[99] It is also clear that certain additional factors may be taken into account which are conceptually distinct from the traditional threefold classification, in particular, the personal and financial circumstances of the parties and their respective **11.049**

[95] *Watts v Story* (1984) 134 NLJ 631 (the NLJ report suggests that benefits received under the will of M were viewed as relevant but the lexis transcript reveals that it was only the rent free accommodation which was expressly taken into account by their Lordships); *E and L Berg Homes Ltd v Grey* (1979) 253 EG 473, CA *per* Brandon L.J. at 479; *Lovett v Fairclough* 1991 61 P&CR 385; *Durant v Heritage* [1994] EGCS 134 and *Appleby v Cowley, The Times,* 14 April 1982.

[96] *Coombes v Smith* [1986] 1 WLR 808.

[97] *Crabb v Arun DC* [1976] Ch 179 CA; *Plimmer v Wellington Corpn* (1884) 9 Ap Cas 699 PC NZ at 414; *Chalmers v Pardoe* [1963] 1 WLR 677; *Griffiths v Williams* (1977) 248 EG 947 CA at 949; *Voyce v Voyce* (1991) 62 P&CR 290 CA; *Stratulatos v Stratulatos* [1988] 2 NZLR 424 at 438; *Pascoe v Turner* [1979] 1 WLR 43 CA at 438f; *Stevens v Stevens* (CA unrep. 1989) lexis transcript and *Habermann v Koehler* (1996) 73 P&CR 515 CA *per* Peter Gibson L.J. at 522.

[98] *Stevens v Stevens* (CA unrep. 1989) lexis transcript *per* Ormrod L.J.

[99] See *Appleby v Cowley, The Times,* 14 April 1982, lexis transcript, and *Sledmore v Dalby* (1996) P&CR 196, CA.

general behaviour.[1] It is possible to characterize such factors as amounting to an additional requirement for establishing a claim in proprietary estoppel, thus reformulating its components into the fourfold classification of assurance, reliance, detriment and absence of bars to the equity. Alternatively, it may be that the threefold test establishes a cause of action in proprietary estoppel, but that relief is discretionary, in the way comparable to equitable remedies such as specific performance or injunctions. We prefer the latter view, but the issue is almost wholly semantic.[2] It has been masked by the use of the language of equities rather than causes of action: a standard approach is to use the orthodox threefold test to establish whether an equity has arisen, followed by an assessment of what is the appropriate way in which to satisfy the equity.[3]

EXERCISE OF THE DISCRETION: GENERAL PRINCIPLES

All the circumstances of the case may be taken into account in deciding which remedy is appropriate.[4] There are two competing views as to the general approach to be taken to quantifying the remedy. One approach is to award W the rights she believed that she had or expected to obtain (the expectation measure). This approach has three significant drawbacks. First, the mechanical fulfilment of expectations may lead to **11.050**

---

[1] As to which see below at paras 11.55–63.

[2] In *Appleby v Cowley, The Times,* 14 April 1982, lexis transcript, Megarry V.-C. understandably declined to consider the issue (*a nice academic point)*, finding it dimension to dismiss the claim in proprietary estoppel. The issue may have a practical dimension in reference to the enforceability of estoppel interests against third parties; if the former approach is correct, it becomes more difficult to justify recognition of any pre-adjudication rights vested in the claimant. See below at paras 11.74–6.

[3] *Plimmer v Wellington Corpn* (1884) 9 Ap Cas 699, PC (New Zealand) at 714; *Inwards v Baker* [1965] 2 QB 29, CA at 36g–7b; *Crabb v Arun DC* [1976] Ch 179, CA at 193a–c where Lord Scarman held that the court must ascertain both the extent of the equity and, secondly, the appropriate way in which to satisfy it. It is not easy to discern the difference between the two but the first issue may concern the general choice between expectation and the reliance measures and the second, the specific choice between particular remedies such as those listed below at paras 11.65–9.

[4] *Plimmer v Wellington Corpn* (1884) 9 Ap Cas 699, PC (New Zealand) at 414; *Chalmers v Pardoe* [1963] 1 WLR 677 at 682; *Habermann v Koehler* (1996) 73 P&CR 515 CA *per* Peter Gibson L.J. at 522; *Smith v Halpin* [1997] 2 IRLM 38; *Griffiths v Williams* (1977) 248 EG 947, CA at 949; *Voyce v Voyce* (1991) 62 P&CR 290, CA; *Stratulatos v Stratulatos* [1988] 2 NZLR 424 at 438 and *Pascoe v Turner* [1979] 1 WLR 43, CA at 438f.

overcompensation of W, for example, where W has spent £100 on building a shed in reliance on the promise that she will be given M's £1 million plot of land.[5] Secondly, where the expectation is generated by M's promise, proprietary estoppel is being used to enforce promises unsupported by consideration, resulting in an obvious conflict with the established principles of contract.[6] Thirdly, since proprietary estoppel is capable of generating property rights binding on third parties,[7] the doctrine may be used as an informal means of creating rights in real property, thus undermining established formality and registration rules. Many,[8] although not all,[9] of older authorities tended to order the fulfilment of the expectation engendered.

The expectation approach was increasingly qualified by reference to equity and fairness. For example, in *ER Ives Investment Ltd v High* Lord Denning, held that the court would not allow the expectation to be defeated '*where it would be inequitable so to do*'.[10] As Professor Finn points out, '*[w]ith Pascoe v Turner, the divorce of equities from expectations is completed . . .*'[11] with its emphasis on the minimum equity to do justice.[12] The modern trend is not to concentrate on the fulfilment of expectations, but on the preventing detriment arising from M's resiling from the assurance: **11.051**

> The unconscionable conduct which it is the object of equity to prevent is the failure of a party who has induced the adoption of the assumption or expectation and who knew or intended that it would be relied on, to fulfil the assumption or expectation or otherwise to avoid the detriment which failure would occasion. The object of the equity is not to compel

[5] The example discussed in *Commonwealth of Australia v Verwayen* [1990] 170 CLR 394 at 441.

[6] Although this defect may be of reduced importance with the increasingly elastic nature of the doctrine of consideration (see *Williams v Roffey Bros & Nicholls (Contractors) Ltd* [1991] 1 QB 1, CA), it is still strongly arguable that if English law is to expand the scope of promises which it is prepared to enforce, this should come from an open appraisal of the law of contract rather than the side wind created by estoppel.

[7] Although in what circumstances and from what point in time are currently unresolved. See generally paras 11.72–83 below.

[8] *Huning v Ferrars* Gilb 85 (1711) 25 ER 59; *Ramsden v Dyson* (1866) LR 1 HL 129, HL (see, particularly, Lord Kingsdown at 170); *Michand v City of Montreal* (1923) 129 LT 417, PC (Canada) and *AG to Prince of Wales v Collom* [1916] 2 KB 193.

[9] *Unity Joint Stock Mutual Banking Association v King (a bankrupt)* (1858) 25 Beav 72, 53 ER 563 and *Foster, Hudson v Foster (No. 2)* [1938] 3All ER 610.

[10] [1967] 2 QB 379 *per* Denning M.R. at 394F–5A; see also his comments in *Inwards v Baker* [1965] 2 QB 29, CA at 37c.

[11] Finn 'Equitable estoppel' Chap. 4 at p. 68.

[12] *Pascoe v Turner* [1979] 1 WLR 431, CA at 437H–8A.

the party bound [it] to fulfil the assumption or expectation: it is to avoid the detriment, which, if the assumption or expectation goes unfulfilled, will be suffered by the party who has been induced to act or abstain from acting thereon.[13]

There is significant support for the detriment based approach. It has been frequently held that the remedy awarded should go no further than the minimum equity to do justice between the parties.[14] Generally, but not invariably, such a remedy will reflect the reliance loss suffered. In the example referred to above, the doctrine should therefore operate to compel the property owner to refund the £100 rather than transfer the promised plot of land. The remedy granted has been confined to reliance loss in a number of cases.[15] In a number of other cases, detriment has been established but a remedy has been denied on the grounds that the claimant has already received sufficient compensation from the property owner, in the form of other benefits[16] (see paragraph 11.47 above for the principles applicable to such benefits). These cases link the extent of relief with the extent of the detriment, since the benefits received might be sufficient to cover the reliance loss but would have been unlikely to equal the value of the property interest expected. In **11.052**

---

[13] *Waltons Stores (Interstate) Ltd v Maher* [1988] 164 CLR 387 at 423 and *Commonwealth of Australia v Verwayen* [1990] 170 CLR 394 at 413.

[14] *Crabb v Arun DC* [1976] Ch 179, CA *per* Scarman at 198g; *Habermann v Koehler* (1996) 73 P&CR 515 CA *per* Peter Gibson L.J. at 522; *Smith v Halpin* [1997] 2 IRLM 38; *Pascoe v Turner* [1979] 1 WLR 431, CA at 437H–8A; *Veitch v Caldecott* (1945) 173 LT 30 *per* Atkinson J. at 34; *Baker v Baker* [1993] 25 HLR 408, CA at 418 and *Burrows and Burrows v Sharpe* [1989] 23 HLR 82, CA at 92.

[15] *Unity Joint Stock Mutual Banking Association v King (a bankrupt)* (1858) 25 Beav 72, (53) ER 563, *Foster, Hudson v Foster (No. 2)* [1938] 3 All ER 610, *Cushley v Seale* (CA unrep. 1986), *Hussey v Palmer* [1972] 1 WLR 1286 CA, *Re Sharp* [1980] All ER 198 (W was promised a right to reside for life but received only a right to reside until her expenditure was refunded) and *Gross v French* (1976) 238 EG 39 CA 41 (it was conceded that the expenditure of the claimant should be refunded but the court refuse to grant the interest expected). In *Savva v Costa and Harrymode Investments Ltd* (1981) 131 NLJ 1114 no estoppel arose because M had not sought to deny W the rights she had expected (namely a right to live in the property). The Court of Appeal considered that had M sought to evict W, there would have been serious issue as to whether '*an interest in the property on her behalf commensurate with the money she has spent on improving its condition should be granted*' *per* Shaw L.J. Reliance loss was awarded in *Burrows v Sharpe* [1989] 23 HLR 82 CA and *Dodsworth v Dodsworth* (1973) 228 EG 1115 CA but seemingly only because the expectation measure was impractical in the circumstances. For academic support for the detriment approach see Hanbury and Martin at p. 886, Hayton and Marshall at p. 66–7 and Lunney, Towards a Unified Estoppel — The Long and Winding Road [1992] *Conv* 239.

[16] *Lovett v Fairclough* (1991) 61 P&CR 385, *Appleby v Cowley, The Times* 14 April 1982, lexis transcript, *Sledmore v Dalby* (1996) P&CR 196 CA.

some cases, however, the only way to prevent detriment may be by fulfilling the expectation. Little guidance has as yet been given by the authorities as to the circumstances which will justify the expectation measure. Mr Justice Mason indicated, in *Verwayen*,[17] that the court might order the expectation to be fulfilled where reliance had taken place for an extended period or where substantial and irreversible detriment would otherwise follow. A further likely example arises where the harm caused by departure from the assumption is intangible and/or hard to quantify. The principles governing the grant of specific performance and injunctions[18] provide an obvious analogy. The *maximum* remedy which the court may award is to make good, in full, the claimant's expectation.[19] The expectation measure will therefore displace the reliance measure where it is the lesser of the two.[20]

The detriment or minimum equity approach has the following advantages. First, it puts the estoppel doctrine on a coherent conceptual foundation[21] and provides a welcome governing principle to control what might otherwise be an arbitrary and idiosyncratic exercise of discretion.[22] Secondly, it ensures that the relief granted is proportional to the harm or potential harm suffered as a result of M's conduct.[23] Thirdly, it better preserves the boundary between contract and estoppel. As Mr Justice Brennan pointed out in *Waltons Stores (Interstate) Ltd v Maher*,[24] so long as this underlying aim of estoppel is kept in mind '*the concern that the general application of estoppel will lead to of the principle of equitable estoppel would make non-contractual promises enforceable as contractual promises can be allayed.*' Although some effect is given to promises unsupported by consideration, they are not automatically enforced in full. Fourthly, it also reduces the conflict with formality and registration rules. Although the doctrine may result in the informal creation of interests in **11.053**

17 *Commonwealth of Australia v Verwayen* [1990] 170 CLR 394 at 416.
18 As to which see specialist texts.
19 *Sledmore v Dalby* (1996) P&CR 196, CA *per* Roch L.J. at 204; *Baker v Baker* [1993] 25 HLR 408, CA at 412, 415; *Watson v Goldsbrough* [1986] EGLR 265, CA; *Dodsworth v Dodsworth* (1973) 228 EG 1115, CA at 1115 and *Lloyds Bank v Carrick* [1996] 4 All ER 630 CA.
20 *Baker v Baker* [1993] 25 HLR 408.
21 As we set out in para. 11.31 above, we consider that the existence or possibility of detriment is the key to liability and therefore it is only appropriate that the relief afforded should be governed by it.
22 See the criticisms in *Introduction to the Law of Restitution*, P.B.H. Birks, Clarendon Press, Oxford, 1988 at pp. 290–291.
23 As to which see Hobhouse L.J. in *Sledmore v Dalby* (1996) P&CR 196, CA at 208–9.
24 [1988] 164 CLR 387 at 423–4.

real property, the content of such rights are determined and circumscribed by the court rather than created by the parties themselves.[25]

Many of the authorities retain an undeniable attachment to an expectation approach[26] albeit frequently qualified by reference to a general fairness requirement. The most common outcome of the cases continues to be the grant of the interest expected or monetary compensation assessed according to the value of that interest.[27] The two competing themes are illustrated by the divergent approaches of majority and minority in *Sledmore v Dalby*;[28] Lords Justice Roch and Butler Sloss held that: '*The extent of the equity is to have made good, so far as may fairly be done between the parties, the expectations of* [W] *which* [M] *has encouraged*'.[29] By contrast, Lord Justice Hobhouse adopted the detriment based approach as the starting point, holding that the court '*. . . may do what is required but no more to prevent a person who has* **11.054**

---

[25] See further Evans 'Choosing the Right Estoppel' [1988] *Conv* 346.

[26] *Burrows v Sharpe* [1991] Fam Law 67, CA at 67; *Watson v Goldsbrough* [1986] EGLR 265, CA at 267; *JT Developments v Quinn* (1991) 62 P&CR 33 at 45; *Lim v Ang* [1992] 1 WLR 113, PC; *Chalmers v Pardoe* [1963] 1 WLR 677 (the expectation was to be fulfilled except where this was impractical, for example, because of the intervention of third party rights); *E and L Berg Homes Ltd v Grey* (1979) 253 EG 473, CA *per* Ormrod J. at 478 (but contrast the approach of Brandon L.J. at 477) and *Smith v Halpin* [1997] 2 IRLM 38 (minimum equity test of *Pascoe v Turner* [1979] WLR 431 CA assumed to require the satisfaction of the claimant's expectation). See also Cooke, 'Estoppel and the Protection of Expectations' (1994) 17 *LS* 258.

[27] *Matharu v Matharu* [1994] 68 P&CR 93 CA, *Crabb v Arun DC* [1976] Ch 179, *Wayling v Jones* [1993] P&CR 170 CA; *Re Basham decd* [1986] 1 WLR 1498; *Lim v Ang* [1992] 1 WLR 113 PC (Brunei); *West Middlesex Golf Club Limited v Ealing London Borough Council* (1993) 68 P&CR 461; *Hammond v Mitchell* [1992] 4 All ER 109 [1991] 1 WLR 1127; *JT Developments v Quinn* (1991) 62 P&CR 33 CA; *Voyce v Voyce* (1991) 62 P&CR 290 CA; *Ungurian v Lessnoff* [1990] Ch 206; *Preston and Henderson v St Helens Metropolitan Borough Bouncil, lands tribunal* [1989] 58 P&CR 500; *Hamp v Bygrave* (1983) 266 EG 720; *Salvation Army Trustee Co Ltd v West Yorkshire Metropolitan County Council* (1981) P&CR 179; *Greasley v Cook* [1980] 1 WLR 1306 CA; *Williams v Staite* [1979] Ch 291 CA; *Jones v Jones* [1977] 1 WLR 438 CA; *Re Vandervelle (No 2)* [1974] 1 Ch 269; *ER Ives Investment Ltd v High* [1967] 2 QB 379; *Smith v Halpin* [1997] 2 IRLM 38 and *Tanner v Tanner* [1975] 1 WLR 1346 CA. Even in Australia, where the detriment based approach has been clearly articulated in the High Court (see para. 11.51 above), the grant of the expectation measure remains the most common outcome: see *Waltons Stores (Interstate) Ltd v Maher* [1988] 164 CLR 387; *Commonwealth of Australia v Verwayen* [1990] 170 CLR 394. Of the later Australian cases assessed by Roberston in 'Satisfying the Minimum Equity: Equitable Remedies after Verwayen' (1996) 20 *MULR* 805, all 24 resulted in an award of the expectation measure.

[28] (1996) P&CR 196, CA.

[29] *Sledmore v Dalby* (1996) P&CR 196, CA at 203, 209, quoting Snell's Equity at p. 576. See also *Inwards v Baker* [1965] 2 QB 29, CA at 37c; *Griffiths v Williams* (1977) 248 EG 947, CA at 949; *Durant v Heritage* [1994] EGCS 134 and *Re Basham deceased* [1986] 1 WLR 1498.

relied on an assumption . . . which [M] *has induced him to hold, from suffering detriment in reliance on that assumption as a result of the denial of its correctness*'.[30] All three members of the court agreed as to the appropriate outcome. In our view, the minimum equity or detriment based approach is the current guiding principle in determining the measure of relief.

EXERCISE OF THE DISCRETION: ADDITIONAL RELEVANT FACTORS

Although there has been a judicial resistance to fettering the flexibility[31] of the wide remedial discretion, certain general principles are discernable. The flexibility of the discretion is such that there may be some losses which are deemed unworthy of compensation.[32] **11.055**

The original expectations of both parties

The general discussion above[33] demonstrates that W's expectation will be an important factor in determining the extent of the remedy. M's intentions are also relevant. In *Stevens v Stevens*,[34] M had allowed W and her children to move into a house he owned and repeatedly told her that '*the house is yours*'. Despite this, W received only a right to occupy for life, partly because M had never intended to transfer the property to her outright, but considered he remained its owner as a custodian of a family asset. **11.056**

[30] *Sledmore v Dalby* (1996) P&CR 196, CA at 208–9, quoting Mason C.J. in *Commonwealth of Australia v Verwayen* [1990] 170 CLR 394 at 413. A similar divergence of opinion can be seen between the judges in *Verwayen* itself with Mason C.J. Brennan J., Dawson J. (at 454), Toohey J. (at 475) and McHugh J. (at 501) taking the detriment based approach and Deane J. (at 441) and Gaudron J. (at 487) favouring the expectation measure.

[31] *Stratulatos v Stratulatos* [1988] 2 NZLR 424 at 438.

[32] *Burrows v Sharpe* [1989] 23 HLR 82 at 92.

[33] At paras 11.50–4.

[34] (CA unrep. 1989) lexis transcript. See also *Dodsworth v Dodsworth* (1973) 228 EG 1115, CA at 1115 and *Price v Hartwell* [1996] EGCS 98, CA at 98.

The subsisting relationship between the parties

11.057 A court is unlikely to grant an order which requires continued cooperation (by way, for example, of co-habitation[35] or coownership[36]) between parties, if the personal relationship between them has broken down.[37] Contrary to this general approach, the court has sometimes confined the remedy to refusing an application for possession or granting W a licence to occupy M's property.[38] In such cases, a degree of continued cooperation is inevitably required.[39]

The general conduct of the parties – the clean hands principle

Pre adjudication misconduct

11.058 Examination of the parties' conduct goes beyond the analysis of assurance, reliance and detriment to look at their general behaviour. No remedy will be granted where W has deliberately or covertly acted on M's assurance with a view to obtaining an interest in his property.[40] Further, W's failure to comply with related contractual obligations may bar her claim to a proprietary estoppel remedy.[41] The court may take into account the conduct of the parties up to[42] and including[43] trial.Examples of misconduct include adducing documents at trial known not to reflect the true position between the parties.[44]

---

[35] *Dodsworth v Dodsworth* (1973) 228 EG 1115, CA and *Burrows v Sharpe* [1991] Fam Law 67, CA, [1989] 23 HLR 82.

[36] *Stratulatos v Stratulatos* [1988] 2 NZLR 424 *per* McGechan J. at 439.

[37] *Pascoe v Turner* [1979] 1 WLR 431, CA.

[38] As to which see below at paras 11.65–6.

[39] *e.g. Matharu v Matharu* (1994) 68 P&CR 93, CA, where the claimant was granted such a right on condition that she pays the mortgage and outgoings, keeps the property in good decorative repair and repays the mortgage payments previously made by M; M was to be responsible for structural repair. See also *Stevens v Stevens* (CA unrep. 1989) lexis transcript.

[40] *Thomas v Fuller-Brown* [1988] 1 FLR 237. Further it is doubtful whether sufficient reliance could be established in such a case — see para. 11.28 above.

[41] *Beaton v McDivett* (1985) 13 NSWLR 134 *per* Kirby P. at 172.

[42] *Crabb v Arun DC* [1976] Ch 179, CA at 199c–e (the Council's conduct in shutting off the promised access route and thus leaving Crabb's property landlocked was 'high handed') and *Pascoe v Turner* [1979] 1 WLR 431, CA (Pascoe had been 'ruthless' in his efforts to evict Mrs Turner).

[43] *Burrows v Sharpe* [1989] 23 HLR 82 at 92 and *J Willis and Son v Willis* [1986] 1 EGLR 62.

[44] *ibid.*

Post adjudication misconduct

In *Williams v Staite,*[45] Lord Denning suggested that post-judgment misconduct might, in an extreme case, deprive the claimant of the rights granted at trial. This proposition was rejected by the majority.[46] Further reservations were subsequently expressed by the Court of Appeal in *J Willis and Son v Willis.*[47] The approach advocated by Lord Denning might be feasible in cases where the remedy previously granted was relatively flexible or undefined, for example, where the court grants a licence or simply refuses M's application for possession. It seems most unlikely, however, that the courts would intervene to divest W of an orthodox, defined and possibly registered proprietary interest such as a fee simple or lease.[48] Post-trial misconduct is more appropriately dealt with using the ordinary principles of criminal law, tort, trespass, nuisance and landlord and tenant.[49] If, which we doubt, Lord Denning's proposition is correct, it is clear that only significant and serious misconduct will cause the court to confiscate rights granted at trial. A greater degree of culpability is required than that sufficient to deprive a claimant of a remedy at trial.[50] **11.059**

The parties' personal circumstances (including financial) and the general effect of the order on them[51]

In *Sledmore v Dalby*, Lord Justices Roch and Butler Sloss[52] reversed an order granting W a life licence to reside in M's property because: '*the* **11.060**

---

[45] [1979] Ch 291, CA *per* Denning M.R. at 298B–C and *J Willis and Son v Willis* [1986] 1 EGLR 62 at 63E–F.

[46] [1979] Ch 291, CA Goff L.J. at 300A–C and Cumming Bruce L.J. at 300D.

[47] [1986] 1 EGLR 62 at 63E–F.

[48] Both *Willis* and *Williams* were licence cases. See generally Thompson 'Estoppel and Clean Hands' [1986] *Conv* 406 on the distinction between remedies which are, and those which are not, meant to amount to a final adjudication of the matter between the parties. The general principles of *res judicata* were considered in neither *Willis* nor *Williams* and might also prove to be a problem.

[49] *Williams v Staite* [1979] Ch 291, CA *per* Goff L.J. at 300A-C.

[50] *J. Willis & Sons v Willis* [1986] 1 EGLR 62.

[51] *Sledmore v Dalby* (1996) P&CR 196, CA at 204, 209; *Pascoe v Turner* [1979] 1 WLR 431, CA at 438F (in comparison to W, M was a rich man); *Baker v Baker* [1993] 25 HLR 408 *per* Dillon L.J. at 412 and *per* Roche L.J. at 419 '*. . . the task of the court here is not to assess loss as though it were awarding damages but to maintain a more flexible approach, designed to achieve justice between the parties'*.

[52] (1996) P&CR 196, CA at 204, 209 respectively; Hobhouse L.J. reached the same decision without reference to M's parlous circumstances.

Recorder should have considered the position of [M] *and her needs and balanced those against the present use of the premises made by* [W] *and his present need for them*'. M had been left a widow living in a house which was too large for her, with mortgage arrears of £6000; interest was being paid with social security; she was dependent entirely on her widow's pension and on welfare benefits; W was employed and used the property for only two nights a week. The Court of Appeal granted M possession of the property. A stricter approach had been adopted in an earlier decision. According to Lord Justice Beldam in *Baker v Baker,*[53] M's financial position could be taken into account only in deciding how the remedy granted by the court may be enforced. In other words, M's position and capacity to pay damages was a relevant consideration neither to the court's decision whether a remedy should be granted (such as a licence, ownership interest or sum of money) nor to the decision as to the extent of that remedy (such as the terms of a licence or amount of money due). It might, however, be relevant in deciding whether money adjudged to be due should be payable immediately or in instalments and, if so, whether a charge on the property should be granted. We consider that the latter, more restrictive, approach is to be preferred since the former creates an unacceptable degree of uncertainty.

Illegality

Where transfer the property in issue is barred by statute, no relief will be granted.[54] Nor will a claim arise where the acts in reliance are unlawful for example by reason of trespass.[55] The same principle may cover a case where the acts in reliance consist of works carried out in breach of planning regulations. Proprietary estoppel cannot be used to undermine the effect of a statute or give a public authority a jurisdiction it would not otherwise have.[56] **11.061**

[53] [1995] 25 HLR 408 at 417. See also *Durant v Heritage* [1994] EGCS 134, lexis transcript.

[54] *Chalmers v Pardoe* [1963] 1 WLR 677. In *Maharaj v Chand* [1986] AC 898, PC this problem was bypassed by resorting to promissory, instead of proprietary, estoppel, as to which see generally Chap. 12 below.

[55] *Hanning v Top Deck Travel Group Ltd*, (1993) 68 P&CR 14, CA at 21–2.

[56] *Western Fish Products v Penwith DC* [1981] 2 All ER 204 CA and *West Middlesex Golf Club Limited v Ealing London Borough Council* (1993) 68 P&CR 461. The principles governing proprietary estoppel and estoppel by representation are the same in this area. Hence, reference should be made to paras 8.121–5 above for further detail on this issue.

Knowledge of the property owner

As we set out in paragraphs 11.21 to 11.22, to establish a claim in proprietary estoppel, it is necessary to satisfy various knowledge requirements. If, as we tentatively conclude, it suffices to show that the property owner ought in all the circumstances to have known the relevant facts, a claim may lie where he does not have actual conscious knowledge of them. The absence of this conscious knowledge might well be taken into account in exercising the remedial discretion. **11.062**

Welfare benefits paid to the claimant

The court will not take into account welfare benefits received by W as a result of M's resiling from the assurance, for example, where W has been rehoused in rent free local authority accommodation as a result of exclusion from M's property. It was held in *Baker v Baker*[57] that: **11.063**

> . . . payments out of scarce public resources which become necessary due to private wrong should not be taken to reduce a private liability for that wrong. . . . The principle on which equity proceeds is that it would be unconscionable for [M] not to satisfy, so far as money payment can do so, the interest which they had promised [W]. I see no reason in conscience why that interest should in part be satisfied at the public expense from housing benefit.[58]

EXAMPLES OF REMEDIES GRANTED

The courts have developed '*a fairly well established remedial menu*'[59] from the wide range of options available. The examples cited may be combined[60] with one another and may be granted subject to conditions, such as payment of a reasonable purchase price for the property,[61] or contributing towards its outgoings and maintenance.[62] They may be **11.064**

---

57 [1993] 25 HLR 408.

58 *Baker v Baker* [1993] 25 HLR 408 *per* Beldam L.J. at 416 (Roch L.J. concurring at 419 and Dillon L.J. dissenting at 413).

59 Gray at p. 531.

60 *Dodsworth v Dodsworth* (1973) 228 EG 1115, CA (award of compensation and right of occupation).

61 *Lim v Ang* [1992] 1 WLR 113, PC (Brunei).

62 *Matharu v Matharu* (1994) 68 P&CR 93 CA.

accompanied by injunctive relief designed to prevent M's interfering with the exercise of the rights granted.[63]

Refusal of the property owner's application to the court

This may take the form of failing to accede to an action in trespass[64] or for breach of a restrictive covenant[65] or for possession.[66] The latter remedial outcome has considerable practical disadvantages. First, the claimant's rights may be vulnerable to third parties.[67] Secondly, they are probably tied to the particular property in question; the claimant cannot move to another without forfeiting them.[68] Thirdly, the rights may not extend to the claimant's family[69] and on death she can pass no rights to dependents. The outcome also has conceptual disadvantages, giving rise to considerable uncertainty.[70] It is unclear, for example, whether a licence for life is been created,[71] with all the potential difficulties which that may involve.[72] Further, W's possession may be adverse, so as to pass legal title after 12 years,[73] leading to the acquisition of a greater right than that contemplated by the parties. **11.065**

63 *Lim v Ang* [1992] 1 WLR 113, PC (Brunei) at 118–9.

64 *Ward v Kirkland* [1966] 1 WLR 601.

65 *Shaw v Applegate* [1977] 1 WLR 970, CA.

66 *Inwards v Baker* [1965] 2 QB 29, CA.

67 If the effect of the order is to grant a mere licence rather than a life interest, as to which see note 71 below and further para. 11.83.

68 As well as the obvious practical inconvenience, the result transgresses the paradigm property law antithesis to arrangements inhibiting the free alienation of land, since W will be encouraged to stay in the property making sale virtually impossible. Neither problem occurs if the arrangement does give rise to a life interest in the property.

69 *Stevens v Stevens* (CA unrep. 1989) lexis transcript.

70 Leading to its rejection in *Stevens v Stevens* (CA unrep. 1989) lexis transcript.

71 *Matharu v Matharu* (1994) 68 P&CR 93, CA at 99, 103 suggests that it does.

72 As to which see para. 000 below. Russell L.J. remarked in *Dodsworth v Dodsworth* (1973) 228 EG 1115, CA at 1115 that the difficulties posed by the Settled Land Act 1925 had been '*overlooked*' in *Inwards v Baker* [1965] 2 QB 29, CA.

73 Limitation Act, s.15: see generally on this point Welstead 'Proprietary Estoppel and the Acquisition of Possessory Title' [1991] *Conv* 280, citing *Cullen v Cullen* [1962] IR 268.

Grant of a right to occupy the property

A licence to occupy may be granted for life or for some other period deemed to be appropriate.[74] Considerable controversy has arisen over whether the grant of a right to occupy for life gives rise to a life interest in property: it seems probable that it did do so under the Settled Land Act 1925.[75] It seems unlikely that this effect has survived the commencement of the Trusts of Land, Appointment of Trustees Act 1996, which governs the operation of all life interest settlements created on or after January 1997. Even if it has, most of the difficulties inherent in such a conclusion have been mitigated by the latter Act. In particular, the power to sell the property is, under the 1996 Act, vested in the trustees, (namely the legal owners) rather than in the life tenant, as was the case under the earlier statute. The powers of the holder of a life interest may, however, even under the new legislation, be more extensive than those originally contemplated by the parties and might be thought to over-compensate W.[76] Given these difficulties, there is little to recommend this remedial outcome. The courts have adopted a pragmatic approach by selecting alternative remedies[77] which give approximately equivalent protection to the claimant. The primary justification for its selection has generally been an attempt to reflect the arrangement actually contemplated by the **11.066**

[74] A life licence was granted in *Ungurian v Lessnoff* [1990] Ch 206, *Matharu v Matharu* [1994] 68 P&CR 93 CA, *Stevens v Stevens* (CA unrep. 1989, lexis transcript) and *Price v Hartwell* [1996] EGCS 98. In *Re Sharp* [1980] All ER 198 and *Dodsworth v Dodsworth* (1973) 228 EG 1115 CA the respective claimants were granted a right to reside until their expenditure was repaid.

[75] *Ungurian v Lessnoff* [1990] Ch 206; *Bannister v Bannister* [1948] 2 All ER 133, CA; *Griffiths v Williams* (1977) 248 EG 947, CA at 949–50; *Dodsworth v Dodsworth* (1973) 228 EG 1115, CA at 1115 and *Habermann v Koehler* (CA unrep.) *per* Millet L.J. (referred to in *Habermann v Koehler* (1996) 73 P&CR 515 CA *per* Evans L.J. at 520). It seems, however, that the court can grant a life licence without creating a life interest so long as it is stated to be personal, non-assignable, non-transmissible and determinable on W's ceasing to live in the property — see the order made at first instance in *Sledmore v Dalby* (1996) P&CR 196, CA at 200 (overturned on other grounds).

[76] For example, the right to move out of the property and let it to someone else. See para. 11.52.

[77] *Griffiths v Williams* (1977) 248 EG 947, CA at 949–50 (tenancy at a nominal rent, determinable on death of W); *Dodsworth v Dodsworth* (1973) 228 EG 1115, CA at 1115 (charge on the property coupled with a right to occupy until the expenditure on it repaid); *Sledmore v Dalby* (1996) P&CR 196, CA at 200 (grant, at first instance, non-assignable, non-transmissible personal licence to occupy, determinable on W's ceasing to live in the property) and Law Commission Report No. 181 of 1989 at paras 1.3 and 4.2.

parties.[78] Once it is recognized that the aim of the remedy should always be the minimum equity rather than the fulfilment of the parties' expectations, any factors in favour of such an order seem to evaporate.[79]

Grant of ownership rights in the property

Such relief has included the grant of a wide range of legal rights and interests such as full fee simple ownership,[80] an easement[81] and a lease[82] (or option to extend or renew an existing lease[83]). An obvious analogy may be drawn between this type of order and one for specific performance of a contract. Alternatively, the claimant may be granted equitable ownership rights in the property,[84] including a life[85] or remainder interest[86]. **11.067**

[78] Although, ironically, the effect of Settled Land Act 1925 was to cause a significant divergence from the expectations of the parties.

[79] Although, it is conceded that a further reason for making such an order was to establish a proprietary interest binding on third parties — see further Law Commission Report No. 181 of 1989 at para. 4.2. See paras 11.50–5 above on the minimum equity principle.

[80] *Dillwyn v Llewellyn* (1862) De G F and J 517, 45 ER 1285; *Pascoe v Turner* [1979] 1 WLR 43; *Re Basham deceased* [1986] 1 WLR 1498; *Voyce v Voyce* (1991) 62 P&CR 290, CA; *Lim v Ang* [1992] 1 WLR 113, PC (Brunei) and *Durant v Heritage* [1994] EGCS 134. The availability of this remedy arguably marks a point of distinction between proprietary estoppel and the common intention constructive trust.

[81] *Crabb v Arun DC* [1976] Ch 179, CA and *Ives v High* [1967] 2 QB 379, CA.

[82] *Huning v Ferrars* (1711) Gilb 85, 25 ER 59; *Stiles v Cowper* (1748) 3 Atk 382, 26 ER 1198; *Gregory v Mighell* (1811) 18 Ves 238, 34 ER 341. *Siew Soon Wah v Yong Tong Hong* [1973] AC 836, PC (Malaysia); *Watson v Goldsbrough* [1986] EGLR 265, CA; *Toogood v Farrell* [1988] EGLR 233, CA (sub-lease granted) and *JT Developments v Quinn* (1991) 62 P&CR 33, CA. See also *Dann v Spurrier* (1802) 7 Ves Jun 232, 32 ER 94, *Ramsden v Dyson* (1866) LR 1 HL 129 HL and *Watkins v Emslie* (1981) 261 EG 1192, CA, where leases were claimed but an estoppel was not established on the facts.

[83] *Taylors Fashions Ltd v Liverpool Victoria Trustees Co. Ltd* [1982] 1 QB 133 (the Olds case) and *West Middlesex Golf Club Limited v Ealing London Borough Council* (1993) 68 P&CR 461. See also *John v George and Walton* (1996) 71 P&CR 375, CA where the landlord was estopped from relying on a valid ground for termination of a lease.

[84] *Jones v Jones* [1977] 1 WLR 438, CA and *Hammond v Mitchell* [1992] 4 All ER 109.

[85] *Ungurian v Lessnoff* [1990] Ch 206 (orthodox life interest) and *Habermann v Koehler* (CA unrep.) *per* Millet L.J. (referred to in *Habermann v Koehler* (1996) 73 P&CR 515 CA *per* Evans L.J. at 520) (interest per autre vie where duration of the right depends on the life of someone other than the holder).

[86] *Smith v Halpin* [1997] 2 IRLM 38.

Compensation and/or charge

In the past, monetary awards were generally made only where the grant of a property interest was impractical[87] or, for some specific reason, undesirable.[88] If the trend towards the detriment based approach continues,[89] such awards are likely to become more common as a simple and accurate way in which to avert harm to W. Payment may be required immediately or over a period.[90] Awards are frequently secured by a charge or lien over the property in issue.[91] Further, the court may grant an occupation right, terminating on final payment.[92] **11.068**

Quantum

No strict principles of quantification have been established. In a number of cases, the award has reflected the value of the share or right expected,[93] thus tending to fulfil the expectations of the parties. As we set out above, however,[94] the prime aim of the remedy should now be confined to avoiding detriment to claimants rather than fulfilling their expectations. According to this approach, quantum should be determined by the nature and extent of W's acts in reliance. Where the acts in reliance consist of improvements to M's property, there remains a choice between two alternative measures. The award may reflect the cost of the works performed or money contributed.[95] Alternatively, it may be **11.069**

[87] *Holiday Inns Inc v Broadhead* (1974) 232 EG 951 and *Wayling v Jones* (1993) P&CR 170, CA where the property in issue had been sold; *Burrows v Sharpe* [1991] Fam Law 67 at 67, CA (where the relationship had broken down between the parties); *Baker v Baker* [1993] 25 HLR 408 (same) and *Tanner v Tanner* [1975] 1 WLR 1346, CA (W left the premises after a possession order was made at first instance).

[88] *Dodsworth v Dodsworth* (1973) 228 EG 1115, CA.

[89] As to which see paras 11.51–4.

[90] *Baker v Baker* [1993] 25 HLR 408 *per* Beldam L.J. at 416.

[91] *Unity Joint Stock Mutual Banking Association v King (a bankrupt)* (1858) 25 Beav 72, 53 ER 563; *Foster, Hudson v Foster (No. 2)* [1938] 3 All ER 610 and *Dodsworth v Dodsworth* (1973) 228 EG 1115, CA.

[92] *Dodsworth v Dodsworth* (1973) 228 EG 1115, CA.

[93] *Holiday Inns Inc v Broadhead* (1974) 232 EG 951 (this measure was the aim of the relief ordered although the means of calculation were fairly rough and ready); *Wayling v Jones* (1993) P&CR 170, CA; *Tanner v Tanner* [1975] 1 WLR 1346, CA and *Baker v Baker* [1993] 25 HLR 408.

[94] At para. 11.50–4.

[95] *Hussey v Palmer* [1972] 1 WLR 1286, CA (this was not strictly a compensation case but the beneficial interest granted was quantified by reference to the amount spent) and *Burrows v Sharpe* [1991] Fam Law 67 (mortgage payments to be refunded).

based on the amount by which the value of the property was enhanced.[96] Whichever method is selected, there are appealing arguments in favour of including a sum for capital appreciation,[97] reflecting overall movements in the market, rather than conventional interest. Arguably, this is necessary in order adequately to compensate W's loss. Such an approach recognizes the social importance of the investment in real property as an effective means of acquisition of wealth by saving. This approach is particularly appropriate where it is likely that the claimant's money would have been invested directly in the property market, were it not for M's conduct.[98] If this analysis is correct, the level of compensation would presumably be reduced were the property market to collapse. This would be consistent with the court's professed aim of achieving a fair result between the parties and would also be justifiable on the basis of causation. Take, for example, the situation where W spends £2000 on a property originally worth £40000 and thereby increases its value by £10000. If the property subsequently halves in value as a result of a market crash, the £5000 reduction in the share of the value attributable to W's work is caused, not by her change of position, but by the fall in the market.[99]

Comment

The increasing maturity of the law of proprietary estoppel should give rise to progressively more certain principles governing the exercise of the remedial discretion. As a cause of action based on detrimental reliance, the modern proprietary estoppel doctrine may give rise to liabilities as onerous as any imposed by tort or contract. It is difficult to justify remedial uncertainty in proprietary estoppel which would be unacceptable in these related areas. The crucial determinant should be the measure of detriment suffered and the importance of factors listed in paras.11.55–63 above should be progressively reduced or eliminated. **11.070**

---

[96] *Stratulatos v Stratulatos* [1988] 2 NZLR 424 at 439.
[97] *ibid.*
[98] *ibid.*
[99] See the approach used in other areas of private law: *South Australia Asset Management Corp v York Montague Ltd* [1996] 3 All ER 365, HL (tort); *Target Holdings v Redferns* [1995] 3 All ER 785, HL (trusts) and *Cheese v Thomas* [1994] 1 All ER 35 (undue influence). See also Chitty at para. 3.118.

EFFECT OF PROPRIETARY ESTOPPEL ON THIRD PARTIES

The outcome of many, though not all, proprietary estoppel cases involves vesting a property right in the claimant.[1] In this section, we attempt to identify the circumstances when rights acquired may be enforced against the property in the hands of third parties. We endeavour to analyse the nature of the rights generated by proprietary estoppel and the point at which they arise. **11.071**

THE BURDEN

An initial distinction must be drawn between the cases under consideration in this part, where an estoppel arises and M subsequently transfers ownership of the relevant property, and those where the conduct of a transferee of property itself gives rise to an estoppel.[2] The latter situation is governed by the ordinary principles of proprietary estoppel, discussed generally in this chapter.[3] **11.072**

Pre-trial

W acquires no enforceable rights before all the three elements of liability are satisfied, namely until she has relied to her detriment on M's assurance.[4] Considerable controversy surrounds the question as to what, if any, interest is generated at this point. The claimant has a sufficient interest to merit compensation in the event of compulsory purchase of **11.073**

---

[1] See, for example, the cases referred to at para. 11.67.

[2] *Taylors Fashions Ltd v Liverpool Victoria Trustees Co Ltd* [1982] 1 QB 133.

[3] The precise borderline between the two types of case is sometimes blurred. See *Salvation Army Trustee Co Ltd v West Yorkshire Metropolitan County Council* (1981) P&CR 179 at 195, where a successor public authority was bound by the proprietary estoppel which arose against, and as a consequence of, the acts of its predecessor. The case against the successor authority was, however, strengthened by the fact that it had itself also been guilty of conduct capable of giving rise to an estoppel — see (1981) P&CR 179 at 195–7.

[4] *Pascoe v Turner* [1979] 1 WLR 43, CA at 435f. We do not agree with the suggestion made by Gray at p. 359, the cause of action is complete only when M seeks to enforce his strict legal rights.

the property.[5] Further, some cases indicate that proprietary estoppel vests an equitable ownership interest in the claimant[6] (or creates a constructive trust in her favour[7]) from the date of detrimental reliance. This would explain the numerous instances where third parties have been bound by rights generated by proprietary estoppel. Specific examples include donees[8] (such as those taking under M's will[9]), a trustee in bankruptcy,[10] a successor public authority,[11] a successor associated company[12] and purchasers with actual notice.[13] It would also explain the dicta in *ER*

---

[5] *Preston and Henderson v St Helens Metropolitan Borough Council, lands tribunal* (1989) 58 P&CR 500 and *Pennine Raceway v Kirklees MBC* [1983] QB 382, CA.

[6] *Unity Joint Stock Mutual Banking Association v King (a bankrupt)* (1858) 25 Beav 72 at 79, 53 ER 563 at 566; *Hamilton v Geraghty* (1901) 1 SRNSW Eq 81 at 86–91; *Pennine Raceway v Kirklees MBC* [1983] QB 382, CA at 390a, 393e (*dicta* since the scope of those entitled to compensation under the statute in issue was wider than those holding proprietary interests in the strict conveyancing sense); *Voyce v Voyce* (1991) 62 P&CR 290, CA at 294 and *Habermann v Koehler* (CA unrep.) *per* Millet L.J. (referred to in *Habermann v Koehler* (1996) 73 P&CR 515 CA *per* Evans L.J. at 520).

[7] *Re Basham decd* [1986] 1 WLR 1498 at 1504a-b, 1504d-e; *Commonwealth of Australia v Verwayen* [1990] 170 CLR 394 at 437; *Sen v Headley* [1991] Ch 425 at 439h–40a and *Re Dale (deceased)* [1993] 4 All ER 129 at 141g–h.

[8] *John v George and Walton* (1996) 71 P&CR 375, CA (the point was conceded).

[9] *Duke of Beaufort v Patrick* (1853) 17 Beav 59, 51 ER 954; *Dillwyn v Llewellyn* (1862) De G F and J 517, 45 ER 1285; *Inwards v Baker* [1965] 2 QB 29, CA 65; *Dodsworth v Dodsworth* (1973) 228 EG 1115; *Griffiths v Williams* (1977) 248 EG 947, CA; *Greasley v Cook* [1980] 1 WLR 1306 CA; *Re Basham deceased* [1986] 1 WLR 1498; *Smith v Halpin* [1997] 2 IRLM 38; *Voyce v Voyce* (1991) 62 P&CR 290, CA and *Wayling v Jones* (1993) P&CR 170, CA. See also *Errington v Errington* [1952] 1 QB 290, CA; the case was decided on contract principles but the Court of Appeal, in *Ashburn Anstalt v Arnold* [1988] 2 WLR 706, CA at 720f-h (*per* Fox L.J.), held that while the contractual analysis was incorrect, the result was justifiable on the basis of an estoppel which was capable binding a third party.

[10] *Re Sharp* [1980] All ER 198, although it is questionable as to whether the finding on estoppel was material to Browne-Wilkinson J.'s decision as to the transmissibility of the right in issue.

[11] *Plimmer v Wellington Corpn* (1884) 9 Ap Cas 699, PC (New Zealand) (although the point was circumvented — all that was material was that the land had been vested continuously in the government 'under whatever form').

[12] *E and L Berg Homes Ltd v Grey* (1979) 253 EG 473, CA.

[13] *Duke of Beaufort v Patrick* (1853) 17 Beav 59, 51 ER 954 and *ER Ives Investment Ltd v High* [1967] 2 QB 379 where the estoppel point formed part of the *ratio* (despite the parallel operation of the benefit and burden principle of *Halsall v Brizell* [1957] Ch 169). Where two reasons are given by the court for reaching its decision, generally both are classified as forming part of the *ratio,* even where one alone would have been sufficient to dispose of the case. Further, the right acquired by Mr High under the benefit and burden principle was precarious. Had E.R. Ives removed their foundations from his premises, Mr High's right would have determined. The easement arising under estoppel principles was not qualified in this way and would have survived such a change of mind by E.R Ives. See also *dicta* in *Lloyds Bank v Carrick* [1996] All ER 630, CA at 642b–c and *Re Sharp* [1980] All ER 198 at 204f.

Ives Investment Ltd v High[14] and *Duke of Beaufort v Patrick*[15] suggesting that proprietary estoppels bind all but the bona fide purchaser for value without actual or constructive notice.[16] There is no case which has directly considered the position of a purchaser with constructive notice.[17] However, in *Lloyds Bank v Rosset*[18] and *Abbey National Building Society v Cann*,[19] the House of Lords assumed, *sub silentio*, that estoppel rights were capable of binding a purchaser with the registered land equivalent of constructive notice, whereby purchasers take subject to the rights of those in actual occupation of the premises.[20] In the former case, Lord Bridge assessed what Mrs Rosset needed to prove in order to establish a right enforceable against the bank. One of the means available to her was proprietary estoppel,[21] although she failed to establish a claim on the facts. In the latter case, their Lordships held that such an estoppel had been made out but was not enforceable against the building society because of the nature of an acquisition mortgage.[22] Unless Mrs Cann had rights capable of binding a purchaser, there would have been no need to consider the various points on which their Lordships based their decision. In *Holiday Inns Inc v Broadhead*,[23] the purchaser, with neither constructive nor actual notice, took free of the estoppel rights.

14 [1967] 2 QB 379.

15 (1853) 17 Beav 59, 51 ER 954. See also *Inwards v Baker* [1965] 2 QB 29, CA *per* Lord Denning at 37f.

16 In both of these cases, the purchaser had actual knowledge of the relevant facts. Even assuming the general principle is correct, it must now be qualified, in respect of real property, by modern statutory modifications made to the doctrine of notice as to which see specialist texts. See also the *obiter* comments of Geoghegan J. in *Smith v Halpin* [1997] 2 IRLM 38. *Dicta* in *Hopgood v Brown* [1955] 1 WLR 213 at 225, 228, 230 (the purchaser had actual notice) indicate that a transferee will be bound regardless of notice. The reasons given for this conclusion are, however, unconvincing and, in any event, may be confined to the estoppel by representation which undoubtedly arose in that case. See 8.136–40.

17 Or its registered land analogue, the purchaser of a property of which the claimant is in actual occupation.

18 [1991] AC 107.

19 [1991] AC 56.

20 Land Registration Act 1925, s.70(1)(g) and see further para. 11.80 below.

21 [1991] AC 107 at 132e–h (approved by the remainder of their Lordships).

22 Admittedly Mrs Cann probably also had an interest under a resulting and constructive trust ([1991] AC 56 at 80–82, 103) but there was no suggestion that her estoppel rights and her trust rights were governed by distinct principles.

23 (1974) 232 EG 951 at 961.

The juristic nature of pre-trial rights

None of the authorities analyse the nature of the rights generated by estoppel with any clarity. As a result of the remedial flexibility of the proprietary estoppel doctrine, there are significant logical difficulties in characterizing such rights as full equitable interests. Prior to the adjudication of the dispute, there is no means of predicting what, if any, proprietary interest may be granted by the court. W cannot insist on a particular interest; she is supplicant for court's discretion and may be granted a lesser interest, compensation or denied any remedy. Further, given the power of the courts to take into account the conduct of the parties up to the date of judgment,[24] the extent of the claimant's rights may fluctuate over time. Such factors have led some[25] to conclude that proprietary estoppel gives rise to a *remedial* constructive trust with the following characteristics. First, W has minimal[26] or no enforceable rights prior to adjudication. Secondly, the court, in tailoring the remedy to fit the wrong, is *creating* new rights rather than upholding existing property interests; its order has, therefore, prospective effect only. Thirdly, whether third parties are bound is a question for the discretion of the court, in each particular case, the determining factor being whether the conscience of the third party is affected. **11.074**

This thesis has undoubted attractions, not the least of which is that it obviates the need to fit estoppel rights into the conveyancing system, a task which is by no means an easy one. The results of many of the cases where third parties have been bound may be susceptible to ex-post facto rationalization as instances where the court has seen fit to exercise a flexible discretion. We are unable, however, to reconcile this thesis with the reasoning used in the cases referred to above where third parties have been bound by rights created by the doctrine. That reasoning involves two stages, first, the recognition of some form of pre-existing property right created by the doctrine and second, the application of **11.075**

---

[24] As to which see para. 11.58–9 above.

[25] Hayton 'Equitable rights of co-habitees' (1990) *Conv* 370; Ferguson 'Constructive Trusts — a Note of Caution' (1993) 109 *LQR* 114, Lord Browne-Wilkinson's 1991 Holdsworth Lecture, 'Constructive Trusts and Unjust Enrichment' and Evans 'Choosing the Right Estoppel' [1988] *Conv* 346. See also *Habermann v Koehler* (1996) 73 P&CR 515 CA *per* Peter Gibson L.J. at 522, where it was suggested, *obiter*, that the fact that the property had been sold to a purchaser with notice of the claimant's occupation of the property but not of its terms, was simply one of a number of circumstances to be taken into account in assessing the appropriate remedy.

[26] If proceedings have been issued in support of a claim to a specific interest in land, the claimant has a right protectable as a pending land action pursuant to the machinery set out below at paras 11.79–80 Underhill and Hayton, at pp. 222–3.

ordinary conveyancing principles to ascertain whether that right binds the current owner of the property.[27] Further, although the path of future development may lie with the remedial constructive trust, Lord Browne-Wilkinson has recently pointed out that the courts have yet to decide what role, if any, the concept will play in English law.[28]

Such rights as W has prior to adjudication are probably too vague and uncertain to amount to fully fledged equitable interests.[29] The most convincing characterization of such rights is as mere equities.[30] Such rights are capable of binding third parties but probably only when attached to some form of orthodox proprietary interest.[31] The only feasible interest with which an estoppel right can form this parasitic relationship, is that granted by the court on trial of the issue. There seems to be a process of relation back whereby the inchoate equity (generated by, and at the time of, acts in reliance) binds retrospectively, when a proprietary interest is granted.[32] This analysis is admittedly somewhat artificial but seems to be the most logical way to explain why such vague and unformed rights can bind third parties in the way made clear in the cases. If this approach is correct, third parties may only ever **11.076**

---

[27] *Re Sharp* [1980] All ER 198 at 203d–4a.

[28] *Westdeutsche Landesbank Girocentral v Islington London Borough Council* [1996] 2 All ER 961, HL at 999a–c. The concept is certainly gaining ground in the English jurisdiction. See [1996] 2 All ER 961, HL 997a–d, 999a–c and *Metall und Rohstoff AG v Donaldson Lufkin and Jenrette Inc* [1990] 1 QB 391 at 478–80.

[29] See the strict approach of the House of Lords in *National Provincial Bank v Ainsworth* [1965] AC 1175 at 1226e–7a, 1238c–e. Such rights are, however, accorded to claimants under specifically enforceable contracts, despite the fact that the courts have a fairly flexible discretion as to whether to grant this equitable remedy: *Lysaght v Edwards* (1876) 2 Ch D 499 at 507. On specific performance generally, see Hanbury and Martin chapter 24.

[30] According to Davis, 'Proprietary Estoppel: Future Interests and Future Property' [1996] *Conv* 193 such an analysis is supported by terminology used in the case law; *viz* those authorities where a *declaration* has been made seemingly recognizing a pre-existing interest. See also those cases which refer to an equity arising out of acquiescence or encouragement. Examples include *Ramsden v Dyson* (1866) LR 1 HL 129, HL at 140–1; *Plimmer v Wellington Corpn* (1884) 9 Ap Cas 699, PC (New Zealand) at 713–14 and *Crabb v Arun DC* [1976] Ch 179, CA at 188b–d and 192–3. Contra. Evans, *Choosing the Right Estoppel* [1988] Conv 346 (references to *satisfying* the equity are inconsistent with the view that it amounts to an enforceable proprietary right prior to court order).

[31] *National Provincial Bank v Ainsworth* [1965] AC 1175 *per* Lord Upjohn at 1238b–g.

[32] See Baughan 'Estoppels Over Land and Third Parties' (1994) 14 *LS* 147. It is conceded that those third party cases where a licence has been granted such as *Plimmer v Wellington Corpn* (1884) 9 Ap Cas 699, PC (New Zealand); *Re Sharp* [1980] All ER 198 and *Pennine Raceway v Kirklees MBC* [1983] QB 382, CA are not explicable on this basis. See para. 11.83 below on the difficulties associated with licence cases.

be bound by estoppel rights if the final order made by the court involves the grant of a property interest. This would seem consistent with both general principles and common sense.

Conveyancing principles

11.077 The principles which deterimine whether a third party will be bound depend on the nature of the claimant's interest prior to trial. As we set out in the preceding paragraphs, there are three views as to the nature of the right generated after detrimental reliance takes place: (i) no property interest, (ii) an orthodox equitable interest, (iii) an inchoate equity. Given the controversy surrounding this question, the priorities principles governing in each of these three situations is assessed. If the remedial constructive trust analysis is adopted, the effect on third parties will be a question of discretion, exercised according to the individual circumstances of the case. There is little guidance as to how such a discretion would be exercised. The oft expressed preference for certainty and predictability in conveyancing matters would seem to require that the discretion be exercised according to clear criteria. The applicable principles would probably be those set out in *Ashburn Anstaldt v Arnold.*[33] A purchaser of property would therefore be bound only where it expressly agreed with the vendor to give effect to the rights in issue or to take the property positively subject to them.[34] It has been suggested that the range on instances where an *Ashburn* constructive trust will arise against a purchaser is much wider.[35] Any purchaser should take the ordinary precaution of consulting occupants as to whether they claim rights in the property; if it fails to take this elementary conveyancing precaution, it deliberately, or recklessly, divests the claimant of opportunity to demand the formal grant of an interest, issue a writ and register a pending land action; such conduct, it is suggested, is sufficiently unconscionable to give rise to an *Ashburn* constructive trust. However, we consider that such an approach

---

[33] [1988] 2 WLR 706, CA.

[34] As opposed to instances where the conveyance is expressed to be subject to the claimant's rights but only in order to discharge the vendor's obligation to reveal possible incumbrances on the title — a negative *'subject to'* clause. It will be seen (from paras 11.79–81 below) that the remedial constructive trust approach grants a lesser degree of protection to the holders of informally created rights in property, than does the equitable interest or mere equity analysis. The practical impact of this conclusion is intensified if proprietary estoppel subsumes and/or displaces the institutional constructive trust presently used to allocate ownership of the family home, as to which see *Lloyds Bank v Rosset* [1991] AC 107.

[35] Underhill and Hayton, at pp. 222–3.

is inconsistent with the strict approach taken in *Ashburn*, where the claimant *was* in occupation of the premises.

11.078 If an orthodox equitable interest is generated as soon as detrimental reliance takes place, ordinary conveyancing principles will govern the position with respect to third parties. For a detailed analysis of the relevant principles, reference should be made to specialist texts.[35a] The principles are largely the same as those which govern the inchoate equity. These are set out immediately below. The principles differ, however, in the following respects. There is some doubt as to whether the inchoate equity is capable of amounting to (i) an overriding interest where its holder is in occupation of the property and (ii) a minor interest in the absence of occupation.[35b] There is no such doubt in respect of an orthodox equitable interests which clearly fall within both categories (i) and (ii).[36] If the correct characterisation of pre-trial rights is that they amount only to an inchoate equity, as we set out above, such an equity is probably incapable of binding third parties unless some property right is eventually granted at trial. Where an equitable or legal ownership interest is granted at trial, and the relation back process is thus triggered, the effect of the equity on third parties is determined as follows.

Unregistered title

11.079 W's rights are not capable of being overreached.[37] Nor are they registerable unless an interest in the land is claimed and litigation has commenced.[38] If the litigation has been so commenced, failure to register the pending land action makes judgment unenforceable against

[35a] See for exmple Gray chapters 6–8 and generally Ruoff and Roper.

[35b] See paras 11.80–1 below.

[36] As to overriding interest see, Land Registration Act 1925 s.70(1)(g) and *Williams and Glyn's Bank v Boland* [1981] AC 487. As to minor interest see Land Registration Act 1925 s.3(xv) and *Williams and Glyn's Bank v Boland* [1981] AC 487.

[37] *Shiloh Spinners v Harding* [1973] AC 691 *per* Lord Wilberforce at 721a–e. This proposition probably remains true even where an orthodox overreachable interest is eventually granted by the court: the overreaching transaction can only operate at the time of sale; its effect cannot extend to the date of court adjudication. See Evans 'The Fall and Rise of the Remedial Constructive Trust' [1989] *Conv* 418 at 427 and Hanbury and Martin at p. 895 but contra. Thompson 'Registration, Fraud and Notice' (1985) 44 *CLJ* 280 at 299 and Baughan 'Estoppels over land and third parties' (1994) 14 *LS* 147 at 154–5. The difficulty in assessing the effect of the overreaching provisions on estoppel rights is an inevitable consequence of the uncertainty surrounding the precise nature of those rights.

[38] Land Charges Act 1972, s.5(1), (3)(a) and 17(1). This seems implicit in the judgment in *Haslemere Estates Ltd v Baker* [1982] 1 WLR 1109 at 119, where registration was inappropriate because the relevant proceedings involved a claim for money rather than interest in land. See Gray at p. 365 n. 13.

a purchaser without actual knowledge of the proceedings.[39] If the assumption relied on by the claimant to found the estoppel amounts to a valid and enforceable contract to grant a legal estate in land, a class C(iv) land charge should be registered: the Court of Appeal declined, in *Lloyd's Bank v Carrick*,[40] in such circumstances, '. . . *to confer on the claimant indirectly and by means of a proprietary estoppel . . . that which Parliament prevented her from obtaining directly by a contract which it has declared to be void*'.[41] Those equities not within these two categories, are presumably governed by the doctrine of notice[42] and will bind all but the bona fide purchaser, for value, of a legal or *equitable*[43] interest or estate, without actual, imputed or constructive notice.

Registered title

Where interest in land is claimed and litigation has commenced, proprietary estoppel rights may be protected by entry of caution on the register of title.[44] The statutory definition of a minor interest is sufficiently wide to cover other equities arising by virtue of this **11.080**

[39] Land Charges Act 1972, s.5(7).

[40] [1996] All ER 630, CA.

[41] *ibid.* at 641j–2a. This pragmatic approach obviates the need to address awkward questions as to the interrelationship of contract and estoppel as to which see para. 11.102–7 below. If the interest granted at trial is one which falls into the categories of those registerable under s.2 of the Land Charges Act 1972, or is a legal interest whose equitable analogue would be so classifiable, there are persuasive arguments to the effect that the 'equity' arising out of the estoppel is registerable under this section as soon as it arises (*viz* from the date of the acts in reliance). If the equity amounts to the final remedy in embryonic form, arguably it should be treated in the same way for registration purposes, on conceptual and analytical grounds, as well as on pragmatic ones. We consider, however, that this approach is not open on the authorities: it was rejected, by the Court of Appeal, in *E.R. Ives Investment v High* [1967] 2 QB 379. Although the case has attracted significant academic criticism, it received judicial approval from the House of Lords in *Shiloh Spinners v Harding* [1973] AC 691 at 721b-d and, more recently, from the Court of Appeal, in *Lloyds Bank v Carrick* [1996] All ER 630, CA.

[42] *Shiloh Spinners v Harding* [1973] AC 691; *ER Ives Investment v High* [1967] 2 QB 379 and *Duke of Beaufort v Patrick* (1853) 17 Beav 59, 51 ER 954. See specialist texts on the operation of the doctrine of notice.

[43] *Phillips v Phillips* (1861) 4 De G F and J 208 at 215–7, 45 ER 1164 at 1166–7. Thus, the protection given to mere equities is less extensive that given to full equitable interests which are vulnerable only to purchasers of a *legal* estate or interest: *Pilcher v Rawlins* (1872) LR Ch App 759; *MacMillan Inc v Bishopsgate Investment Trust* [1995] 1 WLR 1000 at 1014.

[44] Land Registration Act 1925, s.59(1) and Land Charges Act 1972, s.5(1), (3)(a) and 17(1).

doctrine.[45] Therefore, such rights are capable of being protected by caution[46] or, at the discretion of the Land Registrar, by notice.[47] Unless so protected, a minor interest will be void against a purchaser for valuable consideration,[48] unless the latter's conscience is affected according to the principles set out in *Ashburn Anstaldt v Arnold.*[49]

It is not clear whether a right generated by proprietary estoppel is capable of amounting to an overriding interest under Land Registration Act, section 70(1)(g). This section protects the 'rights' of those in actual occupation of property. The concept of 'a mere equity' embraces a range of rights from the purely personal one at issue in *National Provincial Bank v Ainsworth*[50] to the closely defined equity to rectify a document, under consideration in *Blacklocks v J.B. Developments (Godalming) Ltd.*[51] The two cases show that the former clearly is not sufficiently proprietary to qualify as an overriding interest, whereas the latter seemingly is. The question which has yet to be addressed directly in the case law is where estoppel equities fall on the spectrum from personal to proprietary[52]. Although the matter is not entirely free from doubt, proprietary estoppel equities probably have sufficient proprietary character to amount to overriding interests. As we set out above,[53] this was an essential presupposition made in two of the most important modern decisions on registered conveyancing, *Lloyds Bank v Rosset*[54] **11.081**

[45] Land Registration Act 1925, s.3(xv) Ruoff and Roper, para. 8.02. Contra. *dicta* in *Poster v Slough Estates* [1969] 1 Ch 495 at 505 , where Cross J., in concluding that an equitable easement acquired by estoppel could not be protected by caution, must have assumed that an estoppel *per se* is not so protectable — see Baughan *op. cit.* at 155.

[46] Land Registration Act 1925, s.54; Ruoff and Roper, para. 8.02.

[47] Land Registration Act 1925, s.49(1)(f); Ruoff and Roper, para. 35.33 suggest that Cross J. must simply have overlooked the existence of this section in making the comments which he did in *Poster above.*

[48] Land Registration Act 1925, s.3(xxi), 20(1), 23(1), 59(6).

[49] See para. 11.77 above and *Lyus v Prowser Developments* [1982] 1 WLR 1044. contra *Peffer v Rigg* [1977] 1 WLR 285.

[50] [1965] AC 1175.

[51] [1982] Ch 183.

[52] But note that rights generated by equitable forbearance (as to which see chapter 12) are not capable of amounting to overriding interests under s.70(1)(g): *Canadian Imperial Bank of Commerce v Bello* [1992] 64 P&CR 48 CA Dillon L.J. at 52. It was acknowledged in *Habermann v Koehler* (1996) 73 P&CR 515 CA *per* Peter Gibson L.JJ. at 520 that the status of proprietary estoppel rights was still an unanswered question. However, Evans L.J. referred, at 520, to the judgment of Millet L.J. in an interlocutory hearing where he indicated that estoppel rights would arguably fall within the scope of the section.

[53] At para. 11.73 above.

[54] [1991] AC 107.

and *Abbey National Building Society v Cann.*[55] They will therefore bind all purchasers where the claimant is in actual occupation of the property in accordance with the requirements of the section.

Post trial but prior to execution of the order of the court

If the remedy granted by the court is a purely personal one, such as an order for compensation, there is no prospect of its being enforceable against the transferee of the property under dispute. If, however, the court grants an equitable interest in the property under dispute, such interest takes full effect, at the very latest,[56] from the date of the order of the court. Thenceforth, the ordinary priorities principles applicable to the interest in question, apply.[57] Where the court orders that the claimant be granted a legal interest in land, legal title will not pass until the appropriate formality and registration requirements have been met. If title to the disputed land is unregistered, the claimant's interest should be protected, pending such execution, by registration '*as a writ or order affecting land*' under section 6(1) of the Land Charges Act. Failure to register will render the interest void against a purchaser for valuable consideration of any interest in the land in question.[58] If title to land is registered, the claimant has a minor interest which may be protected by entering a caution against dealing[59] or, at the discretion of the land Registrar, by notice[60] or inhibition.[61] Failure to register will render the interest void against a purchaser for value,[62] unless the holder is in actual occupation in which case, it will bind as an overriding interest under s.70(1)(g) of the Land Registration Act 1925. 11.082

Post execution of the court order

After due execution of a court order, by performance of any necessary formality requirements required to vest title in W, priority will be 11.083

---

[55] [1991] AC 56.
[56] And see above at para. 11.76 as to whether such an interest in fact arises at an earlier stage.
[57] As to which see specialist texts on real and personal property. *Quaere* the status of the licence, discussed further at para.11.83 below.
[58] Land Charges Act 1972, s.6(4) and 17.
[59] Land Registration Act 1925, s.54 and s.59(1).
[60] *ibid.* s.49(1)(g).
[61] *ibid.* s.57(1), if the court so orders.
[62] s.20(1) and 59(6).

determined by the ordinary principles applicable to the type of interest granted. An order for the payment of a money sum would therefore be enforceable only against the original party to the litigation, whereas a registered legal fee simple in possession would be enforceable against all. Once the latter right was vested in Mrs Turner, as a result of the court's decision in *Pascoe v Turner*,[63] her rights were as extensive as those of any legal title holder, the origin of her rights being immaterial. Thus, estoppel can be seen, not as a right in itself, but as a means of generating orthodox property interests or other rights.[64] This analysis was thrown into question by those cases that suggested that an estoppel licence is capable of binding third parties,[65] whereas it had long been generally accepted that licences did not confer any such right. The explanation for these cases probably lies in the confusion surrounding the status of the licence and the suggestion that it conferred a proprietary interest.[66] With the return to orthodoxy and the rejection of the latter proposition in *Ashburn Anstaldt v Arnold*,[67] it is to be hoped that principles governing licences created by estoppel will be the same as those for any other right generated by estoppel, namely those applicable to licences in general, with no enhanced or extended rights arising merely because the origin of the legal relationship. It would be preferable to apply the same principles to estoppel as to contractual

[63] [1979] 1 WLR 43, CA.

[64] Battersby, 'Contractual and Estoppel Licences as Proprietary Interests in Land' [1991] *Conv* 36.

[65] *Re Sharp* [1980] All ER 198 and *Williams v Staite* [1979] Ch 291, CA (although the third party point was not taken).

[66] *Errington v Errington* [1952] 1 QB 290, CA; *Binions v Evans* [1972] 1 Ch 359, CA *per* Lord Denning M.R.; *DHN Ltd v Tower Hamlets LBC* [1976] WLR 853 and *Re Sharp* [1980] All ER 198.

[67] *Ashburn Anstalt v Arnold* [1988] 2 WLR 706, CA — see particularly the judgment of Fox L.J. at 718–29. *Re Sharp* [1980] All ER 198 can be explained as being decided on the discredited *Errington* principle (see the disapproval of the case *per* Fox L.J. at 728b–e); although Browne-Wilkinson J. held that the licence arose under both contract and estoppel, he drew no distinction between the effect of two doctrines. Neither does *Williams v Staite* [1979] Ch 291, CA provide any clear authority for the unorthodox view, since the third party point was not taken in the case. More significant difficulties arise from Fox L.J.'s analysis (at 720f–h) of *Errington v Errington* [1952] 1 QB 290, CA. Although rejecting the reasoning used in the case (*viz* that contractual licences could bind third parties), he held that the result was correct and that defendant was bound partly because an estoppel had arisen. Under our analysis this should make no difference. This *dicta* may be reconcilable with our position, however, because in *Errington* the remedy included an orthodox equitable ownership interest in the property under dispute as well as a licence. The former right is capable of binding third parties and therefore the licence may have bound because of the association with it.

licences for two reasons. First, it makes no sense to enforce estoppel rights against a wider range of parties than contractual ones, given that the latter are more certain and arise in clearer and more closely defined circumstances than the former. Secondly, it is possible for a proprietary estoppel and a contract to arise out of the same set of facts (see paragraph 11.106 below). It would undermine the Court of Appeal's restriction on the enforceability of contractual licences in *Ashburn*, if the parties can fall back on estoppel to bind a third party where their contract did not. This is precisely what occurred in *Habermann v Koehler*.[68] The Court of Appeal acknowledged that the estoppel licence question had been left open by *Ashburn*. However, the court was unable to determine the relevant issues because of insufficient evidence. The case was remitted for re-trial. In an earlier interlocutory hearing, Millet L.J.[69] had suggested that the rights of the claimant might bind a third party, but to reach this conclusion, he construed the occupation rights as granting a life interest rather than a mere licence.

THE BENEFIT

Pre-trial

There is clear Commonwealth authority to the effect that the benefit of estoppel rights can be transferred.[70] There is a dearth of English authority on the point but there are isolated examples of such transfers. In *Plimmer v Wellington Corpn*,[71] an estoppel arose in 1856, in P's favour, as a result of works performed by P at the request of the government. P subsequently sold his interest to J who leased to the appellants in the case. In *Unity Joint Stock Mutual Banking Association v King (a bankrupt)*,[72] it was held that a lien for expenditure, acquired by estoppel, had been validly mortgaged prior to trial. The juridical nature of pre-adjudication estoppel rights[73] will determine whether they are transmissible. If a full equitable interest arises, there should **11.084**

[68] (1996) 73 P&CR 515 CA. See in particular the judgments of Evans L.J. at 520 and that of Peter Gibson L.J. at 522–3.

[69] (CA unrep.) referred to in *Habermann v Koehler* (1996) 73 P&CR 515 CA *per* Evans L.J. at 520.

[70] *Hamilton v Geraghty* (1901) 1 SRNSW Eq 81 at 86–91.

[71] (1884) 9 Ap Cas 699 PC (New Zealand).

[72] (1858) 25 Beav 72, 53 ER 563 at 79, 566.

[73] As to which see generally paras 11.74–8 above.

be no restrictions on transmissibility so long as orthodox formality requirements are complied with. If all that vests in W prior to trial is a right to take legal proceedings to request the court to exercise its discretion,[74] such a right cannot be readily transferred. The court's general discretion may be sufficiently flexible, however, to allow it to grant a remedy to a purported assignee, if merited in the particular circumstances of the case. If, as we suggest above, a mere equity arises, the position is less certain. Such an interest is probably sufficiently proprietary in nature as to be capable of transfer, at least where the eventual remedy granted at trial amounts to a transferable interest. This analysis might explain the suggestion in *Fryer v Brook*[75] that estoppel rights are personal and non-transferable, the right claimed there being a personal licence to occupy.[76]

Post trial

Where a claim of proprietary estoppel is successfully made out at trial, any rights granted are transmissible according to the ordinary principles of law governing the particular right. Thus, equitable and legal ownership interests can be freely sold, leased, mortgaged and so on, whereas personal rights to occupy or to demand payment of a sum of money are transferable (if at all) only in limited circumstances. Once the interest has vested, there is no reason to distinguish rights generated by estoppel from those originating from any other legal relationship.[77] **11.085**

[74] See paras 11.74–5 above.

[75] *The Times*, 4 August 1984. Limited weight should be given to the case since the relevant point was immaterial to the result and their Lordships were prepared to assume its correctness without full argument on it.

[76] The transmissibility of licences depends on their particular terms. There is no single rule applicable to all licences. Where the licence arises as a result of estoppel, those terms are set by the court (see, for example, the remedy personal and non-assignable licence awarded at first instance in *Sledmore v Dalby* (1996) P&CR 196, CA at 200). *Fryer* and *Plimmer* above are therefore reconcilable on the basis that the former concerned a non-assignable licence while the latter concerned an assignable one.

[77] See above at paras 11.59 and 11.83.

THE SCOPE OF PROPRIETARY ESTOPPEL

Proprietary estoppel is capable of giving rise to a cause of action.[78] It is not confined to a defensive role and may be used positively to claim property rights. It may be used against both equitable and legal rights.[79] Its effects may be permanent,[80] although they will not invariably be so. The courts' flexible discretion allows a selection from a wide range of outcomes, including both short-term arrangements and the permanent transfer of property rights.[81] **11.086**

THE CLAIMANT FORMED A BELIEF THAT SHE WOULD ACQUIRE RIGHTS OVER THE PROPERTY OF ANOTHER

One of the most controversial aspects of the proprietary estoppel doctrine concerns the subject matter of the belief or assumption formed by W. The doctrine has been described as a manifestation of a wider principle which enables the court to interfere where the assertion of strict legal *rights* is found to be unconscionable.[82] Put simply, the issue is what species of *rights* is M at risk of losing as a result of encouraging or acquiescing in W's expectation or mistake? As currently formulated, the proprietary estoppel doctrine will confiscate or limit only M's property rights.[83] W can only establish a proprietary estoppel if she believed she had, or expected to attain, rights over M's property.[84] **11.087**

[78] *Dillwyn v Llewellyn* (1862) De G F and J 517, 45 ER 1285; *Plimmer v Wellington Corpn* (1884) 9 Ap Cas 699, PC; *Crabb v Arun DC* [1976] Ch 179, CA at 187e; *Pascoe v Turner* [1979] 1 WLR 431, CA at 436f; *Wayling v Jones* (1993) P&CR 170, CA; *Smith v Halpin* [1997] 2 IRLM 38; *Durant v Heritage* [1994] EGCS 134 and *JT Developments v Quinn* (1991) 62 P&CR 33, CA at 45.

[79] *Shaw v Applegate* [1977] 1 WLR 970, CA.

[80] See, for example, *Ives v High* [1967] 2 QB 379 CA; *Crabb v Arun DC* [1976] Ch 179, CA at 187e; *Pascoe v Turner* [1979] 1 WLR 431, CA; *Wayling v Jones* (1993) P&CR 170, CA and *Durant v Heritage* [1994] EGCS 134.

[81] Paras 11.64–8.

[82] *Taylors Fashions Ltd v Liverpool Victoria Trustees Co. Ltd* [1982] 1 QB 133 at 147 and Finn 'Equitable Estoppel' Chap. 4 of *Essays in Equity* ed. Finn (1985) at p. 70.

[83] The flexibility of the remedies available means that this abrogation may take the form of an order for a money payment and is no longer confined to the transfer of property rights to the claimant. See generally paras 11.50–69.

[84] *Ramsden v Dyson* (1866) LR 1 HL 129; *Durant v Heritage* [1994] EGCS 134; *Layton v Martin* [1986] 2 FLR 227 at 238; *Re Sharp* [1980] All ER 198 at 210; *Smith v Halpin*

Hence, general promises to benefit W, such as to provide her with '*financial security*'[85] or '*a roof over her head*'[86] will not give rise to a proprietary estoppel claim unless explicitly or implicitly linked to M's property.[87] It is not sufficient to show that the belief or expectation *related* to M's property. The belief must concern ownership or use rights. Hence a landlord's promise to reduce the rent due on demised premises cannot give rise to proprietary estoppel whereas a promise to extend the lease may do so.[88] Further, a belief formed in relation to W's own property is insufficient.[89] We consider that this general limitation on the scope of proprietary estoppel still forms part of English law, despite *dicta* which might be taken to suggest the contrary. There is some scope for flexibility where the belief is formed in relation to property owned by a person heavily connected with M, such as a company of which he is the sole shareholder. The courts have been inclined to equate M with his company in such circumstances and allow a claim in proprietary estoppel to be made.[90]

Land and other types of property

A qualifying belief may relate not only to outright ownership of the freehold[91] but may encompass any one or more of the numerous ownership rights recognized by the English law of real property. Examples include trust interests,[92] leases,[93] profits *a prendre*,[94] rights of way[95] **11.088**

[1997] 2 IRLM 38; *Western Fish Products v Penwith DC* [1981] 2 All ER 204 CA; *West Middlesex Golf Club Limited v Ealing London Borough Council* (1993) 68 P&CR 461 at 478 and *JT Developments v Quinn* (1991) 62 P&CR 33, CA at 45.

85 *Layton v Martin* [1986] 2 FLR 227 at 238.

86 *Coombes v Smith* [1986] 1 WLR 808 *per* Jonathan Parker Q.C. at 818d–19c.

87 As to whether this link needs to be to a specific asset or to M's property generally, see para. 11.93–5 below.

88 Compare *Central London Property Trust Ltd v High Trees House Ltd* [1947] KB 130 and *Taylors Fashions Ltd v Liverpool Victoria Trustees Co. Ltd* [1982] 1 QB 133. See Treitel at p.129.

89 *Western Fish Products v Penwith DC* [1981] 2 All ER 204, CA and *Lloyds Bank v Carrick* [1996] All ER 630, CA.

90 *Philip Lowe (Chinese Restaurant) Ltd v Sau Man Lee* (CA unrep. 1989) lexis transcript; *Re Schuppan (a bankrupt) (No. 2)* [1997] 1 BCLC 256 at 268g-h and *cf. Windeler v Whitehall* [1990] 2 FLR 505 *per* Millet J. at 516c–e.

91 As in *Pascoe v Turner* [1979] 1 WLR 43 CA.

92 *Lloyds Bank v Rosset* [1991] 1 AC 107 and *Hammond v Mitchell* [1992] 4 All ER 109, [1991] 1 WLR 1127.

93 *Taylors Fashions Ltd v Liverpool Victoria Trustees Co. Ltd* [1982] 1 QB 133 and *JT Developments v Quinn* (1991) 62 P&CR 33, CA.

94 *Lovett v Fairclough* (1991) 61 P&CR 385 (fishing rights); no remedy was granted in

and restrictive covenants.[96] Moreover, the scope of the doctrine extends beyond orthodox ownership interests. It is sufficient to show that W expected to be granted a mere use right over M's property, such as a licence.[97]

11.089 Whether proprietary estoppel can operate in relation to property other than land is by no means clear.[98] The weight of authority now indicates, however, that it can do so. In his discussion of proprietary estoppel principles in *Moorgate Mercantile Co Ltd v Twitchings*,[99] Lord Denning referred both to chattels and to land without drawing any distinction between them. These comments were cited with approval by Lord Justice Megaw, in *Western Fish Products v Penwith DC*,[1] where his Lordship commented that the doctrine might extend to forms of property other than land. There is authority to suggest that the doctrine is applicable to insurance policies;[2] in *Re Vandervelle (No. 2)*[3] the doctrine was applied to shares held in trust, and in *Re Basham*,[4] to furniture and

the case because the claimant had 12 years use of the pool in dispute and therefore had suffered no detriment in contributing to its upkeep.

95 *Crabb v Arun DC* [1976] Ch 179, CA and *Ives v High* [1967] 2 QB 379, CA.

96 *Shaw v Applegate* [1977] 1 WLR 970, CA. In such cases, proprietary estoppel principles tend to blend almost seamlessly into parallel equitable doctrines of acquiescence and laches so that it may be difficult to ascertain the precise juristic basis of the decision.

97 *Baker v Baker* [1993] 25 HLR 408, CA.

98 *West Middlesex Golf Club Limited v Ealing London Borough Council* (1993) 68 P&CR 461 at 478 (applicable to land only).

99 [1976] 1 QB 225 at 242. The weight to be attributed to this authority is limited since the case concerned the highly controversial estoppel by negligence principle. The authorities relied on by Lord Denning to support his proposition also involved estoppel by negligence. It is doubtful whether this doctrine forms part of the law of estoppel at all. It is certainly distinct from the proprietary estoppel doctrine, differing from it in a number of ways. See paras 8.144–160 above.

1 [1981] 2 All ER 204, CA at 218h–j.

2 *Falcke v Scottish Imperial Insurance Co* (1886) 34 ChD 234 CA at 241, 252, 253, though the claimant there failed to establish such a claim. *Foster, Hudson v Foster (No. 2)* [1938] 3 All ER 610 appears to be an example of the application of the proprietary estoppel doctrine to an insurance policy though the judgment contains a puzzling inconsistency: F had paid a number of premiums on a life insurance policy, which he mistakenly thought would accrue to his benefit, whereas in fact it was his father who was so entitled; at 613e, Crossman J. affirmed the general principle that payment by mistake is insufficient to ground a claim unless the property owner knows of his own inconsistent title; curiously, F's estate was granted a lien for his expenditure, despite a finding that '*all parties . . . at all material times*' believed that F was entitled to the policy (614a-b).

3 [1974] 1 Ch 269 *per* Lord Denning M.R. at 321 and *per* Lawton L.J. at 325.

4 [1986] 1 WLR 1498.

other items of personal property. In *Godfrey v John Lees and others,*[5] it was applied to intellectual property rights in a number of musical works and in *Wayling v Jones,*[6] to a hotel business.

Present and future rights in property

As set out above (at paragraphs 11.12–15), it is not necessary for the claimant to show that she believed that she *already had* an interest in M's property, it is sufficient that she believed that she would acquire rights over it at some point in the future.[7] In such cases, the parties often fail to specify when the transfer of the expected interest or right in the property is to occur.[8] Alternatively, they may set a specific date for the transfer or make it conditional on the happening of some future event, commonly the death of the property owner.[9] Frequently, the triggering event occurs prior to adjudication.[10] The court may, however, intervene prior to this point[11] where the property owner indicates that he does not intend to comply with the assurance made. In such circumstances, the court will not accelerate W's entitlement by making an order for the immediate vesting of the anticipated interest. This would breach the principle that the remedy must not exceed the expectation of the parties.[12] Instead, the court may be prepared to grant a future right to W, restricting the owner's powers over the property, pending the occurrence of the triggering event. In *Burrows v Sharpe,*[13] for example, Mrs Sharp agreed with Mr and Mrs Burrows that they could move in with her and would receive her house on her death. The relationship **11.090**

---

[5] [1995] EMLR 307 and *Film Investors Overseas Services SA v The Home Video Channel (trading as the Adult Channel),* [1997] EMLR 347.

[6] (1993) P&CR 170, CA. See also *Windeler v Whitehall* [1990] 2 FLR 505 where a claim to a share in the business M worked in failed for a number of reasons none of which depended on the type of property in issue.

[7] *Crabb v Arun DC* [1976] Ch 179, CA; *Re Basham decd* [1986] 1 WLR 1498; *Durant v Heritage* [1994] EGCS 134 and *Wayling v Jones* (1993) P&CR 170, CA.

[8] In *Crabb v Arun DC* [1976] Ch 179, CA, Mr Crabb knew that further formalities would have to be executed before he would be vested with the right of way promised him by the Council's agents but neither party specified a date by which such execution was to take place.

[9] *Jones v Jones* [1977] 1 WLR 438 CA; *Re Basham decd* [1986] 1 WLR 1498; *Burrows v Sharpe* [1991] Fam Law 67, [1989] 23 HLR 82, CA; *Wayling v Jones* (1993) P&CR 170, CA and *Durant v Heritage* [1994] EGCS 134.

[10] *Jones v Jones* [1977] 1 WLR 438, CA; *Re Basham dec'd* [1986] 1 WLR 1498; *Wayling v Jones* (1993) P&CR 170, CA and *Durant v Heritage* [1994] EGCS 134.

[11] *Burrows v Sharpe* [1991] Fam Law 67, [1989] 23 HLR 82, CA.

[12] See para. 11.52 above.

[13] [1989] 23 HLR 82, CA.

broke down. Lord Justice Dillon held that one of the remedies available was an order that Mrs Sharp hold the property on trust for herself for life, remainder to Mr and Mrs Burrows.[14] It should be noted, however, that hardship to the defendant will be taken into account in assessing the appropriate relief.[15] The owner of the property might well suffer such hardship if his rights to dispose of, and deal with, it were subject to a long-term fetter. Contingencies unforeseen by the parties might make sale or remortgage of property a necessity. This will be particularly important in the type of situation in issue in *Burrows v Sharp*,[16] where an elderly person has promised to leave her home to her relatives in her will. The equity value in such homes is increasingly in demand to pay for the escalating medical and care expenses of the elderly.

No case has yet arisen where the owner has disposed of the property prior to the occurrence of the triggering event. If, as is suggested by a number of authorities, proprietary estoppel vests a full equitable property interest in the claimant as soon as detrimental reliance takes place,[17] a claim for breach of trust should lie against the owner in such circumstances. Further, the claimant would be able to take advantage of equitable tracing rules to claim the property back from third parties other than a bona fide purchaser for value without notice[18] or an innocent volunteer who has changed his position in reliance on receipt of payment.[19] As is set out above[20] however, this analysis of the nature of the claimant's rights prior to adjudication is flawed because it is impossible to reconcile with the remedial flexibility of the proprietary estoppel doctrine. Assuming that these tracing rights are unavailable to the claimant, it is suggested that a claim would in any event lie against M in such circumstances. In *Wayling v Jones*,[21] a claim for proprietary estoppel succeeded where the property in issue had been disposed of after **11.091**

14 *ibid.* at 91. In the event, his Lordship declined to make such an order because it would have been unworkable in the light of the breakdown in relations between the parties. See also *Philip Lowe (Chinese Restaurant) Ltd v Sau Man Lee* (CA unrep. 1989) lexis transcript, where May L.J., (*obiter*), doubted that a promise of entitlement on death could be consistent with an intent to make an immediate grant a future interest in property.

15 See para. 11.60 above.

16 [1991] Fam. Law 67, [1989] 23 HLR 82, CA.

17 See the authorities cited at nn. 6 and 7, para. 11.73.

18 *Re Diplock* [1948] Ch 465, CA at 539.

19 *Lipkin Gorman v Karpnale* [1991] 3 WLR 10, HL at 35.

20 At para. 11.76.

21 (1993) P&CR 170, CA.

the triggering event had occurred but prior to the court hearing. There seems to be no cogent reason for treating an earlier disposal any differently, although admittedly, the prior disposal point was not taken in *Wayling*.

After-acquired property

It seems that no proprietary estoppel will arise where the asset, which is the subject matter of W's belief, has yet to be purchased by M,[22] as there is no property on which the doctrine can bite. W may be able to establish another form of estoppel but this may be of limited practical use given the limitations of the other forms of the doctrine. Where the claimant formed a belief in relation to a specific item of property, a proprietary estoppel claim will arise as soon as the asset is acquired by M.[23] The estoppel is 'fed' by the acquisition. There is no authority on the status of after-acquired, non-specific property.[24] It is probably unnecessary for the actual asset to be specified in advance of the detrimental reliance, if assurance is of such a nature as to make the property readily ascertainable once acquired. For example, if M, prior to selection of any actual property, promises W '*a share in the house I plan to buy*,' the estoppel should be fed by acquisition of a house, in the same way as it would in the case of a promise of an interest in a pre-designated and specified property.[25] Hence, so long as the specific subject property is *eventually* identified, a proprietary estoppel claim is possible.[26] **11.092**

[22] *Abbey National BS v Cann* [1991] AC 56 at 89a-d; *Windeler v Whitehall* [1990] 2 FLR 505 at 516c–e and *Re Goldcorp Exchange Limited* [1994] 2 All ER 806, PC (New Zealand) at 818c–g.

[23] *Abbey National BS v Cann* [1991] AC 56 at 102a–c. There was no doubt that the estoppel was fed by M's acquisition of a property interest: W's failure to establish priority stemmed from that finding that M only ever acquired a *limited* interest in the property, *viz*, one that was subordinate to the security interest granted to the Abbey National, the mortgagee, who lent him the money to complete the transaction. On this and the general principle of 'feeding the estoppel', see para. 10.63–76 above.

[24] In *Abbey National BS v Cann* [1991] AC 56, the detrimental reliance consisted of moving out of a jointly owned property and allowing it to be sold and its proceeds to be used to purchase a new house. By the time these acts took place, the property to be purchased must have been selected. Similarly, in *Re Basham* [1986] 1 WLR 1498, discussed below, no property was purchased after cesser of the acts in reliance, since they continued up until the death of M.

[25] As to which, see above.

[26] See further para. 11.93–5 on the necessity for specific and identifiable property.

Specific property

There is conflicting authority as to whether a proprietary estoppel claimant must establish that she expected to gain an interest over specific items of property or whether it is sufficient that the belief was formed in relation to unspecified items of M's property. Mr Justice Scott held, in *Layton v Martin*,[27] that the former approach was the correct one. The case was not cited in *Re Basham*,[28] in which Nugee Q.C. held that the latter type of belief was sufficient. Mr Justice Scott's comments may have been *obiter dicta*. The proprietary estoppel claim would have failed, even applying Nugee Q.C.'s more flexible approach. M promised W that he would provide her with financial security after his death. The belief formed did not relate to M's property at all, whether specified or unspecified items of it. In contrast, in *Re Basham*, W succeeded in establishing a proprietary estoppel claim on the grounds that M had promised to leave her all his property in his will. She was awarded assets which remained unspecified and unascertained *until* the death of M, which took place after the relevant promise was made and the detrimental reliance had occurred. Nugee Q.C. justified his approach by analysing proprietary estoppel as giving rise to a constructive trust over the whole estate, which consisted of a floating obligation, descending on the specific assets owned on death.[29] The identification of proprietary estoppel with a constructive trust is highly controversial.[30] Scarcely less controversial, is the validity and nature of the so-called floating constructive trust. Of particular difficulty, is the status of M's property prior to death and the extent of the constraints on lifetime dispositions. Nugee Q.C.[31] held that M had been free to deal with his 11.093

[27] [1986] 2 FLR 227 at 238. In *Re Goldcorp* [1994] 2 All ER 806, PC (New Zealand) at 816d–f, the Privy Council clearly held that there was no possibility of establishing a proprietary estoppel in relation to goods which had yet to be ascertained or separated from the general fluctuating stock held by M; however, the case was one where W *expected* an interest only in specific assets. No express comment is made on the position where claimants believe that they are to obtain general rights over all of M's property, viz the situation under discussion here.

[28] *Re Basham decd* [1986] 1 WLR 1498 at 1510c. For criticism of the case see Hayton [1987] CLJ 215; Clarke, *Estoppel interests* [1987] All ER Review 156; Martin, *Estoppel and the Ubiquitous Constructive Trust* [1987] Conv 211 and Davey, *Testamentary Promises* (1988) LS 92.

[29] Applying the mutual wills cases *Re Cleaver decd* [1981] 1 WLR 939 at 946a–7d and *Birmingham v Renfrew* (1937) 57 CLR 666.

[30] See *Stokes v Anderson* [1991] FLR 391.

[31] *Re Basham dec'd* [1986] 1 WLR 1498 at 1505 adopting the approach of Nourse J. in *Re Cleaver* [1981] 1 WLR 939 at 947.

property as he wished (hence, the *floating* nature of the trust), save that he could not make dispositions calculated to defeat the intentions of the parties. These questions were not directly in issue, since the dispute arose only after M's death. Arguably, such a trust would have overcompensated W,[32] since there was no indication that M had made any promises fettering his right to dispose of his property during his lifetime.

The two cases are reconcilable once it is recognized that it is unnecessary for the assets to be specified in advance of the detrimental reliance. It is possible for the belief to relate to property *to be selected* by some triggering event in the future, the obvious example being M's promise to transfer those assets owned at death. Once the triggering event occurs, the assets are ascertained and a proprietary estoppel claim arises. Hence, the result of *Re Basham* may be justified on the basis that, by the date of the hearing, the assets *had been specified*, namely they consisted of the entirety of M's estate on death. The estoppel had been 'fed' by selection of ascertained assets. Arguably, the decision is an authority only for the proposition that a proprietary estoppel may arise in relation to the whole of an estate. In so far as we presume to disagree with the approach of the learned judge, it is with his dicta to the effect that a proprietary estoppel or constructive trust arose *during M's lifetime* and prior to the ascertainment of the relevant property. **11.094**

The better view therefore is that a proprietary estoppel may arise only in relation to specific assets, although the identification may take place after[33] the belief is formed and the detrimental reliance has taken place. Such an approach would obviate the need to resort to the controversial and uncertain concept of the floating constructive trust and would avoid the danger of overcompensation referred to. Further, it would keep the proprietary estoppel doctrine under acceptable constraints.[34] **11.095**

[32] On the principle that the remedy for proprietary estoppel must never exceed the expectation generated — see further para. 11.52.

[33] As in *Re Basham dec'd* [1986] 1 WLR 1498.

[34] See Chitty at para. 3.113 on the merits of such a limitation.

FUTURE DEVELOPMENTS

Can Estoppel Operate on Promises to Confer Benefits Which Are Unrelated to Property?

If W acts to her detriment in reliance on M's promise to give her an interest in his property, estoppel may operate to give her a cause of action against him.[35] If, however, she acts to her detriment in reliance on a promise by M that he will enter a contract to pay her £100, estoppel will not apply.[36] M's conduct would seem to be equally unconscionable in both cases. The anomaly is illustrated by cases concerning negotiations for purchase of property. If a vendor fosters a belief that transfer will take place, a proprietary estoppel claim may lie, if the potential purchaser can demonstrate detrimental reliance.[37] If, instead, it is the purchaser who leads the vendor to assume that the transfer will go ahead, the vendor cannot invoke proprietary estoppel because all that is expected is a contract and money payment rather than a property interest.[38] Hence, had the events leading up to the Australian decision of *Walton Stores v Maher*[39] occurred in the English jurisdiction, the plaintiffs would have been unsuccessful: the owners of the property had commenced building works on it in the expectation that the defendant company would enter the lease which was anticipated by both parties. Had the works been performed by the potential tenant and not the potential landlord, there seems little doubt that English law would have recognized the existence of a proprietary estoppel claim. **11.096**

The issue here is the same as that which has been frequently debated in relation to equitable forbearance, namely whether estoppel can and should operate where one party has promised a benefit to another and **11.097**

---

[35] *Crabb v Arun DC* [1976] Ch 179 and the cases cited at 11.86 above.

[36] *Combe v Combe* [1951] 2 KB 215 and the cases cited at para. 11.87 n. 84 above and 12.62 n. 47 below.

[37] *AG for Hong Kong v Humphreys Estate (Queen's Gardens) Ltd* [1987] 1 AC 114, PC (Hong Kong).

[38] In the comparatively rare case where a land swap is contemplated, such as in *Lim v Ang* [1992] 1 WLR 113, PC (Brunei), both vendor and purchaser may come to expect rights over one another's land and thus proprietary estoppel may be available to both.

[39] [1988] 164 CLR 387, HC of Australia.

the latter relies on the promise to its detriment. If the property qualification is abandoned, the fostering of *any* assumption or belief will be sufficient to trigger proprietary estoppel. Thus, the doctrine could operate to give legal effect to apply to *any* promise which has been relied on to the detriment of the promisor. It would cover the second example posited above as well as the first. This is one route by which English law might move to an assimilation of all types of estoppel since the scope of the expanded proprietary estoppel would subsume virtually all other species of the doctrine. There is some support for the existence of such general equitable estoppel. In *Taylors Fashions Ltd v Liverpool Victoria Trustees Co. Ltd*[40] Oliver J. held:

> Furthermore the more recent cases indicate, in my judgment, that the application of the Ramsden v Dyson, L.R. 1 H.L. 129 principle — whether you call it proprietary estoppel, estoppel by acquiescence or estoppel by encouragement is really immaterial — requires a very much broader approach which is directed rather at ascertaining whether, in particular individual circumstances, it would be unconscionable for a party to be permitted to deny that which, knowingly, or unknowingly, he has allowed or encouraged another to assume to his detriment than to inquiring whether the circumstances can be fitted within the confines of some preconceived formula serving as a universal yardstick for every form of unconscionable behaviour.[41]

This dictum has been cited[42] and applied[43] in a number of contexts where no property was in issue. For example, in *Pacol Ltd v Trade Lines Ltd ('the Henrik Sif')*,[44] Mr Justice Webster applied it to prevent the defendants from denying that they were the proper party to be sued on a bill of lading. This was arguably *dicta* since the prime reason for the decision was estoppel by convention. Further, his Lordship recanted his avowal of 'general equitable estoppel' in a later case.[45] In *Amalgamated* **11.098**

[40] [1982] 1 QB 133.

[41] [1982] 1 QB 133 at 151. See also *Amalgamated Investment & Property Co. Ltd, (in liquidation) v Texas Commerce International Bank Ltd.* [1982] 1 QB 84 *per* Lord Denning M.R. at 122a–d and *Crabb v Arun DC* [1976] Ch 179 *per* Lord Scarman at 193b.

[42] *Kelly v Liverpool Maritime Terminals* [1988] IRLR 310 CA appeal from EAT (notice to extend maternity leave under employment contract). No estoppel was established.

[43] *'The August Leonhardt'* [1984] 1 Lloyd's Rep. 322 *per* Bingham J.; in overturning this decision at [1985] 2 Lloyd's Rep. 28 CA, the Court of Appeal found that no form of estoppel was made out, declining to comment on the validity of 'general equitable estoppel'.

[44] [1982] 1 Lloyd's Rep. 456.

[45] *Shearson Lehman Hutton Inc v Maclaine Watson and Co Ltd* [1989] 2 Lloyd's Rep. 570 at 598.

Investment & Property Co. Ltd., (in liquidation) v Texas Commerce International Bank Ltd.[46] Mr Justice Robert Goff and Lord Denning, applied the *Taylors* principle to a contract of guarantee. Again the case is no more than a straightforward instance of estoppel by convention, as the majority in the Court of Appeal expressly so held. Although Mr Justice Oliver's *dictum* makes no express reference to a property requirement, it must be set against the remainder of the judgment, where he referred to many estoppel principles in orthodox terms;[47] he assessed those authorities which he considered fell within the *Ramsden* principle, all of which involved property. Further, the doctrines which are directly referred to in the *dictum*, all fall within the scope of orthodox proprietary estoppel principles.

Even assuming that it was his Lordship's intention to abandon the property qualification, neither the *dictum* itself, nor the subsequent authorities in which it has been applied, can overturn long established principles of estoppel and contract. The explanation for the restriction is not purely historical.[48] The expectation category of proprietary estoppel[49] frequently though not invariably[50] involves the enforcement of promises which are not supported by consideration. The property limitation is merely one of a number of ways in which the courts have sought to prevent estoppel (in all its various forms) from undermining the principle that English law will not enforce gratuitous promises. The abrogation of this limitation would bring into stark relief the conflict between proprietary estoppel and the doctrine of consideration. Further, it would also conflict with the numerous rules whereby the operation of the various species of estoppel has been carefully circumscribed. In particular, it would breach the principle laid down by the House of Lords in *Jorden v Money*[51] that estoppel by representation can operate only **11.099**

46 [1982] 1 QB 84.

47 For example, by affirming that promissory estoppel can only be used as a defence at 152b–c.

48 Although this is certainly a partial explanation, since the doctrine was developed largely, though not exclusively (see, for example, *Winter v Brockwell* (1807) 8 East 308, (103) ER 359 KB and *Liggins v Inge* (1831) 7 Bing 682, (131) ER 263 CP) in the property oriented court of Chancery.

49 See paras 11.12–5 above.

50 Increasing recognition that the remedy awarded should reflect the *'minimum equity'* to do justice means that the enforcement of the promise is by no means the automatic outcome of a successful claim, it is one which remains available to the court and is still granted in a relatively high proportion of cases: for a recent example see *Durant v Heritage* [1994] EGCS 134. See further paras 11.50–4 above.

51 (1854) 5 HLC 185, 10 ER 868.

on a representation of fact and the principle that equitable forbearance cannot be used to create new rights.[52]

A substantive distinction may be drawn between the two examples posited, which becomes apparent only when the meaning of property is borne in mind. To identify a party as the owner of property is simply a shorthand for asserting that he or she is the holder of a collection of enforceable rights relating to the asset in issue. In the first example, proprietary estoppel may operate to *reduce* those pre-existing rights; in the second, if it operated at all, it would have to impose a *new* and positive obligation on M to pay W the £100. Arguably, the greater safeguards provided by the law of consideration are required in the second but not the first example. Further, it should be recalled that property owners enjoy the privilege of the state's enforcement mechanisms. It may be justifiable to expect those privileges to be exercised responsibly and in a manner which does not lead others to act to their detriment. Proprietary estoppel, like virtually all the other doctrines considered in this work, concerns the *subtraction* of rights from the representor or promisor. Its role is to prevent unconscionable *assertion* of pre-existing rights not the unconscionable failure to confer promised benefits.[53] **11.100**

Arguably, however, to impose a property requirement, is to beg the question. It now seems reasonably clear that any type of property may form the subject matter of a proprietary estoppel claim.[54] The concept of property has proved to be notoriously elastic: it may prove to be a fragile barrier with which to divide proprietary estoppel from the remainder of the English law of promises, particularly given that the benefit of a contract is capable of amounting to a choice in action which is itself a species of property.[55] **11.101**

---

[52] See *Combe v Combe* [1951] 2 KB 215, CA and the discussion below at paras 11.116–7 and 12.61–7. Note, in particular, *Dun & Bradstreet Software Services (England) Ltd v Provident Mutual Life Assurance Association* [1997] EGCS 89 CA, lexis transcript, where Peter Gibson L.J. held that dicta in the '*different context of a proprietary estoppel case*' (*Taylors Fashions Ltd v Liverpool Victoria Trustees Co Ltd* [1982] 1 QB 133) could not have been intended to undermine the established requirements of promissory estoppel (our emphasis).

[53] Finn, Chap. 4.

[54] See above at para. 11.89.

[55] *Fletcher v Fletcher* (1844) 4 Hare 67, 67 E.R. 564 and *Re Cavendish Brown's Settlement* [1916] WN 341.

COMPARISON WITH OTHER DOCTRINES

CONTRACT

Proprietary estoppel cases which involve a unilateral mistake on the part of the claimant followed by acquiescence or encouragement by the property owner,[56] are distinct from contract in that they do not involve the making of a promise as to future entitlement but only an error as to present entitlement. As is set out in paragraphs 11.12 to 11.15 above, however, many and arguably, all those cases in which the relevant assurance concerns an expectation of a rights in property involve a promise by the owner that he will grant those rights to the claimant, on which the latter has relied to her detriment. English law has traditionally regulated promissory liability using the law of contract but it is impossible to assimilate the expectation cases into the latter discipline. There are significant differences between the operation of proprietary estoppel and that of contract. **11.102**

The core distinction between contract and proprietary estoppel lies in the former's requirement of a mutual bargain. Detriment to one party is capable of amounting to consideration, regardless of whether benefit is thereby conferred on the other. Such detriment will not, however, amount to consideration unless it is bargained for by the parties, *viz* W must *promise* to act to her detriment as the quid pro quo or price of the benefit to be conferred by M: **11.103**

> Reliance is, according to [the classical model], only justifiable if it has been paid for or bargained for. A person who relies on another, where such reliance is not actually part of a bargain, is still, according to this theory, acting at his own risk. In the shadow of 19th century individualism, lawyers still pay lip service (and sometimes more) to the fundamental belief that a man should rely on himself and not on others.[57]

---

[56] See paras 11.08–11 above.

[57] Atiyah, 1 at p. 771. According to Atiyah, this model of consideration has never received unqualified acceptance in the English courts (although it has, he concedes, in English universities); he contrasts this position with that of the US, where it emerged as the governing orthodoxy, after the celebrated 1930s dispute between Corbin and Williston on the respective merits of the reliance/bargain based models; the dispute was compromised with an amendment to section 90 of the Restatement to allow reliance based claims to take effect in promissory estoppel. The emergence of a US promissory estoppel doctrine of a more wide ranging and muscular nature than its English counterpart was, according to Atiyah, the direct result of the inflexibility of the American approach to consideration: Atiyah 1 at p. 776.

Thus, Mr Crabb's sale of his land in reliance on Arun DC's promise of an easement did not give rise to a contract: he did not, at any stage, promise or undertake any obligation to the Council to sell the land; it formed no part of the arrangement made between the parties; indeed, the Council were entirely indifferent to whether he did so or not (a fact which would eventually prove to be their downfall). It was only by extending the scope of consideration beyond its conventional, and generally accepted, limits that Atiyah was able to characterize Crabb's case as contractual.[58]

The bargain requirement is not, however, the only point of divergence between the operation of contract and proprietary estoppel. Were the doctrine of consideration to be abolished or altered, for example by extension to cover those acts of detrimental reliance which were the reasonably foreseeable consequence of the promise, proprietary estoppel would continue to operate in a number of cases where no contract exists. First, a promise which is insufficiently certain to give rise to a valid and enforceable contract may give rise to a proprietary estoppel.[59] Secondly, a promise or understanding which is reached without intent to create legal relations may give rise to a proprietary estoppel but not a contract.[60] Thirdly, a promise relating to land, or interest therein, which is not made in writing may give rise to a proprietary estoppel but not a contract.[61] Further, the consequences of contract and proprietary estoppel and contract differ. The remedy in contract cases is enforcement of the promise or full expectation damages.[62] In contrast, the remedy for proprietary estoppel will only extend to the minimum equity to do justice. This measure is arguably confined to the reversal of detriment, extending only to enforcement of the promise where this is the only practical way to attain this end.[63] **11.104**

58 Atiyah 'When is an Enforceable Agreement not a Contract? Answer: When it is an Equity' (1974) 92 *LQR* 174; criticized by Millet in 'Crabb v Arun District Council: a Riposte' [1976] 92 *LQR* 342.

59 *Holiday Inns Inc v Broadhead* (1974) 232 EG 951 at 1087 and *Lim v Ang* [1992] 1 WLR 113, PC (Brunei) where the assumption relied on was contained in the recital of a contract void for uncertainty.

60 *Dodsworth v Dodsworth* (1973) 228 EG 1115 CA; *Voyce v Voyce* (1991) 62 P&CR 290, CA at 296; *Layton v Martin* [1986] 2 FLR 227 (where Scott J. considered the lack of such an intent in relation to the contract claim but not in relation to claim proprietary estoppel). See further para. 11.07 above.

61 Law of Property (Miscellaneous Provisions) Act 1989, s. 2 (or if made before 28 September 1989 but not '*evidenced in writing*': Law of Property Act 1925, s.40).

62 See *Combe v Combe* [1951] 2 KB 215 and specialist texts.

63 See para. 11.52.

A number of the older authorities use contractual terminology[64] to describe estoppel principles, probably because the relevant terms had yet then to acquire the settled and technical connotation to which lawyers now attribute them. However, some of the earlier authorities which are commonly viewed as involving estoppel might be more accurately categorized as contractual.[65] A degree of confusion arises because of the formality requirements for contracts for the sale of land.[66] The court's concentration on the claimant's acts in reliance is explicable on the basis, not of establishing an estoppel, but instead, of providing a justification for dispensing with contract formality requirements. These cases concern the enforcement of bargains where an otherwise binding contract is rendered potentially unenforceable for want of evidence in writing, with the claimant's reliance amounting to an act of part performance. The doctrines of estoppel and part performance were mutually influential, particularly in the earlier stages of their development.[67] The abolition of the latter doctrine in England and Wales[68] has ended this process of cross fertilization but establishing a coherent relationship between the two doctrines remains a task faced in those jurisdictions which retain them both.[69] **11.105**

There is authority to suggest that the same set of facts may give rise **11.106**

[64] A notorious example is provided by Lord Westbury L.C. in *Dillwyn v Llewellyn*: '. . . *if A puts B in possession of a piece of land, and tells him 'I give it to you that you may build a house on it' and B on the strength of that promise, with the knowledge of A, expends a large sum of money in building a house, accordingly, I cannot doubt that the donee acquires a right from the subsequent transaction to call for on the donor to perform that contract and complete the imperfect donation which was made.'* His Lordship later refers to the donee's acts in reliance (building a house on land promised him by the donor) as providing '. . . *the valuable consideration originally wanting*'. The Lord Chancellor is probably using the term consideration in the sense of providing a reason for equity's intervention according to Baughan 'Estoppels Over Land and Third Parties' (1994) 14 *LS* 147.

[65] In *Mcmanus v Cooke* (1887) 35 Chd 631 at 693–7, Kay J. so categorized a considerable number of the early authorities in including *East India Company v Vincent* (1740) 2 Atk 83, 26 ER 451; *Ramsden v Dyson* (1866) LR 1 HL 129, HL and *Plimmer v Wellington Corpn* (1884) 9 Ap Cas 699, PC (New Zealand).

[66] Contracts made before 28 September 1989 must have been *'evidenced in writing'*: Law of Property Act 1925, s.40. Contracts made on or after 28 September 1989 must be *'in writing'*: Law of Property (Miscellaneous Provisions) Act 1989, s.2.

[67] See Matthews, 'Swords and Shields' (1982) *LSG* 662 and Baker 'From Sanctity of Contract to Reasonable Expectation?' (1979) *CLP* 17.

[68] Law of Property (Miscellaneous Provisions) Act 1989, s.2; *United Bank Kuwait v Sahib* [1996] All ER 215, CA.

[69] For example, Australia: see the comments of Nicholson in 'Riches v Hogben: Part Performance and the Doctrines of Equitable and Proprietary Estoppel' (1986) 60 *ALJR* 345.

both to proprietary estoppel and contract.[70] Prior to performance by the promisee, where the contract remains wholly executory, no estoppel analysis is possible because of the absence of reliance. On a trite level, all executed and partially executed contracts are susceptible to being analysed as involving representation and reliance: the promisor represents that she intends to comply with her promise and the promisee relies on the representation, to her detriment, by performing her part of the bargain. Arguably, the mere fact that the relevant acts were specified as the *quid pro quo* of the promise need not prevent their amounting to detrimental reliance for the purposes of proprietary estoppel.[71] To superimpose a proprietary estoppel in every case where the contract contemplated concerns the acquisition of property would obviously undermine, fundamentally, established contract principles, in particular those relating to certainty, legal intent and formality. If the contract claim failed for want of one or more of these three requirements, a claimant might be able to fall back on proprietary estoppel, with the ironic consequence that the more informal and vague arrangement may be upheld where the contractual bargain would have failed. This consequence is averted if it is recognized that detrimental reliance *additional* to mere compliance with the original contract, is required to give rise to an estoppel relationship.[72]

Undeniable difficulties arise in distinguishing proprietary estoppel from contract cases. Proof of extensive acts in reliance may cause the court to conclude that those acts were, in fact, specified as part of the original **11.107**

[70] *Re Sharp* [1980] All ER 198 at 211a–d (the criticism of the case in *Ashburn Anstalt v Arnold* [1988] 2 WLR 706, CA at 728b–f was confined to the constructive trust point); *Errington v Errington* [1952] 1 QB 290, CA (the Court of Appeal in *Ashburn Anstalt* at 720f–h characterized the case as giving rise to both a contract and an estoppel); *Tanner v Tanner* [1975] 1 WLR 1346, CA *per* Lord Denning M.R. at 1350; Moriarty, 'Licences and Land Law: Legal Principles and Public Policies' (1984) 100 *LQR* 376 at 393. See also Battersby 'Contractual and Estoppel Licences as Proprietary Interests in Land' [1991] *Conv* 36 at 45 and Thompson 'Licences: Questioning the Basics' [1983] *Conv* 50; contra. Briggs 'Licences: Back to Basics' [1981] *Conv* 212.

[71] *Habermann v Koehler* (1996) 73 P&CR 515 CA. It should be noted that this analysis is confined to situations where there is no independent, pre-existing duty to perform the acts in issue. If there is (as is commonly the case where promissory estoppel/ equitable forbearance is in issue, as to which see generally paras 12.42–6 below) performance of it probably cannot amount to detriment.

[72] *Ives v High* [1967] 2 QB 379, CA where two neighbours, Westgate and High, entered an enforceable contract to create an easement. Westgate sold to Wright who sold to Ives. The contract was void against Ives for want of registration. Despite this, their Lordships had no hesitation in concluding that the conduct of Westgate and Wright, in standing by while High relied on the contract in building a house and garage accessible only across his neighbour's land, gave rise to an estoppel.

bargain between the parties.[73] The borderline between contractual terms inferred from the conduct of the parties and a fictional imputed agreement is not always an easy one to draw with any clarity.[74] The difficulty has been particularly apparent in respect of licences to occupy residential premises. A number of cases have arisen involving strikingly similar facts: W moves into M's property, having been promised an indefinite right to occupy; she thereby, or subsequently, acts to her detriment in reliance on M's promise. Often such arrangements are made where one of the parties is an elderly family member, wishing to give up living alone. Many such arrangements are made without the benefit of legal advice and without thought to the repercussions of a breakdown of the parties' relationship. Establishing whether the acts of detriment formed part of the original bargain, has proved an awkward forensic exercise;[75] the resulting classification of the licence as based in estoppel or contract (or both) has often appeared to be fairly arbitrary.[76] The law's inability to deal, in a consistent or intelligible way, with such a simple and common social arrangement is to be regretted. Those contemplating such arrangements, in particular where care of an elderly relative is concerned, would be well advised to take legal advice.

---

[73] In *Canadian Pacific Railway v R* [1931] AC 414 at 428–9, Lord Russell characterizes both *Ramsden v Dyson* (1866) LR 1 HL 129 and *Plimmer v Wellington Corpn* (1884) 9 Ap Cas 699, PC (New Zealand) as cases of implied agreement. See also his comments on *Ramsden* in *Ariff v Jadunath Majurndar* (1931) LR 58 Ind App 91 at 102.

[74] Obvious and uncomfortable parallels are provided both by the quasi contract/restitution dichotomy and the mire of confusion surrounding the common intention constructive trust of the family home.

[75] Superficially it might appear that M, in conferring a benefit on W, would be indifferent as to whether it was taken up or not, thus making it unlikely that the act of moving in (or the advantages foregone in so doing) would be likely to have been specified as part of the parties' original bargain. Where, however, M is elderly and encourages a relative to move in, there is a more obvious element of mutual benefit, even where specific caring duties are not stipulated.

[76] *Williams v Staite* [1979] Ch 291, CA (estoppel); *Chandler v Kerley* [1978] 1 WLR 693, CA (contract); *Griffiths v Williams* (1977) 248 EG 947, CA (estoppel); *Tanner v Tanner* [1975] 1 WLR 1346, CA (Browne and Brightman L.JJ. based their decision on contract and Lord Denning M.R., at 1350, on both contract and estoppel) and *Ungurian v Lessnoff* [1990] Ch 206 (estoppel and constructive trust). See generally Moriarty, 'Licences and Land Law: Legal Principles and Public Policies' (1984) 100 *LQR* 376 at 388–98 and Dewar 'Licences and Land Law' (1986) 49 *MLR* 741 (suggesting that a contractual analysis of *Tanner* above was preferred by the majority because Mrs Tanner's re-housing by the local authority would have made a claim less pressing, under the general equitable principles of estoppel).

Pre-contract negotiations

English law imposes no general duty to act in good faith in pre-contract negotiations. The proprietary estoppel doctrine is one of a number of methods by which it is sought to control the *prima facie* right of a party to withdraw from negotiations, at any time prior to entering a binding contract.[77] It is a pre-condition of its application that the contract envisaged would have granted W a right in M's property.[78] Further, it is crucial to show that the property owner indicated, whether explicitly or implicitly, that he considered himself bound to transfer the interest or right expected and that therefore it was safe and risk free to act in reliance on the assumption.[79] He must have expressly or impliedly surrendered his right to withdraw.[80] No proprietary estoppel will arise where the claimant considered the possibility that the interest would not be granted but decided to take a risk[81] and go ahead with the acts in question, *in the hope* that the interest would be granted.[82] **11.108**

It seems that a fairly heavy onus lies on the claimant to establish clearly that such an undertaking has been made; in particular, in a commercial context, the parties might reasonably be expected to require the final agreement of terms and execution of documentation before intending to affect their respective legal positions.[83] It is difficult to establish that the right to withdraw has been surrendered if significant terms have yet to be agreed.[84] If W deliberately refrained from settling a term because **11.109**

---

77 Alternatively, a restitutionary claim may be made for work done in pursuance of an expected contract which never materializes may, where such work enriches the other party: See, for example *British Steel Corporation v Cleveland Bridge Engineering* [1984] 1 All ER 504 and McKendrick 'Negotiations Subject to Contract' [1994] *RLR* 100. Carter notes, in 'Contract, Restitution and Promissory Estoppel' (1989) 12 *UNSWLJ* 30, that whereas the law of restitution throws all the the loss on to one party, a more equitable result may be achieved using estoppel principles. The latter doctrine is sufficiently flexible to enable the loss to be divided between the parties.

78 *Haslemere Estates Ltd v Baker* [1982] 1 WLR 119 at 119g: no proprietary estoppel could be established where anticipated contract involved grant of leases to unascertained third parties rather than the claimant.

79 *Holiday Inns Inc v Broadhead* (1974) 232 EG 951.

80 *Waltons Stores (Interstate) Ltd v Maher* [1988] 164 CLR 387 and *cf. Amalgamated Investment & Property Co. Ltd, (in liquidation) v Texas Commerce International Bank Ltd* [1982] 1 QB 84 *per* Goff J. at 107.

81 *Boxbusher Properties v Graham* (1976) 240 EG 463 at 465 where the claimant took *'a business risk'* knowing that the landlord might enforce his rights at any time.

82 *AG for Hong Kong v Humphreys Estate (Queen's Gardens) Ltd* [1987] 1 AC 114, PC.

83 *JT Developments v Quinn* (1991) 62 P&CR 33, CA at 51.

84 Parkinson 'Equitable Estoppel: Developments after Walton Stores (Interstate) Ltd v Maher' (1990) 3 *JCL* 50, arguing that a distinction should be drawn between the

she wished to postpone becoming legally bound herself, no proprietary estoppel claim will be established.[85] Such surrenders have occurred where an agreement in principle had been reached but where certain 'further processes', including the price, had yet to be agreed,[86] where 'a gentleman's agreement'[87] had been reached and where M indicated that there would be no difficulty in reaching a final agreement.[88] Somewhat surprisingly, in *JT Developments v Quinn*,[89] the making of an offer of a new lease was held to be sufficient. The offer specified the exact terms available and went beyond a mere willingness to negotiate and became a promise that until the defendant was told otherwise, he could rely on being granted such a lease.

'Subject to contract'

Expressly qualifying communications as '*subject to contract*' is likely to protect M because it will generally be taken as a clear indication that M has yet to decide whether or not to grant the interest sought and as reserving the right to withdraw. This provides the explanation for the failure of the government's claim in *AG for Hong Kong v Humphreys Estate (Queen's Gardens) Ltd.*[90] The Privy Council acknowledged, however, that the use of the term '*subject to contract*' would not invariably protect M from an estoppel claim: **11.110**

> The government acted in the hope that a voluntary agreement in principle, expressly made subject to contract would eventually be followed by the achievement of legal relationships in the form of grants and transfers of property. It is possible but unlikely that in circumstances at present unforeseeable, a party to negotiations set out in a document expressed to be subject to contract would be able to satisfy the court that the parties

pre-contract situation and cases such as *Plimmer v Wellington Corpn* (1884) 9 App Cas 699, PC. But see *Crabb v Arun DC* [1976] Ch 179, CA where the contract price had yet to be settled.

85 *Austotal Pty Ltd v Franklin Selfserve Pty Ltd* (1989) 16 NSWLR 582. See Lindgren 'Estoppel in Contract' (1989) 12 *UNSWLJ* 153.

86 *Crabb v Arun DC* [1976] Ch 179, CA at 185g.

87 *Holiday Inns Inc v Broadhead* (1974) 232 EG 951 at 1087.

88 *Central Street Properties Ltd v Mansbrook Rudd and Co Ltd* (1986) 276 EG 414.

89 (1991) 62 P&CR 33, CA.

90 *AG for Hong Kong v Humphreys Estate (Queen's Gardens) Ltd* [1987] 1 AC 114, PC (Hong Kong) and *Canadian Pacific Railway v R* [1931] AC 414 at 429. In *Veitch v Caldecott* (1945) 173 LT 30, Atkinson J. seems to aver, at 33, that the fact that the promise was contractually unenforceable, for want of consideration, was sufficient to negative the possibility of a proprietary estoppel. We consider this position to be untenable in light of the modern formulation of the doctrine.

> had subsequently agreed to convert the document into a contract or that some form of estoppel had arisen to prevent both parties from refusing to proceed. But in the present case the government chose to begin and elected to continue on terms that either party might suffer an change of mind and withdraw.[91]

That the works had been carried out in the hope that the right would be granted was insufficient to raise a proprietary estoppel.[92] In conclusion, although, it is possible for a proprietary estoppel claim to arise out of '*subject to contract*' negotiations, the courts have expressed a marked reluctance to look behind the label[93] and a very clear evidence of that would presumably be required to counter balance the *prima facie* inference to be drawn from it.[94]

EQUITABLE FORBEARANCE

For the reasons set out at para. 12.06 we have used the term equitable forbearance to describe the doctrine frequently referred to as promissory estoppel. Briefly, this doctrine operates where a party to a contract or other legal relationship ('the promisor') makes, to another party ('the promisee'), a clear and unequivocal representation, which is intended to affect the legal relations between them, that the promisor's legal rights under the contract or relationship will not be enforced or will be suspended. If the promisee, to the knowledge of the promisor, alters its position to its detriment in reliance on the representation, the equitable forbearance doctrine may operate to abrogate or extinguish the promisor's right to withdraw the concession.[95] In *Crabb v Arun DC*,[96] Lord Justice Scarman held: **11.111**

[91] *AG for Hong Kong v Humphreys Estate (Queen's Gardens) Ltd* [1987] 1 AC 114, PC (Hong Kong) at 127g–8b.

[92] See also *Boxbusher Properties v Graham* (1976) 240 EG 463.

[93] *Saloman v Akiens* [1993] 1 EGLR 101 CA at 103; *Mecca Leisure v London Residuary Body* [1988] CLYB 1375 and Sutton, *Contract by Estoppel* (1989) 1 JCL 205.

[94] The nearest example to such a case is *Salvation Army Trustee Co Ltd v West Yorkshire Metropolitan County Council* (1981) P&CR 179; this was distinguished by the Privy Council in *AG for Hong Kong* above, at 127, however, on the grounds that the estoppel arose as a result of an undertaking to exercise compulsory acquisition powers, rather than the 'subject to contract' negotiations, for a replacement of the old property with a new one to be purchased from the acquiring authority.

[95] See, generally, Chap. 11 below.

[96] [1976] Ch 179, CA at 193a–b.

> I do not find helpful the distinction between proprietary and promissory estoppel. This distinction may indeed be useful to those who teach or expound the law; but I do not think that, in solving the particular problem raised by a particular case, putting the law into categories is of the slightest assistance.

Examination of the two doctrines demonstrates that, although there are notable similarities between the doctrines, there remain significant differences. Thus, it is still necessary to retain the separate categories criticized by Lord Scarman.

Assurance

The two doctrines operate on different types of assurance. For proprietary estoppel, it is necessary to demonstrate an assurance or promise by M that W has, or will receive, rights over his property.[97] Equitable forbearance will arise where a party promises not to enforce contractual rights.[98] In order to establish equitable forbearance, it is necessary to demonstrate a clear and unequivocal promise that the rights in issue will not be enforced[99] whereas there are no certainty or clarity requirements with respect to proprietary estoppel.[1] It is not even necessary to show a promise. It is sufficient if M acquiesced in or encouraged W's mistaken belief that she owned rights in the property.[2] It is essential to show that the promisor intended to be legally bound in order to establish equitable forbearance[3] but not proprietary estoppel (although a positive intimation that M does not intend to be bound by his assurance may negative the operation of the latter doctrine).[4] 11.112

Detrimental reliance

It is a prerequisite of both doctrines that the claimant has changed her position in reliance on the assurance or promise made.[5] In proprietary estoppel cases, if W demonstrates that M's promise or conduct was 11.113

[97] See para. 11.87 above.
[98] See paras 12.12 and 12.61–2 below.
[99] See para. 12.12–3 below.
[1] See para. 11.07 above.
[2] See paras 11.08–15 above.
[3] See para. 12.23 below.
[4] See para. 11.07 above.
[5] See para. 11.24 above and para. 12.28 below.

calculated to induce her to rely on the assurance, the burden of proof will be reversed, throwing the onus on M to prove that W would have acted in the same way even had no assurance been made.[6] It is possible that the burden will be reversed in similar circumstances in equitable forbearance cases but we consider that this proposition has not yet been validly established.[7] It is clear that in order to establish a proprietary estoppel claim, W must show that, as a result of her change of position, she will suffer detriment if the assurance is withdrawn.[8] Whether such detriment is required for equitable forbearance cases is a matter of some controversy. In our view, it is necessary to establish such detriment[9] and that therefore the doctrines are similar in this respect. Further, neither doctrine will operate unless the party against whom the doctrine is asserted knew of the acts in reliance or intended that the assurance should be so acted upon.[10] However, in neither doctrine is it generally necessary to show that the party against whom the doctrine is asserted knew of his own legal rights,[11] although it may be necessary to do so where his conduct has amounted solely to passive acquiescence.[12]

Relief

Both doctrines may operate permanently or temporarily depending on the nature of the acts in reliance.[13] Both give the courts a flexible remedial discretion.[14] It is increasingly clear that, in proprietary estoppel cases, the guiding principle in exercising this discretion is that the court will seek to grant the minimum necessary to avert detriment.[15] In equitable forbearance cases, the analysis of remedies has tended to revolve around ascertaining whether the doctrine operates to make the forbearance binding permanently or whether it merely precludes its withdrawal before giving reasonable notice. On closer examination, it can be seen, however, that the principles applied are similar to those used in proprietary estoppel. The promisor will only be precluded from withdrawing his promise if this **11.114**

[6] See para. 11.26 above.
[7] See paras 12.30–1 below.
[8] See para. 11.31 above.
[9] See paras 12.34–8 below.
[10] See para. 11.21 above and para. 12.23 below.
[11] See para. 11.20 above and paras 12.23–6 below.
[12] See para. 11.19 above and para. 12.27 below.
[13] See para. 11.86 above and para. 12.51 below.
[14] See para. 11.50 above and para. 12.56 below.
[15] See para. 11.50–4 above.

is the only way to avert detriment to the promisee. The court will permit withdrawal of the forbearance on notice or on conditions, if this is sufficient to avert detriment and restore the promisee to her original position.[16] Thus, neither doctrine operates automatically to enforce the promise made but both may sometimes have this effect.

Scope of the doctrines

Both doctrines are a source of legal obligation. They operate substantively to give legal effects to assurances which they would not otherwise have. In this respect, they differ from traditional estoppels such as estoppel by representation or convention. Equitable forbearance cannot be used as a cause of action but only defensively.[17] Proprietary estoppel is not confined to a defensive role. Not only may it be used to defeat an action by the property owner to enforce his rights, it may be used as a cause of action to claim property rights.[18] Superficially, it is difficult to justify the difference in effect. There seems little conceptual justification for treating property and contractual rights differently in this context. In both cases, the holder of the rights is enjoying the benefit of the state's enforcement mechanisms and so might reasonably be expected to exercise them responsibly. M's conduct would seem to be equally unconscionable whether he encourages W to believe that he, M, will not enforce his contractual rights or his property rights. The anomaly is particularly apparent where contractual and property rights co-exist, for example, in cases concerning leases, restrictive covenants or intellectual property licences. In such cases, promises relating to the duration of the arrangement may give rise to a proprietary estoppel claim whereas promises relating to other terms may only trigger the operation of equitable forbearance.[19] Further, it is sometimes difficult to ascertain which of the doctrines is operating in this context.[20] 11.115

---

16 See para. 12.53 below.
17 See paras 12.61–2 below.
18 See para. 11.86 above.
19 See para. 11.96–101 above.
20 *Saloman v Akiens* [1993] 1 EGLR 101, CA; *Fontana N.V. v Mautner* (1980) 254 EG 199; *Morrow v Carty* [1957] NI 174. A interesting illustration of the overlap of contractual and property issues in estoppel cases is provided by *Film Investors Overseas SA v The Home Video Channel (trading as the Adult Channel)* [1997] EMLR 347. In that case, the authorities cited concerned proprietary estoppel. However, the doctrine operated to deprive the plaintiff of both its property right to restrain infringement of its copyright in a number of films *and* its contractual right to an additional licence fee for the international exploitation of those films.

These factors have led some to argue that the two doctrines would be assimilated, either by removal of the property qualification for proprietary estoppel or by expanding equitable forbearance to cover creation of new rights.[21] However, it may be possible to reconcile the differing approaches. Both doctrines may be said to operate subtractively. Neither creates new rights or obligations in the true sense because both presuppose existing rights of either a proprietary or contractual nature. Both involve a promise not to enforce existing rights rather than to take on a new obligation to confer a benefit. In both cases, the fostering of an assumption on which another has relied to their detriment can operate to deprive a party of its pre-existing rights but cannot to impose new obligations on it. The difference in their effect flows from the distinction between the two types of rights which they concern. In the case of contract, all that is necessary to deprive the promisor of his rights is allowing a defence to the action for breach of contract. There seems no doubt that the promisee in an equitable forbearance case could use the doctrine positively to obtain a declaration that the relevant contractual rights have been suspended or extinguished. Had the remedy in proprietary estoppel remained confined to the refusal of the original owner M's action for possession,[22] or a declaration that no such action would succeed, the operation of the two doctrines would have continued to look very similar. **11.116**

The controversial leap comes with the positive transfer of property rights to the claimant, W. Here it looks superficially as if proprietary estoppel is being used to create new rights and impose new obligations on M. Arguably, however, this distinction between the operation of the two doctrines is illusory. The essence of a property right is that it can be enforced against other people: to say that someone is the owner of property is merely shorthand for asserting that they can enforce a collection of rights to use the property, against other people. Once the court determines that the rights *cannot* be enforced against the claimant, arguably this amounts, in itself, to a transfer of ownership to the claimant.[23] The person who now has the enforceable right to use the property, is W and not M. If M's deprivation of the rights is to be permanent, this **11.117**

[21] The position which has been adopted in Australia. See *Waltons Stores (Interstate) Ltd v Maher* [1988] 164 CLR 387 and *Commonwealth of Australia v Verwayen* [1990] 170 CLR 394.

[22] As in the cases set out at para. 11.65 above.

[23] For example, the grant at a lifetime right to use property probably results in the vesting of a life interest in the grantee, even where the arrangement is phrased in terms of licence rather than ownership: see para. 11.66 above.

amounts to a transfer of absolute title. If it is to be for some shorter period, a lesser property right such as a lease or life interest is transferred. In conferring a positive interest on M, the court is merely enunciating clearly her true status in relation to the property. It thus avoids the ambiguity left by the simple refusal of possession but arguably the substantive legal result is no different. We concede, however, that this argument is controversial, particularly in the light of the uncertainty which does surround those cases where the remedy has been confined to the mere refusal of an owner's action for possession.[24] It appears to us, however, to be an intelligible way in which to explain the apparent differences between the effect of the two doctrines under consideration.

[24] See para. 11.65 above.

Chapter 12

EQUITABLE FORBEARANCE

INTRODUCTION

BACKGROUND

In 1877, in *Hughes v Metropolitan Railway Company*,[1] Lord Cairns held that: **12.01**

> . . . it is the first principle upon which all Courts of Equity proceed, that if parties who have entered into definite and distinct terms involving certain legal results — certain penalties or legal forfeiture — afterwards by their own act or with their own consent enter upon a course of negotiation which has the effect of leading one of the parties to suppose that the strict rights arising under the contract will not be enforced, or will be kept in suspense, or held in abeyance, the person who otherwise might have enforced those rights will not be allowed to enforce them where it would be inequitable having regard to the dealings which have thus taken place between the parties.[2]

The principle was used, some 70 years later, by Lord Denning in *Central London Property Trust Ltd v High Trees House Ltd*[3] as a basis for the following general principle: **12.02**

> . . . where a promise was made which was intended to create legal relations and which, to the knowledge of the person making the promise, was going to be acted upon by the person to whom it was made and which was in fact so acted on . . . the promise must be honoured[4]

These two cases provide the starting point for the development of the modern doctrine of promissory estoppel or equitable forbearance. It will

---

[1] (1877) 2 App Cas 439.
[2] *ibid.* at 448.
[3] [1947] KB 130.
[4] *ibid.* at 134.

be seen, however, that the width of Lord Denning's proposition has been considerably restricted by subsequent cases.

SUMMARY OF ELEMENTS

There are four elements. First, one party to a contract or other legal relationship ('the promisor') makes a clear and unequivocal representation to another party ('the promisee'); that representation being intended to affect the legal relations between them. Secondly, the representation is that the promisor's legal[5] rights under the contract or relationship between the parties will not be enforced or will be suspended. Thirdly, the promisee, to the knowledge of the promisor, in reliance on the representation alters its position to its detriment. Fourthly, the promisor now seeks to withdraw the representation. **12.03**

Once these elements are made out, the doctrine can be invoked to ensure that the promisee is not left, as a result of its change of position, in a worse position than it was in before the representation was made. Three points flow on from this. First, the doctrine's effects will vary according to the way in which the promisee has changed its position in reliance on the representation. Secondly, if it is possible to restore the promisee to its original position and reverse the detriment on reasonable notice, the doctrine will suspend not extinguish the promisor's rights. Thus, the promisor will be permitted to withdraw from the representation on reasonable notice. Thirdly, if that is not possible or it would be highly detrimental or inequitable to allow enforcement, even after notice, the doctrine may operate as a permanent bar on the withdrawal of the representation. **12.04**

TERMINOLOGY AND APPROACH

This doctrine has been referred to as promissory estoppel for various reasons. It is akin to estoppel by representation; both are triggered by detrimental reliance on a representation. It is promissory in the limited sense that it involves a representation as to future intention, *i.e.* a promise that rights will not be enforced. This second element distinguishes it **12.05**

[5] The doctrine affects equitable rights in the same way (see *Goldsworthy v Brickell* [1987] Ch 378, CA) we therefore refer to both 'systems' under the rubric of legal rights.

from estoppel by representation, which will only operate on a representation of fact.[6] The doctrine may be a source of legal obligation: as a result of its operation, certain legal effects are given to promises which they would not otherwise have. In contrast, estoppel by representation does not have this substantive effect: it operates to prevent the denial of the truth of the representation of fact; it thus sets up a state of affairs by reference to which relationships of parties are to be governed.

Notwithstanding the above, we would suggest that it is better to describe this doctrine as equitable forbearance for three reasons. First, the doctrine, by contrast to waiver and variation, originated in equity. Secondly, the term forbearance is apposite because the doctrine is inherently concerned with concession and promises to forbear from enforcing existing rights; it does not operate to create new obligations.[7] Thirdly, equitable forbearance is closely akin to common law waiver; both give rise to limited legal effects and both modify the rights arising from the contract. However, waiver requires knowledge, equitable forbearance does not. Similarly, equitable forbearance requires detriment; waiver does not.[8] The doctrine therefore fills a lacuna between variation, waiver and estoppel and we have adopted the terminology 'equitable forbearance' accordingly. **12.06**

As in the remainder of this work, we have endeavoured to classify and analyse the cases according to the nature of the principles actually applied, rather than the terminology used. Hence, we refer to a number of cases in this chapter which were expressly decided in terms of 'waiver' but involved the application of equitable forbearance principles.[9] This is clear, we would suggest, from their emphasis on the need for reliance **12.07**

[6] *'The Winson'* [1980] Lloyd's Rep. 213, CA at 222; *The 'Superhulls Cover' Case (No. 2)* [1990] 2 Lloyd's Rep. 431 at 448 and *Argy Trading Co Ltd v Lapid Developments Ltd* [1977] 1 WLR 444 at 456g–h. As is set out at para. 12.12, there is some difficulty in reconciling the line of cases based on equitable forbearance with the *ratio* of the House of Lord's decision in *Jorden v Money* (1854) 5 HLC 185 with its strict insistence that estoppel could only operate on representations of fact.

[7] Although it may create the new rights arising from a party's concessions or forbearance, *i.e.* the rights to treat those concessions and forbearances as binding.

[8] See *Waiver — Types and Elements* at para. 4.38 and *Sale of Goods and Shipping* at paras 20.02 and 20.05 ff., for a further discussion of the distinctions.

[9] See, for example, *Bremer Handelsgesellschaft mbH v Vanden Avenne-Izegem* [1978] 2 Lloyd's Rep. 10, HL; *Bremer Handelsgesellschaft mbH v C Macprang JR.* [1979] 1 Lloyd's Rep. 221, CA; *Finagraine SA Geneva v P Kruse Hamburg* [1976] 2 Lloyd's Rep. 508, CA; *Barrett Bros (Taxis) Ltd v Davis* [1966] 1 WLR 1335; *Allen v Robles* [1969] 1 WLR 1193; *Bremer Handelsgesellschaft mbH v Bunge Corpn* [1983] 1 Lloyd's Rep. 477; *Cook v Meunerie Liegeois SA* [1981] Lloyd's Rep. 359 and *Edm.J.M. Mertens v Veevoeder Import Export Vimex* [1979] 2 Lloyd's Rep. 372.

rather than informed election. It should be noted however, that a number of cases may involve the consideration and/or operation of both doctrines.

INTERFACE WITH CONTRACT

12.08 The equitable forbearance doctrine operates to give legal effect to promises which are unsupported by consideration. Detrimental reliance may amount to consideration but only where it is extracted as the price of the promise.[9a] This element of bargain is lacking from the equitable forbearance cases where, so long as detrimental reliance actually took place, all that is necessary is that the promisor knew or intended the promise to be acted upon[10]. Thus it looks as if equitable forbearance is operating as a consideration substitute. The conflict with contract rules has been reduced by two methods: first, equitable forbearance cannot be used to create new rights but only to modify pre-existing ones; secondly, establishing the elements of equitable forbearance does not automatically lead to the enforcement of the promise in issue; the effects will be limited to those necessary to avert detriment to the promisee, with the consequence that it frequently operates only to suspend the withdrawal of the promise.

12.09 There is one qualification to the above. There may be some element of bargain in equitable forbearance cases, the concession being made to encourage the promisee to comply with the reduced obligation under the contract. That this commercial *quid pro quo* could amount to consideration was for many years precluded by *Stilk v Myrick*[11] principles that performance of an existing obligation could not qualify as consideration. Therefore, only equitable forbearance or waiver could be relied upon to give effect to the commercial *quid pro quo*. However, as is set out above,[12] the *Stilk v Myrick* principle has been increasingly qualified and in particular by *Williams v Roffey and Nicholls (Contractors) Ltd.*[13] In *Williams*, it was held that performance of an existing contractual obligation could amount to good consideration if it was such as to render a factual benefit to the promisor. As a more flexible doctrine of consideration is adopted, the courts will inevitably find a greater number of contractual variations

[9a] See paras 11.103 above.

[10] It is sometimes difficult to distinguish the two situations — see, for example, *Re William Porter & Co Ltd* [1937] 2 All ER 361 and *Fenner v Blake* [1900] 1 QB 426.

[11] (1809) 2 Camp 317, 170 E.R. 1168.

[12] See *Variation* at para. 2.18 ff.

[13] [1991] 1 QB 1, CA.

and the operation of equitable forbearance will necessarily decrease. A promisee will generally prefer[14] to put its case in contract because of its more muscular results. In contract, the promisee will be able positively to claim new rights or enforce new obligations and will be entitled to the full measure of expectation damages for breach. It should be noted, however, that equitable forbearance will continue to play an important role where a creditor has promised not to enforce the full debt owed to it and to accept a lesser sum. The expanded *Williams v Roffey Bros* notion of consideration will not assist a promisee in such a case.[15]

ELEMENTS OF EQUITABLE FORBEARANCE

PRE-EXISTING LEGAL RELATIONSHIP

Equitable forbearance operates only on promises to forbear from enforcing existing legal rights; it does not create new obligations.[16] Therefore, there must be some pre-existing enforceable legal right which can be conceded.[17] Consequently, it is essential to demonstrate that the parties were in a relationship giving rise to legally enforceable rights and duties before the relevant promise was made.[18] The standard example of that relationship **12.10**

[14] It may be that a lesser degree of certainty and clarity is required for representations capable of giving rise to equitable forbearance than for those capable of amounting to contractual offers. We doubt that this is the case (see para. 12.15 below). However, if this is the case, there may be forensic attractions in relying on equitable forbearance where a claim based on contractual variation would fail.

[15] See *Re Selectmove* [1995] 1 WLR 474, CA per Lord Justice Peter Gibson at 480C–1D; *Foakes v Beer* (1884) 9 App Cas 605; *Banking* at para. 15.19 and *Variation* at para. 2.24

[16] See para. 12.08 above and 12.61–7 below.

[17] This is a doctrinal and logical necessity.

[18] *Hughes v Metropolitan Railway Company* (1877) 2 App Cas 614 at 448; *Birmingham & District Land Co v London & North Western Rail Co* (1888) 40 ChD 268, CA at 286; *BP Explorations Ltd v Hunt (No. 2)* [1979] 1 WLR 783 at 809f–h (affd on other grounds at [1983] AC 352); *Nippon Yusen v Pacifica Navegacion SA ('the Ion')* [1980] 2 Lloyd's Rep. 245 at 250; *Marseille Fret SA v D. Oltman Schiffahrts GmbH & Co Ltd ('the Trado')* [1982] Lloyd's Rep. 157 at 160–1; *Durham Fancy Goods Ltd v Michael Jackson (Fancy Goods) Ltd* [1968] 2 QB 839 at 846f–g; *Amalgamated Investment & Property Co Ltd (in liquidation) v Texas Commerce International Bank Ltd* [1982] 1 QB 84 *per* Robert Goff J. at 102e–f and 105c–d, *Emery v UCB Bank Plc* (CA, interlocutory hearing, unrep. 1997); *James v Heim Galleries* (1980) 256 EG 819, CA and *Drexel Burnham Lambert International v El Nasr* [1986] 1 Lloyd's Rep. 357 at 365.

is a contract.[19] However, the doctrine extends to other relationships which may potentially give rise to liabilities and penalties[20] including: those of wife and husband,[21] a company customer and company director,[22] an applicant for a statutory pension and the relevant government department,[23] a planning authority and applicant,[24] the victim and perpetrator of undue influence,[25] landlord and tenant (even where there is no privity of contract between them)[26] and a local authority and the owner of land who are negotiating for compensation for proposed compulsory purchase.[27] The doctrine has also been said to apply where contractual and other duties co-exist, for example, it covers an employer's duty to make a redundancy payment,[28] a mortgagee's statutory power of sale[29] and a director's right to remuneration under the articles of a company.[30] There is some doubt as to whether it may apply between landowner and trespasser[31] but

19 See, for example, *Hughes v Metropolitan Railway Company* (1877) 2 App Cas 614 at 448 and *Birmingham & District Land Co v London & North Western Rail Co* (1888) 40 ChD 268, CA at 286.

20 *Durham Fancy Goods Ltd v Michael Jackson (Fancy Goods) Ltd* [1968] 2 QB 839 at 846f–g.

21 *Maharaj v Chand* [1986] AC 898, PC.

22 *Durham Fancy Goods Ltd v Michael Jackson (Fancy Goods) Ltd* [1968] 2 QB 839.

23 *Robertson v Minister of Pensions* [1949] 1 KB 227 (although arguably this case should have been decided on grounds of estoppel by representation rather than equitable forbearance).

24 *Augier v Secretary of State for the Environment* (1979) 38 P&CR 219. Note, however, *Graham v Secretary of the State for the Environment and another* [1993] JPL 353 emphasizing the limited scope for the doctrine in planning matters.

25 *Goldsworthy v Brickell* [1987] Ch 378, CA.

26 *Fontana N.V. v Mautner* (1980) 254 EG 199; *Brikom Investments Ltd v Carr* [1979] QB 467, CA.

27 *Cooperative Wholesale Society v Chester le Street District Council, Lands Tribunal* (1997) 73 P&CR 111.

28 *Evenden v Guildford City Association Football Club Ltd* [1975] QB 917. The case was overruled by the House of Lords in *Secretary of State for Employment v Globe Elastic Thread Co Ltd* [1980] AC 506. The case arguably survives as authority on this point. We think, however, that the better view is that equitable forbearance cannot override or extend the statutory rights created by the Employment Rights Act, 1996. Further, the application of the doctrine on the facts of the case was incorrect: it breached two important principles, namely that equitable forbearance cannot be used to create new rights (see paras 12.61–7) and cannot give a tribunal an authority beyond that granted by statute (see paras 8.121–2).

29 *Braithwaite v Winwood* [1960] 3 All ER 642; *Emery v UCB Bank Plc* (CA, interlocutory hearing, unrep. 1997).

30 *Re William Porter & Co Ltd* [1937] 2 All ER 361.

31 In *Morris v Tarrant* [1971] 2 QB 143, it was held that it could not. Compare Lord Denning M.R.'s minority judgment in *Wallis Holiday Camp v Shell-Mex* [1974] 3 All ER 575 at 580–1.

it is suggested that it cannot. In *Pacol Ltd v Trade Lines Ltd ('the Henrik Sif')*,[32] the court held:

> Whatever the precise meaning of this term, it applies to two parties engaged in an exchange of correspondence in which one intends the correspondence to have legal effect and the other party knows of the intention and makes requests or purports to grant extensions of time which could only be of relevance to the first party if the correspondence between them affected their mutual rights and obligations.[33]

Mr Justice Webster thus seemingly extended the ambit of the equitable forbearance doctrine to all those engaged in litigation against one another. This approach seems hard to justify and has not so far been applied in any other case of which we are aware.[34] The case is controversial and the above proposition was arguably *obiter.*[35]

An additional point arises. Equitable forbearance may, in certain circumstances, operate where the parties are about to enter into a legal relationship. In *Brikom Investments Ltd v Carr,*[36] the defendants were negotiating with the plaintiff with a view to entering into a long lease of the plaintiff's premises; they were concerned about the obligation to contribute to roof repairs contained in the lease; the plaintiff promised that it would not enforce this provision[37] and the defendants were thereby induced to enter the leases. The equitable doctrine allegedly operated to prevent the landlord from resiling from its promise. However, such cases are likely to turn on collateral contract principles and therefore the scope (if any) for the doctrine is limited; it was resorted to in the case only as a somewhat controversial means of extending the landlord's promise to the assignees of the original tenants.[38] **12.11**

[32] [1982] 1 Lloyd's Rep. 456.

[33] *ibid. per* Webster J. at 466 cols 1–2. In *Shearson Lehman Hutton Inc v Maclaine Watson and Co Ltd* [1989] 2 Lloyd's Rep. 570 at 598, Webster J. expressed some doubt as to the correctness of his judgment in *Pacol* but his reservations did not extend to his application of equitable forbearance.

[34] Although the case was approved on another point in '*The Stolt Loyalty*' [1993] 2 Lloyd's Rep. 281.

[35] See para. 12.18 below.

[36] [1979] QB 467, CA. See also *Bank Negara Indonesia v Philip Hoalim* [1973]2 MLJ 3, PC.

[37] It hoped to obtain planning permission to extend the building upwards which would obviously have involved extensive works on the roof anyway.

[38] See para. 12.68 below.

PROMISE OR REPRESENTATION

Central to the operation of equitable forbearance is the requirement that the holder of legal rights has represented[38a] that those rights will not be enforced[39] or will be suspended, at least for a period.[40] The relevant representation thus concerns what the representor intends to do in the future; it is not a representation of present fact.[41] Although it is logically acceptable to use the term representation in the context of equitable forbearance, it is more accurate to characterize the situation as involving a promise[42] or assurance[43] by the holder that it will not enforce its legal rights. Thus it can be seen that an estoppel type doctrine (*i.e.* one triggered by detrimental reliance) is operating on promises or representations as to future intention. This is at odds with the House of Lords decision in *Jorden v Money*.[44] Louisa Jorden was the holder of a bond under which James **12.12**

[38a] The representation may be made directly or through an agent; the ordinary rules on authority applying. See *Fontana v Mautner* (1980) 254 *EG* 19a; Re Wickham (1917) 34 TLR 158 and *Credit Suisse v Allerdale B.L.* [1996] 1 Lloyd's Rep. 315 (affd on other grounds [1996] 2 Lloyd's Rep. 241).

[39] *Hughes v Metropolitan Railway Company* (1877) 2 App Cas 614 at 448; *Birmingham & District Land Co v London & North Western Rail Co* (1888) 40 ChD 268, CA at 286; *Tool Metal Manufacturing Co v Tungsten Electric Co* [1955] 1 WLR 761, HL at 763; *Ajayi v RT Briscoe (Nigeria) Ltd* [1964] 1 WLR 1326, PC at 1331; *Bank Negara Indonesia v Philip Hoalim* [1973]2 MLJ 3, PC at 5; *The Kanchenjunga* [1990] 1 Lloyd's Rep. 391, HL at 399; *The 'Superhulls Cover' Case (No. 2)* [1990] 2 Lloyd's Rep. 431 at 449; *Lark v Outhwaite* [1991] 2 Lloyd's Rep. 132 at 141; *Amalgamated Investment & Property Co. Ltd, (in liquidation) v Texas Commerce International Bank Ltd.* [1982] 1QB 84 *per* Robert Goff J. at 102e–f and 105c-d, *Emery v UCB Bank Plc* (CA, interlocutory hearing, unrep. 1997); *Nippon Yusen v Pacifica Navegacion SA ('the Ion')* [1980] 2 Lloyd's Rep. 245, CA at 250 and *BP Explorations Ltd v Hunt (No. 2)* [1979] 1 WLR 783 at 809f–h (affd on other grounds at [1983] AC 352).

[40] *Hughes v Metropolitan Railway Company* (1877) 2 App Cas 614 at 448; *Birmingham & District Land Co v London & North Western Rail Co* (1888) 40 ChD 268, CA at 286; *Tool Metal Manufacturing Co v Tungsten Electric Co* [1955] 1 WLR 761, HL at 763 and *Bank Negara Indonesia v Philip Hoalim* [1973]2 MLJ 3, PC at 5.

[41] Thus, distinguishing equitable forbearance from estoppel by representation — see further para. 8.29 above.

[42] *Foot Clinics (1943) Ltd v CoopersGowns Ltd* [1947] KB 506 at 510; *Spence v Shell* (1980) 256 EG 55, CA at 63; *James v Heim Galleries* (1980) 256 EG 819, CA at 821–3; *Credit Suisse v Allerdale BC* [1996] 1 Lloyd's Rep. 315 at 370 (affd on other grounds [1996] 2 Lloyd's Rep. 241) and *'The Winson'* [1980] Lloyd's Rep. 213, CA at 222–3. See also *Dun v Bradstreet Software Services (England) Ltd v Provident Mutual Life Assurance Association* [1997] EGCS 89 CA, lexis transcript and *Smith v Lawson* [1997] EGCS 85 CA, lexis transcript (a promise or representation suffices).

[43] *Braithwaite v Winwood* [1960] 3 All ER 642 at 646d–e; *Spence v Shell* (1980) 256 EG 55, CA at 63 and *Lark v Outhwaite* [1991] 2 Lloyd's Rep. 132 at 141.

[44] (1854) V HLC 185, 10 ER 868.

Money was bound to pay her £1200. She repeatedly told him that she would never enforce the debt. When she demanded the money due under the bond, Money argued that she was estopped from so doing because he had relied on her promise not to enforce. The House of Lords rejected the defence on two grounds: firstly there was no intent to create legal relations and secondly estoppel could operate only on representations of fact and not on representations or promises as to future intention. Such promises were only enforceable if given for consideration. In applying the equitable forbearance doctrine in the landmark decision of *Central London Property Trust v High Trees House*,[45] Mr Justice Denning (as he then was) sought to distinguish *Jorden* on the grounds that Louisa Jorden had never intended to be legally bound, whereas the promisor in *High Trees* did so intend. This reasoning is deficient since both of the two reasons given for the decision in *Jorden*, formed part of the ratio, including the assertion that representations of future intention cannot found an estoppel. No case has yet successfully reconciled the existence of the equitable forbearance with the decision in *Jorden*. Even in Australia, where the equivalent doctrine has expanded well beyond the scope of the English version, the majority of the High Court has declined to depart from *Jorden*.[46] The only possible explanation seems now to be a purely pragmatic one. The equitable forbearance doctrine is simply a well established, albeit limited exception to the *Jorden* principle. It is a doctrine distinct and independent from the estoppel by representation principle relied on in *Jorden*, with differing and more limited effects. The conflict between *High Trees* and *Jorden* has been diminished in subsequent authorities which have restricted the scope and effects of equitable forbearance.[47] A further problem caused by the operation of the equitable forbearance doctrine on promises is that it is being used to give certain legal effects to promises unsupported by consideration. In particular, it conflicts with the House of Lords decision in *Foakes v Beer*,[48] where it was held that part payment of a debt cannot amount to a good discharge of the whole. This matter is discussed at para. 12.52 below.

---

45 [1947] KB 130 at 135.

46 See *Waltons Stores (Interstate) Ltd v Maher* [1988] 164 CLR 387 *per* Deane J. and *Commonwealth of Australia v Verwayen* [1990] 170 CLR 394 *per* Deane J. and Mason J. A minority in each case (Deane J. in *Walton* and Deane J. and Mason J. in *Verwayen*) advocated departure from *Jorden v Money* (1854) V HLC 185, 10 ER 868.

47 See in particular, *Combe v Combe* [1951] 2 KB 215 CA (applies to promises to refrain from enforcing existing rights not to promises to create new ones) and *Societe Italio Belge v Palm & Vegetable Oils (Malaysia), The Post Chaser* [1982] 1 All ER 19 at 27 (effect temporary not permanent). See further paras 12.51 and 12.61–2.

48 (1884) App Cas 605.

The promise must be clear and unequivocal

In view of the serious potential consequences of equitable forbearance (namely the suspension or loss of legal rights), a degree of clarity of promise is required.[49] Thus, the promise must be clear and unequivocal.[50] As with waiver, the terms of the contract can make any given promise equivocal by the insertion of a clause prohibiting equitable forbearance.[51] Five further points arise: first, whether the promise must appear to be subjectively or objectively clear and unequivocal; secondly, whether the promise must satisfy the same degree of certainty as is required for a contract; thirdly, whether a promise can be inferred from conduct; fourthly, whether silence or inactivity suffice; and fifthly, whether a failure to object to defective performance will suffice. **12.13**

A subjective or objective test

In *Bremer Handelsgesellschaft Schaft v Vanden Avenne-Izegem,*[52] Lord Salmon held that an objective approach should be taken; it was sufficient **12.14**

---

[49] *The Kanchenjunga* [1990] 1 Lloyd's Rep. 391, HL at 399.

[50] *James v Heim Galleries* (1980) 256 EG 819, CA at 826; *Spence v Shell* (1980) 256 EG 55, CA at 63; *Woodhouse AC Israel Cocoa Ltd v Nigerian Produce Marketing Co Ltd* [1972] AC 741; *Societe Italio-Belge v Palm & Vegetable Oils (Malaysia), The Post Chaser* [1982] 1 All ER 19 at 25c; *Telfair Shipping Corp v Athos Shipping Co SA (The Athos)* [1983] 1 Lloyd's Rep. 127, CA at 134, 141, 145; *Drexel Burnham Lambert International v El Nasr* [1986] 1 Lloyd's Rep. 357 at 365; *Finagrain SA Geneva v P Kruse Hamburg* [1976] 2 Lloyd's Rep. 508, CA at 534; *Cook v Meunerie Liegeois SA* [1981] Lloyd's Rep. 359 at 368; *Goldsworthy v Brickell* [1987] Ch 378, CA at 410; *Allied Marine Transport Ltd v Vale Do Rio Doce Navegacao SA ('The Leonidas D')* [1985] 1 WLR 925, CA at 937; *Mebro Oil SA v Gatoil International Inc* [1985] 2 Lloyd's Rep. 234 at 242; *Cie Francaise Importation et de Distribution SA v Deutsche Continental Handelsgesellschaft* [1985] Lloyd's Rep. 592 at 596; *London and Clydebank Properties v HM Investment Co* [1993] EGCS 63; *Marc Rich & Co AG v Portman* [1996] 1 Lloyd's Rep. 430 at 442. See also *'The Chemical Venture'* [1993] 1 Lloyd's Rep. 509 at 521; *The Kanchenjunga* [1990] 1 Lloyd's Rep. 391, HL at 399 and *The 'Superhulls Cover' Case (No. 2)* [1990] 2 Lloyd's Rep. 431 at 452, *'The Scaptrade'* [1981] 2 Lloyd's Rep. 425 at 430–431 [1983] 1 All ER 301 CA *per* Goff L.J. at 304, (aff. on other grounds [1983] 2 AC 694); *Dun & Bradstreet Software Services (England) Ltd v Provident Mutual Life Assurance Association* [1997] EGCS 89 CA (lexis transcript); *Fraser Shipping Ltd v Colton* [1997] 1 Lloyd's Rep. 586 *per* Potter L.J. at 593 col 2 ('unequivocal'); *'The Shackleford'* [1978] 2 Lloyd's Rep. 155 at 159 ('clear'); *'The Winson'* [1980] Lloyd's Rep. 213, CA ('quite unequivocal'); *Auckland Harbour Board v Kaihe* [1962] NZLR 68 at 90 ('clear and unqualified').

[51] See *Waiver — Complexities* at para. 5.07; *Banking* at para. 15.20 and *Insurance* at para. 19.71.

[52] [1978] 2 Lloyd's Rep. 109, HL *per* Lord Salmon at 126.

to show that the promisee reasonably interpreted the words or conduct of the promisor as amounting to the required promise to forbear, even if such was not the latter's intention. This is difficult to reconcile with the approach taken in *Woodhouse AC Israel Cocoa Ltd v Nigerian Produce Marketing Co Ltd.*[53] There Lord Cross in particular seemed to favour a stricter and more subjective approach.[54] The difficulty is compounded by the fact that Lord Salmon did not refer to *Woodhouse* on the point and Lord Wilberforce indicated that *Bremer* raised no point of principle.[55] On balance, we consider an objective appraisal to be the correct one for four reasons. First, it is consistent with the courts' general approach to promises and representations. Secondly, it has been applied in recent authorities.[56] Thirdly, Lord Cairns, in *Hughes v Metropolitan Railway Company,*[57] held that what is all important is establishing that *the effect* of the conduct of the alleged promisor was such as to lead the other party to suppose that the strict rights arising under the contract would be abrogated. Fourthly, a careful reading of *Woodhouse* reveals that the majority did in fact apply an objective approach, albeit a strict one. A finding that the alleged promisee might reasonably have arrived at that conclusion, is insufficient. There could only have been a clear and unequivocal representation if that party could not reasonably have arrived at any other conclusion.[58]

---

53 [1972] AC 741.

54 *ibid.* at 767–8; see also Spencer Bower at p. 377.

55 *Bremer Handelsgesellschaft v Vanden Avenue-Izegem* [1978] 2 Lloyd's Rep. 109 HL at 116.

56 *Bremer Handelsgesellschaft mbH v C Macprang JR.* [1979] 1 Lloyd's Rep. 221, CA at 228; *'The Chemical Venture'* [1993] 1 Lloyd's Rep. 509 at 521; *'The Scaptrade'* [1983] 1 All ER 301, CA *per* Goff L.J. at 304; *Bremer Handelsgesellschaft mbH v Bunge Corpn* [1983] 1 Lloyd's Rep. 477 *per* Robert Goff L.J. at 483 col 1; *Goldsworthy v Brickell* [1987] Ch 378, CA 410 at 411 and *Societe Italio-Belge v Palm & Vegetable Oils (Malaysia), The Post Chaser* [1982] 1 All ER 19 at 25c-d. See also Chitty at para. 3–068.

57 (1877) 2 App Cas 614 at 448.

58 *Woodhouse AC Israel Cocoa Ltd v Nigerian Produce Marketing Co Ltd* [1972] AC 741 *per* Lord Salmon at 771 and *per* Lord Hailsham at 756. Their Lordships also indicated that the same degree of clarity is required for estoppel by representation and equitable forbearance (contrary to Lord Cross). Hence, further useful insight into the *Woodhouse* test can be found at para. 8.39 above where the same issue is discussed in relation to estoppel by representation. See also *Goldsworthy v Brickell* [1987] Ch 378, CA 410 at 411.

Certainty required

12.15 Although there is some authority to the contrary,[59] it is probable that the promise must be sufficiently clear and certain as to have been capable of giving rise to a contract had it been given for consideration.[60] Whether the promise is sufficiently clear will be decided in light of the surrounding circumstances.[61] Further, once the court has determined that the terms of the promise are sufficiently clear and certain, the mere fact that the promise does not benefit the promisor does not prevent its giving rise to an equitable forbearance.[62]

Promises inferred from conduct

12.16 The promise may be express[63] or may be inferred from conduct.[64] In *Hughes v Metropolitan Railway Company,*[65] for example, a landlord served, on its tenant, a notice to repair within six months; the latter replied by suggesting that the landlord might be interested in purchasing the tenancy, stating that it intended to defer the repairs until the possibility of a sale had been explored. The landlord responded by engaging in negotiations and was held to have thereby promised to extend the period allowed for repairs. Therefore, the six months was to

---

[59] *Hiscox v Outhwaite* [1991] Lloyd's Rep. 524 at 534; *Lark v Outhwaite* [1991] 2 Lloyd's Rep. 132 at 141 and *R & H Electric Ltd and another v Haden Bill Electrical Ltd* [1995] 2 BCLC 280 at 291d–f (no comment was made on the point in the Court of Appeal decision at the same reference).

[60] *Woodhouse AC Israel Cocoa Ltd v Nigerian Produce Marketing Co Ltd* [1972] AC 741 at 757e–g, 762c–d (see also Atiyah 'Consideration and Estoppel: the Thawing of the Ice' (1974) 38 *MLR* 65); *Drexel Burnham Lambert International v El Nasr* [1986] 1 Lloyd's Rep. 357 at 365; *'The Winson'* [1980] Lloyd's Rep. 213, CA at 222–3; *Food Corpn of India v Anticlizo Shipping Corp ('The Anticlizo')* [1987] 2 Lloyd's Rep. 130, CA at 142 (affd on other grounds [1988] 1 WLR 603, HL).

[61] *'The Shackleford'* [1978] 2 Lloyd's Rep 155, CA at 158.

[62] *ibid.*

[63] See, for example, *Central London Property Trust Ltd v High Trees House Ltd* [1947] KB 130; *Tool Metal Manufacturing Co v Tungsten Electric Co* (1950) 69 RPC 108, CA, [1955] 1 WLR 761, HL and *Brikom Investments Ltd v Carr* [1979] QB 467, CA.

[64] *Societe Italio-Belge v Palm & Vegetable Oils (Malaysia), The Post Chaser* [1982] 1 All ER 19 at 25c; *Re William Porter & Co Ltd* [1937] 2 All ER 361 at 363d–h; *Foot Clinics (1943) Ltd v Coopers Gowns Ltd* [1947], KB 506 at 510; *The Kanchenjunga* [1990] 1 Lloyd's Rep. 391, HL at 399 and *The 'Superhulls Cover' Case (No. 2)* [1990] 2 Lloyd's Rep. 431 at 450.

[65] (1877) 2 App Cas 614. Contrast the facts of *Dun & Bradstreet Software Services (England) Ltd v Provident Mutual Life Assurance Association* [1997] EGCS 89 CA, lexis transcript, discussed at para. 12.19, n. 85.

run from the date of the break down in negotiations not from the date of service of the notice. It is difficult to extract general principles from the cases as to what type of conduct will give rise to a sufficiently clear and unequivocal representation. Much will depend on the particular facts in issue. For example, negotiations with a view to an amicable settlement of disputed claim were insufficient in *Braithwaite v Winwood*.[66] By contrast, in *Cooperative Wholesale Society v Chester le Street District Council*,[67] after the Co-op's cause of action had become statute barred, the Council continued to negotiate on the basis that the latter had a potentially enforceable right to compensation. This was held to be a promise to forbear from taking the limitation point. However, a reluctant acceptance that there is an apparently sustainable defence to a claim, does not amount to a promise not to prosecute the claim or inhibit pursuing the claim if the defence proves to be unfounded.[68] Further, a statement that the alleged promisor believed itself to be liable under a contract,[69] or that it had been so advised by its solicitors,[70] does not amount to a promise that it is so liable. A threat to enforce a legal right on the happening of some event, does not amount to a promise to enforce should the relevant event occur.[71]

Promises inferred from silence or inactivity

Subject to one caveat,[72] silence or inactivity may be taken into account in establishing a promise not to enforce obligations but must be *supported* by other factors indicating that such a assurance has been made. Put simply, silence alone is generally incapable of amounting to a sufficiently unequivocal promise and must be buttressed by additional evidence if it is to trigger the equitable forbearance doctrine.[73] A promise **12.17**

---

66 [1960] 3 All ER 642 — see also *London and Clydebank Properties v HM Investment Co* [1993] EGCS 63.

67 Lands Tribunal [1997] 73 P&CR 111 (*dicta*).

68 *James v Heim Galleries* (1980) 256 EG 819, CA at 822 and *Collin v Duke of Westminster* [1985] 2 QB 581 at 599.

69 *Credit Suisse v Allerdale BC* [1996] 1 Lloyd's Rep. 315 (affd on other grounds [1996] 2 Lloyd's Rep. 241).

70 *'The Winson'* [1980] Lloyd's Rep. 213, CA at 223.

71 *Drexel Burnham Lambert International v El Nasr* [1986] 1 Lloyd's Rep. 357 at 365.

72 See para. 12.18 below.

73 *Amherst v James Walker Goldsmith & Silversmith* [1983] Ch 305, CA at 320 and *Vitol SA v Esso Australia Ltd, 'The Wise'* [1989] 2 Lloyd's Rep. 451 CA *per* Mustill L.J. at 461–2. See, however, *Whittal Builders v Chester-Le-Street DC* (1987) 40 BLR 85 *per* H.H. Fox-Andrews Q.C. at 106 (failure to object to defective contractual performance for three years amounted to a representation that the injured party's rights would not be enforced).

may be inferred from a combination of what the alleged promisor said and what it omitted to say.[74] Further, where the promisor can be said to be under a commercial duty to act, delay may in extreme circumstances suffice.[75] However, absent the above, it will be difficult to establish a promise solely from silence: pure inactivity will almost always be equivocal.[76] The reason is that inactivity, even if prolonged, is as likely to be attributable to carelessness as an intentional promise not to enforce a claim.[77] Finally, as a general rule, it is doubtful whether delay in prosecuting a claim can ever amount to a promise not do so in the future; at most it would amount only to an implied representation that the claim was not, *at the time*, being pursued.[78]

The caveat referred to above is that silence or inaction may constitute a promise where the 'promisor' is under a duty to speak.[79] In *Pacol Ltd v Trade Lines Ltd ('The Henrik Sif')*,[80] Mr Justice Webster held that such a duty arose where a reasonable man would expect the person alleged to have made the forbearance, acting honestly and responsibly, to bring the true facts to the attention of the other party where the other party was known by him to be acting under a mistake as to their respective rights. Whilst the statement of the duty may be correct, its application to the facts of *The Henrik Sif* is controversial. The duty to speak in that case was extended to a duty to point out to the opponent in legal **12.18**

---

[74] *'The Chemical Venture'* [1993] 1 Lloyd's Rep. 509 at 521.

[75] See, e.g. *Allen v Robles* [1969] 1 WLR 1193 *per* Fenton-Atkinson L.J. at 1196G-H.

[76] *Mebro Oil SA v Gatoil International Inc* [1985] 2 Lloyd's Rep. 234 at 242; *Allied Marine Transport Ltd v Vale Do Rio Doce Navegacao SA ('The Leonidas D')* [1985] 1 WLR 925, CA at 937; *Cie Francaise Importation et de Distribution SA v Deutsche Continental Handelsgesellschaft* [1985] Lloyd's Rep. 592 at 596; *Food Corpn of India v Anticlizo Shipping Corp ('The Anticlizo')* [1986] 1 Lloyd's Rep. 181 at 187, affd [1988] 1 WLR 603, HL.

[77] *Allied Marine Transport Ltd v Vale Do Rio Doce Navegacao SA ('The Leonidas D')* [1985] 1 WLR 925, CA at 940–1.

[78] See, for example, *Mebro Oil SA v Gatoil International Inc* [1985] 2 Lloyd's Rep. 234 at 242.

[79] *The 'Superhulls Cover' Case (No. 2)* [1990] 2 Lloyd's Rep. 431 at 452 referring to authorities concerning estoppel by representation. See further paras 8.57–63 above for the principles applicable in estoppel by representation. The general principles applicable to equitable forbearance and estoppel by representation appear to be the same in this context (see para. 8.57). However, the result of their application will often differ between the two, given the difference between the assumptions which trigger the respective doctrines: as the remainder of the paragraph shows, the courts will rarely impose a duty to speak where the matter in issue is the *legal rights* and obligations of the parties. Thus the duty to speak arises less often in the context of equitable forbearance.

[80] [1982] 1 Lloyd's Rep. 456 approved in *'The Indian Endurance' (No. 2) Republic of India v India Steamship Company* [1996] 3 All ER 641 CA *per* Staughton L.J. at 654b-d (aff. [1997] 4 All ER 380 HL).

proceedings that it had sought to obtain time extensions from the wrong party. Therefore, the decision has been circumscribed as follows. We would submit that the decision is to be limited to its facts.[81] In '*The Stolt Loyalty*',[82] Mr Justice Clark applied *The Henrik Sif* but stated that each case must be judged on its facts and that opponents in litigation do not normally owe a duty to point out one another's errors. It was appropriate to apply *The Henrik Sif* in *The Stolt Loyalty* because the defendants had responded to the requests for an extension in deliberately equivocal terms to prolong the plaintiff's error.[83] His Lordship further held that, for the duty to arise, the alleged promisor must have at least a suspicion of 'the true position', that is of its own legal rights.

Four points arise. First, silence and delay will constitute a promise where the appropriate duty exists.[84] Secondly, that duty will only arise in limited circumstances. Thirdly, great care must be taken to applying *The Henrik Sif* or *The Stolt Loyalty* to the parties in litigation. The cases must, we suggest, either be seen as being confined to their facts or as being applicable only where one party has employed sharp practice in the conduct of the litigation.[85] Fourthly, the requirement that the **12.19**

[81] *RPPC v Bank Leumi* [1992] Lloyd's Rep. 515 at 542.

[82] [1993] 2 Lloyds 281 at 288–289.

[83] Note the *obiter* divergence of opinions in *Wallis Holiday Camp v Shell-Mex* [1974] 3 All ER 575: the plaintiff had occupied the land for over 11 years when an offer for sale was received from the owners; the plaintiff deliberately failed to respond, in the hope that the 12 year limitation period for adverse possession would elapse before action was taken; Lord Denning M.R. at 580–1 considered such conduct to bring the doctrine into play but Stamp L.J., at 586g–7d, did not (Ormrod L.J. made no comment on the issue).

[84] See *Moorgate Mercantile Co Ltd v Twitchings* [1977] AC 890 *per* Lord Wilberforce at 903; *Pacol Ltd v Trade Lines Ltd ('The Henrik Sif')* [1982] 1 Lloyd's Rep. 456 *per* Webster J. at 465 cols 1–2 and *The Stolt Loyalty* [1993] 2 Lloyd's Rep. 281 *per* Clarke J. at 290 cols 1–2.

[85] In effect, where one party has led the other 'up the garden path'. See also '*The Indian Endurance' (No. 2) Republic of India v India Steamship Company* [1996] 3 All ER 641 CA *per* Staughton L.J. at 654b–d (aff. [1997] 4 All ER 380 HL), discussed at paras 8.57 and 8.63 above. The restrictive approach of the courts in this area is illustrated by *Dun & Bradstreet Software Services (England) Ltd v Provident Mutual Life Assurance Association* [1997] EGCS 89 CA, lexis transcript. The lease between the parties gave the tenant a right to terminate so long as he or she paid a specified penalty rent by a certain date. The landlords deliberately prolonged negotiations for a new lease until after that date, in the hope that the tenant would fail to comply with the terms of the lease. This conduct did not give rise to any promise or representation although it was conceded that it was a borderline case. For a case on the other side of the line, see *Trustees of John Lyon Free School v Mayhem* (1997) 29 HLR 719, although the doctrine in issue was probably waiver rather than equitable forbearance.

alleged promisor must have a suspicion of its rights[86] is an exception to the general rule that such knowledge is not necessary for equitable forbearance.[87] These cases may therefore be regarded as doubly anomalous.

Promises inferred from failure to object to defective performance

The above difficulties are particularly acute where an attempt is made to generate a promise from the alleged promisee's conduct after breach. The courts are generally reluctant to deprive a party of its right to object to breach, merely because that party does not require strict compliance with the contract at all times.[88] There is an undoubted danger that an overly muscular forbearance doctrine will discourage cooperation between contracting parties and force them, prematurely, into litigation. At one level, this result is prevented by the requirement that any representation made must be clear and unequivocal. It will be seen, however, that the doctrine may still provide something of a trap for the unwary litigant; it throws at least some onus on contracting parties to obtain clear legal advice as soon as there is any suggestion of breach. Parties may safeguard their legal position in a number of ways. Continuing to press for full and correct performance of the contract is inconsistent with a promise to forego the right to complain of breaches of it.[89] Likewise, an express reservation of all contractual rights will generally negative the implication of such a promise.[90] Such a reservation does not, however, invariably provide protection if the conduct of the alleged promisee is sufficiently clear.[91] **12.20**

Emphatic reliance on one point of dispute between the parties does not, by itself, necessarily amount to a promise not to enforce other legal **12.21**

---

[86] Which is, of course, a further restriction on the application of these cases.
[87] See below at paras 12.24–8.
[88] As pointed out by Chitty at para. 3–069.
[89] *V. Berg and Son Ltd v Vanden Avenne-Izegem PVBA* [1977] Lloyd's Rep. 499, CA.
[90] *James v Heim Galleries* (1980) 256 EG 819, CA at 826; *Finagrain SA Geneva v P Kruse Hamburg* [1976] 2 Lloyd's Rep. 508, CA at 541; *Peter Cremer v Granaria BV* [1981] Lloyd's Rep. 583 at 588; *Cook v Meunerie Liegeois SA* [1981] Lloyd's Rep. 359 at 368 and contrast the facts of '*The Chemical Venture*' [1993] 1 Lloyd's Rep. 509 at 521 where no such reservation was made.
[91] See, for example, the dubious decision of the majority in *Bremer Handelsgesellschaft mbH v C Macprang JR* [1979] 1 Lloyds Rep. 221, CA and Stephenson L.J.'s dissent on this point at 229.

obligations owed.[92] In *Bremer Handelsgesellschaft mbH v Vanden Avenne-Izegem,*[93] the breach in issue concerned defects in a contractual notice served. The recipient failed to object to the defects in issue but made a number of other criticisms and later demanded performance of part of the contract which would only have been on foot had the notice been valid. The recipient was held to have promised to forego its right to challenge the notice on grounds of the defects in issue. However, the conduct in *Bremer* must be distinguished from mere acceptance of defective documents, without protest or reservation of rights. Such conduct will generally be insufficient, some additional and active conduct is usually necessary, evidencing approval of the documents, for example, by requiring that they be presented to a sub-contractor.[94] Further, although there is no general requirement that the promisor had knowledge of the legal rights it is alleged to have foregone,[95] such knowledge may be relevant in ascertaining whether a sufficiently clear and unequivocal representation has been made. Thus, in cases of the type just described, the alleged promisor's conduct is likely to be equivocal unless it either knew of the defect or the defect was obvious or readily discoverable. Absent such knowledge, it will be difficult to show, in such cases, that the only reasonable interpretation of the conduct in issue was that the right to object to the relevant defect was being foregone.[96]

THE PROMISE MUST HAVE BEEN INTENDED TO AFFECT THE LEGAL RELATIONSHIP BETWEEN THE PARTIES

The courts have frequently stated that the promise must be intended to be legally binding or intended to affect the legal relations between the **12.22**

[92] *Telfair Shipping Corp v Athos Shipping Co SA (The Athos)* [1983] 1 Lloyd's Rep. 127, CA at 136 although see *Vitol SA v Esso Australia Ltd, 'The Wise'* [1989] 2 Lloyd's Rep. 451 CA, *per* Mustill L.J. at 461–462.

[93] [1978] 2 Lloyd's Rep. 109, HL.

[94] *Societe Italio-Belge v Palm & Vegetable Oils (Malaysia), The Post Chaser* [1982]1All ER 19 at 25c–d. This is an illustration of the general principle discussed above at paras 12.16–19, namely that silence alone rarely amounts to a representation but may be relevant where coupled with active conduct.

[95] See para. 12.24 below.

[96] *Avimex SA v Dewulf & Cie* [1979] 2 Lloyd's Rep. 57 *per* Goff J. at 67–8. See also the dissenting judgment of Stephenson L.J. in *Bremer Handelsgesellschaft mbH v C Macprang JR* [1979] 1 Lloyd's Rep. 221, CA at 228.

parties.[97] This requirement is, we would suggest, indistinguishable from the contractual test of intent to create legal relations.[98] Whether the promise was intended to affect legal relations will be decided objectively.[99] The test will be satisfied if a reasonable person would have concluded that the promise was intended to affect the legal position.[1] Further, the House of Lords has averred that 'mere acts of indulgence' will not suffice.[2] Similarly, casual conversations between agents,[3] mere 'gossip'[4] and negotiating with a view to an amicable settlement[5] have also been dismissed as inadequate. By contrast, a statement made 'as a matter of business'[6] was sufficient. This requirement tends to overlap with the need for a clear and unequivocal representation. The purpose of both safeguards is to prevent casual concessions modifying legal obligations. Unfortunately, it is sometimes difficult to establish where the line is to be drawn between such casual concessions and qualifying forbearances.

---

97 *Central London Property Trust Ltd v High Trees House Ltd* [1947] KB 130 *per* Denning J. at 134, 136; *Evenden v Guildford City Association Football Club Ltd* [1975] QB 917 at 924 (same); *Charles Rickards Ltd v Oppenhaim* [1950] KB 616, CA at 622 (same) and *Brikom Investments Ltd v Carr* [1979] QB 467, CA at 482 (same). His Lordship's frequent emphasis on the requirement is understandable in light of his disavowal of the need to show detriment; in the absence of detriment, intention to be bound becomes one of the touchstones of enforceability. For support from other members of the judiciary see *Argy Trading Co Ltd v Lapid Developments Ltd* [1977] 1 WLR 444 at 457a–e and *James v Heim Galleries* (1980) 256 EG 819, CA at 821. Contrast the more flexible approach used in proprietary estoppel, set out at para. 11.07.

98 As to which see specialist texts but note *Vaughan v Vaughan* [1953] 1 QB 762, CA where there could be neither a contract nor a 'promissory estoppel'/equitable forbearance because of the lack of intent to create legal relations.

99 This is consistent with the approach to the nature of the promise made — see para. 12.14 above.

1 *Braithwaite v Winwood* [1960] 3 All ER 642 at 646g–i.

2 *Tool Metal Manufacturing Co v Tungsten Electric Co* [1955] 1 WLR 761, HL *per* Viscount Simonds at 764 and *Morrow v Carty* [1957] NI 174 at 180.

3 *James v Heim Galleries* (1980) 256 EG 819, CA at 822.

4 *Cie Française Importation et de Distribution SA v Deutsche Continental Handelsgesellschaft* [1985] Lloyd's Rep. 592 at 596.

5 *Braithwaite v Winwood* [1960] 3 All ER 642.

6 *Re Wickam* (1917) 34 TLR 158.

THE PROMISOR MUST HAVE INTENDED THE PROMISE TO BE ACTED UPON OR KNOWN THAT IT WAS BEING ACTED UPON

Mere reliance on a promise is insufficient to raise an equitable forbearance, even where it leads to detriment. A key element in establishing the unconscionable conduct or inequity necessary for the operation of the doctrine is establishing the connection between the promisor and the reliance. The promisor's responsibility for the relevant conduct must go beyond the mere making of the promise.[7] This may be done in a number of slightly differing ways. It is clear that a promise may give rise to an equitable forbearance if it was made with the intention that it should be acted upon by the promisee.[8] It is also sufficient if the promisor knew that the promise would be acted upon[9] or was in fact being acted upon.[10] Presumably, however, in the latter case, if the promisor rapidly intervenes and warns the promisee not to rely on the promise, the doctrine will not apply. Although he expressed some doubt about the proposition, Mr Justice McVeigh held, in *Morrow v Carty*,[11] that it might be sufficient if it could be shown that the promisor ought reasonably to have known that its promise was being acted upon. In that case, a contract for the sale of property provided that the deposit was to be paid immediately. On executing the contract, the purchaser asked for time to return home to fetch the money. The vendor granted him an hour's grace. The purchaser thereupon sold his father's farm, allegedly 12.23

---

[7] *cf.* the comparable rule in proprietary estoppel and also the approach of Mason and Wilson in *Waltons Stores (Interstate) Ltd v Maher* [1988] 164 CLR 387 at 406 (Sutton 'Contract by Estoppel' (1989) 1 *JCL* 205 at 212).

[8] *Central London Property Trust Ltd v High Trees House Ltd* [1947] KB 130 *per* Denning J. at 134, 136; *Wallis v Semark* [1951] 2 TLR 222, CA at 226 (same); *Evenden v Guildford City Association Football Club Ltd* [1975] QB 917 at 924 (same); *Charles Rickards Ltd v Oppenhaim* [1950] KB 616, CA at 622 (same); *Brikom Investments Ltd v Carr* [1979] QB 467, CA at 482 (same); *Lyle-Meller v A Lewis & Co* [1956] 1 WLR 29, CA at 36 (same); *Ledingham v Bermejo Estancia Co Ltd* [1947] 1 All ER 749 at 752f–3a (same); *Beesly v Hallwood Estates Ltd* [1960] 2 All ER 314 at 324 (aff. on other grounds at [1961] 1 Ch 105 CA); *James v Heim Galleries* (1980) 256 EG 819, CA at 825; *Augier v Secretary of State for the Environment* (1979) 38 P&CR 219 at 226 and *Goldsworthy v Brickell* [1987] Ch 378 CA.

[9] *Goldsworthy v Brickell* [1987] Ch 378 CA 410 CA at 411; *Re Wickam* (1917) 34 TLR 158 and *James v Heim Galleries* (1980) 256 EG 819, CA at 822.

[10] *James v Heim Galleries* (1980) 256 EG 819 CA at 822 and 825; *Morrow v Carty* [1957] NI 174.

[11] [1957] NI 174.

in reliance on the belief that he had the hour's grace. It was found as fact that he had failed to tender the money within the hour. Even had he performed more timeously, no equity could be raised against the vendor, since the acts in reliance were not ones which *'could reasonably have been contemplated as being done by [the purchaser] on foot of the promise . . . no vendor applying reasonable foresight would think a purchaser who asked for time to go home to get the deposit and who was to be back in a limited period such as an hour, was contemplating a sale of a property in order to obtain the deposit'.*[12] The requisite knowledge or intention may be held via an agent and ordinary principles of attribution will apply.

KNOWLEDGE OF THE PROMISOR'S RIGHTS IS NOT NECESSARY

As is set out in the preceding paragraphs, it is essential that the promisor knew that the promise was being acted upon or intended that it should be so acted upon. We consider that it is unnecessary to show that the promisor was aware of its own legal rights or of the facts giving rise to them. Three points arise: the relationship with waiver; whether equitable forbearance can arise where a party is ignorant of its rights; and the role of knowledge where promises are inferred from conduct. **12.24**

The relationship with waiver

It is on this particular point that equitable forbearance has been most easily confused with waiver. Thus, in *Bremer Handelsgesellechaft mbH v Vanden Avenne-Izegem,*[13] Lord Salmon held that, in assessing whether a contracting party had 'waived' its right to complain of a breach, it was immaterial that, at the relevant time, it had no knowledge of the breach in question. This caused some controversy, given that such knowledge has long been accepted as essential for the operation of the waiver doctrine.[14] Further, in *Bremer Handelsgesellschaft mbH v C Macprang JR*[15] the Court of Appeal were divided as to what the House **12.25**

[12] [1957] NI 174 at 182; *cf.* section 90(1) of the American Restatement, Second, Contracts.

[13] [1978] 2 Lloyd's Rep. 109, HL at 126.

[14] See *Waiver — Types and Elements* at para. 4.44.

[15] [1979] 1 Lloyd's Rep. 221, CA.

of Lords had meant in the earlier *Bremer* case.[16] Lord Denning, held that:

> If a buyer, who is entitled to reject goods or documents on the ground of a defect in the notices or the timing of them, so conducts himself as to lead the seller reasonably to believe that he is not going to rely on any such defect — whether he knows it or not — then he cannot afterwards set up the defect as a ground for rejecting the goods or documents when it would be unfair or unjust to allow him to do so.[17]

Lord Justice Shaw expressed himself to be 'in complete agreement'[18] with the views expressed by Lord Denning, stating:

> I see no reason . . . to limit the effect of waiver to rights known to exist. It may be embracing enough, and so intended as to forego rights which *might* exist in regard to a particular contract or in a particular context[19] (his Lordship's emphasis)

By way of contrast, Lord Justice Stephenson averred that:

> I do not understand Lord Salmon's reference to waiving any defect in the notice . . . 'whether they were aware of it or not' as laying down any general principle that there can be a waiver or equitable estoppel on the part of someone who does not know that his rights have been infringed or has not at the least such obvious means of knowing that his rights have been infringed that the other party can reasonably assume that the party waiving or estopped is acting with knowledge of their infringement. Lord Salmon was I think referring to a patent defect which could only be missed by not reading the notice or not knowing the law[20]

The better view is that Lord Salmon was actually referring to equitable forbearance in *Vanden*, rather than waiver. This is consistent with view of the majority of the Court of Appeal in *Mackprang*, whose allusion to unfairness and injustice, the hallmarks of equitable forbearance, signal that they too were referring to the equitable doctrine. Thus the simple rule emerging from the authorities is that there are two similar doctrines at work, waiver which operates where the promisor has knowledge of its legal rights and equitable forbearance which operates in the absence

[16] *Bremer Handelsgesellschaft mbH v Vanden Avenne-Izegem* [1978] 2 Lloyd's Rep. 109 HL.
[17] [1979] 1 Lloyd's Rep. 221, CA at 225.
[18] *ibid.* at 231.
[19] [1979] 1 Lloyd's Rep. 221, CA at 230.
[20] *ibid.* at 229.

of such knowledge. This view appears to be inconsistent with the judgment of Lord Justice Stephenson. We prefer the view of the majority[21] in *Mackprang* for two reasons. First, the majority decision is supported by Lord Goff's reasoning in *The Kanchenjunga*.[22] In contrasting the principle election and the doctrine here discussed, he asserted that for the latter *'No question of any particular knowledge on part of representor arises'*. In contrast, he asserted that an election requires *'an informed choice made with knowledge of the facts giving rise to the right'*. This conclusion provides a coherent basis for distinguishing waiver from equitable forbearance. It is consistent with the latter's concentration on the promisee and the effect of the promisor's conduct on it. The presence of inequity or detriment, triggered by change of position, provides the justification for judicial intervention, despite the absence of knowledge. Secondly, as argued in detail elsewhere,[23] we would submit that Lord Salmon's approach is entirely consistent with the requirements of equitable forbearance but poses significant difficulties if the case is classified as an example of waiver.

Equitable forbearance and ignorance

Express promises

Due to the fact that knowledge is not required, a party may expressly promise to forbear from enforcing a right which it does not know that **12.26**

[21] In *Cerealmangimi SpA v Toepfer* [1981] 3 All ER 533, Lloyd J. declined to choose between the the majority and minority since he found as a fact that there was sufficient knowledge to satisfy either approach in the case before him.

[22] [1990] 1 Lloyd's Rep. 391, HL at 399; *The 'Superhulls Cover' Case (No. 2)* [1990] 2 Lloyd's Rep. 431 at 449–50; *Auckland Harbour Board v Kaihe* [1962] NZLR 68 (SC of Auckland) at 88 lines 5–30; see also *Telfair Shipping Corp v Athos Shipping Co SA (The Athos)* [1983] 1 Lloyd's Rep. 127, CA and *Ets Soules & Cie v International Trade Development Co Ltd* [1980] Lloyd's Rep. 129, CA at 137–8 where the Court of Appeal rejected a defence based on waiver and election on the basis that there was no knowledge of the relevant right, whereas this fact was wholly ignored in assessing the allegation of promissory estoppel or equitable forbearance. Contra. *Proctor and Gamble Philippine Manufacturing Corp v Peter Cremer GmbH & Co ('the Manila')* [1988] 3 All ER 843 at 853–4.

[23] See *Waiver — Types and Elements* at para. 4.38 ff. and *Sale of Goods and Shipping* at paras 20.02 and 20.05 ff. For a recent example of the failure to distinguish clearly between waiver and equitable forbearance, see *Trustees of John Lyon Free School v Mayhem* (1997) 29 HLR 719. It is acknowledged that the general division which we have adopted is not supported by those cases which aver that there is no distinction between waiver and estoppel: see for example *Vitol SA v Esso Australia Ltd, 'The Wise'* [1989] 2 Lloyd's Rep. 451 CA *per* Mustill L.J. at 461–462 and *Whittal Builders v Chester-Le-Street DC* (1987) 40 BLR 85 *per* H.H. Fox-Andrews Q.C. at 106.

it possesses.[24] In *Bank Negara Indonesia v Philip Hoalim*,[25] for example, a landlord promised its tenant that he could reside in the property for as long as he continued practising as a lawyer. At the time, both parties thought that the tenant had statutory protection and the landlord was therefore ignorant of its legal right to evict the tenant. The Privy Council held, however, that the landlord's promise not to enforce that right was sufficient to give rise to an equitable forbearance.

Inferred promises

Where the relevant promise is not express but is inferred from conduct, the promise may be construed in two different ways. There may be a promise to abandon a *specific right* that is inconsistent with the conduct. The alternative promise is one to abandon *any rights* which the alleged promisor may have which are inconsistent with the course of conduct, whether the alleged promisor is aware of those rights or not.[26] Given the broad nature of the latter promise, knowledge of the relevant right is wholly immaterial — all rights are foregone.[27] However, where a promise to forego a specific right is inferred, certain difficulties arise. It is difficult to infer from conduct an unequivocal promise to forego a specific right unless, as Lord Justice Stephenson pointed out in *Bremer Handelsgesellschaft mbH v C Macprang JR*,[28] the alleged promisee reasonably assumed that the alleged promisor knew of the right. It will **12.27**

---

[24] Contra. *The 'Superhulls Cover' Case (No. 2)* [1990] 2 Lloyd's Rep. 431 at 450 where Philips J. (as he then was) asserted that this was not possible.

[25] [1973] 2 MLJ 3, PC. See also *Cooperative Wholesale Society v Chester le Street District Council*, Lands Tribunal, [1997] 73 P&CR 111 and *Goldsworthy v Brickell* [1987] Ch 378, CA. In *Goldsworthy*, the defendant sought to rely on equitable forbearance to bar a claim to rescission on grounds of undue influence. He did so on the assumption that the equitable defence of acquiescence was not open to him; it being admitted that the plaintiff had no knowledge of his right to rescind at the time when the alleged representation and reliance took place. This ignorance was not considered to impede the equitable forbearance argument. The term acquiescence was there used to refer to the doctrine of cases such as *Holder v Holder* [1968] Ch 353 which may be used to bar an equitable but not a legal claim as opposed to acquiescence in the sense used in proprietary estoppel (as to which see para. 11.8 above).

[26] In *The 'Superhulls Cover' Case (No. 2)* [1990] 2 Lloyd's Rep. 431 at 450.

[27] We would, however, point out it will be extremely difficult to spell out such a wide ranging representation from conduct.

[28] [1979] 1 Lloyd's Rep. 221, CA. See, however, *JT Sydenham & Co Ltd v Enichem Elastomers Ltd* [1989] EGLR 257 *per* H.H. Judge Leonard Bromley Q.C. at 260 col 1, where both a landlord and its tenant mistakenly believed that the level of rent due was lower than it in fact was. The landlord's acceptance of the lower rent without challenge was enough to bring the equitable forbearance doctrine into play.

be difficult, though not impossible, to establish the required clear and unequivocal promise in such cases unless the defect was of the patent type of defect to which his Lordship refers.

Silence and inactivity

In the limited circumstances where a promise or representation may be inferred from silence or purely passive conduct, it is probably necessary that the alleged promisor has knowledge of its legal rights. Without such knowledge, there is nothing to prompt the alleged promisor to intervene to correct the misaprehension of the alleged promisee.[29] **12.28**

RELIANCE

To establish equitable forbearance, it is essential to show that the promisee acted in reliance on the promise that the strict legal rights arising under the relevant legal relationship would not be enforced.[30] It is not necessary to show that the promisee has performed a positive act; proof that it refrained from acting in a particular way as a result of the **12.29**

[29] See para. 12.18–9 above.

[30] *Tool Metal Manufacturing Co v Tungsten Electric* [1955] 1 WLR 761, HL at 764; *Ajayi v RT Briscoe (Nigeria) Ltd* [1964] 1 WLR 1326, PC at 1331; *W. J. Alan & Co Ltd v El Nasr Export and Import Co* [1972] 2 QB 189, CA at 213; *Telfair Shipping Corp v Athos Shipping Co SA (The Athos)* [1983] 1 Lloyd's Rep. 127, CA at 136; *The Kanchenjunga* [1990] 1 Lloyd's Rep. 391, HL at 399; *Edm.J.M. Mertens v Veevoeder Import Export Vimex* [1979] 2 Lloyd's Rep. 372 at 384; *Amherst v James Walker Goldsmith & Silversmith* [1983] Ch 305, CA at 320; *Avimex SA v Dewulf & Cie* [1979] 2 Lloyd's Rep. 57 at 67; *Peter Cremer v Granaria BV* [1981] Lloyd's Rep. 583 at 587; *Fontana N.V. v Mautner* (1980) 254 EG 199 at 205; *Beesly v Hallwood Estates Ltd* [1960] 2 All ER 314 at 324 (aff. on other grounds at [1961] 1 Ch 105 CA); *Smith v Lawson* [1997] EGCS 85 CA, lexis transcript; *Emery v UCB Bank Plc* (CA, interlocutory hearing, unrep. 1997); '*The Scaptrade*' [1983] 1 All ER 301 CA *per* Goff L.J. at 304 and 306 (aff. on other grounds [1983] 2 AC 694); *Bremer Handelsgeselschaft mbH v Bunge Corpn* [1983] 1 Lloyd's Rep. 477 *per* Robert Goff L.J. at 483 col 1; *Mebro Oil SA v Gatoil International Inc* [1985] 2 Lloyd's Rep. 234 at 242; *Allied Marine Transport Ltd v Vale Do Rio Doce Navegacao SA ('The Leonidas D')* [1985] 1 WLR 925, CA at 940–1; *Cie Française Impotation et de Distribution SA v Deutsche Continental Handelsgesellschaft* [1985] Lloyd's Rep. 592 at 596; '*The Multitank Holsatia*' [1988] 2 Lloyd's Rep. 486 at 493; *Ets Soules & Cie v International Trade Development Co Ltd* [1980] Lloyd's Rep. 129, CA at 138; *Wallis v Semark* [1951] 2 TLR 222, CA at 226; *Morrow v Carty* [1957] NI 174 at 181 and *Augier v Secretary of State for the Environment* (1979) 38 P&CR 219 at 226; Spencer Bower at pp. 388–91.

promise received, is sufficient.[31] What is essential is that the promisee has been led to act differently to the way in which it would have done had the promise never been made.[32] This necessarily involves some change of position. The change of position need not fall into any pre-existing category provided that the requirement of detriment or inequity is met.[33] Therefore, any act will suffice so long as it involves a change of position which is such as to give rise to inequity or detriment, in the event of failure to fulfil the promise. However, there are certain restrictions inherent in this apparently flexible approach: some general categories of acts may be incapable of giving rise to inequity or detriment.[34]

It is obviously essential that the promisee knew of the promise. There **12.30**
must be a causative link between that knowledge and the relevant conduct. Therefore, it is necessary to establish that the promise encouraged[35] the promisee to act in the way it did; the fact that the promise was material to the decision so to act is insufficient.[36] This causative link may exist where a belief already held is strengthened or the promisee is lulled into a false sense of security.[37] It is not necessary, however, to show that the actions were caused solely by the promise. It is sufficient if it influenced the promisee's decision to act in the way which it did.[38] Whether reliance has been established is matter of fact.[39]

---

[31] *The Kanchenjunga* [1990] 1 Lloyd's Rep. 391, HL at 399; *Fontana N.V. v Mautner* (1980) 254 EG 199 at 205; *Hughes v Metropolitan Railway Company* (1877) 2 App Cas 614, HL and *Birmingham & District Land Co v London & North Western Rail Co* (1888) 40 ChD 268.

[32] *Finagrain SA Geneva v P Kruse Hamburg* [1976] 2 Lloyd's Rep. 508, CA at 535; *Cook v Meunerie Liegeois SA* [1981] Lloyd's Rep. 359 at 368 and *Re Wickam* (1917) 34 TLR 158.

[33] As to which see below at para. 12.33 ff.

[34] See para. 12.43 ff.

[35] *Brikom Investments Ltd v Carr* [1979] QB 467, CA at 490.

[36] *Credit Suisse v Allerdale BC* [1996] 1 Lloyd's Rep. 315 at 369 (affd on other grounds [1996] 2 Lloyd's Rep. 241). Colman J. was there referring to estoppel by convention but was applying the same test adopted in *Lark v Outhwaite* [1991] 2 Lloyd's Rep. 132 at 142 for equitable forbearance, namely that laid down in *Amalgamated Investment & Property Co. Ltd, (in liquidation) v Texas Commerce International Bank Ltd* [1982] 1 QB 84.

[37] *Lark v Outhwaite* [1991] 2 Lloyd's Rep. 132 at 142.

[38] *ibid.* applying *Amalgamated Investment & Property Co. Ltd, (in liquidation) v Texas Commerce International Bank Ltd* [1982] 1 QB 84 *per* Goff J. at 105a. *cf.* the approach taken in Australia: *Waltons Stores (Interstate) Ltd v Maher* [1988] 164 CLR 387 (HC of Australia) *per* Guadron J. at 463 (the promise must approximate cause of the acts performed); see Sutton, 'Contract by Estoppel' (1989) 1 JCL 205.

[39] *Peter Cremer v Granaria BV* [1981] Lloyd's Rep. 583 at 589.

Burden of proof

There are inherent difficulties in assessing whether reliance has taken place. This is because the court has to ascertain what would have happened had a hypothetical state of affairs occurred, namely one where no promise was made. In consequence, it has been suggested that the normal burden of proof should be reversed. Instead of requiring the promisee to prove the causative link, it has been suggested that the promisor should be required to show that the promisee's actions *were not* caused or influenced by the promise in issue. Thus, in *Brikom Investments Ltd v Carr*,[40] Lord Denning asserted that: **12.31**

> It is no answer for the maker to say, 'you would have gone ahead with the transaction anyway'. That must be mere speculation. No one can be sure what he would or would not have done in a hypothetical state of affairs which never took place . . . .Once it is shown that the representation was calculated to influence the reasonable man the presumption is that he was so influenced[41]

Further, the courts have not always been strict in requiring proof of reliance.[42] If there was a clear indication that the promise was intended to induce the change of position which occurred, it may well be that the burden would be reversed in the way that Lord Denning suggests.

These approaches have much to recommend them but have not yet been adopted by the courts in this area.[43] In *Peter Cremer v Granaria BV*,[44] Mr Justice Goff declined to comment on the issue in the light of an affirmative finding of fact that no reliance had occurred. There are, however, numerous cases where there has been no such presumption and the burden seems to have been placed squarely on the promisee. The promisee then failed to discharge that burden.[45] Indeed, it has been **12.32**

---

40 [1979] QB 467, CA.

41 *ibid.* at 482–3.

42 *Tool Metal Manufacturing Co v Tungsten Electric Co* (1950) 59 RPC 108, CA at 115, 116.

43 As opposed to the doctrine of proprietary estoppel where it is now generally accepted as the applicable rule. See para 11.26. Those cases which aver that equitable forbearance and proprietary estoppel are one and the same doctrine (see paras 11.96–101) might be used to support an argument that the presumption should apply.

44 [1981] Lloyd's Rep. 583 at 589.

45 *Ets Soules & Cie v International Trade Development Co Ltd* [1980] Lloyd's Rep. 129 CA at 137–8; *Bremer Handelsgesellschaft mbH v Bunge Corpn* [1983] 1 Lloyd's Rep. 477 *per* Robert Goff L.J. at 484 col 2; *Mebro Oil SA v Gatoil International Inc* [1985] 2 Lloyd's Rep. 234 at 242; *Allied Marine Transport Ltd v Vale Do Rio Doce Navegacao SA ('The Leonidas D')* [1985] 1 WLR 925, CA at 940–1; *Cie Française*

emphasized that promisees are well advised to call witness evidence to substantiate alleged reliance.[46]

Discharging the burden

The causative link between the promise and the promisor's conduct may be inferred from the circumstances of the case. For example, reliance was inferred where a tenant failed to pay rent following her landlord's promise not to enforce his right to demand rent under the terms of a lease.[47] Significant difficulties face those whose allegation of equitable forbearance rests on an implied promise not to prosecute a disputed claim. In such cases, the promisee will generally believe that it has a good defence to the claim; this will almost certainly be averred in correspondence and/or legal proceedings. In the light of such an averral, it is difficult, to say the least, to establish reliance on any promise; in all likelihood the promisee's actions would have been caused by its belief that the promisor had no valid claim.[48] This category of cases includes those where one of the parties promises not to enforce its right to object to past instances of defective contractual performance.[49] Where it is sought to derive such a promise from delay in prosecuting a claim, it may well be that the actions of **12.33**

Importation et de Distribution SA v Deutsche Continental Handelsgesellschaft [1985] Lloyd's Rep. 592 at 596; *Finagraine SA Geneva v P Kruse Hamburg* [1976] 2 Lloyd's Rep. 508, CA at 535–6; *Raiffeisen Hauptgenossenschaft v Louis Dreyfus & Co* [1981] 1 Lloyd's Rep. 345 at 352 and *Morrow v Carty* [1957] NI 174 at 183. It is admitted, however, that some of these cases might be explicable as instances where there was affirmative evidence that the conduct in question was not caused or encouraged by the promise made.

46 *Telfair Shipping Corp v Athos Shipping Co SA (The Athos)* [1983] 1 Lloyd's Rep. 127, CA at 145.

47 *Smith v Lawson* [1997] EGCS 85 CA, lexis transcript and '*The Scaptrade*' [1983] 1 All ER 301 CA *per* Goff L.J. at 305a (aff. on other grounds [1983] 2 AC 694). See also *Dun & Bradstreet Software Services (England) Ltd v Provident Mutual Life Assurance Association* [1997] EGCS 89 CA, lexis transcript, where it was alleged that a landlord had impliedly assured the tenant that the notice it had served was valid. The fact that no amended notice was served after assurance was made, strongly suggested that assurance was relied on.

48 *Fraser Shipping Ltd v Colton* [1997] 1 Lloyd's Rep. 586 *per* Potter L.J. at 593 col 2. See, for example, *Collin v Duke of Westminster* [1985] 2 QB 581 and *James v Heim Galleries* (1980) 256 EG 819, CA at 825. Similarly, in *Fontana N.V. v Mautner* (1980) 254 EG 199 at 203, the tenant could not demonstrate reliance on a promise that it could remain in the property indefinitely because at all times he believed that he had an independent legal right to remain, regardless of the landlord's wishes.

49 *Ets Soules & Cie v International Trade Development Co Ltd* [1980] Lloyd's Rep. 129, CA at 137–8.

the promisee were performed because of a hope or belief that the action would *'simply disappear'*, rather than in reliance on any promise.[50]

DETRIMENT AND INEQUITY

The equitable forbearance doctrine operates to prevent the peremptory withdrawal of promises where that would be *'inequitable having regard to the dealings which have thus taken place between the parties.'*[51] This requirement of inequity or unfairness has been expressed to be at the heart of the doctrine from its earliest examples.[52] Precisely what types of circumstances give rise to the 'inequity', are a matter of some controversy. We consider that in order to establish inequity it is necessary to show that the change of position, in reliance on the promise, is such as to cause detriment to the promisee, in the event of withdrawal of the promise. **12.34**

Is it necessary to show detriment?

In *Tool Metal Manufacturing Co v Tungsten Electric Co*,[53] one of the few instances where the equitable forbearance principle has been scrutinized by the House of Lords, Lord Simonds emphasized that the promisee must have altered its position. Further, there are a number of authorities which state the promisee must establish that it has suffered detriment[54] or prejudice.[55] However, Lord Denning, disputed this in **12.35**

---

50 *Allied Marine Transport Ltd v Vale Do Rio Doce Navegacao SA ('The Leonidas D')* [1985] 1 WLR 925, CA at 940–1.

51 *Hughes v Metropolitan Railway Company* (1877) 2 App Cas 614 at 448.

52 See *Hughes* itself at 448.

53 [1955] 1 WLR 761, HL at 764. See also *Birmingham & District Land Co v London & North Western Rail Co* (1888) 40 ChD 268.

54 *Alma Shipping Corporation v Union of India ('The Astraea')* [1971] 2 Lloyd's Rep. 494 at 502; *Augier v Secretary of State for the Environment* (1979) 38 P&CR 219 at 226; *Spence v Shell* (1980) 256 EG 55, CA at 63; *Beesly v Hallwood Estates Ltd* [1960] 2 All ER 314 at 324 (aff. on other grounds at [1961] 1 Ch 105 CA); *JT Sydenham & Co Ltd v Enichem Elastomers Ltd* [1989] EGLR 257 *per* H.H. Judge Leonard Bromley Q.C. at 260 col 1; *Je Maintiendrai v Quaglia* [1980] 26 SASR 101; *Emery v UCB Bank Plc* (CA, interlocutory hearing, unrep. 1997); *Morrow v Carty* [1957] NI 174 at 181–2; *Janred Properties Ltd v ENIT* [1989] 2 All ER 444; *Mebro Oil SA v Gatoil International Inc* [1985] 2 Lloyd's Rep. 234 at 242; *Meng Long Development Pte v Jip Hong Trading Pte PC* [1985] AC 511, PC and *Commonwealth of Australia v Verwayen* [1990] 170 CLR 394 at 422.

W. J. Alan & Co Ltd v El Nasr Export and Import Co.[56] In Lord Denning's view, far from being prejudiced in the case, the promisee had received a benefit as a result of the representation. All that was necessary was that the promise should have been acted upon. Lord Salmon expressly left this point open in *Bremer Handelsgesellschaft mbH v Vanden Avenne-Izegem.*[57] In other cases, inequity has been stressed as the key feature of the equitable forbearance doctrine. In *The Kanchenjunga,*[58] Lord Goff held that the doctrine requires '. . . *such reliance by the representee as will render it inequitable for the representor to go back on his representation*'.[59]

As with many of the subjects under consideration in this work, it seems that the confusion in this area is more terminological than substantial. The divergence of view is explicable largely on the basis of differing conceptions of what is meant by detriment. For present purposes,[60] three points should be noted. First, the conduct performed in reliance does not itself have to be onerous, unpleasant or damaging. Nor need it involve spending money or incurring new liabilities (although this type of conduct often typifies detrimental reliance). Secondly, it is true that while the promise is adhered to, the promisee actually enjoys a benefit. **12.36**

---

55 *Amherst v James Walker Goldsmith & Silversmith* [1983] Ch 305, CA at 319–20 and *'The Multitank Holsatia'* [1988] 2 Lloyd's Rep. 486 at 493.

56 [1972] 2 QB 189, CA at 213. See also *Vitol SA v Esso Australia Ltd, 'The Wise'* [1989] 2 Lloyd's Rep. 451 CA *per* Mustill L.J. at 461–462; *Ogilvy v Hope Davies* [1976] 1 All ER 683 at 688b–9a; *Telfair Shipping Corp v Athos Shipping Co SA (The Athos)* [1983] 1 Lloyd's Rep. 127, CA at 135; *Brikom Investments Ltd v Carr* [1979] QB 467, CA at 486 and Stoljar, *Estoppel and Contract Theory* (1990) 3 JCL 1. Those who argue that detriment is not necessary have also cited Lord Denning's judgment in the landmark case of *Central London Property Trust Ltd v High Trees House Ltd* [1947] KB 130. Certainly, detriment was not mentioned as a requirement. However, as we set out below, at para. 12.48, the promisee probably did act to its detriment in the case. *High Trees* was recently approved in *Smith v Lawson* [1997] EGCS 85 CA (lexis transcript). In that case, there was no express mention of detriment but the requirement was clearly satisfied (see further para. 12.40 below).

57 [1978] 2 Lloyd's Rep. 109 at 127.

58 [1990] 1 Lloyd's Rep. 391.

59 *ibid.* at 399. See also *BP Explorations Ltd v Hunt (No. 2)* [1979] 1 WLR 783 at 810d-h (affd on other grounds at [1983] AC 352); *Nippon Yusen v Pacifica Navegacion SA ('the Ion')* [1980] 2 Lloyd's Rep. 245 *per* Mocatta J. at 250; *Civil Aviation Authority v Internationale Nederlanden Aviation Lease VB and the European Organisation for the Safety of Air Navigation (Interveners)* [1997] 1 Lloyd's Rep. 96 *per* Judge Diamond Q.C. at 104 col 2; *'The Scaptrade'* [1983] 1 All ER 301 CA *per* Goff L.J. at 304–6 (aff. on other grounds [1983] 2 AC 694); *Marseille Fret SA v D. Oltman Schiffahrts GmbH & Co Ltd ('the Trado')* [1982] Lloyd's Rep. 157 at 160–1.

60 For a more detailed analysis and citation on this issue see *Proprietary Estoppel* at paras 11.31–47 where the same principles apply.

However, it is not the acts in themselves which must be inherently detrimental, for it is not at the point of performance that detriment is assessed.[61] Rather, it is essential to show that the promisee will suffer some prejudice or detriment *if the promise is withdrawn*.[62] Thirdly, in a trite sense, it may be said that the promisee would always suffer harm as a result of being deprived of the promised advantage. This type of detriment is, however, insufficient. What is necessary is that the promisee's *change of position* will leave it in a worse position than it would have been in, had the promise never been made.[63]

12.37 A useful illustration is provided by *Hughes v Metropolitan Railway Company*[64] where a landlord's conduct led its tenant to believe that a notice to repair would not be enforced; as a consequence the tenant did not bother to carry out the relevant repairs. While the promise was adhered to the tenant did indeed enjoy a benefit, namely not having to perform the repairs. It is not at this point, however, that detriment is assessed. The relevant point at which to analyse the position of the promisee is only *after* the promise has been withdrawn. Thus, it becomes obvious that the tenant in *Hughes* would have suffered such a detriment, had the landlord been permitted to withdraw his implied undertaking with impunity: it would have been liable for breach of covenant and open to proceedings to forfeit the lease.

12.38 Once this definition of detriment is adopted, the boundaries between detriment and inequity tend to collapse. Thus, for example, Mr Justice Hoffman (as he then was) equated the two concepts in *Banner Industrial and Chemical Properties Ltd v Clark Patterson Ltd*.[65] However, Mr Justice Robert Goff (as he then was), seemingly, distinguished them in *Societe Italio-Belge v Palm & Vegetable Oils (Malaysia), The Post Chaser*.[66] We submit, however, that *The Post Chaser* is consistent with

[61] *Fontana N.V. v Mautner* (1980) 254 EG 199 at 205–7, which was heavily influenced by the the analysis of this issue by Spencer Bower at pp. 393–5.

[62] *Je Maintiendrai v Quaglia* [1980] 26 SASR 101 and *Fontana N.V. v Mautner* (1980) 254 EG 199.

[63] See para. 11.31–2 above.

[64] (1877) 2 App Cas 614.

[65] [1990] 2 EGLR 139 at 140d-f ('*. . . estoppel requires that* [the party seeking to raise the estoppel] *should have relied on* [the] *representation to its detriment, in the sense that he has altered his position in a way which would make it unjust for the landlord now to be able to challenge the award*') and *Fontana N.V. v Mautner* (1980) 254 EG 199 at 205–7.

[66] [1982] 1 All ER 19; *The 'Superhulls Cover' Case (No. 2)* [1990] 2 Lloyd's Rep. 431 at 454–5; *Shearson Lehman Hutton Inc v Maclaine Watson and Co Ltd* [1989] 2 Lloyd's Rep. 570 at 598 and *Goldsworthy v Brickell* [1987] Ch 378, CA at 411 (sufficient if promisee acted to its detriment or in some other way which would make it inequitable to allow the promise to be withdrawn).

our position since, in that case, the court was considering the detriment suffered *before* withdrawal of the promise and not afterwards. Mr Justice Robert Goff clearly considered prejudice or detriment in the sense set out above to be highly material: he rejected the claim that the conduct in issue had been inequitable on the following basis:

> In particular . . . I cannot see, that in the absence of any evidence that the seller's position had been prejudiced by reason of their action in reliance on the representation, it is possible to infer that they suffered any such prejudice. In these circumstances a necessary element for the application of the doctrine of equitable estoppel is lacking[67]

Three points emerge. First, the true divergence of opinion is between Lord Denning's view that the mere fact of acting on the promise is sufficient to bring the doctrine into play[68] and those that require prejudice or inequity for its operation. Secondly, although we submit that the latter view is the correct one, the position is uncertain.[69] On the one hand, the language used in the inequity cases is wide enough to embrace a concept which could operate where no detriment is demonstrated. On the other hand, unless the promisee suffers some prejudice as a result of the withdrawal of the promise, it is hard to see why it should be unfair to withdraw the promise.[70] Unless prejudice is essential, it is difficult to ascertain why change of position is necessary at all, let alone understand the emphasis given to it by Lord Simonds in *Tool Metal Manufacturing Co v Tungsten Electric Co.*[71] Thirdly, this analysis is consistent with that of the Privy Council in *Ajayi v RT Briscoe (Nigeria) Ltd*[72] where Lord Hodson stressed that both the existence and the duration of the equity depended on whether the promisee could be restored to its original position: unless prejudice has been suffered as a result of the alteration of position, why should there be any need or justification for the restoration contemplated by their Lordships? We therefore submit that detriment is essential for equitable forbearance preventing an otherwise perilous drift to unstructured concepts of justice and fairness.[73] Further, if a distinction is to be drawn between inequity 12.39

67 [1982] 1 All ER 19 at 27e–g.

68 See para. 12.35 above.

69 Clarification by a higher court would therefore be desirable.

70 *Je Maintiendrai v Quaglia* [1980] 26 SASR 101 *per* King J. at 106.

71 [1955] 1 WLR 761, HL at 764. See also *Birmingham & District Land Co v London & North Western Rail Co* (1888) 40 ChD 268.

72 [1964] 1 WLR 1326, PC at 1331; *Je Maintiendrai v Quaglia* [1980] 26 SASR 101 *per* White J. at 111.

73 See, *e.g. The Mayor and Burgesses of the London Borough of Southwark v Logan* [1996] 29 HLR 40. Note the emphasis placed on detriment by the Australian courts in cases such as *Waltons Stores (Interstate) Ltd v Maher* [1988] 164 CLR 387 and

and detriment in this context, the requirement of inequity should be satisfied *in addition* to the latter threshold test. Put simply, it may be that the existence of detriment is a necessary but sufficient element of the doctrine.

Examples of detriment

Contracting parties may generally protect themselves from becoming bound by equitable forbearance principles by rapid withdrawal of the promise made. This is likely to be effective to prevent the operation of the doctrine as there will have been no time for the promisee to alter its position sufficiently to give rise to detriment.[74] Assuming that rapid withdrawal does not take place, we would identify the following categories of change of position that typically lead to detriment.[75] **12.40**

The promisee fails to safeguard its legal position

The paradigm example is provided by *Hughes v Metropolitan Railway Company*.[76] As set out above, the landlord's conduct led its tenant to refrain from carrying out repairs which it was contractually obliged to perform. Had the landlord been permitted to withdraw his implied **12.41**

Commonwealth of Australia v Verwayen [1990] 170 CLR 394. Given the importance of detriment in relation to the various species of estoppel, as to which see paras 11.96–101, imposing a detriment requirement in equitable forbearance cases should appeal to those who characterize the doctrine as an example of a single unified or federated concept of that doctrine.

[74] *Banner Industrial and Chemical Properties Ltd v Clark Patterson Ltd* [1990] 2 EGLR 139 and *Societe Italio-Belge v Palm & Vegetable Oils (Malaysia), The Post Chaser* [1982] 1 All ER 19.

[75] The categorization adopted is derived, subject to some modifications, from Malcolm Clarke's article 'Banker's Commercial Credits among the High Trees' [1974] *CLJ* 260 at 283.

[76] (1877) 2 App Cas 614. See also *'The Chemical Venture'* [1993] 1 Lloyd's Rep. 509; *Dun & Bradstreet Software Services (England) Ltd v Provident Mutual Life Assurance Association* [1997] EGCS 89 CA, lexis transcript (failing to serve an amended and valid notice under a tenancy in reliance on the landlord's assurance that an earlier notice was valid) and *Smith v Lawson* [1997] EGCS 85 CA, lexis transcript. In the latter case, a landlord agreed to forbear from demanding any rent from the tenant and the tenant thereafter stopped paying. It was held that the landlord could not have claimed possession on the basis of non-payment of rent because the tenant had relied on his promise by failing to pay. The issue of whether arrears could be claimed or whether the old level of rent could be enforced was not considered. Compare *Central London Property Trust Ltd v High Trees House Ltd* [1947] KB 130 (discussed at para. 12.48 below).

undertaking with impunity, the tenant would have suffered the detriment of being exposed to proceedings for breach of covenant and forfeiture. It is important to note that the legal obligations giving rise to the detriment need not have been owed by the promisee to the promisor. The obligations can be owed to a third party. Thus, for example, where a buyer in a string or circle[77] breaches the contract by tendering incorrect documents, the seller may represent that it will not exercise its consequential right to terminate the contract. In reliance on this representation the buyer fails to go into the market to purchase suitable substitute goods. If the promise is then peremptorily withdrawn, the buyer may be sued by subsequent purchasers in the string. Alternatively, the buyer may have been planning to use the goods in fulfilling other types of contracts such as manufacturing or construction and may be sued for late completion under those agreements.[78] In either case, detriment occurs. Further examples include reaching a composition with creditors on the basis that the debt owed to the promisor had been foregone[79] and granting planning permission in circumstances where it was inappropriate.[80]

The promisee foregoes something of value

This typically involves the expenditure of money or marketable labour. **12.42**
The prejudice accruing to the promisee is obvious: the loss of valuable assets. This head of detriment is not without its complications, particularly with respect to assessing whether the expenditure or labour has been truly sacrificed or whether the promisee obtained or retains some benefits, despite withdrawal of the promise. These issues and this type of detriment is discussed extensively in relation to proprietary estoppel where the same

[77] As occurs in the onsale of goods afloat or the futures/derivatives market.

[78] Clarke above asserts that this is the type of detriment which arose in the *W. J. Alan & Co Ltd v El Nasr Export and Import Co* [1972] 2 QB 189, CA. There the seller promised to accept payment calculated in sterling rather than, as specified in the contract, Kenyan shillings. Given the movement in exchange rates, this had the effect of reducing the price; the seller was prevented from withdrawing his promise to accept the reduced price. The difficulty with Clark's analysis is that there was no threat to cancel the contract and thereby deprive the buyer of the goods, the seller was simply demanding the full price for them. It may be that no detriment was suffered in El Nasr; if so, in our view, it was simply not a case where the equitable doctrine should have been applied; it can be justified, if at all, only on the basis of the contractual variation analysis applied by the majority. See also *Wallis v Semark* [1951] 2 TLR 222, CA, where there seems to be no evidence of detriment.

[79] *Re Wickam* (1917) 34 TLR 158.

[80] *Augier v Secretary of State for the Environment* (1979) 38 P&CR 219 at 226.

principles apply.[81] Examples include continuing to trade and incurring liabilities instead of going into liquidation;[82] working on the promotion of various patents and arranging overseas contracts in relation thereto;[83] allowing the promisor to occupy part of a building owned by the promisee;[84] giving up a statutory protected tenancy;[85] paying a statutorily controlled rent assessed on the basis that the landlord was liable for repairs rather then the tenant;[86] and incurring liability for demurrage.[87] Incurring expenditure in legal proceedings will not suffice if the expenditure can be dealt with under the normal costs principles.[88]

Performance of contractual duties

Of particular relevance in the context of equitable forbearance is the situation where the promisor undertakes not to terminate the contract for repudiatory breach. Such a termination would relieve both parties from any further obligation to perform the contract. In such cases, detriment will commonly arise as a result of the promisee's expending money and effort in continuing to perform the contract in reliance on the promise[89] that it will remain on foot. **12.43**

Continued performance of a loss-making contract

The position is different where the right in issue is not termination for breach but the right to insist on strict compliance with contractual obligations.[90] Here the promisee's performance of the reduced obligation cannot normally lead to detriment. The promisee was required by the contract to perform the obligation in any event. Therefore, there is **12.44**

[81] See *Proprietary Estoppel* at para. 11.41–6.
[82] *Re William Porter & Co Ltd* [1937] 2 All ER 361 at 364 and *Ledingham v Bermejo Estancia Co Ltd* [1947] 1 All ER 749.
[83] *Bruner v Moore* [1904] 1 Ch 305.
[84] *J.F. Perrott v Cohen* [1951] 1 KB 705, CA.
[85] *Bank Negara Indonesia v Philip Hoalim* [1973]2 MLJ 3, PC.
[86] *Brikom Investments v Seaford* [1981] 1 WLR 863, CA.
[87] *Cerealmangimi SpA v Toepfer* [1981] 3 All ER 533.
[88] *'The Multitank Holsatia'* [1988] 2 Lloyd's Rep. 486 at 493. Contra. *Shearson Lehman Hutton Inc v Maclaine Watson and Co Ltd* [1989] 2 Lloyd's Rep. 570 at 598, an estoppel by convention case where the limited usefulness of costs orders was adverted to. See also *Cooperative Wholesale Society v Chester le Street District Council*, Lands Tribunal, (1997) 73 P&CR 111.
[89] *Charles Rickards Ltd v Oppenhaim* [1950] KB 616, CA and *Smith v Lawson* [1997] EGCS 85 CA, lexis transcript.
[90] For example, situations where the promisor reduces the obligations to be performed.

no change of position in reliance on the promise.[91] The only argument open to the promisee, in these circumstances, is to suggest that, in reliance on the promise, it refrained from abandoning the contract and paying damages. The promisee therefore continued to perform a loss-making contract. This might be a very real detriment where the promisee has made a particularly bad bargain — the return for the promisee's goods and services on the open market being significantly greater than that yielded under the contract.

There are two supports for this position. First, in *Williams v Roffey Bros and Nicholls (Contractors) Ltd*,[92] the benefit accruing from the continued performance of contractual obligations formed at least some part of the court's findings on consideration.[93] In that case, the defendant had employed the plaintiff to carry out various building works. The latter began to experience problems in carrying out the works, partly because it had underestimated their cost in tendering for the contract. In consequence, the defendant promised the plaintiff an extra payment of £10,300, in addition to the contract price. The Court of Appeal held that the promise was given for good consideration because the defendant obtained factual benefit from the arrangement. Although there was no suggestion of detriment other than of the type under discussion, their Lordships expressed regret[94] that no full argument based on promissory estoppel (*viz* the doctrine to which we refer as equitable forbearance) had been put to them.[95] Further, the fact that continued performance of an obligation represented a benefit to one party suggests that it was also capable of being a detriment to another party. **12.45**

[91] *Fraser Shipping Ltd v Colton* [1997] 1 Lloyd's Rep. 586 *per* Potter L.J. at 593 col 2 (no estoppel claim where the alleged act in reliance was the return of a deposit since the promisee was legally obliged to return it in any event). Contrast *Je Maintiendrai v Quaglia* [1980] 26 SASR 101 *per* White J. at 115. A tenant was having difficulties paying his rent under a 3 year lease. He and his landlord agreed that the rent would be reduced. The reduced rent was paid for some time after which the landlord demanded the arrears. It was held that the tenant had acted to his detriment. One of the reasons given by White J., at p. 115, was that the tenant had refrained from abandoning the premises and taken his chances on being sued for breach of covenant by the landlord. See also *Emery v UCB Bank Plc* (CA, interlocutory hearing, unrep. 1997) (paying increased sums under mortgage agreement to cover a proportion of arrears amounted to detrimental reliance).

[92] [1991] 1 QB 1, CA.

[93] *ibid.* 23a-c.

[94] [1991] 1 QB 1, CA at 13e-g and 17g.

[95] *ibid.* at 13e–g; it should be noted that the plaintiff would have had difficulty in relying on the equitable forbearance doctrine, not just because of the detriment problem adverted to, but also because it would involve using the doctrine aggressively in order to found a positive claim to the promised bonus — see para 12.61 below.

Secondly, there are circumstances in which performance of the reduced obligation almost certainly can amount to detriment. The most obvious is where the buyer and seller enter into a contract for a specific type of goods. The seller tenders non-contractual performance by offering goods which do not conform to specification and the buyer at first promises to accept those goods but then rejects them. If the seller can establish that it would have: (i) sold the goods if they had been rejected immediately; (ii) obtained other goods that complied with the contract; and (iii) in the period between the promise to accept and subsequent rejection, the open market value of the goods fell, it can demonstrate detriment.[96] **12.46**

That said, we would submit that it will be relatively difficult to establish detriment where the promisee simply refrains from breaching its contract for two reasons. First, most courts will be reluctant to hold that a party has suffered detriment by continuing with its bargain. This is consistent with the courts' view that a party that has made a bad bargain will nevertheless be held to it. Secondly, the facts required to establish detriment on the hypothesis, set out at paragraph 12.45, will rarely occur. **12.47**

The promisee alters its budget and expenditure

One of the prime objections to imposing a detriment requirement in equitable forbearance cases stems from the application of the doctrine to promises to forego the full contractual price agreed. As under the other four categories outlined above, while the promise is adhered to, it is clear that no detriment is incurred. When the promise is withdrawn, prejudice is suffered if the contract terms provide for penalties or forfeiture for late payment (see para. 12.42 above). In the absence of such terms, it is superficially hard to discern what detriment the promisee suffers; all that has happened is that its original obligation under the contract has been revived. **12.48**

This apparent absence of detriment can be answered in two ways. First, detriment will be suffered if the promisee has spent its money in a way it would not otherwise have done but for the reduced liability under the contract. If, for example, it has spent its perceived windfall in a one-off dividend to its shareholders, which it would not otherwise have **12.49**

---

[96] *Societe Italio-Belge v Palm & Vegetable Oils (Malaysia), The Post Chaser* [1982] 1 All ER 19 at 26d–e. See also *Bremer Handelsgesellschaft mbH v Vanden Avenne-Izegem* [1978] 2 Lloyd's Rep. 109, HL at 127, where the seller had spent time and money on appropriations which were later rejected by the buyers.

made, withdrawal of the promise would leave it open to an onerous and unexpected liability. That may be sufficient to effect a permanent bar to resumption of the original contractual position. The second, and more likely possibility, is that the promisee has merely rearranged its general day to day budget by, for example, committing itself to larger loan repayments or purchase contracts. Here, peremptory withdrawal of the concession may cause prejudice in the short-term only: income has been committed elsewhere and as a consequence there is insufficient cashflow to meet the demand. The previous contractual position may be reverted to, on giving the promisee reasonable time to make the necessary re-arrangements to its budget. Put simply, it must be given time to revert to the position that it was in, prior to the making of the promise in issue.[97] This seems to be the explanation for the application of the equitable forbearance doctrine in the *High Trees* case.[98] There, the landlord promised to accept a reduced rent for the demised premises for the duration of the war. The landlord was precluded from resiling from that promise without giving the tenant reasonable notice that it would do so.[99] It has been suggested that, given the realities of ordinary

[97] It is well established that spending money may amount to detrimental reliance for the purposes of estoppel by representation, and reference should be made to paras 8.98–101 for further discussion of the relevant principles. There is no reason to believe that the doctrines operate differently as far as this issue is concerned. There are obvious parallels with the defence of change of position in restitution, as to which see *Lipkin Gorman v Karpnale Ltd* [1992] 2 AC 548.

[98] *Central London Property Trust Ltd v High Trees House Ltd* [1947] KB 130, approved in *Smith v Lawson* [1997] EGCS 85 CA and *JT Sydenham & Co Ltd v Enichem Elastomers Ltd* [1989] EGLR 257 *per* H.H. Judge Leonard Bromley Q.C. at 260 col 1. Our explanation of the detriment present in *High Trees* cannot justify Denning J.'s obiter statement that the landlord could not have claimed the arrears due on past payments, even on giving reasonable notice (the arrears were not claimed in the case). Nor can it justify Judge Bromley's decision to deny such back payments when they actually were claimed in the similar case of *JT Sydenham & Co* (above). We suggest that both judges were wrong on this issue. See further at paras 12.52 and 12.57–9 below). The landlord should have been allowed to claim the arrears on giving the tenant reasonable time to re-arrange its affairs and on settling suitable terms for staggered repayment (compare *Je Maintiendrai v Quaglia* [1980] 26 SASR 101 above).

[99] We note that there was no express finding that the promisee had altered its position in any way other than in paying the reduced rent. The account of counsel's argument records the submission that the tenant 'had arranged its affairs on the basis of the reduced rent' *ibid.* at 133. Spencer Bower, at p. 393, identifies the detriment as the promisee's electing to remain as a tenant, liable for the albeit reduced rent. This ignores the fact that it was a 99 year lease; its terms may not have permitted a unilateral right of termination on the part of the tenant (in which case the analysis is open to the objection that the promisee is forced to assert that its failure to breach its legal obligations caused detriment — see paras 12.43–6 above). Assuming,

commercial practice, there will seldom be a case where a promise to accept partial payment will not lead to detriment in this latter sense,[1] but such arguments have by no means always met with a favourable reception.[2]

Other relevant factors in establishing inequitable conduct

As set out above, in establishing whether it would be inequitable to permit the promise to be peremptorily withdrawn, the courts are prepared to take into account a number of factors other than the detriment suffered by the promisee. Although the position is uncertain, it is submitted that, at best, the consideration of these factors amounting to 12.50

however, that the lease contained such termination right, a further fundamental problem rests on the fact that the tenant would have paid a considerable premium for a 99 year lease. Thus, 'staying on' as a tenant was the only way in which they could avoid forfeiting a valuable long term asset and could therefore hardly be viewed as detriment. An alternative view is that the tenant refrained from cutting its losses and assigning the lease (see Gordon, 'Creditor's Promises to Forego Rights' [1963] *CLJ* 222). That might be sufficient to give rise to detriment if the tenant could show that such an assignment was feasible in the difficult wartime conditions then prevailing. A similar argument was put in *Emery v UCB Bank Plc* (CA, interlocutory hearing, unrep. 1997) where borrowers agreed to continue to pay the sums coming due under a mortgage loan, together with a monthly sum to cover a proportion of the arrears. It was held that they had acted to their detriment in refraining from attempting to refinance their loan in reliance on a promise that the lender would not take steps to enforce its security while agreed level of payments were made. The point was left undecided. Had the landlord in *High Trees* sought possession of the premises on grounds of failure to pay the full rent, there is no doubt that detriment could have been shown. The tenant had acted on the promise in such a way as to leave it vulnerable to legal penalties; see further *Smith v Lawson* [1997] EGCS 85 CA and para. 12.40 above.

1 Gordon 'Creditor's Promises to Forego Rights' [1963] *CLJ* 222 and *Tool Metal Manufacturing Co v Tungsten Electric Co* (1950) 69 RPC 108 CA at 115–116 and (1954) 71 RPC 261 CA at 214. See also *Je Maintiendrai v Quaglia* [1980] 26 SASR 101 where a landlord had agreed to accept reduced payments under a 3 year lease. The arrangement continued until the difference between the amounts paid and the amounts due under the letter of the contract amounted to $2392. The landlord then demanded that this sum be paid immediately. It was held that detriment would be caused to the tenant if the landlord was allowed to demand all back payments as a single lump sum.

2 See *Amherst v James Walker Goldsmith & Silversmith* [1983] Ch 305, CA at 319 (where it was conceded that this doctrine could not apply because the tenants had suffered no prejudice as a result of the landlord's protracted delay in issuing rent review proceedings, but in fact had benefited from the use of the money in the interim); *James v Heim Galleries* (1980) 256 EG 819, CA at 822 and *Banner Industrial and Chemical Properties Ltd v Clark Patterson Ltd* [1990] 2 EGLR 139 at 140d–f.

inequitable conduct provides a superadded hurdle which must be satisfied *in addition* to the threshold detriment test. On this analysis, detriment is a necessary but not sufficient requirement for the doctrine to operate. However, we would question whether such an approach is desirable in regulating the concessions made by those in legal relationships. The relevant difficulties might be better dealt with using general legal principles such as duress and breach of contract.

Notwithstanding the above, the courts have suggested that they may take into account all the circumstances in assessing whether to allow the promise in issue to be withdrawn.[3] The following factors have been considered relevant: that the promisee's change of position conferred a benefit on the promisor;[4] that the parties are sophisticated commercial entities;[5] that one of the parties owed obligations to the public at large;[6] and that the promise at issue was extracted under duress.[7] The courts have also examined the general conduct of the parties. Therefore, it will not be inequitable to withdraw a promise if the promisee has failed to comply with its reduced obligations arising under the contract or other legal relationship.[8] Similarly, in *Ogilvy v Hope Davies,*[9] where the vendor of land had promised that it would not enforce its strict right to timeous completion, the fact that the vendor, itself, had been partially to blame for the purchaser's late completion (it had failed to supply relevant documents in good time) was taken into account. Finally, in *Williams v Stern,*[10] the plaintiff was entitled to seize the defendant's goods as a means of payment on a bill of sale. The plaintiff promised not to enforce his entitlement. When the plaintiff sought to resile from that promise, the Court took into account the fact that his decision was prompted by a landlord's threat to distrain against the same goods for arrears of rent. It should **12.51**

---

[3] *BP Explorations Ltd v Hunt (No. 2)* [1979] 1 WLR 783 at 810d-h affd on other grounds at [1983] AC 352; *Nippon Yusen v Pacifica Navegacion SA ('the Ion')* [1980] 2 Lloyd's Rep. 245 at 250 and *Marseille Fret SA v D. Oltman Schiffahrts GmbH & Co Ltd ('the Trado')* [1982] Lloyd's Rep. 157 at 160–1.

[4] *Morrow v Carty* [1957] NI 174 at 183.

[5] In *V. Berg and Son Ltd v Vanden Avenne-Izegem* [1977] Lloyd's Rep. 499, CA at 505, the court held that sophisticated commercial parties would rarely need the protection of equity, being unlikely to 'wilt' under the pressure of international trade.

[6] In *The Mayor and Burgesses of the London Borough of Southwark v Logan* [1996] 29 HLR 40 at 47, Neill J. took into account the housing obligations owed by the authority under this head.

[7] *D & C Builders v Rees* [1966] 2 QB 617, CA.

[8] *Re Selectmove* [1995] 1 WLR 474, CA at 539e.

[9] [1976] 1 All ER 683 at 688b–9a.

[10] (1879) 5 QBD 409, CA.

be noted that equitable forbearance cannot be used to undermine the effect of a statute or give a public authority a jurisdiction it would not otherwise have had.[11]

RELIEF

Suspensory or permanent effect of the doctrines

It has been frequently stated that equitable forbearance generally operates only to suspend temporarily,[12] rather than wholly to extinguish, rights. This is, however, incorrect as an absolute rule. There are occasions when the relief granted is permanent. Some uncertainty surrounds the principles which determine whether the forbearance will operate permanently or temporarily. Few difficulties arise where the forbearance is expressed from the outset to be temporary since it is clear that the maximum extent of relief available is constrained by the terms of the forbearance made. If the forbearance itself was expressly or impliedly temporary, the resumption of the original contractual position will always be possible. In, for example, *Central London Property Trust Ltd v High Trees House Ltd*,[13] the tenant of High Trees House was having difficulty meeting the rent due under the lease because most of the flats in the building were empty as a result of the war. The landlord promised that, for so long as wartime conditions lasted, it was prepared to accept a reduced rent for the property. There was no doubt that the landlord was justified in demanding the full rent once those conditions had ceased. In cases where the forbearance is not so limited, two different methods of selecting between permanent and temporary relief have been suggested in the cases. **12.52**

---

[11] *Secretary of State for Employment v Globe Elastic Thread Co Ltd* [1980] AC 506. The principles governing equitable forbearance and estoppel by representation are the same in this area. Hence reference should be made to paras 8.121–5 above for further detail.

[12] *Societe Italio-Belge v Palm & Vegetable Oils (Malaysia), The Post Chaser* [1982] 1 All ER 19 at 27a–d; *The Kanchenjunga* [1990] 1 Lloyd's Rep. 391, HL at 399; *The 'Superhulls Cover' Case (No. 2)* [1990] 2 Lloyd's Rep. 431 at 449; *'The Chemical Venture'* [1993] 1 Lloyd's Rep. 509 at 521 and *Alma Shipping Corporation v Union of India ('The Astraea')* [1971] 2 Lloyd's Rep. 494 at 502.

[13] [1947] KB 130. See also *Ledingham v Bermejo Estancia Co Ltd* [1947] 1 All ER 749.

The terms of the forbearance

One view is that whether the promise is revocable will depend on its terms. Thus, the effect of the doctrine is the automatic enforcement of the promise to forbear.[14] When the cases are analysed two points arise. First, the cases where the doctrine operated to suspend rights generally concerned promises which were either expressly or impliedly limited in time or where no provision was made for the duration of the forbearance.[15] Thus such cases are consistent with the view advanced. There seems to have been no case where the forbearance was overtly expressed to be permanent but has operated only temporarily. Secondly, there are cases where it is difficult to understand why the doctrine operated permanently, since the promisee could seemingly have been restored to its original position (and detriment thereby averted) by some means other than the extinction of rights.[16] Thus these cases are inconsistent with the alternative remedial approach explained below and seem explicable only on the basis that the terms of the forbearance determine the remedial effects of the doctrine. However, this view characterizes equitable forbearance as a substitute for consideration. As such, it leads to the automatic enforcement of promises unsupported by consideration and to a stark and fundamental conflict with established contract principles. This is particularly so where the forbearance concerns a debt. In those **12.53**

---

[14] *D & C Builders v Rees* [1966] 2 QB 617, CA (*dicta*) *per* Lord Denning at 625a–c; *Smith v Lawson* [1997] EGCS 85 CA (*dicta per* Balcombe L.J.), *Meng Long Development pte v Jip Hong Trading Pte PC* [1985] AC 511 PC Hong Kong *per* Lord Templeman at 524 (*dicta*); Jackson 'Estoppel as a Sword Part 2' (1965) 81 *LQR* 223; Atiyah 'Consideration and Estoppel: the Thawing of the Ice' (1974) 38 *MLR* 65 *cf.* section 90(1) of the American Restatement, Second, Contracts.

[15] See, for example, *Charles Rickards Ltd v Oppenhaim* [1950] KB 616, CA; *Tool Metal Manufacturing Co v Tungsten Electric Co* [1955] 1 WLR 761, HL; *JT Sydenham & Co Ltd v Enichem Elastomers Ltd* [1989] EGLR 257 and *Je Maintiendrai v Quaglia* [1980] 26 SASR 101. In *Central London Property Trust Ltd v High Trees House Ltd* [1947] KB 130 Denning J. made the obiter assertion that the landlord could not have claimed the arrears on giving reasonable notice *i.e.* the right to the shortfall was permanently extinguished, albeit that the landlord could return to demanding the contractual rate in respect of future payments. There are doubts as to what, if any detriment was suffered by the tenant. The only detriment suffered is discussed at para. 12.47–8 above (where the facts are also set out) but it is difficult to see why this should justify permanent extinction of the landlord's rights. See further at paras 12.57–9 below. In *D & C Builders v Rees* [1966] 2 QB 617, CA itself, resumption of the original contractual position was permitted but on the grounds that the concession was extracted by duress and not because of any limitation on the scope of remedial relief available under the equitable forbearance doctrine.

[16] *e.g. W. J. Alan & Co Ltd. v. El Nasr Export and Import Co* [1972] 2 QB 189, CA.

cases, the above approach conflicts with the principle of *Foakes v Beer,*[17] that part payment can never provide good discharge for the whole sum.

Restoration of the promisee to its original position: Prevention of detriment

The second view was set out in *Ajayi v RT Briscoe (Nigeria) Ltd.*[18] There, the Privy Council linked the principle governing the choice of relief to the way in which the promisee has changed its position in reliance on the promise: **12.54**

> . . . when one party to a contract in the absence of fresh consideration agrees not to enforce his rights an equity will be raised in favour of the other party. This equity is, however, subject to the qualifications that (1) the other party has altered his position; (2) that the promisor can resile from his promise on giving reasonable notice which need not be formal notice, giving the promisee reasonable opportunity of resuming his position; and (3) the promise only becomes final and irrevocable if the promisee cannot resume his position.[19]

Therefore, if it is possible for the promisee to resume its previous position, the doctrine will suspend the promisor's rights rather than wholly preclude their enforcement; the suspension will operate so as to give the promisee a reasonable period in which to resume its previous position. In *Hughes v Metropolitan Railway Company,*[20] there was no question of the tenant's being released from its obligation to perform the repairs; the effect of the doctrine was merely to give it a reasonable time to

---

[17] (1884) 9 App Cas 605. The first case where the equitable forbearance doctrine was applied to a promise to accept part payment was *Central London Property Trust v High Trees House* [1947] KB 130 at 135. Denning J. there considered that *Foakes v Beer* was no impediment to the application of the doctrine for two reasons. Firstly, the doctrine was simply not considered in *Foakes*. However, the doctrine had supposedly emerged only seven years beforehand in *Hughes v Metropolitan Railway* (1877) 2 App Cas 439. One would expect the House of Lords to have been aware of its existence and relevance. Secondly, the '*fusion of law and equity*' meant that part payment could now amount to good discharge of a debt. There is no reason to suggest the fusion of the administration of the two jurisdictions should have had any such effect, particularly since the *Foakes* principle was recognized in equity as well as common law. Further *Foakes* actually postdated the Judicature Act of 1975. See further Cartwright 'Extinguishment of Contractual Obligations by Estoppel: High Trees Again' [1990] *CLJ* 13.

[18] [1964] 1 WLR 1326, PC at 1331.

[19] [1964] 1 WLR 1326, PC at 1331.

[20] (1877) 2 App Cas 614. See also *Charles Rickards Ltd v Oppenhaim* [1950] KB 616, CA. See further at paras 12.16 and 12.41 on Hughes.

complete them; thus the tenant was returned to the position that it was in prior to the making of the promise. The third limb of the *Ajayi* test may be illustrated by *'The Chemical Venture'*[21] where the ship owners promised not to enforce their right to object to the charterers docking in an unsafe port. The charterers took the ship into the relevant port where it was damaged as a result of the Iran/Iraq war; the owners permanently lost their right to damages because it was impossible to restore the charterers to their previous position and their detriment could not be reversed. The clock could not be wound back to allow the charterers to take a different decision and proceed to an alternative port. Even if it is possible to restore the promisee to its previous position, the effect of equitable forbearance may be permanent if it would be inequitable to allow the promise to be withdrawn, even on notice.[22]

The relief available is not confined solely to simple choice between suspension or extinction of rights. Thus, in *Brikom Investments v Seaford*,[23] the rent for a statutory protected tenancy was assessed on the basis that the landlord was responsible for repairs. In fact, the lease placed the obligation on the tenant. However, the landlord accepted the rent as assessed (which was greater than that which would have been due had it been appraised on the correct basis). The landlord was permitted to enforce the repairing covenant on giving notice, *but only after* reverting to a proper rent and refunding the past overpayments. Hence, withdrawal of the implied promise was permitted on terms that ensured that the parties were restored to their previous position and that the tenant suffered no prejudice as a result. 12.55

Which view is correct?

Arguably, *Ajayi*'s emphasis on restoration of the original position, is designed to ensure that the promisee suffers no detriment or injustice as 12.56

---

[21] [1993] 1 Lloyd's Rep. 509. In *Ogilvy v Hope Davies* [1976] 1 All ER 683, a vendor promised not to enforce its right to prompt completion; it was prevented from claiming interest on the period of the delayed completion. See also *Nippon Yusen v Pacifica Navegacion SA ('the Ion')* [1980] 2 Lloyd's Rep. 245, CA, where the change of position amounted to allowing a limitation period to elapse; the court thought it most unlikely that the promisee would be granted leave to serve out of time. *Birmingham & District Land Co v London & North Western Rail Co* (1888) 40 ChD 268 and *Bank Negara Indonesia v Philip Hoalim* [1973]2 MLJ 3, PC.

[22] This is seemingly the explanation for *Maharaj v Chand* [1986] AC 898, PC but arguably, it would have been sufficient there to refund the sums spent in reliance on the promise rather than give permanent effect to the forbearance.

[23] [1981] 1 WLR 863, CA; it is not completely clear whether the case was decided on the basis of estoppel by representation or equitable forbearance but it is suggested that it is capable of analysis on either ground.

a result of its change of position.[24] In *Hughes*, this result was secured by suspension of rights, in the *Chemical Venture* by permanent confiscation and in *Brikom v Seaford* by allowing enforcement on terms. There is no need or justification for going beyond this measure of relief. In some cases, the only, or only practical, way in which to effect this result is by enforcing the promise[25] but this is by no means always the case, as is illustrated above. This approach has two advantages. First, it links the remedy with the factors which trigger the operation of the doctrine, namely the change of position of the promisee and the potential detriment.[26] Secondly, it minimises, although does not wholly eliminate the conflict with the law of contract, discussed above.

However, as set out above, there are a number of cases which are difficult to reconcile with this approach. It has, however, been more firmly established as the guiding principle in proprietary estoppel by such cases as *Crabb v Arun District Council*[27] with its emphasis on discerning the 'minimum equity' to do justice. A very similar approach to equitable forbearance was taken in *Roebuck v Mongovin*,[28] where the flexibility of the court's remedial discretion was emphasized. It was alleged that the defendant was prevented from applying to strike out the claim for want of prosecution, on the grounds that it had represented that it did not intend so to do. As a consequence, the plaintiff had incurred some additional legal costs in connection with the claim. Lord Browne-Wilkinson, referring to the doctrine in issue as equitable estoppel, held as follows:[29] **12.57**

> Assuming, for present purposes, that the defendant's conduct does raise such an equitable estoppel (which I think doubtful), such equitable

---

[24] *cf.* the approach of the Australian High Court in *Waltons Stores (Interstate) Ltd v Maher* [1988] 164 CLR 387 and *Commonwealth of Australia v Verwayen* [1990] 170 CLR 394. See also paras 11.31–3 for further discussion of this principle in the context of proprietary estoppel.

[25] A possible example of this is *Brikom Investments Ltd v Carr* [1979] QB 467, CA, which concerned a landlord's promise not to enforce a covenant obliging the tenants to contribute towards roof repairs; an equitable forbearance was established because the tenants and their assignees had entered into the leases in reliance on the forbearance. There was no suggestion that the landlord could revive the tenant's obligation to repair. Permanent extinction or the landlord's rights was the only practical way to avoid prejudice to the tenants and assignees; requiring the landlord to repurchase the leases would be financially onerous and presumably unacceptable to the tenants and assignees.

[26] See para. 12.33 ff.

[27] [1976] Ch 179. See further at paras 11.50–4 above.

[28] [1994] 1 All ER 568, HL at 575d–f.

[29] [1994] 1 All ER 568, HL at 575c–g.

estoppel would not impose an automatic legal bar to obtaining a striking out order. The effect of such an estoppel is to give the court power to do what is equitable in all the circumstances. In *Crabb v Arun District Council* [1976] Ch. 179 the Court of Appeal emphasized that the nature of the relief to be given when an equitable estoppel is raised is extremely flexible. If an equitable estoppel is raised the court's function is to determine what, if anything, is necessary to satisfy that equity in all the circumstances of the case. That is a far cry from saying that, where a defendant has led the plaintiff to incur some additional expense, he is therefore in all circumstances prevented from relying on inexcusable delay by the plaintiff which has seriously prejudiced him. If on the assumption made, the defendant is equitably estopped, then the effect of that estoppel would be to give the court a discretion whether or not to strike out the action (possibly upon terms) depending upon the balance between the harm done to the defendant by the plaintiff's delay and the expense or other detriment incurred by the plaintiff by reason of the defendant's representation.

Payment by instalments

The issue of whether equitable forbearance suspends or eradicates rights **12.58**
is particularly acute where the forbearance of the right to receive periodic payments is concerned. In *Tool Metal Manufacturing Co v Tungsten Electric Co,*[30] Tool Metal was the holder of various patents licensed to the manufacturer, TECO. The contract provided for various fees including a monthly compensation payment. Tool Metal promised to forego their right to this latter fee, pending negotiations for a new contract. Equitable forbearance suspended that right and Tool Metal successfully claimed the compensation payments which had become due, *after* the expiry of the period of reasonable notice. They made no claim to those fees which had accrued during the period of suspension. The question to which no clear answer was given was whether, after giving reasonable notice, Tool Metal could have claimed those back payments. There is *obiter dictum* by Lord Denning, asserting that they could not have done so.[31]

There seems little doubt that if the doctrine only suspends the right **12.59**
to full payment, then the arrears can be claimed as soon as reasonable

[30] [1955] 1 WLR 761.

[31] *Central London Property Trust Ltd v High Trees House Ltd* [1947] KB 130 and *Lyle-Meller v A Lewis & Co* [1956] 1 WLR 29, CA. See also *JT Sydenham & Co Ltd v Enichem Elastomers Ltd* [1989] EGLR 257 and *Je Maintiendrai v Quaglia* [1980] 26 SASR 101.

notice has been given. To deny the claim would be to entail the permanent confiscation of the contractual right to receive full payment during the period of suspension. The position is even clearer where the forbearance concerns the level of instalment payments, rather than[32] a recurring right to receive one-off payments. If the obligation to pay a lump sum is suspended, it is clear that its entirety can be claimed on giving notice. By contrast, if Lord Denning's view is correct, the debtor who is paying reduced sums will be excused forever from meeting at least part of the debt and will therefore be treated more favourably. As Treitel[33] points out, there is no clear reason why such a debtor should receive favourable treatment. It follows that to establish a permanent defence to the claim for arrears, the promisee will have to demonstrate the irreversible or significant change of position necessary to give the equitable doctrine permanent effect.

This difficulty becomes less acute once the remedial flexibility of the equitable forbearance doctrine is appreciated.[34] The court is then not confined to the simple choice between the suspension of rights and their permanent extinction and arguably, the remedy granted will be the minimum necessary to ensure that the promisee suffers no detriment as a result of withdrawal of the promise. Whether back payments are recoverable will depend on the way in which the promisee changed its position in reliance on the forbearance. In most cases, the promisee will merely have altered its day to day budget to take account of the reduced liability; in this situation, all that will be necessary to avoid detriment and restore the promisee to its previous position, is time to re-arrange its finances to take account of the increased liability. Hence, there is no reason why arrears may not be claimed after reasonable notice. **12.60**

Revocation

In many cases the forbearance may be revoked by the promisor, on giving reasonable notice. What period is 'reasonable' is a question of fact for the judge at first instance[35] and in *Tool Metal Manufacturing Co v Tungsten Electric Co*,[36] the House of Lords warned against introducing technical requirements in this area. Consequently, there are no specific **12.61**

32 As in *Tool Metal*.
33 Treitel 1 at p. 122.
34 See para. 12.54 above.
35 *Charles Rickards Ltd v Oppenhaim* [1950] KB 616, CA at 624.
36 [1955] 1 WLR 761, HL at 785.

rules as to the manner or form[37] in which notice must be given and all the circumstances of the case may be taken into account in assessing whether a the notice given is valid and of sufficient duration.[38] Further, it may not even be necessary to give express notice where the concession was originally linked to the continued existence of a particular state of affairs. Such a concession may terminate spontaneously on the cessation of that state of affairs.[39] In other cases, it is necessary for the promisor to intimate to the promisee that it no longer intends or considers itself bound by the forbearance.[40] Sometimes it will be appropriate to specify a date on which the original contractual position is to be resumed but this is not always necessary; it may be sufficient merely to refrain from enforcement for a reasonable period after the intimation is given.[41]

SCOPE OF EQUITABLE FORBEARANCE

The doctrine of equitable forbearance cannot be used to create new obligations. Its ambit is restricted to promises to forego existing rights and it does not extend to promises to create new ones. Hence, if X promises to pay Y £100, Y cannot sue X on the promise even if it has relied on the promise to its detriment. By way of contrast, where a landlord promises not to enforce the tenant's repairing obligation under a lease; if the tenant relies on this promise to its detriment, the doctrine may provide a defence to the landlord's action for breach of covenant and forfeiture. If, however, the landlord went further in its kindness towards the tenant and promised to perform the repairs itself, the tenant will not be able to insist that they are carried out.[42] This proposition was first clearly established in *Combe v Combe*.[43] The court there emphasized that to allow equitable forbearance to be used aggressively to create rights would be to undermine established contract law principles by enabling promises unsupported by 12.62

37 *Ajayi v RT Briscoe (Nigeria) Ltd* [1964] 1 WLR 1326, PC at 1331.
38 *Tool Metal Manufacturing Co v Tungsten Electric Co* [1955] 1 WLR 761, HL at 765, 785.
39 *ibid.* at 785.
40 *ibid.*
41 *Tool Metal Manufacturing Co v Tungsten Electric Co* [1955] 1 WLR 761, HL at 765.
42 Although the tenant's defence to the landlord's action will be as effective here as under example one, assuming the other elements of equitable forbearance are made out.
43 [1951] 2 KB 215, CA.

consideration to be enforced.[44] The *Combe* proposition has been the subject of significant controversy,[45] but in our view, it still represents the current law and has been frequently approved.[46]

The *Combe* principle is commonly said to have the effect that equitable forbearance may be used only as defence[47] and not as a cause of action,[48] that it can be used as a shield but not as a sword. As Lord Justice Ormrod held in *Brikom Investments v Seaford,*[49] however, '*swords with a little ingenuity can be beaten into shields or shields into swords*'. Chitty points out[50] that it is legitimate to apply the doctrine to deprive a party of a defence it would otherwise have had to have an independently existing cause of action based on a pre-existing legal right. For example, if the promisor undertakes not to rely on a time bar, and the requisite detrimental reliance is **12.63**

---

[44] See also *Brikom Investments Ltd v Carr* [1979] QB 467, CA at 486, where Roskill L.J. was concerned to ensure that the doctrine of consideration was not abolished by the back door; compare *Syros Shipping Co SA v Elaghill Trading Co ('The Proodos C')* [1980] 2 Lloyd's Rep. 390.

[45] See, for example, *Re Wyvern Developments* [1974] 1 WLR 1097 and *Evenden v Guildford City Association Football Club* [1975] QB 917, where the *Combe* principle was contravened. In the former case, there was a binding contractual obligation in any event and there was no need to rely on equitable forbearance. The latter case was overruled in *Secretary of State for Employment v Globe Elastic Thread Co Ltd* [1980] AC 506 where Lord Wilberforce held, at 518, that to apply estoppel in the case was to turn the concept on its head. See also *Fenner v Blake* [1900] 1 QB 426. In Australia the principle does not apply: *Waltons Stores (Interstate) Ltd v Maher* [1988] 164 CLR 387.

[46] See cases cited at para. 12.62 nn. 47 and 48 below; see also the Privy Council's support of the doctrine in *Bank Negara Indonesia v Philip Hoalim* [1973] 2 MLJ 3, PC. and those cases which insist on the presence of a pre-existing legal relationship cited at para. 12.10 above, n. 18.

[47] *Lark v Outhwaite* [1991] 2 Lloyd's Rep. 132 at 141–2; *Syros Shipping Co SA v Elaghill Trading Co ('The Proodos C')* [1980] 2 Lloyd's Rep. 390; *Lyle-Meller v A Lewis & Co* [1956] 1 WLR 29, CA *per* Lord Denning M.R. at 36; *James v Heim Galleries* (1980) 256 EG 819, CA at 821; *Morrow v Carty* [1957] NI 174; *Beesly v Hallwood Estates Ltd* [1960] 2 All ER 314 at 324 (aff. on other grounds at [1961] 1 Ch 105 CA), *JT Developments v Quinn* (1991) 62 P&CR 33 CA at *per* Ralph Gibson L.J. at 45; *Argy Trading Co Ltd v Lapid Developments Ltd* [1977] 1 WLR 444 at 457a–e and *Brikom Investments v Seaford* [1981] 1 WLR 863 CA at 868h–869b–d. See also Spencer Bower at pp. 385–8 and *Amalgamated Investment & Property Co. Ltd, (in liquidation) v Texas Commerce International Bank Ltd* [1982] 1 QB 84 at 105.

[48] If the doctrine affords a valid defence then it may be used positively to support a claim for an injunction to prevent seizure of assets to meet the claim — see Chitty at para. 3–76.

[49] [1981] 1 WLR 863, CA at 896b–g, where his Lordship admitted that the doctrine was being used as a shield with a sharp edge but 'a shield none the less'.

[50] At para. 3.076.

established,[51] the doctrine may operate to enable a cause of action to succeed which would otherwise fail. However, Chitty also points out that the forbearance doctrine may not be used to rebut a defence that the promise in issue was not supported by consideration, for this would breach the *Combe* principle.

However, several contrary arguments can be advanced which support the contention that equitable forbearance can generate new rights. First, there are significant difficulties in limiting the concept of the 'pre-existing legal right'. The distinction posited by Chitty and described above has not always been adhered to in the authorities. Thus, in *Pacol Ltd v Trade Lines Ltd ('the Henrik Sif')*,[52] the plaintiffs were the holders of a bill of lading that mistakenly thought that the defendants were parties to the bill and potentially liable on it but in fact they were not. The plaintiff obtained various extensions of time for service of proceedings from the defendants. Mr Justice Webster rejected the defence that the charterers could not be sued on the bill because they were not a party to it. The decision was based on a number of grounds, including that of equitable forbearance. Mr Justice Webster held that the charterers had a legal right to assert that they were not a party to the bill of lading. It was this legal right that the charterers had impliedly promised to forego as a result of their conduct in granting time extensions. Therefore, the court could and did contend that there was the loss of a pre-existing right. 12.64

In *The Henrik Sif* the court appears to be complying with the rule in *Combe v Combe* by finding a pre-existing right which has been foregone. However, on analysis, it is artificial to construct a legal right that permits a party to object that it is not a party to a contract. It follows that the court was in fact using the concept of the 'pre-existing legal right' as a convenient fiction to achieve the result required by the merits, namely the grant of a positive right to sue the defendants on a promise unsupported by consideration. Therefore, *The Henrik Sif* would apparently undermine *Combe v Combe*. We would suggest that *The Henrik Sif* does not in fact undermine *Combe v Combe*. Although the decision was based on a number of grounds, 12.65

[51] *Cooperative Wholesale Society v Chester le Streei District Council*, Lands Tribunal, (1997) 73 P&CR 111.

[52] [1982] 1 Lloyd's Rep. 456. See also *Janred Properties Ltd v ENIT* [1989] 2 All ER 444.

it is clear that the court based its conclusion primarily on estoppel by convention[53] and any statement as to the role of equitable forbearance was therefore *obiter*.[54]

12.66 Secondly, there is authority which suggests that estoppel by representation or convention can create new contractual rights. There are a number of cases where the 'fact' which the representor is estopped from asserting is that no binding contract exists between the parties. Thus, in *Amalgamated Investment & Property Co. Ltd, (in liquidation) v Texas Commerce International Bank Ltd,*[55] the guarantor of loan was prevented from denying that a particular liability (that of its subsidiary) was caught by the loan, all parties having acted on the assumption that the loan was covered by the guarantee. As discussed elsewhere, there are two approaches to the case. First, the estoppel did not give rise to the cause of action. The cause of action flowed from the court's decision as to facts established by the estoppel; that there was a contract of guarantee which covered the loan in issue.[56]. The criticism of this approach is that '*If it is a question of fact whether or not one is legally bound to another, then the maxim that equity is only a shield is meaningless*'.[57] Secondly, *Texas Bank* was a case concerning estoppel by convention which can in reality, although not as a matter of analysis, act as a 'sharp-edged shield'.[58] The fact that detrimental reliance is common to both doctrines is not a sufficient basis, either as a matter of logic or principle, to suggest that equitable forbearance and estoppel by convention are one and the same doctrines, having the same effect. We would therefore suggest that the fact that estoppel by convention can act as a sharp-edged shield does not mean that equitable forbearance can act in a similar way.

---

53 See *Estoppel by Convention* at para. 9.05.

54 A similar logic was adopted in *Hiscox v Outhwaite (No. 3)* [1991] 2 Lloyd's Rep. 524 *per* Evans J. at 534–5. As we have suggested elsewhere (*Estoppel by Convention* at para. 9.05), *Hiscox* was also a case, in our view, turning on estoppel by convention.

55 [1982] 1 QB 84. See also *J.F. Perrott v Cohen* [1951] 1 KB 705 CA; *Harnam Singh v Jamal Pirbhai* [1951] AC 688 at 699; *Farrow v Orttewell* [1943] Ch 480; *Lyle-Meller v A Lewis & Co* [1956] 1 WLR 29 CA; *Robertson v Minister of Pensions* [1949] 1 KB 227 and generally *Estoppel by Representation* at paras 8.28–30.

56 *Amalgamated Investment & Property Co. Ltd, (in liquidation) v Texas Commerce International Bank Ltd* [1982] 1 QB 84 *per* Brandon L.J. at 131–2.

57 Thompson 'From Representation to Expectation: Estoppel as a Cause of Action' [1983] *CLJ* 257 at 274. See further, paras 8.09 and 8.30–3 above for the difficulties encountered in distinguishing representations of fact from promises as to future intention.

58 See *Estoppel by Convention* at para. 9.05 ff.

Thirdly, an analogy may be drawn with proprietary estoppel. It is clear that proprietary estoppel can be used aggressively to transfer rights. The difference in the spheres of operation of the two doctrines is that proprietary estoppel concerns promises[59] that property rights will be foregone whereas equitable forbearance concerns promises to forego contractual rights. It might be thought to be somewhat arbitrary or formalistic to differentiate between these two types of promises. There would seem to be little substantive or juristic difference between contractual and property rights,[60] particularly where they co-exist. Further, there is authority in the proprietary estoppel sphere to suggest that the courts will not permit the assertion of strict legal rights where this would be unconscionable having regard to detrimental reliance on the part the person against whom it is sought to assert them.[61] These authorities have, on occasion, formed the basis of *obiter dicta* in spheres outside those involving property.[62] If there is such an all embracing principle, it would certainly be capable of subsuming equitable forbearance altogether, given the similarity between the components of the two doctrines. Whilst there may be attractions to the creation of such an all embracing doctrine, we would suggest that: (i) it is reasonably clear on the authorities that the property qualification still constrains the scope of aggressive estoppel doctrine; (ii) proprietary estoppel and equitable forbearance are separate and distinct doctrines; and (iii) an analogy with proprietary estoppel cannot assist in assessing the effect of equitable forbearance. In any event, arguably neither doctrine creates new rights, they merely deprive the promisor of pre-existing rights. The effect of such a deprivation in property cases, incidentally involves the vesting of those property rights in the promisee.[63] **12.67**

---

59 The doctrine actually extends beyond the scope of promises to cover acquiescence or encouragement mistakes made by another party but the promissory head of liability is closest to the operation of equitable forbearance. See paras 11.07–15 above.

60 See, further, paras 11.96–101. In *Crabb v Arun DC* [1976] Ch 179 at 193b, Lord Scarman asserted that it was not useful to divide estoppel into the different categories of proprietary and promissory estoppel. This approach is also supported by those cases which suggest that there is a single overarching doctrine covering all estoppels including equitable forbearance, as to which see para. 8.07 above.

61 See para. 11.97.

62 See the authorities cited at 11.98 and 12.65.

63 See para. 11.87, 11.97–9 and 11.115–7 above and *Dun & Bradstreet Software Services (England) Ltd v Provident Mutual Life Assurance Association* [1997] EGCS 89 CA, lexis transcript where Peter Gibson L.J. held that *dicta* in the '*different context of a proprietary estoppel case*' (*Taylors Fashions Ltd v Liverpool Victoria Trustees Co Ltd* [1982] 1 QB 133) could not have been intended to undermine the established requirements of promissory estoppel.

Fourthly, an argument can be constructed using *Waltons Stores (Interstate) Ltd v Maher*.[64] In this case, the Australian High Court averred that it was arbitrary to differentiate between promises to vary existing rights and promises to create new ones. Consequently the court held that it was no longer necessary to show a pre-existing legal relationship. However, under English law, distinctions are still drawn between the creation and modification of obligations. Thus, for example, the doctrine of consideration is still a formidable force in the creation of obligations and rights,[65] whereas its impact on the modification of rights may have been somewhat restricted.[66] Similarly, the law recognizes a substantive difference between restricting the obligations or rights of a party and imposing new and positive obligations on it.[67] Equitable forbearance is concerned only with the modification of obligations, being analogous to waiver where there is insufficient knowledge for the orthodox form of that doctrine to operate. It is therefore appropriate to limit its effect to the restriction of a party's rights. **12.68**

EFFECT OF EQUITABLE FORBEARANCE ON THIRD PARTIES

ASSIGNMENT OF THE CONTRACT

There is a dearth of authority on the impact of equitable forbearance on assignment. In the case of a simple contract, that does not concern **12.69**

[64] [1988] 164 CLR 387.

[65] In *Waltons Stores (Interstate) Ltd v Maher* [1988] 164 CLR 387 and *Commonwealth of Australia v Verwayen* [1990] 170 CLR 394, it was emphasized that the conflict with the consideration rule did not have to be addressed by restricting the doctrine to a defensive role. An alternative means of avoiding direct conflict was by restricting the remedy available under the equitable doctrine. The aim of the remedy was not to enforce the relevant promise in every case (although this might sometimes be appropriate) but restricted to the minimum necessary to avoid detriment to the promisee. This approach is arguably consistent with the remedies available under the English version of equitable forbearance (see para. 12.55) and therefore this is a line of development which is clearly open in this jurisdiction.

[66] *Syros Shipping Co SA v Elaghill Trading Co ('The Proodos C')* [1980] 2 Lloyd's Rep. 390 at 391–2 and *Combe v Combe* [1951] 2 KB 215, CA.

[67] *Combe v Combe* [1951] 2 KB 215 CA *per* Lord Denning at 219, '*The Proodos C*' [1980] 2 Lloyd's Rep. 390 *per* Lloyd J. at 392 col 1, *Hiscox v Outhwaite (No. 3)* [1991] 2 Lloyd's Rep. 524 *per* Evans J. at 534 col 1.

land, there seems to be no reason why assignment should not pass on the rights and obligations, as qualified by the forbearance. In cases where the doctrine operates, the promisor has, by its conduct, reduced its rights under the contract and it is difficult to see why their scope should be re-enlarged if the promisor transfers them to a third party.[68] Similarly, the promisee may be able to pass on the benefits it has obtained as a result of the equitable forbearance doctrine, although it might be sensible to assign those benefits specifically, in addition to the general rights under the contract.[69]

Transfer of Land

Where the contract concerns land, the position is more complicated, as sophisticated rules have emerged to govern which rights and obligations may pass with the transfer of land. It is most unlikely that the equitable forbearance is capable of vesting a property right in the promisee capable of binding third parties purchasing the property that is the subject matter of the agreement. Any benefit generated by equitable forbearance is insufficient to give rise to an overriding interest under section 70(1)(g) of the Land Registration Act 1925, even where the promisee is in actual occupation of the land concerning which the relevant contract was made.[70] **12.70**

There is some authority to suggest, however, that once the components of equitable forbearance are made out, the concession made may bind a party purchasing from the promisor, at least where it had express notice of the concession. In *Birmingham & District Land Co v London & North Western Rail Co*,[71] the plaintiff was in occupation of land under a building lease. The terms of the agreement provided that the lease was to terminate on 30 November 1885 if the works had not been completed. It became apparent that the defendant might be granted a statutory right to build a railway, which would have a material impact on the building **12.71**

---

68 *Re Wickam* (1917) 34 TLR 158.

69 We reach the same conclusion where waiver is concerned — see *Waiver — Complexities* at para. 5.09 ff.

70 *Canadian Imperial Bank of Commerce v Bello* (1992) 64 P&CR 48, CA at 52. In *Beesly v Hallwood Estates Ltd* [1960] 2 All ER 314 at 324 (aff. on other grounds at [1961] 1 Ch 105 CA), it was held that the doctrine could not be used to render enforceable, a land charge void for want of registration or to negative operation of a statute; compare the principles discussed at paras 8.121–5 above and see *per contra. Maharaj v Chand* [1986] AC 898 PC.

71 (1888) 40 ChD 268.

scheme proposed. As a consequence, the landlord, B, told the plaintiff not to start the works until it was clear whether the railway scheme was going to go ahead. The plaintiff accordingly refrained from commencing the works; B sold the part of the land to the defendant, expressly and clearly subject to the plaintiff's rights. The defendant was held to be bound by the forbearance made by its predecessor in title with the result that the plaintiff still had a valid and subsisting lease despite the fact that the time for completion of the works had elapsed. This case may not be very strong authority on the durability of benefits generated by the equitable doctrine. Given the emphasis on the clear notice given to the purchaser, it may well be an instance where the purchaser's conduct was such as to give rise to a constructive trust; such trusts may arise where a purchaser takes expressly and positively subject to the rights of a third party; the obligation arises from the purchaser's conduct rather than as a result of any inherent durability of the third party rights.[72] Alternatively, the case could be analysed as one of proprietary estoppel, which appears to be able to generate rights capable of binding third parties.[73]

Similarly, in *Brikom Investments Ltd v Carr*,[74] the occupiers of a **12.72** building were negotiating with the owners with a view to entering into long leases of the flats it contained. The occupiers were concerned about the obligation to contribute to roof repairs contained in the lease and the owners promised that they would not enforce this provision.[75] As a result, the occupiers were induced to enter the leases; some later assigned their leases. With happy disregard for several hundred years of learning as which rights and obligations pass with the assignment of tenancies, the Court of Appeal held that the equitable doctrine operated to protect both the original tenants and the assignees.[76] *Brikom* could therefore be relied on in theory as authority for the proposition that an equitable forbearance can pass with land. However, given the failure to assess the previous authorities, the case must be questionable, providing only weak authority for this propositon.

[72] *Ashburn Anstalt v Arnold* [1988] 2 WLR 706.

[73] See paras 11.73–83.

[74] [1979] QB 467, CA.

[75] It hoped to obtain planning permission to extend the building upwards which would obviously have involved extensive works on the roof anyway.

[76] Treitel 1 explains the case, at p. 123, as an instance where the collateral contract with the original tenants sufficed to vary the terms of the lease permanently; the old terms could not be revived by transfer of the tenancies.

FORMALITY

Equitable forbearance may affect the legal relationship between the parties without the execution of formal documentation. The promise or representation that strict legal rights will not be enforced probably does not need to comply with the formalities required for the main contract. Thus, an equitable forbearance as to the terms of lease of over three years or the sale of freehold property need not be in writing[77] whereas a contract to create or transfer such property rights must be in writing.[78] It would appear that the injustice of allowing inequitable departure from the promise made outweighs the need for formality. The equitable forbearance doctrine operates outwith the contract and is not constrained by the applicable formality rules.[79] **12.73**

[77] The facts of *Brikom Investments Ltd v Carr* [1979] QB 467, CA are set out above; some of the occupiers were given oral assurances and some were given written ones. Admittedly, the case was decided under s. 40 of the Law of Property Act 1925, which required only that the contract be evidenced in writing; various memoranda were circulated which could probably have satisfied this section; their Lordships might, however, have been expected to comment on the formality issue if it had been deemed necessary to comply with s. 40. See also *Central London Property Trust Ltd v High Trees House Ltd* [1947] KB 130; *Ogilvy v Hope Davies* [1976] 1 All ER 683 at 688b–9a and *Waltons Stores (Interstate) Ltd v Maher* [1988] 164 CLR 387.

[78] Law of Property (Miscellaneous Provisions) Act 1989, s. 2.

[79] The same result is achieved by waiver — see *Waiver — Terminology* at para. 3.03.

Part II

COMMERCIAL LAW APPLICATIONS

Chapter 13

COMMERCIAL LAW — INTRODUCTION[1]

The need for commercial organizations to react to and take advantage of changing market conditions inevitably results in frequent changes, or the desire to make frequent changes, to the obligations assumed by those parties. The doctrines discussed in this book are mechanisms by which those obligations are altered[2] and by which the courts attempt to reconcile the tensions between market conditions with the need for legal certainty in parties' relations. The reconciliation has not been without difficulty, a fact reflected by the conceptual confusion as to the meaning and application of the doctrines outlined and the extent to which these doctrines form an important and difficult part of commercial law.[3] **13.01**

The application of these doctrines to commercial law can be demonstrated in two ways. First, a consideration of the extent to which we have relied on commercial cases in our analysis of these doctrines.[4] Secondly, by considering the application of these doctrines to business transactions, those transactions encompassing not only those areas of law which are traditionally viewed as 'commercial'[5] — banking, insurance, shipping, sale of goods — but also to agency, company, construction and employment law. In each case, each doctrine is considered either when it raises difficulties particular to that area or when it is frequently litigated in that area. We do not consider the application of the doctrines to areas where the analyses outlined above can be applied without **13.02**

---

1 'Commercial Law' is a nebulous and complex area of law. Detailed consideration of all aspects of a particular subject therefore falls outwith this work. Where appropriate we have provided cross references to the relevant specialist work for the detailed consideration of a particular aspect of any given topic.

2 Either as a result of some bilateral or unilateral intentional act (as in variation, waiver and affirmation respectively) or of a response to another party's conduct.

3 See Atiyah/Adams at p. 99.

4 See, for example, *Waiver – Terminology*, Chap. 3; *Waiver – Types and Elements*, Chap. 4 and *The Panchaud Frères 'Doctrine'*, Chap. 6.

5 And therefore designated commercial court business.

difficulty. The result of that approach is that certain doctrines may appear to have particular emphasis in particular areas. That is not necessarily the case, the difference in emphasis is due to the fact that certain doctrines are particularly troublesome in particular areas. Thus, for example, variation receives detailed consideration in the sections dealing with contracts of guarantee,[6] construction[7] and employment law because the application of variation in those areas appears to have created some difficulty.

13.03 Our approach has been affected by three other general considerations. First, due to the frequency in which the point has been argued, much of our general analysis has been drawn from shipping cases. We therefore do not repeat the issues raised in those cases except in general terms. Secondly, a consideration of the case law shows that the area of commercial law in which the most issues raised by the doctrines have been considered most frequently is insurance law. Thus, where a particular issue has not been considered in a particular context, and general principles do not apply, we have relied on analogies drawn from insurance cases to ascertain the result that the courts might reach. Thirdly, any consideration of 'estoppel' in the following chapters is limited to cases of estoppel by representation, estoppel by convention and equitable forbearance. Given its unique nature in English law, proprietary estoppel rarely arises and is rarely argued in the commercial context. To the extent that proprietary estoppel does arise in commercial law, the issues arising have been dealt with in the chapter devoted to proprietary estoppel.

[6] See *Banking* at para. 15.02ff.

[7] Used loosely and in the practitioners' sense.

Chapter 14
AGENCY

WAIVER

Waiver is relevant to the law of agency in two respects — the waiver of breaches of the agency contract between principal and agent; and the agent's authority to waive the principal's rights on the principal's behalf. The former is governed by the general law of waiver[1] and we therefore do not discuss it.[2] The latter is 'not easy'[3] and has generated a considerable amount of confusion and difficulty. **14.01**

Waiver requires an unequivocal representation made with the requisite knowledge. If any one element is not present, there can be no waiver. Therefore, a litigant seeking to establish a waiver must plead and prove both.[4] Where the litigant is alleging that an agent has waived the principal's rights it must establish the elements of waiver *and* plead and prove that: (i) the agent was authorized to make the representations; and (ii) the agent's knowledge binds the principal. If either of the latter two elements is not established, there can be no waiver. It follows that the scope of an agent's *vires* to waive its principal's rights is dependent on whichever of those two elements is most rigidly circumscribed. **14.02**

---

1 See, *e.g. Thornton Hall & Partners v Wembley Electrical Appliances Ltd* [1947] 2 All ER 629.

2 Waiver, as far as knowledge is concerned, is identical to ratification, it therefore follows that as a matter of logical consistency ratification, in all save the most extreme circumstances, will require an unequivocal representation coupled with knowledge of the facts and the principal's legal rights, although such knowledge may be easily imputed to him — see *Bank Melli Iran v Barclays Bank (Dominion, Colonial and Overseas)* [1951] 2 Lloyd's Rep. 367 *per* McNair J. at 376 col. 2–377 col. 2; *Westminster Bank v Banca Nazionale di Credito* (1928) 31 Ll L Rep. 306 at 312 cols 1–2; *Atlantic Bay Shipping v Binham Group of Establishments & Ors* (Comm Ct unrep. 10 October 1996); *Banking* at para. 15.45; Bowstead at para. 2–065, p. 77 and at para. 2–066.

3 *Tenax Steamship Co Ltd v Reinante Transoceanica Navegacion SA ('The Brimnes')* [1973] 1 WLR 386 *per* Brandon J. at 414D–E.

4 See *Peyman v Lanjani* [1985] Ch 457.

AUTHORIZED REPRESENTATION BY THE AGENT

Whether or not a representation made by an agent binds its principal is a question of the agent's actual or ostensible authority.[5] The agent's actual authority will depend on the agreement between it and the principal.[6] The agent's ostensible authority[7] will depend on the representations either expressly or impliedly made by the principal as to the agent's authority.[8] It follows that whether these elements are satisfied must be a question of fact and degree in every case, a detailed examination of which is a matter of agency law proper[9] and lies outside this work.[10] **14.03**

IMPUTATION OF KNOWLEDGE TO THE PRINCIPAL

The circumstances in which English law will impute an agent's knowledge to the principal are poorly defined. This lack of definition arises in part from the fact that the authorities on the point are inconsistent,[11] in part from the English law's failure to draw distinctions between the imputation of notice and the imputation of knowledge to the principal[12] and in part from the fact that any attempts to codify the law in this area are relatively recent.[13] It follows that any attempts to clarify this point must be, at best, tentative. **14.04**

That said, we would suggest that there are two ways in which some guidance can be distilled from the authorities. In so doing, it is important **14.05**

---

[5] See *Nippon Menkwa Kabushiki Kaisha (Japan Cotton Trading Company Ltd) v Dawsons Bank Ltd* (1935) 51 Ll L Rep. 147 *per* Lord Russell at 150 col. 2.

[6] *Freeman & Lockyer v Buckhurst Park Properties (Mangal) Ltd* [1964] 2 QB 480 *per* Diplock L.J. at 502.

[7] Or apparent authority.

[8] See Bowstead at para. 8–017, p. 368.

[9] However, for the application of the doctrine to particular areas see *Insurance Law* at para. 19.59 ff.; *Banking Law* at para. 15.36; *Sale of Goods and Shipping* at para. 20.28 and *Company Law* at para. 16.00.

[10] See Bowstead at para. 8–045, p. 388 for examples.

[11] *Taylor v Yorkshire Insurance Co* [1913] 2 Ir R 1 *per* Palles C.B. at 21.

[12] *cf. Second Restatement on Agency* (American Law Institute) 1958, ss. 9, 268–82 and Bowstead at para. 8.205.

[13] See, *e.g. El Ajou v Dollar Land Holdings plc* [1994] 2 All ER 685.

to note that the key issue for waiver is the imputation of knowledge not of notice. Although there may be substantial overlap between the two,[14] it is submitted that where an agent receives notice it will then possess the appropriate knowledge[15] but not *vice versa*.

General principles

There are three types of case where knowledge will be imputed. First, knowledge will be imputed where the agent is authorized to enter into a transaction in which its own knowledge is material, for example, a broker entering into insurance contracts on behalf of its principal.[16] It has been suggested that this category of case is not one of imputation of knowledge proper[17] but one on which '*the agent's knowledge affects the terms or performance of the contract which he concludes on behalf of his principal*'. Whilst it is submitted that distinction is semantically correct, the issue being merely the type of contract into which the agent is authorized to enter, as a matter of practice, the principal will still be affected by the agent's knowledge. Secondly, knowledge will be imputed where the principal is under a personal duty to investigate and to make disclosure and uses an agent for that purpose.[18] Again, this situation will arise in a broking contract. Thirdly, knowledge will be imputed where the agent has authority to receive[19] or may be reasonably presumed to have authority to receive[20] communications from third parties. **14.06**

Knowledge will not be imputed in two situations. First, knowledge of **14.07**

---

[14] For instance in landlord and tenant cases, the relevant knowledge may be provided by the notice to quit.

[15] On the basis that notice (a specific and formal mechanism of imparting knowledge) *ex hypothesi* includes the lesser requirement of knowledge *simpliciter*.

[16] *El Ajou v Dollar Land Holdings plc* [1994] 2 All ER 685 *per* Hoffmann L.J. at 702c–d.

[17] *ibid. per* Hoffmann L.J. at 702g.

[18] *ibid. per* Hoffmann L.J. at 702h–j.

[19] *ibid. per* Hoffmann L.J. at 703c–d and *Blackley v National Mutual Life Assn of Australia* [1972] NZLR 1038. See also *Re Brewery Assets Corporation, Truman's Case* [1894] 3 Ch 272 *per* Wright J. at 275; *Whitney v Great Northern Insurance* Co [1917] 32 DLR 756; *Beasant v Northern Life Insurance* Co [1923] 2 DLR 1086 *per* Cameron J.A. at 1088–9; *Evans v Employers Mutual Insurance Association Ltd* [1936] 1 KB 505 *per* Greer L.J. at 515 and *Mahli v Abbey Life Insurance* [1995] 4 Re LR 305 *per* Rose L.J. at 310.

[20] *Hadenfayre v British National Insurance Society Limited* [1984] 2 Lloyd's Rep. 393 *per* Lloyd J. at 401 col. 1.

the agent's dishonesty will not be imputed to the principal.[21] Secondly, no knowledge relevant to the commission of a fraud against the principal by the agent will be imputed.[22]

Difficulties with the general analysis

The difficulty with this general analysis is threefold. First, due to the weight and inconsistency of the case law,[23] it is difficult to categorize a particular case under a particular heading. Secondly, there is a considerable overlap between the first and second general categories. On one view, both are articulations of the *Blackburn Lowe & Co v Vigors*[24] test[25] that knowledge will be imputed where, for all intents and purposes, the agent is the principal.[26] On another, both turn on the extent to which the principal has delegated the conduct of a particular transaction to the agent. Delegation must be a question of fact and degree in each case.[27] The result is that in general principles do not assist in deciding the results of specific cases. Further, the reliance on delegation means that the tests for imputation of knowledge and the authorization to make the unequivocal representation are the same. Whilst that makes logical sense enabling the court to apply one test, a reliance on delegation does not assist in deciding individual cases. Thirdly, it follows that one is inevitably driven from a codification of general principles to attempting to generate broad categories of fact in which knowledge has been imputed. **14.08**

Broad categories of fact in which knowledge has been imputed

Adopting an extremely broad factual approach, knowledge will be imputed in two situations. First, where the agent has a broad, wide **14.09**

[21] See *PCW Syndicates v PCW Reinsurers* [1996] 1 Lloyd's Rep. 241 *per* Staughton L.J. at 254 col. 1–247 col. 2.
[22] See *Belmont Finance Corporation Ltd v Williams Furniture Ltd* [1979] Ch 250 *per* Buckley L.J. at 261H–2A.
[23] See Bowstead at paras 8.212–13.
[24] (1887) 12 App Cas 531.
[25] *Per* Lord Halsbury L.C. at 537.
[26] See *Insurance* at para. 19.59.
[27] Compare *Mahli v Abbey Life Insurance* [1995] 4 Re LR 305 with *Evans v Employers Mutual Insurance Association Ltd* [1936] 1 KB 505.

ranging authority to enter into transactions on behalf of the principal,[28] it is relatively likely that the principal will be fixed with the agent's knowledge.[29] Secondly, on company law principles,[30] where the agent is a senior employee of the principal,[31] it is relatively likely that knowledge will be imputed[32] unless the principal can show that the employee was not a guiding mind;[33] had no involvement with the principal's affairs in that regard[34] or in that transaction;[35] or the information was received by the employee or director in another capacity.[36]

---

[28] For example, a sole representative of the principal in a particular area would have this type of authority — see *Farquharson v Pearl Assurance Co Ltd* [1937] 3 All ER 124 *per* Singleton J. at 132G-H (however, on its facts, it appears that the court held that the insurer was estopped).

[29] See *Acey v Fernie* (1840) 7 M&W 151, 151 ER 717 *per* Abinger C.B. and *per* Parke B. at 155 and 719; *Wing v Harvey* (1845) 5 De G & M 265, 43 ER 872 *per* Lord Justice Knight Bruce at 270, 874 and *per* Lord Justice Turner at 271, 875; *Linford v The Provincial Horse and Cattle Insurance Company* (1864) 34 Beav 291, 55 ER 647 *per* Lord Romilly M.R. at 293, 648; *Whitney v Great Northern Insurance Co* [1917] 32 DLR 756; *Ayrey v British Legal and United Provident Assurance Company Ltd* [1918] 1 KB 136 *per* Lawrence L.J. at 140; *Beasant v Northern Life Insurance Co* [1923] 2 DLR 1086 *per* Cameron J.A. at 1088–9; *Evans v Employers Mutual Insurance Association Ltd* [1936] 1 KB 505 *per* Greer L.J. at 515; *Mahli v Abbey Life Insurance* [1995] 4 Re LR 305 *per* Rose L.J. at 310. *Insurance* at para. 19.60 and *Banking* at para. 15.17.

[30] *Société Generale de Paris v Tramways Union Co* (1884) 14 QBD 424 *per* Cotton L.J. at 443; see also *Re Fenwick Stobart & Co* [1902] 1 Ch 507 *per* Buckley J. at 511.

[31] Thus, '*The mind . . . of a company is not reached or affected by information merely possessed by its clerks*' *Houghton & Co v Nothard Lowe & Wills* [1928] AC 1 *per* Lord Sumner at 18 and *Fitchpatrick v Hawkeye Insurance Co* 53 Iowa 335 (1880).

[32] *Re Carew's Estate Act (No 2)* (1862) 31 Beav 39, 54 ER 1051 *per* Lord Romilly M.R. at 42–3, 1053, 46, 1054.

[33] *i.e.* the obverse of *Meridian Global Funds Management Asia Ltd* [1995] 3 WLR 413 *per* Lord Hoffmann at 419.

[34] *Re Carew's Estate Act (No. 2)* above *per* Lord Romilly M.R. at 42, 1053; see also *Bank of Ireland v Cogry Spinning Co* [1900] 1 IR 219.

[35] *Re Peruvian Rlys Co v Thames and Mersey Marine Insurance Co* (1867) 2 Ch App 617 at 618 and *Powles v Page* (1846) 3 CB 16. Thus, where the agent is authorized to deal with a particular transaction and therefore able to appreciate the significance of the information, knowledge will be imputed — see *Evans v Employers Mutual Insurance Association Ltd* [1936] 1 KB 505 *per* Greer L.J. at 515 and *Mahli v Abbey Life Insurance* [1995] 4 Re LR 305 *per* Rose L.J. at 310.

[36] See, *e.g.* *Société Générale de Paris v Tramways Union* (1884) 14 QBD 424 and *Welsbach Incandescent Gas Lighting Co v New Sunshine Incandescent Co* [1900] 2 Ch 1 *per* Rigby L.J. at 12.

ESTOPPEL

The role of estoppel[37] in the law of agency is complex and uncertain. Further, a detailed discussion of that role falls outwith this work.[38] Additionally, much of the law of agency was developed in the nineteenth century and there is a corresponding difficulty in applying Victorian principles and terminology to modern commercial practice. Despite those caveats and for present purposes, estoppel is relevant to the law of agency in three ways: the relationship between estoppel and ostensible authority; the additional[39] effect that estoppel may have on relations between the principal, agent and third party; and the circumstances in which an estoppel can arise against a third party. **14.10**

ESTOPPEL AND OSTENSIBLE AUTHORITY[40]

Where a principal 'holds out' X as its agent having authority to carry out a particular function, the principal may be unable to argue, against third parties that have relied on the holding out, that X is not its agent. This 'ostensible authority' is therefore: **14.11**

> a legal relationship between the principal and the contractor created by a representation, made by the principal to the contractor, intended to be and in fact acted upon by the contractor, that the agent has authority to enter on behalf of the principal into a contract of a kind within the scope of the "apparent" authority, so as to render the principal liable to perform any obligations imposed upon him by such a contract[41]

[37] As pointed out elsewhere (*Commercial Introduction* at para. 13.04), estoppel for present purposes does not comprise proprietary estoppel. Even the wide ranging concept of estoppel in the agency context enunciated in *Pacol Ltd v Trade Lines Ltd ('The Henrik Sif')* [1982] 1 Lloyd's Rep. 456 *per* Webster J. at 466–7 probably does not suggest that proprietary estoppel has a role to play. We therefore use the term as including estoppel by representation, estoppel by convention and equitable forbearance.

[38] Readers requiring a detailed exposition should refer to Bowstead.

[39] *i.e.* in addition to the issues arising from ostensible authority.

[40] Our approach is limited to questions of principle. For a detailed exposition of the circumstances in which ostensible authority will arise, reference should be made to Bowstead, Articles 74 ff.

[41] *Freeman & Lockyer v Buckhurst Park Properties (Mangel) Ltd* [1964] 2 QB 480 *per* Diplock L.J. at 503.

14.12 Expressed in those terms, ostensible authority has much in common with an estoppel by representation.[42] The ostensible authority can arise from either an express oral or written representation or by the principal's conduct[43] on which the third party must have relied or have been induced to act to its detriment.[44] Additionally, and subject to one caveat,[45] ostensible authority will not alter the substantive relations between the parties. Like estoppel by representation,[46] ostensible authority cannot be used, for example, to bypass the *ultra vires* doctrine: the fact that an agent represents that a particular act is within its principal's power does not render the act *intra vires*.[47] Further, as with an estoppel by representation in agency cases, the courts may be relatively quick to find that the third party has acted to its detriment. Thus, provided that the third party has acted in a way which it otherwise would not have done,[48] the requirement of detriment will frequently be satisfied.[49]

14.13 These similarities have led the courts to three conclusions. First, ostensible authority is nothing more than an estoppel.[50] Secondly, that ostensible authority arises as a result of an estoppel by representation:

---

[42] The estoppel could also be an estoppel by convention and, in extreme circumstances, an equitable forbearance. However, the most likely 'candidate' for the link between ostensible authority and estoppel is estoppel by representation and we refer, for the most part, to that doctrine.

[43] *Freeman & Lockyer v Buckhurst Park Properties (Mangel) Ltd* [1964] 2 QB 480 *per* Diplock L.J. at 506. Where one party owes the other a duty to speak, the ostensible authority may be created by silence or in action on the part of the principal (see *Wilson & Meeson v Pickering* [1946] KB 422 *per* Lord Greene M.R. at 425; contra. *Phoenix Insurance Co Ltd v Berechee* (1906) 3 CLR 946 at 959–60; *Tobin v Broadbent* (1947) 75 CLR 378; *Press v Mathers* [1927] VLR 326; *Rockland Industries Inc v Amerada Minerals Corp of Canada* (1978) 95 DLR (3d) 64; *Daniell v Paradiso* (1991) 55 SASR 359; *Norfolk County Council v Secretary of State for the Environment* [1973] 1 WLR 1400 *per* Lord Widgery C.J. at 1405F-G).

[44] *George Whitechurch Ltd v Cavanagh* [1902] AC 117 at 129–31; *Farquharson Bros v King & Co* [1902] AC 325 *per* Lord Halsbury L.C. at 330–1; *Mac Fisheries v Harrison* (1924) 93 LJKB 811 *per* Swift J. at 815–16 and *Wilson & Meeson v Pickering* [1946] KB 422 *per* Lord Greene M.R. at 426.

[45] See *Ostensible authority and title* at para. 14.17 below.

[46] *York Corporation v Henry Leetham & Sons* [1924] 1 Ch 557 *per* Russell J. at 573; *Rolled Steel Products (Holdings) Ltd v British Steel & Corp* [1985] 3 All ER 52 *per* Slade L.J. at 86g-h.

[47] *Freeman & Lockyer v Buckhurst Park Properties (Mangel) Ltd* [1964] 2 QB 480 at 506.

[48] *Cleveland Mfg Co Ltd v Muslim Commercial Bank Ltd* [1981] 2 Lloyd's Rep. 646 *per* Robert Goff J. at 650 col. 2–651 col. 1 and *Polish SS Co v AJ Williams (Overseas Sales) Ltd (The Suwalki)* [1989] 1 Lloyds Rep. 511 *per* Steyn J. at 514 col. 1–515 col. 2.

[49] See, *e.g. Freeman & Lockyer v Buckhurst Park Properties (Mangel) Ltd* [1964] 2 QB 480.

[50] *Rama Corporation Ltd v Proved Tin and General Investments Ltd* [1952] 2 QB 147 at 149 *per* Slade J.; *Freeman & Lockyer v Buckhurst Properties (Mangel) Ltd* [1964] 2 QB 480 at 503 and *R v Charles* [1977] AC 177 at 183. Although the general term 'estoppel' is used, it is clear that the courts were considering an estoppel by representation.

the principal by its conduct being estopped from denying that X is its agent and therefore an agency relationship arises.[51] Thirdly, that any debate as to the difference between estoppel by representation and ostensible authority is 'academic'.[52] However, it is submitted that there are differences between estoppel by representation and ostensible authority that suggest that their superficial similarity is based on supposed links that are, in fact, at best tenuous.[53]

Those differences can be analysed under three categories: the circumstances which give rise to ostensible authority; the relationship between ostensible authority and agency by estoppel; and the effect that ostensible authority can have on title. **14.14**

The circumstances creating ostensible authority

The circumstances which may give rise to ostensible authority are many and varied.[54] However, three particular points arise. First, ostensible authority may arise where there has been no representation other than the fact that X occupies a particular office[55] or carries out a particular role.[56] The obvious difficulty with such cases is that there is no obvious representation as would be required for an estoppel by representation.[57] Secondly, a distinction has been drawn between the ostensible authority which arises from X's ordinary authority and an estoppel binding the principal where it expressly represents that X is its agent.[58] **14.15**

---

51 *Egyptian International Foreign Trade Co v Soplex Wholesale Supplies Ltd ('The Raffaella')* [1985] 2 Lloyd's Rep. 36 *per* Browne-Wilkinson L.J. at 41 cols 1–2 '*Ostensible authority comes about where the principal, by words or conduct, has represented that the agent has the requisite actual authority, and the party dealing with the agent has entered into a contract and relied on that representation. The principal in these circumstances is estopped from denying that the actual authority existed*'; *Armagas Ltd v Mundogas SA (The Ocean Frost)* [1986] AC 717 *per* Lord Keith at 777A-B. See also *Crabtree-Vickers PTY Ltd v Australian Direct Mail Advertising and Addressing Co Pty Ltd* (1975) 133 CLR 72 and *Northside Developments Pty v Registrar General* (1990) 170 CLR 146.

52 *Polish SS Co v AJ Williams (Overseas Sales) Ltd (The Suwalki)* [1989] 1 Lloyd's Rep. 511 *per* Steyn J. at 514 col. 1.

53 See Bowstead at para. 8.029.

54 See Bowstead, Articles 74 ff.

55 *Hely — Hutchinson v Brayhead* [1968] 1 QB 549 *per* Lord Denning M.R. at 583D–F.

56 *Waugh v HB Clifford & Sons* [1982] Ch 374.

57 See Bowstead at para. 8.018 for a discussion of this point.

58 *Ebeed v Soplex Wholesale Supplies Ltd and PS Refson & Co Ltd* [1985] BCLC 404 *per* Browne-Wilkinson L.J. at 411f–h and *Armagas Ltd v Mundo Gas SA* [1986] AC 717.

Under the first head, where any agent is clothed with the trappings of authority, the agent will possess the concomitant ostensible authority and *vice versa*.[59] The very existence of this distinction suggests that the two doctrines are not the same. Thirdly, ostensible authority cannot arise from any statements made by X[60] but can only arise from statements made by the principal or a person authorized by the principal to make statements of that kind.[61] That limitation arises not from considerations of equity but from the need to find some form of authority. If estoppel by representation and ostensible authority were the same doctrine, it would be reasonable to expect that any limitation would arise from the considerations of equity and not from the need for authorization.

Ostensible authority and agency by estoppel

Further complexities arise from the existence of the doctrine of 'agency by estoppel'. An agency by estoppel will arise where the principal as a result of its representations or conduct cannot deny that X is its agent.[62] That, at first sight, would appear to be nothing more than an occasion on which estoppel and ostensible authority were one and the same.[63] However, the courts have made it clear that an agency by estoppel is not agency.[64] By way of contrast, ostensible authority and agency are axiomatically one and the same. Four results flow. First, agency by estoppel and ostensible authority cannot be one and the same doctrine. If they were, agency by estoppel would be agency. Secondly, there must **14.16**

[59] *First Energy (UK) v Hungarian International Ltd* [1993] BCC 533 *per* Steyn L.J. at 540E-G and *British Bank of the Middle East v Sun Life Assurance of Canada* [1983] 2 Lloyd's Rep. 9 *per* Lord Brandon at 17 col. 2–18 col. 1.

[60] There being no such thing as a self-authorizing agent — see *Ebeed v Soplex Wholesale Supplies Ltd and PS Refson & Co Ltd* [1985] BCLC 404 *per* Browne-Wilkinson L.J. at 414a–g.

[61] *Freeman & Lockyer v Buckhurst Park Properties* [1964] 2 QB 480; *IRC v Ufitec Group Ltd* [1977] 3 All ER 924 *per* May J. at 937c–8c; *British Bank of the Middle East v Sun Life Assurance of Canada* [1983] 2 Lloyd's Rep. 9 *per* Lord Brandon at 17 col. 2 and *Rhodian River Shipping v Halla Maritime* [1984] 1 Lloyd's Rep. 373 *per* Bingham J. at 379 col. 2.

[62] *Pole v Leask* (1863) 33 LJ CH 155.

[63] *Rama Corporation Ltd v Proved Tin and General Investments Ltd* [1952] 2 QB 147 *per* Slade J. at 149; *Freeman & Lockyer v Buckhurst Properties (Mangel) Ltd* [1964] 2 QB 480 at 503 and *R v Charles* [1977] AC 177 at 183.

[64] *Pole v Leask* (1863) 33 LJ CH 155 *per* Lord Cranworth at 161–2.

therefore be some distinction between agency by estoppel and ostensible authority. Thirdly, agency by estoppel must therefore be, as the name suggests, a form of estoppel. Fourthly, estoppel[65] must therefore be distinguished from ostensible authority.

Ostensible authority and title

Where the principal clearly represents to a third party[66] that X has the principal's authority to sell the goods, and the third party relies on that representation,[67] the principal will be precluded from denying the third party's title to those goods. That result would appear to be based on traditional estoppel by representation principles. However, in contrast to 'traditional' estoppel,[68] the effect of the estoppel in this context is to transmit title enabling the third party to sell on the goods.[69] This anomaly can be explained in two ways. First, title passes not as a result of an estoppel but of the doctrine of ostensible authority. A further distinction is therefore drawn between the two doctrines. Under estoppel by representation,[70] title cannot pass, under ostensible authority title does pass. Secondly, ostensible authority forms part of a general exception to the *nemo dat* principle;[71] that is, commercial expediency[72] has led the courts to recognize that title should pass by virtue of this general **14.17**

[65] As above, the most obvious form of estoppel would be estoppel by representation. However, we would suggest that all types of estoppel can be so distinguished.

[66] Thus, for example, the handing over of a log book on the sale of a car was not a sufficiently clear representation — see *Central Newbury Car Auctions Ltd v Unity Finance Ltd* [1957] 1 QB 371 *per* Hodson L.J. at 390 and *per* Morris L.J. at 398. The principal must also be the owner of the goods — *Sargent (J) (Garages) Ltd v Motor Auctions (West Bromwich) Ltd* [1977] RTR 121; *Rimmer v Webster* [1902] 2 Ch 163 and *Abigail v Lobin* [1934] AC 491.

[67] The reliance must be clearly established. Therefore, where X's and the third party's interests are contradictory, there will be no reliance by the third party — see *Heane v Rogers* (1820) 9 B & C 577, 109 ER 215 *per* Bayley J. at 586–7, 218–9 followed in *Richards v Johnston* (1859) 4 H&N 660, 157 ER 1000 *per* Martin B. at 664, 1002.

[68] Where title does not pass —see *In re Goldcorp Exchange Ltd* [1995] 1 AC 74 *per* Lord Mustill at 93F–4G.

[69] *Eastern Distributors Ltd v Goldberg* [1957] 2 QB 600 *per* Devlin J. at 611.

[70] And we would suggest estoppel by convention. Rights may be conferred by proprietary estoppel but we would suggest that the cases at issue are plainly not cases where proprietary estoppel was in play.

[71] See s. 21(1) of the Sale of Goods Act 1979.

[72] See, for instances, the transactions at issue in *Mercantile Credit Co v Hamblin* [1965] 2 QB 242 *per* Pearson L.J. at 275A–D approved in *Moorgate Mercantile Co Ltd v Twitchings* [1977] AC 890 *per* Lord Edmund-Davies at 918F–19A.

exception[73] and in this particular case where an agent has been given authority to sell.[74] Although both explanations are plausible, we would submit that the better view is the latter, the passing of title forming part of an exception that runs throughout commercial law.[75]

We would seek to draw out three points from the above analysis. First, as a matter of practice, in the vast number of cases there will be no distinction between estoppel by representation and ostensible authority. Secondly, although ostensible authority may arise from the same facts as an estoppel, it will also arise from a wider set of circumstances and have more far reaching and possibly irrevocable[76] effects. Thirdly, as a matter of theory ostensible authority must therefore be a distinct doctrine either deriving from the special nature of the agency relationship or from the particular application of estoppel principles to the agency context. **14.18**

ESTOPPEL AND THE RELATIONSHIP BETWEEN PRINCIPAL, AGENT AND THIRD PARTY

Provided that the elements of an estoppel[77] are established, an estoppel will have the same effect on the relationships between principal, agent and third parties as it does elsewhere. Thus, for example, a principal **14.19**

[73] See Benjamin at para. 7.007 ff. This exception is referred to as an 'estoppel'. However, as we suggest elsewhere the courts are in fact using the term 'estoppel' wrongly to cover an exception to the *nemo dat* principle (see *Sale of Goods and Shipping* at para. 20.20; Benjamin *op. cit.*).

[74] See Bowstead at para. 8.109. This is the analysis adopted in the Commonwealth — see *Motor Credits (Hire Finance) v Pacific Motor Auctions Pty Ltd* (1963) 109 CLR 87 at 97, 103; *Curtis v Perth & Freemantle Bottle Exchange Co* (1914) 18 CLR 17 at 23, 38 and *Thomas Australia Wholesale Vehicle Trading Co Pty Ltd v Marac Finance Australia Ltd* (1985) 2 NSWLR 452. This argument has very rarely succeeded — see *Mercantile Bank of India v Central Bank of India* [1938] AC 287 at 302; *Henderson v Williams* [1895] 1 QB 521; *Eastern Distributors Ltd v Goldring* [1957] 2 QB 600; see Benjamin at para. 7.008, n. 64 and cases there cited.

[75] This would still follow if we are wrong in asserting that there is a general exception to *nemo dat* (see *Sale of Goods and Shipping* at para. 20.20) and the title passes purely as a result of ostensible authority.

[76] Thus, for example, ostensible authority may be irrevocable either where the authority has arisen to provide the agent with a security (*Smart v Saunders* (1848) 5 CB 895) or where, arguably, the special circumstances of the case require it to be so (*Society of Lloyds v Leighs & Ors* Coleman J. (Comm Ct unrep. 21 February 1997 — upheld on different grounds (CA) unrep. 31 July 1997).

[77] Used to mean estoppel by representation, estoppel by convention and equitable forbearance unless otherwise stated.

can be estopped from ratifying its agent's acts or estopped from denying that it has ratified its agent's acts.[78] On standard principles, the estoppel will arise where the principal makes an express representation[79] or where the principal was aware[80] that the third party believed that there had been ratification, did nothing to correct that belief and the third party suffered detriment as a result.[81] In such cases, the fact that the estoppel has arisen in an agency context creates no particular difficulties. However, the courts have applied the doctrine of estoppel to the agency relationship in four additional situations. In each situation, the basis on which it can be said that an estoppel in the correct sense of the word is operating is unclear. The elements identified as being necessary for the estoppel being absent. Therefore, we would suggest that these 'estoppels' are anomalous, the courts using the label of estoppel as a means of defining the necessary adjuncts of the agency relationship imposed by the courts to preserve the commercial efficacy of that relationship.

Estoppel and election between suing the principal or agent

Except where the agent is acting solely as the principal's disclosed agent,[82] a third party will be able to choose between suing the principal or the agent for the loss and damage it has suffered. If, however, the third party represents that it will sue, for example, only the principal, and the agent relies on that representation, the third party will be estopped from then suing the agent. The same result will flow if the third party initially represents that it will only sue the agent.[83] Although **14.20**

[78] *McEvoy v Belfast Banking Co Ltd* [1935] AC 24 *per* Lord Atkin at 45.

[79] For example, receipt of the funds generated by the agent's acts *The Bonita; The Charlotte* (1861) 1 Lush 252, 167 ER 111 at 265, 118.

[80] Therefore, there will be no estoppel where the principal is unaware of the third party's state of mind — see *Marsh v Joseph* [1897] 1 Ch 213 *per* Lord Russell C.J. at 246–7.

[81] The courts will impose on the principal a duty to inform the third party in such circumstances, the failure so to inform constituting the representation required for the estoppel — see *Suncorp Insurance and Finance v Milano Assicurazioni SpA* [1993] 2 Lloyd's Rep. 225 *per* Waller J. at 241 col. 1; contra. *Yona International Ltd and Heftsiba Overseas Works Ltd v La Reunion Francaise Société Anonyme d' Assurancees et de Reassurances* [1996] 2 Lloyd's Rep. 84 *per* Moore-Bick J. at 103 col. 1 where no estoppel arose on the facts of that case.

[82] In which case, the principal becomes solely liable — see Bowstead Article 99.

[83] See *Second Restatement on Agency* (American Law Institute 1958), s. 337.

this appears to be an estoppel, in the vast majority of cases[84] the third party has first and foremost elected to sue the principal and its cause of action against the agent has merged in the judgment obtained against the principal.[85] Therefore, before an estoppel can arise the third party must make the informed choice required for an election.[86]

Estoppel and the principal's title to goods or funds

The courts have held that an agent is 'estopped' from alleging that it has better title to the principal's goods than the principal and from alleging that the third party has a better title to funds held by the agent on the principal's behalf.[87] As with certain cases of ostensible authority, the express representation necessary to found an estoppel is frequently missing in these cases. Further, as the agent-bailee will not be estopped from denying the principal's title in an action to recover the goods, we would suggest that the courts are in fact using estoppel to cloak policy decisions.[88] **14.21**

Estoppel and forgery

As discussed elsewhere,[89] the doctrine of 'estoppel by negligence' will, in certain circumstances, preclude a person from alleging that a particular document has been forged.[90] Thus, the holder of a bank account that **14.22**

[84] There will, of course, be rare cases where the elements for an estoppel are made out but there is no election.

[85] This will usually take place when judgment is entered; see para. 14/8/2 *Rules of the Supreme Court* Sweet & Maxwell, London 1997; *Neilson v Betts* LR 5 HL 1.

[86] See *Island Records Ltd v Tring International Ltd* [1995] 3 All ER 444 *per* Lightman J. at 447 and *Bonus Garment Company v Karl Rieker GmbH & Co KG* [1995] 3 HKC 721.

[87] See Bowstead at paras 6.111–13 and cases cited.

[88] Although this has been described as an 'estoppel' the elements required for an estoppel are usually missing. Therefore, it may be more appropriate to analyse the rule as an anomaly arising from the agency relationship (see Bowstead at paras 6.111–13), a view strengthened by the fact that the agent-bailee of the principal's goods will not be estopped from asserting that a third party has better title to the goods in an action for their recovery.

[89] See *Banking* at para. 15.55 ff.

[90] *Swan v North British Australasian Co* (1863) 2 H&C 175, 159 ER 73 at 189–90, 79; *London Joint Stock Bank v Macmillan* [1918] AC 777 *per* Lord Finlay L.C. at 793–4; *per* Lord Finlay at 811 and *per* Viscount Haldane at 817–18 and *Greenwood v Martins Bank Ltd* [1933] AC 51 *per* Lord Tomlin at 57–8, 59. See also *Tina Motors Pty Ltd v Australia and New Zealand Banking Group Ltd* [1977] VR 205 at 208 ll 45–50; Paget at pp. 316– 317.

carelessly presents a forged cheque or allows a series of fraudulent cheques to be cashed will be estopped as against the bank which cashes the cheque from denying that the cheques are forged or fraudulent. This doctrine also applies in the sphere of agency.[91] Therefore, a principal can be estopped from denying the forgeries of its agent where the principal represents to a third party that the forgeries are genuine and the third party relies on that representation.[92]

Estoppel and undisclosed principals

An undisclosed principal directly suing the third party with which its agent contracted may be bound by any defences which the third party may have had against the agent.[93] This limitation on the undisclosed principal's ability to sue has been described as an estoppel preventing the undisclosed principal from asserting that it was, in fact, the principal.[94] Three points arise. First, the commercial logic supporting the limitation is clear. A third party may have deliberately chosen to contract with the agent as opposed to the principal because, for example, the third party wished to exercise a right of set-off against the agent, there being no similar right against the undisclosed principal. The third party should therefore not be deprived of that benefit by being sued by the undisclosed principal. Secondly, the legal logic supporting the limitation is far from clear. An undisclosed principal is, by its very nature, undisclosed; it does not play a part in the transaction between the third party and the agent. Therefore, it is difficult to see how the undisclosed principal can make any representation on which the third party could rely. Thirdly, the status of this limitation is uncertain. On one view, it is arguable that the cases in which the undisclosed principal was bound were extreme ones and the limitation should be confined to the facts of those cases. The alternative, and far more difficult view, is to suggest that the term 'estoppel' is again being used as cover for policy decisions.[95] **14.23**

---

91 As to whether the doctrine can be properly described as an estoppel see *Banking* at para. 15.56 ff.

92 See Bowstead at paras 2.055, 2.057.

93 *Cooke & Sons v Eshelby* (1887) 12 App Cas 271 *per* Lord Aktin at 278–9.

94 *Fish v Kempton* (1849) 7 CB 687, 137 ER 272 *per* Wilde C.J. at 691–2, 274 and *Ramazotti v Bowring* (1859) 7 CB (NS) 851; 141 ER 1050 at 856; 1052 per Erle C.J.

95 See Bowstead at para. 8.109, 8.111.

ESTOPPEL AND THIRD PARTIES

Again an estoppel will arise as against third parties[96] where the requisite elements are established. However, two particular circumstances should be noted. First, where the third party requests payment from a disclosed principal's agent, the third party will be precluded from then suing the principal where the principal has settled its account with the agent on the basis of that request.[97] There is a clear representation by the third party that is acted on by the principal to its detriment. Secondly, the third party will be similarly precluded where it leads the principal to believe that the agent has paid for goods and the principal settles its account with the agent on the basis of that belief.[98] **14.24**

[96] In the sense of parties who are neither principal nor agent.
[97] *Smyth v Anderson* (1849) 7 CB 21, 137 ER 9 *per* Maule J. at 40–2, 17–8.
[98] *Horsfall v Fauntelroy* (1830) 10 B & C 755, 109 ER 630 *per* Lord Tenterden C.J. at 759, 632; *Wyatt v Hereford* (1802) 3 East 147, 102 ER 553 *per* Lord Ellenborough C.J. at 148, 553 and Bowstead at para. 8.119.

Chapter 15

BANKING LAW[1]

VARIATION

In the main, the variation of contracts in the banking context will be uncontroversial.[2] Difficulties may arise, however, where a variation is made either to the terms of a bank guarantee or to the terms of the facility being guaranteed.[3] **15.01**

VARIATION OF THE GUARANTEE

A contract of guarantee falls within section 4 of the Statute of Frauds and therefore must be in writing to be enforceable. Similarly, all consensual variations[4] to that contract must be in writing if they are to be enforceable. Three points flow. First, if the contract of guarantee is orally varied, the creditor will be unable to sue on the contract as varied.[5] However, the guarantor will be permitted to rely on the terms of the 'variation' to defeat any claim by the creditor on the unvaried contract.[6] Secondly, a waiver of the terms of the guarantee does not have to be in writing.[7] Thirdly, the **15.02**

---

1 This chapter considers the operation of variation, waiver and estoppel in traditional paper based banking. The potential application of the doctrines to paperless banking (*i.e.* through EFT, ATM and EFTPOS see Paget, Chap. 19 *passim*) is not considered in detail. However, we would suggest that the principles set out in this chapter will apply to paperless banking although the physical means by which any variation or unequivocal representation is made may be different from those set out below.

2 Provided that care is taken to ensure that any variation or provision allowing for variation does not fall foul of the Unfair Contract Terms Regulations 1994 (1994/3159) — see Paget at p. 315.

3 Many of these difficulties can be avoided by careful drafting and have therefore led to the rise of standard form guarantees — Paget at pp. 617, 621, 638 ff.

4 See para. 15.03 and n. 13 below.

5 See, *e.g. Barclays Bank plc v Caldwell* (25 July 1986, unrep. Harman J.).

6 *Re A Debtor (No. 517 of 1991)* (1991) TLR 25 November.

7 See by analogy *Ogle v Earl Vane* (1868) LR 3 QB 272 *per* Kelly C.B. at 278–9; *Hickman v Haynes* (1875) LR 10 CP 598; *Levey & Co v Goldberg* [1922] 1 KB 688 and *Besseler Waechter Glover & Co v South Derwent Coal Co Ltd* [1938] 1 KB 408.

courts have adopted two mechanisms to bypass the formal requirements as to writing: drawing a distinction between a 'variation' which merely alters one particular aspect of the guarantee and a 'variation' which goes to the root of the contract;[8] and deciding that the effect of some changes is to create a new contract superseding the guarantee and which can be relied on.[9] Either mechanism creates uncertainty with it being open to the court to decide that there is a new contract, a subsisting contract of guarantee with immaterial alterations or no contractual relationship between the parties. As pointed out elsewhere,[10] one resolution to such difficulties is to suggest that any *enforceable* variation will serve to discharge the contract in its entirety and replace it with the contract as varied. It follows that any variation to a guarantee which is not in writing and is therefore unenforceable will have no effect[11] other than to generate an waiver/estoppel/equitable forbearance defence preventing the creditor from suing on the unaltered contract.

In the above we, of course, draw a distinction between variation and **15.03**
waiver. It is submitted that any waiver of the terms of the guarantee should have effect as there can be no difficulty with section 4 of the Statute of Frauds.[12] We also stress that the above only applies to variations of the guarantee in the true sense of the word; that is consensual variations of the terms of the guarantee which are supported by consideration.[13] It is important to note that none of the above applies a material, physical, and unilateral alteration of the document containing the contract of guarantee. Such a material, physical and unilateral alteration of the document will automatically discharge the surety.[14]

---

[8] See *Morris v Baron & Co* [1918] AC 1; *United Dominions Corp (Jamaica) Ltd v Shoucair* [1969] 1 AC 340 and the cases discussed at *Variation* para. 2.30.

[9] *Hunt v South Eastern Rly Co* (1875) 45 LJ QB 87 *per* Lord Hatherley at 94 col. 2–96 col. 1; *Williams Bros v ET Agius Ltd* [1914] AC 510 *per* Lord Atkinson at 527; *Raggow v Scougall & Co* (1915) 31 TLR 564 *per* Darling J. at 565 and *Rose and Frank Co v JR Crompton & Bros Ltd* [1925] AC 445 *per* Lord Phillimore at 456.

[10] See *Variation* at para. 2.30.

[11] See also the analogy with position that an unenforceable variation of the principal contract will not discharge the guarantor — see *Holland Commercial Mortgage Co v Hutchings* [1936] SCR 165; *Manulife Bank of Canada v Corbin* 120 DLR (4th) 234 (1994); *Ankhan Pty Ltd v National Westminster Finance* (1987) 162 CLR 549 *per* Mason A.C.J., Wilson, Brennan, Dawson JJ. at 559 and *Corumo Holdings v Itoh* (1991) 5 ACSR 720 at 729, 753.

[12] *Credit Suisse v Borough Council of Allerdale* [1995] 1 Lloyd's Rep. 315 *per* Coleman J. at 370–2; a finding not disturbed on appeal at [1996] 3 WLR 894; *Kok Hoong v Leong Cheang Kweng* [1964] AC 993 *per* Viscount Radcliffe at 1015.

[13] See *Variation* at para. 2.02.

[14] *Pigot's Case* (1614) 11 Co Rep. 26b; *Lombard Finance v Brookplain Trading Ltd* [1991] 1 WLR 271 *per* Dillon L.J. at 274B-F; for examples see *Aldous v Cornwall*

VARIATION OF THE FACILITY

A material variation to the facility will discharge the guarantor unless it is apparent, without inquiry, that the alteration is unsubstantial and/or cannot be otherwise than of benefit to the guarantor.[15] The guarantor itself will be the sole judge of whether it will consent to remaining liable notwithstanding the alteration.[16] The reason for the rule is that if the guarantor pays any sums due and owing under the facility, it will be able to recoup those sums against the borrower. That right is a valuable right which may be destroyed or reduced in value by alterations to that facility.[17] It follows from the above that an alteration may be material even if it is not, in fact, prejudicial to the guarantor.[18] It will be sufficient if as at the date of the variation[19] it appeared to the guarantor that its rights might be affected. **15.04**

The guarantor's right to be discharged is circumscribed in two important ways. First, if the variation to the facility is unenforceable or void, the guarantor will not be discharged[20] — a variation in that form cannot affect the guarantor's rights against the borrower. Secondly, if the guarantor authorizes the variation of the facility or consents to it, the guarantor will not be discharged.[21] Therefore, the prudent bank will[22] include in the terms of the guarantee a provision that the guarantor authorizes in advance all alterations, whether they be variations or concessions, made to the terms or the operation of the facility. A clause of that nature will protect the bank from the guarantee being discharged **15.05**

(1868) LR 3 QB 573; *Suffell v Bank of England* (1882) 9 QBD 555; *Ellesmere Brewery v Cooper* [1896] 1 QB 75; *Bishop of Crediton v Bishop of Exeter* [1905] 2 Ch 455 and *CIBC v Hardy Bay Inns Ltd* [1985] 1 WWR 405.

15 See *Holme v Brunshill* (1878) 3 QBD 495 *per* Cotton L.J. at 505–6.

16 *ibid.* Brett L.J. at 508.

17 See *Polak v Everett* (1876) 1 QBD 669 *per* Blackburn J. at 673–4 and *National Bank v Awolesi* [1964] 1 WLR 1311.

18 *Egbert v National Crown Bank* [1918] AC 903 *per* Lord Dunedin at 908–9.

19 *Credit Suisse v Borough Council of Allerdale* [1995] 1 Lloyd's Rep. 315 *per* Coleman J. at 365 col. 2–366 col. 1; [1996] 2 Lloyd's Rep 241, CA issue not raised on appeal.

20 *Holland Commercial Mortgage Co v Hutchings* [1936] SCR 165; *Manulife Bank of Canada v Corbin* 120 DLR (4th) 234 (1994); *Ankhan Pty Ltd v National Westminster Finance* (1987) 162 CLR 549 *per* Mason A.C.J., Wilson, Brennan, Dawson JJ. at 559 and *Corumo Holdings v Itoh* (1991) 5 ACSR 720 at 729, 753.

21 *Stewart v M'Kean* (1855) 10 Exch 675, 156 ER 610 *per* Alderson B. at 688, 616 and *per* Parke B. at 691, 618; *British Motor Trust v Hyams* (1934) 50 TLR 230; *Woodcock v Oxford and Worcester Railway Co* (1853) 1 Drew 521 *per* Kindersley V.C. at 529–30, 61 ER 551 at 555.

22 And in most modern guarantees, does so include — Paget at pp. 637–8.

if it is enforceable,[23] and, on its proper construction, it covers the events which have taken place.[24]

WAIVER

The doctrine of waiver has particular relevance to five areas of banking law and practice: in the operation of loan facilities; in the maintenance of security for those facilities; in the syndication of such loan facilities; in the use of bills of exchange and cheques; and in the use of documentary credits. **15.06**

THE OPERATION OF LOAN FACILITIES

The offer and subsequent operation of a loan facility will, axiomatically, necessitate a close and continuing relationship between the lending bank and the borrower. If the facility is large, the prudent banker will have carried out due diligence checks on the borrower; the grant of the facility will probably entail the opening and operation of other accounts; operating accounts will require the bank to decide whether or not to honour cheques or bills on presentation; interest repayments will be staggered over a period of time and more than one draw down may be permitted. The result is that the lending bank and borrower will be engaged in a continuing relationship in which the lending bank will, as a matter of prudence, know both the financial stability of the borrower and whether the borrower is complying with the terms of the facility. Therefore, it may well be relatively straightforward to establish that the lending bank has waived its rights; the bank has numerous occasions on which it can make an unequivocal representation — for example, by accepting payment under the facility — and will also in the normal course of events possess the appropriate knowledge to found a waiver.[25] **15.07**

[23] However, the Unfair Contract Terms Regulations 1994 may apply to such clauses (see reg. 3(2)(a); Sched. 3, categ. (b)) rendering them unenforceable if, on the facts of the particular case, the clause is unfair (see reg. 4 and Sched. 2).

[24] See, *e.g.* *Cowper v Smith* (1838) 4 M&W 519, 150 ER 1534; *Perry v National Provincial Bank of England* [1910] 1 Ch 464; also *Moschi v Lep Air Services* [1973] AC 331 *per* Lord Diplock at 349C and *per* Lord Reid at 344G. See also *Wood Hall Ltd v Pipeline Authority and another* [1979] 24 ALR 385.

[25] The position can be contrasted with, for example, that between ship owners and charterer during the period of a charterparty. The owners may know little of the charterer's affairs unless and until notified by the charterer under the terms of the charterparty.

Pure and unilateral waiver

15.08 The doctrines of pure and unilateral waiver apply to loan facilities in the same manner as they do to any other contract. As the borrower's obligations under a loan facility will usually be to repay the principal and interest, it will normally be the provisions in the facility as to mechanism[26] or place[27] of repayment which are waived in this matter. Those terms will usually be waived by the lending bank accepting a repayment which does not conform to the provisions of the facility. Further, as the non-conforming payment will be, on its face, contrary to the terms of the lending bank's own facility, the bank will have the necessary knowledge.[28] However, a distinction must be drawn between an offer to pay by the borrower which does not conform with the terms of the facility and payment in a non-conforming manner. In the former case, acceptance of the offer by the lending bank may constitute either a variation[29] or a unilateral or a pure waiver by the bank. In the latter case, as the borrower will have already performed its obligations, there will be no consideration to support a variation and no future performance under the contract which the lending bank can waive. Thus, the lending bank will be waiving rights arising from a breach of the terms of the loan; that is, there will be a waiver by election.[30]

Waiver by election

15.09 Waiver by election most commonly arises where a borrower who has defaulted in the repayment of interest or capital or who has committed an event of default under the facility attempts to argue that the lending bank has waived the breach.[31] The borrower will succeed in that contention if the lending bank has made an unequivocal representation to that effect whilst possessing the appropriate knowledge.

26 *Cubitt v Gamble* (1919) 35 TLR 223 *per* McCardie J. at 224 col. 1; *Cohen v Roche* [1927] 1 KB 169 *per* McCardie J. at 180.
27 *Gyles v Hall* (1726) 2 P Wms 378, 24 ER 774 *per* Lord King L.C.
28 Subject to points made on the accepting agent's authority below.
29 See *Variation* at para. 2.15.
30 Further, the acceptance of the non-conforming payment will, in all likelihood, generate an estoppel/equitable forbearance defence if the borrower suffers detriment.
31 Waiver by election may also occur where there is acceptance of a non-conforming payment under the facility — see para. 15.08 above.

Unequivocal representation

Three areas must be considered: the effect of the acceptance of payments under the facility; whether silence or inaction is sufficient; and whether the lending bank can reserve its rights so as to prevent a waiver from taking place. **15.10**

Accepting payment under the facility

The most likely form of unequivocal representation by the lending bank will be the acceptance of payments under the facility. It follows that the acceptance of interest payments by the lending bank, notwithstanding the fact that it could call-in the facility, may be evidence that it has waived its rights.[32] However, it must be remembered that, if there is to be waiver, the lending bank will be responding to a breach which would entitle it to call-in and determine the facility. Calling-in the facility will usually accelerate the future repayment of interest and capital by the borrower but has no effect on obligations of the borrower which have already accrued. It follows that as the lending bank is allegedly waiving its rights to call-in the facility, the unequivocal representation must relate to those future obligations of the borrower. Therefore, the acceptance of *accrued* interest will not, without more,[33] found a waiver[34] nor will the acceptance of interest payments after the facility has been called-in.[35] It is only if the lending bank accepts interest payments in advance or as confirmation of a continuing, future relationship between itself and the borrower without calling-in the facility, will a waiver definitely occur.[36] **15.11**

Silence or inaction

As with other areas of law, silence or inaction will not be sufficient to found a waiver.[37] However, the lending bank should not delay in either calling-in the facility or reserving its rights. If it does so delay and the **15.12**

---

[32] See *Seal v Gimson* (1914) 110 LT 583 *per* Coleridge J. at 584 col. 2.

[33] The position may be different, for example, if the lending bank makes some other representation to the borrower.

[34] See Cresswell, *Encyclopaedia of Banking Law* Butterworths, London loose-leaf at para. F–3643 and *Oceanic Freighters Corp v MV Libyaville Reederei und Schiffarhts Gmbh The Libyaville* [1975] 1 Lloyd's Rep. 537.

[35] See *Keene v Biscoe* (1878) 8 Ch D 201 *per* Fry J. at 203.

[36] See *Re Royal British Bank, Mixer's Case* (1859) 4 De G & J 575, 45 ER 223 *per* Lord Campbell L.C. at 586, 228 and *per* Turner L.J. at 587, 228.

[37] See *Waiver — Types and Elements* at para. 4.14 Cresswell *op. cit.* F–3647.

borrower suffers prejudice as a result, there is a risk that the court will find that the bank has lost its rights.[38]

Reservation of rights

A lending bank faced with an event of default by the borrower may seek to reserve its rights. If the lending bank does so, it should do so clearly but need not state in terms that it is 'reserving its rights'.[39] A reservation of rights should, in theory, be effective to protect the bank's position should it later wish to call in the facility. The reservation of rights will have the effect of making any unequivocal representation by the bank as to its future conduct equivocal.[40] **15.13**

However, as with an insurer[41] or ship owner[42] the lending bank must not act inconsistently with that reservation of rights. If the bank does so, the general rule will not apply and the reservation will have no effect.[43] It is submitted that banks must exercise particular caution in this respect. A bank will normally have close contact with the borrower and the more contact the bank has with the borrower, the more opportunity it will have for acting inconsistently with the reservation of rights and, therefore, the less protection that reservation of rights will offer. Further, the lending bank will usually be faced with a stark choice — to accept the breach or call-in the facility. Where the bank does not call-in the facility, it will be difficult for the bank's subsequent actions not to be some form of unequivocal representation that it has waived its rights.[44] Therefore, it is submitted that a reservation of rights may only offer the bank temporary protection and the prudent bank should decide what action it wishes to take as soon as may be practicable. **15.14**

---

[38] See *Allen v Robles* [1969] 2 Lloyd's Rep. 61 *per* Fenton-Atkinson L.J. at 63–4. As pointed out above (*Insurance*, para. 19.53), the better analysis of such cases is that the lending bank has affirmed the facility or is estopped from denying liability.

[39] *Hill v Citadel Insurance Co Ltd* [1995] LRLR 218 *per* Cresswell J. at 239 col. 2.

[40] See *Waiver — Types and Elements* at para. 4.11 ff.

[41] See *Insurance* at para. 19.82.

[42] See *Sale of Goods and Shipping* at para. 20.16.

[43] See *Davenport v R* (1877) 3 App Cas 115 *per* Sir Montague E Smith at 132; *Croft v Lumley* (1856) 5 E & B 648 at 652; *Stone v Stringer* (1880) 61 LT 470; *R v Paulson* [1921] 1 AC 271 *per* Lord Atkinson at 286; *Haynes v Hirst* (1927) 27 SR (NSW) 480 *per* Long Innes J.; *Carter v Green* [1950] 2 KB 76; *Antaios Naviera SA v Salen Rederierna AB* [1983] 1 WLR 1362 *per* Lord Donaldson M.R. at 1370H–1C and *per* Fox L.J. 1377A–C.

[44] The position can be contrasted with that of an insurer — the investigation by an insurer of the claim may well be a 'neutral' act which is not inconsistent with the reservation of rights.

Knowledge

The borrower will have to prove that the lending bank had knowledge of the fact of breach[45] and of its rights.[46] In the main that requirement will create two difficulties for the borrower. First, the borrower will have to establish that the lending bank *qua* principal is fixed with the knowledge of its employees or agents.[47] Secondly, in syndicated loan facilities, the borrower may have to establish that the syndicate was fixed with the agent bank's knowledge.[48] **15.15**

Imputing knowledge

As pointed out elsewhere,[49] the question of when, and in what circumstances, the knowledge of an agent or employee will be imputed to the principal/employer is a difficult one. The court will in each case seek to ascertain whether the agent is under a duty to transmit the information to the principal. If it is, then the principal will be fixed with knowledge. However, as the authorities are expressly confined to the facts of the individual case, it is difficult to distil the general principles governing the decisions.[50] **15.16**

In the banking context, five points should be considered. First, in a complex transaction, the lending bank will deal with the borrower through an authorized loan officer or loan review committee. In most cases, the authorized loan officer or committee will be expressly authorized to waive breaches of the facility and therefore the knowledge of the officer or the committee will be that of the bank. By parity of reasoning, there will be no waiver where the officer does not have the requisite express authorization.[51] Secondly, absent fraud, the loan officer will be the bank's delegated agent for dealing with the facility and the bank will be fixed with that officer's knowledge even if there was no **15.17**

[45] Or was put on inquiry as to such facts to a sufficient degree.
[46] See *Waiver — Types and Elements* at para. 4.22.
[47] As a waiver is an unequivocal act committed in light of the requisite knowledge, if the knowledge of the agent is not to be imputed to the bank, then the agent will not have authority to waive breaches on the bank's behalf and *vice versa*.
[48] The borrower will only have to do so where the decision to call in the facility rested with the syndicate or a majority of the banks involved as opposed to with the agent.
[49] See *Agency* at paras 15.04, 15.08.
[50] See *Agency*, Chap. 14 *passim*.
[51] See by analogy *Mardorf Peach & Co Ltd v Attica Sea Carriers Corp of Liberia, The Laconia* [1977] AC 850 and Paget at p. 304 (in the context of EFT).

express authorization.[52] Thirdly, if the knowledge was passed on to a senior director or employee of the bank, then the bank will be fixed with that director's or employee's knowledge[53] unless the bank can show: that the director or employee had no involvement with the bank's affairs in that regard;[54] that the director or employee had no involvement or awareness of that particular transaction;[55] or that the information was received by the employee or director in another capacity.[56] Fourthly, where the director or employee is perpetrating a fraud on the bank, the bank will not be fixed with that director's or employee's knowledge if the bank's possession of that knowledge would mean that it was also aware of the fraud.[57] Fifthly, where the bank's employees have represented that they are authorized to take messages and pass them on to the loan officer or senior management, the bank will be fixed with the knowledge given to those employees[58] — the bank will not be able to rely on the breakdown of its internal communications to defeat the allegation that it was aware of the breach.

Effect of the waiver

In accord with standard principles and subject to one caveat, waiver by election is usually irrevocable; pure and unilateral waivers are suspensory unless and until acted upon. **15.18**

The caveat to the above is that the lending bank cannot waive part of a debt; that is the lending bank cannot by making an unequivocal **15.19**

---

[52] See by analogy *Whitney v Great Northern Insurance Co* [1917] 32 DLR 756; *Beasant v Northern Life Insurance Co* [1923] 2 DLR 1086 *per* Cameron J.A. at 1088–9; *Evans v Employers Mutual Insurance Association Ltd* [1936] 1 KB 505 *per* Greer L.J. at 515 and *Mahli v Abbey Life Insurance* [1995] 4 Re LR 305 *per* Rose L.J. at 310.

[53] *Re Carew's Estate Act (No. 2)* (1862) 31 Beav 39, 54 ER 1051 *per* Lord Romilly M.R. at 42–3, 1053, 46, 1054.

[54] *ibid. per* Lord Romilly M.R. at 42, 1053; see also *Bank of Ireland v Cogry Spinning Co* [1900] 1 IR 219.

[55] *Re Peruvian Rlys Co v Thames and Mersey Marine Insurance Co* (1867) 2 Ch App 617 at 618 and *Powles v Page* (1846) 3 CB 16.

[56] *Société Generale de Paris v Tramways Union Co* (1884) 14 QBD 424 *per* Cotton L.J. at 443; see also *Re Fenwick Stobart & Co* [1902] 1 Ch 507 *per* Buckley J. at 511.

[57] *Re European Bank, ex p. Oriental Commercial Bank* (1870) 5 Ch App 358 *per* Sir G.M. Giffard L.J. at 361–2; see also *Belmont Finance Corporation Ltd v Williams Furniture Ltd* [1979] Ch 250 *per* Buckley L.J. at 261H–2A; *PCW Syndicates v PCW Reinsurers* [1996] 1 Lloyd's Rep. 241 *per* Staughton L.J. at 254 col. 1–247 col. 2.

[58] *Re Brewery Assets Corporation, Truman's Case* [1894] 3 Ch 272 *per* Wright J. at 275.

representation waive its rights to claim the full amount due and owing under the facility.[59] This accords with the rule in *Pinnel's Case*[60] and is therefore subject to the same exceptions. Therefore, a waiver of part of the amounts due under the loan facility may be permissible where: the borrower has offered additional non-monetary consideration;[61] there has been an alteration in the place or mechanism of payment under the facility;[62] a third party promise to pay some of the debt has been accepted;[63] there has been a composition of creditors; and, in cases where the facility is being paid by means of a bill of exchange, there has been a renunciation of the bill under section 62 of the Bills of Exchange Act 1882.[64]

Practical responses

The prudent bank has two mechanisms of protecting itself. First, a 'non-waiver' clause can be inserted into the facility. That clause will offer some protection but will be strictly construed against the bank.[65] Secondly, the bank should react to all defaults by the borrower as quickly as possible reaching a conclusion as to whether to call-in the facility or continue with the transaction. If the bank decides to accept further repayments under the facility, then unless it has taken unusual steps to protect its position, it should be prepared to be held to have waived its rights. 15.20

THE MAINTENANCE OF SECURITY

Where the principal security backing the loan is a contract of guarantee, that contract can be affected in three ways by waiver: a waiver of the terms of the guarantee itself; the effect of a waiver of the terms of the 15.21

[59] See *Re Selectmove* [1995] 1 WLR 474, CA *per* Lord Justice Peter Gibson at 480C–1D; *Foakes v Beer* (1884) 9 App Cas 605; *Variation* at para. 2.24 and *Equitable Forbearance* at para. 12–09.

[60] (1602) 5 Co Rep. 117a; see also *Foakes v Beer* (1884) 9 App Cas 605.

[61] See *Pinnel's Case* (1602) 5 Co Rep. 117a.

[62] See *Vanbergen v St Edmunds Properties Ltd* [1933] 2 KB 223 *per* Lord Hanworth M.R. at 232–3.

[63] *Kemp v Watt* (1846) 15 M & W 672, 153 ER 1020 *per* Parke B. at 680–1, 1024; *Henderson v Stobart* (1850) 5 Exch 99; *Hirachand Punamchand v Temple* [1911] 2 KB 330 *per* Fletcher Moulton L.J. at 339.

[64] See para. 15.29 below.

[65] See *R v Paulson* [1921] 1 AC 271 *per* Lord Atkinson at 280. See also *Insurance* at para. 19.71.

facility on the guarantee; and a waiver of the guarantor's rights of subrogation against the borrower.

Waiver of the terms of the guarantee

The courts have used waiver as a mechanism for bypassing the complexities arising from section 4 of the Statute of Frauds.[66] As a result, it is now clear that the provisions of the guarantee can be waived without difficulty and without attracting the formal requirements laid down by section 4. If there is to be a waiver of the provisions of the guarantee, the requirements set out elsewhere will have to be complied with.[67] **15.22**

Waiver of the terms of the principal contract

By contrast with the established view that a material variation of the principal contract discharges the guarantor,[68] it is unclear whether a waiver of the terms of the principal contact has the same effect. It might be said that as both variation and waiver modify the obligations set out in the principal contract, the guarantor should be discharged in either event. Thus, where the effect of the waiver has been to alter substantially the day to day operation of the guarantee, the courts have held that the alteration is tantamount to being a variation of the contract and has the effect of discharging the guarantor.[69] This approach makes practical sense but, first, avoids the issue and, secondly, tends to confuse the doctrines of waiver and variation. **15.23**

The alternative approach is to consider the nature of the bargain entered into by the guarantor. Here the guarantor assumes the risk that it will become liable as a result of the lending bank's business practices. Therefore, as a waiver arguably is no more than an example of those business practices,[70] the guarantor has assumed the risks associated with waiver and should not be discharged.[71] On this analysis, a variation is **15.24**

---

66 See para. 15.02 above.

67 See *Waiver — Types and Elements passim.*

68 See para. 15.04 above.

69 See *Bank of Baroda v Patel* [1996] 1 Lloyd's Rep. 391 *per* Potter J. at 396 col. 2.

70 For example, the effectiveness of the lending bank's due diligence tests or the extent to which the lending bank is risk averse.

71 See Johan Steyn (as he then was) 'Guarantees: the Co-extensiveness Principle' (1974) 90 *LQR* 246 at 256–8; 260–1.

to be distinguished from a waiver on the basis that variation is a bilateral, permanent alteration of the principal contract, and waiver may not be. The guarantor does not accept the risks associated with a variation because the permanent nature of the alteration and the involvement of the borrower increase the risk of prejudice to the guarantor. Thus, the guarantor will be discharged by the variation and not by the waiver. This approach may make commercial sense in ensuring that concessions granted in the ordinary course of business do not vitiate the contract. However, the approach fails to take into account the similar practical effect that waiver and variation may have on the principal contract — both may alter the future performance of the principal contract and do so irrevocably.

On balance, we would tentatively submit that the proper approach is the former. One should therefore consider the practical similarities between waiver and variation. If, as is often the case, the application of the two doctrines has similar results, then there is no reason why the two doctrines should be treated differently. Additionally, the historical reason for the guarantor being discharged — that it is being deprived of its rights against the borrower or that the risk it is guaranteeing has substantially altered — holds good in either case. It follows that the guarantor should be discharged whenever there is a material modification to the terms or operation of the principal contract, whether that modification is effected either by a waiver or by a variation. **15.25**

Waiver of the right to subrogate

In the normal course of events, the guarantor will be able, after it has paid on the guarantee, to subrogate against the borrower to recoup monies paid to the lending bank. As with all rights, the right to subrogate can be waived. However, given that the right to subrogate represents a valuable benefit to the guarantor, the court will be reluctant to find that the guarantor has foregone its rights. Thus, the court will find that the right was waived only in the clearest cases (and not by a mere course of dealings between the parties[72]) or when it can be shown that the guarantor, with full knowledge of the right that it is losing,[73] has received **15.26**

[72] *Re Bulmer, ex p. Johnson* (1853) 3 De GM & G 218, 43 ER 86 *per* Lord Cranworth L.C. at 235, 93.

[73] *Lake v Brutton* (1856) 8 De GM & G 440, 44 ER 460 *per* Knight Bruce L.J. at 452, 465.

a comparable benefit in lieu of the rights it is losing, for example, an indemnity from the lending bank.[74]

SYNDICATION

The syndication of large or high risk loan facilities will inevitably create an agency relationship between the lead or agent bank and the members of the syndicate. In most cases, the syndication agreement will set out the agent's powers including the circumstances in which the agent bank can waive breaches of the facility.[75] If the syndication agreement makes no provision for waiver whatsoever, whether or not the agent bank can waive breaches will be decided on normal agency principles, namely whether the agent is authorized to make the representation and whether its knowledge will be imputed to the syndicate.[76] If the syndicate has delegated the running of the facility to the agent bank, it is likely that the agent will have authority to waive breaches of the loan facility. **15.27**

BILLS OF EXCHANGE[77]

The interaction between waiver and bills of exchange is complex, a complexity which arose from the status of bills of exchange under the law merchant and which is now reflected in the provisions of the Bills of Exchange Act 1882. The result is that a distinction must be drawn between a waiver of the terms of the bill itself, renunciation,[78] and a **15.28**

---

[74] *Cooper v Jenkins* (1863) 32 Beav 337, 55 ER 132 *per* Lord Romilly M.R. at 339–40, 133.

[75] Usually the agent bank will be permitted to waive minor breaches of the facility and less minor breaches where its actions have been approved by a certain proportion of the syndicate, that proportion being calculated by reference to the ratio between the amounts advanced by each voting bank and the overall amount of the facility. For a typical waiver provision see Cresswell *Encyclopaedia of Banking Law* Butterworths, London loose-leaf at F-5300. Where powers are conferred on the majority of the syndicate that majority will be able to bind and waive the rights of the minority — see, by analogy, *Re Dominion of Canada Freehold Estate and Timber Co Ltd* (1886) 55 LT 347 and *Follit v Eddystone Granite Quarries* [1892] 3 Ch 75.

[76] See para. 15.11 above.

[77] A cheque is a bill of exchange (see ss. 73 and 3(1) of the Bills of Exchange Act 1882). However, as cheques are no longer, in the main, negotiable instruments, many of the points raised here do not apply to cheques. The following paragraphs should therefore be treated as dealing with bills of exchange *simpliciter* unless we expressly state otherwise (see, *e.g.* n. 92 below).

[78] Governed by s. 62 of the Bills of Exchange Act 1882.

waiver of the formalities associated with payment of the bill namely waiver of notice of dishonour and presentment.

Renunciation

Bills of exchange traditionally formed an exception to the common law doctrine that whilst a contract could be mutually discharged prior to breach,[79] discharge after breach could only be by way of accord and satisfaction.[80] A bill could be discharged at any time[81] for two reasons. First, a bill, being an internationally recognized instrument, was used in countries where there was no need for accord and satisfaction post breach; and secondly, a party informed of a renunciation would either act to its detriment or would change its position giving it a cast iron estoppel/equitable forbearance or restitutionary defence to an action on the bill.[82] The Bills of Exchange Act reflected this state of affairs by allowing for the renunciation of a bill. **15.29**

Section 62 of the Act provides: **15.30**

> (1) Where the holder of a bill on or after its maturity absolutely and unconditionally renounces his rights against the acceptor the bill is discharged.
> The renunciation must be in writing, unless the bill is delivered up to the acceptor.
> (2) The liabilities of any party to a bill may in like manner be renounced by the holder, before, at, or after its maturity; but nothing in this section shall affect the rights of a holder in due course without notice of the renunciation.

The effect of the renunciation is firstly, to release the acceptor of the bill from the obligations accrued under the bill and, secondly, to release *all* parties to the bill.[83] The act of renunciation therefore operates as a pure or unilateral waiver of the holder's rights[84] under the bill, the unequivocal representation being made by the written communication of the renunciation to other parties. The renunciation is unconditional.[85] However, the act of renunciation is potentially more wide ranging than **15.31**

---

[79] *Dobson v Espie* (1857) 26 LJ Ex 240 *per* Pollock C.B. and Martin B. at 241.
[80] *Foster v Dawber* (1851) 6 Ex 839, 155 ER 785 *per* Parke B. at 851, 790–1.
[81] *ibid. per* Parke B. at 852, 791.
[82] *ibid.*
[83] Subs. (2); *Jones & Co v Whitaker* (1887) 3 TLR 723.
[84] To present the bill and receive payment.
[85] *Abrey v Crux* (1869) LR 5 CP 37.

a pure or unilateral waiver: parties other than the holder and acceptor can be affected by it . Therefore, limits are imposed on the circumstances in which a bill can be renounced. Thus, as between holder and acceptor, the bill can only be renounced after maturity;[86] the renunciation must be in writing — written evidence will not suffice[87] although the renunciation may be spelt out from more than one document.[88] It follows that mere delivery of the bill is insufficient to constitute a renunciation,[89] some additional act will be required.

Waiver of formalities

It is important to note that whilst renunciation is a specialized form of waiver, other rights accruing under the bill are also subject to the doctrine. Thus, the formalities required for payment on the bill are capable of being waived. Further, unlike a renunciation, a waiver of these formalities[90] does not have to be communicated to a particular party to the bill or indeed to any party to the bill.[91] 15.32

The Bills of Exchange Act provides that the formalities of entitlement to a notice of dishonour and to presentation of the bill[92] can be waived. A notice of dishonour[93] can be waived by any unequivocal act;[94] the presentation of the bill for payment can be either be waived 15.33

[86] *Dod v Edwards* (1827) 2 C & P 602.

[87] *In re George. Francis v Bruce* (1890) 44 Ch D 627 *per* Chitty J. at 632.

[88] *Dickinson v Lucas* (1909) 101 LT 27 *per* Eve J. at 29.

[89] *Midland Bank v Harris* [1963] 1 WLR 1021 *per* Megaw J. at 1025; *Cohn v Warner* (1891) 8 TLR 11 *per* Collins J.; contra. *Rimalt v Cartwright* (1925) 132 LT 40 at 42.

[90] Except of course where the waiver is effected by means of an indorsement to the bill under s. 16 of the Bills of Exchange Act 1882.

[91] *Potter v Rayworth* (1811) 13 East 417, 104 ER 432 *per* Lord Ellenborough C.J. and Bayley J. at 418–19, 433 and *Gunson v Metz* (1823) 1 B & C 193, 107 ER 72 at 195, 73.

[92] Waiver of presentation was the way by which cheque truncation, the process in electronic banking by which *physical* presentation of the cheque to the paying bank can be avoided, had to take place (see Paget at p. 279). However, given the coming into effect of the Deregulation (Bills of Exchange) Order 1996 (1996/2993) presentation of the cheque can now take place by notification of the essential details of the cheque by electronic means. Waiver is therefore no longer required.

[93] In theory, the drawer on a cheque is entitled to a notice of dishonour (s. 48 of the Bills of Exchange Act 1882) and if it is not given or is not required in the circumstances, no liability will accrue. However, in practice, notices of dishonour are normally not required on cheques either because the bank on which the cheque is drawn is under no obligation to pay (s. 50(2)(c) of the Bills of Exchange Act 1882) or because the drawer has countermanded payment (see Paget at p. 244).

[94] s. 50(2)(b) of the Bills of Exchange Act 1882.

expressly or impliedly.[95] In the main, those provisions will bite as between the holder of the bill requesting payment and the payor. However, any indorsor of the bill can by indorsing the bill waive any of the holder in due course's duties under it.[96] Those duties include presentation and the giving of a notice of dishonour. Although the wording adopted by the Bill of Exchange Act does vary, it is submitted that a waiver of formalities to a bill may either be a waiver by election (where the formalities have not been met and the waivor pays on the bill) or a pure waiver (where the waivor excuses the future performance of the formalities). In either event, the elements of an unequivocal representation with requisite knowledge will in all probability be required.

Unequivocal representation

The clearest form of unequivocal representation will either be a promise by the waivor that it will pay on the bill in any event or the waivor meeting any obligation to pay imposed by the bill. Such a promise will act as a waiver of any entitlement to notice of dishonour[97] (even if the time for giving the notice has expired)[98] and of any entitlement to presentation of the bill.[99] It also appears that an entitlement to a notice of dishonour can be waived by the waivor assuming the burden of discovering if the bill has been dishonoured[1] or intimating that it is aware that the bill will be dishonoured and that he will therefore be liable on it. **15.34**

However, care must be taken to define exactly the representation made and whether any rights have in fact been waived.[2] Thus, if, on analysis, the promise to pay is conditional upon the giving of notice or presentment, there will be no waiver.[3] Further, it may well be that the waivor **15.35**

---

[95] s. 46(2)(e) of the Bills of Exchange Act 1882.

[96] s. 16 of the Bills of Exchange Act 1882; see also *Blou v Georgiades* (1959) (1) SA 219 (waiver of requirement of notice of dishonour).

[97] *Cordery v Colville* (1863) 32 LJCP 210 *per* Byles J. 211 col. 1.

[98] *Woods v Dean* (1862) 32 LJQB 1 *per* Cockburn C.J. at 5.

[99] See *Vaughan v Fuller* (1746) 2 Stra 1246, 93 ER 1159; *Hopley v Dufresne* (1812) 15 East 275; 104 ER 848; *Hodge v Fillis* (1813) 3 Camp 462; 170 ER 1447 at 465; 1447 *per* Ellenborough C.J. (promise to pay or partial payment on account); *Newman v Browne* [1925] 1 DLR 676 (payment of interest due under the bill).

[1] *Phipson v Kneller* (1815) 4 Camp 285, 171 ER 91 *per* Lord Ellenborough C.J. and *Burgh v Legge* (1839) 5 M & W 418, 151 ER 177 *per* Parke B. at 402–2, 178–9.

[2] *Coulcher v Toppin* (1866) 2 TLR 657 *per* Lord Herschell L.C. at 658 col. 2.

[3] *Pickin v Graham* (1833) 1 Cr & M 725, 149 ER 591 *per* Vaughan B. at 727–30, 592–3 and *Prideaux v Collier* (1817) 2 Stark NPC 57, 171 ER 571.

has in fact only waived part of its rights and therefore will only be liable for some of the monies covered by the bill.[4]

Knowledge

Four points arise. First, it may well be that knowledge of the facts[5] giving rise to the right to avoid payment is sufficient to found the waiver.[6] It would follow that bills of exchange would be anomalous in this respect. However, it is submitted that in line with the more modern approach to waiver,[7] knowledge of the relevant legal rights will be required to found a waiver but, in most cases, the courts will be extremely willing to find that the waivor had the requisite knowledge. The court will do so either on the basis that a party using a bill of exchange will be familiar with its rights or as a result of the court's willingness to find that the technical formalities in this area have been waived.[8] Secondly, the requisite knowledge will be imputed to the waivor in accordance with the rules of agency.[9] Thus, for example, an attorney or clerk who has management of the case can make a promise to pay on the bill and that promise will be an effective waiver of the formalities.[10] Thirdly, it is important to note that it is *knowledge* that is required not *notice*.[11] It follows that the relevant principles to be applied are not those which govern the transmission of the notice of dishonour to the principal but those which govern imputation of knowledge.[12] Fourthly, once a *prima facie* case of an unequivocal act coupled with knowledge is made out, the waivor will be required to show that it was ignorant of its rights[13] or that the **15.36**

---

4 *Fletcher v Frogatt* (1827) 2 C& P 569, 172 ER 259 *per* Abbott C.J.; contra. *Standage v Creighton* (1832) 5 C & P 406, 172 ER 1029 *per* Denman C.J. at 1030.
5 As opposed to knowledge of the *rights* arising from the known facts.
6 *Stevens v Lynch* (1810) 12 East 38, 104 ER 16.
7 See *Waiver — Types and Elements* at para. 4.22.
8 See, *e.g. Lombard Banking Ltd v Central Garage and Engineering Co Ltd* [1963] 1 QB 220 *per* Scarman J. at 233.
9 Discussed in the banking context at para. 15.16 above. See also *Agency passim.*
10 *Standage v Creighton* (1832) 5 C & P 406, 172 ER 1029 *per* Denman C.J. at 1030.
11 *Pickin v Graham* (1833) 1 Cr & M 725, 149 ER 591 *per* Vaughan B. at 727, 592; *Carter v Flower* (1847) 16 M & W 743, 1553 ER 1390 *per* Parke B. at 749, 1392 and *Byles* p. 181.
12 Assuming that there is a distinction in English law *cf.* Bowstead at para. 8.205.
13 *Taylor v Jones* (1809) 2 Camp 105, 170 ER 1096 *per* Bayley J. at 106, 1096 and *Swift Canadian Co v Duff* (1916) 38 OLR 163.

unequivocal act was made as a result of a mistake of fact[14] or that there was inexcusable delay in presenting the bill[15] to avoid liability.

Effect of the waiver

15.37 In general, the waiver will have the same effect as in the general law. However, two particular issues arise in relation to bills of exchange. These issues arise from the fact that bills of exchange are negotiable instruments and will therefore be passed down a chain from holder to holder or from indorsee to indorsee. First, where the entitlement which has been waived is the entitlement to a service of a notice, all subsequent holders of the bill will be entitled to rely on the waiver and claim monies on the bill[16] the reason being that if that were not the case, the obligation to provide a notice of dishonour would change from holder to holder as the bill was negotiated depending on their relationship with the waivor. Similarly, where a defence to a claim on the bill, for example, laches, is waived by a party to the bill paying the holder, the waivor cannot sue those who negotiated the bill prior to him;[17] they are entitled to be discharged.[18]

15.38 Secondly, any waiver by the plaintiff of execution against one party to the bill will not prevent the plaintiff from executing against another party to the bill. Therefore, a waiver of a writ of *fieri facias* against the acceptor is no bar to execution against the drawer of the bill.[19]

DOCUMENTARY CREDITS

15.39 The accepted course of business in the international transactions is that the goods or services will be paid for by a banker's documentary credit.[20] The result of that practice is the creation of four autonomous[21] and

---

[14] *Blesard v Hirst* (1770) 5 Burr 2670, 98 ER 402 *per* Lord Mansfield at 2671–2, 403.

[15] *Taylor v Jones* (1809) 2 Camp 105, 170 ER 1096 *per* Bayley J. at 106, 1096 and *Swift Canadian Co v Duff* (1916) 38 OLR 163.

[16] *Coulcher v Toppin* (1866) 2 TLR 657 *per* Lord Herschell L.C. at 658 col. 2 and *Bank of Toronto v Bennett* (1925) 57 OLR 326.

[17] *Turner v Leech* (1821) 4 B & Ald 451, 106 ER 1002 *per* Abbott C.J. at 452–3, 1003.

[18] *Smith v Mullett* (1809) 2 Camp 208, 170 ER 1131.

[19] *Pole v Ford* (1816) 2 Chit Rep. 125.

[20] *Ian Stach v Baker Bosley Ltd* [1958] 2 QB 130 *per* Diplock J. at 137–8.

[21] See *Hamzeh Malas & Sons v British Imex Industries Ltd* [1958] 2 QB 127 *per* Jenkins L.J. at 129 for an early statement relating to the autonomy of such contracts. Autonomy is central to the use and need for documentary credits — see Paget at

interrelated contracts — the underlying contract (usually a contract of sale between buyer and seller);[22] the contract between the buyer and the issuing bank for the issue of the documentary credit; the contract/agency relationship[23] between the issuing bank and the confirming bank for the transmission of documents and funds against those documents; and the contract between the confirming bank and the seller for the provision of the documents by the seller and transmission of the funds to the seller.[24] A 'paper transaction'[25] is created in which payment is made against documents of sale by means of the documentary credits.[26] It follows that the actual condition of the goods is irrelevant as far as the banks are concerned. Therefore, for present purposes, we are concerned solely with the documentary aspects of the contracts[27] and the application of waiver to each.

As the transaction is based purely on the presentation and transfer of the documents;[28] a party to the transaction will only be able to refuse payment or refuse to accept payment if the documents[29] presented are defective or do not conform with the contractual provisions.[30] If the **15.40**

p. 656; Uniform Customs and Practice for Documentary Credits 1993 Revision ICC 500 (UCP 500) Art. 3. Most UCP provisions can be overridden by the express requirements laid down in the credit.

22 For ease we therefore refer to the parties to the underlying contract as the buyer and seller.

23 *Bank Melli Iran v Barclays Bank (Dominion, Colonial and Overseas)* [1951] 2 Lloyd's Rep. 367 *per* McNair J. at 376 col. 2.

24 *United City Merchants (Investments) Ltd v Royal Bank of Canada* [1983] 1 AC 168 *per* Lord Diplock at 182H–3D; *Bankers Trust Co Ltd v State Bank of India* [1991] 2 Lloyd's Rep. 443 *per* Lloyd L.J. (as he then was) at 445 col. 1.

25 As to which see UCP 500 Art. 14(b); Paget at pp. 667 ff., 685 ff.

26 It must be remembered that two categories of documents are at issue — those relating to payment, the documentary credit(s), and those relating to the underlying transaction, most usually those relating to the transfer of goods, the shipping documents and/or documents relating to title. We refer to the former as documentary credits and the latter as the documents of sale.

27 For the relationship between the non-documentary elements of the sale/carriage of goods contract and waiver see *Sale of Goods and Shipping* para. 20.13.

28 We use the word 'documents' to refer to all the documentary elements of the transaction.

29 For a consideration of the relevant documents see Paget at p. 667 ff.

30 Compliance with the contractual requirements is strict — see *Equitable Trust Co of New York v Dawson Partners Ltd* (1927) 27 Ll L Rep. 49; *Skandinaviska Akt v Barclays Bank* (1925) 22 Ll L Rep. 523; *Kydon Compania Naviera SA v National Westminster Bank* [1981] 1 Lloyd's Rep. 68 and *Glencore International AG v Bank of China* [1996] 1 Lloyd's Rep. 135 *per* Lord Bingham M.R. (as he then was) at 150 cols 1–2.

documents are defective,[31] then the party has the right to reject the documents and to proceed no further with the transaction. It follows that the doctrine of waiver will be invoked where it appears that a party has not rejected defective or non-conforming documents. It also follows that we are dealing, subject to one possible exception,[32] with waiver by election.

Unilateral waiver by the bank?

15.41 This possible exception relates to the relationship between the issuing bank and the buyers. The provision or acceptance of the documentary credit may be linked into a long standing loan facility offered by the issuing bank and supporting the buyers' trading activities. If so, the bank may require the loan facility to be secured by the bank having the documents of sale made out to its order enabling it to have first recourse to those goods. It is arguable that such a requirement would operate solely for the issuing bank's benefit and therefore could be subject to a unilateral waiver.[33] However, as we have suggested elsewhere, there are conceptual difficulties with any unilateral waiver, difficulties which are increased in this context for three reasons. First, all obligations under the loan facility will be bilateral, the provision of adequate and enforceable security by the buyer being, in most cases, a condition precedent to draw down. Therefore, the existence of adequate security is for both parties' benefit. Secondly, a unilateral waiver of rights arising from defects in the documents of sale would be contrary to the Uniform Customs and Practice for Documentary Credits 1993 Revision ICC 500 ('UCP 500').[34] Thirdly, any change to the documents of sale may affect the last three contracts forming the overall transaction and referred to above. The UCP 500 and the relationships between the banks and the buyers/sellers are structured to prevent such unilateral changes from happening.[35] If a bank were able to alter unilaterally in advance the documents of sale elements of the transaction, uncertainty would be introduced into the transaction. As one of the main practical reasons

---

[31] As they are in a significant number of cases — see *Banque de l'Indochine et de Suez SA v JH Rayner (Mincing Lane) Ltd* [1983] QB 711 and Clive Schmitthoff 'Discrepancy of Documents in Letter of Credit Transactions' [1987] *JBL* 94.

[32] Which relates to the possibility of a unilateral waiver.

[33] *Guaranty Trust of New York v Van Den Berghs Ltd* (1925) 22 Ll L Rep. 447 *per* Scrutton L.J. at 454.

[34] See Jack at para. 4.19, p. 74.

[35] See para. 15.48 ff below and the express UCP 500 provisions governing waiver.

for this type of transaction is commercial certainty, anything which erodes that certainty would run counter to the UCP 500, the banking relationships between the banks and the buyers/sellers and the rationale of the transaction.

We would therefore suggest that there can be no unilateral waiver by the bank. It follows that a bank can only waive the rights arising from defects in the documents after non-conforming or defective documents have been presented to it. It follows that with documentary credits there can only ever be a waiver by election by the bank which is subject to the rules and practices set out below. **15.42**

Waiver by election

Unequivocal representation

The requirements to found this type of waiver are the same as those under the general law. Thus, a party will make an unequivocal representation by the acceptance of the non-conforming or defective documents or by shipping the goods[36] or by asking for an extension of time for delivering the goods.[37] However, a party may also lose the right to reject by delay in checking the documents and giving its grounds for its rejection.[38] If that process were a waiver, it would appear to be inconsistent with the general law. It is submitted, however, that the principle is consistent with the rule that delay may lead to loss of rights if the other party suffers prejudice.[39] In commercial transactions of this nature 'time is of essence' and any unnecessary delay will almost automatically therefore be to the prejudice of the other party. **15.43**

Knowledge

The requisite knowledge again is that which is required under the general law.[40] However, it is important to note that a court may well be willing to presume that the parties to the transaction have knowledge of the facts — having been provided with the documents which will be either **15.44**

[36] See *Cape Asbestos Co Ltd v Lloyd's Bank Ltd* [1921] WN 274.
[37] *Enrico Furst & Co v WE Fischer Ltd* [1960] 2 Lloyd's Rep. 340.
[38] *Bank Melli Iran v Barclays Bank* [1951] 2 TLR 1057.
[39] This rule is based on estoppel or equitable forbearance principles — see *Allen v Robles* [1969] 1 WLR 1193 *per* Fenton-Atkinson L.J. at 1196G–H and *Waiver — Types and Elements* at para. 4.10.
[40] See *Waiver — Types and Elements* at para. 4.22.

good or bad on their face,[41] and of their rights, being experienced commercial men and banks. Where an agency relationship is involved, knowledge will be imputed in accordance with the rules of agency. Thus, for example, the parties are entitled to assume that another party's representatives will pass on information to the relevant person.[42]

The one difficulty which arises in this area relates to the loss of rights as between the issuing and confirming banks. The relationship between these banks is that of principal and agent[43] and it has been said that any loss of rights to reject as between those banks arises by way of the defects being ratified not by any waiver of rights.[44] If the test for knowledge in the case of ratification is different from that applicable in cases of waiver, then the knowledge required will vary according to the parties involved. However, as argued elsewhere,[45] we would suggest that in fact the courts will apply the same test whether ratification or waiver is at issue. It follows that there is, at most, a semantic difference between the loss of rights as between the issuing and confirming banks and the loss of rights as between the other parties to the transaction. **15.45**

Relevance of waiver to documentary credits

Waiver has relevance to the transaction in three ways: what defects in the documents can found a waiver of a party's rights; the interaction between waiver and the UCP 500; and the effect of the waiver on the relationships between the parties. **15.46**

Defects capable of founding a waiver

It is now clear that any defect in the documents is capable of leading to a waiver of a party's rights. Thus, for example, requirements that the documentary credit be confirmed and irrevocable[46] or be in a particular **15.47**

[41] See the analogous position and its associated difficulties in sale of goods and shipping — *Sale of Goods and Shipping* at para. 20.02, 20.05.

[42] *Midland Bank v Seymour* [1955] 2 Lloyd's Rep. 147 *per* Devlin J. at 169 col. 1.

[43] *Bank Melli Iran v Barclays Bank (Dominion, Colonial and Overseas)* [1951] 2 Lloyd's Rep. 367 *per* McNair J. at 376 col. 2.

[44] *Bank Melli Iran v Barclays Bank (Dominion, Colonial and Overseas)* [1951] 2 Lloyd's Rep. 367 *per* McNair J. at 376 col. 2–377 col. 2 and *Westminster Bank v Banca Nazionale di Credito* (1928) 31 Ll L Rep. 306 at 312 col 1–2.

[45] See *Agency* at para. 14.01, n. 2.

[46] *Panoutsos v Raymond Hadley Corporation of New York* [1917] 2 KB 473 and *Enrico Furst & Co v WE Fischer Ltd* [1960] 2 Lloyd's Rep. 340.

currency[47] or that the documentary credit be opened at a particular time can all be waived. However, it is important to note the acceptance of a defective documentary credit on one occasion does not necessarily mean that future defective documentary credits will also be accepted.[48] The courts will only infer such a waiver of futuie obligations if there is a repeated acceptance of defective documentary credits so as to spell out a course of dealing[49] which can only be resiled from if appropriate notice is given to the other parties to the transaction[50] or if there is a variation of the contract.[51]

Relationship with the UCP 500

Article 14c of the UCP 500 provides: **15.48**

> If the Issuing Bank determines that the documents appear on their face not to be in compliance with the terms and conditions of the Credit, it may in its sole judgment approach the Applicant for a waiver of the discrepancy (ies).

The Article has importance in two respects. First, the numbers of transactions where the documents of sale do not comply is very high. Therefore, some mechanism must be in place for obtaining the buyer's consent to the acceptance of the non-complying documents.[52] Secondly, the issuing bank will need to recoup the monies, expended by and under the documentary credit, from the buyer. The bank will usually do so under an indemnity given to it by the buyer. If the buyer felt that the issuing bank had wrongly waived its rights arising from discrepancy, it might refuse to pay on the indemnity. Article 14c provides a mechanism for legitimizing the bank's actions and avoiding such difficulties.

However, Article 14c does not mean that the banks are absolved **15.49**
from responsibility for examining the documents of sale and deciding whether or not to waive rights arising from any defects found on

---

47 *WJ Alan & Co Ltd v El Nasr Export* [1972] 2 QB 189.
48 See *Cape Asbestos Co Ltd v Lloyd's Bank Ltd* [1921] WN 274 *per* Bailhache J. at 275.
49 As in *WJ Alan & Co Ltd v El Nasr Export* [1972] 2 QB 189 at 218, 221.
50 *Panoutsos v Raymond Hadley Corporation of New York* [1917] 2 KB 473.
51 See, *e.g.* *WJ Alan & Co Ltd v El Nasr Export and Import Co* [1972] 2 QB 189 *per* Megaw L.J. at 217.
52 See the findings of fact in *Bankers Trust Co v State Bank of India* [1991] 2 Lloyd's Rep. 443. In fact, 90 per cent of the approaches under Art. 14c lead to a waiver of the discrepancy.

examination. As far as the issuing bank is concerned, it must still examine the documents of sale although after examination the bank may pass the documents to the buyer for the buyer to make a commercial decision as to whether to accept or reject the documents.[53] The buyers will not be permitted to carry out the bank's examination for it, nor will it be appropriate for the buyers to search through the documents of sale searching for discrepancies.[54] The distinction between the buyers and the issuing bank in this regard is made clear by the fact that the buyers can unilaterally waive their rights (usually a waiver relating to the provisions of the underlying contract which triggers payment via the documentary credit);[55] the bank may not.[56]

To ensure that the transaction is not stultified by the referral back to the buyers, the issuing bank must identify the defects on which it will rely within a reasonable time; if it does not, the right to reject will be lost by either under UCP 500 Article 14(e)[57] or by lapse of time.[58] Further, under the UCP 500,[59] if the issuing bank fails to state all the defects on which it will rely, it will lose the right to rely on any further defects at a later date.[60] By way of contrast, under English common law and as with the general law of waiver, the issuing bank will be able to rely on additional grounds of rejection even if it fails to raise those grounds first time around.[61] The position will be different if the issuing **15.50**

---

53 *Bankers Trust Co v State Bank of India* [1991] 2 Lloyd's Rep. 443 *per* Farquharson L.J. at 455 col. 1.

54 *ibid. per* Lloyd L.J. at 449 col. 2.

55 *ibid. per* Lloyd L.J. at 451 col. 1.

56 See para. 15.41 above.

57 Paget (at p. 688) states that said preclusion is '*akin to an estoppel*'. However, we would suggest that, given the above and the fact that no detrimental reliance is required, the preclusion is founded on waiver. There is an additional debate as to whether the result achieved by Art. 14(e) is in fact a ratification by the issuing bank of the defects (see Paget at p. 688, n. 14 and *Westminster Bank Ltd v Banca Nazionale di Credito* (1928) 31 Ll L Rep. 306 *per* Roche J. at 312). However, given that the elements and effect of ratification and waiver are identical for present purposes, in practice little turns on the distinction.

58 *Bank Melli Iran v Barclays Bank* [1951] 2 TLR 1057.

59 See Art. 14(d)(ii).

60 *Hip Hing Hip Fat Co Ltd v Daiwa Bank* [1991] 2 HKLR 35.

61 *Kydon Compania Naviera SA v National Westminster Bank Ltd 'The Lena'* [1981] 1 Lloyd's Rep. 68 *per* Parker J. at 79 cols 1–2; *Skandinaviska Akt v Barclays Bank* (1925) 22 Ll L Rep. 523 *per* Greer J. at 525; *Westminster Bank v Banca Nazionale di Credito* (1928) 31 Ll L Rep. 306 *per* Roche J. at 311 col. 1. In the US, a failure to state all the discrepancies relied on will be a waiver of other grounds — see *Barclays Bank DCO v Mercantile National Bank* [1973] 2 Lloyd's Rep. 541 *per* Ingraham L.J. at 549 col. 1 relying on *Bank of Taiwan v Union National Bank* 1 F 2d 65 at 66 (3rd Cir 1924) and *Continental National Bank v National City Bank* 69 F 2d 312, 318–9 (9th Cir 1934).

bank requests the confirming bank to remedy certain defects, a request which will generate an estoppel preventing the issuing bank from relying on additional grounds at a later date.[62]

Effect on waiver on the relationship between the parties

The UCP 500 is narrowly worded and will bite only on the waiver of defects as between the issuing bank and the buyers. Where the UCP 500 does not apply, the general law applies.[63] Three particular points arise. First, as a matter of practice, a waiver by a confirming bank will be rare. If the confirming bank discovers that the documents are defective, it should refer the documents back to the seller allowing the defects to be remedied in time.[64] Secondly, the issuing bank examining the documents must take care that the result of any waiver which it might give is not the discharge of the indemnity given to it by the buyer.[65] Therefore, the issuing bank should ensure that the indemnity will apply even if it does not refer the documents back to the buyer under Article 14c of the UCP 500. By way of contrast, the buyer will wish to ensure that the indemnity will only apply if there is reference back. Thirdly, where the issuing bank has acted outwith its mandate in waiving defective documents, the buyers may waive the issuing bank's breach of mandate.[66] The effect of that waiver will be, subject to the drafting of the indemnity, to waive any rights which the buyer may have to avoid the indemnity or to treat itself as discharged from liability thereunder. **15.51**

---

62 *Floating Dock Ltd v Hong Kong and Shanghai Banking Corporation* [1986] 1 Lloyd's Rep. 65 *per* Evans J. at 76 col. 1–2 and *Astro Exito Navegacion SA v Chase Manhattan Bank NA, the Messiniaki Tolmi* [1986] 1 Lloyd's Rep. 455 *per* Leggatt J. at 458 col. 2–459.

63 Thus, for example, a waiver of the failure to open a documentary credit in time (by a request for the credit after the time for its opening has passed) will not waive the requirement that time is of the essence in opening that credit — see *Ian Stach v Baker Bosley Ltd* [1958] 2 QB 130 *per* Diplock J. at 144.

64 See Jack at para. 5.37 at pp. 94–5.

65 *Skandinaviska Akt v Barclays Bank* (1925) 22 Ll L Rep. 523 *per* Greer J. at 525 col. 1.

66 *Midland Bank v Seymour* [1955] 2 Lloyd's Rep. 147 *per* Devlin J. at 168 col. 2–171 col. 1 (*obiter*).

ESTOPPEL

The same principles apply to estoppel[67] in the sphere of banking law as elsewhere, there being no mitigation in this sphere[68] of the requirement that the party seeking to rely on an estoppel must establish that there was a representation on which it relied to its detriment.[69] A party will therefore seek to rely on estoppel principles in the banking context where it cannot establish that the bank had the appropriate knowledge to found a waiver or that the person making the representation relied on was not the bank's agent for the purposes of waiver.[70] Estoppel therefore arises in many of the contexts discussed above and we consider its application to: the mandate between customer and bank; guarantees; syndication; bills of exchange and securities; documentary credits; and restitutionary claims brought by the bank. 15.52

THE MANDATE

Apart from the estoppels which may arise on the facts of individual cases as a result of representations made by the bank, the role of estoppel in the operation of the mandate gives rise to two specific issues: whether an estoppel can be created by documents issued by the banks and the role of the so-called estoppel by negligence. 15.53

Estoppel and bank documents

Where the bank issues the customer with a pass book or statement of account, the bank may be estopped by the representations it makes in and by the pass book or statement provided that the other elements 15.54

[67] As stressed in the *Commercial Introduction* (para. 13.04), estoppel is used in the sense of estoppel by representation, estoppel by convention and equitable forbearance, unless otherwise stated.

[68] Contrast *Agency* at para. 14.20 ff.

[69] See Cresswell *Encyclopaedia of Banking Law* Butterworths, London loose-leaf at para. C:611; it is 'scarcely necessary' to point out that the elements of estoppel are necessary in this area.

[70] *Overbrooke Estates Ltd v Glencombe Properties Ltd* [1974] 1 WLR 1335 *per* Brightman J. at 1341B-C; see also *TSB Bank of Scotland plc v Welwyn Hatfield District Council* [1993] 2 Bank LR 267.

necessary for an estoppel are present.[71] Whether or not the bank is estopped will primarily depend on exactly what representation the bank has made. Thus, for example, where the bank credits an account with the sums due under a forged cheque, if that forgery was not detectable by the bank on a reasonable inspection, there will be no estoppel. The representation that the bank made in crediting the account was not that the customer was entitled to the sums but that the bank believed that the cheque was good on a reasonable inspection; a representation from which the bank can resile.[72]

Estoppel by negligence

Under the mandate, the bank is required to debit the customer's bank account on receipt of a payment instruction[73] from the customer provided that the instruction is valid and the account is in credit. Where the bank debits the account as a result of a false or forged instruction, the customer may sue the bank for breach of the mandate. In such a claim, the bank can, in limited circumstances, argue that the customer should not succeed, the customer being precluded from denying that the instruction was valid and an essential element of the customer's cause of action being missing.[74] The alleged basis of the preclusion is an 'estoppel by negligence'. This 'estoppel' will arise where the customer[75] owes the bank a duty in presenting the instruction, the customer is in breach of that duty in presenting the instruction, the bank relies on the presentation and acts to its detriment. It is an 'estoppel' which can be both **15.55**

---

[71] *Holland v Manchester and Liverpool District Banking Co Ltd* (1909) 25 TLR 386 *per* Alverstone C.J. at 387 col. 1 and *United Overseas Bank v Jiwani* [1977] 1 All ER 733.

[72] *National Westminster Bank v Barclays Bank International* [1975] QB 654.

[73] Whether cheque, other bill of exchange or use of a PIN.

[74] See *Swan v North British Australasian Co* (1863) 2 H&C 175, 159 ER 73 at 189–90, 79; *London Joint Stock Bank v Macmillan* [1918] AC 777 *per* Lord Finlay L.C. at 793–4 and *Greenwood v Martins Bank Ltd* [1933] AC 51 *per* Lord Tomlin at 57–8, 59. See also *Tina Motors Pty Ltd v Australia and New Zealand Banking Group Ltd* [1977] VR 205 *per* Crockett J. at 208 ll 45–50 and Paget at pp. 316–17 and Byles at pp. 275–6.

[75] Customer in this sense may include the presentor of a bill (*M'Kenzie v British Linen Co* (1881) 6 App Cas 82); the holder of a promissory note (*William Ewing & Co v Dominion Bank* [1904] AC 806; *Ogilvie v West Australian Mortgage and Agency Corpn Ltd* [1896] AC 257 *per* Lord Watson at 268) but not consecutive holders of a bill (*Scholfield v Earl of Londesborough* [1986] AC 514). We therefore use the word 'customer' as a generic term to cover such persons.

prospective and retrospective[76] and gives rise to two issues: what is the basis of estoppel by negligence and what duty gives rise to the 'estoppel'.

The basis of estoppel by negligence

15.56 In *London Joint Stock Bank v Macmillan*,[77] the House of Lords articulated two bases for the doctrine. First, in presenting the instruction in circumstances in which the customer should have known that the instruction was invalid, the customer owed a duty to the bank to inform it of that fact. Therefore, in not so informing the bank, the customer made a representation that the instruction was valid. The bank relied on that representation by paying under the instruction and suffered a detriment when the customer sought to recover the monies wrongly paid out.[78] The second was that the presentation of the instruction constituted a breach of the customer's duty. The bank suffered loss as a result of that breach — namely paying out under the instruction. That loss was in the same amount as the customer sought to recover from the bank. The customer's claim therefore failed for circuity of action.[79]

15.57 There is authority to support both approaches.[80] However, we would suggest that the better view is that in most cases the customer's claim fails for circuity rather than as a result of an estoppel for four reasons. First, spelling out the appropriate representation to found the 'estoppel by negligence' is extremely tortuous.[81] Apart from the difficulties in showing that silence on the part of the customer amounts to a representation, there are the difficulties in establishing exactly what representation is made. Further, given the supposed estoppel may apply to bank customers and the holders of bills[82] or presentors

[76] *Brown v Westminster Bank Ltd* [1964] 2 Lloyd's Rep. 187 *per* Roskill J. at 200 col. 1–203 col. 2. Therefore, where the customer only discovers the last in a series of forged instructions but has previously made a very clear representation that all the instructions were to be treated as valid, the customer will be precluded from arguing that any of the instructions were forged.

[77] [1918] AC 777.

[78] *ibid.* at 834.

[79] *ibid. per* Lord Finlay at 811.

[80] As to estoppel by negligence see *e.g. Greenwood v Martins Bank Ltd* [1933] AC 51 *per* Lord Tomlin at 57–8, 59 and *Brown v Westminster Bank Ltd* [1964] 2 Lloyd's Rep. 187 *per* Roskill J. at 200 col. 1–203 col. 2. As to circuity see *Swan v North British Australasian Co* (1863) 2 H&C 175, 159 ER 73 at 189–90, 79.

[81] See *Wilson & Meeson v Pickering* [1946] KB 422 *per* Lord Greene M.R. at 425 for a criticism of the reliance on estoppel.

[82] *M'Kenzie v British Linen Co* (1881) 6 App Cas 82.

of promissory notes,[83] it is difficult to spell out a common representation made by all three categories of person. Secondly, it appears that the bank must show that the customer caused the bank to pay on the false instrument as a result of some element of misleading conduct.[84] Put another way, the bank must establish a causative link between the conduct and the loss.[85] That requirement suggests that the proper approach is circuity, arising as it does from a duty/breach/damage analysis not from an estoppel analysis.[86] Thirdly, under the mandate, the bank is entitled to an indemnity from the customer where the customer has caused the bank loss. Where the customer's breach of duty causes the bank to pay on an invalid instruction, the indemnity would operate. That indemnity would, of course, equal and defeat the customer's claim in the same way as circuity would do.[87] Fourthly, given the existence of the mandate and the reciprocal obligations owed by the parties to it, the simplest and most natural analysis would be to argue that there has been a breach of that mandate rather than to search for an estoppel.[88]

There are three counter arguments to the above. First, clearly an estoppel could apply where the customer made an express oral or written representation at the time of giving the instruction that the instruction **15.58**

[83] *William Ewing & Co v Dominion Bank* [1904] AC 806 and *Ogilvie v West Australian Mortgage and Agency Corpn Ltd* [1896] AC 257 *per* Lord Watson at 268.

[84] *The Guardians of Halifax Union v Wheelwright* (1875) LR 10 Exch 183 *per* Cleasby B. at 191 and *Lewes Sanitary Steam Laundry Co v Barclay & Co Ltd* (1906) 95 LT 444 *per* Kennedy J. at 447 col. 1, 448 col. 2.

[85] Thus, where the bank is itself in breach of the mandate or has concealed a material fact, that breach will break the chain of causation and prevent circuity of action from arising — see *George Whitchurch Ltd v Cavanagh* [1902] AC 117 *per* Lord Brampton at 145; *National Westminster Bank Ltd v Barclays Bank International Ltd* [1975] QB 654 *per* Kerr J. at 676; *Secretary of State for Employment v Wellworthy Ltd (No. 2)* [1976] ICR 13 *per* Nield J. at 25A and *Varker v Commercial Banking Co of Sydney Ltd* [1972] 2 NSWLR 967 *per* Macfarlan J. at 976A–B.

[86] This analysis is particularly clear in the Sale of Goods context — see *Sale of Goods and Shipping* at para. 20.21.

[87] *Bank of England v Vagliano Bros* [1891] AC 107 *per* Lord Halsbury L.C. at 114; *per* Lord Selborne at 126–7; *per* Lord Watson at 134 and *per* Lord McNaghten at 159 and *Farquharson Bros & Co v King & Co* [1902] AC 325.

[88] For the contractual analysis see *Commonwealth Trading Bank of Australia v Sydney Wide Stores Pty Ltd* (1981) 35 ALR 513 at 519 ll 30–5, 520 l 5–521 l 15; *Bad Boy Appliances and Furniture Ltd v Toronto Dominion Bank* (1972) 25 DLR (3d) 257 at 261 ff., and *Arrow Transfer Co Ltd v Royal Bank of Canada* (1972) 27 DLR (3d) 81 *per* Martland J. at 87.

was valid.[89] However, such an estoppel would be simple estoppel by representation rather than the more complicated estoppel by negligence. Further, the effect that the estoppel had would depend on the terms of the representation made.[90] Secondly, there is authority to suggest that the English courts adopt a more limited view of the banking mandate than those of the Commonwealth.[91] On such a restrictive view, it is difficult to imply terms into the mandate which oblige the customer to check instructions.[92] However, any difficulty that there may be in establishing such implied terms would not affect the cross-indemnity nor the implied and recognized duties in tort, both of which would also create circuity of action and defeat the claim. Thirdly, it could be said that the bank merely has to suffer detriment, not establish that it has suffered loss and damage. If there was only detriment and no loss, then the bank would be relying on an estoppel not circuity. The difficulty with that approach is that the bank must clearly establish some pecuniary injury in the sense of loss and damage to itself.[93] In all cases that will be the payment out of the monies and, in some cases, the loss of a right to reclaim the monies from the forger or of the right to take steps to protect itself.[94] Each of these losses would found a claim for damages in contract or tort and therefore can form the basis of circuity.

The extent of the duty

The duty on the customer was clearly set out in *Tai Hing Cotton Mill v Liu Chong Hing Bank Ltd.*[95] The duty extends to: (i) conducting 15.59

---

[89] *Bank of England v Vagliano Bros* [1891] AC 107 *per* Lord Halsbury L.C. at 117 and *per* Lord Selborne at 123–4.

[90] *Tina Motors Pty Ltd v Australian and New Zealand Banking Group Ltd* [1977] VR 205 *per* Crockett J. at 210 ll 5–30. Therefore the 'estoppel' might not automatically defeat the customer's claim.

[91] *Joachimson v Swiss Bank Corporation* [1921] 3 KB 110 at 127.

[92] See *Tai Hing Cotton Mill v Liu Chong Hing Bank* Ltd [1986] AC 80 *per* Lord Scarman at 106E–7A.

[93] *M'Kenzie v British Linen Co* (1881) 6 App Cas 82 *per* Lord Watson at 109, 111, 112.

[94] The fact that those proceedings might hypothetically have failed is irrelevant for these purposes — see *M'Kenzie v British Linen Co* (1881) 6 App Cas 82 *per* Lord Watson at 110; *Ogilvie v West Australian Mortgage and Agency Corpn Ltd* [1896] AC 257 *per* Lord Watson at 270; *Knights v Wiffen* (1870) LR 5 QB 660 *per* Blackburn J. at 666; *Brown v Westminster Bank* [1964] 2 Lloyd's Rep. 187 *per* Roskill J. at 200 col. 1–203 col. 2; *Ontario Woodsworth Memorial Foundation v Grozbord* (1969) 4 DLR (3d) 194 at 202; but *cf. Imperial Bank of Canada v Bank of Hamilton* [1903] AC 49 *per* Lord Lindley at 57.

[95] [1986] AC 80.

mandate so that fraud might not occur; and (ii) notifying the bank as and when suspicious circumstances arise. That duty can be extended by the express wording of the mandate provided that such wording is sufficiently clear.[96] The first limb of the duty will therefore include: avoiding the insertion of unusual blank spaces in the cheque as to prevent interpolation;[97] and assisting the bank to recover against forger.[98] However, the duty will not extend: to ensuring that there are no blanks in the cheque;[99] to ruling lines on both sides of payee's name to prevent further names from being added;[1] to monitoring the activities of the joint account holder unless there is something to suggest that the joint account holder is forging checks;[2] to avoiding employing particular persons as the customer's agent;[3] to exercising general care in the conduct of its business;[4] or to checking and verifying all bank statements.[5]

GUARANTEES

As discussed above, one effect of the Statute of Frauds is to make the alteration of guarantees difficult. That difficulty is reflected in part by **15.60**

[96] See *Tai Hing per* Lord Scarman at 108G–10C. A bank can arguably therefore protect its position by inserting into the mandate a clear requirement that its customer verify all debits to the account and notify the bank as soon as discrepancy occurs — see *Bad Boy Appliances and Furniture Ltd v Toronto Dominion Bank* (1972) 25 DLR (3d) 257 at 261 ff. and *Arrow Transfer Co Ltd v Royal Bank of Canada* (1972) 27 DLR (3d) 81 *per* Martland J. at 87.

[97] *London Joint Stock Bank v Macmillan* [1918] AC 777 *per* Lord Finlay at 810.

[98] *Fung Kai Sun v Chan Fui Hing* [1951] AC 489, PC at 506. Therefore, the customer will be in breach if its silence gives the forger the chance to escape and the customer was aware of the potential dangers associated with the forger — see *Ogilvie v West Australian Mortgage and Agency Corp* [1896] AC 257 at 269, 270.

[99] Therefore, where a cheque was properly drawn, save for one space, there was no breach — *Colonial Bank of Australia v Marshall* [1906] AC 559 and *London Joint Stock Bank v Macmillan* [1918] AC 777 *per* Viscount Haldane at 814–15.

[1] *Slingsby v District Bank Ltd* [1931] 2 KB 588 *per* Wright J. at 602.

[2] *Brewer v Westminster Bank* [1952] 2 All ER 650 *per* McNair J. at 655E-G, 656E-F and *Welch v Bank of England* [1955] Ch 508 *per* Harman J. at 537.

[3] *Lewes Sanitary Steam Laundry Co v Barclay & Co Ltd* (1906) 95 LT 444 *per* Kennedy J. at 448 cols 1–2.

[4] *Keptigalla Rubber Estates v National Bank of India* [1909] 2 KB 1010 *per* Bray J. at 1023–6 and *Morison v London County and Westminster Bank* (1913) 18 Com Cas 137 *per* Lord Coleridge J. at 145.

[5] *Wealden Woodlands (Kent) Ltd v National Westminster Bank Ltd* (1983) 133 NLJ 719 (unless the customer is a sophisticated commercial entity that is expected to monitor its finances strictly *Canadian Pacific Hotels Ltd v Bank of Montreal* (1981) 122 DLR (3d) 519 *per* Mongomery J. at 532).

the fact that the courts will be unwilling to allow a plea of estoppel[6] to be used as a mechanism for bypassing the Statute of Frauds.[7] Therefore, although there is no absolute bar on an estoppel being used in that fashion, the circumstances in which the court will permit such an exercise will be limited to those where denying one party the benefit of the estoppel would be manifestly unjust.[8]

SYNDICATION

It is common practice for the agent bank in a syndication to insert into the syndication bible non-reliance clauses. These clauses constitute statements by the members of the syndication that in entering into the arrangement they were not induced by any representation by the agent bank. A clause of this nature will be enforceable because it generates an estoppel. Therefore, the clause must be clear and the agent must have relied on the clause to its detriment.[9] **15.61**

BILLS OF EXCHANGE AND SECURITIES

As with waiver, estoppels may arise under statute or at common law. Under statute the estoppel is created by the express wording of the Bills of Exchange Act 1882 and is, by and large, unproblematic. At common law, the doctrine has given rise to the idea that a bill or security can become negotiable by estoppel. Under either head it is important to note that in modern commercial practice, these estoppels are rare and that where cheques are concerned, it is relatively unlikely that an estoppel will arise.[10] **15.62**

[6] The plea could be one of either estoppel by convention or estoppel by representation.

[7] *Bank of Scotland v Wright* [1991] BCLC 244 *per* Brooke J. at 265a–b.

[8] *Bank of Scotland v Wright* [1991] BCLC 244 *per* Brooke J. at 266d–g applying *Kok Hoong v Leong Cheong Kweng Mines Ltd* [1964] AC 993 *per* Viscount Radcliffe at 1015.

[9] *Lowe v Lombank Ltd* [1960] 1 WLR 196 *per* Diplock J. at 205–6 (for CA).

[10] Thus, for example, an estoppel will not arise between the collecting and issuing bank of a cheque — *Marquess of Bute v Barclays Bank Ltd* [1955] 1 QB 202 *per* McNair J. at 213–4 and *Orbit Mining and Trading Co v Westminster Bank Ltd* [1963] 1 QB 794 *per* Harman L.J. at 827–9. Similarly, it is not possible to suggest that the operation of clearing houses is assisted by estoppel (see *Barclays Bank v Bank of England* [1985] 1 All ER 385 *per* Bingham J. at 391e–h, 392d–g, 394b–e).

Under statute

The Bills of Exchange Act 1882 creates three 'statutory estoppels'. First, the acceptor is precluded from denying to a holder in due course that the drawer's signature is valid;[11] an indorser is precluded from denying to the holder in due course that the drawer's signature and all previous endorsements are valid;[12] and the acceptor for honour is precluded from denying that he is liable on the bill where he has accepted the bill for payment and the bill has been protested for non-payment.[13] In each case, although all the elements required for an estoppel at common law are missing, an 'estoppel' arises by virtue of the statute. 15.63

At common law

There is authority to suggest that a bill or security can become negotiable as a result of an estoppel[14] and that title to the bill or security passes to third parties as a result of an estoppel.[15] This estoppel arises when a principal gives a completed or signed bill[16] or security to its agent with the express purpose of allowing the agent to sell or negotiate the bill or security. There are two possible bases to the estoppel. First, as discussed elsewhere,[17] this is not an estoppel at all but is either a general exception to the *nemo dat* principle or an anomalous rule arising out of the agency relationship as a means of bypassing the *nemo dat* principle. Therefore, whether or not title is created will depend on whether or not the principal authorized the agent to deal with the bill or security[18] and, because the rule applies to preserve the commercial 15.64

---

[11] s. 54(2).

[12] s. 55(2).

[13] s. 66(1).

[14] *Goodwin v Roberts* (1876) 1 App Cas 476 *per* Lord Cairns L.C. at 489–90 and *Easton v London Joint Stock Bank* (1886) 34 Ch D 95 *per* Bowen L.J. at 113–14.

[15] *Easton v London Joint Stock Bank* (1886) 34 Ch D 95 *per* Bowen L.J. at 113 and *Colonial Bank v Cady and Williams* (1890) 15 App Cas 267 *per* Lord Herschell at 285.

[16] *France v Clark* (1884) 26 Ch D 257 *per* Lord Selborne L.C. at 262; *Lloyds Bank v Cooke* [1907] 1 KB 794 *per* Lord Collins M.R. at 800 ff. and *per* Cozens-Hardy L.J. 804–5 and *Lilly v Farrar* (1908) 17 QRBR 554.

[17] See *Agency* at para. 14.17.

[18] *Farquharson Bros & Co v King & Co* [1902] AC 325 *per* Lord Halsbury at 330. See also *Brocklesby v Temperance Permanent Building Society* [1895] AC 173; *Rimmer v Webster* [1902] Ch 163; *Lloyds Bank v Cooke* [1907] 1 KB 794 and *Smith v Prosser* [1907] 2 KB 735.

efficacy of the transaction, the rule only applies to negotiable instruments.[19] Secondly, that a representation is created by the handing over of the bill which is repeated each time the bill or security is sold.[20] This representation creates a purely personal estoppel preventing the principal and subsequent vendors from denying the agent's authority to negotiate the bill.[21]

Of the two bases, it is submitted that the former is the better explanation of the principle for two reasons. First, there is authority to suggest that the mere negotiation and handing over of the bill or security cannot create an estoppel.[22] If that is correct, then it becomes difficult to spell out the repeated representation required to generate the purely personal estoppel against the subsequent vendors preventing them from denying that title has passed. Secondly, it is difficult in any event to spell out the repeated representation necessary to generate the personal estoppel. Given that a personal estoppel cannot create title,[23] it is possible that at a particular stage in the on-selling of the bill or security the requisite representation would be missing and title would pass no further. The commercial purpose of the agency relationship and of negotiable instruments would therefore be frustrated. **15.65**

DOCUMENTARY CREDITS

As discussed above,[24] Article 14(e) of the UCP 500 determines the circumstances in which an issuing bank will be deemed to have lost the right to reject defective documents in a documentary credit transaction. That loss of rights covers both waiver and estoppel. Where the UCP 500 does not apply, questions of estoppel will be decided under the common law. There, the issuing bank does not lose its rights to rely on other grounds for rejecting the documentation by initially stating that it wished to rely on one particular ground.[25] **15.66**

[19] *Smith v Prosser* [1907] 2 KB 735 *per* Vaughan-Williams L.J. at 749, *per* Fletcher Moulton L.J. at 752–3 and *per* Buckley L.J. at 755.

[20] *Colonial Bank v Cady and Williams* (1890) 15 App Cas 267 *per* Lord Herschell at 285 and *Fuller v Glyn Mills & Co* [1914] 2 KB 168 *per* Pickford J. at 176–7.

[21] See Paget at pp. 578–9.

[22] *Smith v Prosser* [1907] 2 KB 735 *per* Vaughan Williams L.J. at 746.

[23] See *In re Goldcorp* [1995] 1 AC 74 *per* Lord Mustill at 94G–H.

[24] See para. 15.48.

[25] *Kydon Cia Naviera SA v National Westminster Bank Ltd, The Lena* [1981] 1 Lloyd's Rep. 68 *per* Parker J. at 79 col. 2–80 col. 1 and *European Asian Bank AG v Punjab and Sind Bank* [1983] 1 WLR 642 *per* Robert Goff L.J. at 661.

RESTITUTIONARY CLAIMS

Where a bank has paid out monies by mistake, it will be able to bring a claim in restitution to recoup those monies.[26] The courts long recognized that the party that received those monies could rely on estoppel as a defence to that claim.[27] This estoppel was based on estoppel by negligence principles[28] and therefore suffered from the complexities associated with that doctrine. Further, the application of estoppel by negligence principles to the restitutionary context created three particularly acute difficulties. First, as estoppel by negligence is in fact a doctrine based on circuity of action,[29] the estoppel was believed to operate as a complete defence to the claim.[30] The obvious difficulty that arose was that in certain circumstances it would be inequitable for the defendant to retain all the monies paid to him. Therefore, what purported to be an equitable doctrine had an inequitable result. Secondly, particular care had to be taken in determining what representation had been made to the defendant. Thus, unless the bank had clearly stated to the defendant that it was entitled to treat the monies as its own,[31] the defendant might be in difficulties in establishing its defence.[32] Thirdly, different results could emerge depending on whether the court examined the case from the perspective of which duty was owed to whom or from the perspective of which party was at fault.[33] **15.67**

These difficulties have now been mitigated by the House of Lords' **15.68**

---

[26] *Lipkin Gorman v Karpnale Ltd* [1991] 2 AC 548.

[27] *Skyring v Greenwood* (1825) 4 B&C 281, 107 ER 1064 *per* Abbott C.J. at 289–90, 1066–7.

[28] See *National Westminster Bank Ltd v Barclays Bank International Ltd* [1975] QB 654 *per* Kerr J. at 662F–G and at para. 15.55 above.

[29] See para. 15.56 ff., above.

[30] See *Avon CC v Howlett* [1983] 1 WLR 605 *per* Slade L.J. at 624D-E. However, it is important to note that *pro rating* was not argued in *Howlett* and that all three Lord Justices reserved the question of whether *pro rating* might occur in an appropriate case — see *per* Everleigh L.J. 611C-D, 611G–12B, *per* Slade L.J. at 620H–1A, *per* Slade L.J. at 622B–C and *per* Cumming Bruce L.J. at 609E–F.

[31] See, for example, *Skyring v Greenwood* (1825) 4 B&C 281, 107 ER 1064 *per* Abbott, C.J. at 289–90, 1066–7 and *Holt v Markham* [1923] 1 KB 504 *per* Bankes L.J. at 511 and *per* Scrutton L.J. at 514–15.

[32] Thus, for example, in *National Westminster Bank Ltd v Barclays Bank International Ltd* [1975] QB 654, the court held that no representation capable of founding an estoppel was made where a bank pays on forged instrument (*per* Kerr J. at 672D–F) even where the cheque was presented for special collection (*per* Kerr J. at 675).

[33] See *Lloyds Bank v The Hon Cecily K Brooks* (1950) 6 Legal Decisions Affecting Bankers 161 *per* Lynskey J. at 169 (where the comparative blameworthiness of the parties was examined) and *United Overseas Bank v Jiwani* [1976] 1 WLR 964 at 968, 970 (where a duty based analysis was applied).

decision in *Lipkin Gorman v Karpnale Ltd*[34] which recognized that there were two defences to such restitutionary claims — estoppel and a separate and additional defence of change of position.[35] A party will be said to have changed its position where as a result of the receipt of the monies, the defendant has done something which it would not have otherwise done[36] it therefore being unjust to require the defendant to repay the monies.[37] Mere receipt of the monies will not suffice.[38]

Six points arise.[39] First, change of position does not operate as a complete defence but permits *pro rating*. That flexibility allows estoppel to remain as a complete defence and to be confined to those circumstances where it is properly applicable — where there is a clear representation that the defendant may retain all of the monies.[40] Secondly, the confusion which arises from applying the anomalous principles of estoppel by negligence to restitutionary claims is avoided. Thirdly, there is no longer a confusion between considerations of blame[41] and considerations of duty,[42] a confusion which has led to conflicting cases.[43] Considerations of duty are no longer relevant. Fourthly, the courts now consider whether or not it would be unjust to compel the defendant to repay all or part of the monies[44] balancing the comparative injustice of depriving the bank of its monies and of requiring the defendant to repay.[45] Fifthly, this greater flexibility means that the scope and application of the defence are unclear and must be developed on a case by case basis.[46] Sixthly, greater flexibility has been achieved at the expense of clarity. **15.69**

[34] [1991] 2 AC 548.

[35] *ibid. per* Lord Goff at 578G–9E.

[36] For example, payment to a third party from whom no recovery can be made *Deutsche Bank (London Agency) v Beriro & Co* (1895) 73 LT 669 or investment in company which has gone into liquidation *Holt v Markham* [1923] 1 KB 504.

[37] [1991] 2 AC 548 *per* Lord Goff at 580F–G and *South Tyneside MBC v Svenska International plc* [1995] 1 All ER 545 *per* Clarke J. at 565f–g.

[38] *Larner v LCC* [1949] 2 KB 683 *per* Lord Denning M.R. at 688–9 (an analysis based on estoppel by negligence reasoning which, however, accords with the rules applicable to change of position).

[39] For more detailed consideration, reference should be made to the standard restitution textbooks — in particular Goff & Jones.

[40] [1991] 2 AC 548 *per* Lord Goff at 579E.

[41] Necessary in deciding whether or not it is just for the defendant to retain the monies.

[42] Necessary to establish that there was an estoppel by negligence.

[43] See *Lloyds Bank v The Hon Cecily K Brooks* (1950) 6 Legal Decisions Affecting Bankers 161 *per* Lynskey J. at 169 and compare *United Overseas Bank v Jiwani* [1976] 1 WLR 964 at 968, 970.

[44] See *Westdeutsche Landesbank Girozentrale v Islington London BC* [1994] 4 All ER 890 *per* Hobhouse J. at 948.

[45] See *Lipkin Gorman v Karpnale Ltd* [1991] 2 AC 548 *per* Lord Goff at 579F.

[46] *ibid. per* Lord Goff at 580C.

Chapter 16

COMPANY LAW

WAIVER

The term 'waiver' can be used in two senses in company law: the voluntary relinquishment of a right or the bypassing of the statutory requirements applicable to companies. 16.01

VOLUNTARILY RELINQUISHING A RIGHT

The same principles[1] apply in company law as they do elsewhere. Thus, a waiver can arise between the company and its shareholders[2] or directors[3] or other third parties[4] and can affect both substantive and procedural[5] rights. Similarly, the shareholders to a company can waive the directors' breaches of its articles[6] or can, by adopting particular provisions in the Articles of Association,[7] or by prior agreement,[8] waive restrictions on the directors acting for other companies or in their own interest.[9] Any waiver 16.02

---

1 See *Waiver — Types and Elements passim.*

2 See, *e.g. Bank of New Zealand v Logan* (1899) 18 NZLR 117; 641

3 See, *e.g. Re Arigina Iron Mining Co* (1853) 1 Eq Rep 269.

4 For example, potential shareholders in relation to statements made in the company's prospectus — see *Greenwood v Leather Shod Wheels Co* [1900] Ch 421; *Cackett v Keswick* [1902] 2 Ch 456 and *Watts v Bucknell* [1903] 1 Ch 766.

5 As, for example, a waiver of the right to claim or to dispute a claim for security for costs — *Re North of England Banking Co, Hutchinson's Case* (1849) 1 De G & Sm 563, 63 ER 1196; *Re Home Assurance Association (No. 2)* (1871) LR 12 Eq 112; *Re Oro Fino Mines* (1900) 7 BCR 388 — or the waiver of improper service on the company *Pearks, Gunston & Tee Ltd v Richardson* [1902] 1 KB 91.

6 See, *e.g. Northern Crown Bank v Great West Lumber Co* (1914) 6 WWR 528.

7 See, *e.g.* Art. 85 of Table A, Companies (Tables A to F) Regulations 1985 (1985/805).

8 *New Zealand Netherlands Society 'Oranje' Inc v Kuys* [1973] 1 WLR 1126.

9 Where there is such a provision, its terms must be strictly complied with if the clause is to have effect (*Imperial Mercantile Credit Association v Coleman* (1873) LR 6 HL 189 and *Guinness plc v Saunders* [1988] 1 WLR 863) and such a provision will not release a director from compliance with his fiduciary obligations (see Birds, *The Permissible Scope of Articles Excluding the Duties of Company Directors* (1976) 39 MLR 394).

will be subject to the same limitations as apply elsewhere. Thus, an unequivocal representation[10] made with the requisite knowledge[11] must be pleaded and proved. Further, any waiver will be case specific, limited to those party to the unequivocal representation at issue.[12]

However, particular difficulties result from the fact that a company can only act via its agents. Thus, issues may arise as to when and in what circumstances the knowledge or actions[13] of its agents will be attributed to the company; the company seeking to avoid the loss of its rights by arguing that there was no attribution of knowledge or that the relevant acts were authorized. As discussed in detail elsewhere, it is difficult to draw out any precise guidance from the case law as to when the company will succeed on such an argument; attribution and authorization being a question of fact in each case.[14] **16.03**

Bypassing Statutory Requirements[15]

The Companies Act 1985 provides that notice of company meetings must be given to all shareholders. Thus, 21 days' written notice must be given of an annual general meeting.[16] All other meetings require seven days' notice in unlimited companies[17] and 14 days' notice in all other companies.[18] However, those requirements can be waived. Thus, all the members entitled to attend and vote at an annual general meeting may agree at that annual general meeting to waive the requirement.[19] Similarly, members representing 95 per cent of those shareholders **16.04**

---

[10] See, *e.g. Re Joint Stock Discount Co, Shipman's Case* (1868) LR 5 Eq 219 (delay not sufficient) and *Glass v Pioneer Rubber Works of Australia* [1906] VLR 754 (mere concurrence not sufficient).

[11] See, *e.g. Southland Frozen Meat & Produce Export v Nelson Bros* (1895) 13 NZLR 704; *Pegge v Neath & District Tramways Co Ltd* [1898] 1 Ch 183 and *Re Melbourne Brewery & Distillery* [1901] 1 Ch 453.

[12] *Westfall v Schmalz Agencies Ltd* (1958) 12 DLR (2d) 86.

[13] See, *e.g. In re The Vale of Neath and South Wales Brewery Co* (1853) 3 De GM & G 272, 43 ER 107 *per* Knight Bruce L.J. at 280, 110.

[14] As to which see *Waiver — Complexities* at para. 5.08; *Insurance* at para. 19.58; *Banking* at para. 15.16 and *Agency passim.*

[15] For the position at common law see *Browne v La Trinidad* (1887) 37 Ch D 1; *Southern Counties Deposit Bank Ltd v Rider & Kirkwood* (1895) 73 LT 374; *Henderson v Bank of Australasia* (1890) 45 ChD 330 and *Excel Footwear Co, ex p. Nova Scotia Trust Co* [1923] 3 DLR 212.

[16] s. 369(1).

[17] s. 369(1)(a).

[18] s. 369(1)(b).

[19] s. 69(3)(a).

entitled to attend and vote[20] or 95 per cent of the total voting shares[21] may agree at any other meeting to waive the applicable notice requirements.[22]

ESTOPPEL

As with agency, many of the cases concerning the operation of estoppel[23] in the company law context originate in the nineteenth century. Two points follow. First, there is the difficulty of applying Victorian principles to modern commercial situations. Secondly, the lack of clarity of much of the authority means that it is essential to bear in mind that, under the modern law, an estoppel in the true sense of the word cannot alter the substantive position between the parties. In the context of company law therefore an estoppel in the true sense of the word[24] will not vest title in a third party;[25] will not bypass the doctrine of *ultra vires*;[26] and will not render a forged[27] document valid.[28] Similarly, an estoppel cannot bind the liquidator of the company unless it made the statement allegedly giving rise to the estoppel.[29] **16.05**

---

[20] s. 369(4)(a).

[21] s. 369(4)(b).

[22] s. 369(3)(b).

[23] As stressed in the *Commercial Introduction* (at para. 13.04), the term 'estoppel' is used to include equitable forbearance, estoppel by convention and estoppel by representation, unless we have stated otherwise.

[24] However, reference should be had to the bypassing of the *nemo dat* rule by an alleged estoppel discussed at *Agency* at para. 14.17 ff. and *Banking* at para. 15.64 ff.

[25] *Simm v Anglo American Telegraph* (1879) 5 QBD 188 *per* Brett L.J. at 206–7 and *In re Goldcorp Exchange Ltd* [1995] 1 AC 74 *per* Lord Mustill at 93F–4G.

[26] *Freeman & Lockyer v Buckhurst Park Properties (Mangel) Ltd* [1964] 2 QB 480 at 506.

[27] And therefore void.

[28] See *Ruben v Great Fingall Consolidated* [1906] AC 439 *per* Lord Loreburn at 443. The company may be estopped from denying validity (see *Gore-Brown on Companies*, ed. Boyle & Sykes (44th ed., Jordans, London) loose-leaf at para. 5.7) or, more usually, the director's authority to sign the document — it being difficult for someone to forge his own signature.

[29] See *Re Exchange Securities & Commodities Ltd* [1987] 2 All ER 272 *per* Harman J. at 280g–h. To do so would be to give an estoppel force against parties other than the representor. The position may be different where representations are made as to the title of shares where the representation is made in and by the share certificate, the liquidator arguably adopts that representation and is bound (see *Re Victoria Silicate Brick Co ex p Martin* [1912] VLR 442 *per* Hood J. at 445; *Re British Farmers Pure Linseed Cake Co* (1878) 7 ChD 533; *Bloomenthal v Ford* [1897] AC 156 and *Re London Celluloid Co* (1888) 39 ChD 190 and para. 16.10 below).

With those limitations in mind, the estoppel has appeared to play a role in the following areas: the power of the company's agents to bind the company; the company's compliance with statutory requirements; the issue of securities and shares by the company. **16.06**

ESTOPPEL AND COMPANY AGENTS

Many of the difficulties associated with estoppel and the agents' authority to bind the company arise from the interrelationship of estoppel and ostensible authority which is discussed elsewhere.[30] However, two points, specific to the company law context, should be noted. First, a common occurrence in company law is the *de facto* 'appointment' of a Managing Director without the requisite compliance with the procedures for appointment laid down in the company's Memorandum and Articles of Association. Where there are no procedures for delegating to the Managing Director, the Managing Director so appointed cannot bind the company,[31] the delegation being *ultra vires* the company.[32] Further, there is authority to suggest that where the third party does not know whether or not there is a power to delegate in the company's Memorandum and Articles of Association, there can be no ostensible authority,[33] reliance on any representation as to the director's powers being presumably unreasonable. However, given that parties dealing with the company are now under no obligation to enquire as to the company's *vires* to act,[34] it is submitted that the circumstances in which it will be unreasonable for a third party to rely on any representation as to the director's powers will be very limited.[35] **16.07**

Secondly, as pointed out elsewhere,[36] the representation as to the director's powers to act must be made by the company — there being **16.08**

[30] See *Agency* at para. 14.11 ff.

[31] *Mercantile Bank of India v Chartered Bank of India* [1937] 1 All ER 231 *per* Porter J. at 238D–G.

[32] The third party dealing with the company in such circumstances cannot rely on s. 35A of the Companies Act 1985 which is limited to the powers of the board of directors to bind the company.

[33] *Houghton & Co v Nothard, Lowe & Wills* [1927] 1 KB 246 *per* Sargeant L.J. at 266.

[34] s. 35B of the Companies Act 1985.

[35] Therefore, *Houghton & Co v Nothard, Lowe & Wills* [1927] 1 KB 246 would be confined to its particular facts.

[36] See *Agency* at para. 14.15.

no such thing as a self-authorizing agent.[37] As the company can only act via its agent, the representation must be made by another agent of the company authorized to make that particular representation.[38] That authorization can either be explicit (the other agent is expressly appointed to manage the affairs of the company in that respect) or arise as a result of the company's Memorandum and Articles of Association.[39]

COMPLIANCE WITH STATUTORY REQUIREMENTS

Section 349(1) of the Companies Act 1985 provides that the company's name must be clearly shown on all cheques and bills of exchange issued by the company. A director who completes a cheque which violates section 349(1) will be personally liable on the cheque and is liable to a fine.[40] Where a company sues the director who is personally liable on a cheque, the company may be estopped from so doing if the elements of an estoppel are made out.[41] However, given that the Companies Act imposes criminal penalties for breach of section 349(1), a court will only find that there has been an estoppel in extreme cases.[42] **16.09**

THE ISSUE OF SHARES AND SECURITIES

The issue of shares

In and by the share certificate, the company makes a representation — either that the shares are fully paid up or that a particular person is **16.10**

[37] *Ebeed v Soplex Wholesale Supplies Ltd and PS Refson & Co Ltd* [1985] BCLC 404 *per* Browne-Wilkinson L.J. at 414a–g.

[38] See *Freeman & Lockyer v Buckhurst Park Properties* [1964] 2 QB 480; *IRC v Ufitec Group Ltd* [1977] 3 All ER 924 *per* May J. at 937c–8c; *British Bank of the Middle East v Sun Life Assurance of Canada* [1983] 2 Lloyd's Rep. 9 *per* Lord Brandon at 17 col. 2 and *Rhodian River Shipping v Halla Maritime* [1984] 1 Lloyd's Rep. 373 *per* Bingham J. at 379 col. 2.

[39] See Arts 107, 109 of Table A Companies (Tables A to F) Regulations 1985 (1985/805).

[40] s. 349(4) of the Companies Act 1985.

[41] *Rafsanjan Pistachio v Reiss* [1990] BCLC 352 *per* Potter J. at 360a–e.

[42] See *Durham Fancy Goods Ltd v Michael Jackson (Fancy Goods) Ltd* [1968] 2 QB 839 *per* Donaldson J. at 845–6 (company fills out bill of exchange and passes it to director for signature — company estopped); but compare *Lindholst & Co A/S v Fowler* [1988] BCLC 166 at 168–9 and *Rafsanjan Pistachio v Reiss* [1990] BCLC 352 *per* Potter J. at 360a–e.

entitled to the shares. Therefore, where a company refuses to register X, a purchaser of the shares that is named on the certificate, on its register of members because the shares which X has allegedly purchased were subject at some time to a forged transfer, the company will be estopped from denying that X is entitled to the shares as set out in the certificate.[43] Five points flow. First, in such cases, X must show that it has suffered some detriment — whether that be the loss of the right to sue the broker[44] or the loss of the ability to sell on the shares. Secondly, the estoppel will arise where X is named as the holder of the shares but only becomes the holder of the shares at some later date.[45] Thirdly, as a result of the estoppel, X does not obtain the shares[46] but compensation from the company[47] or an indemnity in respect of loss and damage arising from the on-sale of the shares.[48] Fourthly, where X is the person that presented the forged transfer, no estoppel will arise and X will be liable to compensate the company for any loss it suffers.[49] Further, where X knew that it was not entitled to the shares[50] or there were facts that would have put X on inquiry as to its entitlement to the shares[51] no estoppel will arise.[52] Fifthly, because the representation is made in and by the share certificate, the representation is continuing and, arguably, will be adopted by subsequent agents of the company. Therefore, a liquidator may well

43 *Re Bahia and San Francisco Rly Co* (1868) LR 3 QB 584; *Re Ottos Kopje Diamond Mines Ltd* [1893] 1 Ch 618 *per* Lindley L.J. at 625–6 and *per* Bowen L.J. at 628–9 and *Daily Telegraph Newspaper Co v Cohen* (1905) 5 SR (NSW) 520.

44 *Dixon v Kennaway & Co* [1900] 1 Ch 833 *per* Farwell J. at 839, 842.

45 *Burkinshaw v Nicholls* (1878) 3 App Cas 1004; *Bloomenthal v Ford* [1897] AC 156; *Re Phillip-Stephan Photo, Litho and Typographic Process Co Ltd* (1891) 12 LR (NSW) Eq 4 and *Re Bonang Gold Mining Co Ltd* (1897) 18 LR (NSW) Eq 141.

46 There being no shares to which X is entitled.

47 *Re Bahia and San Francisco Rly Co* (1868) LR 3 QB 584 *per* Cockburn C.J. at 595 and *per* Blackburn J. at 596–7.

48 *Balkis Consolidated Co Ltd v Tomlinson* [1893] AC 396 *per* Lord Herschell L.C. at 403–5, 408.

49 *Sheffield Corp v Barclay* [1905] AC 392 *per* Lord Halsbury L.C. at 397 and *Yeung v Hong Kong and Shanghai Bank* [1981] AC 787 *per* Lord Scarman at 796F–8G.

50 *Re Eddystone Marine Insurance Co (No. 2)* [1894] WN 30 *per* Stirling J. at 30 col. 2.

51 *Balkis Consolidated Co Ltd v Tomkinson* [1893] AC 396 *per* Lord Field at 411–2; contra. *Bloomenthal v Ford* [1897] AC 156 *per* Lord Halsbury L.C. at 161 and *per* Lord Herschell at 168.

52 The court will therefore carefully consider X's knowledge — see *Re African Gold Concessions and Market Development Co, Markham and Darter's Case* [1899] 1 Ch 414 *per* Wright J. at 430.

be bound by this type of estoppel, notwithstanding that the estoppel arose prior to the liquidator's appointment.[53]

16.11 A similar principle will arise where the company represents that the shares are fully paid-up.[54] However, as representations of this category may not be made in and by the share certificate, an estoppel may not arise because the representee fails to establish that the appropriate representation was made[55] or because X had already agreed to purchase the shares before the representation was made.[56]

16.12 Although the principles governing both types of representation are, in essence, the same, a distinction may have to be drawn between the two types. Where there is a representation that the shares are fully paid-up, there is authority to suggest that the estoppel will operate for the benefit of X where X whilst a purchaser for value knows that the shares are in fact not fully paid-up.[57] Three possible analyses flow. First, X paid for the shares as if they were fully paid-up. Therefore, X had a contractual and legal right to the shares as if they were fully paid-up, notwithstanding the fact that equity would not intervene to protect X.[58] Secondly, the authority is analogous to the conferring of title by ostensible authority[59] where substantive rights are granted as part of an exception to the *nemo dat* principle. The difficulty with that analysis is that no issue as to title arises. X has the right to the shares but is aware that it is liable to calls for further contributions from the company. No *nemo dat* issue arises. We would therefore suggest that the analogy is inappropriate. Thirdly, the authority is at least at odds with the modern approach to estoppel[60] and therefore is no longer good law.[61]

---

53 See *Re Victoria Silicate Brick Co, ex p. Martin* [1912] VLR 442 *per* Hood J. at 445; *Re British Farmers Pure Linseed Cake Co* (1878) 7 ChD 533; *Bloomenthal v Ford* [1897] AC 156; *Re London Celluloid Co* (1888) 39 ChD 190; contra. see *Re Exchange Securities & Commodities Ltd* [1987] 2 All ER 272 *per* Harman J. at 280g-h.

54 *Burkinshaw v Nicholls* (1878) 3 App Cas 1004 *per* Lord Cairns L.C. at 1017 (policy behind the rule) and *per* Lord Blackburn 1026–7 and *Re British Farmers' Pure Linseed Cake Co* (1878) 7 ChD 533 *per* Lord Jessel M.R. at 538 and *per* James L.J. at 538–9.

55 Some care must therefore be taken in ascertaining the precise representation that was made — compare *Re Celluloid Co* (1888) 39 Ch D 190 *per* Cotton L.J. at 202; *Re Building Estates Brickfield Co, Parbury's Case* [1896] 1 Ch 100 *per* Vaughan-Williams J. at 106.

56 *Re Vulcan Ironworks Co* [1885] WN 120 col. 2 *per* Pearson J.

57 *Re Stapleford Colliery Co, Barrow's Case* (1880) 14 ChD 432.

58 This appears to be the analysis in *Re Stapleford Colliery Co, Barrow's Case* (1880) 14 ChD 432 *per* Lord Jessel M.R. at 445 — see also *Re MacDonald Sons & Co* [1894] 1 Ch 89 *per* Lindley L.J. at 104–5.

59 See *Agency* at para. 14.17 and *Banking* at para. 15.55 ff.

60 See *In re Goldcorp Exchange Ltd* [1995] 1 AC 74 *per* Lord Mustill at 95G–H.

We submit that the last view is the best of the three. It is therefore strongly arguable that no distinction is to be drawn between the two types of representation, *Re Stapleford Colliery Co, Barrow's Case*[62] being confined to its particular facts.

The issue of securities

16.13 The courts have used estoppel in two ways where the issue of securities is concerned. First, as discussed elsewhere,[63] the company may be 'estopped' from asserting title to particular securities where it permits an agent to deal with those securities.[64] The fact that the 'estoppel' created appears to give good title to the world[65] has led us to treat such cases as not involving estoppel in the true sense of the word but forming part of an exception to *nemo dat*.[66] Secondly, where the company acts *ultra vires* in issuing a security, there is authority to suggest that the company can be 'estopped' from denying that it was acting *ultra vires*.[67] We would submit that such authority is doubtful for two reasons. First, the cases on which the court relied in support of its decision were not ones in which 'estoppel' overrode *ultra vires*. Secondly, it is clear that estoppel, in the true sense of the word, cannot override *ultra vires* being purely evidentiary.[68]

[61] It may also be arguable that the case was not good law at the time the decision was given — see *Re Celluloid Co* (1888) 39 Ch D 190 and *Re Railway Time Tables Publishing Co* (1889) 42 ChD 98 *per* Stirling J. at 110.

[62] (1880) 14 ChD 432.

[63] *Banking* at para. 15.55.

[64] *Colonial Bank v Cady* (1890) 15 App Cas 267 *per* Lord Herschell at 285.

[65] See, *e.g. Fuller v Glyn Mills & Co* [1914] 2 KB 168 *per* Pickford J. at 176–7.

[66] See *Agency* at para. 14.17 ff. and *Sale of Goods and Shipping* at para. 20.20 for further discussion of this exception.

[67] *Webb v Herne Bay Cmrs* (1870) LR 5 QB 642 *per* Cockburn C.J. at 650–1.

[68] *York Corporation v Henry Leetham & Sons* [1924] 1 Ch 557 *per* Russell J. at 573; *Rolled Steel Products (Holdings) Ltd v British Steel & Corp* [1985] 3 All ER 52 *per* Slade L.J. at 86g–h and *Re Exchange Securities and Commodities Ltd* [1987] 2 All ER 272 *per* Harman J. at 276j.

Chapter 17
CONSTRUCTION LAW

INTRODUCTION

Many of the cases in this area turn on the terms of the standard form contracts widely used by the industry. As such, the cases do not raise points of general principle. Further, a consideration of the terms of the standard form contracts falls outwith the present work[1] which examines the extent to which the principles we have sought to deduce above[2] are elucidated by the cases. **17.01**

VARIATION

The issues raised in and by the construction cases are threefold: the meaning to be given to 'variation'; the necessary elements of any variation; and the mechanisms by which any variation takes place. **17.02**

THE MEANING OF VARIATION

Two levels or categories of obligations may be identified in construction contracts. First, the contractor accepts a general obligation to carry out 'the works' in a given period and to a given standard. These obligations will usually be set out in the main body of the contract and will be subject to the standard process of agreement between the contractor and the employer. Secondly, a specification drafted by an architect or engineer and incorporated into the contract will set out in technical detail **17.03**

---

1 For a full discussion of the difficulties, reference should be made to Hudson at pp. 876 ff.

2 See *Variation passim.*

what 'the works' are to be.[3] The specification may be agreed at a different date and may not be subject to the standard process of agreement. Further, alterations to the specification, and thus to the second level or category of obligations, will usually be expressly governed by clauses in the main body of the contract.[4] Such clauses will contain the manner in which the specification may be altered and the extent to which the contractor will be remunerated for carrying out the altered obligation.[5] These differences between alteration of the main contract and alteration of the specification have led some commentators[6] to suggest that the modification of the two categories of obligation is to be treated differently[7] with only modification of the second level or category of obligation being treated as variation within the true meaning of the term.

However, we would suggest that that distinction is incorrect for a number of reasons. First, and axiomatically, both sets of obligations will be contractually binding, the contractor being liable for breach if, for example, he delivers late or he does not carry out the works as per the specification.[8] Secondly, on analysis, the requirements for the modification of either category of obligation match those required for a variation. Thirdly, the distinction is in fact between a variation of a particular element of the contract, an item in the specification, said variation being governed by the terms of that contract;[9] and a variation of the terms of the contract for which no advance contractual provision has been made. Therefore, useful though the distinction drawn may be for practical purposes,[10] it is submitted that the distinction is one without a difference. Thus, for the purposes of the **17.04**

---

[3] Hudson at para. 1.209, at p. 110. For example, the specification will set out the depth at which the foundations have to be laid or refer to the drawings from which the works will be carried out.

[4] By way of contrast, the contract will rarely set out a mechanism by which the general obligations assumed the contract may be altered.

[5] See, *e.g.* clause 51(1) of the Fourth and Fifth Editions ICE Conditions.

[6] See Hudson at para. 1.091, p. 46, para. 7.001 ff., p. 877 and Keating at pp. 86–7, which appears to refer to 'Varied Work' as synonymous with 'Extra Work' and therefore not a contractual variation.

[7] See Hudson at para. 7.002, in which the author suggests that variations *stricto sensu* are modifications of the secondary category of obligations which are instructed by the employer's architect or engineer.

[8] See, *e.g.* *Williams v Fitzmaurice* (1858) 3 H & N 844 and *Re Walton on the Naze Urban District Council and Moran* (1905) *Hudson on Building Contracts* (4th ed.) Vol. 2, p. 376.

[9] See *Variation* at para. 2.38.

[10] For example, as a mechanism for approaching the considerable case law in this area.

following discussion we utilize one term to cover the modification of either category of obligation.

THE REQUIREMENTS FOR VARIATION

Therefore, for all purposes relating to construction contracts, we would suggest that the requirements are as set out below.[11] **17.05**

(1) The variation must alter the obligations of the parties. Therefore, where the scope of the works is concerned, the variation must increase or decrease the actual or implied obligations[12] of the contractor to carry out the works.
(2) The work should have been at the employer's request.
(3) The contractor should have agreed to carry out the work, *i.e.* accepted the employer's request.
(4) Consideration should be provided for the work. That consideration, as set out above, can take two forms — either an express or implied acceptance by the contractor that it will carry out the work and an express or implied acceptance by the employer that it will pay for the work[13] or the receipt of a benefit by one of the parties.[14]

Two consequences flow from the above. First, absent any agreement allowing subsequent variation of the scope of the works, each and every variation will have to be agreed by the parties or their agents. Secondly, as each change will be a variation, on the analysis set out above,[15] each change discharges the performance of the old contract and substitutes a new in its place. Therefore, where a variation to the scope of the works **17.06**

[11] See Hudson at para. 7.006, pp. 880–1 and Keating at pp. 86–7.

[12] *i.e.* where the contractor has agreed to carry out a particular set of works, it will be taken to have impliedly agreed to carry out all works necessary to carry out those works and to have assumed the risks associated with said carrying out (see, *e.g. Tharsis Sulphur & Copper Co v McElroy & Sons* (1878) 3 App Cas 1040 *per* Lord Blackburn at 1054). Therefore, where the contractor agrees to construct a railway for a lump sum, it will be taken to have agreed to carry out the excavation works required to build that railway even if those works are far greater than originally envisaged — see *Sharpe v San Paulo Rly* (1873) LR 8 Ch App 597.

[13] Therefore, subject to *Williams v Roffey* [1991] 1 QB 1 discussed at *Variation* at para. 2.19, the work to be carried out cannot be remedial. As remedial works, *ex hypothesi*, are to remedy the defective performance of the contract, a contractor agreeing to carry out remedial works is merely agreeing to carry out that which it was already obliged to carry out namely to complete the works in a good and workmanlike fashion.

[14] *Watson Lumber Co v Guennewig* 226 NE (2d) 270 (1967) Ap Ct IL.

[15] See *Variation* at para. 2.30.

takes place, the parties will be required to ascertain in what way the contract price has altered as a result of that particular variation. It follows that where there are multiple variations, it is not appropriate to compare the initial price under the unvaried contract with the price under the multiple varied contract and generate a 'global' or 'total cost' claim.[16] The effect on price, reflecting each new bargain, should ideally be ascertained at each stage.[17] However, in difficult cases the courts may be willing to accept a 'rolled up' plea setting out the overall effect of the variations.[18]

MECHANISMS FOR VARIATION

In practice, the parties bypass the requirements of variation by agreeing a contractual mechanism by which variations to the scope of the works will take place. This mechanism is an agreement permitting variation[19] and has two main benefits — the theoretical, avoiding any difficulties with consideration; and the practical, allowing the employer to delegate the technical management of the works to the architect or engineer which prepared the specification. However, the disadvantage of such a mechanism is that the parties may fail to comply with it. Thus, for example, in *Russell v Viscount SA da Bandiera*[20] the plaintiff had contracted with the defendant to construct a warship as per the then English design and to be ready to sail on completion for a fixed sum. Variations to the design of the warship were to be agreed in writing. However, during construction, the design of the warship was altered without written agreement and recovery of the associated costs was sought. The plaintiff sued for its costs incurred as a result of the alteration and failed, the court holding: 17.07

[16] This conclusion is subject to there being some provision in the contract allowing for such a claim.

[17] See *McAlpine Humberoak Ltd v McDermott International* (1992) 58 BLR 1 at 28 and *Boyajian v US* 423 F (2d) 1231 (1970).

[18] *Imperial Chemical Industries plc v Bovis Construction Ltd* (1992) 32 Con LR 90; *Mid-Glamorgan County Council v Devonald Williams & Partners* (1991) 29 Con LR 24, 129 *per* Mr Recorder Tackaberry Q.C. at 154; *Bernhard's Rugby Landscapes Ltd v Stockley Park Consortium Ltd* (1997) 82 BLR 39; and *John Holland Construction & Engineering Pty Ltd v Kuaerner RJ Brown Pty Ltd* (1996) BLR 81.

[19] See *Variation* at para. 2.38.

[20] (1862) 13 CBNS 149, 143 ER 59.

> The contractor has no right to complain if he loses the price of extras and additions which, in disregard of the stipulation which he has entered into, he furnishes without authority.[21]

Whilst it is submitted that *Russell* is correct as a matter of analysis, that analytical rigour does create difficulty in the face of the day to day reality on construction sites where instructions may be given without regard to the formalities laid down. The courts have attempted to resolve this difficulty by three main routes.[22] First, the court may imply that there has been offer and acceptance by reason of the employer's awareness that the works were being carried out and a subsequent failure to order the contractor to cease carrying out those works.[23] Secondly, the court may find that the parties have in fact entered into two contracts running concurrently, a contract for the works and a contract for extra work.[24] Thirdly, the court may find that the employer has been unjustly enriched by the receipt of the benefit of the work and therefore should make restitution to the contractor on a *quantum meruit* basis.[25] Each of these paths has its difficulties: whether that be the overriding of an express written agreement by an implied contract (whatever that might be);[26] or of showing that there are two co-existent contracts which do not conflict or of having a *quantum meruit* claim alongside the main contract;[27] or of having any restitutionary claim at all.[28] Those difficulties can be resolved, it is submitted, by a consideration of the true nature of variation. If any variation constitutes a discharge by agreement of the previous contract and an entry into a new contract in similar terms, the variation must affect the scope of the works and the agreement permitting variation. In most cases, the agreement permitting variation will be in identical terms to that previously agreed. However, it may well be that the intention of the parties was such that the formalities of **17.08**

---

21 *ibid. per* Byles J. at 199–200, 80–1. See also *Attorney-General v McLeod* (1893) 14 NSWLR 246 at 251.

22 The courts may also find that the employer has waived its rights arising from the non-compliance with the contractual provisions governing variation — see para. 17.12 below.

23 See *Liebe v Molloy* (1906) 4 CLR 347 at 354.

24 See *Lamprell v Billericay Union* (1849) 18 LJ Ex 282 and *Blue Circle Industries Plc v Holland Dredging Co* (1987) 37 BLR 40.

25 See Hudson at para. 7.099, pp. 942–3.

26 See *Brown v Lord Rollo* (1831) 10 S 667.

27 See *The Olanda* [1919] 2 KB 728; see also Goff & Jones, pp. 45–6.

28 The difficulty being that if the contractor carries out work, the employer may be physically unable to refuse to accept the benefit of that work. Thus, the employer's conduct may not be unjust so as to found a restitutionary claim.

the original agreement permitting variation have been dispensed with and the contractor is therefore entitled to be paid.

Adopting the above analysis also resolves two other problems which have arisen in the area. First, the clauses permitting variation in the main contract will provide for the amounts to be paid to the contractor in respect of modifications to the scope of the works. In changing markets, the contractor may wish to claim higher prices than those allowed for in those clauses and will therefore argue that the works carried out were not 'modifications' but extra work outwith the contract. To resolve that issue, the court must commence a detailed analysis of the works undertaken comparing them against the specification and then apply a subjective judgment as to whether the two are comparable.[29] Further, where there is a chain of contracts by which the main contractor has hived off its obligations to subcontractors, differences will occur depending on the obligation hived off and the work undertaken.[30] The simpler task is to examine the parties' intent (whether actual or deemed) to see whether in fact the parties were agreeing to enter into a different kind of agreement permitting variation.[31] **17.09**

Secondly, the analysis sheds some light on 'multiple variations'. The courts have apparently held that the repeated consensual[32] variation can repudiate the bargain between the parties allowing each to sue on a *quantum meruit* basis as if no contract existed. Thus, in *Pepper v Burland*[33] Lord Kenyon held: **17.10**

> . . . if a man contracts to work to a certain plan, and that plan is so entirely abandoned that it is impossible to trace the contract, and to what part of it the work shall be applied, in such a case the workman shall be permitted to charge for the whole work done by measure and value, as if no contract at all had been made . . .

Evidential and conceptual difficulties arise. Evidentially, it appears that the court in *Pepper* compared the performance of the parties before **17.11**

---

[29] See, *e.g. Watson v O'Beirne* (1850) 7 Up Can QB 345. *Air-a-Plane Corp v US* 408 F.(2d) 1030 at 1033, '*The basic standard . . . is whether the modified job was essentially the same work as the parties bargained for when the contract was awarded.*'

[30] See, *e.g. Hansen and Yuncken v Chadmix Plastics* [1985] BCLR 52, where a variation to the scope of the works repudiated the subcontract.

[31] It may be said that the effect of this argument is to bypass the established provisions of, for example, the ICE or JCT Contracts. It is submitted that since these cases only arise where the ICE and JCT requirements have not been complied with, that objection has more form than substance.

[32] A non-consensual variation, whether repeated or not, may also constitute a repudiation of the contract — see, *e.g. Employment* at para. 18.05 ff.

[33] (1792) 1 Peake NP 139 at 140.

and after the alteration and deduced from the difference that the parties no longer intended to be bound by the original or any contract. We would suggest that such a process of comparison generates confusion between qualitative changes[34] and quantitative changes.[35] Thus, for example, *Pepper* does not assist the court in deciding whether or not a given change abnegates the contract. Conceptually, it is difficult to see how a consensual variation, which constitutes a new agreement,[36] can destroy all contractual relations between the parties. We would therefore suggest that the better approach would be for the court to consider whether the elements of variation set out above have been complied with and then ascertain which terms of the contract have been moderated and to what extent. If, on analysis, the new agreement operated as a consensual discharge of all obligations under the contract with one party continuing to perform, then it would be appropriate to adopt restitutionary principles to ascertain the extent of that party's recovery.

WAIVER

In considering waiver in this context, care must be taken as it is common for standard form construction contracts to contain express provisions as to when and in what circumstances a party will be taken to have waived its rights. However, absent express provision, the various types of waiver, as defined above,[37] apply equally to construction law.[38] Thus, rights accruing from a non-compliance with agreed mechanisms governing the formation of contracts[39] or the approval or certification of variations[40] are capable of being waived. In the former case, the waivor loses the right to argue that there was no concluded contract and in the latter the right to contest payment where the works had not been certified as per the contract.[41] Similarly, the employer can waive **17.12**

[34] That is the importance that may attach to a change to any one obligation.
[35] That is the number of obligations which have changed.
[36] Which occurs in all variations — see *Variation* at para. 2.30.
[37] See *Waiver — Types and Elements passim.*
[38] However, see Hudson at para. 1.255, where the author appears to suggest that for there to be a waiver there must be a change of position on the part of the representee.
[39] *MR Hornibrook v Eric Newham* (1971) 45 AJLR 523.
[40] *Meyer v Gilman* (1899) 18 NZLR 129.
[41] Indeed, a court may well readily find that the employer is precluded from relying on non-compliance with the contractual mechanism for approving variations as a defence to a claim by the contractor for monies arising from those variations — see Hudson at para. 7.042.

its rights to repudiate the contract for late completion of the works[42] and in extreme cases, its right to claim liquidated damages for the late completion of the works.[43] All such waivers can be categorized either as pure waivers or waivers by election. In each case, the elements of an unequivocal representation coupled with knowledge must be made out.[44] However, care must be taken in two respects — whether rights accruing from defective works can be waived by mere inspection on the part of the employer's architect or engineer and whether a particular breach of contract is continuing.

WAIVER OF DEFECTS

It is standard practice for the works to be inspected and certified by the employer's architect or engineer. That process of inspection has led defaulting contractors (or their sureties and bondsmen) to argue that any defective works are waived by that inspection. Whilst there can be little doubt[45] that the act of certification would count as the necessary unequivocal representation,[46] whether or not the architect or engineer has the authority to waive defects or the requisite knowledge are more difficult. We would suggest that the architect or engineer has neither. **17.13**

As far as authority is concerned, it is clear that the architect or engineer is appointed to supervise the works on the employer's behalf. Further, it is possible, though unlikely, that an employer could expressly authorize its architect or engineer to waive defects on its behalf. However, in most cases, the contractor will be forced to argue that the architect or engineer had ostensible authority to waive defects in the works. The weakness of that argument is that the architect or engineer is appointed to ensure that only the employer's interests are protected and the contractor will be aware of that fact. The architect or engineer cannot instruct the contractor how to carry out its works[47] nor does it owe an obligation to the contractor to inform it that its works are defective.[48] Thus, by **17.14**

---

[42] See Hudson at para. 9.012.

[43] *Thornhill v Neats* (1860) 8 CB NS 831.

[44] See *Mitsui Babcock Ltd v John Brown Engineering Ltd* (1997) 51 ConLR 129 *per* H.H.Judge Esyr Lewis Q.C. at 185 ff.

[45] Absent express agreement to the contrary.

[46] See *Waiver — Types and Elements* at paras 4.08, 4.26 for analogous examples.

[47] See *Clayton v Woodman & Son Ltd* [1962] 1 WLR 585.

[48] See Hudson at para. 5.021 and *AMF International Ltd v Magnet Bowling* [1968] 1 WLR 1028 *per* Mocatta J. at 1053. Thus, the fact that the architect or engineer fails to notice defective works and is thereby in breach of its obligations to the employer

parity of reasoning, the architect's or engineer's authority is strictly limited and does not extend to confer the benefit of its expertise on the contractor.[49] The contractor will normally be aware of that fact and thus there can be no ostensible authority to confer the benefit of waiving rights accruing from defective works.[50]

Further difficulties arise as far as knowledge is concerned. We have already pointed out that knowledge of the facts and of the rights consequent on those facts is necessary for there to be a waiver.[51] Further, any waiver will be limited to the rights accruing from the facts which were known at the time of the alleged waiver. Thus, a successful plea of waiver will not preclude the waivor from relying on its rights accruing from unknown breaches of contract.[52] The architect or engineer certifying the works may be aware of some of the alleged defects or facts but not all. Similarly, the architect or engineer may not be aware of hidden defects. If so, either there will be no waiver — the loss of the employer's rights being dependent on all the facts being known — or there will only be a limited waiver in relation to those patent breaches or defects.[53] **17.15**

CONTINUING BREACHES

A distinction is to be drawn between a breach which occurs once and a breach which is continuing. Thus, a failure to complete the works[54] on time will be a breach which occurs once[55] whereas a failure to exercise due diligence during the currency of the works may well be a continuing breach.[56] A breach which occurs once can be waived by, for example, **17.16**

cannot confer the benefit on the contractor of exempting that contractor from liability *East Ham Corporation Council v Bernard Sunley* [1966] AC 406 *per* Lord Reid at 444.

[49] It is to be noted that the limit on the architect or engineer's authority arises more as a matter of policy than of strict legal analysis.

[50] The alternative, and more difficult, way of putting this argument is to suggest that the architect or engineer is not the employer's agent to know for this specific purpose. Therefore, the architect's or engineer's knowledge of the defects will not be imputed to the employer and there will be no waiver of the employer's rights — see *Agency* at para. 14.04 ff.

[51] See *Waiver — Types and Elements* at paras 4.28 ff.

[52] See *Waiver — Complexities* at para. 5.05.

[53] See Hudson at para. 5.021.

[54] Or a section of them.

[55] See *Platt v Parker* (1886) 2 TLR 786.

[56] See Hudson at paras 4.128, 9.022, 9.032, 12.050.

the employer continuing to act as if the contract remained on foot whilst possessing the requisite knowledge.[57] However, where the breach is continuing, the employer will be able to rely on the continued failure to remedy the breach as grounds for repudiating the contract even if it has previously acted as if the contract remained on foot. Thus, where there is a continuing failure to remedy defective works, the employer will not be taken to have waived its rights even if it, for example, makes payments under the terms of the contract.[58] Similarly, where the employer gives notice under the contract requiring the contractor to remedy its defective performance and the contractor does not remedy its performance, the employer will, subject to agreement to the contrary,[59] be able to treat the contract as repudiated.

ESTOPPEL

Given the strong contractual basis of construction law, it would be reasonable to expect that contractors and employers would frequently rely on the doctrine. That is indeed the case. However, it is the relatively rare case in which a plea of estoppel[60] will succeed.[61] This arises, not because the elements of estoppel differ in construction law, but there are three particular difficulties in construction law in raising an estoppel. 17.17

First, it is of the nature of construction projects that the works are ongoing and that defects in those works may not be immediately noticeable. Therefore, it is most unlikely that defects will be specifically drawn to the attention of the architect/engineer enabling the architect/engineer to represent that those specific defects have been approved.[62] Therefore, no estoppel by representation can arise.[63] Further, the fact that the architect/engineer approves certain defective items of construction does not preclude the employer from arguing that items constructed later 17.18

[57] See, *e.g.* *Walker v North Western Railway* (1876) 1 CPD 518 and *Ex p. Newitt re Garrud* (1881) 16 ChD 522.

[58] See *Cooper v Uttoxeter Burial Board* (1864) 11 LT 565.

[59] See *Election* at para. 7.08.

[60] As pointed out in the *Commercial Introduction* (at para. 13.04), estoppel is used in the sense of estoppel by representation, estoppel by convention and equitable forbearance, unless the contrary is expressly stated.

[61] See Hudson at para. 1.247.

[62] See Hudson 1.249.

[63] Indeed, given the facts it is difficult to see why this type of estoppel could arise.

constructed to the same standard are defective.[64] This conclusion flows from the fact that no representation was made as to the later items of construction. Similarly, any representation made will not preclude the employer from arguing that there were hidden defects in the construction, the presence of which entitles it to damages.[65]

Secondly, where the architect/engineer has approved a particular set of defective works, the contractor will wish to argue that the approval constituted an estoppel by representation. The contractor will then seek to rely on that estoppel as a defence to a claim for damages brought against it by the employer. The effect of that defence is that as a result of the architect/engineer's representation the contractor was entitled to provide defective goods or services and is not obliged to remedy any damage which the employer had suffered as a result. The contractor will therefore be using an estoppel by representation to deprive the employer permanently of its right to proper performance of the contract. An estoppel by representation cannot have that effect and therefore the contractor's defence must fail. **17.19**

Thirdly, it may be difficult for the contractor to establish that it has suffered any detriment. Where the architect/engineer has approved defective works, the contractor will either fail to remedy those works or will continue to perform defectively. Both courses of action amount to a continued breach and a court will be extremely reluctant to find that a continued breach of contract can amount to detriment. We would therefore suggest that the contractor will only succeed in establishing detriment if, as a result of the approval, it has removed labour from site and the employer requests the contractor to remedy the defect immediately. By analogy with the repayment of loans,[66] as a result detriment would be suffered in the short-term but not in the long-term and would therefore be insufficient to defeat a claim by the employer for damages. **17.20**

Notwithstanding the above caveats, an estoppel will arise and will be particularly powerful in two types of case. First, where a contractor represents that it has concluded a contract with the employer or that its tender is valid and binding, the contractor cannot subsequently argue that there was no concluded contract[67] nor that it is entitled to withdraw **17.21**

---

[64] *Ata Ul Haq v City Council of Nairobi* (1985) 28 BLR 29.

[65] See Hudson at paras 5.021–4, 8.116 and *AMF International Ltd v Magnet Bowling* [1968] 1 WLR 1028 *per* Mocatta J. at 1053.

[66] See *Equitable Forbearance* at para. 12.47.

[67] See *Mitsui Babcock Energy Ltd v John Brown Engineering Ltd* (1997) 51 ConLR 129 *per* H.H.Judge Esyr Lewis Q.C. at 185 ff.

its tender[68] provided that the other elements required for an estoppel, in particular that of detriment/fairness,[69] are made out.[70] Secondly, again where representation and detriment are established, an estoppel may be made out in respect of defective works[71] and non-compliance with contractual notification provisions.[72]

---

68 *MJ Peddlesden Ltd v Liddell Construction* (1981) 128 DLR (3d) 260 and *Northern Construction v Gloge Heating and Plumbing* (1986) 27 DLR (4th) 265.

69 In *Mitsui Babcock* an estoppel of the most general kind was relied on (at 186) making analysis of the type of estoppel in play difficult (the court may have been applying principles set out in *Panchaud Frères* — see *The Panchaud Frères 'Doctrine'* at para. 6.06 ff.) and placing particular emphasis on the question of fairness.

70 We would suggest that this type of estoppel would be an estoppel by convention. However, *Mitsui Babcock* would suggest that a more wide ranging estoppel is in play.

71 *Acme Investments v York Structural Steel* (1974) 9 NBR (2d) 699 — employer's agent represents that a steel roof can be altered to make cost savings, the employer is estopped from claiming damages arising from said alteration.

72 *Update Construction Ltd v Rozelle Child Care Centre* (1990) 9 ACLR 66 — variations to works to be in writing, the employer's agent is notified of variations orally and agreed that payment would be made — employer is estopped from denying liability to pay for the variations.

Chapter 18

EMPLOYMENT LAW

VARIATION

Due to the intervention of statute,[1] the arguably special nature of the employment relationship[2] and the inequality of bargaining powers between the parties, contracts of employment raise particular complexities where the modification of their terms is concerned. Those complexities can be broken down into: **18.01**

(1) the method by which the proposed variation is to be accepted;
(2) the effect of an unaccepted variation;
(3) the effect of the ERA; and
(4) the effect of the Transfer of Undertakings (Protection of Employment) Regulations (TUPE) 1981.

ACCEPTANCE OF THE VARIATION

Variations of contracts of employment will, in most cases, be contentious with each side attempting to reap the maximum benefit from the variation. Employers generally adopt one of three paths — negotiation and maintaining good industrial relations, dismissing the work force and re-engaging it on different terms or unilateral modification of the terms.[3] In the former two cases, no issue for present purposes should **18.02**

---

1 The Employment Rights Act ('ERA') 1996.

2 See para. 18.14 below.

3 It should be noted, however, that in extreme circumstances a unilateral variation will amount to a withdrawal of the previous contract and its replacement with a new contract and not a repudiatory breach to be accepted or rejected — see *Alcan Extrusions v Yates* [1996] IRLR 327 and *Raggow v Scougall & Co* (1915) 31 TLR 564 *per* Darling J. at 565.

arise.[4] Where there has been a unilateral modification, the employee has two choices — accept or reject. As far as the acceptance is concerned, the employee can explicitly accept the variation. However, such an occurrence in practice is rare outside of formal negotiations between the employer and the employee's representatives. Therefore, an employee will be deemed to have accepted a variation by his or her continued presence at work after that variation[5] and the consideration supporting that variation will be the continued provision of work by the employee. This solution makes it difficult to say with certainty when the employee has or has not accepted the variation by continuing to work. The employer is therefore left with the possibility that the employee will complain of the variation at some future and unknown date.[6]

The difficulties are demonstrated by *Aparau v Iceland Frozen Foods*.[7] **18.03**
In *Aparau*, the respondent introduced a mobility clause into all its employees' contracts. There was an express stipulation that the employees were to sign the contract, that signature constituting acceptance of the terms. Ms Aparau refused to sign the contract and continued to work for the respondent for one year. At the end of that time, the respondent, pursuant to the mobility clause, instructed Ms Aparau to work at another of its stores, she refused, resigned and claimed constructive dismissal, a claim which was upheld by the Industrial Tribunal and EAT. The EAT held that the mobility clause did not have an immediate effect on Ms Aparau. Therefore, she was not deemed to have accepted the clause by continuing to work for the respondent. The EAT supported its conclusion by referring to those clauses which would have an immediate effect (relating for instance to pay) and those which did not. Variations of the former could be accepted by a continuation to work whereas the latter would not.

4 But note *Greenaway Harrison v Wiles* [1994] IRLR 380, in which the employer intimated to the employee that it intended to dismiss and re-engage her on different terms at some point in the future. The employee resigned and claimed constructive dismissal. The Employment Appeal Tribunal ('EAT') held that there had been a repudiatory breach of contract which entitled her to resign. Although the decision is arguably wrong (as to which see *Haseltine Lake & Co v Dowler* [1981] ICR 222), the dismissal and re-engagement route is not without its own difficulties and, further, could lead to an argument that the employee's terms and conditions had in fact altered.

5 See *Western Excavating (ECC) Ltd v Sharp* [1978] QB 761 and *Bashir v Brillo Manufacturing Co* [1979] QB 295.

6 See *GW Stephens & Son v Fish* [1989] ICR 324; *Post Office v Roberts* [1980] IRLR 347 (six weeks whilst employee examines employer's conduct, there was no waiver of the breach) and *WE Cox Toner (International) Ltd v Crook* [1981] ICR 823 (four weeks' delay constituted a waiver of the breach).

7 [1996] IRLR 119.

Aparau has three unfortunate effects. First, the employer seeking to vary contracts must first decide whether or not the variation will have 'immediate effect'. It would appear that 'immediate effect' involves both a subjective analysis of the term (for some employees the proposed variation will not have immediate effect, and for others it will) and a certain amount of hindsight (often the effect of a variation of a contract of employment will only be clear some time after the event). Secondly, once the employer has reached its decision as to the effect of the variation, it must allow a 'reasonable time'[8] for its employees to accept or reject the variation from the time that it has effect. If the variation does not have immediate effect, then the employer's only longstop will be a reasonable time after the clause is operated against a particular employee. Again, the process of variation will be haunted by uncertainty. Thirdly, ideally where there is negotiation between the employer and employees' representatives, the new contract of employment will be a compromise between the two parties where concessions have been made on both sides. The terms of the new contract will therefore represent an entire bargain which cannot be separated out into particular terms which may or may not have an immediate effect. Both parties to the negotiations may be reluctant to accept 'cherry-picking' whereby individual terms are rejected at some later and unascertainable date. *Aparau*, it is submitted, introduces unwelcome uncertainty into the affairs of both parties. **18.04**

One additional complexity requires consideration. In deciding whether there has been acceptance of variation, the courts have examined the cases solely in the context of constructive dismissal. Therefore, the courts have analysed the position in terms of the employee waiving its rights to claim of a repudiatory breach and therefore losing its rights to claim constructive dismissal. Put another way, in both cases, the courts examine whether the employee has accepted the conduct complained of and affirmed the contract.[9] It is submitted that unfortunate results flow.[10] First, a suggested variation by the employer can only be actionable if it constitutes a repudiation by the employer.[11] The result is that **18.05**

---

8 Subject to the difficulties set out above as to what constitutes a 'reasonable time'.

9 See *Western Excavating (ECC) Ltd v Sharp* [1978] QB 761 *per* Lord Denning M.R. at 769A–C. The conflation arises, in part, from the fact that both the employee complaining of a variation and the employee alleging that there has been a repudiatory breach will bring a claim for constructive dismissal before the Industrial Tribunal.

10 For a consideration of waiver see at para. 18.13 below.

11 See *Industrial Rubber Products v Gillon* [1977] IRLR 342 (unilateral variation to reduce wages was repudiation); *Pederson v Camden LBC* [1981] ICR 674 (unilateral change in job duties was variation) and *Courtaulds Northern Spinning Ltd v Sibson and TGWU* [1988] ICR 451 (unilateral transfer of employee to factory more than reasonable distance from the present workplace was repudiation).

employees may only complain of unilateral variations in extreme circumstances.[12] Secondly, further uncertainty may be generated, for while it may be analytically correct to categorize certain variations as repudiations,[13] it is difficult in some cases to advise either party as to whether the proposed variation will constitute a repudiatory breach of contract.

THE EFFECT OF AN UNACCEPTED VARIATION

In theory, an unaccepted variation has no contractual force[14] and the parties can continue with the contract as previously agreed. However, in employment contracts, due to the imbalance in bargaining power, the employer may insist on minor variations to the contract and expect the employees to accept the same.[15] If the employee does not accept the changes, he or she cannot adhere to the terms previously agreed as the employer will not permit such a course of action. Therefore, the employee is left with two options: resign and claim constructive dismissal hoping to establish that the employer's conduct was repudiatory or apply for a statement of the terms of the contract.[16] It is submitted that either course is unattractive as is the fact that the employer's greater bargaining power has been legitimized by the case law. The better course would be, it is submitted, to comply with the logic of the doctrine of variation and, absent express agreement, to give no effect to variations of employment contracts. **18.06**

THE EFFECT OF THE ERA

Under sections 1 to 6 of the Employment Rights Act 1996, an employer is obliged to issue a written statement of the key terms of the contract between itself and its employees. The obligation has two elements. First, there is an obligation to issue an initial statement within two months of **18.07**

[12] Subject to para 18.08 below.
[13] See *Western Excavating (ECC) Ltd v Sharp* [1978] QB 761.
[14] See *Burdett-Coutts v Hertfordshire County Council* [1984] IRLR 91.
[15] This is consistent with the courts' approach to variations of employment contracts within the context of constructive dismissal and therefore only being concerned with such variations if they constitute repudiatory breaches of the contract — see para. 18.05 above.
[16] See para. 18.07 below.

the commencement of employment.[17] That statement must include the names of the parties to the employment contract, the dates on which the employment began and the date on which continuous employment began[18] together with particulars as to the hours of work, amount and timing of payment and notice periods.[19] Secondly, if the particulars given under section 1 change during the course of employment, the employer must provide a written statement setting out the changes to the particulars.[20] It is important to note that any written statement provided does not form the contract of employment[21] and a written acceptance (short of express bilateral agreement)[22] of the terms will not transubstantiate the statement into a contract.[23] It follows that, absent an express bilateral agreement making the statement the contract of employment, any changes to the particulars given will not in itself constitute a variation of the contract of employment. What the statement will provide, however, is a clear and possibly conclusive indication that the terms of the contract have been varied.

The employee has a right to force the employer to provide a statement.[24] That right, coupled with the indication that the contract has been varied, permits an employee some remedy, short of resigning and claiming constructive dismissal, in the face of the variation of the contract. The employee can apply to the Industrial Tribunal and the tribunal could find: that there had been a variation but that the employer had failed to issue a new written statement of the terms; that by reason of the variation the terms were incomplete;[25] or that by reason of the variation the statement was inaccurate.[26] To avoid such an application, in all cases where there is a variation, the employer must reduce the terms of the contract as varied into writing. **18.08**

There are both technical and substantial limitations on that remedy. Technically, the drafting and effect of section 11, setting out the employee's right, are unclear. The section appears to draw a distinction between: (i) the failure to provide a statement; (ii) the failure to provide **18.09**

---

17 s. 1(2) of the ERA.
18 s. 1(3) of the ERA.
19 s. 1(4) of the ERA.
20 s. 4(1) of the ERA.
21 *Turriff Construction v Bryant* (1967) 2 ITR 292; *Parkes Classic Confectionery v Ashcroft* (1973) 8 ITR 43 and *Robertson and Jackson v British Gas Corporation* [1983] ICR 351.
22 *Gascol Conversions Ltd v Mercer* [1974] ICR 420.
23 *System Floors (UK) Ltd v Daniel* [1982] ICR 54.
24 s. 11 of the ERA.
25 s. 11(1) of the ERA.
26 s. 11(2) of the ERA. See also *Mears v Safecar Security Ltd* [1982] ICR 626.

a complete statement; and (iii) the failure to provide an accurate statement. Where an employee is solely concerned with (iii), as the law currently stands, it should bring an application under section 11(2);[27] otherwise the application must be brought under section 11(1). However, the division between (ii) and (iii) above in practice may be very fine. Therefore, as a matter of caution an employee should make an application under both subsections. Further, even if that procedural hurdle is overcome, the Industrial Tribunal can only find what the terms of the contract actually agreed were. There is no power to interpret the terms[28] nor, other than by a process of implication at common law, to insert terms required by section 1(4) but not agreed between the parties.[29] Therefore, the employee's remedy, in any event, will be limited.

Substantively, a section 11 application is only a mechanism by which the employee can ascertain the terms of her contract. In the face of a variation, an ability to discover *merely* what the terms of the contract are does not assist the employee. Where the variation is of a key term of the contract of employment, the more natural remedy will be to resign and claim constructive dismissal. Where the variation is not of a key term, there may be little point in instituting legal proceedings to obtain a formal declaration that the term has changed. Section 11 might be of use, however, where the employer is surreptitiously and gradually changing the terms of the contract of employment. In such case, the employee would be able to fix the terms of the contract at a particular point providing a potential benchmark for the future. The sole difficulty with such a course of action would be if the employer were unilaterally varying the terms of the contract, those unilateral variations not being accepted by the employee and therefore axiomatically not forming part of the contract of employment.[30] The employee would therefore gain nothing more than a statement of the terms as originally agreed and, potentially, an investigation of the employer's conduct by the Industrial Tribunal. Initiating adversarial legal proceedings merely to trigger an investigation could be seen as tactically short sighted. **18.10**

---

[27] *Mears v Safecar Security Ltd* [1982] ICR 626.

[28] *Cuthbertson v AML Distributors* [1975] IRLR 228; *Construction Industry Training Board v Leighton* [1978] 2 All ER 723 and *Mears v Safecar Security Ltd* [1982] ICR 626.

[29] See *Eagland v British Telecommunications plc* [1990] ICR 248; affd [1992] IRLR 323.

[30] If the employee did not accept the changes, the changes would not become part of the contract of employment — see *Variation* at para. 2.36.

THE EFFECT OF TUPE[31]

18.11 TUPE protects the employee's rights on the transfer of the undertaking in which the employee is involved from one employer to another. The regulations will only bite where there is a relevant transfer[32] of a relevant undertaking[33] and events unconnected with the transfer are not caught. Once TUPE does apply, the common law position as to variation of the contracts of employment[34] may be altered. In *Wilson v St Helens Borough Council*[35] the Employment Appeal Tribunal[36] considered the combined effect of regulations 5(1), 12 and the European Court of Justice's case law on the parties' ability to vary the contract of employment. Regulation 5(1) of TUPE provides that the contract of employment of any person, A, employed in the undertaking of X by X shall have effect on transfer of that undertaking to Y as if the contract had been originally made between A and Y. Thus, A's rights and obligations transfer to Y in full. Further, any agreement connected with the transfer which seeks to curtail the operation of regulation 5(1) is void[37]

---

[31] The meaning and application of TUPE raises complex and difficult issues which fall outside this work. For a detailed consideration of this area, reference should be made to Harvey Division F and specialist works.

[32] Defined in reg. 3.

[33] An undertaking meaning any economic entity as opposed to the narrower concepts of company or firm. It was originally thought the Industrial Tribunal will adopt a broad brush approach to the definition of undertaking which would be satisfied provided that it were possible to identify the assets and activities comprising the undertaking after transfer — see, *e.g. Schmidt v Spar-und Leihkasse der früheren Ämter Bordesholm, Keil und Croshagen* [1994] IRLR 302; *Dines v Initial Health Care Services* [1995] ICR 11; *Kelman v Care Contract Services Ltd* [1995] ICR 260; *Council of the Isles of Scilly v Brintel Helicopters Ltd* [1995] ICR 249 and *Betts v Brintel Helicopters Ltd and KLM ERA Helicopters (UK) Ltd* [1996] IRLR 45. However, the ECJ considerably curtailed that broad brush approach in *Ayse Suzen v Zehnacker Gebaudereinigung* GmbH [1997] ICR 662 in which it held that the mere transfer of an activity from one body to another could not constitute the transfer of an undertaking. This is a significant retreat from *Schmidt* (see also *Betts v Brintel Helicopters Ltd* (on appeal) [1997] IRLR 361 and the previously thought to be anomalous cases – *Rygaard v Strø Mølle Akustik A/S* [1996] IRLR 51 and *BSG Property Services v Tuck* [1996] IRLR 134 and *Harvey* F 83.05.

[34] See *Variation* at para. 2.07

[35] [1996] IRLR 321 and *Wilson v St Helens BC; Meade and Baxendale v British Fuels Ltd* [1997] IRLR 505.

[36] This 'pure' *Wilson* point was not considered by the Court of Appeal on appeal which decided that in *Wilson* itself there was an ETO dismissal and therefore any question of variation did not arise *Wilson v St Helens BC; Meade and Baxendale v British Fuels Ltd* [1997] IRLR 505. The point therefore remains open.

[37] Reg.12 of TUPE.

and it is not open to A to waive the rights granted by regulation 5.[38] Therefore, any attempt to alter the terms of A's contract which is connected with the transfer will be void. The logical result the Employment Appeal Tribunal held was that TUPE will prohibit consensual variations of A's contract of employment if those consensual variations take place as a result of the transfer.

That conclusion makes significant inroads into the parties' freedom to contract where there has been a transfer. However, it is important to note that there are two limits on that analysis. First, *Wilson* will only apply where the variation is a '*direct effect*' of the transfer. Thus, variation of the contract of employment which is not a direct effect of the transfer will be valid and *Wilson* will only catch employers seeking to purchase and reorganize the undertaking in one go. It would follow that *Wilson* will adversely affect those transferees with short-term goals and probably not those that plan to restructure the transferred undertaking over the longer term. Put another way, the longer that Y waits before attempting to vary the terms of the contract, the less likely it is that regulation 12 will vitiate that variation.[39] Secondly, where A's contract of employment ceases, for a reason unconnected with the transfer, and Y re-engages A, Y can re-engage A on whatever terms are appropriate.[40] Thus, arguably, *Wilson* would not apply.[41] To this extent it would appear that TUPE reflects the common law position on the variation of contracts in requiring the contract to subsist on both sides of the transfer.[42] **18.12**

WAIVER

On the simplest level, the doctrine of waiver applies to contracts of employment as it does elsewhere. Thus, an employee may waive its entitlement to a particular period of notice under the contract by **18.13**

---

[38] *Foreningen AF Arbejdsledere I Danmark v Daddy's Dance Hall A/S* [1988] IRLR 315.

[39] See *Meade and Baxendale v British Fuels Ltd* [1996] IRLR 541 affirmed sub nom. *Wilson v St Helens BC; Meade and Baxendale v British Fuels Ltd* [1997] IRLR 505.

[40] *ibid.*

[41] This was the solution adopted by the Court of Appeal in *Wilson v St Helens BC; Meade and Baxendale v British Fuels Ltd* [1997] IRLR 505. Compare, however, *Rostart de Herlaing v J Benoidt SA* TLR 25 November 1996.

[42] See *Variation* at para. 2.07.

accepting a different termination package.[43] It is also clear that, in employment law as elsewhere, waiver is capable of distinction from a consensual variation of the contract. Therefore, an employee can accept a variation by silence or delay[44] but silence or delay cannot by themselves constitute a waiver.[45]

However, as with variation, particular difficulties arise due to the unique nature of employment contracts. Apart from the conceptual difficulties associated with the issue of knowledge[46] and the possibility that contracts of employment automatically terminate on breach,[47] there are additional practical difficulties. First, any waiver in the employment context will be total. Where there has been a repudiatory breach of contract, the employee has a stark choice. It can either elect whether to accept the repudiation and terminate the contract[48] or to continue with the contract and waive any right to claim damages.[49] Secondly, contrary to general contractual principles, an employee may not be put to its election in certain limited circumstances. If the employer repudiates the contract by instituting unfounded disciplinary proceedings, it is possible that the employee can remain in employment and contest the disciplinary proceedings, without electing to waive the breach. The logic behind that distinction is that if the employee leaves without contesting the disciplinary proceedings, it may find it difficult to find work due to the resulting stigma.[50] Thirdly, where an employee has allegedly waived benefits accruing to it under the contract, it will find it difficult to argue that it did not have the requisite knowledge to found a waiver — the court will readily find that it was aware of the contract terms.[51] Fourthly, in exceptional circumstances, an employer may be taken to have 'waived' its rights to be informed by the employee that she wishes to exercise **18.14**

[43] *Griffiths v Buckinghamshire CC* [1994] ICR 265.

[44] Although an acceptance of a variation by silence or delay is often colloquially referred to as a 'waiver of the right to claim unfair dismissal' it is submitted that, on analysis, there is no waiver in the true sense.

[45] *WE Cox Toner International Ltd v Crook* [1981] ICR 823 *per* Browne-Wilkinson J. at 828. Although the courts have also suggested that a waiver can be made out in such circumstances (see *Allen v Robles* [1969] 1 WLR 1193) it is submitted that those cases turn on equitable forbearance principles — see *Waiver — Types and Elements* at para. 4.24 ff.

[46] See para. 18.15 below.

[47] Discussed at para. 18.17 below.

[48] Subject to the points made relating to automatic termination below.

[49] *Western Excavating (ECC) Ltd v Sharp* [1978] QB 761 *per* Lord Denning M.R. at 769A–C.

[50] *Bliss v South East Thames Regional HA* [1987] ICR 700 *per* Dillon L.J. at 715F–H.

[51] *Griffiths v Buckinghamshire* CC [1994] ICR 265 *per* David Steel Q.C. at 276D–G.

rights conferred on her by statute. This alleged waiver arises from the employer's obligation to inform an employee of her rights under contract or statute.[52] It is in fact not a waiver, in the true sense, at all but waiver being used as a device to achieve a desired outcome.

KNOWLEDGE

In *Bliss v South East Thames Regional Health Authority*,[53] Lord Justice Dillon considered a submission (based on *Peyman v Lanjani*[54]) that the party waiving its rights must be aware both of the facts and its rights consequent on those facts and stated: **18.15**

> This is a formidable argument, and the acceptance of it could have considerable repercussions in employment law. But I do not find it necessary to express any opinion on it in the present case . . . [55]

The repercussions are obvious — the courts, faced with claims by employees who may well be ignorant of their rights, will find it difficult to accept that the employee has waived those rights. Further, the requirement of knowledge might be said to impose too great a degree of legal formalism on what has traditionally been seen as a flexible relationship.

We would accept that those concerns are valid, however, we would also suggest that there is no reason why employment law should not be consistent with the general law of contract in this respect. If arguing that there has been a waiver of rights is a 'serious step' in insurance law,[56] there is no reason why it should not also be a serious step in employment law. Further, as an employer who actually suffers detriment can rely on estoppel, there is no reason why an employee should lose rights of which it is unaware. Finally, it may be said that the requirement of knowledge will prevent the employee from being held to have 'waived' its rights in constructive dismissal cases. However, where the constructive dismissal is triggered by a repudiatory breach by the employer (other than a variation of the terms of the employment contract),[57] the employee will be aware of its ability to resign and has a choice whether or not to withdraw its labour in the face of the repudiation. **18.16**

---

[52] See *Scally v Southern Health and Social Services Board* [1991] ICR 771 and *Gray v Smith* (EAT unrep. 2 July 1996) IDS Brief 584, 14–15 March 1997.

[53] [1987] ICR 700.

[54] [1985] 1 Ch 457 — discussed in detail at *Waiver — Types and Elements* at para. 4.18 ff.

[55] [1987] ICR 700 at 717F–G.

[56] *Brook v Trafalgar Insurance Co Ltd* (1947) 79 Ll L R 265 at 367 and *Insurance* at para. 19.01.

[57] See para. 18.06 above.

AUTOMATIC TERMINATION

18.17 There is some debate as to whether, contrary to the general law, the employment contract terminates automatically on repudiatory breach by either party.[58] This concept of automatic termination means that the employee can dismiss herself[59] losing all rights against the employer in the process[60] without the employer having to elect to terminate the contract. Similarly, on this argument, it would be impossible for the employee to elect to continue the contract of employment after a repudiatory breach by the employer, the contract already having determined. The argument has three bases. First, it is not open to either party to specifically enforce the contract of employment. However, an election by one party to keep the contract alive would be obtaining specific performance by another route. Secondly, the existence of mutual obligations in a contract of employment is paramount.[61] A party's repudiation of the contract destroys that mutuality and *ipso facto* the contract of employment. Thirdly, and more pragmatically, allowing the innocent party an unfettered right of rejection creates considerable practical difficulties with employees arriving for work when the employer has clearly intimated that it will not accept their offer to serve.

18.18 Although the law in this area is unclear and unsatisfactory,[62] it is submitted that the better view is that a repudiatory breach does not automatically terminate the contract of employment.[63] On the conceptual level, we would submit that there is no reason in principle why contracts of employment

[58] See also the possibility that a contract of employment may automatically terminate, in extreme circumstances, on unilateral variation of the contract of employment — see *Alcan Extrusions v Yates* [1996] IRLR 327.

[59] See *Sanders v Ernest A Neale* [1974] ICR 565; *Thomas Marshall v Guinle* [1979] 1 Ch 227 *per* Megarry V.C. at 239F and *London Transport Executive v Clarke* [1981] ICR 355 *per* Templeman L.J. at 367E.

[60] *London Transport Executive v Clarke* [1981] ICR 355 *per* Lord Denning M.R. at 363D–E.

[61] *Nethermere (St Neots) Ltd v Taverna & Gardiner* [1984] ICR 612 at 623; *McLeod v Hellyer Brothers Ltd* [1987] IRLR 232 at 239 and *Carmichael v National Power* (EAT/1160/95 unrep.).

[62] Compare *Gunton v Richmond upon Thames LBC* [1981] 1 Ch 448 and *Boyo v Lambeth LBC* [1994] ICR 727. See also *Shook v Ealing BC* [1986] ICR 314 *per* Waite J. at 325 in comparison with *Marsh v NAS* [1993] ICR 453 *per* Ferris J. at 456B–9E.

[63] See *Gunton v Richmond Upon Thames LBC* [1981] 1 Ch 448; *Boyo v Lambeth LBC* [1994] ICR 727; *Shook v Ealing BC* [1986] ICR 314 *per* Waite J. at 325D; *Dietmann v Brent LBC* [1987] ICR 737 *per* Hodgson J. at 755D; *Rigby v Ferodo Ltd* [1988] ICR 29 *per* Lord Oliver at 34F–G; *Ali v Southwark LBC* [1988] ICR 567 *per* Millett J. at 576H–8C and *Marsh v NAS* [1993] ICR 453 *per* Ferris J. at 459E.

should differ from the general law of contract in this one respect; a submission which was supported by the House of Lords in *Rigby v Ferodo Ltd.*[64] Further, it may well be[65] that a contract of employment can be split into two categories of obligation: those relating to personal service[66] and all other obligations.[67] Whilst a repudiation might eliminate the obligations relating to service, those other obligations would remain on foot. The alternative view would be that the fact that an equitable remedy, specific performance, is unavailable, does not necessarily impact on the relationship at law between the parties. Therefore, the fact that specific performance is unavailable does not necessarily mean that the contract is determined.

Turning to the alleged practical difficulties standing in the way of an unfettered right to reject, we would suggest that they can be, and have been, resolved by two routes. First, the courts have indicated that they will readily infer that the repudiation has been accepted[68] and may well assume that the issue of a writ claiming damages for wrongful dismissal[69] will amount to an acceptance of the repudiation.[70] Therefore, in most cases, the innocent party will be taken to have elected to terminate the contract. Secondly, contracts of employment require the cooperation of both parties.[71] Therefore, if the innocent party wishes to keep the **18.19**

[64] [1988] ICR 29 *per* Lord Oliver at 34 F–35 C.

[65] *cf.* in *Rigby* the House of Lords considered the point without deciding upon it. However, see *Decro-Wall International SA v Practitioners in Marketing* [1971] 1 WLR 361 *per* Salmon L.J. at 369–70.

[66] i.e. the minimum mutual obligation of an offer of service and payment for that offer.

[67] This approach is consistent with the test adopted in cases relating to whether casual workers are engaged under a contract *simpliciter* or a contract of service where it may be accepted that there is a contract but there is no contract of service — see *Wiltshire County Council v NAFTE* [1980] ICR 455 *per* Lord Denning M.R. at 460 A–C and *per* Ackner L.J. 462H. It is also consistent with the court's approach to garden leave injunctions where, notwithstanding the termination of service, the other terms of the contract remain in effect — see *Evening Standard v Henderson* [1987] ICR 588 and *Provident Financial Group Ltd v Hayward* [1989] ICR 160.

[68] *Gunton v Richmond Upon Thames LBC* [1981] 1 Ch 448 at 469A–B.

[69] The position may be different where all that the employee is claiming is an injunction to keep the contract on foot pending conclusion of a disciplinary procedure — see *Dietmann v Brent LBC* [1987] ICR 737 *per* Hodgson J. at 755D.

[70] *Gunton v Richmond Upon Thames LBC* [1981] 1 Ch 448 at 467B. The position may well be different where proceedings are issued in the Industrial Tribunal, any deemed election may be postponed until after the conclusion of those proceedings — see *Shook v Ealing LBC* [1986] ICR 314 at 325. If the position is different, it is submitted that the difference arises from the statutory rights which an applicant has before an Industrial Tribunal, in particular, the right to claim reinstatement. A deemed election to terminate would run contrary to the claim for reinstatement.

[71] See *Clea Shipping Corp v Bulk Oil International (No. 2) (The Alaskan Trader)* [1984] 1 All ER 129 *per* Lloyd J. at 138.

contract on foot in the face of the other party's refusal to cooperate, the cooperation exception to the innocent party's rights of election will apply.[72]

ESTOPPEL

As a result of the statutory overlay, estoppel[73] has little role to play in employment law; the reason being that estoppel cannot give rise to substantive rights and therefore cannot give the employee rights under the statutory scheme of the ERA. Therefore, even where the elements of an estoppel are made out,[74] that estoppel cannot give the employee rights under the statutory scheme or the Industrial Tribunals, albeit that the employee could rely on the estoppel in an ordinary civil action.[75] **18.20**

[72] The innocent party will therefore be precluded from electing to keep the contract in being — see *White and Carter (Councils) v McGregor* [1962] AC 413 at 429 discussed at Election, para. 7.09.

[73] As pointed out elsewhere (*Commercial Introduction* at para. 13.04), estoppel is used in the sense of estoppel by representation, estoppel by convention and equitable forbearance.

[74] Care must be taken in the employment context not to confuse variation with estoppel. As the continued offer of services may constitute consideration, it is relatively easy to establish that any alteration of the terms of the contract is supported by consideration (see cases discussed at Harvey at paras CI:631–651).

[75] See *Secretary of State for Employment v Globe Elastic Thread Co Ltd* [1980] AC 506 *per* Lord Wilberforce at 518G–H; 519A–B. Even if, as Harvey suggests (see para. CI:619), *Globe* could have been confined to a finding that any estoppel as between employer and employee would not bind the Secretary of State thereby permitting an employee to rely on an estoppel in the Industrial Tribunals, the employee would be using estoppel to create substantive rights and therefore her claim would fail.

Chapter 19

INSURANCE LAW

INTRODUCTION

19.01 As pointed out above,[1] the result of a successful plea of waiver or estoppel[2] will be to bar another party from relying on its rights or defences under a contract or common law. Therefore, although such a plea is a 'serious step,[3] it is the obvious step for an insured to take in replying to an insurer's denial of liability on the basis of material non-disclosure, a breach of warranty by the insured or failure of condition precedent. Thus, waiver[4] and estoppel, and the issues raised by them, are considered as a matter of common practice in insurance litigation. Three unfortunate results have followed. First, allegations of waiver and estoppel are sometimes raised without any detailed consideration of whether it is appropriate to make such allegations. Secondly, in a series of conflicting and sometimes confused decisions the courts have reached apparently differing conclusions as to the circumstances in which an insurer is precluded from raising defences to a claim by the insured. Thirdly, the application of the doctrines in insurance law are unnecessarily unclear and complicated.

WAIVER

19.02 A degree of clarification and simplification can be created by considering five issues: what is the meaning of the waiver as applied to insurance

---

[1] See *Waiver — Terminology, Waiver — Types and Elements* and *Waiver — Complications passim.*

[2] Estoppel is used in the sense of estoppel by representation/equitable forbearance/estoppel by convention.

[3] *Brook v Trafalgar Insurance Co Ltd* (1947) 79 Ll L Rep. 265 at 367 a *dictum* on waiver which, it is submitted, is of general application.

[4] Often pleaded and argued as if it were synonymous with estoppel.

law; when and in what circumstances will an insured succeed in arguing that the insurer has waived its rights; what are the particular difficulties which arise in considering waiver in this context; what is the effect of an allegation that the insurer has waived its rights; and how can the difficulties associated with the doctrine can be resolved by practitioners, claims managers and underwriters in practice.

THE MEANING OF WAIVER

Generally

At root, the doctrine of waiver in this context has the same meaning as it does in the general law of contract.[5] Logically, it therefore follows that the analysis of the meaning of waiver set out in Chapters 3 and following will apply. Waiver is distinguishable from estoppel and can broadly be defined as the voluntary relinquishment of a right.[6] In insurance law, a waiver will be based on '*the insurer's unequivocal conduct, knowingly contrary to the claim provisions of the contract, that betrays the insurer's purpose to relinquish its right to rely on the contractual language*'.[7] Further, the insurer's conduct must be so unequivocal that it cannot be consistent with any other interpretation than that the insurer is foregoing its legal rights.[8] An estoppel, on the other hand, relates to the conduct of both parties and will be made out where there is a representation on the part of the insurer which is inconsistent with its strict legal rights and detrimental reliance on the part of the insured.[9] **19.03**

The application of general contract principles to this area has two other results. First, the difficulties that the general law of contract has **19.04**

---

[5] See MacGillivray para. 803, pp. 331–2 and *Barratt (Bros) v Davies* [1966] 2 Lloyd's Rep. 1 *per* Lord Denning M.R. at 5.

[6] See *Waiver — Terminology* at para. 4–13. In an insurance context see, *e.g. Shapiro v Shapiro* 701 SW 2d 205 (Mo.App.1985) at 206.

[7] *Brown v State Farm Automobile Insurance* Co SW 2d 384 (Mobanc 1989) *per* Robertson J. at 387.

[8] See *Saunders v Lloyd's of London* 779 P 2d 249 (Wash.1989) *per* Utter J. at 254 col. 2; see also *Pitts v American Security Life Insurance Co* 931 F2d 351 (5th Cir 1991) *per* Duhé C.J. at 357; *Intel Corp v Hartford Accident and Indemnity Co* 692 F Supp 1171 at 1179 (ND.Cal.1988) and *Federated Service Insurance Co v Granados* 889 P 2d 1312 (1995).

[9] *Mississippi-Fox Drainage District v Plenge* 735 SW 2d 748 (Mo.App.1987) at 754; *Farm Bureau Mutual Automobile Insurance Co v Houle* 118 Vt 1545; 102 A 2d 326 (1954) at 330; see also *Buchanan v Switzerland General Insurance Co* 455 P 2d 344 (1969) and *McDaniels v Carlson* 738 P 2d 2554 (1987) and see also Clarke at para. 26–4A1.

experienced in defining waiver[10] have been transposed into insurance law. Thus, there is authority to suggest that an insured which has been 'misled' by the insurer can rely on waiver;[11] that 'waiver is a branch of estoppel';[12] that a waiver only has any relevance as and when it becomes an estoppel[13] and that waiver is in fact nothing more than estoppel.[14] Further, as in the general law of contract, the courts have adopted a broad brush approach looking at the merits of the case and articulating broad policy-based arguments. Thus, in the United States, the courts are generally reluctant to allow the insurer to avoid, or in American terms forfeit, the policy as:

> Our well established general rule . . . is 'Forfeitures are not favoured in law' and that 'courts are always prompt to seize hold of any circumstances that indicate an election to waive a forfeiture, or an agreement to do so on which the party has relied and acted.' Any agreement, declaration, or course of action on the part of an insurance company which leads a party insured honestly to believe that, by conformity thereto, a forfeiture of his policy will not be incurred, followed by due conformity on his part, will estop, and ought to estop, the company from insisting on a forfeiture, though it might be claimed under the express letter of the contract.[15]

The result is that the courts, on occasion, look to the end to be achieved — preventing insurers from approbating and reprobating the policy – and view the means, waiver and estoppel, as synonymous.

However, as argued at length elsewhere, it is submitted that to confuse or to fuse waiver and estoppel is an error which only leads to further **19.05**

---

10 See *Waiver — Terminology passim.*

11 *Beatty v Mutual Reserve Fund Life Association* 75 F 65 (1896) *per* Hawley D.J. at 69.

12 *Teasdell v Sun Life Assurance Co of Canada* [1927] 2 DLR 502 *per* Riddell J.A. at 509 and *DS Ashe Trucking Ltd v Dominion Insurance Corp* (1966) 56 DLR (2d) 730 *per* Tysoe J. at 745.

13 See, *e.g.* *Alexander v Standard Accident Insurance Co Detroit Michigan* 122 F 2d 995 (1941) *per* Huxman C.J. at 997 col. 2; '*Strictly speaking, the inability of a party to an action to assert as a defense a right given by a contract does not arise from a waiver thereof, but from estoppel resulting from a waiver. Mere failure to insist on a right or taking affirmative steps which would not be required until the other party to the contract had performed a condition required of him will of itself work an estoppel. It is only when the waiver causes the other party to the contract to change his position to his detriment which he would not have done save for his reliance upon the conduct of the other party, that an estoppel results*'.

14 *Equitable Life Assurance Society v McElroy* 83 F 631 (1897) *per* Sanborn C.J. at 683; *Spoeri v Massachusetts Mutual Life Insurance* Co 39 F 752 (1889) *per* Thayer J. at 753 and *Barratt (Bros) v Davies* [1966] 2 Lloyd's Rep. 1 *per* Lord Denning M.R. at 5.

15 *Union Life Insurance Co v Brewer* 309 SW 2d 740 (1958) *per* Holt J. at 743 col. 2–744 col. 1; see also *American Life Assocation v Vaden* 261 SW 320 at 324 and *American Insurance Union v Benson* 291 SW 1007 at 1011.

confusion. Thus the correct (and more recent) approach of the courts is to view waiver and estoppel as 'different legal doctrines'[16] and to formulate 'clear definitions' to 'lift' the 'mist of confusion' which has haunted insurance law in this regard.[17]

Secondly, the linkage between waiver and affirmation, less apparent elsewhere, is apparent.[18] An insurer seeking to avoid a policy on the grounds that the insured has failed to disclose a material fact or has misrepresented a fact will be seeking to exercise its rights to rescind the policy. The insured can respond in two ways — by alleging first that the insurer has waived its rights to avoid the policy or second that the insurer has affirmed the policy and therefore lost the right to rescind. Either case will be made out on the same facts and will have the same result. Thus, the Courts have held that the right to avoid for non-disclosure arises and continues until the insurer with full knowledge, affirms by a unequivocal act.[19] In other words, the courts apply the same test for waiver and affirmation/loss of the right to rescind and will do so even when the insurer is seeking to avoid for reasons other than misrepresentation or non-disclosure. Thus, where the insurer was seeking to rely on the insured's breach of a claim notification provision in the policy, the Court of Appeal held that whether or not the right to avoid had been waived was to be decided on parallel principles as loss of the right to rescission.[20] Applying those principles, there could be no loss of the right to by mere lapse of time or silence, as no unequivocal representation can be spelled out from the insurer's doing nothing.[21] **19.06**

[16] See *Craine v Colonial Mutual Fire Insurance Co* (1920) 28 CLR 305 *per* Isaacs J. at 327; *Brown v State Farm Mutual Automobile Insurance Co* SW 2d 384 (Mobanc 1989) *per* Robertson J. at 386 col. 2 and *Motor Oil Hellas (Corinth) Refineries SA v Shipping Corporation of India ('The Kanchenjunga')* [1990] 1 Lloyd's Rep. 391 *per* Lord Goff. at 399 col. 2.

[17] See *Brown v State Farm Mutual Automobile Insurance Co* SW 2d 384 (Mobanc 1989) *per* Robertson J. at 388 col. 1.

[18] See *e.g. Insurance Corporation of the Channel Islands v Royal Hotel Ltd* (unrep. 30 July 1997 Comm Ct Mance J).

[19] *Liberian Insurance Agency Inc v Mosse* [1977] 2 Lloyd's Rep. 560 *per* Donaldson J. at 565. Mr Justice Donaldson then went on to suggest that there could be a deemed affirmation of the policy by reason of the insured suffering prejudice as a result of the insurer's delay in rescinding the policy, an articulation, it is submitted, of equitable forbearance principles not waiver/affirmation.

[20] *Allen v Robles* [1969] 1 WLR 1193 *per* Fenton-Atkinson L.J. at 1196G–H.

[21] The court then went on to hold that the insured had suffered a detriment as a result of the silence and delay and as a result the insurer was to be taken to have 'waived' its rights (*per* Fenton-Atkinson L.J. at 1196G–H). As we have suggested elsewhere (see *Waiver — Types and Elements* at para. 4.24) the court was in fact applying equitable forbearance principles.

19.07 It follows that whether one reaches the conclusion by the route of affirmation, loss of the right to rescind by affirmation or waiver, the elements required are the same — at least knowledge of the facts giving rise to the right of the right itself and an unequivocal representation that the insurer is foregoing its rights will be required.[22] It also follows that, in the majority of cases, the insurer will be responding to a breach by the insured and the courts will be considering 'waiver by election'.[23] We therefore concentrate on the application of that doctrine to insurance law. However, there are two occasions in which the doctrines of pure and unilateral waiver will operate.

Pure waiver and unilateral waiver

19.08 As discussed above,[24] pure waiver, and usually unilateral waiver, will take place where X, the party alleged to have waived its rights, has indicated that it would not require the future performance of some of Y's, the other party to the contract, obligations. Similarly, an insurer can waive its rights under, and in relation to, the contract of insurance *in futuro*. The insurer will do so in two main ways. First, the insurer may represent that the traditional methods of contract formation need not be complied with in the particular case, thereby waiving its rights to argue that there is no concluded contract of insurance at a later date. Secondly, the insurer may waive the insured's obligations which exist to protect the insurer, for example, the insured's common law obligation to give full disclosure of all material facts prior to entry into the contract of insurance. In both cases, there has been no breach of contract by the insured, axiomatically as in both cases there is no concluded contract of insurance, and therefore no waiver by election. The waiver is either a unilateral waiver[25] of obligations which solely benefit the insurer, or the pure waiver[26] by which the insurer divests itself of its rights to argue that there is no contract of insurance or no such contract was ever concluded. In either event, the elements required to found the waiver will be the same as discussed above,[27] – namely an unequivocal act by the insurer possessing the appropriate knowledge.

---

[22] See *Insurance Corporation of the Channel Islands v The Royal Hotel Ltd* (Mance J Comm Ct unrep. 30 July 1996); *National Insurance and Guarantee Corp Plc v Imperio Reinsurance Co (UK) Ltd* (Coleman J Comm Ct unrep. 30 September 1997).

[23] See *Waiver — Types and Elements* at para. 4.01 above.

[24] *ibid.* at para. 4.27 ff., above.

[25] Defined *ibid.* at para. 4.27 above.

[26] *ibid.* at para. 4.35 above.

[27] See *ibid.* at para. 4.44.

The means by which the contract of insurance is formed

Most insurance contracts will be formed by a traditional process of offer and acceptance. Thus, on the Lloyd's market, the insurer by its scratch on the slip agrees to insure, the slip containing the material terms of the contract. In home and motor insurance, the insurer will accept the risk by sending a cover note to the insured. In either event, it is necessary to show some exchange leading to a *consensus ad idem*, both parties being taken to be aware of the terms of the policy. However, that practice can alter in three ways. **19.09**

First: **19.10**

> Where the circumstances are such that it must have been within the contemplation of the parties that, according to the ordinary uses of mankind, the post might be used as a means of communicating the acceptance of an offer, the acceptance is complete as soon as it is posted.[28]

Here, the insurer will be taken to have waived its right to receive the acceptance prior to conclusion of the contract. The requisite knowledge to found the waiver will be taken from the insurer's traditional conduct of its business or market practice. The waiver will also mean that the insurer has waived its rights to contend at some future date that there is no concluded contract.

Secondly, in motor insurance, dependent on the particular facts, the receipt of a temporary cover note may be construed as an offer to insure for the future. If so, that is an offer which can be accepted by conduct. The insured will be taken to have so accepted the offer by taking a car out on the roads relying on the temporary cover note.[29] The unequivocal act of sending the cover note therefore acts as a waiver of the insurer's right to argue that there was no concluded contract.[30] **19.11**

Thirdly, there may be occasions in which the slip as scratched is insufficiently clear or precise to form a concluded contract[31] or the slip constitutes nothing more than an agreement to agree the eventual terms of the policy.[32] In those limited circumstances, the contract of insurance will only come into being on the signing of the policy wording by the insurer. Therefore, if the policy wording is not issued, the insurer will be free to disclaim liability on the slip. However, the insurer will be **19.12**

---

[28] *Henthorn v Fraser* [1892] 2 Ch 27, CA *per* Lord Herschell at 33.
[29] See *Taylor v Allon* [1966] 1 QB 305 *per* Lord Parker C.J. (*obiter*) at 311.
[30] The waiver described would probably also be an estoppel — the detrimental reliance being taking the car out onto the road.
[31] For instance, if it fails to state the risk assumed or the period of insurance.
[32] See, *e.g.* Walford v Miles [1992] 2 AC 128.

precluded from so doing if it has waived the point. Thus, in the Lloyd's market, it is standard practice for subscribers to a line led by another underwriter to mark the policy 'TBA L/U'. In so doing, the subscribers unequivocally state that they will be bound by the Lead Underwriter's wording. As the subscriber will be deemed to have knowledge of the practice of the Lloyd's market, the subscriber will be taken to have waived their rights to object to the terms of the policy as and when the Lead Underwriter agrees those terms.

Waiver of non-disclosure

It is trite law that an insurance contract is an *uberrimae fides* contract and that, as a result, the insured is under a duty to disclose all facts which a reasonable business man would have disclosed and which were material to the insurer.[33] The difficulty arises in deciding what is material for those purposes, whether or not the insurer has waived performance of the duty and therefore whether the insurer has waived its rights to avoid for material non-disclosure. That difficulty can be analysed in three main ways — the effect of the proposal form; whether or not the insured has to disclose facts of which the insurer is or should be aware; and the effect of the answers given by the insured. **19.13**

The effect of the proposed form

Usually the insurer will request specific information relating to the risk from the insured in the proposal form. The insurer will also make the truth of the insured's responses the basis of the policy and/or seek a warranty from the insured warrants as to the truth of the information given. On either basis, if the insured answers any of those questions incorrectly, absent a waiver or estoppel, the insurer will be entitled to avoid the policy. The difficulty is whether in requesting specific information the insurer waives its rights to avoid the policy for a material non-disclosure of facts, details of which were not sought in the proposal in the form. In English law,[34] except for cases of fraud and moral hazard **19.14**

[33] As to which see *Pan Atlantic Insurance Co v Pine Top Ins Co* [1995] AC 501. The duty arises before the contract of insurance is formed, when the policy renews and when a claim arises — *New Hampshire Insurance Co v MGN Ltd* (CA unrep. 6 September 1996) disapproving *Black King Shipping Corp v Massie (The Litsion Pride)* [1985] 1 Lloyd's Rep. 437; see also *Manifest Shipping Co Ltd v Uni-Polaris Shipping Co Ltd (The Star Sea)* (CA unrep. 20 December 1996)

[34] In US law, a failure to ask questions will constitute a waiver — see, *e.g. Allesina v London & L & G Insurance Co* 78 P 392 (1904).

where the insurer is taken never to have waived its rights,[35] there are two conflicting streams of authority.

General duty of disclosure

On the one hand, the courts have held that the insured owes a duty to disclose all relevant facts. That duty cannot be limited or curtailed by action by the insurer. Thus: **19.15**

> It does not matter whether [the insured] . . . is asked questions about [the facts]; he must tell every material fact . . .[36]

On that basis, the courts have held that the contents of the proposal form do not release the insured from the duty to disclose those facts which the reasonable business man would have disclosed.[37] Further, where the proposal provides that the answers to certain questions will form the basis of the contract of insurance, the courts have concluded that such a provision does not relieve the insured of its general obligation to disclose.[38] On that approach

> it is only if . . . the insurers are put on enquiry about some particular matter that it can be said that they have waived the obligation[39]

Waiver by the insurer

On the other hand, it appears that in certain cases the courts have also used the questions asked in the proposal form to curtail the insured's duty of disclosure. Thus, in *Court v Martineau*,[40] the insured was the part owner of a vessel which salvaged a brig and ship off the coast of Ireland. The insured, based in Liverpool, required insurance for the prize and therefore sent a written request for insurance to its broker in London stating that the insured was concerned that the salved ship might be a total loss. The broker took out insurance on receipt of that letter **19.16**

---

[35] Clarke at para. 23.12C and see also discussion in *Insurance Corporation of the Channel Islands v Royal Hotel Ltd* (Mance J Comm Ct unrep. 30 July 1997).

[36] *McCormick v National Motor Accident Insurance Union Ltd* (1934) 49 Ll L Rep. 361 *per* Scrutton L.J. at 363.

[37] *Becker v Marshall* (1922) 11 Ll L Rep. *per* Salter J. at 117 col. 2, 119 col. 1; *Glicksman v Lancashire & General Assurance Company Ltd* [1927] AC 139 *per* Lord Dunedin at 143; see also *Taylor v Eagle Star Insurance Co Ltd* (1940) 67 Ll L Rep. 136 *per* Macnaghten J. at 140 col. 1–141 col. 2.

[38] See *Schoolman v Hall* [1951] 1 Lloyd's Rep. 139 *per* Cohen L.J. at 142 col. 2–143 col. 1.

[39] *Arterial Caravans Ltd v Yorkshire Insurance Co Ltd* [1973] 1 Lloyd's Rep. 169 *per* Chapman J. at 180 col. 2–181 col. 1.

[40] (1782) 3 Doug 1161, 99 ER 591.

disclosing the insured's concerns, the premium being rigged to reflect the fact that the ship had not arrived and those concerns.[41] However, subsequent to the sending of the first letter, the insured discovered that the ship was a total loss and wrote to the broker informing it of the fact. That letter did not arrive before the broker took out the insurance. The insurer refused to pay alleging that the broker had failed to disclose the fact that the insured was communicating by letter and therefore there would be a delay in receiving news of the ship. On those facts, Lord Mansfield found that there was a fair presentation of the risk overall and then stated that:

> If the underwriter had wished to know by what means the broker acquired his information that the ship had not arrived, he should have made inquiry; but he waived the inquiry by putting no questions to him, though they naturally arose from the subject.[42]

The approach in *Court v Martineau* has been supported by subsequent authority. Thus, in *Joel v Law Union and Crown Insurance Company*[43] Lord Justice Vaughan Williams stated that: 19.17

> the insurance office may, by the requisitions for information of a specific sort which it makes of the proposer, relieve him partially from the obligation to disclose by an election to make inquiries as to certain facts material to the risk to be insured against itself

Further, in *Hair v Prudential Assurance Co Ltd*[44] Mr Justice Woolf, as he then was, stated that if a reasonable reader would infer from the insurer's questions that the insurer was only concerned with the specific matters referred to in the form, then there would be a waiver of materiality. Therefore, if the insurer wished to avoid the possibility of a waiver's being found against it, the insurer should state that it required disclosure of matters additional to those specifically referred to in the proposal form.[45]

---

41 See finding of fact (1782) 3 Doug 1161, 99 ER 591 at 162, 592.
42 (1782) 3 Doug 1161, 99 ER 591 at 163, 592.
43 [1908] 2 KB 863 at 878.
44 [1983] 2 Lloyd's Rep. 667 at 673 cols 1–2.
45 See also *Laing v Union Marine Insurance Company* (1865) 1 Comm Cas 11 *per* Mathew J. at 15: the insured '*is not bound to give information which the underwriter waives or as to which the assured may reasonably infer that the underwriter is indifferent.*' This approach would be consistent with the judging of materiality by reference to the prudent underwriter's view of the facts not what the prudent insured believed it should disclose. Thus the prudent underwriter will know what is material and ask questions accordingly – see *March Cabaret Club & Casino Ltd v The London Assurance* [1975] 1 Lloyd's Rep. 169 at 176 per May J; *The Insurance Corporation of the Channel Islands v The Royal Hotel Ltd* (Mance J Comm Ct unrep. 30 July 1997).

Difficulties and potential solutions

There are difficulties with both approaches. The former may be seen as imposing onerous obligations on the insured especially if that insured is not an experienced commercial party but an inexperienced consumer. Thus, the Insurance Ombudsman has argued strongly in favour of the latter approach as a mechanism for protecting the consumer. The latter approach raises conceptual difficulties. It is difficult to see how there can be a waiver when the insurer may not have the requisite knowledge; in some cases the insurer will not have knowledge of the facts or type of facts of which it is allegedly waiving the materiality.[46] Further, it is submitted that *Court* turns on the finding that there was an overall fair presentation of the risk and *Hair*, in which the insured was a consumer, was motivated by Mr Justice Woolf's view that the inequality of bargaining between the two parties was such that the insurer should not be permitted to rely on the onerous duty of disclosure.[47] It follows that it may not be right to apply *Court* or *Hair* across the board. **19.18**

It is submitted that there are two ways in which the difficulties can be resolved. The first is to view insurance contracts with consumers as different to commercial insurance contracts. An extreme example of this approach is *Dyck v Poirer*.[48] *Dyck* concerned car rental contracts which also contained obligatory insurance provisions. Mr Justice Walker held[49] that a car rental contract was not an *uberrimae fides* contract because of the special circumstances in which it was entered into. Insurance was arranged as a matter of course by the rental agency to comply with the insured's statutory obligations, the insurer did not examine the risk at all and the entire transaction was carried out at high speed. Further, and in any event given the nature of the relationship, Mr Justice Walker held the insurer would be taken to have waived the materiality of any facts not the subject of specific inquiry. However, absent the extreme **19.19**

---

[46] However, an experienced insurer will find it difficult to argue that it was unaware of a fact or category of facts which was material to the placing of the risk. In the normal course of events, an insurer will be aware of what categories of fact will be material to the risk — see para. 19.20 below.

[47] The questions in *Hair* were widely drawn and the insurer had also inserted a very wide warranty into the proposal and policy so that, on one construction, the truth of the facts in the proposal was warranted at the date on which the proposal was completed and the future truth of the facts was also warranted. Unsurprisingly, Woolf J. rejected that construction and construed the questions narrowly (at 672 col. 2 *per* Woolf J).

[48] (1988) 47 DLR (4th) 193.

[49] *ibid.* at 206–209.

facts of *Dyck* it is difficult to see how a distinction between consumer and insurance contracts can be drawn.

The second, and it is submitted preferable, approach arises from the standard nature of many consumer insurance contracts. It is settled law that an insurer is taken to know, or to be put on inquiry as to, those facts which inevitably arise from the subject matter of the contract of insurance. Therefore, if the insurer fails to make inquiry in the proposal form as to those facts, it will be taken to have waived the materiality of those facts.[50] In the vast majority of consumer contracts, the insured will be seeking to protect standard risks against standard perils. It follows that the facts which will be material may fall within a predictable span. It therefore follows that in a standard consumer insurance contract, the insurer will be aware of the type of facts which should be disclosed and, if the proposal form is silent on the point, the insurer can safely be taken to have waived further disclosure. The insurer can avoid that result by expressly stating that questions in the proposal form are 'without prejudice' to the insured's duty to disclose all material facts. By contrast, in the less predictable world of commercial insurance, the risks being insured against fall into a wider span and the material facts are less predictable. Therefore, the insurer is less likely to have sufficient knowledge to found a waiver and should not be taken to have waived further disclosure by the questions it has asked in the proposal form. It therefore follows that the proposal form should have less effect in commercial insurance than it does in consumer insurance provided that the consumer insurance at issue relates to a standard risk. 19.20

Disclosure of facts of which the insurer should be aware

In certain types of risk, irrespective of the contents of the proposal form,[51] the insurer is deemed to know the facts relating to the risk or is put on inquiry as to those facts. If the insurer fails to make further inquiry as to those facts, it will be taken to have waived its rights to avoid the policy in the event of non-disclosure. Frequently, the waiver will arise from the market practice[52] or the facts being '*common notoriety or* 19.21

---

[50] See, *e.g. Asfar & Co v Blundell* [1896] 1 QB 123; *Cantiere Meccanico Brindisino v Janson* [1912] 3 KB 452; *Mann, Macneal and Steeves v Capital and Counties Insurance Co* [1921] 2 KB 300; *Roselodge Limited v Castle* [1966] 2 Lloyd's Rep. 113 and *Roberts v Plaisted* [1989] 2 Lloyd's Rep. 341.

[51] See para. 19.14 ff., above.

[52] See *Pacific Queen Fisheries et al v L Symes ('The Pacific Queen')* [1963] 2 Lloyd's Rep. 201 *per* Barnes Ct. J. at 208–9 (US Court of Appeals, Ninth Circuit) — the insurer will be taken to know that which is in general usage and universally known to all engaged in the relevant trade.

knowledge'.[53] Thus, in marine insurance, if the insurer agrees a 'seaworthiness admitted' clause, it will be deemed to know whether the particular risk being insured is of a type which is seaworthy and the insured will only be required to disclose defects which are particular to that particular vessel, such as corrosion or design defects.[54] Again in hull insurance, the insurer will be taken to know of the particular perils associated with a particular type of hull and be put on inquiry as to whether the cargoes proposed whilst the insurer is on risk are of such a type as to create those particular perils.[55] In reinsurance, the reinsurer will be taken to be aware of the standard clauses in the insurance policies which it is reinsuring.[56] Finally, in the Lloyd's market, a managing agent seeking reinsurance is under an obligation to disclose all material facts as well as all those facts which might possibly give the reinsurer cause to avoid the contract.[57] It follows that if the managing agent does so, and the reinsurer makes no further inquiry, the reinsurer, by virtue of market practice, will be taken to have waived its rights to argue that there were additional facts which the managing agent should have disclosed.

As well as market practice, the waiver can also arise from the court taking a common sense view of the risk and the activities normally associated with that risk. Thus, where the insured sought to insure its hotel, the court held that the running of a discotheque was ancillary to the running of the hotel and the insurer would be aware of that fact. If the insurer then made no inquiry as to the existence of a discotheque, it **19.22**

---

53 *Marc Rich & Co v Portman* [1997] 1 Lloyd's Rep. 225 *per* Leggatt L.J. at 232 col. 2.

54 See *Cantiere Meccanico Brindisino v Janson* [1912] 3 KB 452 *per* Vaughan Williams L.J. at 461 and *per* Fletcher Moulton L. J. at 466; *North British Fishing Boat Insurance Co Ltd v Starr* (1922) 13 Ll L Rep. 206 *per* Rowlatt J. at 210.

55 See *Carter v Boehm* (1766) 3 Burr 1905 *per* Lord Mansfield at 1910 see also 1915. *Mann, Macneal and Steeves v Capital and Counties Insurance Co* [1921] 2 KB 300 *per* Bankes L.J. at 309; *cf. Asfar & Co v Blundell* [1896] 1 QB 123 *per* Lord Esher M.R. at 129. However, if one proposed cargo has a particularly perilous and not immediately apparent nature or has a problematic history, the insured must disclose that cargo to the insurer *Greenhill v Federal Insurance Company Limited* [1927] 1 KB 65 *per* Lord Hanworth M.R. at 73; *per* Scrutton L.J. at 84.

56 *Charlesworth v Faber* (1900) 55 Comm Cas 408 *per* Bigham L.J. at 412; *Sumitomo Marine & Fire Insurance Co Ltd v Cologne Reinsurance Company of America* 552 NYS 2d 891 (Ct App, 1990) *per* Kaye J. at 896 col. 1. The reinsurer may also be obliged to accept all risks underwritten by the insured and falling within the terms of the treaty thereby waiving its rights to have disclosure of the specific facts relating to those risks (see Clarke at para. 23.12C and fn 352).

57 See *Aiken v Stewart Wrightson Members' Agency Limited* [1995] 3 All ER 449 *per* Potter J. at 481a–e.

would be taken to have waived the materiality of the insured's failure to disclose that it was running a discotheque. Consequently, the insurer waived its rights to avoid the policy for non-disclosure.[58] Similarly, where the broker/insurer is informed that the risk to be insured is a particular cargo which is by its very nature perilous but the insurer is not told, does not know and does not ask whether the particular cargo is perilous, the insurer will be taken to have waived the non-disclosure of the perilous nature of that cargo.[59]

There are three important caveats to this rule. First, as with the proposal form, the insurer cannot waive the insured's failure to disclose facts relating to a fraud on the insurer nor to any moral hazard. The simple reason is that the insurer cannot be taken to be aware of facts which are of their very nature abnormal. Secondly, the insured will only establish that the insurer has waived non-disclosure of a particular set of facts if, apart from those facts, there has been an overall fair presentation of the risk.[60] Again the caveat makes practical sense. If there was no overall fair presentation of the risk the insurer would, absent waiver or estoppel, be entitled to avoid the policy even if there was a waiver of the materiality of certain facts in and by the proposal form. Thirdly, care must be taken to define the category of facts which the insurer is deemed to know as a result of market practice or common sense. Therefore, in marine insurance, the insurer will not be deemed to know the specific facts relating to one particular charterer or line.[61] **19.23**

The effect of answers given by the insured

An insured often responds to the proposal either by leaving sections of it blank or partially completed or by supplying the insurer with documents. Each creates its own difficulty for the insurer. Thus, if the insurer issues on the policy on the strength of partial or no answers **19.24**

---

[58] *Roberts v Plaisted* [1989] 2 Lloyd's Rep. 341 *per* Purchas L.J. at 347 col. 2–348 col. 1. See also *St Paul Fire & Marine Insurance Co v McConnell Dowell Constructors Limited* [1993] 2 Lloyd's Rep. 503 and *Newbury International v Reliance National Insurance Co* [1994] 1 Lloyd's Rep. 83.

[59] *Greenhill v Federal Insurance Co Ltd* [1927] 1 KB 65 *per* Scrutton L.J. at 84.

[60] See *Harrower v Hutchinson* (1870) LR 5 QB 584 *per* Kelly C.B. at 592–3; *per* Willes J. at 594; *Container Transport International Ltd v Oceanus Mutual Underwriting Association (Bermuda) Ltd* [1984] 1 Lloyd's Rep. 476 *per* Parker L.J. at 511; *Newbury International v Reliance National Insurance Co* [1994] 1 Lloyd's Rep. 83 *per* Hobhouse J. at 90 col. 1 and *Marc Rich & Co AG v Portman* [1997] 1 Lloyd's Rep. 225 *per* Leggatt L.J. at 233 col. 2–234 col. 1.

[61] *Marc Rich & Co v Portman* [1997] 1 Lloyd's Rep. 225 *per* Leggatt L.J. at 231 col. 1–232 col. 2 — insurer did not have deemed knowledge of the extensive demurrage claims being made against Marc Rich.

to the questions in the proposal form, the insurer will have waived the materiality of the facts left incomplete or blank[62] unless it is clear from the context[63] or the proposal form expressly provides[64] that the blank answers signify an assertion that the insured has nothing to disclose in relation to those questions, said assertion potentially forming the basis of a non-disclosure.[65]

As for disclosure by documents, the rule appears to be that the insurer is put on inquiry as to the contents of the documents and other events or documents referred to them[66] provided that there are 'significant indications' of the true position so that the insurer may be fairly said to be put on inquiry.[67] Thus, for example, if the insured refers to admission to hospital, that will be sufficient to put the insurer on inquiry as to what happened when the insured was admitted to hospital and to make a request for the relevant hospital records.[68] Similarly where the broker provides the insurer with both a summary and a full version of the insured's claim record and the insurer reads only the summary, the insurer will be taken to have waived the materiality of the facts set out in the full record.[69] **19.25**

---

62 *Roberts v Avon Insurance Company Ltd* [1956] 2 Lloyd's Rep. 240 *per* Barry J. at 249 cols 1–2 and *Marcovitch v The Liverpool Victoria Friendly Society* (1912) 28 TLR 188 at 189.

63 Which will only happen rarely (*Marcovitch v The Liverpool Victoria Friendly Society* (1912) 28 TLR 188 at 189).

64 See, *e.g. Saunders v Queensland Insurance Co Ltd* (1931) 45 CLR 557 and *Calder v Batavia Sea and Fire Insurance Co Ltd* [1932] SASR 46.

65 In American law, the rule appears to be that a failure to answer a question with subsequent issue of policy is a waiver of the materiality of the answer or of the requirement to answer that question *Mutual Reserve Fund Life Association v Farmer* 47 SW 850 (1898) *per* Bunn C.J. at 852 col. 2; *Bowles v Mutual Benefit Health and Accident Association* 99 F 2d 44 (1938) *per* Parker C.J. at 46 col. 1 and *Transamerica Premier Insurance Co v Miller* 41 F 3d 438 (1994). In Australia, unless there is express provision in the proposal (see *Saunders v Queensland Insurance Co Ltd* (1931) 45 CLR 557 and *Calder v Batavia Sea and Fire Insurance Co Ltd* [1932] SASR 46) a parallel rule applies — see *London and Lancashire Insurance Co Ltd v Honey* (1876) 2 VLR (L) 7 and *Calder v Batavia Sea and Fire Insurance Co Ltd* [1932] SASR 46.

66 See *Freeland v Glover* (1806) 7 East 457 103 ER 177 *per* Lord Ellenborough C.J. at 462, 179 and *Ellingwood v NN Investors Life Insurance Company Inc* 805 P 2d 70 (NM 1991) *per* Ransom J. at 77 col. 2.

67 See *Asfar & Co v Blundell* [1896] 1QB 123 at 129–130; *Kreglinger and Fernau Ltd v Irish National Insurance Co Ltd* [1956] IR 116 *per* Davitt P. at 151; see also *Duren v Northwestern National Life Insurance Co* 5581 So 2d 810 (Ala 1991) *per* Almon J. at 816 col. 1 and *Steptore v Masco Construction Co Inc* 643 So 2d 1213 (1994).

68 See, *e.g. Prudential Insurance Co v Saxe* 134 F 2d 16 (1943) *per* Rutledge J. at 29.

69 See *Pan Atlantic Ins Co Ltd v Pine Top Insurance Co Ltd* [1992] 1 Lloyd's Rep. 101.

WHEN WILL THERE BE A WAIVER BY ELECTION?

In summary and applying the principles set out in Chapter 4,[70] for a waiver by election there must be a repudiatory breach by the insured of its obligations. Additionally, those elements necessary to establish a pure or unilateral waiver must be present; an unequivocal act by the insurer or its agent,[71] that act being committed when the insurer or its agent had the appropriate knowledge[72] and after the insurer had been given a reasonable time to consider its position in light of its knowledge.[73] It is important to note that all three elements must be present, thus even if there is a representation of the most unequivocal kind — the issue of the policy — if there is nothing to suggest that the insurer possessed the appropriate knowledge, there will be no waiver.[74] It is also important to note that there must be some unequivocal act by the insurer — silence, without the intervention of statute[75] or estoppel,[76] will not suffice.[77] **19.26**

[70] See, in particular, *Waiver — Types and Elements* at para. 4.01 ff.

[71] As to which see *Agency passim* and para. 19.58 below.

[72] See *Waiver — Types and Elements* at paras 4.14 ff and 19.31 below.

[73] *McCormick and another v National Motor and Accident Union Ltd* (1934) 49 Ll L Rep. 361 *per* Scrutton L.J. at 365 col. 2; see also *Melik & Co v Norwich Union* [1980] 1 Lloyd's Rep. 523 *per* Woolf J. at 534 col. 1.

[74] *P Samuel v Dumas* [1924] AC 431 at 476; *per* Lord Sumner at 483.

[75] *cf* in New York and Missouri, state law requires an insurer to state all the grounds on which it seeks to avoid the policy as soon as possible after discovery of said grounds, absent such a statement, silence will equate to a delay which will prevent the insurer from raising those points — see *Allstate Insurance Company v Flaumenbaum* 308 NYS 2d 447 *per* M.M. Levy J. at 456–8; *Consolidated Electrical Cooperative v Employers Mutual Liability Insurance Co* 106 F Supp 322 (1952) *per* Hulen D.J. at 331 col. 1; *Salerno v Western Casualty & Surety Co* 336 F 2d 14 (1964) *per* Ridge C.J. at 17 col. 2; *Boston Old Colony Insurance v Lumbermans Mutual Casualty Company* 889 F2d 1245 (2nd Cir, 1989) *per* Feinberg J. at 1247 col. 2; *Dependible Janitorial Services Inc v Transcontinental Insurance Co* 622 NYS 632 (1995) and *In re Balfour Maclaine International Ltd* 873 F Supp (1995).

[76] See *Allen v Robles* [1969] 1 WLR 1193 *per* Fenton-Atkinson L.J. at 1196G–H. It is submitted that the reference to the insured being 'prejudiced' by the delay shows that the court was, in fact, stating that the insured was estopped by its silence from relying on the breach — see *Waiver — Types and Elements* at para. 4.10.

[77] *Accident Insurance Co v Young* (1891) 20 SCR 280; *State Farm Mutual Automobile Insurance Co v Elgot* 369 NYS 2d 719 (1975) *per* Stevens P.J. at 721; see also *Scali McCabe Sloves Inc v North River Insurance Co* 532 F Supp 203 (1981) *per* Sweet D.J. at 207 and *FDIC v Duffy* 47 F 3d 146 (1995).

Repudiatory breach of the insured of its obligations

There are three types of breach which can be committed by the insured — breach of condition, breach of the duty of good faith and breach of warranty. The burden of proving breach will lie on the insurer. Practically, however, in cases of plain breach, the insured may adopt the course of admitting the breach and concentrating on allegations of waiver and estoppel. In that case the burden will pass to the insured.[78] If the insurer fails to prove breach, it will be unnecessary to consider waiver. **19.27**

Breach of condition

Whether or not there has been a breach of a condition of the policy will be a question of construing the policy using the standard canons of construction and then adducing evidence of breach. In deciding whether or not the term of the policy at issue is a condition, the court will have the commercial purpose of the clause firmly in mind.[79] Thus, in financial risk insurance, the insurer will usually require some form of due diligence on the part of the insured before entry into the transaction being insured. The court will consider that transaction, the nature of the risk and the market practice in deciding whether the term is a condition and, if so, the precise nature of the due diligence required by the term.[80] **19.28**

Breach of duty of good faith

Again the insurer will have to prove that there were material facts which remained undisclosed. Materiality must be proved by both the individual underwriter and by expert evidence as to that which the reasonable underwriter would have done.[81] **19.29**

---

78 See para. 19.84 below.

79 See *Charter Reinsurance v Fagan* [1996] 2 WLR 76; *Arbuthnott v Fagan* (1993) CA unrep. Transcript 1024 per Sir Thomas Bingham M.R. and Steyn L.J. and *The Antaios* [1985] AC 191 *per* Lord Diplock at 200–1; *Reardon Smith Line v Hansen Tangen* [1976] 1 WLR 989 *per* Lord Wilberforce at 996 and *Wickman Machine Tool Sales Ltd v L Schuler AG* [1974] AC 235 *per* Lord Reid at 251.

80 See, *e.g. Svenska Handelsbanken v Sun Alliance and London Insurance plc* [1996] 1 Lloyd's Rep. 519.

81 *Pan Atlantic Insurance Co Ltd v Pine Tops Insurance Co* [1995] AC 501.

Breach of Warranty

As with the above, the insurer will have to establish that there was a warranty, the scope of the warranty and that it has been breached. However, unlike breaches of the duty of good faith and of condition, the application of the doctrine of waiver to breaches of warranty creates two complex issues: the extent to which any breach of warranty can be waived and the circumstances in which the breach of warranty can be waived. **19.30**

Waiver of a breach of warranty?

In *The Good Luck*[82] the House of Lords considered the interrelationship of insurance warranties with section 33(3) of the Marine Insurance Act 1906 and held that, on the plain meaning of the section, the insurer was automatically discharged from liability under the policy from the date of breach of the warranty. The logical result of such a finding could be that it would be impossible for the insurer to waive the breach of warranty as the insurer had already been discharged from liability. Therefore, the insurer could only be liable if it agreed afresh to be bound by the terms of the policy, that is, there was reinstatement of the policy.[83] This logical impasse has led commentators to suggest that the effect of *The Good Luck* is that insurers can now only be estopped from alleging that there has been a breach of warranty;[84] that all warranties are now to be considered as exceptions to the policy[85] which cannot be waived;[86] that marine insurance is now to be treated differently to non-marine insurance — it being impossible to waive a breach of warranty in marine insurance but not in non-marine insurance;[87] and that, at its lowest, all cases in this area should be reconsidered in light of *The Good Luck*.[88] **19.31**

However, it is submitted, albeit with some degree of caution, that the effect of *The Good Luck* is not to make it impossible to waive a breach **19.32**

---

82 [1992] 1 AC 233.

83 Birds, 'The Effect of Breach of an Insurance Warranty' (1991) 107 *LQR* 540 at 542.

84 Clarke at para. 20.7A.

85 *ibid.* at para. 19.1B.

86 As the effect of the waiver would be to extend the cover beyond that which was actually agreed and a waiver cannot enlarge the terms of a contract — see Clarke at para 19.1B2 and below.

87 See Kluwer *Insurance Law* at para B.2.3–42. It is submitted that this view is incorrect — it now being well established that the principles which apply to marine insurance also apply to non-marine insurance and had their Lordships intended to reverse that principle they would have done so explicitly. See also Clarke at para. 20.6C, fn 207.

88 See *Reinsurance Practice and the Law*, (1993, LLP, London) at para. 24.6.4.6.

of warranty for three reasons. First, section 34(3) of the Marine Insurance Act 1906 expressly provides that the insurer may waive a breach of warranty. Nothing in *The Good Luck* suggests that their Lordships were intending to erode the plain words of that section. Secondly, their Lordships did not overrule previous authority holding that a breach of warranty could be waived. Thus, where there was a right to avoid the policy on the basis of the breach of a warranty as to the amount insured:

> [that] right may be waived either by express words or by conduct inconsistent with the continuance of the right . . .[89]

Thirdly, the phrasing of Lord Goff's judgment suggests that he did not intend to suggest that it was impossible to waive a breach of warranty. Lord Goff stated: **19.33**

> if a promissory warranty is not complied with, the insurer is discharged from liability as from the date of the breach of warranty, for the simple reason that fulfilment of the warranty is a condition precedent to the liability of the insurer. This moreover reflects the fact that the rationale of warranties in insurance law is that the insurer only accepts the risk provided that the warranty is fulfilled. This is entirely understandable; and it follows that the immediate effect of a breach of a promissory warranty is to discharge the insurer from liability as from the date of breach . . . where we are concerned with a promissory warranty, i.e. a promissory condition precedent, contained in an existing contract of insurance, non-fulfilment of the condition does not prevent the contract from coming into existence. What it does (as section 33(3) makes plain) is to discharge the insurer from liability as from the date of breach. Certainly, it does not have the effect of avoiding the contract ab initio. Nor, strictly speaking, does it have the effect of bringing the contract to an end. It is possible that there may be obligations of the insured under the contract which will survive the discharge of the insurer from liability, as for an example a continuing liability to pay the premium. Even if in the result no further obligations rest on either party, it is not correct to speak of the contract being avoided; and it is, strictly speaking, more accurate to keep to the carefully chosen words in section 33(3) of the Act . . .[90]

Lord Goff then went on to consider section 34(3) of the Marine Insurance Act 1906 stating:

> When, as section 34(3) contemplates, the insurer waives a breach of promissory warranty, the effect is that, to the extent of the waiver, the insurer cannot rely upon a breach as having discharged him from liability.

[89] *P Samuel & Co v Dumas* [1924] AC 431 *per* Viscount Cave at 442.
[90] [1992] J AC 233 at 262H–3E.

> This is a very different thing from saying that the discharge of the insurer from liability is dependent upon a decision by the insurer.[91]

It is clear, it is submitted, that Lord Goff was giving a literal and limited meaning to section 33(3), namely that the sole effect of the section was to discharge the insurer from liability — the contract remaining on foot. In that context, the word 'automatic' means that the insurer is discharged without its electing to be so discharged. Therefore, there is nothing to prevent an insurer, possessing the appropriate knowledge and after the appropriate time for reflection, from electing that to continue to provide cover under the contract and thereby being unable to rely on the particular breach as discharging it from liability. **19.34**

There are two alternative views to that we have expressed above. First, that the insurer affirms the contract of insurance, as Lord Justice Kerr has suggested: **19.35**

> the correct analysis of a breach of warranty in an insurance contract may be that, upon the true construction of the contract, the consequence of the breach is that the cover ceases to be applicable unless the insurer subsequently affirms the contract, rather than to treat the occurrence as a breach of contract by the insured which the insurer subsequently accepts as a wrongful repudiation.[92]

The insurer will thus waive its rights to argue at a later date that it was discharged from liability by the particular breach of warranty at issue. As the tests for affirmation and waiver by election are identical[93] this analysis may be logically correct but is somewhat over complicated. Secondly, it is potentially arguable that the effect of waiver in insurance law is to reinstate the contract of insurance on the same terms save for the terms which been waived.[94] If so, then as all waivers are reinstatements of the policy, there is no logical difficulty created by *The Good Luck* — the policy is discharged and then reinstated by the waiver. The difficulty with this analysis is that it gives the waiver the force of a variation,[95] which may be overstating the position.

We would therefore tentatively reject both alternatives and suggest **19.36**

[91] *The Good Luck* at 263E.
[92] *State Trading Corporation of India Ltd v M Golodetz Ltd* [1989] 2 Lloyd's Rep. 277 at 287 col. 2.
[93] *Allen v Robles* [1969] 2 Lloyd's Rep 61 *per* Fenton-Atkinson L.J. at 63.4. See also *Election, Affirmation and Acquiescence* at para. 7–02 ff.
[94] *Block v Guaranty Co* 290 SW 429 (1926) at 437; see also *Union Life Insurance Co v Brewer* 309 SW 2d 740 (1958) *per* George Rose Smith J. at 745 col. 1. (dissenting from the conclusions reached by the remainder of the court).
[95] See analysis of Implied Discharge, *Variation* at para. 2.30 ff.

that *The Good Luck* does not affect the law relating to waiver. It follows that, provided that the requirements for a waiver by election are met, a breach of warranty is capable of being waived.

The circumstances in which a breach of warranty will be waived

As set out above, whether there is a breach of warranty will depend on the terms of the warranty allegedly breached. Similarly, the terms of the warranty may affect whether or not there is a waiver of a particular breach. Thus, in *Mint Security Ltd v Blair*[96] there was a breach of the warranty that the facts stated in the proposal form were true, the warranty being a condition precedent to the insured's recovery under the policy. The insurer, with the appropriate knowledge, repudiated the insured's claim but not the policy. Mr Justice Staughton, as he then was, decided that the insurer had not waived its rights to repudiate the claim. His conclusion appeared to be based on a threefold categorization of the insurer's actions in relation to breach. First, the insured can simply affirm the policy by relying on all its terms, by, for example, giving 30 days' notice of cancellation of cover under the policy.[97] Secondly, where the warranty was a condition precedent to any liability under the policy, any action by the insurer under the terms of the policy with the appropriate knowledge would be a waiver.[98] Thirdly, where the warranty is a condition precedent to the insured's recovery under the policy in that instance, the insurer's actions on the policy will not waive its rights to repudiate liability.[99] This last category applied and therefore the insurer was not precluded from repudiating. Whilst this analysis may offer an insurer some comfort, we would suggest that it will only apply in cases where the policy wording is the same as that in *Blair* and that no general principle, other than that care should be taken to examine the wording of the policy, can be extracted from the case. **19.37**

---

[96] [1982] 1 Lloyd's Rep. 188.

[97] *ibid.* at 198 col. 1.

[98] [1982] 1 Lloyd's Rep. 188 at 198 col. 2–199 col. 1; *West v National Motor and Accident Insurance Union Ltd* [1954] 1 Lloyd's Rep. 461; [1955] 1 All ER 800, CA where insurer purported to repudiate the claim but not the policy on the basis of a material non-disclosure. The Court of Appeal held that the insurer could not do so — it had a stark choice either to repudiate the policy *in toto* or pay the claim (per Lord Goddard C.J. at 463).

[99] [1982] 1 Lloyd's Rep. 188 at 198 col. 2 – 199 col. 1.

Unequivocal representation by the insurer

In English law, the insurer must make an unequivocal representation that it considers the policy to be valid. Depending on the alleged breach,[1] the types of unequivocal acts which will suffice to give rise to a waiver can be divided as follows: those relating to the premium; those relating to the issue of the policy; those relating to the investigation of claims; and those relating to the conduct of litigation by the insurer. **19.38**

Premium

Assessing the premium payable,[2] accepting the premium,[3] failing to give notice of late payment of the premium,[4] issuing a receipt stating that the premium has been received,[5] declining an offer of payment in the expectation of being paid by another[6] and demanding payment of premium from the insured and payment being tendered by the insured,[7] will all be sufficiently unequivocal to found a waiver.[8] However, the fact that the insurer has accepted late payment in the past will not be sufficiently unequivocal to waive the insured's future obligations to make prompt payment of the premium, especially if the insurer has given notice to the insured that it will in future require prompt payment.[9] Further, **19.39**

[1] And in the case of warranties, assuming that the wording in *Mint Security v Blair* has not been adopted.

[2] *Beatty v Mutual Reserve Fund Life Association* (1896) 75 F 65 *per* Hawley D.J. at 72; see also *Phoenix Mutual Life Insurance Co v Raddin* 120 US 183 at 196.

[3] *Wing v Harvey* (1845) 5 De G & M 265, 43 ER 872; *Hemmings v Sceptre Life Ass Ltd* [1905] 1 Ch 365 *per* Kekewich J. at 369–70; *Armstrong v Turquand* (1858) 9 Ir CL Rep. 32 and *General Accident v Campbell* (1925) 25 Ll L Rep. 151 at 158. Similarly, acceptance of a cheque payment will amount to a waiver of the right to be paid in cash – see *e.g. Bell Bros v Hudson Bay Ins Co Ltd* (1911) 44 SCR 419.

[4] *Simpson v Accidental Death Co* (1857) 2 CB (NS) 257 at 292.3.

[5] See *e.g. Farquharson v Pearl Assurance Co Ltd* [1937] 3 All ER 124 *per* Singleton J at 132.

[6] See *Tennant v Travellers Insurance Co* (1887) 31 F 322.

[7] This waiver could be either of the failure to pay the premium or of the right to avoid for a material non-disclosure. Note, however, there will be no waiver if premium is accepted *after* formal notice of cancellation see *Back v National Ins. Co of NZ Ltd* (1996) 9 ANZ Insurance Cases 76, 560.

[8] *Edge v Duke* (1848) 18 LJ Ch 183; *Neal v Gray* 52 SE 622 and *London & Lancs Life Ass v Fleming* [1897] AC 499.

[9] See *Laing v Commercial Union Assurance Co Ltd* (1922) Ll Rep. 54; *Tankexpress A/S v Cie Financière Belge des Pétroles SA* [1949] AC 76 at 98. See also *Redmond v Canadian Mutual Aid Association* (1891) 18 OAR 335 *per* Burton J.A. at 340. However, in certain US States, acceptance of late payment in one year will constitute a waiver of the insurer's right to avoid for late payment in future years — see *Saunders v Lloyd's of London* 779 P 2d 249 (Wash 1989) *per* Utter J. at 254 col. 1. See also Clarke at paras 11.40, 13.11A (a)–(f).

receipt of the premium relating to a past period of cover may not constitute a waiver. So where the policy contains a clause which accelerates the payment of all premium on default/maturity, on default, all the premium under the policy becomes due and owing and relates to past cover. Acceptance of that premium may not constitute waiver.[10]

Issue of the policy

Whether or not issue of the policy will constitute a waiver of any breach is unclear. If the issue of the policy was a purely ministerial act, then it is possible that there would be no waiver. Thus in *Morrison v The Universal Marine Insurance Co*,[11] the insurer between the scratch and issue of the policy had discovered that the insured had failed to disclose material facts. The insurer then issued the policy. The judge allowed the question of whether the issue of the policy constituted a waiver by election to go to the jury. However, the judge stated that he attached no weight to the stamping and issue of policy, that is that it did not in his view constitute an unequivocal act. On appeal, the argument that the judge, in saying that he attached no weight to the stamping and issue of the policy, was guilty of a misdirection failed.[12] **19.40**

However, we would suggest that *Morrison* is an unusual case which revolves, in part, around the function of the jury. It is submitted that the issue or reissue of the policy will in many circumstances be an unequivocal act sufficient to found a waiver.[13] That will certainly be the case if the issue of the policy also coincides with the tender and acceptance of premium.[14] Further, the issue of a policy by deed may be representation as to a certain state of facts which the insurer will not be allowed to controvert. Thus, if the policy is by deed and recites that the premium has been paid, the insurer will be prevented either by waiver or estoppel by deed from avoiding on the basis of non-payment of premium.[15] **19.41**

---

[10] *Duncan v Missouri State Life Insurance Co* (1908) 160 F 646 *per* Hook C.J. at 648.

[11] (1872) LR 8 Ex 197.

[12] *ibid. per* Honyman J. at 205.

[13] *The Sulphite Pulp Company Limited v Faber & Another* (1895) 1 Comm Cas 143 *per* Lord Russell C.J. at 153–4 and *Svenska Handelsbanken v Sun Alliance and London Assurance plc* [1996] 1 Lloyd's Rep. 519 *per* Rix J. at 569 col. 1.

[14] *Hadenfayre v British National Insurance Society Limited* [1984] 2 Lloyd's Rep. 393 *per* Lloyd J. at 400 col. 2.

[15] *Roberts v Security Company Ltd* [1897] 1 QB 111 *per* Lord Esher M.R. at 114–5 and *per* Lopes L.J. at 115, 116.

19.42 The prudent insurer will therefore, on discovery of a material non-disclosure, put a halt to any further action on the slip or policy unless it wishes to waive the non-disclosure. Further, if, for example, the insurer wishes to ensure that cover will not commence until the premium is paid, as well as inserting the standard term that cover will not incept until the premium is paid,[16] the insurer should not issue any policy by deed nor contain in its policy wording any recital that the premium has been paid.[17] Finally, the prudent insurer must take care that there are no terms in the issued policy which it knows the insured cannot comply with. If it does issue the policy with that knowledge it may be taken to have waived compliance with those terms.[18]

19.43 In the American market the insurer must exercise additional caution for two reasons. First, given the courts' policy in relation to forfeitures,[19] the issue of the policy may in itself constitute a waiver.[20] Secondly, in New York, any insurer seeking to rescind the policy must serve a notice of rescission as soon as possible after discovery of the breach. If it does not, the insurer will be unable to avoid the policy. Therefore, issue of the policy may be symptomatic of delays which will deprive the insurer of its right to avoid.[21]

19.44 It follows that in those cases where the insurer has issued the policy, the insurer's only defence to an allegation of waiver will be to suggest that the issue of the policy was a ministerial or formal act which either could not constitute any form of representation[22] or was carried out without the necessary knowledge.[23]

---

16 *Western Assurance Company v Provincial Insurance Company* (1880) 5 OAR 190 *per* Burton J.A. at 192–3.

17 One effect of such clauses should prevent the issue of the policy from constituting any form of unequivocal representation sufficient to found any type of waiver or estoppel — see discussion in Clarke at para. 13.11A.

18 *Forsikringsaktieselskapet Vesta v Butcher (No. 1)* [1989] 1 All ER 402 *per* Lord Lowry at 413.

19 See *Union Life Insurance Co v Brewer* 309 SW 2d 740 (1958) and para. 19.04 above.

20 *Phoenix v Flemming* 67 Am SR 900 (1898).

21 See *Sumitomo Marine & Fire Insurance Co Ltd v Cologne Reinsurance Co of America* 552 NYS 2d 891 (Ct. App 1990) and para. 19.54ff. below.

22 This appears to be the basis of the judge's direction in Morrison. See also *Sumitomo Marine & Fire Insurance Co Ltd v Cologne Reinsurance Co of America* 552 NYS 2d 891 (Ct. App 1990) *per* Kaye J. at 896.

23 See para. 19.54 below and *Waiver — Types and Elements* at para. 4.18 ff. and Clarke at para. 26.4D.

Investigation

An investigation of the claim may constitute a waiver of the breach of any requirement in the policy that the insured notify the insurer of any claims or potential claims as soon as possible. That will be so where the insurer appears to represent that it has decided that nothing more will be required of the insured to prove its claim. Put another way, there will be a waiver if the insurer's actions unequivocally suggest that it has assumed liability to the insured.[24] The rule appears to be that the more extensive the investigation is by the insurer, the more likely it is that the insurer has waived its rights. Thus, carrying out a post-mortem of the insured[25] and extensively investigating the claim[26] will operate as a waiver of any notification requirements in the policy. However, in general terms merely requesting the insured to fill out a claim form will not constitute any form of waiver.[27] Further, if the insurer is required to carry out detailed investigations, for example, into fraudulent conduct, a more protracted period of investigation will be permitted before the insurer will be held to have waived its rights.[28] **19.45**

The conduct of litigation

The conduct of litigation may be relevant to waiver in two ways. First, the insurer may rely on a term in the policy giving it the right to assume control of any litigation arising in relation to an insured peril or risk. Secondly, the insurer and insured may enter into litigation as to whether a claim will be met by the insurer. In either event, the insurer may make unequivocal representations as to its view of the policy and/or the insured's compliance with its obligations. **19.46**

---

24 *Alexander v Standard Accident Insurance Co Detroit Michigan* 122 F 2d 995 (1941) *per* Huxman J. at 997 col. 1, 998 col. 1; *Boyer v American Casualty Company* 332 F 2d 708 (1964); see also *Globe Savings Co v Employers' Liability Assurance Co* (1900) 13 Man R 531.

25 *Donnison v Employer's Accident and Life Stock Insurance* (1897) 24 R 681.

26 *King v Commercial Union Insurance Company of New York* 306 F Supp 9 (1969) *per* Woodward D.J. at 11. See *Sproul v National Fire Insurance Co* [1925] 1 DLR 1152 *per* Harris C.J. at 1155–8.

27 *James v Royal Insurance Co* (1907) 10 NZ Gaz LR 244; *Canada Landed Credit v Canada Agricultural* (1870) 17 Grant 418 and *Kiamie v Equitable Life Insurance Co* 44 NYS 2d 510 (1943).

28 See by analogy *Southland Corporation v Mir* 748 F Supp 969 (1990) — a two month investigation by the franchisor into a credit card fraud on the part of the franchisee was not a waiver of the franchisor's right to terminate the franchise.

Assuming control of litigation

In *Soole v Royal Insurance Co Ltd*,[29] the insurer defended a claim made against the insured, relying on a term of the policy which provided: 19.47

> in the event of any claim being made against the Insured which is covered by this Policy the Company shall be entitled at its own expense and in the name of the Insured to take or defend legal proceedings . . .

In a subsequent coverage dispute the insured contended that if the insurer undertakes the defence of an action on behalf of the insured, the insurer waives its rights against that insured to avoid the policy.[30] Mr Justice Shaw held that the insured's contention was too widely drawn.[31] He held that if the claim against the insured was defeated there never was a claim under the policy and that the policy wording must be construed in light of that fact. Therefore, the policy wording covered both claims made against the insured and which were covered by the policy and claims made against the insured which *might be* covered by the policy. It followed that in defending the litigation against the insured, the insurer was representing that there might be a claim under the policy which it might meet. There was no unequivocal representation that the insurer regarded:

> the claim which [was] . . . the subject matter of the proceedings as one which *must* give rise to a liability to indemnify the insured

only a representation that the claim

> may give rise to such liability

It followed that there was no unequivocal representation and no waiver.[32]

The other potential mechanism by which an insurer might waive its rights is if during its conduct of litigation on behalf of the insured it becomes aware of facts which would entitle it to avoid the policy or would discharge it from liability. It is relatively clear that the insurer will have a reasonable time upon discovery to decide whether or not it should cease to defend on the insured's behalf.[33] It is also relatively strongly arguable that the insurer is entitled to continue the litigation to 19.48

---

[29] [1971] 2 Lloyd's Rep. 332.
[30] A contention drawn from the then current edition of MacGillivray.
[31] [1971] 2 Lloyd's Rep. 332 at 339 col. 2.
[32] *Ibid.* at 339 col. 2–340 col. 1.
[33] *McCormick and another v National Motor and Accident Union Ltd* (1934) 49 Ll L Rep. 361 *per* Scrutton L.J. at 365 col. 2.

a conclusion so as to ascertain whether there is a claim under the policy.[34] That would accord with the logic of *Soole* and would make practical and commercial sense; there would be little point in souring relations with the insured if the dispute as to whether a claim could be made against the insurer by the insured was academic.

It is therefore submitted that in English law, an insurer may protect itself from waiving its rights in defending litigation on behalf of the insured by the appropriate policy wording. However, even with the benefit of the appropriate policy wording, the insurer must act with caution if it decides to conduct litigation on the insured's behalf particularly if facts come to light which suggest that there is or may be a coverage dispute. It follows that the insurer should be astute to reserve its position either at the outset or as soon as potentially damaging facts come to light. **19.49**

The above is to be contrasted with the position under US law. In most states, an insurer who conducts litigation on behalf of the insured with the appropriate knowledge of breach will be taken to have waived its rights[35] unless in fact the insurer acting on behalf of the insured is not in the insured's best interests.[36] In the states which operate that principle, the insurer will not be able to prevent there being a waiver by reserving its rights.[37] **19.50**

Litigation against the insured

In English law, the insurer that resists the claim by the insured under the policy on a particular ground will not generally waive its rights to resist the insured's claim on other grounds. Therefore, if an insurer objects to the claim on the basis of fraud but fails on that allegation at trial, it will be permitted to resist the insured's claim on the basis of breach of condition.[38] Similarly, an insurer that generally reserves its rights cannot be said to have waived its rights to resist the claim on a particular ground.[39] In America and Canada, the insurer must act with **19.51**

---

[34] *ibid. per* Greer L.J. at 369 col. 1.

[35] *Beatty v Employers' Liability Assurance Corp* 168 A 919 (1933); *Insurance Company of North America v Atlantic National Insurance Co* 329 F 2d 769 (1964) at 775 col. 2–776 col. 1 and cases there cited *per* Boreman C.J. and *Commercial Union Insurance Co v International Flavors & Fragrances Inc* 633 F Supp 646 (SDNY, 1986) *per* Milton Pollack S.D.J. at 650 col. 21–1651 col. 2.

[36] *Matia v Carpet Transport Inc* 888 F 2d 118 (11th Cir, 1989).

[37] Contrast the position in Louisiana where an insurer becomes a party to litigation — there will be no waiver even if there is a considerable delay before it does so *FDIC v Duffy* 47 F 3d 146 (1995); as to reservation of rights see *Turner Liquidating Co v St Paul Surplus Lines Insurance Co* 638 NE 2d 174 (1994).

[38] *Welch v Royal Exchange Assurance* [1939] 1 KB 294 *per* Slesser L.J. at 305–6.

[39] *McCormick v The Royal* 163 Pa 184 (1894); *Cleaver v Trader's Insurance* 40 F 711 (1989) and *Lugo v AIG Life Insurance Co* 852 F Supp 187 (1994).

more caution, since resisting the claim on one ground may constitute a waiver of other grounds.[40]

19.52 However, the above position will change if the insurer takes a positive step in the action which indicates that it will only rely on one ground. Thus, where there has been a breach of procedural conditions, for instance the claim being brought too soon, and the insurer makes an unconditional payment in without allocation between those elements of the claim which had been brought at the correct time and those which had not, the insurer was taken to have waived its rights to rely on the procedural conditions.[41] Similarly, if the insurer enters into without prejudice agreements with the insured that define the matters in dispute, the insurer may be taken to have waived its rights to rely on matters not contained in the without prejudice agreements.[42] Finally, if the insurer enters into settlement negotiations that are not without prejudice to its rights, then there will be a waiver of its rights.[43]

Silence or delay

19.53 As pointed out elsewhere,[44] silence will not constitute an unequivocal representation such as to found a waiver. However, the courts have held that silence accompanied by a delay which prejudices the insured, may found a 'waiver.[45] Given the basic principles set out above, it is submitted that the reference to the insured suffering 'prejudice' as a result of the inaction suggests that the better analytical[46] view is that the delay triggers an equitable forbearance precluding the insurer[47] from denying

40 *Appell v Liberty Mutual Insurance Co* 255 NYS 2d 545; *Pensky v Aetna Life & Cas Co* 375 NYS 2d 780; *Consolidated Electrical Cooperative v Employers Mutual Liability Insurance Co* 106 F Supp 322 (1952) *per* Hulen D.J. at 331 col. 1, 332 col. 1 and *Fowlie v Ocean Accident and Guarantee Corporation Limited* (1902) 4 OAR 146.

41 *Harrison v Douglas* (1835) 3 Ad & E 394, 111 ER 463 *per* Lord Denman C.J. at 403, 466–7.

42 *Vitol SA v Esso Australia Ltd ('The Wise')* [1989] 2 Lloyd's Rep. 451 *per* Mustill L.J. at 460 col. 2.

43 *Lee v Casualty Corporation of America* 90 Conn 202 (1916) and *United States Fidelity & Guarantee Co v Bimco Iron & Metal Corp* 464 SW 2d 353 (1971).

44 See *Waiver — Types and Elements* at para. 4.24.

45 *Allen v Robles* [1969] 1 WLR 1193 *per* Fenton-Atkinson L.J. at 1196G–H.

46 The practical result will, in all probability, be identical.

47 An estoppel by representation could be generated if the insurer was under a duty to inform the insured that it was avoiding cover. In most circumstances, it is unlikely that such a duty would be imposed.

liability or, possibly, the insurer may be taken to have affirmed the policy.[48] It appears that the courts will be willing to find evidence that the insured was prejudiced by the delay on very slight grounds.[49]

Appropriate knowledge

For any of the unequivocal acts considered above to constitute a waiver, the insurer must have the appropriate level of knowledge.[50] The requirement of knowledge is separate and distinct from the need for an unequivocal representation and as a matter of analysis even the most unequivocal representation will not allow the court to find that there was a waiver by the insurer absent the requisite knowledge.[51] Establishing that the insurer had the requisite knowledge at the time of the unequivocal act will be one of the more difficult evidential hurdles for the insured to overcome.[52] However, the more unequivocal the representation is, the more likely it is that the insurer will be precluded from asserting its rights by estoppel/equitable forbearance, there being no need to establish knowledge to found an estoppel/equitable forbearance.[53] Two issues arise: what type of knowledge is required and who must possess that knowledge. **19.54**

---

48 See *Svenska Handelsbanken v Sun Alliance and London Assurance plc* [1996] 1 Lloyd's Rep. 519 *per* Rix J. at 569 cols 1–2. Contra. 19–06, fn. 19 above.

49 See *Svenska Handelsbanken v Sun Alliance and London Assurance plc* [1996] 1 Lloyd's Rep. 519 *per* Rix J. at 569 col. 2 — where the possibility that the insured would have conducted its affairs differently coupled with the fact that the insured's options were decreasing all the time sufficed.

50 However, in US law the requirement in some states that the insurer notify the insured of its grounds of avoidance as soon as possible, may circumvent the requirement of knowledge — see *In re Balfour Maclaine International Ltd* 873 F Supp (1995). Where state law does not incorporate such a requirement, knowledge is required — see *Norrington v Wright* 115 US 188 (1885).

51 *P Samuel v Dumas* [1924] AC 431 *per* Lord Sumner at 483; but see *the Insurance Corporation of the Channel Islands v Royal Hotel Ltd* (Mance J Comm Ct unrep. 30 July 1997). As a matter of merit, it may be very difficult for an insured to persuade a court that an insurer is estopped where the insurer had no knowledge whatsoever of the facts giving rise to the alleged estoppel.

52 At least where waiver by election is concerned where the insurer is responding to the insured's act. In pure and unilateral waiver, the insurer will presumably be aware of its own rights.

53 It is therefore respectfully submitted that cases in which the courts have found that there was a 'waiver' but made no finding as to the insurer's knowledge relying instead on the prejudice or detriment suffered by the insured were in fact cases of estoppel — see *Toronto Railway Company & Ors v National British & Irish Millers Co* (1914) 111 LT 555 at 563 per Scrutton L.J.; *Burridge and Son v Haines and Sons* (1918) 118 LT 681 *per* Avory J. at 685.

Type of knowledge required

As per general contractual principles, the insurer will normally have to be aware of the facts and the rights arising from those facts. Put another way, the insurer must be aware that there has been a breach and that, as a result, certain rights have become vested in the insurer.[54] Similarly, the knowledge must be knowledge in the mind of the insurer at the appropriate time. If the insurer has been told of the relevant facts at some time previously, there will be no waiver if the insurer has since forgotten those facts.[55] However, it is important to note that in certain cases, the insurer will be deemed to possess the appropriate knowledge. Thus, the insurer does not have to be actually aware of the insured's breach but will be deemed to have the appropriate knowledge if it has information which if investigated would lead that insurer[56] or the reasonable man[57] to discover the breach. By parity of reasoning, in reinsurance, if the reinsurer is aware that an insured syndicate has carried out investigations and that the syndicate is therefore aware of its rights, that reinsurer will have the knowledge necessary to found a waiver even if it has no actual knowledge of the facts.[58] **19.55**

Whatever the position may be in the United States,[59] there is no requirement in English law[60] that the insurer, in making the unequivocal **19.56**

---

[54] See *The Insurance Corporation of the Channel Islands v Royal Hotel Ltd* (Mance J Comm Ct unrep. 30 July 1997); *National Insurance and Guarantee Corp Plc v Imperio Reinsurance Co (UK) Ltd* (Coleman J Comm Ct unrep. 30 September 1997); *Waiver — Types and Elements* at para. 4.22 but compare Clarke at para. 26.4C.

[55] *Kelly v Solari* (1841) 9 M&W 54; 152 ER 24 at 58; 26 *per* Abinger CB; see, *e.g. Keehn v Excess Insurance Co of America* 129 F2d 503 (1942) *per* Major C.J. at 506 col. 1 and *Deaves v CML Fire and General Insurance Co Ltd* [1979] 53 AJLR 382 *per* Gibbs A.C.J. at 389 col. 1.

[56] *Dalzell v Northwestern Mutual Insurance Company* 32 Cal.Rptr 125 (1963) *per* Schottky J. at 128 col. 1 and *Bailey v Robert V Neuhoff Ltd Partnership* 665 So 2d 16 (1995).

[57] See *The Insurance Corporation of the Channel Islands v Royal Hotel Ltd* (Mance J Comm Ct unrep. 30 July 1997).

[58] *Simner v New India Assurance Co Ltd* [1995] LRLR 240 *per* Judge Diamond Q.C. at 260 col. 1.

[59] *Boyer v American Casualty Company* 332 F 2d 708 (1964) *per* J.J. Smith C.J. at 711; *Richmond v Grabowski* 781 PP 2d 192 (1989); *Shane v WCAU-TV, CBS Televisions, Div of CBS Inc* 719 F Supp 353 (1989) and *Lone Mountain Production Co v Natural Gas Pipeline Co of America* 710 F Supp 305 (1989). However, problems may arise where a waiver is alleged to have taken place as a result of X's conduct — see, e.g. *Community Convalescent Center of Naperville Inc v First Interstate Mortgage Co of Illinois* 537 NE 2d 1162, appeal denied 545 NE 2d 106 (1989) and *Ebrahimi v EF Hutton & Co Inc* 794 P 2d 1015 (1989).

[60] In Australia and New Zealand, the position is confused. There is authority to suggest that intention is required but will be simply spelt out from the insurer's conduct (see

representation, must intend to waive its rights.[61] This position undoubtedly arises from the fact that English civil law rarely relies on a party's subjective intent, preferring instead to extrapolate any intent from the party's actions as viewed by an objective, reasonable third party observer.[62]

Finally, in this context, it is extremely important to note that knowledge is only required to establish a waiver. Therefore in cases of estoppel, the courts will be less concerned in establishing what the insurer knew. Thus, in *In re Economic Fire Office Limited*[63] the court held that provided that the insured acted on what appeared to be legitimate representation by the insurer then the insurer would be precluded from resiling from that representation.[64] In doing so, the court expressly distinguished those cases in which the agent's authority (and therefore its ability to fix the insurer with knowledge) was considered as not being cases of estoppel.[65] **19.57**

Whose knowledge

The knowledge[66] must be that of the insurer.[67] Therefore, where an agent receives knowledge as the agent of the insured, that knowledge will not, without more, be imputed to the insurer.[68] As the insurer will **19.58**

Watson v Healy Lands Ltd [1965] NZLR 511 *per* Woodhouse J. at 514 – ll 33–5) but the better view is that intention is not required *Tropical Traders v Goonan* (1964) 111 CLR 41 *per* Kitto J. at 55; *Sargent v ASL Developments* (1974) 131 CLR 634 *per* Stephen J. at 646 and *Champtaloup v Thomas* [1976] 2 NSWLR 264 *per* Glass J.A. at 268E. See *Waiver — Types and Elements* at para. 4.25.

[61] *Webster v General Accident Fire and Life Assurance Corporation Ltd* [1953] 1 QB 520 *per* Parker J. at 532.

[62] See *Watson v Healy Lands Ltd* [1965] NZLR 511 *per* Woodhouse J. at 514 ll 33–5 and *Waiver — Terminology* at para. 4.23.

[63] (1896) 12 TLR 142.

[64] *ibid. per* Vaughan-Williams J. at 142 col. 2.

[65] *ibid. per* Vaughan Williams J. at 142 col. 2–143 col. 1 expressly distinguishing *Acey v Fernie* (1840) 7 M&W 151; 151 ER 717; see also *Ayrey v British Legal and United Provident Assurance Company Ltd* [1918] 1 KB 136 *per* Atkin L.J. at 142.

[66] Again in cases of estoppel, the mechanism by which the insurer has any relevant knowledge will be less important. See para. 19.57 above.

[67] *Billington v Provincial Insurance* (1877) 2 OAR 1558; *Western Assurance Company v Provincial Insurance Company* (1880) 5 OAR 190 *per* Burton J.A. at 192–3; *Wheeler v Waterton Fire* 131 Mass 1 (1881); *Atlas Assurance Co v Brownell* (1899) 29 SCR 537; *Bible v John Hancock Mutual Life Insurance Co* 176 NE 838 (1931); *Connecticut Fire Insurance Co v Fox* 361 F 2d 1 (1961) and *Jackson v National Flood Insurers Association* 398 F Supp 1383 (1974) at 1388 col. 2.

[68] *Newsholme Bros v Road Transport & General Ins Co Ltd* [1929] 2 KB 356 doubting *Bawden v London Edinburgh & Glasgow Ass Co* [1892] 2 QB 534; *Hough v Guardian Fire & Life Ass Co* (1902) 18 TLR 273 and *Holdsworth v Lancashire and Yorkshire Insurance Company* (1907) 23 TLR 521 on this point.

usually be a corporation, it will only be fixed with knowledge if the information is passed on to the appropriate natural person; one expressly or impliedly authorized by the insurer to waive breaches and therefore possessing sufficient authority to fix the insurer with knowledge. Cases of an insurer giving an agent express authority to waive breaches will be extremely rare.[69] Therefore, the courts are faced with the difficult task of spelling out the appropriate authority from the facts of the case; the difficulty of the task being demonstrated by the confused and contradictory authorities on the point.[70] Thus, although there is authority to suggest that the knowledge possessed by a loss adjustor[71] or by a soliciting agent[72] will also be the insurer's knowledge, there is also authority to suggest that the knowledge of an agent authorised to make the original contract will not be that of the insurer.[73] It follows that this issue cannot be resolved by the application of previous authority but by the loose application of general principles to the facts of each case. The immediate difficulty that arises is that of identifying the operative general principles.[74] We can at best only tentatively identify general guidelines which may be applied to particular cases.

The applicable principles were summarized in *Blackburn Lowe & Co v Vigors:*[75] **19.59**

> Where a person is the agent to know his knowledge does bind the principal .... Some agents so far represent the principal that in all respects their acts and intention and their knowledge may truly be said to be the intentions and knowledge of the principal. Other agents may have so limited and narrow an authority both in fact and in the common understanding of the form of their employment that it would be quite inaccurate to say that such an agent's knowledge or intentions are the knowledge and intentions of his principal . . .[76]

[69] The simple reason being that to do so would unnecessarily restrict the insurer's business operations. The insurer would have to select a particular person at any branch to take over dealings with insureds when any issue of its knowledge arose.

[70] *Mahli v Abbey Life Insurance* [1995] 4 Re LR 305 *per* Balcombe L.J. at 313 (agreeing with Rose L.J. — McCowan L.J. dissenting).

[71] *United States Fidelity and Guaranty Co v Bimco Iron Corp* 464 SW2d 353 (Tex 1971).

[72] *Splents v Lefevre* (1864) 11 LT 114.

[73] *Blair v National Reserve Insurance Co* 199 NE 337 (1936).

[74] See *Agency* at paras. 14.04 and 14.08. As to specific difficulties in the insurance context see Bowstead at para. 8–213(11), p. 538, n. 6.

[75] (1887) 12 App Cas 531.

[76] *ibid. per* Lord Halsbury L.C. at 537.

Two points flow from *Blackburn*. First, the general law of agency will apply in deciding whether or not the insurer is fixed with knowledge.[77] Therefore, the issue is whether the insurer is fixed with knowledge. Once the appropriate person has fixed the insurer with knowledge, a subsequent breakdown in communication will not prevent the insurer from being held to have waived its rights.[78] Secondly, the court will examine the actual and intended relationship between the insurer and agent to ascertain whether the agent *is* the insurer when making the unequivocal representation. Any consideration of the actual and intended relationship between insurer and agent will centre on the tasks which the agent is authorized to perform and its role in the insured's organisation.

Considering the acts which the agent is authorized to perform

In considering the tasks which the agent is authorized to perform, the fewer tasks that the agent can perform, the less likely it is that the insurer will be fixed with the agent's knowledge. Put another way, the greater general authority that the agent has, the more likely it is that the authority to waive breaches will be ancillary to or a corollary of that authority. Therefore, if the agent did not have authority '*to grant or contract to grant, policies*'[79] or if the agent was authorized to accept premiums on extremely limited terms,[80] the insurer will not be fixed with the agent's knowledge. By way of contrast, where the agent is the district manager and is entitled to accept premiums, enter into contracts[81] and run the branch, the insurer may well be fixed with the agent's knowledge.[82] **19.60**

The agent's role and status in the insurer's organization

In a direct analogy with company law,[83] the court will also consider how important the agent was. Thus, if important information is passed **19.61**

[77] See *Meridian Global Funds Management Asia Ltd v Securities Commission* [1995] 3 WLR 413 *per* Lord Hoffman at 418F–G.

[78] *Holdsworth v Lancashire and Yorkshire Insurance Company* (1907) 23 TLR 521.

[79] *Linford v The Provincial Horse and Cattle Insurance Company* (1864) 34 Beav 291, 55 ER 647 per Lord Romilly M.R. at 293, 648.

[80] *Acey v Fernie* (1840) 7 M&W 151, 151 ER 717 *per* Abinger C.B. and *per* Parke B. at 155, 719.

[81] See contra. *Ayrey v British Legal and United Provident Assurance Company Ltd* [1918] 1 KB 136 *per* Lawrence L.J. at 140.

[82] *Wing v Harvey* (1845) 5 De G & M 265, 43 ER 872; *per* Lord Justice Knight Bruce at 270, 874 and *per* Lord Justice Turner at 271, 875.

[83] Where, for example, an executive director's authority will be much wider than that of an employee.

on to the insurer's clerks[84] or to someone who is unable to '*appreciate its significance*'[85] then the insurer will not be fixed with that person's knowledge. However, if the information is passed to: an agent delegated to investigate the risk[86] or claim;[87] an agent who, as part and parcel of the normal working practice of the insurer, would, or it was reasonable to presume would, pass the information onto the relevant person;[88] the sole representative of the insurer in a particular area;[89] then the insurer will be fixed with that person's knowledge.

On either approach, it is important to note that the insurer will not be fixed with its agent's knowledge in two circumstances. First, any collusion between the agent and insured, or knowledge on the part of the insured that the agent does not have authority to waive the insurer's rights, will prevent there being a waiver.[90] Secondly, the insurer will not be fixed with knowledge of the agent's own dishonesty[91] nor will the insurer be fixed with any knowledge of the agent relevant to the commission of a fraud against the insurer by that agent.[92] **19.62**

---

84 *Houghton & Co v Nothard Lowe & Wills* [1928] AC 1 *per* Lord Sumner at 18: '*The mind . . . of a company is not reached or affected by information merely possessed by its clerks*'; *Fitchpatrick v Hawkeye Insurance Co* 53 Iowa 335 (1880).

85 *Mahli v Abbey Life Insurance* [1995] 4 Re LR 305 *per* Rose L.J. at 309.

86 *Whitney v Great Northern Insurance Co* [1917] 32 DLR 756 and *Beasant v Northern Life Insurance Co* [1923] 2 DLR 1086 *per* Cameron J.A. at 1088–9.

87 *Evans v Employers Mutual Insurance Association Ltd* [1936] 1 KB 505 *per* Greer L.J. at 515 and *Mahli v Abbey Life Insurance* [1995] 4 Re LR 305 *per* Rose L.J. at 310. Notwithstanding suggestions to the contrary (see Bowstead at para. 8.210, n. 86, p. 535), we would suggest that *Mahli* did not distinguish *Evans* and each remains good law on its facts.

88 *Hadenfayre v British National Insurance Society Limited* [1984] 2 Lloyd's Rep. 393 *per* Lloyd J. at 401 col. 1.

89 *Farquharson v Pearl Assurance Co Ltd* [1937] 3 All ER 124 *per* Singleton J. at 132G-H — a district manager can waive payment of premium by the insured. However, on its facts, it appears that the court held that the insurer was estopped from claiming payment of the premium.

90 *O'Brien v Prescott Insurance Co* 134 NYS 28 (1892); *Levy v Scottish Employers Insurance* (1901) 17 TLR 229 and *John Hancock Mutual Life Insurance Co v Luzio* 176 NE 446 (1931) — such knowledge of the part of the insured would prevent the agent from possessing ostensible authority. It follows that the insured's knowledge of the agent's vires would be irrelevant where the agent has actual authority.

91 See *PCW Syndicates v PCW Reinsurers* [1996] 1 Lloyd's Rep. 241 *per* Staughton L.J. at 254 col. 1–247 col. 2.

92 See *Belmont Finance Corporation Ltd v Williams Furniture Ltd* [1979] Ch 250 *per* Buckley L.J. at 261H–2A.

PARTICULAR DIFFICULTIES WHICH ARISE FROM THE APPLICATION OF WAIVER TO INSURANCE LAW

19.63 There are two particular difficulties which arise from the application of waiver to insurance law: can cover under the policy ever be extended by the operation of a waiver and can an insurer protect its position by entering into a 'non-waiver' agreement with the insured.

Waiver and extension of cover

19.64 Explicit in our definition of waiver is that waiver is not a modification of the terms of the contract.[93] It follows that whilst waiver can prevent a party from relying on the terms of a bargain, it cannot alter the bargain. In most cases, that distinction will have little practical effect. However, in insurance law, the position would appear to be more complex.

19.65 The complexity arises from the relationship between the warranties, exclusions and conditions, to the policy and waiver. Applying basic principles, the effect of a contractual exclusion is that the parties agree that the insurer will never be liable in respect of a particular category of risk. By contrast, the effect of a condition or warranty is that the insurer agrees to be liable if certain preconditions are met. It follows that an insurer can agree to waive a condition or a warranty — the insurer is agreeing to excuse performance of a condition of liability. However, an insurer cannot waive an exclusion to the policy as the insurer would thereby be extending cover and altering the scope of the parties' bargain.[94] Put another way, the insurer would be extending cover when it had not received a premium in respect of that extended cover.[95] It follows that in analysing whether a particular term can be waived, the court must decide whether the term is, on its proper construction, an exclusion to liability under the policy.[96] If the term is an exclusion clause, then the term cannot be waived.

---

93 See *Waiver — Terminology* at para. 3.08 and the contrast with variation.

94 *Proper v Oswego County Fire Relief Association* 190 NY 12 (1907) and *Harrison v Liberty Mutual Insurance Co* 290 F 2d 900 (1961) at 903–4.

95 *Zappone v Home Insurance Co* Ct App 447 NYS2d 911 *per* Meyer J. at 914 col. 1.

96 *Conner v Union Automobile Insurance Co* 9 P 2d 863 (1932) at 865 and *Insurance Company of North America v Atlantic National Insurance Co* 329 F 2d 769 (1964) *per* Boreman C.J. at 775 cols. 1–2.

19.66 Two objections may be made to the above. First, there is no real difference between a warranty /condition to the policy and an exclusion clause. Secondly, there is authority to suggest that cover under the policy can be extended by a waiver.

No distinction between warranties and exclusions

19.67 The argument is based on two premises. First, an assertion that in reality there is no difference between a warranty and an exclusion — both clauses have the effect that the insurer will not be liable if X is the case and both clauses serve to 'define' the risk.[97] Whilst we would accept that if the insurer relies on an exclusion or a warranty, the same end result is achieved — the insurer is not liable; we would suggest that there is a difference between the two. A warranty renders performance under the policy conditional; an exclusion is an absolute rejection of liability for that particular type of risk. Secondly, a suggestion that Lord Goff in *The Good Luck*[98] recognized that warranties only defined the risk when he stated that:

> The rationale of warranties in insurance law is that the insurer only accepts the risk provided that the warranty is fulfilled.[99]

The result would be that both exclusion clauses and warranties were definitional, they state the circumstances in which the insurer will not be liable. However, we would suggest that this premise does not support the argument contended for. Assuming that both warranties and exclusions are definitional, they are definitional in different ways. As set out above, an exclusion clause lays down the parameters of cover, a warranty sets out the preconditions to liability or cover. Put simply, by an exclusion, an insurer states that it will not be liable for X; by a warranty, the insurer states that it will be liable provided that X does not occur. It follows that this argument fails.

Authority for the proposition

19.68 In the United States, there are numerous authorities which appear to suggest that cover under the policy can be extended by waiver and therefore that exclusion clauses can be waived. However, on close

97 See Clarke at para. 19.1B2.
98 [1992] 1 AC 233.
99 *ibid.* at 263B.

reading, we would suggest that authorities either relate to statutory exceptions to that principle or fall within the general principle outlined above.

Statutory exceptions

The statutory exceptions take two forms. First, several states[1] require an insurer to raise all its defences to a claim on the policy 'as soon as possible'. If the insurer does not, then the insurer will be precluded from relying on any defences not so raised.[2] Thus, if the insurer wishes to argue that the policy does not cover the claim, it must do so as soon as possible, if it is not to lose that right. The effect of the statutory rule could be described as a waiver. However, the authorities themselves regard the principle as one of 'estoppel'[3] and suggest that the effect of that rule is only to deprive the insurer of a defence, there is no actual extension of cover.[4] Secondly, other states[5] provide that an insurer's defence of an action on behalf of the insured will operate to extend cover. However, the rationale behind that extension is not that the cover is extended by a process of waiver but that the statutory rules have modified the contract of insurance so as to extend cover.[6] **19.69**

Application of the general principle

The remaining cases where the insurer's unequivocal act has apparently extended cover fall into two main categories. First, where the courts have drawn a fine distinction between a waiver that might extend cover **19.70**

1 For example, New York and Missouri.

2 *Consolidated Electrical Cooperative v Employers Mutual Liability Insurance Co* 106 F Supp 322 (1952) *per* Hulen D.J. (Missouri) at 331 col. 1.

3 *Salerno v Western Casualty & Surety Co* 336 F 2d 14 (1964) *per* Ridge C.J. at 17 col. 2; *Boston Old Colony Insurance v Lumbermans Mutual Casualty Company* 889 F 2d 1245 (2nd Cir, 1989) *per* Feinberg J. at 1247 col. 2; *Bucon Inc v Pennsylvania Manufacturing Association Insurance Company* 547 NYS 2d 925 (AD 3 Dept, 1989) *per* Levine J. at 927 cols. 1–2; *Lumbermans Mutual Casualty Insurance Co v Aggesen* 618 NYS 2d 441 (1994); *Presbyterian Hospital of New York v Empire Insurance Co* 633 NYS 2d 339 (1995) and *Dependible Janitorial Services Inc v Transcontinental Insurance Co* 622 NYS 632 (1995).

4 *Calocerinos & Spina Consulting Engineers PC v Prudential Reinsurance Co* 856 F Supp 775 (1994); *Lumbermans Mutual Casualty Co v Peaceful* 638 So 2d 1026 (1994); *Emscor Manufacturing Inc v Alliance Insurance Group* 879 SW 2d 894 (1994) and *Steptore v Masco Construction Co Inc* 643 So 2d 1213 (1994).

5 For example, Wisconsin.

6 *Insurance Company of North America v Atlantic National Insurance Co* 329 F 2d 769 (1964) *per* Boreman C.J. at 775 col. 2. – 779 col. 1 and cases there cited; see also *Challoner v Pennings* 94 NW 2d 654 (1959); *Henthorn v MGC Corp* 83 NW 2d 759 (1957) and *Behringer v State Farm Mutual Insurance Co* 82 NW 2d 915 (1957).

and, for example, one precluding the insurer from asserting that cover under the policy had been suspended and have rejected the former.[7] As with warranties, terms which suspend cover do not extend the parties' bargain to take in perils or risks which were never contracted for. As the label suggests, such terms merely suspend cover until certain conditions are met. Therefore, a suspension of cover can be waived without violating the general principle set out above. Secondly, there are cases where the courts have extended cover but have made it clear that they are applying the doctrine of estoppel not waiver.[8] It is submitted that there is little difficulty in suggesting that cover can be extended by means of an estoppel which is not, unlike waiver, purely a contractual doctrine and which operates in a far broader range of circumstances.[9]

A 'non-waiver' agreement

In the United States, it is relatively common practice for an insurer to seek a 'non-waiver' agreement from the insured. The courts will uphold such agreements and their effect, subject to certain caveats, will be to preserve the status quo between the parties and all conditions precedent to liability in the contract of insurance.[10] Further, after entry into a **19.71**

[7] See, *e.g. Reliance Insurance Co v The Escapade* 280 F 2d 482 (1960); *Albert J Schiff Associates Inc v Flack* Ct App 435 NYS 2d 972 *per* Fuchsberg J. at 975 col. 1; *Kaminer v Franklin Life Insurance Co* 472 F 2d 1073 (1973) *per* Rives C.J. at 1077 col. 1.; *Matia v Carpet Transport Inc* 888 F2d 118 (11th Cir, 1989) at 121 col. 1; *Aetna Casualty and Surety Co v Richmond* App, 143 Cal Rptr 75 *per* Hanson A.J. at 79 col. 2–80 col. 1; *Rhinebeck Bicycle Shop v Sterling Insurance* 546 NYS 2d 499 (AD 3 Dept 1989) *per* Levine J. at 501 col. 2 and *Budget Rent-A-Car Systems Inc v Shelby Insurance Group* 541 NW 2d 178 (1995).

[8] *Draper v Oswego County Fire Relief Association* 82 NE 755 (1907) *per* Cullen C.J. at 756 col. 2: '*The rule prevailing in this state, that an insurance company will not be permitted to defeat recovery on a policy issued by it by proving the existence of facts which render it void where it had full knowledge of the facts when the policy was issued . . . . rests rather on the doctrine of estoppel than on that of waiver*'; see also *Robbins v Springfield Fire & Marine Insurance Co* 44 NE 159 (1896) *per* Martin J. at 161 col. 1.

[9] Thus, if insurer misrepresents the scope of cover, then an estoppel will operate to expand cover to comply with representation if the elements required for an estoppel are made out — *Standard Fire Insurance Company v Marine Contracting and Towing Company* 392 SE2d 460 (SC 1990) *per* Finney J. at 462 col. 1 and *Anderson v Minnesota Insurance Guaranty Association* 520 NW 2d 155 (1994). An estoppel will operate (at least in New Hampshire) despite clear policy wording to contrary — see *Trefethen v New Hampshire Insurance Group* 645 A 2d 72 (1994); but see contra. *Bailey v Robert V Neuhoff Ltd Partnership* 665 So 2d 16 (1995); *Black v Aetna Insurance Co* 909 SW 2d 1 (1995).

[10] *Connecticut Fire Insurance Co v Fox* 361 F 2d 1 (1966) *per* Hill C.J. at 7 col. 1.

non-waiver agreement, the insured will be unable to rely on any waiver by the insurer[11] provided that the waiver is caught by the terms of the agreement.[12]

It follows that a 'non-waiver' agreement provides a useful tool for regulating the parties' arrangements whilst investigating a claim. However, its use is subject to certain caveats. First, the agreement will be strictly construed against the insurer.[13] Therefore, care must be taken in drafting the clause to ensure that it is clear which of the insurer's acts are caught by it and which are not. Secondly, a non-waiver agreement will, in all probability, be an agreement which operates solely for the benefit of the insurer and therefore can be subject to a unilateral waiver on the part of the insurer.[14] Thirdly, the agreement will only operate up to the moment at which the insurer repudiates liability under the policy. The rationale for such a limitation is that the non-waiver agreement will depend for its existence on the continuation of the policy. If the policy is avoided, there will be nothing to continue. Further, once the insurer has repudiated, there will be no commercial purpose for the continuation of the agreement.[15] Fourthly, the entry into a non-waiver agreement or the request that the insured do enter into a non-waiver agreement will constitute an unequivocal act. Therefore, if the insurer seeks a non-waiver agreement after breach, the insurer will waive its rights to be discharged from liability or avoid the policy as a result of that breach.[16] **19.72**

Some use of non-waiver agreements is made in the English market. This is particularly the case in marine insurance.[17] Subject to three **19.73**

---

11 *Keehn v Excess Insurance Co of America* 129 F2d 503 *per* Major C.J. at 505.

12 In the US, an insured's refusal to enter into a non-waiver agreement will also relieve the insurer of any requirement that it defend actions for and on behalf of the insured — see *Ezell v Hayes Oilfield Construction Co Ltd* 693 F2d 489 (1982) *per* Goldberg C.J. at 494 col. 2. and *Clement v Marathon Oil Company* 724 F Supp 431 (ED La, 1989).

13 *Connecticut Fire Insurance Co v Fox* 361 F 2d 1 (1966) *per* Hill C.J. at 7 col. 1.

14 *Phenix Insurance Co v Grove* 74 NE 141 (1905) and *Knickerbocker Life Insurance Co v Norton* 96 US 234 (1878). See *Waiver — Types and Elements* at para. 4.27 above for an explanation of unilateral waiver.

15 *Federal Insurance Co v Matthews* (1956) 3 DLR (2d) 322 *per* Clyne J. at 340–1 citing *Beattie v US Fidelity & Guaranty Co* [1933] 2 DLR 133 *per* Harvey C.J. at 162–3.

16 *King v Commercial Union Insurance Company of New York* 306 F Supp 9 at 11 (1969) *per* Woodward D.J.

17 For example, a sue and labour clause is frequently accompanied by a non-waiver clause. Non-waiver clauses are also found in Institute Cargo Clauses (A) clause 17; Institute Cargo Clauses (C) clause 17 (both in respect of any waiver of notice of abandonment); Institute War Clauses (Cargo) clause 12; Institute Strikes Clauses clause 12; Institute Time Clauses (Hulls) clause 20 and Institute Voyage Clauses (Hulls) clause 20 (in respect of waiver of claims for freight).

caveats, we can see no reason why insurers should not make wider use of non-waiver agreements. First, an English court will construe the terms of such an agreement against the insurer.[18] Care must be taken therefore to avoid any ambiguity which might attract the *contra proferentem* and deprive the agreement of effect. Secondly, if such clauses became part of the insurer's standard terms, they would attract scrutiny under the Unfair Contract Terms Directive[19] and Regulations.[20] Thirdly, an English court might well feel that the use of such agreements in the non-commercial context would unnecessarily tilt the balance between the parties in the insurer's favour. In the commercial context, where the insurer is dealing with experienced and astute financial organizations or traders, that imbalance would not arise.[21] Therefore, we would suggest that it would appropriate to use such agreements where they have been individually negotiated and in commercial insurance contracts only.

THE EFFECT OF A WAIVER

The effect of a waiver in insurance law will be similar to its effect in the general law of contract. Thus, as set out above, a waiver by election will usually be an irrevocable waiver of the right to avoid the policy or be discharged from liability.[22] By contrast, provided that notice is given before performance of the relevant obligation, pure and unilateral waivers will be revocable waivers of the performance of that obligation.[23] **19.74**

Similarly, a waiver will be case specific[24] and care must be taken to ascertain which unequivocal acts by the insurer constitute a waiver of which rights. Each case will depend on its facts. However, for example, waiving the requirement that the insurer be notified of a claim, by investigating the claim, will not be a waiver of a requirement that suits/ **19.75**

18 See, by analogy *R v Paulson* [1921] 1 AC 271 *per* Lord Atkinson at 280.
19 93/13/EEC. See Clarke at para. 19.5A and Chitty at para. 14.088.
20 (1995/3169).
21 This, of course, is the case in marine insurance.
22 *Compagnia Tirrena Di Assicurazioni v Grand Union Fire Insurance Co Ltd* [1991] 2 Lloyd's Rep. 143 *per* Waller J. at 153 cols 1–2, 154 cols 1–2; see also para. 19.89 in relation to reinstatement.
23 See *Waiver — Complications* at para. 5.02 ff.
24 See *Waiver — Complications* at para. 5.05 ff.

claims be brought within one year from the insured peril occurring;[25] nor of limitation generally;[26] investigating the claim will not constitute a waiver of a condition requiring the insured to provide an honest estimate of loss or proof of loss;[27] and waiving the requirement that notice of a claim be given within a certain time will not waive a requirement that the insured must make an honest claim nor will it operate as a general extension of time allowing claims to be brought some considerable time after the event.[28]

Finally, in English law, the fact that the insurer has previously waived a breach of a particular term does not mean that the insurer has waived any future breach of that term.[29] The position is to be contrasted with that in the United States where the courts are more astute to spell out a general course of dealing from the past waiver of breaches of particular terms so as to hold that there is a waiver of the future breaches of those terms.[30] **19.76**

PRACTICAL MECHANISMS FOR DEALING WITH THE ISSUES RAISED BY WAIVER

Prior to litigation

Both insurer and insured

Both insurer and insured should be aware at all times of the potential impact the doctrine of waiver can have on their dealings. Further, a general rule for both parties would be that the greater informality there **19.77**

---

[25] *Washington v Allstate Insurance Co* 901 F 2d 1281 (5th Cir 1990) *per* Duhé C.J. at 1288 col. 1.

[26] See Clarke at para. 26.5 C.

[27] *Maple Leaf Milling Co v Colonial Assurance Co* (1917) 36 DLR 202 *per* Perdue J.A. at 204–5.

[28] *In re an arbitration between Carr and the Sun Fire Assurance Company* (1897) 13 TLR 186 *per* Lord Esher M.R. at 186.

[29] See *Laing v Commercial Union Assurance Co Ltd* (1922) 11 Ll L Rep. 54; see also *Howell v Kightley* (1856) 21 Beav 331, 152 ER 887 *per* Sir John Romilly M.R. at 335–6, 889.

[30] See *Beatty v Mutual Reserve Fund Life Association* (1896) 75 F 65; *Thompson v Knickerbocker Life Insurance Co* (1881) 104 US 252 at 259–0; and *Spoeri v Massachusetts Mutual Life Insurance Co* (1889) 39 F 752 at 753 *per* Thayer J.; *cf.* in Canada if insurer accepts persistently late payments it can later demand timeous payment of the premiums (*Whitehorn v Canadian Guardian Life Insurance Co* (1909) 19 OLR 535).

is in their dealings, the more potential there will be for an allegation of waiver to be made out[31] and the more difficult it will be to predict whether or not those allegations will succeed. Both parties should therefore be astute to record their acts, the reasons for their acts and the knowledge that they possessed at the time of making those acts.

Insurer

The best mechanism an insurer can adopt to avoid being held to have waived its rights is to exercise extreme caution at all stages of its relationship with the insured. Further, the insurer should organize its affairs so that it and its employees are aware which of them is authorized to waive breaches and to ensure that information is always passed on to the employees who are so authorized. **19.78**

Prior to entry into the policy

The insurer should consider what information will be material and ask for detailed information on those topics. Further, the insurer should include a provision in proposal form which expressly states that the questions asked do not relieve the insured of its duty of good faith. If the insurer is aware of anything which suggests that the insured has acted in breach of its obligations, the insurer should either raise the point or accept that it may well have waived its rights. **19.79**

Issue of the policy

The insurer should consider whether it wishes to adopt the clauses used in *Mint Security v Blair*[32] and *Soole v Royal Insurance Co Ltd*[33] to afford it some measure of protection. As issue of the policy is, in all probability, an unequivocal act founding a waiver, the insurer must again consider any information that it may have as to the insured's conduct and on that basis reach a commercial decision as to whether it wishes to issue the policy, make enquiries or refuse to proceed further. **19.80**

---

[31] See, for example, the closer and more informal the relationship between the insurer and the insured, the more likely it is that the insurer will fail actively to seek information in and by the proposal form, the more likely it is that the insurer has waived the materiality of the issues not raised in and by the proposal form — see *Taylor v Eagle Insurance Co* (1940) 67 Ll L Rep. 136.

[32] [1982] 1 Lloyd's Rep. 188.

[33] [1971] 2 Lloyd's Rep. 332.

During the life of the policy

19.81 The insurer should consider what knowledge it has of the insured's conduct and, if necessary, reserve its rights before it takes any action or makes any request of the insured[34] if it appears that there has been a breach. Further, the insurer should consider the representations that it has made to the insured in the past. If any of those representations could be taken to be continuing representations, and if the insurer becomes aware of facts the result of which is that the insurer wishes to resile from those representations, it should so resile as soon as it becomes aware of those facts.[35] In the interests of both parties, the insurer should not wait until there is a claim before notifying the insured that it considers that there has been a breach of the insured's obligations. If at any time the insurer is uncertain of its position and decides to investigate, it should reserve its rights generally.[36] If the insurer is unsure of its rights whilst investigating a claim, again it can either reserve its rights or carry out only the standard inquiries which are carried out on every claim irrespective of whether or not the insurer meets the claim at the end of the day.[37]

Reservation of rights

19.82 If the insurer reserves its rights, it must do so clearly. However, there is no need for the insurer to state in terms that it is 'reserving its rights'.[38] Once there has been a reservation of rights, the insurer must take care to ensure that any of its subsequent conduct is not inconsistent with its reservation of rights. Thus, if the insurer impliedly or expressly accepts a claim under the policy, the fact that it has also reserved its rights will not prevent it from being held to have waived its rights.[39] By contrast, it appears that a mere acceptance of a payment under the policy will not be inconsistent with the insurer's reservation of rights.[40] Given that uncertainty, the prudent insurer will not accept payments under the

---

[34] See, *e.g. Svenska Handelsbanken v Sun Alliance and London Assurance plc* [1996] 1 Lloyd's Rep. 519 *per* Rix J. at 569 col. 1 — requesting the insured to alter the terms of a facility insured under a Commercial Mortgage Indemnity Policy will amount to waiver.

[35] *Simner v New India Assurance Co Ltd* [1995] LRLR 240 *per* Judge Diamond Q.C. at 260 col. 1.

[36] *National Trust v Sterling Accident* (1916) QR 551 SC 481.

[37] *Gillis v Bourgard* (1983) 145 DLR (3d) 570 at 571–2.

[38] *Hill v Citadel Insurance Co Ltd* [1995] LRLR 218 *per* Cresswell J. at 239 col. 2; (aff'd CA unrep. 5 December 1996).

[39] *Reid v Campbell Wallis Moule & Co Pty* [1990] VR 859 *per* Tadgell J. at 874 1 30.

[40] *Barber v Imperio Reinsurance Co (UK) Ltd* (CA 15 July 1996 unrep.).

policy even if it has reserved its rights and in most cases the best course of action will be for the insurer to decide swiftly whether it wishes to remain on risk and act accordingly. If the insurer does decide to repudiate liability, the insurer should return the premium.[41]

Insured

The insured will wish to ensure that the insurer waives as many of its rights as possible. However, the insured faces the pragmatic difficulty that if the insured attempts to 'manufacture' a waiver, the court will react unfavourably.[42] The most prudent course of conduct that the insured can adopt will be to pass on in writing all information relating to breaches of the policy, ensure that the information is communicated to the appropriate underwriter/claims manager and request the insurer to state its position in response. If the insurer fails to reserve its position or repudiate liability within a reasonable time, the insured may well be able to argue that the insured waived its rights. The insured should also ensure that it answers all queries raised by the insurer after breach. If it does not do so, or delays in so doing, it may prevent the insurer from possessing the knowledge to found a waiver and lose the ability to argue that the insurer has waived its rights.[43] **19.83**

After the commencement of litigation

The burden of pleading and proving that there has been a waiver is on the insured.[44] The plea is a 'serious step' and should only be made where there are good grounds for supporting that plea.[45] If there are such **19.84**

[41] *Simon Haynes Barlas & Ireland v Beer* (1946) 78 Ll L Rep. 337 at 369 *per* Atkinson J. at 369 col. 2–370 col. 1.

[42] Further, if the insured pleads waiver and estoppel in the alternative, any attempt to manufacture a waiver will preclude a claim in estoppel.

[43] *Hill v Citadel Insurance Co Ltd* [1995] LRLR 218 *per* Cresswell J. at 239 col. 1; (aff'd CA unrep 5 December 1996).

[44] See *Locker & Woolf v W Australian Insurance Co* [1936] 1 KB 408; *Busteed v West of England Fire and Life Insurance Co* (1857) 5 Ir Ch R 553; *Phillips v Grand River Farmers' Mutual Fire Insurance Co* (1881) 46 UCR 334 and *De Maurier v Bastion Insurance* [1967] 2 Lloyd's Rep. 550.

[45] See *Brook v Trafalgar Insurance Co Ltd* (1947) 79 Ll L Rep. 265 at 367.

grounds, the plea should be made in the insured's reply to the insurer's defence and counterclaim[46] alleging that it has avoided the policy. The plea should set out the alleged unequivocal representations made by the insurer and particulars of knowledge possessed by the insurer at the time of making the representation.[47]

To support the plea, the insured will, in all probability, be forced to rely on cross examining the insurer's witnesses at trial as to the knowledge they possessed. However, if the insured can establish a *prima facie* case of knowledge, the burden will be reversed. Thus where the insurer sought to rely on a 'no other insurance' clause to repudiate the policy and the other insurances had been at all material times taken out with that insurer, there was a *prima facie* case that the insurer was aware of the other insurances and waived the breach arising on their being taken out.[48] **19.85**

The insurer facing allegations of waiver will, in all likelihood, allege that it did not have the appropriate level of knowledge. However, the insurer could adopt two other paths. **19.86**

First, the insurer should check the information revealed on discovery very carefully. It may well be that new information arises on discovery which allows the insurer to avoid or be discharged on other grounds or which suggests that any knowledge which the insurer possessed prior to discovery was incomplete and therefore was not sufficient to waive its rights. Axiomatically, there cannot have been a waiver if the insurer's knowledge arises on discovery. On that basis, the insurer will escape liability as a result of the information revealed on discovery.[49] **19.87**

Secondly, the insurer may be able to argue that whilst there was a waiver by election, there was not a total waiver. Thus, the insurer may have waived its rights to avoid the policy but not waived any right to claim damages for breach of the terms. In every case therefore, the insurer may be able to recover damages if it can establish that the breach of the **19.88**

---

46 The counterclaim will arise as the prudent insurer will seek declarations as to the status of the policy and may argue that if the terms of the policy were not conditions entitling it to avoid the policy, they were terms which were breached allowing it to claim damages. The damages will be the sums claimed by the insured in the action and the insured's claim will fail for circuity. See *The Brede* [1974] 1 QB 233 and in the Lloyd's context *Society of Lloyd's v Leigh & Wilkinson* (unrep. 30 July 1997 CA).

47 See *Peyman v Lanjani* [1985] Ch 457 and *Waiver — Types and Elements* at para. 4.18.

48 See *Marcovitch v The Liverpool Victoria Friendly Society* (1912) 28 TLR 188.

49 See *Hill v Citadel Insurance Co Ltd* [1995] LRLR 218 *per* Cresswell J. at 238 col. 2; (aff'd CA unrep 5 December 1996) and *Svenska Handelsbanken v Sun Alliance and London Assurance plc* [1996] 1 Lloyd's Rep. 519 at 560 col. 1 *per* Rix J.

terms of the policy caused it loss. In most cases, the damage caused will be nominal. However, if the breach of the term was directly related to the existence of the insurance policy or to the claim, the damages caused would be the sums claimed. Therefore, the insurer will be entitled to counterclaim the same amount of damages arising from breach of the policy as the insured claims from it under the policy. The insured's claim will therefore be bad for circuity and must fail. The difficulty with such an argument will be that a term which goes to the root of the policy will probably be a condition, breach of which allows the insurer to be discharged and will rarely sound in damages as well. Therefore, the waiver of that term may well be a waiver of a right to claim damages.

ELECTION

Where a claim is made and the insurer has the power under the terms of the policy to reinstate the damaged property, in the normal course of events, the insurer will be put to its election whether to reinstate or to indemnify; an election which must be made within a reasonable time.[50] Three issues arise: can the right to elect be modified by the policy; in what ways can the election be made; and what is the effect of the election. 19.89

MODIFICATION BY THE POLICY

A right to elect can be altered or curtailed by the terms of a contract.[51] 19.90
Therefore, an insurer can by the wording of the policy grant itself the right to reinstate in part and indemnify in part.[52] This is the case even though the obligations assumed by the insurer form an entire contract elements of which cannot be in severed. However, in such cases there will be a presumption in favour of the insurer's having made an election between the two.[53] It follows that if the insurer wishes to preserve its right to both reinstate and indemnify it should do so by clear wording in the policy and informing the insured that it is not making its election even though it is reinstating or indemnifying to some extent.

[50] Clarke at para. 29.2A.
[51] See *Election, Affirmation and Acquiescence* at para. 7.08.
[52] *Allwright v Queensland Ins Co Ltd* (1966) 84 WN (Pt 1) (NSW) 378 at 391.
[53] *Bowes v National Fire & Marine Ins Co of New Zealand* (1888) 7 NZLR 27 *per* Williams J. at 30, 33.

MEANS BY WHICH THE ELECTION CAN BE MADE

19.91 Where the terms of the policy do not provide otherwise,[54] an election will usually be made where the insurer states that it intends to reinstate and not indemnify or *vice versa*.[55] However, where the offer to reinstate or indemnify is clearly made for an ulterior motive (for example as the first step in negotiations[56]) and is refused, the insurer will then be left to a free election.[57] By way of contrast, an election may occur irrespective of any action on the part of the insurer if reinstatement becomes impossible before the insurer elects.[58]

THE EFFECT OF THE ELECTION

19.92 In *Brown v Royal Insurance Co*,[59] the court stated that the effect of the election was that the insurer is '*in the same position as if he had originally contracted to do the act which he has elected to do*'[60] a statement that has led to some confusion. Thus, in Canada, the courts have tended to give a wide meaning to the statement and hold that the effect of the election is to replace the contract of indemnity with a contract for reinstatement *in toto*.[61] Therefore, once election has taken place, it is not possible for the insurer or insured to resile from that position and select the alternative mode of performance. However, in England, the position appears to be that if, after election, reinstatement becomes impossible, the obligation to reinstate revives.[62] This position, it is submitted, can be justified by three routes. First, if the insurer refuses to reinstate and cannot rely on frustration,

---

54 See para. 19.90 above and *Election Affirmation and Acquiescence* at para. 7.08.

55 *Scottish Amicable Heritable Securities Assn Ltd v Northern Assurance Co.* (1883) 11 R 287.

56 As part of such negotiations, the insured could, of course, accept less than 'perfect' reinstatement by way of compromise of the claim under the policy — see Clarke at para. 29–2A.

57 *Sutherland v Sun Fire Office* (1852) 14 D 775 at 777.

58 *Anderson v Commercial Union Assurance Corp* (1885) 55 LJQB 146 *per* Bowen L.J. at 150.

59 (1859) 1 El&El 853, 120 ER 1131.

60 *ibid. per* Lord Campbell at 858–9, 1133.

61 *Maher v Lumbermen's Mutual Casualty Co* [1932] 2 DLR 593 at 600–1 and *Carlyle v Elite Ins Co* (1984) 56 BCLR 331 *per* Wood J. at 335.

62 See Clarke at para. 29–2C, n. 36.

the insurer's secondary obligation to pay damages accrues,[63] that obligation will be the same as the obligation to indemnify. The obligation to indemnify is therefore effectively resuscitated.[64] Secondly, the election to indemnify or to reinstate is an election as to the means by which the insurer will perform the contract. Under English law, where one means of performance of the contract becomes impossible, the party must perform by the other means[65] as to do otherwise would be to deprive the parties of the full benefit of their contract. Thirdly, as pointed out elsewhere,[66] an election may only suspend the right to be indemnified in damages[67] and in any event an election will not amount to a total waiver. In either eventuality, the election to reinstate does not release the insurer from the obligation to indemnify.

ESTOPPEL

Estoppel[68] operates in insurance law in the same way as it does elsewhere. Therefore, the party seeking to establish an estoppel must show that there was a representation/promise/mutual assumption on which it acted to its detriment.[69] Similarly, as elsewhere, an estoppel **19.93**

63 *Robophone Facilities Ltd v Blank* [1966] 1 WLR 1428 *per* Diplock L.J. at 1446A–C; *C Czarnikow Ltd v Koufos* [1966] 2 QB 695 *per* Diplock L.J. at 730F–1B; *RV Ward Ltd v Bignall* [1967] 1 QB 534 *per* Diplock L.J. at 548B–E; *Banning v Wright* [1972] 1 WLR 972 *per* Lord Simon at 990C–D; *Moschi v Lep Air Services* [1973] AC 331 *per* Lord Diplock at 350C–D and *per* Lord Simon at 355G; *Photo Production Ltd v Securicor Transport Ltd* [1980] AC 827 *per* Lord Diplock at 848–50; *Bremer Vulkan Schiffbau und Maschinenfabrik v South India Shipping Corp Ltd* [1981] AC 909 *per* Lord Diplock at 982C–E; *Sudbrook Trading Estate Ltd v Eggleton* [1983] 1 AC 444 *per* Lord Diplock at 478F–G; *Paal Wilson & Co A/S v Partenreederei Hannah Blumenthal* [1983] 1 AC 854 *per* Lord Diplock at 915D–E; *Afovos Shipping Co v Pagnan* [1983] 1 WLR 195 *per* Lord Diplock at 203C–G and *State Trading Company of India v M Golodetz Ltd* [1989] 2 Lloyd's Rep. 285 *per* Kerr L.J. at 285 col. 2–286 col. 1.

64 See also *Johnson v Agnew* [1980] AC 367 *per* Lord Wilberforce at 392E–3E and *per* Lord Wilberforce at 398E–H.

65 *Vantol v Fairclough Dodd & Jones Ltd* [1955] 1 Lloyd's Rep. 546 *per* McNair J. at 552 cols 1–2; *Agricultores Federados Argentinos v Ampro SA* [1965] 2 Lloyd's Rep. 157 *per* Widgery J. at 167 col. 2.

66 See *Waiver — Complexities* at para. 5.03 and *Election, Affirmation and Acquiescence* at para. 7.01.

67 See *Hickman v Hayes* (1875) LR 10 CP 598 at 607.

68 As pointed out elsewhere (*Commercial Introduction* at para. 13.04), estoppel is used in the sense of estoppel by representation, estoppel by convention and equitable forbearance unless explicitly stated otherwise.

69 See *Newbon v City Mutual Life Assurance Society Ltd* (1935) 52 CLR 723 and *Yovich v Collyer* [1972] WAR 143. For authority that no distinction is to be drawn

may come into play where the party seeking to rely on waiver is unable to show the level of knowledge required to establish any form of waiver.[70] Four particular areas require consideration: the greater flexibility of estoppel as opposed to waiver; the representations triggering an estoppel; the reliance/detriment necessary; and rights that can be lost by an estoppel.

Greater flexibility of estoppel

Estoppel (provided that the elements can be established) will operate in three areas where a waiver will not. First, where there are difficulties in establishing that the other party or its agents had the requisite knowledge or that the knowledge is to be imputed to the other party,[71] an estoppel will arise and a waiver will not. Secondly, it is strongly arguable that, unlike with waiver,[72] an estoppel may preclude an insurer from relying on exceptions to the cover under the policy notwithstanding the fact that the estoppel is operating as a 'variation under another name'[73] by extending cover beyond the terms originally agreed without the support of consideration.[74] However, an estoppel extending cover, because it modifies the extent of cover without being supported by consideration, will only occur rarely. Thirdly, an insurer may be estopped from alleging that the premium due under the policy has not been paid.[75] Put another way, an estoppel can be used to incept cover where, in contract, cover cannot incept. **19.94**

Representations triggering an estoppel

The representations that give rise to an estoppel[76] will be the same as those for a waiver.[77] Thus, for example, issuing the **19.95**

between waiver and estoppel in the insurance context see *Mowie Fisheries Pty Ltd v Switzerland Insurance Australia Ltd* (1996) 140 ALR 57 *per* Tamberlin J. at 79–80.

70 See *Morrison v Universal Marine* (1873) LR 8 Ex 197 at 204–5.

71 See para. 19.56 above.

72 See para. 19.64 above.

73 *Hiscox v Outhwaite (No. 3)* [1991] 2 Lloyd's Rep. 524 *per* Evans J. at 535 cols 1–2.

74 *Hully v Aluminium Co of America* 143 F Supp 508 at 512–3 *per* District Judge Davies (SD Iowa, 1956).

75 *Balent v National Insurance Co of New Zealand Ltd* (1959) SR (NSW) 275 at 280–1.

76 Here the estoppel is estoppel by representation.

77 See para. 19.38 ff.

policy[78] or accepting further premiums[79] will suffice. As with waiver, there is some doubt as to whether the insurer conducting the insured's defence will constitute a sufficient representation. However, the position in English law[80] rests on two principles: that set out in *Soole v Royal Insurance Co*[81] and a requirement that the requisite elements for an estoppel must be present.[82]

RELIANCE/DETRIMENT NECESSARY

For an estoppel to arise there must be reliance/detriment. As a matter of logic, there must be reliance before there can be a detriment[83] and this reliance must be reasonable.[84] Reliance will not be established, for example, where the alleged representation was made by an agent that lacked both ostensible and actual authority to make it. Reliance in those circumstances would not be reasonable[85] and would not be such as to attract the intervention of equity. However, pure reliance is not sufficient, there must be detriment[86] which may comprise the payment of further premiums;[87] not seeking alternative cover;[88] or losing the ability to settle an action brought by a third party against the insured.[89] The loss of a pure right (that is without any harm being suffered) will probably not be sufficient to establish detriment.[90] **19.96**

[78] *Jones v Bangor Mutual Shipping Ins Sy Ltd* (1889) 61 LT 727 *per* Mathew J. at 729 col. 1 and *Keeling v Pearl Assurance Co* (1923) 129 LT 573.

[79] *Jones v Bangor Mutual Shipping Ins Sy Ltd* (1889) 61 LT 727, 729 and *Hemmings v Sceptre Life Assn Ltd* [1905] 1 Ch 365 *per* Kekewich J. at 369–70.

[80] Under US law, the position is different — see para. 19.50 above.

[81] [1971] 2 Lloyds Rep. 332 — see para. 19.47 above.

[82] MacGillivray at para. 2004.

[83] If there were not the detriment suffered would not be connected to the representation complained of.

[84] Clarke at para. 20.7E esp. n. 296.

[85] *M'Millan v Accident Ins Co* 1907 SC 484, PA.

[86] *Western Canada Accident and Guarantee Ins Co v Parrott* (1921) 61 SCR 595 *per* Idington J. at 600.

[87] *Wing v Harvey* (1854) De G M & G 265, 43 ER 872 *per* Knight Bruce L.J. at 270, 874; *Holdsworth v Lancashire & Yorkshire Ins Co* (1907) 23 TLR 521 *per* Bray J. at 523.

[88] *Hargett v Gulf Ins Co* 55 P 2d 1258 at 1261.

[89] *Western Canada Accident and Guarantee Ins Co v Parrott* (1921) 61 SCR 595 *per* Anglin J. at 603 and *per* Mignault J. at 605.

[90] *Hansen v Marco Engineering (Aust) Pty Ltd* [1948] VLR 198 at 211; compare *Territory Insurance Office v Adlington* (1992) 2 NTLR 55.

RIGHTS LOST AS A RESULT OF AN ESTOPPEL

In general, the rights lost as a result of an estoppel will be the same as those lost by a waiver — the right to repudiate, the right to avoid and the right to avoid liability as a result of a failure of a condition precedent. However, three additional rights may be lost by an estoppel which will not be lost by a waiver: the right to rely on a policy exclusion;[91] the right to recover monies paid by the insurer under a mistake of fact;[92] and the right to subrogate.[93] **19.97**

[91] See para. 19.94 above.

[92] Discussed at *Banking* at para. 15.66 ff.

[93] Where the insured is estopped from pursuing the claim, the insurer will also be estopped — the insurer being unable to place itself in a better position than the party to whose rights it is subrogating — see *Northern Assurance Co Ltd v Wolk* (1944) 49 NYS 2 d 754 at 756.

Chapter 20

SALE OF GOODS AND SHIPPING

INTRODUCTION

Due to the close relationship between the sale of goods and shipping elements in international trade contracts, similar issues arise in applying the doctrines to sale of goods and shipping law. As a result principles applicable to one area can and have been applied to the other. **20.01**

TERMINOLOGICAL DIFFICULTIES ASSOCIATED WITH WAIVER[1]

In these two areas, the case law on 'waiver' must be analysed with particular care.[2] A party seeking to establish the waiver can face difficulty in establishing the requisite level of knowledge on the part of the party alleged to have lost its rights. That difficulty was circumvented in *Bremer Handelsgesellschaft v Vanden Avenne-Izegem*[3] by the court finding that there had been a 'waiver' comprised of the making of the innocent party making unequivocal representation which has been relied upon by the other party to its detriment.[4] Ostensibly the court did not appear to find that knowledge was required. However, in subsequent cases,[5] a **20.02**

---

[1] See also *Waiver — Types and Elements* at para. 4.38 ff; *Equitable Forbearance* at paras. 12.26–7.

[2] We are solely concerned with those cases dealing with international trade or shipping in which terminological difficulties have arisen. For a general consideration of the terminological difficulties see *Waiver — Terminology passim*.

[3] [1978] 2 Lloyd's Rep. 109.

[4] Discussed at *Waiver — Types and Elements* at para. 4.26 ff.

[5] See *Avimex SA v Dewulf & Cie* [1979] 2 Lloyd's Rep. 57 *per* Robert Goff J. at 67–8 and *Cook Industries v Tradax Export SA* [1985] 2 Lloyd's Rep. 454 *per* Kerr L.J. at 462 col. 1 — col. 2.

party relying on waiver in the *Bremer* sense was met with the successful argument that, absent knowledge, there could be no waiver.

20.03 It is submitted that the confusion can be resolved in two ways. First, to argue that in *Bremer* and the subsequent cases, the defects being waived were obvious — the documents were defective on their faces.[6] This, it is submitted, is clear from Lord Salmon's speech in *Bremer* where, having pointed out that the relevant document — a *force majeure* notice as required by clause 22 of GAFTA 100[7] — was defective and served out of time, his Lordship then went on to hold that whether or not the buyers had any knowledge of their rights was irrelevant.[8] It is submitted that it is arguable that the buyers, a sophisticated commercial organization, would have known, on receipt of the notice, both of its patent defects and of their rights. Therefore, the question of knowledge was 'irrelevant' because, as a matter of fact, there was no need to consider it; the buyers had the requisite knowledge. The difficulty with that analysis is that it does not explain why their Lordships also stated that detrimental reliance was an element of waiver. If the case turned on issues of waiver in the true sense of the word, this second element was not necessary.

20.04 The second route is to argue that *Bremer* and the subsequent cases were cases where the doctrine of equitable forbearance was in play. Equitable forbearance, as we have suggested elsewhere,[9] does not require knowledge. Analytically, this is the better view and mitigates the effects of the use of confused terminology.

20.05 The practical effect of the above is threefold. First, *Bremer* and the subsequent cases can, it is submitted, be relied on with some degree of confidence where a party cannot establish knowledge but has suffered detriment and therefore wishes to rely on equitable forbearance. Secondly, and more controversially, *Bremer* can be relied to support a plea of waiver where the defects are obvious to all concerned. That course of action would only be justified where a documentary requirement patently had been not complied with. Even in such circumstances we would suggest that to do so would be to confuse two radically different types of 'waiver' and that the proper

---

6 See also *Bremer Handelsgesellschaft mbH v C Macprang JR* [1979] 1 Lloyd's Rep. 221 at 226 col. 1, 229 col. 1, 231 col. 1.

7 See *Variation* 2.39 ff., for an explanation of the GAFTA 100 contract.

8 *Bremer Handelsgesellschaft v Vanden Avenne-Izegem* [1978] 2 Lloyd's Rep 109 at 127 col. 1.

9 See *Waiver — Types and Elements* at para. 4.16.

approach would be to plead equitable forbearance. Thirdly, it follows that the prudent litigant wishing to avoid the consequences of *Avimex*[10] will decide at an early stage of proceedings whether or not it can establish knowledge. If it can, the obvious plea will be one of waiver by election, if it cannot, it will be safer to plead the case in the alternative as one of equitable forbearance rather than waiver *simpliciter*.

SALE OF GOODS — WAIVER

It is possible to identify cases of all four types of waiver in this area. However, as with shipping law, and, it is submitted, for the same reasons,[11] the majority of cases relate to waiver by election and we therefore concentrate on that area. **20.06**

TOTAL WAIVER

Notwithstanding the theoretical complexities arising from the relationship between accord and satisfaction and waiver,[12] we have suggested elsewhere[13] that a party can waive both the right to reject goods[14] and the right to claim damages in respect of those goods.[15] However, apart from where the buyers waive late delivery of the goods[16] cases of total waiver will be rare.[17] **20.07**

---

[10] *Avimex SA v Dewulf & Cie* [1979] 2 Lloyd's Rep. 57 *per* Robert Goff J. at 67–8 and *Cook Industries v Tradax Export SA* [1985] 2 Lloyd's Rep. 454 *per* Kerr L.J. at 462 col. 1—col.2.

[11] See *Shipping* at para. 20.19 below.

[12] See *Waiver — Types and Elements* at para. 4.29.

[13] See *Waiver — Types and Elements at paras* 4.33, 4.34.

[14] *Hain SS Co Ltd v Tate and Lyle Ltd* [1936] 2 All ER 597 at 608 and *Bentsen v Taylor, Sons & Co* [1893] 2 QB 274.

[15] But *cf. Kwei Tek Chao v British Traders and Shippers Ltd* [1954] 2 QB 459 at 477 and *The Democritos* [1975] 1 Lloyd's Rep. 368 at 398 for the contrary view.

[16] *Hartley v Hyams* [1920] 3 KB 475 *per* McCardie J. at 495 and *Charles Rickards Ltd v Oppenhaim* [1950] 1 KB 616 *per* Denning L.J. at 624.

[17] See Benjamin at paras 12.034 and n. 77.

PURE AND UNILATERAL WAIVER

It is clear that any right possessed by one party to the contract can be waived.[18] However, with the exception of the sellers' lien, it is as difficult in this area as in others, to identify rights which belong solely to the buyers or the sellers. Thus, although there is authority to suggest that conditions precedent are capable of being unilaterally waived[19] it is submitted that the better view is that they are not; a condition precedent forms an essential part of the bilateral bargain which must be complied with if there is to be contractual performance. It follows that the more prudent classification of such cases would be as ones of waiver by election or pure waiver. **20.08**

Sellers' lien

That difficulty does not arise with the sellers' lien over goods which have not been paid for. That lien is a right existing for the sellers' unique benefit and can be waived as such.[20] Thus, provided that there is the requisite knowledge, the lien can be waived by giving credit;[21] by the sellers seeking the buyers' permission to retain the goods as a temporary loan;[22] by refusing a tender of the price by the buyers;[23] by refusing to deliver the goods for reasons other than the buyers' failure to pay the price of those goods;[24] by allowing the buyers to take delivery;[25] by agreeing a sub-sale;[26] or by acting in any manner inconsistent with the continuation of the lien or with the buyers' rights.[27] **20.09**

---

18 See *Waiver — Types and Elements* at paras. 4.27; 4.35.

19 See *Napiers FE v Dexters* (1926) 26 Ll L R 62; 63 col. 2 – 64 col. 1 *per* Roche J; 184; 187 col. 2 – 188 col. 1 per Bankes L.J.

20 See s. 43(1)(c) of the Sale of Goods Act 1979.

21 This proposition derives from the relationship between s. 41(1)(b) and 43(1)(c) of the Sale of Goods Act 1979 (see Benjamin at paras. 15.033–035; 15.056; Atiyah & Adams at p. 407). The lien will be suspended for so long as the credit lasts.

22 See Atiyah & Adams at p. 407.

23 *Jones v Tarleton* (1842) 9 M & W 675, 152 ER 285 *per* Parke B. at 677, 286, *per* Alderson B. at 678, 286.

24 Thus, retaining the goods and demanding payment in respect of other goods will waive the sellers' lien in respect of the particular goods — see *Boardman v Sill* (1808) 1 Camp 410(n), 170 ER 1003 *per* Lord Ellenborough C.J.; *Weeks v Goode* (1859) 6 CBNS 367, 141 ER 499 *per* Cockburn C.J. at 370, 500 and *White v Garnier* (1824) 2 Bing 23, 130 ER 23.

25 *Bank of S Africa v Salisbury Gold Mining Co Ltd* [1892] AC 281 *per* Lord Watson at 284.

26 See Benjamin at paras 15.56; 15.060; 15.092–6.

27 *Mulliner v Florence* (1878) 3 QBD 484 and see Benjamin 15.057; 15.058.

PURE WAIVER

The best example of pure waiver is allowing the buyers time to pay. The sellers, in such circumstances, permit the future obligations of the contract to alter. As a result, although the right to call for payment at that time is lost,[28] time will remain of the essence[29] and the seller will remain free to fix a further time for payment on reasonable notice.[30] **20.10**

WAIVER BY ELECTION

The cases where there has been a waiver by election can be broken down into those relating to: late or incorrect delivery of the goods; a failure to tender proper documents; a failure to give proper notice under the contract; and a failure to pay in accord with the contract. **20.11**

Defective delivery

It is trite that time is of the essence in sale of goods contracts. It follows that a late delivery of goods will amount to a repudiatory breach of the contract which can be waived.[31] Similarly, the delivery of incorrect goods; delivery in instalments where one delivery was required[32] and excessive delivery[33] can be waived. **20.12**

---

[28] *The Scaptrade* [1983] 2 QB 529.

[29] *Buckland v Farmer & Moody* [1979] 1 WLR 221 *per* Buckley L.J. at 231D.

[30] *Charles Rickards Ltd v Oppenhaim* [1950] 1 KB 616 and *State Trading Corp of India v Compagnie Francaise d'Importation et de Distribution* [1983] 2 Lloyd's Rep. 679 at 682 cols 1–2.

[31] See Benjamin at para. 8.027 and cases there cited and in particular *Ogle v Earl Vane* (1868) LR 3 QB 272 *per* Kelly C.B. at 278–9; *Hickman v Haynes* (1875) LR 10 CP 598; *Levey & Co v Goldberg* [1922] 1 KB 688 and *Besseler Waecheter Glover & Co v South Derwent Coal Co Ltd* [1938] 1 KB 408.

[32] *Bentsen v Taylor & Sons & Co* [1893] 2 QB 274 and *Cobec Brazilian Trading and Warehousing Corporation v Toepfer* [1983] 2 Lloyds Rep. 386. *Champion v Short* (1807) 1 Camp 53, 170 ER 874 *per* Lord Ellenborough C.J. at 54, 874 and *Tarling v O'Riordan* (1878) 2 LR Ir 82 at 86 have been cited as authority for this proposition, it is submitted, however, that these cases are cases where the courts assumed that there was a presumption that delivery would not be by instalments, said presumption being rebutted by the parties' conduct.

[33] See Benjamin at para. 8.064.

Tender of non-conforming documents

International trade contracts normally contain three elements — the payment by way of documentary credit,[34] the shipping of the goods under a charterparty or similar arrangement[35] and the contract for the sale of the goods. The sale and banking contracts normally proceed by and against documents, therefore in both cases there is the potential for the tender of documents which do not conform with the contract. In the case of the banking contract, a tender of non-conforming documents is the main form of defective performance.[36] By way of contrast, under the sale contract both the documents and the goods themselves can be defective and a defect in either may give rise to a right to terminate the contract by rejecting either. A distinction must therefore be drawn between the right to reject arising from defects in the goods and that arising from defects in the documents.[37] Thus, in theory, the acceptance by the buyers of non-conforming documents will not necessarily waive any rights that they may have in respect of the goods themselves. However, by and large, an acceptance of non-conforming documents will waive the right to reject the goods either because it is the documents only (and not the goods) which are defective[38] or because the defect in the document is also the defect in the goods. Thus, for example, where a bill of lading patently shows that the goods were shipped late and therefore neither the bill nor the goods are as per contract, the buyers' acceptance of the bill of lading will waive their rights to reject the bill and the goods themselves.[39] **20.13**

In considering the above, it is also important to note two points. First, **20.14** the acceptance of non-conforming documents could also be categorized as a variation of the terms of the contract of sale. However, as the elements required for waiver and variation are quite distinct, care must

[34] See *Banking* at para. 15.39 ff.
[35] See *Shipping* at para. 20.21 below.
[36] See *Banking* at para. 15.47 ff.
[37] *Kwei Tek Chao v British Traders and Shippers* [1954] 2 QB 459 *per* Devlin J. at 480 and *Procter & Gamble Philippine Manufacturing Corp v Kurt A Becher* [1988] 2 Lloyd's Rep. 21 *per* Kerr L.J. at 30 cols 1–2.
[38] *Shipton Anderson & Co v John Weston & Co* (1922) 10 Ll L R 762 *per* Greer J. at 763 col. 2 and *Procter & Gamble Philippine Manufacturing Corp v Kurt A Becher* [1988] 2 Lloyd's Rep. 21 *per* Kerr L.J. at 30 cols 1–2.
[39] *Kwei Tek Chao v British Traders and Shippers* [1954] 2 QB 459 *per* Devlin at 481; *Bremer Handelsgesellschaft mbH v Deutsche Conti-Handelsgesellschaft mbH* [1983] 2 Lloyd's Rep. 45 and *Avimex SA v Dewulf & Cie* [1979] 2 Lloyd's Rep. 57 *per* Robert Goff J. at 67–8.

be taken to ascertain which doctrine applies[40] and the case pleaded and proved accordingly. Secondly, as pointed out above,[41] there will be no waiver by election unless the buyers have knowledge of the defects and their rights.[42] The former *may* be supplied if the documents are defective on their faces and the latter *may* be presumed when one is dealing with an experienced commercial organization.[43] In this respect, it is important to note that a waiver of any rights arising from defective documents can take place if the buyers acquire knowledge of the defect after acceptance of the documents but before taking up the goods and with that knowledge take up the goods.[44]

Failure to give proper notice under the contract

Sale contracts may provide for notices to be issued to the buyers and sellers; typical examples being notices appropriating goods to a particular contract in the sale of generic/bulk goods or notices of supervening events under a *force majeure* clause. Defects in the notices will be waived by acceptance of the notice[45] after the recipient has had a reasonable time to consider the contents of the notice.[46] Waiver will not arise in the normal course of events, however, if the recipient has expressly reserved its rights.[47] Further, a distinction must be drawn between notices which are patently defective, where arguably there will be presumed or deemed **20.15**

40 *WJ Alan & Co Ltd v El Nasr Export and Import Co* [1972] 2 QB 189 *per* Megaw L.J. at 217.

41 At para. 20.02.

42 *Suzuki & Co v Burgett and Newsam* (1921) 8 Ll L Rep. 495 *per* Shearman J. at 496 col. 2–497 col. 1 and (1922) 10 Ll L Rep. 223 *per* Bankes L.J. at 225 col. 2.

43 However, see difficulties pointed out at para. 20.05 above.

44 *Kwei Tek Chao v British Traders and Shippers Ltd* [1954] 2 QB 459 *per* Devlin J. at 477 where the learned judge rejected a submission that the acceptance of the goods in such circumstances could be a total waiver but did not appear to reject the idea that the acceptance could be a waiver by election.

45 *Avimex SA v Dewulf & Cie* [1979] 2 Lloyd's Rep. 57 *per* Robert Goff J. at 67–8 and *Cook Industries v Tradax Export SA* [1985] 2 Lloyd's Rep. 454 *per* Kerr L.J. at 462 col. 1– col. 2.

46 *Bremer Handelsgesellschaft mbH v Deutsche Conti-Handelsgesellschaft mbH* [1983] 2 Lloyd's Rep. 45 *per* Goff L.J. at 49 col. 2. Therefore, there will be no loss of rights if the innocent party fails to take the point immediately — see *V Berg & Son v Vanden Avenne-Izegem PVBA* [1977] 1 Lloyd's Rep. 499 *per* Roskill L.J. at 504 col. 2.

47 *Bremer Handelsgesellschaft mbH v Deutsche Conti-Handelsgesellschaft mbH* [1983] 2 Lloyd's Rep. 45 *per* Goff L.J. at 49 col. 1.

knowledge,[48] and less obvious defects where explicit knowledge of the facts and rights will be required.

Incorrect payment or tender of payment

20.16 The contract of sale will provide for the time, manner and place of payment and each of those requirements may be waived. It is submitted that, as a matter of practice, all such waivers are waivers by election as the innocent party has accepted performance which differs from that agreed and which would therefore constitute breach. Thus, the requirement that payment be made at a particular time can be waived by accepting a late payment;[49] a requirement as to place of payment can be waived by accepting payment elsewhere[50] and arguably by delivery of the goods.[51] Both waivers are final.[52] Similarly, a requirement for the tender of the price can be waived by delivering the goods prior to tender and will be final.[53]

ELEMENTS COMMON TO ALL TYPES OF WAIVER

20.17 Four points are to all the types of waiver set out above. First, we stress that knowledge is required.[54] However, as a matter of practicality, provided that the differing elements of pleading and proof are met, the result achieved by a waiver or estoppel[55] will be the same. This practical similarity is echoed by the courts' apparent tacit approval of the overlapping of waiver and equitable forbearance in this area.[56] Secondly, care must be taken where the innocent party reserves its rights. We have

---

48 See paras 20.04–20.05 above.

49 See, in the shipping context, *China Trade Corporation v Evlogia Co (The Mihalios Xilas)* [1979] 1 WLR 1018.

50 *Gyles v Hall* (1726) 2 P Wms 378, 24 ER 774 and *Caine v Coulton* (1863) 1 H&C 764, 154 ER 1092 *per* Pollock C.B. at 767, 1093 and *per* Martin B. at 768, 1093.

51 *Gordon v Strange* (1847) 1 Exch 477, 154 ER 203 *per* Pollock C.B. and Parke B. at 478, 204.

52 The time for performance having passed.

53 *Cohen v Roche* [1927] 1 KB 169.

54 Benjamin at para. 19.131.

55 In the sense of estoppel by representation, estoppel by convention and equitable forbearance.

56 See *Bremer Handelsgesellschaft v Vanden Avenne-Izegem* [1978] 2 Lloyd's Rep. 109 and para. 20.02 ff above.

already suggested that in most cases a reservation of rights will protect the innocent party by rendering subsequent communications equivocal.[57] However, the court may conclude that the innocent party has waived its rights, notwithstanding the express reservation if the innocent party subsequently acts inconsistently with that reservation.[58] Further, it appears that the courts are relatively willing to reach this conclusion in this context.[59] Thirdly, a waiver will only apply in a limited fashion. Thus, the waiver will only operate to extinguish rights arising in relation to a particular shipment or particular goods.[60] There will be no 'general waiver' of non-specific rights. Fourthly, the representation relied on in all cases must be unequivocal. Therefore, for example, calling for proof of *force majeure* will not waive defects in the notice as the proof should validate the notice[61] and any representation made with an obvious ulterior motive will not found a waiver of rights.[62]

ESTOPPEL

The fact that estoppel is a vague doctrine incapable of juridical formulation[63] has not prevented it from being used in two ways in this area. First, an estoppel[64] can be relied on where the requisite knowledge for **20.18**

---

[57] See *Waiver — Types and Elements* at para. 4.11 ff.

[58] See *Davenport v R* (1877) 3 App Cas 115 *per* Sir Montague E Smith at 132; *Croft v Lumley* (1856) 5 E & B 648 at 652, 680–2; 119 ER 622 at 624, 635; *Stone v Stringer* (1880) 61 LT 470; *R v Paulson* [1921] 1 AC 271 *per* Lord Atkinson at 286; *Haynes v Hirst* (1927) 27 SR (NSW) 480 *per* Long Innes J; *Carter v Green* [1950] 2 KB 76 and *Antaios Naviera SA v Salen Rederierna AB* [1983] 1 WLR 1362 *per* Lord Donaldson M.R. at 1370H–1C and *per* Fox L.J. 1377A-C.

[59] *Nichimen Corp v Gatoil Overseas Inc* [1987] 2 Lloyd's Rep. 46 *per* Kerr L.J. at 51 and *Vitol SA v Esso Australia Ltd (The Wise)* [1989] 2 Lloyd's Rep. 451.

[60] *Bremer Handelsgesellschaft mbH v Deutsche Conti-Handelsgesellschaft mbH* [1983] 2 Lloyd's Rep 45 *per* Goff L.J. at 48 col. 2 and *Peter Cremer v Granaria* [1981] 2 Lloyd's Rep. 583 *per* Robert Goff J. at 590 col. 1.

[61] *Bremer Handelsgesellschaft mbH v Deutsche Conti-Handelsgesellschaft mbH* [1983] 1 Lloyd's Rep. 339.

[62] Thus, accepting an appropriation of goods to obtain an export licence will not waive defects in the notice see *Bremer Handelsgesellschaft mbH v Bunge Corp* [1983] 1 Lloyd's Rep. 476 *per* Goff L.J. at 483 col. 2. *Bremer* is an equitable forbearance case but it is submitted that the principle will apply in cases where the motive is sufficiently obvious to render the representation equivocal.

[63] *Colley v Overseas Exporters* [1921] 3 KB 302 *per* McCardie J. at 311–2.

[64] Estoppel means estoppel by representation, estoppel by convention and equitable forbearance unless otherwise stated as, for example, in the last sentence of this paragraph.

a waiver cannot be established. Estoppel in this sense will apply in the situations set out above where that knowledge is absent and detriment is present. Secondly, 'estoppel' has been used as a mechanism for passing title to goods.

ESTOPPEL AND TITLE TO GOODS

'Estoppel' has been used as a mechanism for passing title in two ways; **20.19**
both of which are either exceptions to the *nemo dat* principle or differing aspects of the same exception to the *nemo dat* principle. The exception in any event exists for reasons of commercial expediency and runs throughout commercial law.[65] It is important to note that neither are estoppels in the true sense of the word, where title does not pass,[66] and that a plea based on these exceptions will rarely succeed[67] not least because of the potential that both have for destroying subsequently concluded bargains.[68]

Estoppel by representation

Where a seller expressly represents to a buyer that title to the goods has **20.20**
passed, the seller will subsequently be 'estopped' from arguing that title has not passed. Further, the buyer will be able to sell the goods on to third parties giving goods apparently title as it does so. Axiomatically, therefore, this type of 'estoppel by representation' is not a true estoppel by representation, what amounts to good title being created.[69] It is or is part of an exception to the *nemo dat* principle that also permits title to be transmitted as a result of ostensible authority.[70] Three points arise. First, the title created must relate to ascertained goods or an existing bulk that is sufficiently large to satisfy *all* relevant claims to title. The

---

[65] Both are discussed at *Agency* at para. 14.17 ff., and *Banking* at para.15–64 ff.
[66] *In Re Goldcorp* [1995] 1 AC 75 Lord Mustill at 94G-H.
[67] See *Mercantile Bank of India Ltd v Central Bank of India Ltd* [1938] AC 287; *Henderson v Williams* [1895] 1 QB 521; *Eastern Distributors Ltd v Goldring* [1957] 2 QB 600 and Benjamin at para. 7.007 and cases there cited.
[68] *Commonwealth Trust v Akotey* [1926] AC 72 at 76 and *Jerome v Bentley & Co* [1952] 2 All ER 114 *per* Donovan J. at 118A–B.
[69] This rule also applies to the allocation of specific goods. From goods in bulk – see Benjamin at para. 7–103; *Simms v Anglo-American Telegraph Co* (1879) 5 QBD 188 *per* Cotton LJ at 215.
[70] See *Agency* at para. 14.17 ff.

estoppel will not create a title where there are insufficient extant goods.[71] Secondly, the elements for an estoppel by representation are required — there must be an express representation as to title. Therefore, delivery,[72] handing over of a receipt or documents of title,[73] acceptance of delivery or entry of goods into the buyer's books, will not suffice to create the estoppel.[74] Similarly, an attornment, a promise to deliver, will not generate an estoppel,[75] a mere promise failing the basic *Jorden v Money*[76] requirement that there be a representation of fact. To establish the estoppel there must be a clear, additional representation that title has passed.[77] Thirdly, the estoppel will only confer limited rights on the party seeking to raise it. Therefore, the estoppel will only create rights as between the representor (or principal of the representor) and the representee. Third party purchasers for value of the goods without notice will not be affected.[78]

Estoppel by negligence

The true owner of goods can pass good title to those goods as a result of an 'estoppel by negligence'. The 'estoppel' will arise where the true owner sues a buyer for the return of the goods and the buyer establishes that the true owner owed a buyer a duty of care, was negligent and that negligence was causative of the buyer purchasing the goods.[79] Three points arise. First, the buyer must establish that a **20.21**

[71] See *In re Goldcorp* [1995] 1 AC 74 *per* Lord Mustill at 93E–F.
[72] *Colley v Overseas Exporters* [1921] 3 KB 302 *per* McCardie J. at 311–2.
[73] *Mercantile Bank of India Ltd v Central Bank of India Ltd* [1938] AC 287 *per* Lord Wright at 303.
[74] *Laurie & Morewood v Dudin & Sons* [1926] 1 KB 223.
[75] *Coventry & Co v GE Rly* (1883) 11 QBD 776 and *Alicia Hosiery Ltd v Brown Shipley & Co Ltd* [1970] 1 QB 195 *per* Donaldson J. at 206A–B.
[76] (1854) 5 HL Cas 185.
[77] *Knights v Wiffen* (1870) LR 5 QB 660; *Simm v Anglo American Telegraph Co* (1879) 5 QBD 188 at 215 and *Capital and Counties Bank Ltd v Warriner* (1896) 12 TLR 216. Contra. *In re Goldcorp* [1995] 1 AC 74 *per* Lord Mustill at 92F–5E in which *Knights v Wiffen* was distinguished, their Lordships holding that: (i) title could not pass by an estoppel; (ii) that for title to pass there must be at least sufficient goods to satisfy all claims by buyers to have title ie the doctrine would not create title where the goods were not extant.
[78] See *Re London Wine Co (Shippers) Ltd* [1986] PCC 121; *In Re Goldcorp Exchange Ltd* [1995] 1 AC 74
[79] *Mercantile Credit v Hamblin* [1965] 2 QB 242 *per* Pearson L.J. at 271; *Moorgate Mercantile Co Ltd v Twitchings* [1977] AC 890 and *Gator Shipping Corp v Trans-Asiatic Oil Ltd* [1978] 2 Lloyd's Rep. 357 *per* Kerr J. at 377 col. 1–378 col. 2.

duty of care was owed[80] and this is an onerous burden. Therefore, a failure to take precautions to prevent theft;[81] a merely careless loss;[82] or a failure to report the theft,[83] will not suffice. Secondly, the buyer must establish causation.[84] Thirdly, it follows that estoppel by negligence in this context is one of two things. First, as in banking law, 'estoppel by negligence' is here the application of the principles of circuity of action.[85] The buyer has an equal and opposite claim to that of the true owner arising from the true owner's breach of duty and buyer's loss. Secondly, estoppel by negligence in the sale of goods context is either another example of the *nemo dat* exception or another *nemo dat* exception.[86] On balance, as title can be passed, the latter view would appear to be correct. However, in either event, the courts are not applying the doctrine of estoppel in any proper sense of the word.

SHIPPING

As pointed out elsewhere,[87] shipping law has been responsible for many of the developments in the doctrines of waiver, election and estoppel.[88] In part, this is due to the historically high volume of litigation. It is also due to the notification and documentary provisions which attach to most forms of shipping transactions. The complexity and number of those provisions offers parties more opportunities to make errors or to make the unequivocal representations necessary to trigger the three doctrines. **20.22**

---

[80] See Benjamin at para. 7.015 n. 85 and cases cited.
[81] *Farquharson Bros & Co v King & Co* [1902] AC 325 *per* Lord McNaghten at 335 and *Jerome v Bentley & Co* [1952] 2 All ER 114 *per* Donovan J. at 118G.
[82] *Farquharson Bros & Co v King & Co* [1902] AC 325 *per* Lord McNaghten at 335–6.
[83] *Debs v Sibec Developments Ltd* [1990] RTR 91.
[84] See Benjamin at para.7–016.
[85] See *Banking* at para. 15.55.
[86] Discussed at para. 20.20 above.
[87] See Chap. 13, '*Commercial Introduction*'.
[88] Apart from the creation of variation by necessity (see *Variation* at para. 2.39 ff), shipping law has had little impact on the law of variation, the cases being decided on established principles.

WAIVER

PURE AND UNILATERAL WAIVER — SHIPOWNERS' LIEN

There is no difference between the doctrine of waiver which is of general application and the doctrine of waiver as applied to shipping law. Thus, the doctrines of pure and unilateral waiver apply here as elsewhere. The clearest example of their application is the waiver of the shipowners' lien in respect of freight by the unequivocal acts of accepting of the bill of lading[89] or of requiring that the freight be paid after delivery.[90] In both cases, a right which is particular to the shipowner is lost[91] and the future performance of the parties' rights and obligations under the charterparty is altered. It follows that the loss of the shipowners' lien can be categorized as both a unilateral and a pure waiver. **20.23**

WAIVER BY ELECTION

The majority of the case law relates to waiver by election. This, it is submitted, arises from the fact that the shipowners or charterers will most frequently be reacting to a discovered breach rather than altering the future performance of a charterparty governed by standard terms. We therefore concentrate on examining the breaches of shipping contracts which are capable of waiver; the manner in which those breaches can be waived; and the effect of the waiver. **20.24**

BREACHES CAPABLE OF WAIVER

The types of breach can be split into two categories: breaches of conditions of the charterparty, for example as to suitability of the ship,[92] or as to the shippers' inability to deviate from the course,[93] or as to the **20.25**

---

89 *Tamvaco v Simpson* (1866) LR 1 CP 363 *per* Pollock C.B. and Blackburn J. at 371–2.
90 *Foster v Colby* (1858) 3 H&N 705, 157 ER 651 *per* Watson B. at 718, 657.
91 As opposed to the charterer's loss of the right to call for the freight.
92 *The Aegean Dolphin* [1992] 2 Lloyd's Rep. 178 *per* Hobhouse J. at 186 col. 1.
93 Deviation is 'repudiation in an extreme form' (*Woolf v Collis Removal Service* [1948] KB 11 *per* Asquith L.J. at 16–17 and *Astro Vendecor v Mabanaft* [1971] 2 QB 588).

quantity or quality of goods shipped;[94] and breaches which trigger a particular right under the charterparty, for example, late payment of hire for the vessel which would normally trigger the right to withdraw the vessel.[95] Both types of breaches are capable of waiver. Therefore, a deviation from the allotted course can be waived[96] as can the late payment of hire.[97]

MANNER IN WHICH THE BREACHES CAN BE WAIVED

Unequivocal representation

For there to be a waiver, the innocent party must make an unequivocal representation whilst possessing the appropriate knowledge. The types of unequivocal representation which will found the waiver are on one level unproblematic. The representation must be 'unequivocal, definite, clear, cogent and complete'.[98] Thus, for example, the right to withdraw can be lost by accepting a late tender of hire[99] or by allowing the ship to proceed to port.[1] Further, although there is authority to suggest that a reference to arbitration may not be sufficiently unequivocal to found a waiver,[2] we would suggest that a party facing a repudiatory breach may, in limited circumstances,[3] waive that breach by seeking a reference to arbitration. However, on another level, this simple overview must be qualified by the presence of three issues which require consideration. **20.26**

94 *Chandris v Isbrandtsen-Moller* [1951] 1 KB 240.
95 For example, under Clause 5 of the New York Produce Form or clause of Baltime Charterparty.
96 *Compagnie Primera de Navagaziona v Compania Arrendataria de Monopolio de Petroleos SA* [1940] 1 KB 362 *per* McKinnon L.J. at 375.
97 See, *e.g. China Trade Corporation v Evlogia Co (The Mihalios Xilas)* [1979] 1 WLR 1018 at 1024C–G.
98 *McCormick v National Motor Insurance* (1934) 40 Com Cas 76 *per* Slesser L.J. at 93.
99 See *Tenax Steamship Co Ltd v Brimnes (Owners) The Brimnes* [1975] QB 929 and *Mardorf Peach & Co v Attica Sea Carriers Corporation of Liberia (The Laconia)* [1977] AC 850 *per* Lord Wilberforce at 872D–E. However, the late tender must be in complete not part payment of the hire — see *The Mihalios Xilas* above.
1 *Dimech v Corlett* (1858) 12 Moo PC 199, 14 ER 887 *per* Lord Coleridge at 227, 897 explained *Behn v Burness* (1863) 32 LJQB 204 *per* Williams J. at 208.
2 *US Shipping Board v Bunge y Born* (1924) 41 TLR 73 *per* Bankes L.J. at 74 col. 2.
3 For example, where the reference to arbitration is consistent only with the continued existence of the contract.

20.27 First, where a breach has triggered a party's rights under the charterparty, that party will be allowed time to investigate the breach.[4] After investigation, the party's rights must be exercised within a reasonable time[5] if they are not to be lost.[6] It follows that mere silence and delay under a charterparty can 'waive' rights accruing under it; a conclusion which is, at first sight, contrary to the general law. It is submitted, however, that the loss of rights in such circumstances is in fact consistent with the general rule for the simple reason that the silence and delay with the concomitant uncertainty as to the charterers' rights and potential difficulties with the practical organization of the charterparty inevitably result in the charterer suffering prejudice. It is therefore submitted that the above position is consistent with the rule laid down in *Allen v Robles*[7] and the operation of equitable forbearance principles. It also follows that the charterer alleging that the owners have 'waived' the breach by silence or delay should in fact formally plead and prove its case on equitable forbearance principles. Thus, the charterer must show that it has suffered some detriment albeit that the court may readily infer that it has.

20.28 Secondly, the courts will place any allegedly unequivocal act in its context to ascertain whether or not it is truly unequivocal. If the act is not sufficiently clear and unequivocal, there will be no waiver.[8] Thus, where the alleged act was the loading and sailing of the vessel, the court examined whether that act occurred on the instructions of the charterers (the party in breach) or the owners. Where the act was on the instructions of the charterers, acquiescence by the owners was not sufficient to found a waiver.[9] Further,

---

4 *China Trade Corporation v Evlogia Co (The Mihalios Xilas)* [1979] 1 WLR 1018 *per* Lord Scarman at 1036B.

5 *Mardorf Peach & Co v Attica Sea Carriers Corporation of Liberia (The Laconia)* [1977] AC 850 at 872E and *China Trade Corporation v Evlogia Co (The Mihalios Xilas)* [1979] 1 WLR 1018 *per* Lord Salmon at 1030H.

6 The rights will only be waived if the party has acted unreasonably. Thus, if a party has acted *slowly* but within a reasonable time, there will be no 'waiver' of its rights (see *The Balder London* [1980] 2 Lloyd's Rep. 489 *per* Mocatta J. at 494 co. 2).

7 [1969] 1 WLR 1193. It should be noted that, as a matter of analysis, the courts are not utilizing waiver in its strict sense in such cases, the reasoning appears to be closer to that of an estoppel being created — see *Waiver — Types and Elements* at para. 4.10.

8 See *United States Shipping Board v JJ Masters & Co* (1922) 10 Ll L R 573 *per* Atkin L.J. at 578 col. 2 — indorsement of the bill of lading is not a sufficiently unequivocal act to waive any defects in the bill.

9 Compare *Tyrer v Hessler* (1902) 7 Com Cas 166 (there was a seven day delay in which the owners did nothing and the master telegraphed for new cargo on the charterers' instructions: held — no waiver *per* Vaughan Williams L.J. at 170; approved in *Vsesojuznoje Objediheni Sovfracht of Moscow v Temple Steamship Co Ltd* (1945) 62 TLR 43 *per* Lord Porter at 46 col. 1) with *Nova Scotia v Sutherland* (1899) 5 Com Cas 106 (there was a two day delay in which the master acting as the owners' agent loaded cargo and therefore waived their rights *per* Bigham J. at 109–10).

it is also arguable that if the owners are acting with an ulterior motive, there will be no waiver. Therefore, where there has been a deviation, allowing the ship to load and sail to prevent a further deviation[10] or endorsing a bill of lading to obtain perishable freight,[11] may not be sufficiently equivocal to found a waiver.

Thirdly, the courts will examine with care any agency relationship between the person making the alleged unequivocal representation and the party alleged to have waived its rights. If the person who made the representation did not have actual or ostensible authority to waive any rights, there may well be no waiver. Thus, an acceptance of a late tender of hire by the owners' banks will not constitute a waiver if the bank's instructions are limited by a requirement for the owners' approval of the acceptance.[12] Similarly, if the master of the vessel does not have authority to waive the terms of the charterparty, his actions will not waive the owners' rights.[13] **20.29**

Knowledge

As pointed out above,[14] the courts have used the term 'waiver' to mean 'equitable forbearance.'[15] The reason for their doing so, it is submitted, has been the difficulty of showing that the party alleged to have waived its rights possessed the requisite knowledge as at the date of the unequivocal representation. A party considering whether the right to terminate the contract has been lost must, as suggested above, analyse whether the right has been waived or whether the party is precluded from taking the point as a result of an equitable forbearance. **20.30**

EFFECT OF THE WAIVER

The theoretical effect of the waiver does not differ from the general law. **20.31**
However, two particular points should be noted. First, where there has

[10] *Vsesojuznoje Objediheni Sovfracht of Moscow v Temple Steamship Co Ltd* (1945) 62 TLR 43 *per* Lord Porter at 46 col. 1 (in that case, however, there was a subsequent breach on which owners could rely).

[11] *SS Ardennes (Cargo Owners) v SS Ardennes (Owners)* [1951] 1 KB 55 *per* Lord Goddard C.J. at 60.

[12] *Mardorf Peach & Co v Attica Sea Carriers Corporation of Liberia (The Laconia)* [1977] AC 850 *per* Lord Wilberforce at 871G.

[13] *Chandris v Isbrandtsen-Moller* [1951] 1 KB 240 at 242; see also *Steven v Bromley & Son* [1919] 2 KB 722 *per* Bankes L.J. at 725.

[14] See para. 20.02 above and ff.

[15] See *Waiver — Types and Elements* at para. 4.38 ff., and cases there cited.

been a deviation, the contract will only be terminated when there has been an election to treat the deviation as repudiatory.[16] If the right to repudiate is waived, then both parties will be able to rely on all the terms of the contract with the waivor being limited to a limited claim for damages arising from the deviation.[17] However, if the right is not waived, then all the terms of the contract will cease to have force and effect.[18] Thus, a holder of a bill of lading where there has been a deviation will rarely be aware of the deviation until the voyage is completed. Further, as a waiver of the right to terminate may expose the holder to a claim for general average or freight, the holder has little to gain by waiving its rights and the claimant much to gain from arguing that there has been a waiver.[19] The issue of knowledge and the precise effect of the waiver therefore are crucial. Secondly, in common with the negotiation of bills of exchange,[20] a cargo afloat may be onsold many times sometimes with the bill of lading being endorsed to that effect. It is therefore important to remember that a waiver will only affect the parties to it. Therefore, any waiver as between the sellers and shipowners or charterers, or original sellers and purchasers in a string, will not affect subsequent purchasers and sellers in the string or endorsees of the bill of lading.[21]

ELECTION

As pointed out above, certain breaches of charterparties will automatically give rise to the right to terminate the charterparty. Under the common law, the innocent party would therefore be forced to its election. Whether or not the innocent party had so elected would be decided **20.32**

---

[16] *Hain SS Co v Tate & Lyle* (1936) 41 Com Cas 350 *per* Lord Atkin at 355; *Hirju Mulji v Cheong Yue SS Co* [1926] AC 497 *per* Lord Sumner at 509–10.

[17] *Hain SS Co v Tate & Lyle* above at 354–5 *per* Lord Atkin; *per* Lord Wright at 363 and *per* Lord Maugham at 371–2.

[18] *Balian v Joly, Victoria* (1890) 6 TLR 345 *per* Lord Esher M.R. at 345 col. 2; *The Dunbeth* [1897] P 133; *Joseph Thorley v Orchis* [1907] 1 KB 660 *per* Lord Collins M.R. at 667–8 and *Paterson Steamships v Robin Hood Mills* (1937) 58 Ll L R 33 at 39. For the similar view of the US courts see *The Tregenna (Farr v Hain SS Co)* 121 Fed. Rep. (2d) 940 (1941).

[19] The party claiming for general average or freight will, of course, be unable to rely on estoppel as that would be using estoppel as a sword and not as a shield.

[20] See *Banking* at para. 15.37.

[21] *Leduc v Ward* (1888) 20 QBD 475 *per* Fry L.J. at 485.

under the normal rules.[22] This position has been altered by 'anti-technicality' clauses in the charterparty. These clauses usually either provide that the charterparty can only be terminated after compliance with a notification process[23] or that the charterparty cannot be terminated for merely formal breaches.[24] The effect of such clauses will be to prevent the innocent party from exercising rights to repudiate arising from breach unless it complies with notification provisions set out in the clause or there is another substantial breach of the charterparty.[25]

ESTOPPEL

As is clear from the above,[26] a party may have recourse to an estoppel where it is unable to establish knowledge. First and foremost, recourse will be to equitable forbearance, however, estoppel by representation and estoppel by convention both may apply. Thus, for example, the charterers may be precluded from arguing that a notice of readiness was premature.[27] As pointed out above, that preclusion can be categorized as waiver or equitable forbearance.[28] However, in *Transgrain Shipping BV v Global Transporte Oceanico SA (The Mexico I)*,[29] Lord Justice Mustill, as he then was, doubted where the 'elusive concept of waiver' had any role to play in relation to notices of readiness[30] **20.33**

[22] Thus, for example, if there is no provision in the charterparty as to notification of the party in breach that the other has exercised its right of election, normal common law rules will apply (see *Tyrer v Hessler* (1902) 7 Com Cas 166 *per* Romer L.J. at 171.)

[23] See, *e.g.* *Afovos Shipping Co SA v Pagnan* [1983] 1 WLR 195 at 198A–B.

[24] For example, where payment is required by close of business on Friday, receipt of funds on Monday will not constitute breach.

[25] See *Election, Affirmation and Acquiescence* at para. 7.08.

[26] See paras. 20.02 ff., and 20.30.

[27] *Surrey Shipping Co Ltd v Compagnie Continentale (France) SA (The Shackleford)* [1978] 1 Lloyd's Rep. 191.

[28] *Sofial SA v Ove Skou Rederi (The Helle Skou)* [1976] 2 Lloyd's Rep. 205 *per* Donaldson J. at 214. The learned judge referred to the doctrine applied as 'waiver'. However, as the charterers had no knowledge of the facts, the doctrine being applied must have been equitable forbearance.

[29] [1990] 1 Lloyd's Rep. 507. See also *Galaxy Energy International v Novorossiys Shipping Co (The Petr Schmidt)* Longmore J. (Comm Ct unrep. 5 December 1996).

[30] *The Mexico I* at 514 *per* Mustill L.J.

deciding that the better analysis in notice of readiness cases was estoppel by convention.[31]

Bearing in mind the above, estoppel[32] may arise in three particular situations: in relation to bills of lading; in relation to salvage and in relation to demurrage. **20.34**

BILLS OF LADING

At common law,[33] representations[34] made in and by the bill of lading will create an estoppel by representation provided that the elements of that estoppel are established. Therefore, a statement that the goods are shipped in good order will preclude the shipowner/carrier from arguing the contrary when sued by an indorsee for value of the bill[35] or the lawful holder of the bill on presentation.[36] A similar estoppel will arise from the description of the goods in the bill of lading.[37] As the bill of lading is passed from carrier to carrier, the bill will estop successive carriers on a through carriage from arguing that the goods differ from the description in the bill[38] unless those successive carriers make some statement to the contrary. **20.35**

Three points arise on this estoppel. First, there will be no estoppel where the representor had no authority to make the representation and the representee is aware of that fact. Therefore, an estoppel will not arise where the master makes a representation as to goods which are not on board ship[39] or as to the commercial quality of the goods.[40] Both such representations are clearly outwith his authority. Secondly, the shipowner can avoid creating an estoppel by making vague representations.[41] Such representations will be insufficiently certain to amount to the requisite representation but do not offend against the **20.36**

[31] On the facts of the case there was no estoppel.
[32] Used in the sense of equitable forbearance, estoppel by representation and estoppel by convention — see *Commercial Law — Introduction* at para. 13.04.
[33] As opposed to under statute — see para. 20.37 below.
[34] As to the absolute nature of those representations see *Trade Star Lines Corp v Mitsui Ltd* (CA unrep. 4 July 1996).
[35] *Compania Vascongada v Churchill* [1906] 1 KB 237; *The Skarp* [1935] P 134 and *The Tromp* [1912] P 337.
[36] *Brandt v Liverpool* [1924] 1 KB 575.
[37] *Parsons v New Zealand Shipping Co* [1901] 1 KB 548.
[38] *Crawford & Law v Allan Line SS Co* [1912] AC 130.
[39] *Grant v Norway* (1851) 10 CB 665.
[40] *Cox, Patterson & Co v Bruce & Co* (1886) 18 QBD 147.
[41] For example, 'quantity unknown' or 'quantity believed to be'.

Hague-Visby rules. The carrier's response in such circumstances would be to call for a bill which complies with Article III, rule 3 of the Hague-Visby rules.[42] Thirdly, it could be possible to argue that as the buyer is already bound to complete the sale, the buyer does not rely on the representation as to the quality of the goods made in the bill. However, in reality, the effect of the obligation to complete is to prevent any presumption of reliance from arising from the mere taking up of documents.[43] Reliance/detriment will still arise, however, as the shipowner will be taken to have intended that the representation be relied on and the buyer will either permit its bank to pay against documents or pay for the goods itself.[44]

A result analogous to a common law estoppel is achieved by two other routes: by statute and by the rules governing bills of lading. By statute, section 4 of the Carriage of Goods by Sea Act 1992 provides that a bill of lading issued after the coming into force of the act[45] which (i) represents goods have been shipped or received for shipment and (ii) is signed by the master or person having authority of carrier to sign the bill; is conclusive evidence in favour of the lawful holder of the bill of the fact of shipment or receipt for shipment. A similar effect is achieved by the rules which normally govern bills of lading.[46] **20.37**

SALVAGE

During the negotiations for salvage, the shipowner may be estopped from denying that it is liable to the salvor for the salvage due by the representations made during the negotiations. Thus, for example, the appointment of arbitrators to determine what salvage is due or the deposit of monies to pay salvage are both sufficient representations to generate an estoppel.[47] As elsewhere, the salvor must establish detriment. Further, the estoppel created will not operate as a sword. No cause **20.38**

[42] *Noble Resources Ltd v Cavalier Shipping Corporation (The Atlas)* [1996] 1 Lloyd's Rep. 642 *per* Longmore J. at 646 col. 2.

[43] *Cremer v General Carriers SA* [1974] 1 WLR 341 *per* Kerr J. at 352F–H.

[44] *Brown Jackson v Percy Dalton* [1957] 2 QB 621; *Silver v Ocean SS Co* [1930] 1 KB 416; *V/O Rasnoimport v Guthrie* [1966] 1 Lloyd's Rep. 1 at 14 and *Evans v Webster* (1928) 34 Com Cas 172.

[45] *Yemen Bank for Reconstruction v Owners of the Future Express* (unrep. 29 July 1993).

[46] See Art III, r. 4 of the Hague-Visby rules in the Schedule to the Carriage of Goods by Sea Act 1971 and Benjamin at para. 8–012. See also r. 7(b) of the Comite Maritime International Uniform Rules for Sea Waybills.

[47] *The Prinz Heinrich* (1888) 13 PD 31 at 34.

of action is being created but, as with estoppel by convention, a party is being precluded from denying that a contract was entered into.

DEMURRAGE

The failure to place a demurrage indorsement on a bill prior to the signing of the bill will preclude a claim for demurrage. The bill is clear representation to the holder as to the status of the cargo at shipment. By parity of reasoning, no estoppel will arise in a claim against the charterer because no representation is made to the charterer in or by the bill.[48] Further, no estoppel will arise unless there is reliance/detriment.[49] Once a claim for demurrage is made, the claimant may be estopped from altering that claim.[50] **20.39**

[48] See Tiberg, *Law of Demurrage* (4th ed., Sweet & Maxwell, London, 1995) at p. 655.

[49] *Love & Stewart v Rowtor* [1916] 2 AC 527 *per* Lord Sumner at 539–40.

[50] Tiberg, *Law of Demurrage* (4th ed. Sweet & Maxwell, London, 1995) at p. 657.

BIBLIOGRAPHY

STANDARD WORKS REFERRED TO

'Andrews/Millet'—*Law of Guarantees*, G Andrews & R Millett, 2nd Ed., FT Law & Tax, London, 1995.

'Aitiya 1'—*The Rise and Fall of the Freedom of Contract*, PS Atiyah, Clarendon Press, Oxford, 1979.

'Atiyah/Adams—*Sale of Goods* PS Atiyah & J Adams, 9th ed., Pitman Publishing, London, 1995.

'Benjamin'—*Benjamin on Sale of Goods*, A Guest Q.C. (General ed..), 5th ed., Sweet & Maxwell, London, 1997.

'Bowstead'—*Bowstead & Reynolds on Agency*, F Reynolds Q.C., 16th ed., Sweet & Maxwell, London, 1996.

'Byles'—*Byles on Bills of Exchange*, F Ryder & A Bueno, 26th ed., Sweet & Maxwell, London, 1988.

'Chitty'—*Chitty on Contracts* A Guest Q.C. (General ed.), 27th ed., Sweet & Maxwell, London, 1994 (& Suppl 1996).

'Clarke'—*Law of Insurance Contracts*, M Clarke, 3rd ed., Lloyds of London Press, London, 1997.

'Finn'—*Essays in Equity*, ed. PD Finn, The Law Book Co. Ltd, Sydney, 1985.

'Goff & Jones'—*The Law of Restitution*, G Jones, 4th ed., Sweet & Maxwell, London, 1993.

'Gray'—*Elements of Land Law*, K Gray, 2nd ed., Butterworths, London, 1993.

'Harvey'—*Harvey on Industrial Relations and Employment Law*, B Perrins (General ed.), Butterworths, London (loose-leaf).

'Hanbury & Martin'—*Modern Equity*, J Martin, 15th ed., Sweet & Maxwell, London, 1993.

'Hayton & Marshall'—*Commentary and cases on the Law of Trusts and Equitable Remedies*, D Hayton, 10th ed., Sweet & Maxwell, London 1996.

'Hudson'—*Hudson's Building and Engineering Contracts* I Duncan Wallace Q.C., 11th ed., Sweet & Maxwell, London, 1995.

'Jack'—*Documentary Credits*, I Jack Q.C., 2nd ed., Butterworths, London, 1993.

'Keating'—*Keating on Building Contracts*, Sir Anthony May (General ed.), 6th ed., Sweet & Maxwell, London, 1995.

'MacGillivray'—*MacGillivray and Parkington on Insurance Law*, M Parkington (General ed.), 8th ed., Sweet & Maxwell, London, 1988.

'Meagher'—*Equity Doctrines and Remedies*, Meagher, Gummow & Lehane, 3rd ed., Butterworths, Sydney, 1992.

'Paget'—*Paget's Law of Banking*, Mark Hapgood Q.C., 11th ed., Butterworths, London, 1996.

'Pawlowski'—*The Doctrine of Proprietary Estoppel*, M Pawlowski, 1st ed., Sweet & Maxwell, London, 1996.

'Ruoff and Roper'—*The Law and Practice of Registered Conveyancing*, TB Ruoff, RB Roper, EJ Pryor, C West, R Fearnley Loose-leaf ed., Sweet & Maxwell, London, 1996.

'Snell'—*Snell's Equity*, P Baker Q.C. and P St J Langan, Sweet & Maxwell, London, 1991.

'Spencer Bower'—*The Law Relating to Estoppel by Representation*, Sir Alexander Kingcombe Turner, 3rd ed., Butterworths, London, 1977.

'Treitel 1'—*The Law of Contract* GH Trietel Q.C., 9th ed., Sweet & Maxwell, London, 1995.

'Treitel 2'—*Frustration and Force Majeure*, GH Trietel Q.C., Sweet & Maxwell, London, 1994.

'Underhill and Hayton'—*Underhill and Hayton 'The Law of Trusts and Trustees'*, D Hayton, 15th ed., Butterworths, London, 1995.

SUBJECT INDEX

Index compiled by Indexing Specialists, Hove